Global Human Resource Development

"*Global Human Resource Development* is an excellent book on the ins and outs of human resource development across almost 100 countries. The chapters are written by experts in the countries represented following a common format. The book can be used effectively in courses on global training and development, global talent management, and global leadership."
—*Randall S. Schuler, Rutgers University, USA*

Drawing on contributions from leading academics in the field, this volume within the Routledge Series in Human Resource Development specifically focuses on global human resource development (HRD). The volume provides an overview of 17 regions, 85 countries, and includes one emerging market grouping, CIVETS. This book examines the role of the state in HRD, the relationship between HRD and the level of economic development in the country or region, the influence of foreign direct investment within the country or region, and firm-level HRD practices within countries or regions.

Employing a comparative perspective, *Global Human Resource Development* makes it possible to analyze trends across countries and regions and to draw conclusions about the contemporary nature of the field of HRD in a global context. The ground covered is diverse, encompassing both policy and practice aspects of HRD around the world.

Thomas N. Garavan is Research Professor in Leadership at Edinburgh Napier Business School, Scotland.

Alma M. McCarthy is Head of the Management Department and Senior Lecturer in Human Resource Management at the National University of Ireland, Galway, Ireland.

Michael J. Morley is Professor of Management at the Kemmy Business School, University of Limerick, Ireland.

Routledge Studies in Human Resource Development

Edited by Monica Lee, Lancaster University, UK

HRD theory is changing rapidly. Recent advances in theory and practice, how we conceive of organizations and of the world of knowledge, have led to the need to reinterpret the field. This series aims to reflect and foster the development of HRD as an emergent discipline.

Encompassing a range of different international, organisational, methodological, and theoretical perspectives, the series promotes theoretical controversy and reflective practice.

Global Human Resource Development

Regional and Country Perspectives

Edited by Thomas N. Garavan, Alma M. McCarthy and Michael J. Morley

Routledge
Taylor & Francis Group

NEW YORK AND LONDON

First published 2016
by Routledge
711 Third Avenue, New York, NY 10017

and by Routledge
2 Park Square, Milton Park, Abingdon, Oxon OX14 4RN

First issued in paperback 2018

Routledge is an imprint of the Taylor & Francis Group, an informa business

© 2016 Taylor & Francis

Library of Congress Cataloging-in-Publication Data
Names: Garavan, Thomas N., editor. | McCarthy, Alma, editor. |
    Morley, Michael, editor.
Title: Global human resource development : regional and country perspectives /
    edited by Thomas N. Garavan, Alma M. McCarthy, and Michael J. Morley.
Description: First Edition. | New York : Routledge, 2016. | Series: Routledge
    studies in human resource development ; 24 | Includes bibliographical
    references and index.
Identifiers: LCCN 2015036731 | ISBN 9780415737227 (hardback : alk. paper) |
    ISBN 9781315818177 (ebook)
Subjects: LCSH: Personnel management. | International business enterprises—
    Personnel management.
Classification: LCC HF5549 .G53875 2016 | DDC 658.3—dc23
LC record available at http://lccn.loc.gov/2015036731

ISBN 13: 978-1-138-61714-8 (pbk)
ISBN 13: 978-0-415-73722-7 (hbk)

Typeset in Sabon
by Apex CoVantage, LLC

Contents

Tables and Figures

TABLES

FIGURES

1 Global Human Resource Development

Landscaping the Anatomy of An Evolving Field

Thomas N. Garavan,
Alma M. McCarthy and
Michael J. Morley

INTRODUCTION AND THE ORIGIN OF THE VOLUME

This volume is the culmination of a substantial cooperative effort by a global team of individuals with whom we have had the pleasure of collaborating with over the past several years. As co-editors, we have had the good fortune to have a sustained and mutually rewarding research collaboration stretching back over a considerable number of years. This volume is vested partly in this historical engagement, along with an on-going professional interest in the evolving field of human resource development from a comparative and cross-cultural perspective.

Beyond our own immediate academic relationship, we have also had the good fortune to encounter and connect with all of the chapter contributors, either individually or as an editorial team, as part of our own academic journeys over several years. In so doing, we became enthusiastic about the possibility and the prospect of creating a platform for the gathering and articulating of a collective set of ideas that underscore the field of human resource development (HRD) from a comparative perspective. In particular, we were excited about the prospect of augmenting our "Western" thinking with insights and lessons from emerging economies and territories previously underrepresented in the HRD literature but which offered the prospect of providing fresh insights on the field of HRD and its evolving nature.

That said, our initial collective enthusiasm inevitably gave way to periods of doubt about our enterprise, most likely because there is something slightly unnerving about the preparation of a volume, no matter what the topic, worthy of being labeled a "global perspective". It has the connotation of seeking to provide an all-encompassing, grand view vested in a vision perhaps somehow broader than that offered by others and possessed of a deeper insight on each quarter and territory that the volume focuses on. In light of this, it is important at the very outset to set the record straight on this front regarding the genesis of this volume and our underlying motivation for preparing it. Far from starting from the perspective that we as an editorial team were somehow possessed of more privileged insight than others, rather the opposite point of departure was the order of the day and served as our basic motivation. We were gradually becoming aware of gaps in our knowledge of the basic elemental building blocks of HRD in many territories that were on a significant developmental trajectory, territories that are marked by distinct institutional and cultural tenets, and that have witnessed a growth in indigenous enterprise along with emerging as important locations for foreign direct investment. This dearth of knowledge, insights, and research in the extant literature on many of these locations and territories persuaded us of the importance of a volume which might garner diverse contextual insights on HRD from a range of countries and territories, many of which were historically underrepresented in the existing literature, but all of which offered the prospect of generating insights on unique idiosyncratic elements governing the HRD system in different territories and countries. These insights, which of necessity might span the national level, along with organizational-level policy, practice, and preferred approaches could, we felt, when set opposite each other, allow the reader to judge what they would consider to be elements of commonality and difference at play in each territory and system, elements of stability and change in response to internal or external forces, along with elements of adaptation and transition, depending on the genesis of the forces for change and the manner in which HRD and institutional systems change being brought about.

Adopting this basic comparative approach as the architecture for the volume would, we felt, have a number of advantages. First, it would allow for a basic landscaping of regions and territories, some documented in the HRD literature heretofore, but many that are also undergoing deep change, such as, for example, in the major emerging markets, but which remain significantly underrepresented in the literature, relative to their counterparts in Western developed economies. Akbar (2006) highlights that, from an academic perspective, the emerging markets, as a heterogeneous group of societies, offer an important testing ground for our existing theories, models, and concepts. They also represent a potential source of new theories and new approaches, which call into question the value and sustainability of simply imposing Western approaches and solutions in these territories (Horwitz, Budhwar, and Morley, 2015). The HRD literature has to date been very USA and Euro centric. Second, allied to this, we were persuaded by the view that such dynamic contexts provided an important opportunity for scholars not just to observe the nature and shape of the HRD system in the territory being examined but also to observe whether and how core tenets of HRD are unfolding as part of the broader developmental trajectory being experienced by that location. Third, it would, we felt, afford us the opportunity to at least speculate as to the antecedents of similarities and differences between territories and allow the reader to make a judgment about the explanatory power of different factors at different levels of analysis as the likely root source of differences or indeed similarities. Fourth, implicitly or otherwise, the exercise would also allow for a further explication of the convergence thesis found in the organization and management literatures (see for example, McGaughey and DeCieri, 1999; Guillén, 2001; Brewster et al., 2004; Mayrhofer et al., 2011) in terms of whether HRD systems were becoming more similar as a result of globalization or indeed remaining different and embedded in distinct institutional, socio-cultural, economic, and labor market idiosyncratic elements. Finally, given that much of the effort to date has been focused on more micro- or meso-level perspectives on the field, we set ourselves the task of establishing a more macro, regio-comparative perspective as our initial point of departure for the book, although in addition to such regional clusters forming the comparative architecture of the majority of the chapter contributions, on occasion we also do include single country accounts of the prevailing national HRD system. We do so on the basis of the degree of dynamism characterizing those countries and the inherent lessons for other countries and territories that may be garnered from a deeper contextual account of their particular experience.

Of necessity, the ground that we cover is diverse and variable, covering HRD as a field of policy and practice and crossing different levels of analysis. Importantly though, despite the breadth of our endeavor, in as much as is practicable when commissioning chapters that have an inherent contextualism underlying their preparation, we sought to ensure that each chapter had a similar basic structure. Here we invited authors to provide an account of the historical, political, economic, institutional, social, and cultural context of the territory under consideration. This was followed by an outline of the general vocational and educational base for HRD, including consideration of key actors, such as government and government agencies, employer bodies, labor unions, nongovernmental agencies, etc., in addition to the legislative and policy context within the territory, including how regulated, integrated, and coherent the HRD system is. We also encouraged contributors to provide an account of HRD systems and practices at the organizational level. In the situation where the chapter was covering a number of countries, we asked for a discussion of the strengths and weaknesses of HRD in that region, along with similarities and differences between countries within the region. Finally, we encouraged authors to speculate about potential future challenges that HRD was likely to encounter in that territory, region, or country. Importantly, given the varying conceptualizations of HRD across the diverse territories covered, along with significant variations both in the level of maturity of the field along with the actual research base from a scientific point of view that authors in each territory could utilize, we had of course to allow a degree of flexibility on how the overall chapter framework was interpreted and developed in order to ensure that the authors were afforded the opportunity to provide coverage of contextually important elements.

In the remainder of this overarching chapter, we briefly introduce the field of HRD, we call attention to its evolving nature, its growth as a field of investigation, and we discuss several contiguous themes underscoring the development and promulgation of a more global understanding of HRD. First, we call attention to the importance of bringing certainty to the research trajectory or route that one embarks on and that serves to position the line of inquiry one pursues. Allied to this, we highlight the importance of the overarching paradigm or archetype guiding the research effort and the ongoing debate on convergence and divergence. We also call attention to emerging patterns of global mobility, talent development, and human capital accumulation as potential drivers of fresh conceptualizations and a novel discourse in HRD. Additionally, we point to the reemergence of the social role of HRD, an emphasis that had partially waned in the field in recent years in favor of a more rational economic perspective. Finally, we provide an introduction to each of the contributions in the volume.

HRD AS AN ACADEMIC FIELD

McGuire (2014) in explicating the origins of the field proposes that HRD has three major concerns: the development and enhancement of human potential, the enhancement of organizational effectiveness, and overall societal development. The combination of these concerns emphasizes the multidisciplinary nature of HRD (Swanson and Holton, 2001; Chalofsky, 2004) and despite variations in emphases in early scholarly contributions from different countries, these three basic tenets of the field have been largely consistent. Heretofore, scholarship has been most significantly influenced by US and UK discourse, with European and Asian contributions being more visible in recent times. Such traditions have inevitably led to variations in how HRD is conceptualized, what level of analysis is emphasized, the nature of whom it is it serves and whether HRD is good for organizations and society. Early writings in the US in particular (e.g., Nadler 1970; Knowles, 1998) proposed a conceptualization of HRD focused on individual development and betterment with a strong emphasis on education as an instrument toward achieving those outcomes. In contrast, a retrospective examination of the origins of the field of HRD in the UK yields an account vested in the role and value of training to the primacy of learning as an underlying process of HRD (Tjepkema, Stewart, Sambrook, Mulder, and Schwerens, 2002). A particularly strong feature of European approaches is their espousal of humanistic and philosophically rooted notions of HRD (Kenney, Donnelly and Reid, 1979) and the use of training to develop the job skills required to achieve economic growth. This early emphasis was to eventually culminate in the opening of a new line of inquiry on the strategic value and import of a best practice approach to HRD (Garavan, 1991). Subsequent European contributions were to emphasize a composite blend of individual, organizational, and national systems concerns.

In the early writings, the primary focus was on the individual. This level of analysis was reflected in writings about motivation to learn, learner readiness, personal development, and skills development. This subsequently shifted to an organizational level of analysis with an emphasis on the business contribution of HRD and in particular the performance contribution. More laterally, community, national, and societal concerns have been emphasized (Garavan, McGuire, and O'Donnell, 2004). There has also been a significant evolution in the field in recent years toward examining different systemic approaches to HRD and engaging in a discourse on preferred national models and approaches (Cho and McLean, 2004), although it is of relatively recent vintage. Allied to this, there is the debate on globalization as a driving force for the spread of ideas and practices, which, as a phenomenon, has acted as a trajectory for the promotion of international and global HRD as a field of inquiry (Wang and McLean, 2007; Garavan and Carbery, 2012). Arising from the unique set of conditions that gave rise to the recent global financial crisis, a line of inquiry has commenced on whether HRD has indeed contributed to its emergence (MacKenzie, Garavan, and Carbery, 2012), and regardless of what we conclude on that matter, there are those who suggest that the crisis has resulted in a shift in emphasis in the field whereby it has disengaged from its earlier roots in humanistic social science to a new found overemphasis on economic pressures and concerns (Ardichvili, 2013). Finally, providing evidence of the growing maturity of the field is the emergence of critical perspectives on HRD (Fenwick, 2005; Lawless, Sambrook, and Stewart, 2012; Fenwick, 2013). These critical perspectives question the purpose of HRD, its underpinning ideologies, its representationalist organization perspectives, and its humanistic assumptions. They suggest that there is an inherent tension between the needs of individuals and organizations. The emergence of critical perspectives is a signal that the field has reached a point of maturity whereby it can engage with its foundations, assumptions, and practices in a critical way.

GLOBAL HRD AS AN EMERGING FIELD OF INVESTIGATION

A noted above, global perspectives, vested in more macro comparative approaches to HRD are less common, although growing in popularity. The literature contains a small number of contributions that take as their starting point the 'global' view of HRD through the lens of globalization and internationalization (Garavan and Carbery, 2012; Kim and McLean, 2012). There are several reasons underscoring the emergence of a global perspective on HRD. Morley (2007) describes three distinct, but overlapping, research trajectories that are helpful to positioning lines of inquiry in management research that span national boundaries, namely an international, a comparative, and a cross-cultural trajectory, a classification that has been utilized to understand the construct of global HRD (Garavan and Carbery, 2012). In this approach, the concept of 'trajectory' is used to denote the existence of a distinctive line of inquiry. This distinctiveness may be observed both in terms of differing points of departure in the original research effort and consequently unique developmental paths for the major themes investigated.

It is suggested that *international* can be conceptualized as a field of inquiry dedicated to charting the anatomy of practice in the multinational corporation (MNC) and the unearthing of the strategies, systems, and practices pursued in the context of internationalization. The overlapping *comparative* trajectory, it is suggested, shows a preference for exploring the context, systems and content, and national patterns as a result of the distinctive developmental paths of different countries and their subsequently idiosyncratic institutional and economic regimes. A long-established tradition, it is based on the premise that many relevant insights into organizational processes and systems in a global era will come from studying them in a comparative context (Poole, 1993; Strauss, 1998; Evans et al., 2002). New locations, especially in the emerging markets that are on a significant development trajectory through the securing of significant foreign direct investments, are now proving fertile ground for generating insights in this comparative tradition. Within this comparative trajectory in the HRD field, there is a focus on national systems elements (Cho and McLean, 2002) as a basis for legitimate comparison and, as indicated earlier, whereas the focus until relatively recently has largely been on economically successful and developed economies, there is a growing emphasis in recent years on emerging economies as a testing ground for existing concepts or theories or indeed as a source of new theories (Horwitz et al., 2015). The final trajectory, labeled as *cross cultural*, is conceived of as a research tradition dedicated to explicating tenets of national culture as the dominant paradigm for conditioning what is acceptable organizational practice in that socio-cultural context. In this genre, significant explanatory power is accorded to tenets of societal culture in accounting for similarities and differences in the conceptualization and practice of management. Much of the empirical effort in this trajectory has been focused on the issue of dimensionalizing these cultural tenets and replicating inquiry in an array of contexts. And, as with the other trajectories outlined earlier, the range of contexts is continuously expanding with the relationship-rich cultures in the emerging markets once again proving especially fruitful locations for opening up new lines of inquiry (Akbar, 2006; Gammeltoft, et al., 2010; Horwitz, et al., 2015).

Against the backdrop of these distinct trajectories, which may prove instructive in determining and pursuing a research agenda within the field, we also want to summarily present a number of additional background themes that may help in explicating the contemporary nature of the field of HRD. First, there is the fundamental question of the appropriate paradigm necessary to conceptualize and understand the field. Mayrhofer et al. (2000), among others, identify two paradigms, namely a universalist and a contextual paradigm, that are a mainstay of the human resources management (HRM) field and which can be considered relevant to the HRD field, although they have received considerably less attention in the latter domain. The universalist paradigm dominant in theorizing in the US, but also widely used in other countries, is essentially, they argue, a nomothetic approach using evidence to test generalizations of an abstract character. Research conducted within this perspective contributes significantly to theory development. The contextual paradigm, Mayrhofer et al. argue, stands in contrast and offers an alternative perspective that is essentially idiographic in nature. It stresses the importance of understanding what is contextually unique in explaining and understanding phenomena under investigation. In the context of HRD, this will involve understanding what is different between and within HRD systems and practices in various contexts and understanding the antecedents of those differences in practices.

Second, the debate on convergence and divergence is relevant (McGaughey and DeCieri, 1999; Woodall, 2005). The questions of whether HRD globally is subject to convergence or ongoing and enduring divergence provides an important backdrop to debates on the evolving nature of the field and in particular notions of global HRD. Convergence-divergence is a well-established debate in the management literature, although it has not crossed over to the extent that one may expect to HRD. Those who argue for convergence propose that the effects of increasing internationalization in general will eventually give rise to an increasing similarity of systems, approaches, and practices. At the organization level, this will be manifest in a common set of strategic requirements resulting in a convergence of approaches regardless of cultural or national institutional differences (McGaughey and DeCieri, 1999; Mayrhofer et al., 2011). The logic of this argument is that the impact of the national origin on HRD practices will progressively decline due to globalization and lead to more generic, standardized HRD practices, irrespective of the cultural and institutional context. Divergence theorists reject the notion of convergence. They argue that national, institutional, cultural, and in some cases regional contexts are slow to change, because they have their foundations in deep-seated beliefs and value systems and are subject to ongoing ideational legacies. The consequence for HRD is that practices within different countries will have unique, idiosyncratic elements.

A third cross-cutting theme that has relevance in explaining the emergence of a global HRD perspective can be found in debates on global mobility and global talent management (Kim and McLean, 2012; Cascio, 2014). Increasingly, labor markets are viewed as global in nature and organizations, irrespective of their geographic location, need access to a skilled workforce and talent pool (Morley et al., 2015). The emergence of global labor markets combined with significant shifts in global mobility resulted in many emerging and developed economies striving to ensure that they have the appropriate mix of skills in their national talent pool. This theme has its antecedents in trends such as shifting patterns of foreign direct investment; growing international mobility and increasing workforce flux; an increased emphasis on global talent sourcing, development, and utilization; the development of global competencies and mind-sets; and the importance of international human capital. Global HRD, therefore, plays a key role in the development of cross-cultural competencies, diverse cognitive perspectives to facilitate decision making in different cultural contexts, and specialized knowledge about international markets (Kim, Pathak, and Werner, 2015). A well-developed talent pool helps organizations to operate in different time zones and achieve international competitiveness.

A fourth cross-cutting theme of particular relevance here concerns the reemergence of the social role of HRD. This theme has reemerged as a response to commentators who have argued that HRD has departed from its humanistic and developmental focus. The argument goes that HRD has a major role to play in strengthening state institutions, dealing with major social problems such as poverty, the strengthening of anticorruption regimes, capacity building, and enhancing the work of nongovernmental organizations (Berman, 2015). HRD is increasingly viewed as a set of practices that can benefit society as a whole (Kania and Kramer, 2011); facilitate large-scale social change through bringing together multiple social actors; and prevent, reduce, and alleviate poverty. Global HRD in this context is a fundamentally positive phenomenon that generates benefits for society.

INTRODUCING THE CONTRIBUTIONS IN THIS VOLUME

We landscape the nature and state of human resource development from a regio-comparative perspective. Such a perspective as our basic platform for analysis, we are conscious that several trade-offs relating to breadth and depth had to be made in pursuing this approach. There is little doubt that a within-country systems perspective with a sharp focus on national HRD would clearly have afforded more treatment of actors, interactions, and developments within the context of the country or system under examination. There is a long history within business and social science literature of this country comparative perspective, which "shows a preference for exploring the landscape, contours and national patterns of management as a result of the distinctive developmental paths of different countries and their subsequently idiosyncratic institutional and economic regimes" (Morley, Heraty, and Michailova, 2009: 5). On this occasion, we opt not for this well-trodden path as the point of departure of our analysis, but rather we opt for a regio-comparative perspective, realizing that adopting this approach is underscored by trading 'within-systems' depth for 'across-systems' scope and coverage. Importantly, however, our regional perspective also affords us the opportunity to cast particular light on different aspects of HRD less emphasized in scholarship heretofore. In particular, it allows for the calling of attention to the unique characteristics of regions, the emergence of clusters of countries with similar approaches to HRD, and the development of a cross-regional perspective on HRD. Regio-comparative perspectives are also valuable in developing theory about HRD that takes a broader, societally embedded approach and the development of new theories and models of HRD using inductive approaches that are cognizant of institutional and sociopolitical contexts and relationships.

Each of the chapters that follow is presented as a contextual account that may be read individually in order to provide insights into developments in the territory under study or comparatively in order to elucidate commonalities and differences between territories in a particular region or indeed more globally in order to judge the extent of globalization and its shaping influence on HRD from a policy and practice perspective.

SECTION 1: HRD IN ASIA AND OCEANIA

Turning to the chapter contributions, our first set of five chapters is focused on providing contextual insights from Asia and Oceania, along with the significant impact of state of development and dynamic pressures on the emergence and sedimentation of the HRD system.

In the chapter on Australia and New Zealand, McGraw and Kramar call attention to the parallel development of HRD and the economic and social development of both countries. They highlight the emergence of an Australasian HRD system, which is closely connected to underlying institutional processes, including social, political, and economic concerns. In both countries, they observe a profound historical shift from state models based on government invention to a more liberal, economic model.

The East Asia chapter by Rasdi and Ismail, focusing on Japan, South Korea, and Taiwan, notes the unifying impact of a strong foundation of human development and resultant high growth. Although late developers as capitalist economies, they note that they represent among the first Asian success stories in terms of their economic development. An important unifying theme in these countries is their collective commitment to investment in human capital and the expansion in vocational education and training.

The chapter on South Asia, including India, by Pandey, Hewapathirana, and Pestonjee focuses on a group of countries that are significantly less developed than their Asian Tiger economies and are characterized by political uncertainty, poor governance, poor investment climate, and underlying poverty and inequality. Against this backdrop, the authors argue that HRD is multifaceted and multilayered and heavily dependent on the state of economic development. They note that whereas they share many similarities, they also display unique features, which must be appreciated as part of the conceptualization of HRD.

In our chapter on China and North Korea, Sun and Wang provide a unique insight into contrasting economies in vastly different stages of their transition to more market-oriented socialist economies. While China has featured significantly in recent literatures in HRD, the insights here on North Korea and the misinterpretations of elements of its development in Western literature are especially valuable. They note that both countries have adopted similar institutional policies in developing their human resources (framed as *hukou* in China and *songbun* in North Korea) whereby development and career choices are not governed by personal decision making but by state regulation and intervention.

The contribution on Malaysia and Singapore by Ismail and Rasdi highlights the role of HRD in achieving and sustaining a growth trajectory. In this way, HRD has been used as a conduit to transformation, something that was recognized early in the development of these economies. The chapter also calls attention to the central role of government in planning education and investment in HRD, along with strong leadership and administration of HRD institutions. They also note that both countries have realized that the rich cultural context that pertains must be given expression to in the conceptualization of HRD in order to ensure its legitimacy.

SECTION 2: HRD IN AFRICA AND THE MIDDLE EAST

In the next section, we turn to Africa and the Middle East. Here we offer three chapters that call attention to the role of deep cultural traditions, strongly held religious beliefs, and a distinctly localized and unique conceptualization of HRD, often arising from the preponderance of family-owned enterprises and the significance of network relationships.

The chapter on sub-Saharan Africa by Nafukho and Muyia locates HRD within the broader debate on nation building and the important role of education and training as fundamental drivers of social, economic, and health development. Capacity building is a central leitmotif in this chapter. Nafukho and Muyia note the diversity of the region under consideration and move to focus on the Southern African Development Community Region in order to illuminate the role of HRD in enhancing employment and labor mobility, education and skills development, science and innovation, and children and youth. In this way, they underscore the significant social role of HRD.

The second chapter in this section stands in contrast to the other two contributions within the North Africa and Middle East section. In their treatise of the Middle East, Alhejji and Garavan focus on six countries that are part of the Gulf Cooperation Council, which acts as a unique supranational-shaping influence on country-level developments. In combination, these countries rely heavily on natural resources and the use of a largely expatriate talent pool to sustain growth and development. Their significant youthful population and high unemployment among the youth, especially among females, serve as particular challenges for the relative HRD systems.

Our final chapter in this section landscapes HRD in North Africa with a focus on Algeria, Morocco, and Tunisia. Here Alhejji and Garavan note that whereas these countries have different political systems, they are unified by a relatively underdeveloped HRD system, a youthful population, significant gender imbalances in society and the workplace, the predominance of Islamic law, and the power of tribes. They share a highly centralized approach to the management of the HRD system. Importantly, these countries have acted as hosts for foreign direct investment from outside multinationals, but the majority of enterprises are family-owned enterprises, which results in a significant role for networks and personal relationships as inputs to understanding HRD.

SECTION 3: HRD IN THE AMERICAS

Turning to the Americas, we offer insights on Canada and the USA, Latin America, and Brazil.

The chapter on the USA and Canada by McLean and Budhwani explores how each of these countries differs in the HRD domain, even though they share one of the longest international borders in the world. Often conceived of as the cradle of the discipline of HRD, the influence of the US system on the Canadian system is less than might be expected. McLean and Budhwani note particular differences in the role of stakeholders. For example, in Canada, the strong role of unions is noted, the variations between provinces is highlighted, and the unifying role of adult education in developing the profession of HRD is emphasized. Conversely, in the US context, they call attention to the role of HRD specific programs as drivers of the growth of the profession, as well as the prominent role of individuals investing in their own HRD or indeed corporate universities in taking responsibility and in funding HRD activity.

Our chapter on Latin America by Waight, Rangel Delgado, and Lopez commences by calling attention to key influences on HRD in Latin America, such as inequality, political ideologies, divergent economic policies, and major social challenges. The vocational and technical education system, often the backbone of national HRD initiatives, remains fragmented and underfunded. They also highlight the shaping influence of culture and heritage in conceptualizations of HRD. Here relationships, status, hierarchy, and religion are all considered important. At the political level, they highlight the short-termism of HRD policy making as a result of political instability.

Beyond the comparative analysis of Latin America, we also have a specific chapter focused on developments in Brazil by Leitão Azevedo, Ardichvili, Casa Nova, and Cornacchione. They note that whereas it has similarities and differences with its Latin American neighbors, the HRD system does have particularly unique elements vested in its language, its racial diversity, its postcolonial status, and its very significant recent economic trajectory. Despite its power as a major economic entity, its low level of education attainment may act as a constraint on its future development. Its approach to HRD is dominated by a unique approach to getting things done referred to as *jeitinho*. The case of Brazil serves as an example of a relationship-rich culture.

SECTION 4: HRD IN CENTRAL AND EASTERN EUROPE, RUSSIA AND THE FORMER SOVIET UNION

Our analysis of developments in Central and Eastern Europe (CEE), Russia and the former Soviet Union proceeds in two chapters. One chapter focuses on Central and Eastern Europe, with an emphasis on the Czech Republic, Estonia, Hungary, Latvia, Lithuania, Poland, Slovakia, and Slovenia. The second chapter focuses on Russia and the former Soviet Union. One area that has recently received increasing attention covers the ex-communist states of Central and Eastern Europe; the "transition economies" (Stark and Bruszt, 1998; Morley et al., 2009). Whereas it is clear what they are transitioning from, it is not clear exactly what they are transitioning to or whether, in fact, they represent a new Variety of Capitalism (Amable, 2003). This geographic territory is not historically well documented in the literature, and contemporary developments occur against the backdrop of large-scale political, economic, and socio-cultural shifts. In our chapter on CEE, Sheehan and Buchelt argue that these countries are the most transformed of these economies in transition and that the significant influence of joining the EU cannot be underemphasized in bringing much of this about. Nonetheless, the historical legacy of communism has resulted in them lagging somewhat behind their Western European neighbors. They note that these eight countries in particular illustrate the nuanced interaction of historical, social, political, and economic factors in shaping preferred approaches to HRD.

In our chapter on Russia and the former Soviet Union by Ardichvili, Zavyalova, and Tkachenko, consideration is given to the development of HRD in the post-socialist context and its importance as an ideational legacy in governing contemporary arrangements in Russia, Ukraine, Azerbaijan, and Kazakhstan. All four countries have experienced radical restructuring. They also suffer from significant underinvestment in education, and their vocational education and training system is considered unresponsive to the requirements of the market. At the firm level, HRD is confined to the large national resource industries and to the banking and high-tech sectors. There appears to be lack of a tradition of HRD as a profession, although this is changing.

SECTION 5: HRD IN WESTERN EUROPE

In our treatise on Western Europe, we offer four chapters based on regional/cultural clusters. We offer significant coverage to the Western European context on the basis of what can be perceived as an underlying socio-cultural and institutional heterogeneity that characterizes this geographic space and that results in distinct ideational legacies and different business traditions at the cultural level, which outlive individual leaders, technological changes, and dominant product lifecycles.

McCarthy focuses on the HRD systems in operation in the Republic of Ireland and the UK (England, Scotland, Wales, and Northern Ireland). Geographic neighbors, with a shared Anglo-Saxon tradition, they are characterized by a slowly evolving liberal political system and a concern for the social and the economic as complementary dual paths to development and its sustainability. The VET system in the Republic of Ireland developed in a similar way to that in the UK with a shared emphasis on HRD for competitiveness and development. Whereas there are, however, major sectoral variations with the result that there is a manifest unevenness in the provision of HRD, importantly a good balance is struck between state and private HRD provision.

Our chapter on the Nordic countries by Heidl and Dusoye highlights the uniqueness of the Nordic countries as among the top 20 most affluent in the world. The role of the Nordic Council in the HRD landscape is highlighted. The five countries under consideration enjoy strong contemporary cooperation vested in deep historical ties. Highly developed education systems characterize this cluster along with sophisticated HRD systems serving as inputs to their sustained levels of innovation. In this sense, they are often highlighted as exemplars on the HRD front.

Our chapter dealing with the Germanic countries in Europe by Mulder and Nieuwenhuis analyzes HRD in Germany, Austria, the Netherlands, and Switzerland. Among the most developed economies in the world, they comprise highly developed VET systems, both at corporate and state level.

Turning to Southern Europe, the chapter by Tomé calls attention to the explanatory power of culture in this Latin cluster comprising France, Greece, Italy, Portugal, and Spain. He notes that, in recent years, several have found themselves in a uniquely challenging position vis-à-vis their emergence from the global economic crisis and their post-crisis relationship with the EU. Referring to them as the "South of the North" based on their particular attitudes and values, France stands out in the cluster due to its "French singularity," resulting in a greater focus on HRD as part of a sustained competitiveness drive.

SECTION 6: HRD IN THE EMERGING MARKETS

Our final chapter in the volume focuses on a comparison of the CIVETS countries, which include Colombia, Indonesia, Vietnam, Egypt, Turkey, and South Africa. Our logic here is governed not by the explanatory power of similarities between systems lying in cultural or institutional determinants but rather by whether aspects of explanation may be unearthed in the level of economic development of the countries and their associated economic trajectories. Horwitz, Budhwar, and Morley (2015) argue that the very notion of the emerging markets represents something of a portmanteau term built on a series of layered insights garnered from several academic fields and multiple levels of analysis. In the final chapter landscaping HRD in this volume, Garavan and Akdere explore the complexities of HRD and the extent of similarity and difference they reveal in CIVETS, a group of emerging economies. They note that how HRD has developed is largely in response to the aggressive developmental trajectory and to their positioning as significant hosts for foreign direct investment. In addition, they share a conceptualization of HRD that focuses significantly on the individual and the capacity for HRD to eliminate inequality and poverty. Nonetheless, their HRD systems are embryonic, highly fragmented, and under-resourced. In addition, waves of political instability in some quarters have resulted in questions being raised about their likely capacity to sustain a growth trajectory.

REFERENCES

Akbar, Y. H. (2006). A research agenda. *International Journal of Emerging Markets*, 1(1).

Amable, B. (2003). *The Diversity of Modern Capitalism*. Oxford: Oxford University Press.

Ardichvili, A. (2013). The role of HRD in CSR, sustainability, and ethics: A relational model. *Human Resource Development Review*, 12: 456.

Berman, E. (2015). HRM in development: Lessons and frontiers. *Public Administration and Development*, 35(2): 113–127.

Brewster, C., Mayrhofer, W., & Morley, M. (Eds.). (2004). *Human Resource Management in Europe. Evidence of Convergence?* Oxford: Butterworth-Heinemann.

Cascio, W. F. (2014). Leveraging employer branding, performance management and human resource development to enhance employee retention. *Human Resource Development International*, 17(2): 121–128.

Chalofsky, N. (2004). *Human and Organization Studies: The Discipline of HRD.* Online Submission.

Cho, E. S., & McLean, G. N. (2002). National human resource development: Korean case. In U. Pareek, A. M. Osman-Gani, S. Ramnaravan, & T. V. Rao (Eds.), *Human resource development in Asia: Trends and challenges* (pp. 253–260). New Delhi, India: Oxford & IBH.

Cho, E., & McLean, G. N. (2004). What we discovered about NHRD and what it means for HRD. *Advances in Developing Human Resources*, 6(3): 383–393.

Evans, P., Pucik, V., & Barsoux, J. L. (2002). *The Global Challenge: Frameworks for International Human Resource Management*. New York: McGraw-Hill/Irwin.

Fenwick, T. (2005). Conceptions of Critical HRD: Dilemmas for Theory and Practice. *Human Resource Development International, 8*(2), 225–238.

Fenwick, T. (2013). Work and learning: Perspectives from Canadian adult educators. In T. Nesbit, S. M. Brigham, N. Taber, & T. Gibb (Eds.), *Building on Critical Traditions: Adult Education and Learning in Canada*, 289–302. Toronto: Thompson.

Gammeltoft, P., Barnard, H., & Madhok, A. (2010). Emerging Multinationals, Emerging Theory: Macro- and Micro-Level Perspectives. *Journal of International Management, 16*(2), 95–101.

Garavan, T. N. (1991). Strategic human resource development. *Journal of European Industrial Training, 15*(1): 17–30.

Garavan, T. N., & Carbery, R. (2012). A review of international HRD: Incorporating a global HRD construct. *European Journal of Training and Development, 36*(2/3): 129–157.

Garavan, T. N., McGuire, D., & O'Donnell, D. (2004). Exploring human resource development: A levels of analysis approach. *Human Resource Development Review, 3*(4): 417–441.

Guillén, M. F. (2001). *The Limits of Convergence. Globalization and Organizational Change in Argentina, South Korea and Spain*. Princeton: Princeton University Press.

Horwitz, F., Budhwar, P., & Morley, M. J. (2015). Future trends in human resource management in emerging markets. In F. Horwitz, & P. Budhwar (Eds.), *Handbook of Human Resource Management in Emerging Markets*, 470–488. Cheltenham: Edward Elgar.

Jacobs, R. L. (2014). Systems theory and HRD. In N. E. Chalofsky, T. S. Rocco, and M. L. Morris (Eds.), *Handbook of Human Resource Development*, 21–39. Hoboken, NJ: John Wiley & Sons.

Kania, J., & Kramer, M. (2011). Collective impact. *Stanford Social Innovation Review*, (4): 36–41.

Kenney, J. P. J., Donnelly, E. L., & Reid, M. A. (1979). *Manpower Training and Development*. London: IPM.

Kim, K. Y., Pathak, S., & Werner, S. (2015). When do international human capital enhancing practices benefit the bottom line? An ability, motivation, and opportunity perspective. *Journal of International Business Studies*, 46: 784–805.

Kim, S., & McLean, G. (2012). Global talent management: Necessity, challenges, and the roles of HRD. *Advances in Developing Human Resources*, 14(4): 566–585.

Knowles, M. S. (1998). *The Adult Learner: The Definitive Classic in Adult Education and Human Resource Development*. Houston, TX: Gulf Publishing Company.

Lawless, A., Sambrook, S., & Stewart, J. (2012). Critical HRD: Enabling alternative subject positions within an MA HRD 'community'. *Human Resource Development International*, 15(3): 31–336.

MacKenzie, C. A., Garavan, T. N., & Carbery, R. (2012). Through the looking glass: Challenges for human resource development (HRD) post the global financial crisis—business as usual? *Human Resource Development International*, 15(3): 353–364.

Mayrhofer, W., Brewster, C., & Morley, M. (2000). The concept of strategic European human resource management. In C. Brewster, W. Mayrhofer, & M. Morley, *New Challenges for European Human Resource Management*, 3–37, London: Palgrave Macmillan.

Mayrhofer, W., Brewster, C., Morley, M. J., & Ledolter, J. (2011). Hearing a different drummer? Convergence of human resource management in Europe—a longitudinal analysis. *Human Resource Management Review*, 21(1): 50–67.

McGaughey, S., & DeCieri, H. (1999). Reassessment of convergence & divergence dynamics: Implications for international HRM. *International Journal of Human Resource Management*, 10(2): 235–250.

McGuire, D. (2014). *Human Resource Development.* London: Sage.

Morley, M. J. (2007). *Of Infants and Adolescents: Progress and Pessimism in the Development Trajectory of International Human Resource Management.* Keynote Presentation to the 9th Conference on International Human Resource Management, June 12th-15th. Estonia: Tallinn.

Morley, M. J., Heraty, N., & Michailova, S. (2009). *Managing Human Resources in Central and Eastern Europe.* London: Routledge.

Morley, M., Sculion, H., Collings, D., & Schuler, R. (2015). Talent management: A capital question. *European Journal of International Management,* 9(1): 1–8.

Nadler, L. (1970). *Developing Human Resources.* Houston, TX: Gulf Publishing Company.

Poole, M. (1993). Industrial relations: Theorising for a global perspective. In R. Adams and N. Meltz (Eds.), *Industrial Relations Theory: Its Nature, Scope and Pedagogy,* 185–199. Metuchen, NJ: The Scarecrow Press.

Stark, D., & Bruszt, L. (1998). *Postsocialist Pathways: Transforming Politics and Property in East Central Europe.* Cambridge, MA: Cambridge University Press.

Strauss, G. (1998). Regional studies of comparative international industrial relations: Symposium introduction. *Industrial Relations,* 37(3): 273–281.

Swanson, R. A., & Holton, E. F. (2001). *Foundations of Human Resource Development.* Oakland, CA: Berrett-Koehler Publishers.

Tjepkema, S., Stewart, J., Sambrook, S., Horst, H., Mulder, M., & Scheerens, J. (2002). The role of human resource development practitioners in learning oriented organizations. *HRD Research Monograph Series.*

Wang, X., & McLean, G. N. (2007). The dilemma of defining international human resource development. *Human Resource Development Review,* 6(1): 96–108.

Woodall, J. (2005). Convergence and Diversity in HRD. *Human Resource Development International,* 8(1), 1–4.

Section I
Asia and Oceania

2 Human Resource Development in Australia and New Zealand

Peter McGraw and Robin Kramar

INTRODUCTION

HRD is not a static process but evolves as the economic and broader environment changes and organizations respond accordingly (Mankin, 2001). Although often viewed mainly as an organizational process, HRD initiatives and policies are also enacted at various levels of government to facilitate and support broader economic and societal changes. Different industry sector representatives, employer bodies, educational institutions, and trade unions also play a role in developing and facilitating HRD. This is especially true in Australia and New Zealand where governments and other stakeholders have traditionally had an active role in labor markets and related policy areas, such as industrial relations and HRD. Also, an understanding of these dynamics helps us to understand the reasons why stakeholders have different views of HRD and have changed their views over time. In this chapter, the examination of HRD in Australia and New Zealand demonstrates the way HRD has evolved in two countries as they have moved away from their traditionally centralized, regulated labor markets toward more decentralized models. During the last four decades, both Australia and New Zealand have responded to volatile, unpredictable external contingencies such as globalization by reducing the direct role and support of government in HRD initiatives alongside broader economic reform policies. Consequently, many HRD activities, such as vocational training, are increasingly privatized and influenced by direct market forces within a broad policy framework established at the government level. In this context, an examination of HRD in Australia and New Zealand provides insights into the evolution of HRD in two countries moving, at different speeds and on different paths, toward more neoliberal economies.

The approach taken here implicitly adopts both an institutional and neo-institutional perspective (Meyer and Rowan, 1977; Di Maggio and Powell, 1983) to understand the development of HRD in Australia and New Zealand. These perspectives argue that formal institutions in society interact and influence organizational practices through direct and indirect mechanisms. In relation to HRD, the formal institutions are wide ranging and include employers and their associations, governments, trade unions, economic, political, social, cultural, and legislative bodies. Such an approach also recognizes that these institutions are interdependent, are influenced by evolving norms and ideology, as well as formal mechanisms operating at the macro/national/regional level, at the meso/organizational level, and at the micro/workplace level. In order to understand HRD in Australia and New Zealand, it is essential to understand the interaction within and between institutions at all three levels and to also understand the historical traditions informing the operation of the institutions.

This chapter outlines the key influences shaping HRD practices in Australia and New Zealand with a particular emphasis on how contemporary practice reflects a profound historical shift. The first section illustrates how concepts of HRD have evolved in Australia and New Zealand alongside the economic and social development of the nations. Later sections illustrate HRD systems and outcomes in various organizational contexts as well as the contributions made by governments, employment tribunals, and education and training providers. After documenting contemporary HRD mechanisms and practices, the chapter concludes with observations about the overall role of HRD in Australia and New Zealand and its contributions to economic and broader societal outcomes.

THE HISTORICAL, POLITICAL, ECONOMIC, INSTITUTIONAL, SOCIAL, AND CULTURAL CONTEXT IN THE REGION

Both New Zealand and Australia can trace their recent history back to settlement and colonization by the British in the late nineteenth century. Whereas both countries had significant indigenous populations and history before white ('Pakeha' in New Zealand) settlement, nevertheless, widespread modernization, economic, and population growth is commonly traced back to the colonial starting point. Australia is an island continent with a population of over 23 million people of whom approximately 15 million are formally designated as part of the workforce according to the Australian Bureau of Statistics (2012). New Zealand comprises two main islands and has a current population of approximately 4.5 million people with the majority living on the North Island. Both countries have very significant and economically important agricultural sectors, especially New Zealand, although in both countries these employ less than 10% of the overall working populations. Both countries are ethnically diverse and have become distinctly more so in recent times, although there are differences between the two countries: whereas Australia has a formal policy of multiculturalism (in recognition of the almost 140 ethnic identities that have been recorded in the Australian population), New Zealand has a policy of biculturalism, which specifically notes the position of the Māori in New Zealand society and culture. In recent times, both countries, but especially Australia, have received significant migration inflows from Asia and China in particular.

Australia has sometimes been referred to as a 'Lucky Country' because of its abundance of natural resources and land. Throughout much of its history, since colonial settlement over 200 years ago, it has enjoyed sustained prosperity, high employment, and high levels of GDP per capita with average incomes. This trend has continued, despite the challenging period of the last two decades with a doubling of GDP, a 50% increase in employment, and a quadrupling of nominal household wealth (Australian Workforce and Productivity Agency, 2013). By early 2015, however, the 'once in a lifetime' resources boom associated with rapid Chinese economic growth had slowed significantly and the prices of key export minerals had declined; both factors suggest more difficult economic times ahead.

New Zealand enjoyed enormous prosperity on the basis of agricultural exports (especially refrigerated meat and wool) from the 1880s to the early 1970s when it was colloquially referred to as the 'UK's farm'. Since then it has experienced over three decades of economic turbulence, as will be outlined later in this chapter. However, unlike Australia, New Zealand experienced a protracted recession following the global financial crisis with unemployment levels of up to 7% during 2012. Interestingly, the New Zealand economy has rebounded since 2012 as the Australian economy has started to slow. Indicative of this is the fact that, while for several decades, New Zealand suffered from a significant 'brain drain' with nearly 25% of its highly skilled workers living and working overseas, this trend has reversed since the global financial crisis. Now the term 'brain gain' has become common as expatriate workers return to work in the healthy economy of their homeland.

Because of their relatively late industrialization, general prosperity, early democratization, and perhaps isolation, both Australia and New Zealand developed unique labor systems in the decades before and after the turn of the twentieth century. These factors significantly impacted their respective HRD practices. Until the early 1980s, the domestic economies of both countries, under what broadly might be referred to as an Australasian model, demonstrated high levels of state involvement: regulated labor systems with compulsory arbitration, combined with strong protection from international competition. During the last four decades, however, both countries have been through significant programs of economic reform and liberalization with concomitant deregulation of the labor markets and dismantling of government-sponsored arbitration systems. Although the trajectories of change have varied between the two countries, with Australia evolving and New Zealand undergoing more radical and faster changes, HRD systems and mechanisms in both countries have changed accordingly.

The Australian HRD Backdrop and History

Australia was colonized as an English penal settlement in 1788, although it had an existing indigenous population that has been estimated to go back over 40,000 years. After a difficult and turbulent period of early colonial history, the various colonies (now states) developed and grew significantly throughout the nineteenth century via successive waves of mainly, but not exclusively, British migration. Colonial social and economic institutions were built on the Anglo-Celtic model and mentality, and as a result, there developed early on a strong trade union consciousness with emphasis on workers. With Federation in 1901, the regulation of industrial conditions was enshrined into the constitution and came to characterize the Australian system of labor relations for the remainder of the twentieth century. HRD practice in Australia occurred within the context of a centralized and bureaucratically rigid industrial relations system characterized by high levels of union influence and enormous complexity. The results were narrowly defined and fragmented occupational skill categories, inflexible working arrangements, and managerial control consistent with an economy based on protectionism. The combined effect of these factors generally led to underinvestment in HRD (Holland et al., 2007).

However, the sourcing of labor, particularly skilled labor, was solved at the macrolevel by migration. Following the Second World War and during the 1950s and 1960s with widespread migration from various parts of Europe, there was widespread concern about skill shortages. At the micro- and meso-levels, training was rare in manufacturing and other industries with employers typically obtaining the skills they needed from the external labor market (McKeown and Teicher, 2006). Employees typically learned on the job under the supervision of a foreman, whereas larger organizations often had apprenticeship schemes involving classes provided by technical colleges and work experience during the day (Wright, 1995). Some large banks, retail stores such as David Jones, the public services, and especially the NSW Railways established internal labor markets that provided training and career opportunities. However, these applied to supervisory, technical, and managerial staff rather than to lower level employees (Wright, 1995).

Despite the influx of immigrants, labor shortages continued in Australia until the 1970s. A small number of employers developed systematic training procedures to deal with these shortages that included: in-plant apprenticeship training schemes that formalized systems of training semiskilled workers, the adoption of Training Within Industry programs that trained 'trainers' to teach employees about how to correctly do a job, and the adoption of specialized 'off-the-job' training schemes (Wright, 1995). However, the external labor markets typically continued to provide skilled employees to organizations.

In the 1980s, the economy began to be opened up to international competition as the ability to compete in Australian industry grew. This resulted in the introduction of major reforms by successive federal governments from the mid-1980s onward, such as extensive deregulation, which in turn resulted in significant changes to the pattern of HRD. These reforms began at the macrolevel with the dismantling of trade and protection barriers, the floating of the Australian dollar, and labor market deregulation (Smith and Hayton, 1999). Later the focus shifted to micro-economic reforms in the labor market and attempts to create 'new workplace cultures' in which HRD emerged as a potential key source of competitive advantage (Hutchings and Holland, 2007). Further changes also included radical reforms to the national vocational education and training system, various policies to encourage employers to invest in HRD, the introduction of competency-based skill frameworks, the creation of a competitive market for training provision, and a host of related progressive reforms.

Developments in the 1980s stimulated changes in employer, trade union, and industrial tribunal policies. The industrial tribunal, the Conciliation and Arbitration Commission, sought to improve productivity in workplaces by adopting the 'restructuring and efficiency principle' in 1987, the 'structural efficiency principle' in 1988, and in 1989, the National Wage Cases. Among the changes in employment practices contributing to greater productivity were initiatives resulting from increased training, such as skill-related career paths and greater multiskilling. Under the Labor Government 'Accord' agreement, Australian trade unions generally supported these changes, which also included increased training, career structures, and consultation.

In the 1980s too, a series of reviews of the Australian vocational and educational systems were undertaken with input from governments, trade unions, employers, and industrial tribunals. These reviews indicated that education and training were essential for increasing the competitiveness of Australian organizations. Among the recommendations in the joint report by the Australian Council of Trade Unions (ACTU) and the Trade Development Council (Department of Trade, ACTU and TDU, 1987) was increased recognition of the importance of training and skill development. The 1988 Dawkins report, *Industry Training in Australia: The Need for Change* (1988), claimed there was a need for multiskilling, broader job structures, and career paths, whereas a white paper higher education policy statement claimed the university sector needed to be reformed to increase skills to cope with international competitiveness.

The Australian government developed a number of initiatives in the area of HRD in the last couple of decades. The Australian Best Practice Demonstration Program identified and disseminated best practice HRD based on a broad approach that sought to build a learning culture facilitating continuous improvement and a highly skilled and flexible workforce (Rimmer et al., 1996, p. 22). Under this program, training and communication initiatives were developed. Establishing standards for competency by industry with associated curriculum development to reflect outcomes was also a government initiative, which included the development of an Australia-wide Standards Framework for vocational education and training credentials and the establishment of a National Training Board (NTB). There was agreement on a National Framework for the Recognition of Training (NFROT) and a number of reports on issues related to the training implications of industrial relations changes, young people's participation in post-compulsory education and training, and the need for curricula to take into account a number of general or core competencies. The Australian Vocational Certificate Training System (AVCTS), whose purpose was to provide a number of pathways in the transition from school to work, was also a key initiative within the education and training context. Establishment of the Australian National Training Authority to oversee the allocation of government resources to the publicly funded Technical and Further Education (TAFE) sector was also a key milestone in the development of education and the skills agenda in Australia.

The federal government also enacted legislation to encourage increased training and development. The Training Guarantee Scheme began in 1990. It required employers with payrolls of over $200,000 to spend at least 1.5% of payroll per year or pay an equivalent amount to the payroll. Judgments about the success of the schemes differed, with some arguing it was unsuccessful in achieving an increase in training (Teicher, 1995; DEETYA, 1996), whereas others argue it did increase expenditure on training (Hall, 2011). The scheme was discontinued in 1996.

Notwithstanding these initiatives, there was also a trend for employers to focus on increased flexibility through workforce reduction and greater work intensification; increased labor flexibility through the introduction of casual, part-time, and contract employment; and working time and remuneration changes (Wright, 1995; Hall, 2011). These employer priorities mitigated the intention for greater training and development of the workforce and employer reactions to training and career development were varied during this period. Some organizations did invest in training, career development, the systematic analysis of training needs, and the establishment of internal labor market structures, whereas others did not. Training, therefore, was not always seen as a means of developing organizational commitment. Rather, training was regarded in a highly instrumental way. Managers considered it should be highly relevant to the specific problems faced by the organization (Smith and Hayton, 1999). This could help explain the predominantly 'ad hoc' approach that was adopted to training in Australia (Kane et al., 1994).

Between the mid-1990s and 2009, the Strategic Human Resource Management (SHRM) approach to employee management became more widespread in Australia (Kramar, 2012). Training and development of employees is an important component of the 'developmental humanism' approach to SHRM, which emphasizes treating employees as valued assets. Expenditure on training for different groups of employees, professionals, managers, clerical, and manual employees remained fairly constant during this period at about 4% of payroll. Similarly, the number of training days per employee remained much the same remaining at between four and eight days for the different groups of employees (Kramar, 2012).

Evaluation of the outcomes of HRM policies is a key component of SHRM. According to the Australian Cranet data, during the 1996–2009 period, there was a dramatic decline in the evaluation of training from 82% to 56% (Kramar, 2012). Where organizations continued to engage in some form of training evaluation during the 1996–2009 period, the evaluation methods employed changed. Evaluation, in terms of behavior change following training (or level 3 in the Kirkpatrick evaluation model), increased from 68% to 82%, whereas evaluation in terms of reactions and results declined from 78% and 56% to 48% and 14%, respectively. In 2009, almost half the organizations evaluated training in terms of whether it met the objectives in the training and development plan and by gaining feedback from line managers and employees (Kramar, 2012).

As mentioned in chapter 1, HRD involves not only training and development but also career development. Internal labor markets provide employees with the opportunities to move up a career ladder and develop a career within an organization. During the 1996–2009 period, there was substantial growth in the use of career planning and methods, such as career paths, development centers, succession plans, planned job rotation, and high-potential schemes. The use of planned job rotations increased by 70% and the use of development centers increased by 400% during this period (Kramar, 2012). Further support for the development of internal labor markets came from the increasing use of internal recruitment for managerial, professional, clerical, and manual employees and the increasing use of leave and career-break schemes (Kramar, 2012). In addition, HRD at the organizational level, includes not just training, development, and career development but also job structures, rewards, recognition policies, and feedback. HRD therefore has resulted in better utilization of skills of employees and increased productivity. There is little evidence of the extent of skill utilization policies in Australian organizations, although the Australian Workforce Productivity Agency (AWPS) suggests 37% of employers report their employee skills are underutilized (AWPS, 2013, p. 54).

The New Zealand HRD Backdrop and History

New Zealand had a long history of settlement before Europeans arrived in sustained numbers from around the 1800s. It was first occupied by the Moriori population who gradually became extinct after the Polynesian Māori peoples began to settle in the country from around 1250 onward. From 1788 until the signing of the Treaty of Waitangi in 1840, New Zealand was mostly administered as part of the British colony of New South Wales. With the signing of the treaty and declaration of sovereignty, the number of immigrants, particularly from the UK, began to increase, which eventually led to the land wars of the 1860s and 1870s. In the late 1800s, New Zealand led the world in socially progressive policies for its citizens. For example, in 1893, New Zealand was the first country in the world to give women the right to vote and the following year introduced a pioneering compulsory arbitration system between unions and employers.

New Zealand almost literally 'lived off the sheep's back' in the first seven decades of the twentieth century, such was the significance of the meat and wool industry to the economy. The associated prosperity of this period allowed New Zealand to build up a highly protected domestic economy servicing other sectors and highly regulated and inefficient systems of industrial relations and associated labor market mechanisms. However, it has experienced significant economic upheaval and declining economic fortunes since then after losing much of its traditional export markets when the UK joined what is now the European Union in 1973.

After a period of stagnation and crisis in the late 1970s and early 1980s, the New Zealand economy has since been transformed from one with high levels of economic protectionism to one of the most liberal free-market economies in the world. Unlike Australia, which evolved more gradually toward deregulation, New Zealand went for the 'big bang' when in 1984 the newly elected Labour government embarked on a radical economic reform program that removed controls on wages, prices, and interest rates; introduced tight monetary policies; drastically reduced fiscal deficits; and removed a raft of agricultural and other industry subsidies. Colloquially known as 'Rogernomics', after the then treasurer Roger Douglas, the long-term economic outcomes of this radical experiment in monetary, as opposed to the more traditional Keynsian economics, are still controversial to this day. However, for the labor market, the effects were immediate and profound. Around 70,000 jobs in manufacturing were lost from the mid to late 1980s (Bell, 2006); employers became more adversarial in relation to wage bargaining and union recognition, and there was a widespread decline in trade union membership and power. By 2013, trade union membership in New Zealand among the working population had fallen to 16.6% (New Zealand Government, 2013) from around 50% in the late 1980s.

In relation to HRD and technical education for skilled employees, New Zealand had underdeveloped formal systems until the early 1900s and relied mainly on skilled migration, primarily from the UK, to fill the gaps. From the start of the twentieth century, New Zealand started to establish technical schools and colleges in major urban areas and developed an apprenticeship system similar to that in the UK and Australia. However, New Zealand traditionally lagged behind Australia in technical training because of the lack of a large-scale mining or manufacturing sector to provide impetus to technical skills development. Also, up until the 1940s, most technical college classes had to be taken part time in the evenings, which limited access. After the Second World War, technical training for apprentices became more systematic with the passing of the Apprentices Act in 1948 and, for the first time, daytime attendance at classes and a theoretical component within the curriculum became mandatory, as well as formal examination before certification.

By the 1960s, technical training had become more mature and extensive and was centered around technical schools and polytechnics for higher-level courses. Student numbers at these institutions rose steadily during the 1960s and 70s, and by 1981, constituted almost half of the student population enrolled in tertiary education. In addition to the technical schools and poly-technics, New Zealand had five universities in the early 1980s. Alongside wider economic reform, New Zealand's technical and tertiary education was extensively reformed during the late 1980s. Uniform central control of cur-riculum and courses was removed and educational institutes were allowed more freedom to develop new courses under the auspices of the New Zea-land Qualifications Authority. As a result, the old polytechnics started to offer degree-level courses in competition with established universities paral-leling developments in Australia and the UK after their changes to the dual system of higher education. Further changes during the 1990s also saw the emergence of an extensive private-sector involvement in sub-degree-level vocational training, and there is now extensive competition in the sector.

Because of the generally small size of New Zealand organizations, there has been a marked tendency in the last two decades to outsource HR func-tions to specialist consultancies. This has been particularly the case with regard to HRD (Toulson and Defryn, 2007). Most large private- and pub-lic-sector organizations in New Zealand organize their own enterprise-level training and development and employ HRD specialists to organize and coordinate this activity in conjunction with private-sector providers. Employers of all sizes and types in New Zealand also interact with the voca-tional education and training (VET) sector as part of their capability devel-opment initiatives.

THE CURRENT VOCATIONAL AND EDUCATIONAL BASE FOR HRD

Current New Zealand VET Framework

Today, New Zealand has very different systems of vocational education than those discussed in the previous section and attempts to be more cohe-sive and integrated. According to the New Zealand Ministry of Education (2013), technical and vocational education and training (TVET) can start at school and be continued at the tertiary level via institutes of technology and polytechnics (ITPs), industry training organizations (ITOs), wānanga (publicly owned tertiary institutions that provide education in a Māori cul-tural context), private training establishments (PTEs), and in the workplace. Some programs are also available in government training establishments and several universities.

New Zealand's 'Youth Guarantee' comprises a set of vocational path-ways that bring together the standards and skills recommended by indus-try in five broad sectors—manufacturing and technology, construction and infrastructure, primary industries, social and community service, and service industries—and links these to study and employment possibilities. Within this, system learners can progress through different training and education levels and vocational pathways developed through consultation between government agencies, the industry training sector, secondary and tertiary education representatives, and industry and employer representatives.

In total, there are currently 22 trade academies administered through schools and other providers that deliver trades and technology programs to students in years 11 to 13 (ages 15 to 18). They take account of local and national workforce needs and are also aligned to allow students to achieve secondary and tertiary qualifications. Trades include such areas as tourism, primary industries, building and construction, hospitality, engineering, business, and computing.

At the next level, there are 18 ITPs that provide professional and vocational education and training on a wide range of subjects up to full-degree level. New Zealand also has around 40 industry training organizations, which are government and industry-funded bodies that represent particular industry sectors such as agriculture, building and construction, and automotive trades. These teach national standards and qualifications for their sector, facilitate on-the-job training, and contract training providers to offer off-job training and courses. Working alongside the ITPs are nearly 600 private training establishments, which offer specific vocational courses at certificate and diploma level for various occupations and include language training for overseas students. Finally, New Zealand now has eight universities, many of which have multiple campuses.

Current Australian VET System

In Australia, there are three main educational sectors: school education, higher education in universities, and the vocational education training (VET) sector. In total, according to the Australian Bureau of Statistics, almost 60% of Australians now have a non-school qualification, such as a degree or certificate (ABS, 2012). The current framework for post-school education is the Australian Qualifications Framework (AQF), which sets out national policy standards and definitions for recognized qualifications. The AQF, which is nationally and internationally recognized, has ten levels in all, ranging from the most basic at level 1 (certificate 1) up to the most advanced at level 10 (doctoral degree level). In the AQF framework, levels 1–5 are distinctly in the VET sector, and the top-four levels are in the higher education sector. Articulation is possible through different parts of the system, and level 6 (advanced diplomas/associate degree) is transitional between sectors.

In the last two decades, the educational sector has expanded dramatically in Australia, partly because of a big increase in the participation rates in post-school education and partly because of a big influx of international students to the higher education sector. Projections of demand for the next decade reflect continued year-on-year growth in the educational sector ranging from 2.8% to 4.0% in AQF levels 3 and 4 (certificates 3 and 4) and 3.9% to 4.9% in AQF level 9, (postgraduate university), according to the Australian Workforce and Productivity Agency (AWPA, 2013).

In 2012, nearly 2.8 million people were enrolled in study for a qualification, with two-thirds of these students studying full time. Approximately 1.2 million (42%) of these enrolled people were attending a higher education institution, 764,000 (27%) were at school, 518,200 (18%) were at Technical and Further Education (TAFE) institutions, and 363,600 (13%) were at other educational institutions (ABS, 2012). Participation rates were slightly higher for women (53%) than for men (47%) overall, especially in the university sector, but men were still overrepresented in certain areas. For example, out of the 220,000 apprentices or trainees, 77% were men. Significantly, the highest number of apprentices and trainees, nearly 70,000, worked in the male-dominated construction industry.

All of the aforementioned sectors have relevance for HRD, but the VET sector is arguably the most relevant for HRD because of its size, and it is also the most distinctively Australian. The VET sector draws largely, but not exclusively, on public funds and has the goal of developing the vocational skills of the Australian workforce. The VET system evolved from the old apprenticeship system common in many Anglo-Saxon countries, and apprenticeships still form a big part of the system. Most occupations now have VET qualifications and competency standards in the AQF associated with them. Within the VET, training packages include elements such as competency standards and assessments guidelines based on minimum standards for competency requirements across different occupations. Typically, competence is assessed in the workplace and/or vocational setting. In all, more than 80 training packages have been introduced via tripartite industry bodies (industry training advisory bodies). While much of the delivery of training in the VET system is provided by the traditional, publicly funded, TAFE institutes, there has been a big growth in accredited private-sector providers since the 1990s. Overall, the training of workers in the VET system is a major element of HRD for the Australian economy. Most medium to large organizations in Australia participate in the VET system as training sites and employ significant numbers of graduates from the system.

INSTITUTIONS RESPONSIBLE FOR MACROLEVEL HRD IN AUSTRALIA AND NEW ZEALAND

New Zealand

In New Zealand, the Tertiary Education Commission (TEC), Te Amorangi Matuauranga Matua, is responsible for funding tertiary education, assisting people in reaching their full potential, and contributing to the social and economic well-being of the nation (The Tertiary Education Commission,

2013). The TEC has overall responsibility for funding tertiary education and training provided by universities, polytechnics, colleges of education, wānanga, private training establishments, industry training organizations, foundation education agencies, and adult and community education providers. The TEC coordinates its work with all other relevant stakeholders, such as industry and community groups, with the broad goal of developing knowledge and skills in New Zealand.

The work of TEC includes advising on tertiary education policies and priorities, providing guidance to organizations that wish to receive funding, gathering and publishing performance information, and undertaking reviews and consultations with the sector on aspects of tertiary education (TEC, 2013). Other government agencies that TEC liaises with and their roles include: the Ministry of Education, which advises on the government's budget, leads the development of the government's tertiary education strategy, and collects and publishes tertiary education statistics; the New Zealand Qualifications Authority (NZQA), which administers the NZQF, including registration of tertiary education organizations, and is the body primarily responsible for quality assurance matters in the sector; Creers New Zealand, which provides support and assistance to learners; the Ministry of Social Development, which funds employment training; StudyLink, which administers student allowances and student loan schemes; the Ministry of Business, Innovation, and Employment (formerly the Department of Labor), which provides labor market information to assist tertiary providers; and Immigration New Zealand, which provides migrant funding for ESOL programs (TEC, 2013).

The strategy and goals of the TEC are defined within the Education Act 1989. Under this law, and guided by the Minister for Education, Skills, and Employment, the TEC is required to issue a tertiary education strategy that sets out the government's long-term goals for tertiary education, as well as its current and medium-term priorities for tertiary education. This strategy sets the long-term direction and addresses economic, social, and environmental goals, as well as the development aspirations of Māori and other population groups.

The tertiary education strategy is used to guide investment decisions so as to maximize tertiary education's contribution to national goals and acts as a reference point for the government's policy making and in relationships with the sector. The formal strategy for 2010–2015 outlines the government's broad objectives in four key areas (TEC, 2013):

- Provide New Zealanders of all backgrounds with opportunities to gain world-class skills and knowledge.
- Raise the skills and knowledge of the current and future workforce to meet labor market demand and social needs.
- Produce high-quality research to build on New Zealand's knowledge base, respond to the needs of the economy, and address environmental and social challenges.
- Enable Māori to enjoy education success as Māori.

New Zealand is served by 39 industry training organizations that purchase training, set standards, and aggregate industry opinion about skills in the labor market. Under these industry training organizations, training has evolved from just apprenticeships to more lifelong learning for workers of all ages, some of whom might need retraining.

Trade unions in New Zealand play an important role in advocating for HRD both within individual workplaces and more broadly as key stakeholders with regard to HRD policy matters. The New Zealand Council of Trade Unions (NZCTU) also manages the Learning Representatives Program Akoranga Ngātahi (NZCTU, 2015), which is an initiative to work with employers and government to develop core workplace skills, especially language, numeracy, and literacy. The program's core is training and supporting over 400 elected learning representatives to advocate learning among their peers and build learning cultures in workplaces through work with peers, unions, employers, and other relevant stakeholders. The program is funded by the TEC and is also supported by Business New Zealand to train and support learning representatives from a wide variety of industries to advocate a learning culture within the workplace.

The NZCTU established the role and purposes of learning representatives in accordance with the fact that over 40% of the workforce in New Zealand does not have sufficient foundational learning skills to engage in continuing education and training. As noted, the country has a long-standing and extensive vocational learning framework, yet training has been inaccessible and disconnected from the needs of many in the workforce. Learning representatives are therefore expected to work with existing agencies to promote learning that is reflective of workers' general needs and cultural backgrounds, workplace needs, and focused on industry training programs.

The guiding principles behind the roles and responsibilities of learning representatives are to work in partnership with key stakeholders, to enhance productivity at the workplace, and to stimulate economic growth. Specific functions of these representatives include the following: promoting learning in general and industry-specific training in particular; providing information and advice about learning and training to workers; advocating for the learning needs of workers and the accessibility of training; working with coworkers to identify and access appropriate support for language, literacy, and numeracy issues in learning; working with others to explore additional learning issues, including those related to more effective participation at work and beyond; working in cooperation with employers, unions, industry training organizations (ITOs), and apprenticeship coordinators to promote training and learning and to facilitate first contact for new learners; maintaining a link with the appropriate ITO as part of its stakeholder group; coordinating activities with local ITO agents and assessors and with union representatives on ITO boards and standards committees; advocating and advising workers on the National Qualifications Framework (NQF) and pathways toward qualifications (NZCTU, 2015).

Australia

In Australia, there are a number of federal government agencies that have a role in influencing HRD policy and practice. These are currently undergoing restructuring after the election of the Liberal National Government in the second half of 2013 and are in a state of transition. On 18 September 2013, two new departments, the Department of Education (2014) and the Department of Employment (2014), were created to replace the former Department of Education, Employment, and Workplace Relations. In relation to HRD, the Department of Education is responsible for national policies and programs that help Australians access early childhood education, school education, post-school and higher education, as well as other policy areas, such as access to childcare. The Department of Employment, on the other hand, is responsible for HRD-related national policies and programs that assist people in finding and keeping work as well as industrial relations matters. In addition, the Australian Workforce and Productivity Agency (AWPA) also plays a key role in HRD by providing advice to the government on current, emerging, and future skills and workforce development needs. The AWPA consults with industry and education providers and conducts research and workforce studies to provide advice on skills and workforce issues, including demand for and supply of skills, particularly in specialized occupations and in priority industries; productivity and participation; the reform of the tertiary education sector; better use of skills in workplaces; and advice to the Australian government on the use of the National Workforce Development Fund (AWPA, 2014).

Another important Australian government department with a key HRD role is SkillsConnect (Skills Connect, 2014) which oversees key elements of enterprise training and skill development, including the apprenticeship system. SkillsConnect is the agency that links enterprises with support for skills and workforce development. In 2013–2014, it had a budget of $1.5 billion to support growth in skills, qualifications, productivity, more effective workforce planning and development, and, ultimately, social inclusion. Currently, SkillsConnect has four key areas of focus and activity: enterprise-based funding that provides government co-funding so that enterprises can meet their skills needs, skilling of the workforce and apprenticeship development by providing support for apprenticeships and international graduates, improving access to training and providing support for building foundation skills in the workforce, support for the National Training System by providing support for training agencies and vocational education and training information to the sector (Skills Connect, 2014).

In addition, SkillsConnect also administers eleven long-running Industry Skills Councils in key areas of the economy, such as automobiles, agriculture, and energy. These skills councils develop and implement workforce development strategies and relevant nationally endorsed qualifications to meet the current and emerging needs of enterprises, employees, and students in the sector that they represent. A key function is also to coordinate the goals of multiple stakeholders, including businesses, regional communities, research organizations, registered training organizations, the tertiary sector, industry bodies, trade unions, and representatives from the three tiers of government in Australia (SkillsConnect, 2014).

Another key role of SkillsConnect involves the administration of HRD-related support services to business. An example of this is a program called EnterpriseConnect, which provides expert assistance via consultants, business reviews, and funding opportunities to help small- and medium-sized businesses to reach their full potential. According to the AWPA, EnterpriseConnect has assisted more than 19,000 organizations through a range of services since 2008 (AWPA, 2014).

HRD FOR DIFFERENT SOCIOECONOMIC GROUPS AND LEVELS

According to the United Nations Human Development Index (UNHDI), Australia ranks second (behind Norway) and New Zealand ranks sixth among the top-ten developed countries in the world. The UNHDI measures health, education, and income indicators. Australia and New Zealand have populations with average life expectancies over 80 years. New Zealand scored particularly highly on education with mean years of schooling for adults of 12.5 years compared to 12.0 years in Australia, but incomes were significantly higher in Australia (UNHDI, 2013). So at a general level, the macro indicators suggest that HRD systems in Australia and New Zealand, in tandem with other economic and social policy initiatives, produce outcomes that are broadly beneficial to the respective populations.

Beyond aggregate measures, a number of characteristics associated with individuals have been found to influence access to employer-provided training in Australia. Data involving almost 14,000 employees and almost 1,500 workplaces reveals that, unlike other countries, there was little evidence of discrimination on the grounds of sex, parenthood, place of birth, and being an aboriginal or Torres Strait Islander. However, people on part-time and fixed-term contracts, people with low-potential experience, low-current job tenure, low-educational levels, and low-skilled vocational training were less likely to receive training (Almeida-Santos and Mumford, 2004).

Despite these findings, there is a need for more expenditure on training and development to equip Australians with the skills required to operate in a global economy. Research by the Australian Workforce and Productivity Agency (AWPA) has found, for example, that many Australians have poor language, literacy, and numeracy (LLN) skills. Specifically, 54% of Australians in the age range of 15 to 74 years were found to possess inadequate prose literacy skills. A similar percentage did not possess the necessary documentary literacy skills, and 47% had inadequate numeracy skills (ABS, 2012 and AWPA, 2013). Such skills are critical for building labor force participation and ongoing economic health, and the AWPA is particularly concerned that an OECD 2009 Program for International Student Assessment revealed that school students in Australia achieved a greater range of scores than the OECD average. The results are particularly poor for students from lower socioeconomic groups. As discussed earlier in the chapter, similar trends regarding inadequate levels of literacy and numeracy have also been identified in New Zealand (Industry Training Federation, 2007).

There is a strong relationship between the attainment of post-school qualifications and labor force participation. People who leave school in the early years of high school, such as years 9 or 10, are more likely to have lower workforce participation than other groups. Both men and women with degrees or higher qualifications enjoy the highest rate of participation (AWPA, 2013).

A number of groups have been identified as requiring training and development to improve labor force participation and skills. These include women and men engaged in gendered occupations and older workers. Women make up 80% of the workforce in traditional female industries, such as health care and social assistance, whereas men dominate mining, construction, and posts in the electricity, gas, water, and waste services (AWPA, 2013,p. 73). Industry initiatives are in place to increase the participation of women in the mining and resources sector and in manufacturing.

Older employees with lower skills are vulnerable to unemployment. The Australian government has implemented the Experience + Program, the Corporate Champions Program, and the Job Bonus Program. Experience + assists mature workers, who are classified as 45 years and over, to develop their skills so they can more effectively apply for a job, as well as providing training in IT and job-specific training. The Corporate Champions Program provides good examples of mature-age worker strategies in organizations, whereas the Job Bonus Program provides funding for employers who provide continuing employment to mature-age workers.

As discussed earlier in this chapter, the VET sector provides vocational training. In this sector, particular groups of people have been identified as disadvantaged learners. These include people with low LLN skills, people with a disability, mental health issues, low socioeconomic backgrounds, low incomes, and those in juvenile justice centers (AWPA, 2013). In South Australia, initiatives have been put in place to case manage disadvantaged learners.

As mentioned previously, there is a lack of training opportunities for casual and part-time employees and self-employed people. Approximately 25% of women are employed in casual positions that provide them flexibility but can also disadvantage their access to training and career progression (ACTU, 2012), so indirectly, women are disadvantaged with their access to training.

ORGANIZATIONAL TRENDS, SIMILARITIES, AND DIFFERENCES IN THE REGION

In a recent review of the Cranet data looking at organizational-level trends in Australian HRD over the last two decades, McGraw (2014) noted several key themes. First, the amount of training, as measured by training days, had remained relatively steady. Second, there was a marked decline in attempts to measure the utility of HRD programs themselves but a marked increase in the direct measurement of individual employee performance measures to target HRD. Initiatives such as formal career development plans, succession plans, job rotations, and individualized high-potential schemes had all increased substantially and there was a corresponding increase in the use of individual performance measurement. Third, the trends noted earlier were relatively consistent in both the public and private sectors. Fourth, larger enterprises were found to use more formal and sophisticated HRD methods than smaller entities. Fifth, there were marked differences in the level of HRD between organizations from different industries that reflected the evolution of activity in the Australian economy overall. Whereas, for example, civil engineering with mining and banking had increased HRD effort over the period under study, there had been a decline in the 'old economy' sectors, such as manufacturing.

The McGraw (2014) study also looked at differences in HRD between indigenous companies and foreign multinationals. There was some evidence that foreign firms manage HRD more intensively, but the differences were relatively minor and both groups were moving in the same direction in relation to overall HRD practices.

In New Zealand, there have been very few recent studies looking at overall HRD trends, although Pio (2007) is an exception. In her review, Pio (2007) notes that some form of training had become common in New Zealand enterprises. Using 2003 data, she reported that organizations spent an average of 3.7% of payroll on training but that the amount varied considerably depending on organizational size, with bigger firms spending more. Furthermore, whereas larger businesses had the scale to conduct formal in-house training, smaller firms tended to be more ad hoc and reliant on some of the government-sponsored industry training initiatives discussed earlier.

DISCUSSION

This chapter has highlighted the emergence, especially during the twentieth century, of an 'Australasian' HRD system, which was closely connected to broader institutional mechanisms in both countries relating to industrial relations and wider social and political outcomes. Despite broad similarities, many differences were also noted between the two countries.

In documenting the emergence of contemporary HRD mechanisms in both countries, the chapter has noted a profound historical shift away from the old models comprising high levels of state intervention and control toward new models, which are more economically liberal in character. Although the paths to modern practice were different, with New Zealand taking a more radical path, there are still broad similarities between institutional mechanisms in the two countries with ongoing legacies from the old models.

The overall outcomes of the HRD systems in both countries were noted to be generally positive using the broad measure of the UN Human Development Index. although challenges remain in both countries with regard to overall educational standards, workforce literacy, and social groups suffering from long-term economic disadvantage.

HRD challenges for the future in Australia and New Zealand can be found in a number of areas and are probably similar to those facing other developed countries: the changing nature of employing organizations that are increasingly likely to outsource work and invest less in HRD, the declining propensity and ability of governments to fund expensive HRD initiatives, the challenge associated with managing intergenerational workforces, and the increasing fragmentation of HRD with the growth of private providers in the area.

More specific HRD challenges for Australia and New Zealand can be found in three key areas. First, in responding to continuing rapid change and uncertainty with economies that are highly export dependent and integrated into the global economy. For example, an immediate challenge for the Australian economy in 2015 is adjusting to the pronounced downturn in terms of trade and overall demand for its key mineral exports after several years of boom and the resulting loss of employment and development opportunities in the sector. Second, and related to the aforementioned, is the requirement for large sections of the population in both countries to learn new skills as traditional sectors, such as manufacturing, continue to decline in overall employment terms. This challenge will be compounded for the most affected sections of the populations by the low literacy and numeracy levels discussed earlier. A third major challenge for both countries relates to their aging populations. Large numbers of 'baby boomers' are expected to retire within the next decade, leaving key skills gaps within both workforces, increasing burdens on social services, and shrinking taxation revenues to fund necessary provisions. Here though, perhaps there is some room for optimism, because in both countries there is scope for larger populations and hence the possibility, once again, for inward migration to help mitigate this problem.

Notwithstanding these challenges, the overall pattern of HRD in Australia and New Zealand from the start of the colonial era to the present day has shown systems that adapt well to their external environments. As such, there are reasons for optimism concerning the ability of both countries to overcome current challenges and continue to have HRD outcomes that are at or near the top of those in the rest of the developed world.

REFERENCES

ACTU (2012). *ACTU Women's Committee Submission to the Secure Jobs Inquiry* (2012), p 4. At http://securejobs.org.au/submissions/22_feb_2012/ACTU%20 Women's%20Committee.pdf (viewed 18 June 2015).

Almeida-Santos, F., & Mumford, K. A. (2004). Employee training in Australia: Evidence from AWIRS. *Economic Record*, 80: 553–564.

Australian Bureau of Statistics. (2012). *Education and Work Australia*, Catalogue No. 6227.0, May, ABS, Canberra.

Australian Workforce and Productivity Agency. (2013). *Future Focus: 2013 National Workforce Development Strategy*, Australian Government Publishing Service. Accessed 19 April 2015. (http://www.awpa.gov.au/our-work/Workforce%20develop ment/national-workforce-development-strategy/Pages/default.aspx)

Australian Workforce and Productivity Agency. (2014). Accessed 18 April 2015. (http://www.awpa.gov.au/Pages/default.aspx)

Bell, J. (2006). *I See Red*. Wellington: Awa Press.

Dawkins, J. S. (1988). *Industry Training in Australia: The Need for Change*. Australia Department of Employment, Education and Training (DEET), Australian Government Publishing Service, Canberra.

Department of Education. (2014). Accessed 12 December 2013. (http://education.gov.au)

Department of Employment. (2014). Accessed 12 December 2013. (http://employment.gov.au)

Department of Employment, Education, Training and Youth Affairs (DEETYA). (1996). *The Training Guarantee: Its Impact and Legacy, 1990–1994*. Main Report, AGPS, Canberra.

Di Maggio, P. J., & Powell, W. W. (1983). The iron cage revisited: Institutional isomorphism and collective rationality in organisational fields. *American Sociological Review*, 48(2): 147–160.

Hall, R. (2011). Skills and skill formation in Australian workplaces: Beyond the war for talent. In M. Baird, K. Hancock and J. Isaac (Eds.), *Work and Employment Relations: An Era of Change*, 78–92. Sydney: The Federation Press.

Holland, P., Sheehan, C., & De Cieri, H. (2007). Attracting and retaining talent: Exploring human resources development trends in Australia. *Human Resource Development International*, 10: 247–262.

Industry Training Federation. (2007). *Business New Zealand Skills and Training Survey*, 2007.

Kane, R. L., Abraham, M., & Crawford, J. D. (1994). Training and staff development: Integrated or isolated? *Asia Pacific Journal of Human Resources*, 32(2): 112–132.

Kramar, R. (2012). Trends in Australian human resource management: What next?, *Asia Pacific Journal of Human Resources*, 50(2): 133–150.

Mankin, D. P. (2001). A model for human resource development. *Human Resource Development International*, 4(1): 65–85.

McGraw, P. (2014). A review of human resource development trends and practices in Australia: Multinationals, locals, and responses to economic turbulence. *Advances in Developing Human Resources*, February, 16: 92–107.

McKeown, T., & Teicher, J. (2006). HRD in a deregulated environment. In H. DeCieri and P. Holland (Eds.), *Contemporary Issues in Human Resource Development: An Australian Perspective*, 25–51. Melbourne: Pearson.

Meyer, J. W., Rowan, B. (1977). Institutionalized organizations: Formal structure as myth and ceremony. *American Journal of Sociology*, 83: 340–363.

New Zealand Council of Trade Unions. (2015). Accessed 19 April 2015. (http://union.org.nz)

New Zealand Government. (2013). Accessed 10 December 2013. (http://www.societies.govt.nz/cms/registered-unions/annual-return-membership-reports/union-membership-return-report-2013/UnionMembershipNumbers2012.pdf/)

New Zealand Ministry of Education. (2013). *Technical and Vocational Education.* Accessed 16 December 2013. (http://www.minedu.govt.nz/NZEducation/EducationPolicies/InternationalEducation/ForInternationalStudentsAndParents/NzEdOverview/Technical_and_Vocational_Education.aspx)

Pio, E. (2007). International briefing 17: Training and development in New Zealand. *International Journal of Training and Development*, 11: 71–83.

Rimmer, M., Lee Rimmer, M., Chenhall, R., Langfield-Smith, K., & Watts, L. (1996). *Reinventing Competitiveness: Achieving Best Practice in Australia.* South Melbourne: Pitman Publishing.

Skills Connect Australia. (2014). Accessed 18 April 2015. (http://skillsconnect.gov.au/home/industry-skills-councils/)

Smith, A., & Hayton, G. (1999). What drives enterprise training? Evidence from Australia. *The International Journal of Human Resource Management*, 10(3): 251–272.

Teicher, J. (1995). The training guarantee: A good idea gone wrong. In F. Ferrier & C. Selby-Smith (Eds.), *The Economics of Education and Training*, 105–112. Canberra: Australian Government Publishing Service.

The Tertiary Education Commission. (2013). Accessed 18 December 2013. (http://www.tec.govt.nz)

Toulson, P. K., & Defryn, M. K. (2007). The development of human resource management in New Zealand. *New Zealand Journal of Human Resources Management*, 7: 75–103.

United Nations Human Development Index. (2013). Accessed 10 December 2013. (http://hdrstats.undp.org/en/countries/profiles)

Wright, C. (1995). *The Management of Labour: A History of Australian Employers.* Melbourne: Oxford University Press.

3 Human Resource Development in East Asia

Roziah Mohd Rasdi and Maimunah Ismail

INTRODUCTION

East Asia covers about 28% of the Asian continent and is one of the world's most populated places with more than 1.5 billion people. The population comprises 38% of the population of Asia and 22% of the world. This part of Asia has by far the strongest overall Human Development Index (HDI) improvement of any region in the world, nearly doubling its average HDI attainment over the past 40 years. Using Japan, South Korea, and Taiwan as samples, this chapter aims to analyze human resource development (HRD) components for East Asia. These countries, well known as the Asian Tigers, have developed into advanced and high-income economies. They also are notable for maintaining exceptionally high growth rates and rapid industrialization. They feature the growth of the East Asian economies and reflect the emergence of the Asian Economic Miracle.

This chapter presents the reviews of HRD components for Japan, South Korea, and Taiwan. The introductory section follows with the historical, social, and cultural context; the training and education system; the institutional context of HRD; organizational-level HRD; and summary comparisons between the countries. Indicators such as GDP per capita, years of schooling, gender inequality, labor force participation rates, Research and Development (R&D) percentage relative to GDP, and phases of development experienced by each country are briefly examined to highlight similarities and differences between the countries. The concluding section discusses HRD issues and challenges, as well as key similarities and trends within the countries. The reviews in this chapter are based mostly on data available from online sources and supplemented with data collected from empirical studies and national sources of information.

HISTORICAL, SOCIAL, AND CULTURAL CONTEXT

Japan

Japanese history has a wide span: from the ancient history of the golden age of classical Japanese culture with its development of strong centralized government; fractured government where political power was subdivided into the control of hundreds of local daimyo (samurai leaders); the prosperous and peaceful Edo period where the shogun was appointed by the emperor in 1603 and the closed-door policy was practiced; to the Meiji period, starting in the 1860s, which ended feudalism, as well as transformed an isolated, underdeveloped island into a world power that closely followed Western models. Subsequently, there was a full-scale war with China in 1937; the Soviet invasion of Manchuria; the attack on Pearl Harbor in December 1941, which led to war with the US and its allies, followed by the atomic bombings of Hiroshima and Nagasaki in August 1945. All have influenced Japan's future development. Under US occupation, a recovery strategy was successfully conducted in 1947–1948, and post-war inflation was terminated. After 1955, Japan enjoyed very high economic growth rates, becoming a world economic power, especially in engineering, automobiles, and electronics, accompanied by a significant increase in the standard of living and life expectancy. In the 1970s, economic growth slowed down to about 4%, followed by the Bubble Economy in the 1980s, and the New Growth strategy in the 2000s (Table 3.1). Japan is also referred to as a major economic power, has the world's third largest economy by nominal GDP, and the world's fourth largest economy by purchasing power parity.

A long history in such a challenging environment has had a profound effect on Japanese culture; people developed very strong cooperative ties as a collective survival mechanism. Japan's social stability is contributed to by the strong sense of family solidarity combined with lifetime employment of workers from the time they enter the company after completing education right up to retirement. Traditionally, layoffs and dismissals of employees were rare, even during times of recession. With Japan's economic downturn of the early 1990s, however, companies were forced to downsize. During the last 150 years of industrialization and economic development, the population has grown from around 30 million to its present size. The main cultural and religious influences came from China.

South Korea

South Korea experienced remarkable economic turnover during Park's rule in the early 1960s. The colonial era lasted from 1910 to 1945 and resulted in Korea becoming an underdeveloped country in the 1950s and early 1960s because of the added legacy of the Korean War (1950–1953), its agriculture-oriented economic structure, its limited availability of natural resources, and its small territory size (Kim, Kwon, & Pyun, 2008). Korea's economy, after passing through a full-scale, government-led industrialization period, resulted in a GDP per capita increase of almost 40 times from US$67 in 1953 to US$20,050 in 2007 Suh and Chen, 2007, p. 6). Domestic demand has led the growth with private consumption and facility investment having posted excellent figures. Exports have increased with a rise in overseas

Table 3.1 Human Development Index of Japan, South Korea, and Taiwan

HDI Rank	Countries (Land Area/ Population)	Years	HDI Indicators				5*			Phases of Development		
			1	2	3	4	F	M	6	1960s–1970s	1980s–1990s	2000s–2010s
10	Japan (377,944 km²; 126,659,683)	2000	0.878	28,889	14.6					Post-war reconstruction (Post-war High/ rapid Economic Growth)	Bubble Economy (Stable Growth) 1975–1996	New Growth Strategy
		2005	0.896	30,441	15							
		2012	0.912	30,660	15.3	0.131	49.4	71.7	3.26			
12	South Korea (100,210 km²; 50,219,669)	2000	0.742	10,209	11.9					Agriculture-based economy (basic input factors—land and labor)	Resource-led economy (infrastructure, risked-free capital, labor)	Innovation-led economy (knowledge-based factors— technology market
		2005	0.742	11,544	12.6							
		2012	0.769	13,672	12.6	0.153	49.2	71.4	3.74			
101	Taiwan (36,193 km²; 23,340,136)	2000	0.59	2,667	9.5					Factor-driven economy (import-export, education)	Factor-driven economy (capital-and-technology intensive)	Factor-driven economy (expansion of industries)
		2005	0.637	4,115	10.5							
		2012	0.699	7,418	11.7	0.213	67.7	80.1	1.76			

HDI Indicators: 1 – HDI Value, 4 – Gender Inequality Index (Data as of 2012)

2 – GDP per capita, 5*– Labor Force Participation Rate – F: Female, M: Male (Data as of 2011)

3 – Expected Years of Schooling, 6 – R&D% to GDP (2005–2010)

Note: Based on the UNDP Report (2013), data for Korea include South Korea and North Korea, and data for Taiwan include Taiwan and China.

Sources: Human Development Report (2013, p. 144–159) and (http://hdr.undp.org/en/).

demand amid the global economic recovery and backed by increased competitiveness of Korean products. Thus Korea has leaped ahead to become the world's eighth-largest exporting nation in 2012 with trade volume of US$1,080 billion, while achieving a trade surplus of over US$25 billion for the fourth year in a row.

Korean society is highly influenced by Confucianism, which emphasizes individual morality and ethics, political power by rulers, and the cultivation of the individual's mind rather than the development of technical skills (Kim et al., 2008). Politically, it practices a presidential representative democratic republic in which the president is the head of state, elected by direct popular vote for a single five-year term. Executive power is exercised by the government. Legislative power is vested in both the government and the National Assembly.

Intensive investment in education, particularly with substantial capital investment in 1960s' primary education, seemingly led to the rapid and sustained economic growth of South Korea. In the mid-1970s, the well-targeted industrial policy resulted in a major shift in the development of heavy and high-tech industries (e.g., chemicals, shipbuilding) and progress in science and technology. Policies were also directed toward technological capabilities and improving access to and quality of technical and vocational training. Accordingly, the focus of the Korean economic structure shifted in 1980s from imitation to innovation. The National Research and Development Program was established in the 1980s to develop a higher education system through investment in research and development capabilities geared to indigenous high-technology innovation. This expansion of the higher education system promoted an increase in the skilled labor force in the 1990s. Consequently, a knowledge-based economy was created with priority on learning alongside the establishment of a lifelong learning infrastructure. This transformation was led by private companies and universities with embedded knowledge/technology and human and social capital as the engine of growth.

Taiwan

Historically, up to 1945, royal Chinese bureaucrats and Japanese colonial administrators ruled Taiwan. Since 2008, the Nationalist Party of Taiwan, called the 'Kuomintang', has been in power. Members of the Nationalist Party ruling Taiwan are not natives of the land but belong to the Chinese regions. Their rule indeed has an immense effect on the whole of Taiwan society. Traditional religions include Buddhism, Taoism, and various folk beliefs. Christianity was introduced to Taiwan in the early seventeenth century by Spanish and Dutch missionaries. Due to its multicultural history and the existence of religious freedom, numerous other religions such as Bahá'í, Islam, and Tienlichiao (a Japanese religion) find prominent places among the Taiwanese. Confucian philosophy still spreads its roots, conferring

Taiwanese civilization with a specific view of life, and fostering a harmonious labor-management relationship in Taiwanese firms (Lin and Ho, 2009).

Taiwan's economic development was initially hampered by a scarcity of natural resources, shortages of capital and foreign exchange, technological backwardness, and lack of entrepreneurial skills. The government began to press forward with economic development plans around the 1950s, starting with advancing sweeping changes in agricultural production technologies while actively developing labor-intensive essential goods industries. The government's implementations of economic plans have provided the infrastructure and incentives needed to forward its policies for the rapid development of industrialization. Other major initiatives include the formulation of investment programs, the provision of low-interest loans, the establishment of industrial zones, export-processing zones, a science-based industrial park, the Ten Major Development Projects, the Twelve New Development Projects, and the Fourteen Key Projects in the 1970s and 1980s. The government also adopted various supplementary fiscal, financial, foreign-exchange, and trade-promotion measures to quicken the pace of industrialization (Fei, 1995). As a result of a long-term evolutionary process of entrepreneurial vision by the government, careful policy experimentation and market selection, Taiwan has been referred to by the World Bank as one of the East Asia's 'economic miracles'. The flexibility of Taiwan's government policy made it possible to abandon ineffective programs and devise new ones to meet changing conditions (Li, 1995).

PHASES OF DEVELOPMENT

Table 3.1 shows the phases of development experienced by each country. Japan, South Korea, and Taiwan have each experienced substantial phases of development. During the 1960s and 1970s, these countries struggled to reconstruct their nation's economies according to their focus and needs at that time. Japan and South Korea's developmental period started after WWII, reconstruction being a lengthy prerequisite to any increase in economic size, whereas each government worked very aggressively in industrial promotion and infrastructure building. As a result, Japan and South Korea managed to achieve steady economic growth in the 1970s, due also to effective strategies taken to repair the damage caused by the war. On the other hand, Taiwan had invested in education to provide skilled manpower for the progressing economy. Education and training were the leading factors of human development that contributed to economic expansion. Taiwan's intense focus on capital development led to better economic growth and stability. Japan experienced an economic bubble specifically from 1986 to 1991, bringing rapid expansion and acceleration of asset prices and of the economy. This bubble was closely associated with an excessive policy of monetary easing at that time but which did indeed increase Japan's economic size. Nevertheless, the Japanese asset-price bubble's collapse happened gradually within the Japanese economy starting from the year 1991 and continuing to 2000, sometimes called Japan's Lost Decade.

The current phase of development, from the 2000s to the present, has witnessed the emerging economies entering a more advanced national development. Due to the effect of globalization, all countries have to attune to the current demand caused by the interaction between domestic and foreign forces. These countries' modernization period, which began in the nineteenth century, has been marked by the various powerful strategies taken during the period from 2000 to the present. Japan introduced the New Growth strategy for revitalizing the nation, which sets forth strategies for achieving a strong economy. South Korea's scarcity in natural resources has motivated the country to look at its human capital as its biggest endowment: the country has invested heavily in education, science and technology, and more recently in a knowledge-based economy during the current phase of development. Taiwan, which had previously a manufacturing-based economy, involved itself rapidly in the knowledge-based industry through a phenomenal expansion of the semiconductor industry, particularly from 1994 to 1996. The Taiwanese government has in fact been implementing the Asia-Pacific Operations Centres (APROC) plan since 1996, aimed at liberalizing and modernizing Taiwan's outmoded service sectors (Chen, Chen, & Liu, 2001). As a result of this effort, the service industry has become increasingly important to Taiwan's economy.

EDUCATION AND TRAINING SYSTEMS

Japan

Japan's Basic Act on Education (March 1947), later revised in December 2006, clearly sets out principles for education, such as placing value on public-spiritedness and other forms of the normative consciousness that the Japanese people possess, as well as respecting the traditions and culture that have fostered this said consciousness. The basic national principles of education are equal opportunity, compulsory education, co-education, school education, social education, plus the prohibition of partisan political education, religious education, and the improper control of education.

The modern school system in Japan stems from the promulgation of the school system in 1872. Japan has an established 6–3–3–4-year system of school education aimed at realizing the principle of equal opportunity. Six years are spent in elementary school, three in lower secondary, three in upper secondary, and four or more in university. Upper secondary schools established, in 1948, offered full-time and part-time courses; and in 1961, correspondence courses were added to the system. The new system for universities began in 1949. Colleges of technology were initiated as an educational institution in 1962 to provide lower secondary school graduates with a five-year consistent education. At first, special schools were established separately based on types of disability but were then turned into a system of schools for special needs education that could accept several types of disabilities. Additionally, there were kindergartens for preschool children, specialized training colleges, and other miscellaneous vocational schools that offered technical courses or courses designed for various practical purposes. The upper secondary school courses are classified as: (i) General (providing mainly general education suited to the needs of both those who wish to advance to higher education and those who are going to get a job but have chosen no specific vocational area); (ii) Specialized (providing vocational or other specialized education for those students who have chosen a particular vocational area as their future career); (iii) Integrated (providing a variety of subject areas and subjects from both the general and the specialized courses to satisfy students' diverse interests, abilities, aptitudes, and future career plans.

The Japanese dual-style system has also been introduced where classroom lectures at educational/training institutions and practical training in companies are being implemented in parallel. The implementation ranges from short-term training (standard five-month period) to long-term training (one to two years). These model projects, implemented in special high schools, are offered in 20 regions; development of educational programs for special training schools are being implemented in 10 prefectures (Ministry of Education, Culture, Sports, Science and Technology).

The government and prefectures are obliged to provide vocational training for workers who intend to change their jobs as well as other persons who need special assistance for the development and improvement of their vocational abilities (Table 3.2). In Article 4–2 of the Human Resources Development Promotion Act, public human resources development facilities are to be established to provide various types of vocational training to meet individual worker's needs. The persons eligible for these facilities are unemployed workers, employed workers, and graduates.

Table 3.2 Public HRD Facilities in Japan

Category	Type of Vocational Training	Establishing Entity
Polytechnic Universities	Advanced vocational training for senior high school graduates, etc. (specialized course) More advanced, specific and practical vocational training for those who finished advanced course (applied course)	Japanese Organization for Employment of the Elderly, Persons with Disabilities and Job Seekers

(Continued)

Table 3.2   (Continued)

Category	Type of Vocational Training	Establishing Entity
Polytechnic Colleges	Advanced vocational training for senior high school graduates, etc. (specialized course)	Japanese Organization for Employment of the Elderly, Persons with Disabilities and Job Seekers Prefectures
Polytechnic Centers	Short-term vocational training for unemployed workers and employed workers	Japanese Organization for Employment of the Elderly, Persons with Disabilities and Job Seekers
Advanced Polytechnic Centers	Advanced and innovative vocational training in production-related fields mainly for middle-career engineers	Japanese Organization for Employment of the Elderly, Persons with Disabilities and Job Seekers
Polytechnic Schools	Vocational training for junior and senior high school graduates, unemployed workers, and employed workers, etc.	Prefectures Municipalities
Polytechnic Schools for Persons with Disabilities	Vocational training according to the ability and aptitude of persons with disabilities	The government (cf. Note) Prefectures

South Korea

South Korea's schooling system comprises six years of elementary school (primary education), three years of middle school, three years of high school (secondary education), and college/university and TVET (Figure 3.1). The compulsory and national common education (basic curriculum necessary for every citizen) consists of a nine-year education in primary and secondary schools. The beginning of vocational education in high school provides an option either to choose general or vocational high school among middle school graduates. High schools are geared to university entry and vocational high schools to employment after graduation. There are special-purpose high schools and autonomous private high schools that aim at providing advanced general and specific education on the basis of middle school education. The higher educational institutions are divided into four categories: four-year colleges and universities, two- to three-year vocational junior colleges and polytechnic colleges, the Air and Correspondence University, polytechnic universities, and other schools (including theological colleges and seminaries). The majority of higher educational institutions are under the supervision of the Ministry of Education, which manages student quotas, qualifications of teaching staff, and curriculum and degree requirements (Chung, 2013).

There are two categories of TVET in South Korea: vocational education from vocational high schools to vocational colleges, and vocational training from vocational training institutes of private/public sector and training centers within companies. Formal vocational education institutes include specialized high schools and vocational colleges, such as Korea Polytechnics. Students of polytechnics include school dropouts, unemployed people, and disadvantaged groups. As of 2012, there are 653 vocational high schools with 423,544 students in Korea accounting for 22.1% of total high school students (Chung, 2013).

The effective contribution of TVET, to meet rising labor demands by providing initial training for large populations of learners, has contributed to Korea's economic growth for the last 40 years. The enactment of the Vocational Training Law in 1967 expanded the volume of the vocational training institutes (Chung, 2013). In the 1980s, TVET was upgraded to raise the skills levels of workers. The integration of the Employment Insurance Act with the expansion of TVET institutions helped Korea grow out

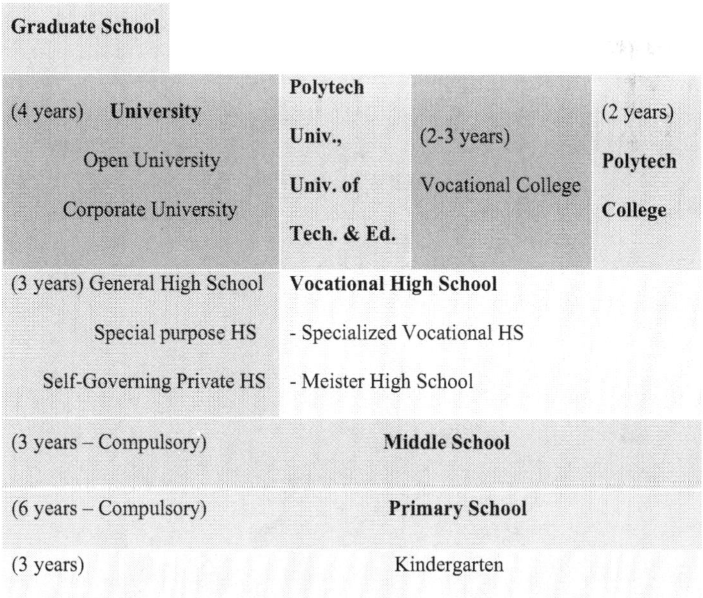

Graduate School				
(4 years) **University**	**Polytech Univ.,**	(2-3 years)	(2 years)	
Open University		Vocational College	**Polytech**	
Corporate University	**Univ. of Tech. & Ed.**		**College**	
(3 years) General High School	**Vocational High School**			
Special purpose HS	- Specialized Vocational HS			
Self-Governing Private HS	- Meister High School			
(3 years – Compulsory)	**Middle School**			
(6 years – Compulsory)	**Primary School**			
(3 years)	Kindergarten			

Figure 3.1   The Schooling System in South Korea

of the Asian financial crisis in the 1990s. Since 2000, the goal has been to streamline the division of roles and responsibilities and strengthen collaboration among TVET stakeholders. In order to overcome the skills and talent mismatch, wide-ranging efforts have been made to reform the TVET framework and its policies. The current agenda is to overhaul the TVET system to allow industries to take greater initiative and to be able to respond to the demand of industry by training and equipping learners with the necessary technological expertise and skills. Hence the TVET is being transformed into a consumer-led system (Eom, n.d.).

In 1965, changes in parents' confidence in education resulted in almost a 20-fold increase in the number of college students, plus a 15-fold increase of middle and high school students. Consequently, Korea's HRD level exceeded what would be the norm for a country with three times Korea's median per capita Gross National Product (GNP). The education explosion continued after the early 1960s right through to the '90s, well above the standards of the Organization for Economic Cooperation and Development (OECD). The expansion of secondary and primary school enrollments with the improvement in higher education has contributed greatly to the expansion of Korea's economy and its per capita growth. The effects of education on per capita growth are seen through: (i) increases in skills and productivity; (ii) investment in higher levels of R&D as a result of higher education and, specifically, the training of R&D personnel for firms as part of endogenous technical change; and (iii) the ability to transfer technology from more advanced countries by practicing them on the job. The entrance rate to tertiary education from general and vocational high schools has increased from 27.2% in 1980 to 82.5% in 2004 (Jang, n.d.). There remains, however, an increasing need for continuing education and lifelong education in the labor market. A society based on knowledge and information technology needs employees who are creative and able to adapt to rapid changes in society and that employees be given ample opportunity to study constantly via self-directed learning.

Taiwan

Taiwan's education system has undergone tremendous changes in line with economic development. In the 1960s, Taiwan moved into an expansionary period of import-export business, witnessing a rapid growth in the number of small and medium enterprises, all thirsting for skilled labor. In 1968, Taiwan started a nine-year compulsory education policy, abolished the junior vocational schools, and in their place rapidly expanded senior vocational schools and junior colleges. With a view to advancing the scale and quality of industries, the Ministry of Education encouraged private sectors to participate and establish their own schools in those areas necessary to provide an even more qualified middle-level labor force.

After the 1970s, Taiwan's traditional industries began the transition into capital-and-technology-intensive industries; and the demand for labor, while continuing to emphasize quantity, also started to look into quality. In order to continually increase the supply of better-educated manpower, the country focused investment in vocational and technical education. To elevate the quality of higher-level technological and vocational education, the Ministry of Education established the first technological college (Taiwan Institute of Technology), which was the forerunner of a now comprehensive TVE system that consists of vocational high schools, junior colleges, and colleges/universities of technology.

In the early 1980s, the government gradually increased the ratio between senior vocational schools and general high schools, finally reaching the goal of 7:3 with a view to supplying the labor requirements of the thirsting industry and allowing Taiwan's economy to quickly expand. By the mid-1980s, internationalization and the open market had significantly escalated demand for a higher level of technological and business personnel. Quality junior colleges were upgraded to colleges of technology, and quality colleges of technology were upgraded to universities of technology. Comprehensive high schools, offering curricula for both TVE and general high schools, were added, and the ratio between the number of students in senior vocational high schools and general high schools was increased. By the year 2010, this ratio reached 5.5:4.5, which mirrored the needs of market and time, reflecting a more effective education system.

Taiwan's educational system begins with nine years of free compulsory education. The system, in effect since 1968, starts with three years at the preschool level. This level is divided into two grades: preschool playgroup and kindergarten. Compulsory education in Taiwan takes place in both public and private schools. Individuals are required to spend six years in elementary school passing through six grades. The learning process continues at high school, which consists of two levels: junior and senior high school, three years for each. Education continues at the college or university level, which takes around four years. Both graduate and adult education programs have been expanding steadily, entrance being by examination given by individual departments within universities. Taiwan's special education schools cater to students with mental or physical disabilities, which vary depending on the different stages of education (includes kindergarten, primary school education for six years, junior high education for three years, and senior high/vocational education for three years). Supplementary education, on the other hand, is divided into five levels (supplementary primary school, junior high, senior high/vocational school, junior college, and open university) and is provided by both private and government institutions. Supplementary and continuing education institutions provide extensive and comprehensive learning opportunities for the general public, but graduates of supplementary education have to pass an additional qualification test before they can obtain a diploma.

INSTITUTIONAL CONTEXT OF HRD

Japan

In Japan, the HRD Bureau, which comes under the Ministry of Health, Labor, and Welfare, aims to establish an ability-based society, whereby an educational level is completed when people have acquired the skills needed for the job they desire and which best meets their skill set. People can upgrade their skills by availing of opportunities to do so, and the vocational skills they acquire are then appropriately evaluated, encouraging them to acquire even more.

In July 2006, the Ministry of Health, Labor, and Welfare formulated the Eighth Basic Plan for HRD. Based on this plan, it works on measures and policies, such as the provision of diversified vocational training opportunities; the establishment of labor-market infrastructure (socioeconomic infrastructure), including the enhancement of ability evaluation systems and vocational career support; the provision of sustainable career development support throughout workers' lives; reinforcement of 'in the field excellence'; and skills inheritance and advancement. Moreover, the plan covers:

(i) A practical system for HRD, established to develop and improve practical vocational abilities;

(ii) Provision was made for reducing working hours and for taking leave in order to prepare for reemployment as well as other measures. These measures were proposed to employers as ways to promote spontaneous development and improvement of vocational capabilities in workers;

(iii) Regulations of these established.

Other measures were taken through the "Law for Partial Amendment of the HRD Promotion Law and the Act on the Promotion of Improvement of Employment Management in Small and Medium-Sized Enterprises for Securing Manpower and Creating Quality Jobs".

In addition, the Ninth Basic Vocational Ability Development Plan has been established with future directions, such as:

(i) The urgent task of cultivating human resources in fields with potential for growth, especially in manufacturing, which is the fundamental industry in Japan with international competitiveness;

(ii) Establishing a framework that allows job seekers who are not covered by unemployment insurance smooth access to vocational training as a part of the employment safety net;

(iii) Improving the vocational ability evaluation system connected to educational training to contribute to the formation of a labor market based on individual abilities;

(iv) Providing vocational ability development assistance to individuals and companies;

(v) National and local governments, private educational training organizations, companies sharing roles, and consideration of the need of companies and regions for the provision of necessary vocational training.

South Korea

Essential areas of HRD in Korea include: education and training; deployment of human resources in the labor market and re-education and retraining; necessary infrastructure, such as communication channels for effective development and deployment of human resources; and the increased demand for innovative manpower. Korean National Human Relations Development (NHRD) aspires to improving individuals' quality of life and to strengthening national competitiveness in order to achieve the goal of becoming one of the world's top-ten knowledge powers. NHRD has successfully redesigned the national HRD system in order to cultivate people's basic competence, to develop talents with competitive advantage, and to establish an infrastructure for national HRD.

Government ministries place great emphasis on harnessing HRD effort and its implementation at the higher level; they also apply macro HRD to strengthen national competitiveness. Enterprise has taken charge of micro HRD in the form of organizational reform, company policy revisions toward greater productivity, and by incentive programs aimed at boosting performance by individuals, groups, and organizations. Figure 3.2 presents the ministries that contributed significantly to Korean HRD.

Korean policies act as a driving force of national development for a fast growth economy, including the improvement of social security, which plays a central role in active labor market policy, and leading the transformation of training governance from a government-led public training to a market-led paradigm marked by voluntary participation and government support (Uh, 2013). The direction of Korea's policy has changed significantly every decade or so, which has helped to drive the economy toward a brighter and more prosperous future. The Asian financial crisis in 1997 made Korea take on bold reforms to bring about a speedy recovery. Increased transparency, meeting global standards, and policies to facilitate start-ups were initiated by Korean businesses. Since 2000, innovation has topped the national agenda. Korea is promoting business-friendly policies and policies enhancing cooperation between large companies and small and medium enterprises (SMEs). The current economic policies that have underpinned Korea's significant growth have emphasized the development of a vigorous, export-oriented manufacturing industry, with a progressive shift toward high technology.

The enactment of the Korea Vocational Training Management Corporation Act in December 1981 led to the establishment of the Korea Vocational

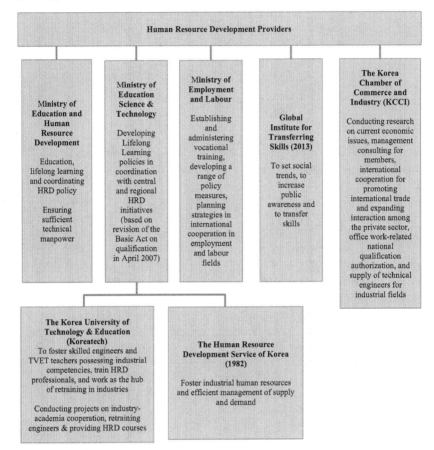

Figure 3.2   HRD Providers in South Korea

Training Management Corporation in March 1982 and the establishment of the Korea University of Technology and Education in July 1989. The Labor Vocational Training Promoting Act, a government statute, regulates organizational and financial support. Other acts related to TVET are: the Vocational Training Act (January 1967), which initiated the vocational training system and established many vocational training institutes; the National Technical Qualifications Act (amended December 1973), established to clarify standards and to develop the qualification system consisting of five levels (craftsman, industrial engineer, engineer, master craftsman, and professional engineer), 27 job fields, 180 job types, and 556 items; and the Framework Act on Qualifications (amended March 1997), which designates qualifications as national or private and defines the basic articles of the qualification system.

To strengthen its policy measures for meeting the challenges and changing trends of HRD, government launched communications campaigns to increase public interest in science and technology, built a state-sponsored system for developing human resources, and ensured its effective application in the corporate sector.

Taiwan

The Taiwan government's intervention and commitment to HRD has not only supported enterprise training and employee development but also transformed the workforce from labor intensive to skill intensive. A range of organizations significantly contribute to Taiwan's HRD, including government departments, the Workforce Development Agency, and the Occupational Safety and Health Administration. The government's emphasis on HRD has led Taiwan to becoming one of the most powerful economies in the world. Although other factors such as government financial policies and market forces have influenced Taiwan's economic growth, the government policies that highly value human capital point to the contribution of HRD in this growth. The role of the government in Taiwan has been a most controversial issue (Yu, 2007). Not only has the Taiwan government not pursued a noninterventionist or neutral policy, it has rather intervened extensively in the economy by actively promoted the development of many new industries, including many that have become internationally competitive (Yu, 2007). Starting from the 1950s, the government developed supportive HRD policies to promote vocational training nationwide for the highly skilled technical workforce. For instance, the fourth four-year economic development plan (1965–1968) explicitly included a chapter on HRD for the first time.

One of the most dramatic government policies putting the HRD concept into action is the legislation referred to as the Civil Servant Lifelong Learning Act enacted by the Legislative Yuan in 2002. The vision of this legislation is to build an integrated human resource system by promoting innovation, continual learning, and self-management learning in order to improve the quality of civil services in terms of effectiveness and efficiency, with an ultimate goal of building a learning government (Chen, Holton, & Bates, 2005). The promotional work of the Taiwan TrainQuali System is one of the major national employee training and development policies that motivates and even forces the corporations to cultivate their manpower.

Taiwan's midterm administrative plans from 2009 to 2012 focused on moving toward the following goals: a high-quality labor force, strengthening job security, implementing of humane labor conditions and a labor insurance annuity system, promoting workplace equity, strengthening workplace democracy, expanding dialogue mechanisms with society, and establishing a secure and healthy work environment to promote labor safety and health.

To implement a humane labor force and to promote workplace equity, the following acts were reviewed, modified, or enacted:

- Labor Standards Act: encourages employer-employee negotiation on shorter working hours and flexible hours to safeguard sensible labor rights.
- Gender Equality in Employment Act: creates a gender-friendly work environment with equal working rights, strengthens awareness of gender quality in the workplace, and enhances the authentic equality in gender.
- Employment Services Act: promotes antidiscrimination in employment through enhancing functions of the Employment Discrimination Review Committee and by raising awareness of antidiscrimination and rights protection in employment among employers, labor, and the general public.
- Labor Insurance Act: promotes a labor insurance annuity system and establishes a labor insurance annuity system for the elderly, disabled, and survivors in order to secure the life of laborers and their families in the long run.
- Labor Pension Act: focuses on voluntary participants in terms of reviewing the entry barriers to starting annuity insurance and to improving related laws and regulations.
- Labor Education Act: establishes a Labor Education Fund specifying educational scope, fund sources, fund allocation methods, etc., to improve the labor education laws and regulations.
- Group Employer-Employee Relations Act: establishes a ruling mechanism regarding improper laboring and sets up the Ruling Committee for Improper Laboring to secure solidarity, negotiation, and dispute rights for labor.
- Vocational Safety and Health Act: promotes labor safety and health laws and regulations to create a work environment that is safe, healthy, and conformable.

In addition, the Ministry of Education announced a number of policies with a view to: counteracting Taiwan's deficiencies that have contributed to raising the number and quality of researchers, enhancing science and technology education, revising the current income tax system for the purpose of encouraging lifelong studies, boosting part-time and recurrent education opportunities, improving foreign language capabilities, and encouraging exchange research (Chien, 2007).

ORGANIZATIONAL-LEVEL HRD

Japan

Japanese training and development practices are characterized by the systematic use of on-the-job training and the content of employee on-the-job learning. Training and development tends to be planned and executed in a diligent and disciplined manner at every level in the organization. The job-card system is important in Japan and is a system in which vocational training is provided at enterprise workplaces in association with education/training institutions that provide certificates after completion of the training for utilization in job-seeking activities. They aim to enhance skill recognition and transferability across employers and sectors.

South Korea

Organizational-level HRD in Korea focuses on developing job-related knowledge and skills and on molding current and future managers to fit into corporate culture. The role and outcome of training and development is linked closely to the evaluation and promotion of employees. These initiatives generally promote a skills-development framework with a view to realizing a competency-oriented society. The main context includes skills development throughout working life, skills development as a universal right, expansion of a competency-oriented system and culture, maintenance of a TVET advancement system, reinforcement of workplace competency, harmonization of work and education, and support for 'employment first, university later' choice. Korean organizations focus on both structured training programs and unstructured informal learning experiences to cultivate the learning climate.

HRD functions in organizations are as follows:

(i) Employee resourcing: include recruitment on demand, selection, and contracts; job mobility (lifetime career) and development of professional.

(ii) Annual employee rewards: based on individual ability or performance; merit pay based on competence and performance used; evaluation for pay increases; appraisal feedback; 360-degree appraisal of supervisors, subordinates, customers, and suppliers.

(iii) Employee development: classified as new recruits and existing employees; in-house and external; language proficiency, job ability, character building; and basic and advanced courses. Emphasis on training, including overseas programs; differentiated training; numerical flexibility context.

(iv) Employee relations: include enterprise-based union and federations, more freedom, involvement of knowledge workers, information sharing.

Taiwan

In Taiwan, organizational-level practices of HRD are mainly concentrated on training. Increased training efforts are emerging to facilitate the shift from traditional labor-intensive and cost-based industries to more knowledge-intensive sectors. In training and development practices, job rotation is generally perceived to be most effective, followed by in-house training and outside training (Drost, et al., 2002). Jean (1993) concluded that training in large-scale enterprises is mainly focused on in-service specialized training, orientation for new employees, and leadership training for potential heads. Orientation for new employees in small- and medium-size enterprises constitutes the major element of training, followed by safety and hygiene training, and on-the-job specialized training. Other significant components of Taiwan-organizational HRD are career development, organizational development, continuous learning, and self-management learning, with an ultimate goal of building a learning government.

SIMILARITIES AND DIFFERENCES IN SELECTED COUNTRIES

Table 3.3 shows a summary comparison of HRD in Japan, South Korea, and Taiwan. It is based on reviews of the literature.

Table 3.3   Comparisons of HRD in Japan, South Korea, and Taiwan

	Japan	South Korea	Taiwan
Historical Context	Four major periods: that in which emperors held real power, the period of samurai governments, that of modernization and military invasion, and that of the period of post–World War two growth. Japan absorbed successive external shocks and used them positively for change and new growth. The country retained its national identity throughout the process. There was a lack of natural resources.	Differences between political, economic, and social systems led to the Cold War from 1948, which divided Korea into South and North Korea. In 1950, the United Nations recognized South Korea as the sole legal government of Korea. The country has limited natural resources and high population density.	Since 1624, Taiwan has been ruled by foreign regimes, such as the Dutch, Koxinga, Ching, Japan, and the Republic of China, which led to modernized society. In 1945, Taiwan was liberated from colonial rule, experienced an economic miracle, and introduced political democracy achievements. Since 2008, it is governed by the Nationalist Party of Taiwan called the 'Kuomintang'. The country has limited natural resources.

	Japan	South Korea	Taiwan
Development context	From a weak, agricultural backward country with low technology to a New Growth strategy.	From a typical labor surplus economy, transformed into agriculture-based economy, to an innovation-led economy.	From import-export and education to expansion of industries.
Scope of HRD	Includes working adults, undergraduate and graduate students, handicapped adults, and new graduates. Focuses on vocational training for the public, supports vocational ability development in the private sector, establishes systems to evaluate vocational ability, and promotes international cooperation in the field of HRD.	Innovation of a national HRD system involving development of globally competitive core talent, empowerment of all citizens for lifelong learning, and facilitation of social integration and educational and cultural welfare.	Training oriented. Government intervention, vocational and technical education, social network, and organizational structures are the key factors that influence the training and development process.

CONCLUSION: SIMILARITIES, TRENDS, ISSUES, AND CHALLENGES

Japan, South Korea, and Taiwan have all successfully entered a period of high growth using HRD strategies. Based on the reviews of these developed economies in East Asia, some common trends can be identified. These countries demonstrate their unique history in HRD despite their deficiencies in natural resources. Their late development as capitalist countries has given them considerable advantages. They also share many similar cultural features and a strong work ethic.

The three countries have experienced significant economic and sociopolitical growth over the past ten years. Starting from very low levels of development in the 1950s and early 1960s, these countries have enjoyed tremendous success in human capital formation, which further contributed to economic miracles, social development, and political transformation. The main factors that account for the countries' extraordinary performance is their undivided commitment to human capital investment. The role of education in developing and unleashing human capital potential is highly significant. The expansion of education and training in these countries was also dramatic during the same period.

These countries experienced rapid development in primary education, followed by an intense growth in higher education. A typical characteristic of the education and training systems in these countries is the strong focus on vocational education in order to supply for the ever-increasing demands of skilled manpower needed for industrial growth. All three countries emphasized vocational education, starting at the high school level and leading on to colleges, institutes of private/public sector, and training centers within companies. Today, the education and vocational developments at all levels in these countries are very high.

All of these countries (Japan, South Korea, and Taiwan) have limited natural resources. In addition, Taiwan possesses only a small area of land that can be utilized for nation development (23,340,136 people; 36,193 km^2) (Table 3.1). These factors have compelled these countries to concentrate on HRD, reaping thereby rich benefits: both their strong HRD systems and their high-quality educated and skilled workforce have caused them to flourish economically in the region, despite their limited natural resources. This swift development is due to expansionist policies in higher education, allowing rapid growth combined with public or private investments.

Investment in human capital is regarded as the cornerstone of nation building and the key factor of economic development for Japan, South Korea, and Taiwan. Such development is made possible by several factors: rapid economic growth, a declining rate in population growth, increase in the aging population, plus cultural and political factors. These elements not only allow the countries to spend more and more on education and training but also to restructure their education system for improvements in quality and equity. Among the important cultural factors that contribute to this success are the Confucian values of knowledge and education, especially in Korea, Taiwan, and Japan. On the political side, the commitment of government and other HRD providers provides essential support to continuous effort in developing and sustaining human capital. All these factors have been considerably related to the HRD process and have positively influenced both the demand and supply factors relating to human capital investment, thus transforming human capital into a potentially significant asset of development.

The phases of development for the three countries indicate the close relationship between HRD, productivity, and competitiveness. A knowledge-driven society requires a significant increase in the number of highly trained people to manage those in technical, professional, and managerial positions. HRD is fundamental to this development. It must remain coherent with developmental policies and form an integrated part of comprehensive economic, labor market, and social policy by providing programs that promote economic and employment growth (Khan, 2005). The experience of these countries through several phases of development clearly shows that these nations have exhibited the economic conditions necessary for high growth trajectories as promoted by the World Bank. Precursors to such results are macroeconomic stability, sustained growth in productivity, significant investment in technology, and continued investments development. However, these qualities only work because of specific government guidance, planning, policies, and interventions, especially in developing the human capital of the nations. These countries did achieve rapid growth because of their deliberate and planned actions, not by chance or accident, and a significant part of those actions were the skills formation policies linked to sector development policies. HRD investment through education and training plus the equipment of these countries with skilled manpower have provided the necessary ingredients for development.

ISSUES AND CHALLENGES

Despite all of these successes, Japan, South Korea, and Taiwan still experience several issues and challenges that occasion setbacks for HRD in each country. With regards to the Japanese, they recognized the issues they currently face are due to structural changes in labor supply and demand that are significant against the background of changes in the social and economic environment, such as the declining birth rate, an aging population, and changes in industrial structure and globalization. Japan's population remains roughly unchanged but recently has entered into a declining phase. It is projected that by 2060, the total population will drop below 90 million, while the aging population ratio will be about 40%. In addition, the increase in the number of non-regular employees who lack opportunities for vocational ability formation has accelerated. In order to establish a sustainable and vital economic society, it is essential to improve their working abilities and productivity for all individuals in society, including the young generation, females, the elderly, the disabled, and non-regular employees.

As for Korea, it is facing challenges in terms of an increasing the aging population and the proportion of women workers (Kim et al., 2008). As life expectancy increases, the percentage of the population over 65 is consistently increasing as a result of health-care quality and a low national birth rate. It is expected that the population of over 55 years will have increased from 19% in 2000 to 30% in 2020, while the active working population will have decreased from 48% in 2000 to 37% in 2020. Meanwhile, the percentage of those in age group 15–29 will have declined from 32% in 2000 to 18% in 2020 (Kim, 2005). The Aging Index reveals that 47.4% of all adults were 65 years old or older in 2005 (Korea National Statistical

Office, 2005). The index presents overall patterns of the aging population by comparing population numbers: for every 100 children there are 47.4 senior citizens, and this is expected to rise to 124.2 senior citizens by 2020. This could be problematic for corporations, because it reflects the decline in the available human resource (Kim et al., 2008).

The number of working women is steadily increasing. The population graph of female employment resembles an M-curve, meaning that most employed women are either fresh college graduates or women in their 40s, whereas the number of employed women in their 30s is relatively small (Koh, 2005). The number of employed women workers aged between 25 and 29 stands at 63.7%, between 30 and 34 at 50.3%, and from 40 to 49 at 64.1% (Korea National Statistical Office, 2005). The "double workload" seems to be the reason for this phenomenon among women. Most female workers often suffer hardships balancing home and work and, consequently, leave their job to pursue family life. Moreover, although the number of women in the workforce has continuously increased in Korea, the majority are low-educated women who are employed in sales or service industries, such as 'pink collar' workers, operators, or laborers (Jang and Merriam, 2004). Likewise, women in this category partake in only marginal, supportive, and even repetitive work with a low possibility of promotion to higher positions (Kim et al., 2008). These challenges raise national concern about sustaining HRD, which consequently effect national economy and development.

In Taiwan, there are many changes that have brought significant challenges to HRD practices. Globalization has fuelled the competitive environment, making organizations' ability to successfully attract, develop, and retain talent in competition with other countries a paramount priority. Concurrently, organizations in Taiwan also face challenges in changing workforce demographics and related skill gaps. During the past decade, this change was represented by a trend of nearly zero growth population, a decline in birth rate, increase in the aging population, and in new immigrants, mainly from Southeast Asia (Wang, 2008).

Globalization has resulted in Taiwan becoming part of one interdependent global market place characterized by worldwide competition. The education and skills of the workforce will be the key competitive weapon for organizations (Chien, 2007). Changing organizational structures and work patterns necessitate HRD focusing on a small core of professionals, technicians, and managers and on more investment in the management and training of part-time and temporary workers. All these factors, plus technological changes, have led to the flexibility and more customized production of goods and services rather than mass production in long production lines. As the workforce becomes more mobile in response to changing organizational structures, one impact on work patterns is the emergence of relationship organizations, known also as virtual corporations. These kinds of corporations need workers who are highly skilled, reliable, and educated; able to understand the new forms of information; adaptable; and able to work efficiently with others without face-to-face contact. These work-pattern changes are increasingly taking place in Taiwan. HRD policies and programs will have to change in response to these changes (Chien, 2007).

REFERENCES

Chen, H., Holton III, E. F., & Bates, R. (2005). Development and validation of the learning transfer system inventory in Taiwan. *HRD Quarterly*, 16(1): 55–84. doi:10.1002/hrdq.1124

Chen, T. -J., Chen, S. -H., & Liu, M. -C. (2001). *Implications, Challenges, and Prospects for Taiwan in the Knowledge-Based Economy*. East-West Center Working paper (no. 35, September 2001). Honolulu, Hawaii: East-West Center.

Chien, M. -H. (2007). A study of HRD and organisational change in Taiwan. *Journal of American Academy of Business, Cambridge*, 11(1): 309–314.

Chung, J. (2013). Vocational education system. In Y. -B. Park & J. Chung (Eds.), *Vocational Education and Training in Korea*, 32–68. Korea Research Institute for Vocational Education and Training (KRIVET). (http://www.krivet.re.kr)

Drost, E. A., Frayne, C. A., Lowe, K. B., & Geringer, J. M. (2002). Benchmarking training and development practices: A multi-country comparative analysis. *Human Resource Management*, 41(1): 67–86.

Eom, J. C. (n.d.). *TVET System in Korea*. (http://www.hrdkorea.or.kr/)

Fei, J. C. H. (1995). Introduction. In K.-T. Li (Ed.), *The Evolution of Policy Behind Taiwan's Development Success* (2nd ed.), 29–52. Singapore: World Scientific.

Human Development Report. (2013). *The Rise of the South: Human Progress in a Diverse World*. New York: United Nations Development Programme (UNDP). (http://www.hdr.undp.org)

Jang, C. W. (n.d.). *Human Resources Development System, Policy and the Contribution of HRD to Economic Growth in South Korea*. (http://eng.krivet.re.kr/eu/index.jsp)

Jang, S. Y., & Merriam, S. B. (2004). Korean culture and the reentry motivations of university graduated women. *Adult Education Quarterly*, 54(4): 273–290.

Jean, J. Z. (1993). A survey and analysis of 1,000 large scale enterprises: HRD training status in Taiwan. *Journal of Labour Studies*, 121(10): 1–18.

Khan, M. A. (2005). HRD, competitiveness and globalization: A South Asian perspective. *Journal of HRD*, 1(1): 15–54.

Kim, H., Kwon, D. B., & Pyun, C. (2008). Korean corporate HRD in transition: Issues and challenges. *HRD International*, 11(1): 81–89. doi:10.1080/13678860701782428

Kim, M. H. (2005). *HRD for Knowledge Economy: Reforming the Role of Government*. (http://www.adbi.org/conf-seminar-papers/2005/11/01/1468.hrd.policy.korea/)

Koh, H. W. (2005). Yeosung injukjawongaebal-kwa yeosung koyong changchul [HRD for women and the employment of women]. *The HRD Review*, 8(1): 76–83.

Korea National Statistics Office. (2005). *Korean Statistical Information Service*. (http://www.kosis.kr).

Li, K,-T. (1995). *The Evolution of Policy behind Taiwan's Development Success* (2nd edition). Singapore: World Scientific.

Lin, L., & Ho, Y. (2009). Confucian dynamism, culture and ethical changes in Chinese societies: A comparative study of China, Taiwan, and Hong Kong. *The International Journal of Human Resource Management*, 20(11): 2402–2417.

Suh, J. & Chen, D. H. C. (2007). *Korea as a Knowledge Economy: Evolutionary Process and Lessons Learned.* Washington, DC: World Bank. (http://hdl.handle.net/10986/6755)

Uh, S. (2013). *Vocational Education and Training in Korea: A Historical Approach.* (https://www.kdevelopedia.org)

Wang, C. (2008). Enhancing the interactive relationship between lifelong learning and social changes to carry out a learning society in Taiwan. *International Journal of Lifelong Education,* 27(5): 535–542.

Yu, F. -L. T. (2007). The architect of Taiwan's economic miracle: Evolutionary economics of Li Kuo-Ting; Global economic review: Perspectives on East Asian economies and industries. *Global Economic Review,* 36(1): 53–67. doi:10.1080/12265080701217249

4 Human Resource Development in South Asia

Satish Pandey, Gertrude I. Hewapathirana and Dinyar M. Pestonjee

INTRODUCTION

Understanding HRD in Southeast Asia cannot be complete without look-ing at prominent global and regional economic, political, and technological trends. Among these, the most critical are the globalization of economies, accelerated technology and innovation, the information and communication revolution, rapid organizational change and outsourcing of manufactur-ing/services operations of multinational corporations (MNCs). The role of HRD has been invaluable in preparing a diversified workforce by unleash-ing human expertise to face the challenges arising from the rapidly changing global business environment. However, South Asian countries often suf-fer from ineffective government policies, political uncertainty, and lack of trained HRD experts to initiate effective HRD practices at multiple levels. Inadequate emphasis of respective governments on enhancing employee pro-ductivity and organizational change has made most South Asian countries vulnerable to rapid global changes, thereby increasing poverty combined with social, political, and economic inequality. Slow economic growth and increasing youth unemployment (9.6% compared to global youth unem-ployment of 4.2%) has aggravated this situation (ILO, 2012). Even though globalization has influenced expansion of international markets, the acceler-ated speed of business transactions, aided by information communication technologies, and internationalization of MNCs, South Asian countries still lag behind compared to their neighboring Asian Tigers: Singapore, Taiwan, and South Korea.

As a region, South Asia is unique in the world. It consists of eight coun-tries: Afghanistan, Bangladesh, Bhutan, India, Maldives, Nepal, Pakistan, and Sri Lanka, all of which are currently members of the South Asian Asso-ciation of Regional Cooperation (SAARC), a regional cooperative associa-tion founded in 1985 in Kathmandu, Nepal. These countries have historical, political, social, and cultural linkages that connect them with each other. India is the largest country of the region (in terms of its geography, econ-omy, and population) and quite ahead of its neighbors in terms of HRD policies and practices at different levels. It also has the largest workforce available for its industries and the largest pool of educational and scientific research institutions. It is the most culturally diverse country in the region followed by Pakistan, Sri Lanka, and Afghanistan, whereas Nepal, Bhutan, Bangladesh, and Maldives are relatively homogenous. Political uncertainty, poor governance, corruption, violation of human rights, poverty and poor investment are important factors that cannot be ignored when discussing HRD policies and practices in South Asia. Compared with other regional associations (e.g., ASEAN, EU, GCC) SAARC has yet to reach its goals of developing a regional free-trade zone, inward investment, and mutual business partnerships, all of which are crucial for optimal utilization of human resources of member countries. At the Fourth SAARC Summit (December 29–31, 1988) the heads of the states and governments of the member countries agreed to establish the SAARC Human Resource Development Centre (SHRDC) in Islamabad, Pakistan, with the objective of developing knowledge and skills by undertaking research, imparting training, disseminating information on HRD issues, and to advise the member states on HRD-related policies and strategies. To promote management education, training, research, and professional collaborations among scholars, researchers, and industry practitioners of South Asian countries, leading management institutes and university departments of the SAARC countries launched a pan-SAARC association of management professionals called the Association of Management Development Institutions of South Asia (AMDISA) in 1988. Recognizing the importance of HRD at the twelfth SAARC Summit, (January 4–6, 2004) held in Islamabad, SAARC member countries decided to establish a network of centers of higher learning, training, and skills development institutes (SDIs) across all the member countries. The main objective behind establishing these network organizations was to share the indigenous knowledge and human resources of the different countries in the region, as well as to work on its economic and social development.

The different knowledge and practice landscape of HRD in South Asia differs greatly from Western regions with its multifaceted and multilayered philosophies and practices (Walton, 2003). The contribution of HRD to the broader goals of economic, political, and social development in South Asian countries is heavily dependent on the understanding of social and political environments, demographic changes, and stages of economic development (McLean and McLean, 2001). Although there are some similarities in HRD across the South Asian nations, their socio-cultural and economic variations have impacted differently in shaping the HRD philosophies and practices in each nation. Therefore, studying each country is important to understand the uniqueness of their national HRD practices (McLean, 2004; Cho and McLean, 2009). Hence a multilevel approach that includes region, nation as a whole, organization, individuals, and society will provide knowledge central to understanding varying HRD philosophies and practices in these countries (Garavan et al., 2004). Equally important aspects to examine are the complex interactions between cultures, institutions, societal norms, and government regulations. With these we gain understanding of this field (ILO, 2002; Stiglitz, 2002; Edward and Kuruvilla, 2005).

This chapter attempts to reflect on the historical evolution of HRD philosophies, policies, and practices in South Asian countries in order to see how they influence national development at different levels. Moreover, this chapter reflects on similarities and differences in HRD philosophies, policies, practices, and the role of national stakeholders in specific sociopolitical contexts of South Asian countries.

THE HISTORICAL EVOLUTION OF HRD PHILOSOPHIES, POLICIES, AND PRACTICES IN SOUTH ASIAN COUNTRIES

The South Asian experience supports the ongoing debate that it is difficult to define the boundaries of international or global HRD due to differences in practices, values, beliefs, behaviors, and philosophical underpinnings of the different countries (Ruona, 2000; McLean and McLean, 2001; Wang and McLean, 2007). Since HRD is used in many different contexts, it can apply to a range of widely differing activities, organizational development, and human behavior (Garavan et al., 1995). In terms of developing workforce vocational and technical skills, HRD policies and practices of South Asian nations are primarily the responsibility of respective governments. During the past couple of decades, South Asian countries experienced a change in the meaning and scope of HRD practices. Different layers of evolutionary HRD practices in South Asian countries since the 1950s to date are summarized below in Table 4.1.

Table 4.1 Evolving Trends in National HRD Philosophies and Policies of South Asian Countries

Decade	Focus of HRD Policies of the National Governments
1950–60	Poverty alleviation, literacy and education, providing basic health services to people through government funds
1960–70	Economic development through agriculture and industries, human capital development through education, creating employment opportunities through public-sector companies
1970–90	Social equality, economic empowerment, and well-being of the people through strong public-sector and socialistic economy
1990–2000	Economic reforms, faster economic growth, new technologies and industrial development, emergence of new private-sector players, encourage public-private partnership in national infrastructure development
2000 onward	Globalization and regional economic equality, democracy, good governance and growth, technology and innovation, and social well-being of the people (Millennium HRD goals in line with the UN Millennium developmental goals)

1950s: Developing countries across the world and in South Asia began focusing on formulating economic policies to achieve economic equilibrium. The primary focus of education was *to alleviate the poverty of their citizens.*

1960s: With the donor funding from UN, World Bank, and developed countries, most countries such as Sri Lanka, Bangladesh, Pakistan, and India were forced to focus on employment creation to improve the 'quality of life' of their citizens. Governments of South Asian countries started supporting indigenous industries and entrepreneurship through subsidies, loans, and other means. In India, success of the cooperative movement in agriculture and small-scale industries resulted in the 'Green Revolution', high agricultural output; the 'White Revolution', high milk production and growth of dairy industry; and fast growth of Khadi and Village industries, leading to rural employment across the country.

1970s: With economic liberalization, most countries focused on improving GDP growth rate, employment, income distribution, poverty alleviation, and achieving balance of payment equilibrium.

1980s: The key policy areas of the 1970s continued with a shift of focus slightly toward stabilization of countries, balance of payment equilibrium, fiscal and monetary equilibrium, structural adjustment, and efficiency. During this period, foreign donors (World Bank, International Monetary Fund (IMF), International Labor Organization (ILO), and United Nations Development Fund (UNDP)) influenced developing SMEs as a means of poverty alleviation and economic development. The Indian government's initiative has been cited as a success story for reduction in poverty by increasing access to education and health to empower people as part of its new economic policy.

1990s: During the Asian crisis, most governments focused on structural adjustment, institutional construction, global capitalism, liberalization, and deregulation. Foreign donors influenced these countries to achieve good governance as a way of economic and societal success. Democracy and good governance were considered as means of poverty alleviation. India started its economic reforms in 1991 and promoted public-private partnership (PPP) models across industries, which resulted in speedy growth in the later years. Bangladesh, despite its effort to reduce poverty, has achieved mixed success. In the case of Sri Lanka and Nepal, governmental actions remain critical for empowering its people. Pakistan has also taken similar actions through its Eighteenth Amendment to the Constitution and the seventh National Finance Commission. However, due to implementation issues, it was not very successful.

2000s: The new millennium saw a change toward focus on human development, the alleviation of poverty and inequality, and work toward achieving Millennium Development Goals. These trends reflect changes in HRD philosophies and thought processes. Thus free-market thinking impacted on some of those countries (India) to develop science and technology. In 2000, UN member countries committed themselves to the attainment of the Millennium Development Goals (UN website, 2015).

These Millennium Development Goals have influenced the national HRD policies and practices of South Asian countries, governments having realized

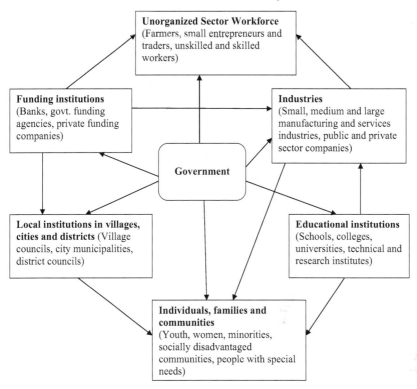

Figure 4.1   Relationships Among Various Stakeholders and Beneficiaries of National HRD Policy in South Asian Context

the importance of social well-being of their people, of sustainable development, as well as economic growth. National governments have been major stakeholders in national HRD policies designed to deliver social benefits to different stakeholders/beneficiaries in South Asian countries. The success of HRD in the South Asian region is highly dependent on individual governments' efforts to empower people through good political, economic, and civic governance. Developing human capabilities, transforming institutions, and making resources and assets accessible for all communities are considered as essential characteristics of good governance, which has become the key requirement for HRD in these countries. Figure 4.1 sets out the different kinds and levels of relationships among various stakeholders and beneficiaries of effective national HRD policies implemented by governments.

NATIONAL POLICIES ON EDUCATION AND VOCATIONAL TRAINING IN SOUTH ASIAN COUNTRIES

National policies on education and vocational training in South Asian countries have recognized the importance of HRD in a nation's economic growth and social development. The government of India created its Ministry of Human Resource Development on 26 September 1985 (earlier known as Ministry of Education) to strengthen citizens of the country through school education, literacy, higher education, technical education, and vocational education (Ministry of HRD, Government of India website, 2015). It is unfortunate that the country with the largest youth population in the world (356 million 10–24 years old, per (The Economic Times, Nov 18, 2014)), is suffering from problems of poor educational infrastructure at the grass-roots level: quality of delivery at primary, secondary, higher, and vocational education; and quality of employability of qualified graduates and skilled diploma holders (The Economic Times, Nov 18, 2014). India has just 2% skilled workers compared to 70% in the UK, 74% in Germany, 80% in Japan, and 96% in South Korea (The Hindu, Jan 13, 2015). Indian universities and vocational training institutes have failed to deliver a skilled workforce to industry. To overcome these shortcomings, and with the objective of building a national human resource capable of promoting a knowledge society, the government of India set up the National Knowledge Commission in 2005. There have been a number of challenges and hurdles. Struggle with internal political conflicts, poverty, and numerous social problems have meant that resources in these countries are expended on less productive measures, hence education and vocational training of youth has suffered a lot due to a lesser share in the national budget compared to other sectors. However, each country is trying to build its own national human resource capability by improving its national HRD policy to meet the changing needs of socioeconomic and political realities. The positive sign in the case of India is that Prime Minister Narendra Modi has listed employment, growth, and skill development in his top priorities to handle challenges of the upcoming young workforce (The Hindu, Jan 13, 2015; SiliconIndia News, Feb 4, 2015).

Governments of South Asian countries set up a range of different institutions to improve the quality of education and vocational training. For example, in India, the University Grants Commission (UGC), Council of Scientific and Industrial Research (CSIR), National Knowledge Commission (NKC), National Council of Educational Research and Training (NCERT), National Council on Skill Development (NCSD), National Council of Vocational Training (NCVT), All India Council of Technical Education (AICTE), Indian Council of Social Science Research (ICSSR), Rehabilitation Council of India (RCI), and Medical Council of India (MCI) are some of the institutions at the national level that play regulatory roles in education and training across different disciplines. These bodies support other institutions, such as schools, colleges, universities, and technical institutes in preparing skilled workers for different industries. Other South Asian countries also have similar institutions, e.g., the Higher Education Commission (Pakistan), the National Human Resource Development Council (Sri Lanka), which promote educational and vocational training. However, these institutions in

South Asia have been plagued by inefficient bureaucratic structures and are slow in delivering their objectives (Asrar-ul-Haq, 2015). They have focused more on the administrative regulation of universities, technical institutes, and other educational bodies rather than facilitating excellence in education, training, and research. This has led to the loss of talented professionals and skilled workers from South Asia to countries with developed economies where they can find better career opportunities. Currently, South Asian countries provide a huge migrant workforce (both skilled/knowledge workers and semiskilled/unskilled) to Gulf countries, UK, USA, Canada, Australia, and many other developed countries. Consequently, there are not enough employment opportunities for qualified, trained, and capable people within the region (Abbasi and Burdey, 2008; Ozaki, 2012). According to the UN-DESA Report (2013): of the 36 million international migrants from South Asia, 13.5 million migrated to the oil-producing countries of West Asia; however, India itself became home to 3.2 million Bangladeshi migrants in 2013 (The Times of India, Sept. 13, 2013). Though India has demonstrated the highest economic growth of countries in South Asia in the past, it has failed to generate enough employment opportunities for its own qualified/trained people, although unemployment has risen with slow economic growth since 2009. Conditions are no better in other South Asian countries, as unemployment rates are very high in Pakistan, Bangladesh, Bhutan, Nepal, Sri Lanka, and the Maldives (World Bank, 2011). Smaller countries such as Nepal, Bhutan, and the Maldives have very few universities, colleges, or vocational training institutes. Pakistan, Bangladesh, and Sri Lanka are better off in terms of public and private universities/colleges/technical institutes and a number of foreign university campuses. Recognizing the need for effective technical and vocational education and training for the youth of Pakistan, Mustafa, Abbas, and Saeed (2005) drew attention to the inefficient technical and vocational education infrastructure in Pakistan and lamented the poor quality of training delivered as a result.

THE EVOLUTION OF HRD PHILOSOPHIES, POLICIES, AND PRACTICES AT THE LEVEL OF INDUSTRY IN SOUTH ASIA

The history of HRD practices in South Asian countries can be traced back to the British colonial era when the entire region was under the influence of the British administrative and education systems. After gaining independence, India, Pakistan, and Sri Lanka started focusing on strengthening their industries by promoting public-sector companies (supported by governments) and supporting private industries through various means. India has always been ahead compared with its neighbors, being the largest country in the region; having the legacy of some of the best institutions established by the British; and some philanthropic business houses, royal families, and visionary leaders of India during the pre-1947 era (e.g., Jamshedji Tata, Jamnalal

Bajaj, Madan Mohan Malaviya, Rabindranath Tagore, Sir Syed Ahmad Khan, Maharaja Sayajirao Gaikawad). National policy initiatives by respective governments and regional economic trends influenced HRD practices at the industry level. In India, earlier governments strongly supported public-sector companies, but in the post-90s, private-sector companies grew at a faster pace. Concurrently, other South Asian countries have also established initiatives (e.g., attracting foreign investments) to support their industries in order to generate employment opportunities for their citizens. Table 4.2 presents a chronological overview of emerging trends in prevailing HRD philosophies, policies, and practices at the level of industry in South Asian countries; however, it should be noted that these trends were more visible in India than in other countries. In India, evolution of HRD practices in government organizations, public- and private-sector companies has been very similar to international trends emerging in the developed countries, whereas other neighbor countries achieved slower progress. The next section discusses country-specific HRD practices.

India

The concept of HRD in India came into existence in 1973–1974 when Professors Udai Pareek and T. V. Rao, and faculty members of Indian Institute of Management in Ahmedabad took an organiational development (OD) assignment as an intervention at Larsen and Toubro Ltd. (L&T), a large engineering company. The project was deemed a success and led to the

Table 4.2   Evolving Trends in HRD Philosophies, Policies, and Practices at Industry Level in South Asian Countries

Decades	Focus of HRD Policies in Industries Prevailing in Public- and Private-Sector Companies
1950–70s	Personnel management era; trade unionism; rise of government-owned, public-sector companies; workers' participation in management
1970–90s	Shift from personnel management to human resource management approach, emergence of HRD movement, focus on maintaining good industrial relations between trade unions and management, stronghold of public-sector companies as major employers
1990–2000s	Emergence of knowledge economy and new strong private-sector companies, strengthening of HRD movement, shift from HRM to Strategic HRM, IT influence on HRD practices
2000 onward	Emergence of new communication technologies, internationalization of some South Asian companies, shift of focus from Strategic HRM to Global HRD, focus on developing diversified talented workforce

establishment of the first HRD department in an Indian corporation. Pareek and Rao suggested fourteen basic principles and six subsystems of HRD. The project developed into a large-scale HRD movement in India (Pareek and Rao, 1998). In 1985, T. V. Rao, Udai Pareek, D. M. Pestonjee, and Fr. E. Abraham launched the National HRD Network (NHRDN), a professional association committed to the development of the field of HRD, with the support of L&T top management. Later this association got the support of most of the leading corporate groups of India, and currently NHRD has collaborations with other professional associations, such as the Confederation of Indian Industries. To enable professional education in the field of HRD, NHRDN founded the Academy of HRD, India (AHRD) in 1990, three years ahead of the US AHRD. Through AHRD, India started offering diploma programs, management development programs, and in-company training programs, which focused on HRD and later offered a doctoral program in HRD, the first of its kind in India. In collaboration with XLRI, it also published several books and monographs on HRD research in India. Today it conducts conferences, workshops, and publishes newsletters regularly (Rao, 2003; Pareek and Rao, 2008). NHRDN, Indian Society for Training and Development (ISTD), and SHRM are functioning successfully as professional associations of HRD academics and professionals in India.

Rao (2003) argues that HRD philosophy in Indian corporations has not been as successful as hoped. In his book, *Future of HRD*, he argues that the blame for failure of HRD in Indian corporations should be taken by CEOs who fail to understand the potential of HRD specialists in contributing to organizational success; rather, they reduce the role of HR managers to an administrative function instead of a developmental one. In most companies in India, the meaning of HRD is understood as 'human resource department' not 'human resource development'. There are also issues with the curriculum of MBA/PGDM programs offered by Indian management institutes/ business schools. The curricula of HRD specializations offered on MBA/ PGDM programs emphasize the building administrative skills required of 'an effective HR manager' rather than developing the person as 'a true HRD professional'. The 'development' focus seems to be lost in the overload of administrative/functional roles in most Indian corporations. High economic growth during 2001–2007 led to rampant hiring in 'booming industries' (including IT, organized retails, aviation, BPO, automobile, pharmaceuticals, and many other services industries), which later resulted in downsizing, layoffs when the economy slowed down after 2008, with a consequent increase in unemployment in most sectors. Currently, Indian corporations do not seem to have a focused strategy to address upcoming HRD challenges for developing a skilled and talented workforce for the future. Job losses and reduced employment opportunities for qualified and skilled people have resulted in poor employer-employee relationships in organizations. However, some well-known companies (for example, L&T, State Bank of India, Bank of Baroda, Bharat Earth Movers Ltd., Bharat Heavy Electricals Ltd.,

Indian Oil Corporation, Steel Authority of India Ltd., Crompton Greaves, TVS Group) where the top management team has taken an active interest in developing human capital (in terms of talent acquisition and talent retention) seem to have achieved desired goals through investment in HRD (Pareek and Rao, 1998,p. 350–374 & 2008; Rao, 2003). There are many Indian corporations and leaders who are regularly applauded in the popular media for their effective HRD systems and practices, including N. M. Desai and A. M. Naik (L&T), Ratan Tata (Tata Group), Aditya Vikram Birla and Kumar Managlam Birla (Aditya Virkam Birla Group), K. V. Kamat (ICICI Bank), Anil Khandelwal (Bank of Baroda), O. P. Bhatt (State Bank of India), Subir Raha (ONGC), N.R. Narayanmurthy and Nanadan Nilkeni (Infosys Technologies), Azim Premjee (Wipro Technologies), and Deepak Parikh and Aditya Puri (HDFC Bank) (Brockbank and Prabhakar, 2013). All of the aforementioned organizations are now global market players in different geographical regions and continuously contribute to innovations in global HRD practices.

Bangladesh

The history of HRD in Bangladesh starts with the Bangladesh Institute of Management (BIM), set up for human resource development activities in the country in 1971. Initially, the BIM conducted training programs for government employees but later widened its remit to include both public and private-sector companies and NGOs (Chowdhury and Hasan, 2009). Chowdhury and Hasan (2009) argue that the apathy of government agencies toward HRD, a shortage of qualified trainers in the country, and the lack of investments in HRD have acted as barriers to the development of focused HRD policies and practices in Bangladesh. The scenario is not very different in industry or in the private sector where HRM/HRD practices are neglected in most of the companies. Some recent studies have reported on the extremely poor commitment to HRM practices in the pharmaceutical (Rehman et al., 2013), higher education (Islam and Alam, 2013), and the ready-made garments (Huda, Karim and Ahmad, 2007) sectors in Bangladesh. The situation is a bit better in the professions where Bangladesh has professional associations, such as the Bangladesh Society for Training & Development (BSTD) established in 1980, and the Bangladesh Society for Human Resource Management (BSHRM) founded in 2001 for promoting HRD professionals in the country.

Bhutan

The Royal Government of Bhutan is perhaps the first government in the world to include a Gross National Happiness (GNH) Index as a measure of the country's progress in its National HRD Policy (National HRD Policy of the Kingdom of Bhutan, 2010). The Royal Government of Bhutan has accepted that it is the responsibility of the government to create conditions that enhance the happiness of citizens and recognize that happiness is not possible if people lack requisite knowledge and skills for gainful employment and future employability (National HRD Policy of the Kingdom of Bhutan, 2010). To assit with the achievement this goal of gross national happiness, the Ministry of Labor and Human Resources has decided to mobilize national resources for strengthening education at every level, primary, secondary, tertiary, technical, vocational; to promote a national network of HRD professionals; to promote public-private partnership; and to continuously monitor the national labor market. However, the report does not mention anything about any future initiatives from the government to increase employment opportunities for the people of Bhutan. As an agrarian rural economy with a very traditional culture, Bhutan needs transformation from traditional methods of production to modern technology and requires considerable investment to develop physical and human infrastructure for sustainable development (Ansari, 2009). According to the *Country Strategy Paper of Royal Government of Bhutan 2007–2013* (2013), Bhutan's overall performance on social development indicators (gender equality, primary education and literacy, public health, conservation of natural resources and environment) is far better than other South Asian countries. However, *Bhutan's Living Standards Survey* (BLSS, 2012), while recognizing the Bhutan government's achievements of Millennium Development Goals (MDGs), identified poverty, poor access to school education, and lack of employment opportunities as the biggest challenges for the country into the future (BLSS, 2012). This report suggested the Bhutan government creates more employment opportunities in the private sector for Bhutanese youth by developing policies and programs.

Maldives

The Maldives government has focused on HRD initiatives for its public service division, which include in public services reforms, good governance guidelines, and the efficient management of national resources as a part of its Vision 2020 (Asim, 2004). The government also introduced the new performance appraisal system in the public service department (PSD). These initiatives were received well and employees called for more focused efforts on HRD initiatives (Asim, 2004). Continuing these reforms, the Maldives government set up the Civil Service Commission in 2007 with the focus on quality services, quality performance, and quality people; hence it emphasized heavily "HRD & training" along with "organizational development & performance" (Maldives Civil Service Strategic Plan 2011–17, 2013). Though the Maldives is a very small country, its commitment and initiatives to build quality human capital for government departments are laudable, but it needs to create more employment opportunities for its educated and trained young workforce in the private sector in the future.

Nepal

The condition of HRM/HRD is significantly underdeveloped in Nepal if we consider prevailing practices in Nepalese companies (Adhikari and Muller, 2001; Bania, 2004; Gautam and Davis, 2007; Adhikari, 2010). Bania (2004) reported that most Nepalese business organizations invest little money on HRD, do not have full-time personnel managers to look after HR and HRD affairs, nor do they allocate budgets to HRD. Some professional HRM practices were reported in a handful of organizations, such as the Nepal Bank and multinational companies working in Nepal (Adhikari and Muller, 2001; Gautam and Davis, 2007; Adhikari, 2010). Slowly, Nepalese companies are trying to learn and adopt globally prevalent HRD practices and integrate HRD with organizational strategy to develop competitive advantage. Nepal also suffers from the migration of its talented professionals to countries such as India, the Middle East, the UK, the USA, and East Asian countries for better employment opportunities. There are only a few professional associations, e.g., the Management Association of Nepal (MAN) and the Federation of Nepalese Chambers of Commerce and Industry (FNCCI), which are working to bring professionalism to HRM/HRD practices in Nepalese organizations (Adhikari and Muller, 2001). A large proportion of aspiring youth migrate to India for better education and employment opportunities. The government of India offers equal employment opportunities for qualified people from Nepal and Bhutan in military services, government departments, and public and private-sector companies.

Pakistan

Human resource management (HRM) and human resource development (HRD) have both suffered from neglect in the state of Pakistan (Khilji, 2001; Abbasi and Burdey, 2008; Qadeer et al., 2011). Although Pakistan has a Ministry of Human Resource Development and a Ministry of Labor to address issues on HRD, labor affairs, education, and training, HRD practices are neglected in private companies. High politicization of administration in government and public-sector companies has resulted in unproductive, inefficient systems and a demoralized workforce in most organizations (Abbasi and Burdey, 2008). Khilji (2001) points out that the focus on human resource management was not recognized as important in Pakistan until 1997 when the government of Pakistan increased efforts to improve the working conditions of Pakistani companies by appointing professional managers at the top level to bring the best HRM practices of multinational companies to indigenous Pakistani organizations. Khilji (2001) also highlights the positive contributions of a few successful management institutes that have focused on developing human capital, including the Institute of Business Administration in Karachi (set up with support of the Wharton Business School in 1970), the Lahore University of Management

Sciences (set up with the support of Harvard Business School and McGill University in the late 1980s), and the Pakistan Institute of Management (set up with support of the Ford Foundation and Harvard Business School). In that way, American management philosophy and the British legacy can be considered very influential on HRM/HRD practices in Pakistani companies (Khilji, 2001).

Pakistan has two professional associations working for the promotion HRD research and programs: The Human Resource Development Network (HRDN) and Human Resource Development Society (HRDS). However, both public and private-sector universities and institutes are not very much different in terms of their HR policies and practices (Qadeer et al., 2011). Khilji (2001) attributed five important cultural factors (*Islam religion, Indian origins, British inheritance, American influence* and *military intervention*) that influence HR policies and practices in Pakistani public and private-sector organizations. Although Pakistan has seen many democratically elected governments at different periods, the strong influence of the military has always been there. Pakistan has received huge foreign aid from different countries for its social development activities, but its problems are very similar to India: unemployment, lack of a skilled workforce, migration of talented people to other developed countries, few opportunities for entrepreneurship ventures, and lack of access to education by common people (Asrar-ul-Haq, 2015). Asrar-ul-Haq (2015) argues that if Pakistan wants to grow as a progressive nation in the future then it needs to include various stakeholders, such as academics, NGOs, industry, and research institutions in national human capital development and to build bridges between these various groups. He further argues that to achieve these goals, government should commit itself to develop human capital for global employability (Asrar-ul-Haq, 2015).

Sri Lanka

In Sri Lanka, HRM education, training, and research is promoted by the Institute of Personnel Management (IPM), Sri Lanka. The Association of Human Resource Professionals (AHRP) was formed in 2000 to promote best HR practices in Sri Lanka. IPM acts as the authority on HR training and development as it offers several diploma courses to develop competencies to identify and analyze training and development needs at the organizational level. The India-Sri Lanka HR professional exchange program serves to share knowledge and best practices, build relationships between NIPM India and IPM Sri Lanka. Sri Lanka has recently revised its National Human Resources and Employment Policy (NHREP, 2011), which includes policy on HRD in agriculture, tourism, manufacturing, SME, education, health, IT, and other sectors. The NHREP is guided by the core values of 'Mahinda Chintana-Vision for the Future Framework', which was accepted by the Sri Lankan government in 2005. This framework states: "All persons of working age become globally competitive and multiskilled, and enjoy full, decent and productive employment with higher incomes in conditions of freedom, equity, security and human dignity". The NHERP emphasizes increasing collaboration among government agencies, universities and colleges, NGOs, and national chambers/associations of industries for training and skills development of youth and the enhancement of national productivity and employment opportunities.

HRD PRACTICES IN THE SOCIAL DEVELOPMENT SECTOR

The notion of HRD as social and community development in the South Asian region has existed since the early 1960s with the intervention of international developmental partners such as World Bank, UNDP, ILO, bi-lateral and multilateral donors, and international NGOs from various countries. South Asian countries have been characterized as having high unemployment and poverty rates, low literacy, high incidence of disease and elevated maternal and infant mortality rates, inequality in income and nutritional intake, lack of access to basic services, and absence of freedom (Mankin, 2011; World Bank, 2011). At the same time, poor governance; weak institutions; lack of local and national level policy formulation; and enforcement, favoritism, and corruption have been critical factors impeding human and economic development (Baniya, 2004; Gandhi et al., 2011; World Bank, 2011 and 2013). These unfavorable conditions prompted many donors to invest with a view to improving the quality of lives of people in the region and reducing social inequalities. Thus a variety of initiatives have been implemented by respective governments, NGOs, community development organizations, and local groups by using various techniques other than HRD, some of which have a HRD remit, e.g., facilitation, social counseling, training, skills, competency and leadership development, poverty alleviation, health education, and human rights (World Bank, 2013). Thus Western HRD concepts have been adopted in these countries in the guise of social and community development. There is evidence that HRD principles and theories have been used for social development; and such HRD practices as National HRD (NHRD) and HRD are given a broader context including community, nation, and region (Demartis et al., 2012; McLean et al., 2011).

South Asian countries have demonstrated better results in human resource development and capability building processes in the social development sector where NGOs have proven their capabilities in educating and training deprived communities, minorities, marginalized groups, disabled people, women, elders, and children. Several NGOs, e.g., SEWA, CRY, PRIA (India), Aga Khan Rural Support Program (Pakistan), Grameen Bank (Bangladesh), HomeNet South Asia have set up models of excellence in human capability building (Smillie and Hailey, 2001; Rao, 2003, p.164; Khan, 2006; Lewis and Ravichandran, 2008; Mustaghis-ur-Rahman, 2008; Pandey, 2011). Most NGOs functioning in South Asian countries are largely dependent on international donor agencies, government funds, and corporate support in the form of corporate social responsibility (CSR) funding. SEWA and HomeNet South Asia collaborated to set up a company for home-based women workers of South Asia, called 'SABAH' (SAARC Business Association of Home-Based Workers), initially working in Nepal and Pakistan and later spreading its operations to other SAARC countries (Jhabvala and Donane, 2011). SEWA has also contributed to women empowerment initiatives in Afghanistan with support of the governments of India and Afghanistan (Nanavaty, 2011). In Sri Lanka, the Sarvodaya movement (started in 1986) and the Agromart Foundation (established in 1989), the International Center for Training of Rural Leaders (ICTRL), and the Rural Economy Advancement Program (REAP, established in 2009) are a few examples of successful collaborations between government, community organizations, and international donors. HRD practices of most of the NGOs functioning in South Asian countries have been strongly influenced by the HRD policy guidelines of international donor agencies, UN guidelines, and the national regulatory framework of respective countries. With the dawn of the twenty-first century, involvement of business corporations in social development projects in South Asian countries is more highly visible. Better collaboration is needed among these stakeholders for effective implementation of national HRD policy at different levels in the country. In India, the Aadhar Card Project (a unique identification card for all residents of India) has proven very effective by linking the Mahatma Gandhi National Rural Employment Guarantee Scheme (MNERGA) payments through direct cash transfers to people's bank accounts, empowering poor rural people in India to find employment opportunities within their localities. This project is an example in which not only public-sector banks and state governments but also private-sector banks and IT companies collaborate, thereby delivering results at the grassroots level (The Hindu BusinessLine, Jan 6, 2013; The Economic Times, April 30, 2013). Demartis, Matthews, and Khilji (2012) proposed NHRD to be simultaneously used by the Afghan government and the United Nations Development Program (UNDP) as an effective strategic approach to progressing Afghanistan's nation-building strategy. This is very important, as Afghanistan is a war-torn country attempting to build itself with the support of international development agencies, governments, and NGOs. Demartis et al. (2012) go on to argue that NHRD and HRD are critical levers achieving the goals of improving organizational and workforce performance, achieving human development, abatement of social injustices, and building a democratic society. The Afghanistan government has launched its first Decent Work Country Program (DWCP) to boost employment opportunities in the country, with the support of international agencies, such as ILO, UNHCR, UNDP, UNICEF, and UNOPS and in partnership with employers' and workers' organizations (ILO, 2012). Neighboring countries (India and

Pakistan) are also partners with the Afghanistan government in its social and economic development projects. Smaller countries such as Bhutan and the Maldives have achieved significant milestones in their social development initiatives as guided by UN Millennium Development Goals and have demonstrated better performance than big neighbors, such as India and Pakistan. Overall, these projects aimed to improve the well-being of citizens (Knight and Wasty, 1991). Their programs have been diverse in nature and were often influenced by global changes, such as rapidly advancing technology, expanding global links, improving competitiveness, and enhancing social equity (Knight and Wasty, 1991).

HRD AT THE ORGANIZATIONAL LEVEL IN SOUTH ASIA

Organizations across different sectors are important stakeholders of any government's national HRD policy and serve to develop the human resources of individual countries (Rao, 2003, p. 159–184). To ensure sustainable economic growth, countries need high-performing organizations across different sectors. This need has also been realized by governments of South Asian countries and has motivated them to formulate a national HRD policy for educating their people and preparing a skilled workforce for the industries/organizations functioning on their soil. India, the largest country in the region, has been well ahead of its neighbors in terms of investing in government institutions, universities, technical/research institutes, colleges, public-sector companies, small/medium enterprises, and in creating investment opportunities for MNCs. India can also take the credit for establishing HRD departments in large private and public-sector companies, sharing with each other HRD best practices as India grew economically post-1991 liberalization (Rao, 2003; Ghosh and Barman, 2014). Indian companies best known for their HRD systems are L&T, Tata Group, State Bank of India, Indian Oil Corporation, Life Insurance Corporation of India, Hindustan Aeronautics Ltd., Rashtriya Chemicals & Fertilizers Ltd., ICICI Bank, Infosys, Wipro, Bank of Baroda, ONGC, and Axis Bank (Rao and Pareek, 1992, p. 350–374; Haldar and Sarkar, 2012, p. 743–755; Ghosh and Barman, 2014). In other SAARC countries, e.g., Pakistan, Bangladesh, and Sri Lanka, HRD systems are stronger in MNCs functioning in those countries than government organizations and private companies, because they implement their global HRD practices with local adaptation to the region. Examples of some organizations that have invested in strengthening their HRD systems especially in training and development activities are: National Bank of Pakistan, Indus Motor Company, COMSATS Institute of IT, Aga Khan Foundation (Pakistan), Grameen Bank (Bangladesh), and Nepal Bank (Nepal). Small countries such as Bhutan and the Maldives have also invested in training of their government officials, technical and academic workforce for their skill development through international training programs (Asim,

2004; Sofo, 2007). A follow-up research study conducted at the behest of Ministry of Education, Royal Government of Bhutan found that international exposure to training of the employees of the Ministry of Education was very successful in terms of increased self-confidence and acceptance of effective transfer of training (Sofo, 2007).

Unlike large public organizations or private companies, small medium enterprises (SMEs) in SAARC countries are not very resourceful in terms of HRD. For example, SMEs in India have neither HRD policies nor resources to invest in HRD activities, although there is a lot of scope in terms of adapting HRD practices to SMEs from MNCs and large corporations (Singh and Vohra, 2005). SMEs across South Asian countries face similar economic environments, the constraints of government agencies, lack of a skilled workforce and lack of resources to invest in training and development activities; however, the support of large public and private organizations to SME training activities could be very beneficial to both sides in terms of skill development, knowledge development, technology innovation, and organizational learning (Ahmad et al., 2011).

In a HRD audit study of 12 large Indian organizations, Rao (2003) found that out of 12 participant organizations, less than 50% have full-time HRD staff and only two HRD subsystems (training and development, as well as performance appraisal) have been implemented well across all organizations. These organizations were not found to be effective in implementing organizational development, potential appraisal, career planning, and development subsystems. Rao (2003) identified the following reasons for the failure of HRD in Indian organizations: (i) lack of understanding and appreciation of HRD by top management, (ii) lack of competent HRD staff, (iii) lack of professional development of HRD staff, and (iv) inadequate understanding and weak implementation of MNCs' HRD models without proper adaptation to Indian/Asian culture. These findings suggest that many successful Indian organizations have a long way to go for effective implementation of HRD systems.

SIMILARITIES AND DIFFERENCES ACROSS THE REGION

South Asia benefits from beautiful geographical and cultural diversity from the Himalayas to the Indian Ocean. Each country in the region has its own unique natural, historical, and cultural heritage that differentiates it from other neighbors. As a region, it is of immense historical importance (the Indus Valley civilization in the Bronze Age through the Vedic, Aryan, and Dravidian periods; onto the periods of Buddhism, Maurya, and Gupta kings; the Mughal era; and finally to the period of British colonization), and all the countries in the region share these historical roots. It is not an easy task to identify similarities and differences across SAARC countries while discussing human resource development issues that matter for the region as a unique entity. The biggest problem for all SAARC countries is their population growth, which has resulted in surplus labor in every country, whereas industries face a huge skills deficit in the workforce for their business needs (Ahmad et al., 2011). Moreover, talented professionals migrate to developed countries for better employment opportunities (Ahmad et al., 2011). In addition, political uncertainty and terrorism are two major challenges facing all the countries as they implement their national HRD policy. India, Afghanistan, Pakistan, Bangladesh, Sri Lanka, and Nepal are currently struggling with homegrown and externally supported terrorist groups. Bhutan is the most peaceful state in the region, known more for its achievement of "Gross National Happiness" than GDP. Another similarity across SAARC countries is that the majority of their workforce is employed in agriculture and unorganized sector jobs rather than in industries, government jobs, or other organized sector jobs. To create more jobs in industries and the organized sector, all SAARC countries see the need to attract foreign direct investments in their economic and HRD policies (Bhushan, 2005; Khan, 2007). MNCs working in SAARC countries have strong HRD systems in their local units because of their strong global HRD policy and practices adapted to the local culture of the country. Many local companies in India, Pakistan, Bangladesh, and Sri Lanka have also benefited from learning some HRD practices from MNCs. However, across all the SAARC countries, government organizations and large public organizations face bureaucratic inertia as a major hurdle in improving HRD systems and organizational learning. India is somewhat better off in spreading technology innovations across industries. Other neighbors are also catching up, and we are happy to see emerging SMEs in many niche industries in Pakistan, Bangladesh, and Sri Lanka (Ahmad et al., 2011).

DISCUSSION

The success of HRD in the South Asian region is highly dependent on individual governments' efforts to empower people through good political, economic, and civic governance. Developing people's capabilities, transforming institutions, and making resources and assets accessible for all communities are considered essential characteristics of good governance, which has become the key requirement for HRD in these countries. Poverty, nutrition, health, access to education, skills development, and employment opportunities are still major challenges for all the South Asian countries, despite the increase in economic growth. HRD initiatives at the government level are dependent on foreign direct investments and funds from international agencies, such as the World Bank, UN agencies, and other international donor agencies. Recent economic growth in South Asian countries has also prepared many South Asian business corporations to join in partnership with their governments in social development projects. Rao (2003, p. 163–167) suggests 12 key guidelines for national-level human resource capability building that the governments of South Asian countries need to consider carefully. The process should start with conducting a national HRD audit to analyze human development indices for the country, region, states, cities, and villages. It should further evaluate the functioning of political institutions, administrative machinery, and governance systems and attempt to develop competency indices for the aforementioned systems. This process should also include corporations and NGOs through public-private partnerships with government institutions (Rao, 2003, p.178). Rao (2003, p. 163–167) emphasizes specifically the importance of increasing government investment in educational infrastructure (schools, colleges, universities, technical and research institutes), educating girls and women, grassroots-level entrepreneurship, strengthening agriculture for rural employment, improving efficiency and effectiveness of government agencies, and mobilizing resources for social support to marginal communities. Effective intersectoral collaboration among industry, agricultural entrepreneurs/farmers, government agencies, and NGOs is critical if South Asian countries are to develop effective social support systems for their people. No country can become a stronger nation until it builds its human capabilities through education, training, and employment opportunities and delivers quality of life in organizations, cities, and villages.

CONCLUSION

In this chapter, we have attempted to provide an overview of the HRD landscape in the South Asian context. The historical and cultural contexts are quite different from other regions and countries and have naturally had an impact on the development of HRM and HRD within the region. Its roots in the ancient traditions of the Indus Valley where a sophisticated civilization thrived in the Bronze Age, which developed learning and teaching in mathematics and sciences as well as urban planning, is an important backdrop. On the other hand, feudal traditions of 'casteism' and 'narrow nationalism' have hindered the development of enlightened HRD practices. Most modern HRD practices are based upon Western values of equality and egalitarianism and, at times, the socio-cultural values of this region are in conflict with these Western values. This leads to a certain resistance of HRD processes and practices at the level of individual countries and in the region. This acts as an impediment to imbibing HRD values, whether at the national or the organizational level in the South Asian context. In this chapter, we have argued that in order to adopt contemporary global HRD practices, South Asia needs to work harder and with stronger commitment from individual governments if it wants to reach integration at the level of individual countries. In light of what we have observed in this chapter, it seems highly likely that HRD in this region will undergo major changes and modifications into the future.

REFERENCES

Abbasi, Z., & Burdey, M. B. (2008). The changing paradigm of human resource in the economic development of Pakistan. *Journal of Management and Social Sciences*, 4(1): 1–11. Accessed September 20, 2013. (http://www.biztek.edu.pk/downloads/research/jmss_v4_n1/1%20The%20Changing%20paradigms.pdf)

Adhikari, D. R. (2010). Human resource development (HRD) for performance management: The case of Nepalese organizations. *International Journal of Productivity and Performance Management*, 59(4): 306–324.

Adhikari, D. R., & Muller, M. (2001). Human resource management in Nepal. In P. S. Budhwar and Y. A. Debrah (Eds.), *Human Resource Management in Developing Countries*, 98–101. London: Routledge.

Ahmad, V., Wahab, M., & Mahmood, H. (2011). *Effectiveness of HRD in Developing SMEs in South Asia*. SAARC Human Resource Development Center, Islamabad, MPRA Paper no. 30780. Accessed June 22, 2015. (http://mpra.ub.uni-muenchen.de/30780/)

Ansari, M. (2009). Economic growth and agricultural transformation in Bhutan: An exploration into the political economy of Eastern Himalayas. *SAARC Journal of Human Resource Development*, 2009: 1–17. Accessed September 22, 2013. (http://www.shrdc.org/doc/sjhrd/2009/8.%20Mahmood%20Ansari.pdf)

Asrar-ul-Haq, M. (2015). Human resource development in Pakistan: Evolution, trends and challenges. *Human Resource Development International*, 18(1): 97–104.

Bania, L. B. (2004). Human resource development practice in Nepalese business organizations: A case study of manufacturing enterprises in Pokhara. *The Journal of Nepalese Business Studies*, 1(1): 58–68. Accessed September 22, 2013. (http://www.nepjol.info/index.php/JNBS/article/view/39)

Bhushan, S. (2005). Changing global and regional scenario and human development efforts in South Asia. *SAARC Journal of Human Resource Development*, 1(1): 77–89. Accessed June 22, 2015. (http://www.shrdc.org/doc/sjhrd/2005/05.SudhanshuBhushan.pdf)

Bhutan Living Standards Survey. (2012). *Asian Development Bank and National Statistical Bureau of Bhutan*. Accessed September 20, 2013. (http://www.adb.org/publications/bhutan-living-standards-survey-2012)

Brockbank, W., & Prabhakar, L. (2013). India. In David Ulrich, Wayne Brockbank, Jon Younger and Mike Ulrich (Eds.), *Global HR Competencies: Mastering Competitive Value from the Outside In*, 135–153. New Delhi: McGraw-Hill.

Cho, Y., & Mclean, G. N. (2009). Leading Asian countries HRD practices in the IT industry: A comparative study of South Korea and India. *Human Resource Development International*, 12(3): 313–331.

Chowdhury, M. T., & Hasan, F. (2009). Role of training institutes in human resource development—A study on Bangladesh Institute of Management. *Asian Affairs*, 31(3): 5–25. Accessed September 20, 2013. (http://www.cdrb.org/journal/2009/3/1.pdf)

Country Strategy Paper 2007–13. *Royal Government of Bhutan*. Accessed on September 20, 2013. Accessed September 20, 2013. (http://eeas.europa.eu/bhutan/csp/07_13_en.pdf)

Demartis, W., Matthews, C. D., & Khilji, S. E. (2012). Analyzing HRD and NHRD: The road ahead for Afghanistan. *South Asian Journal of Global Business Research*, 1(1): 128–142.

Edwards, T., & Kuruvilla, S. (2005). International HRM: National business systems, organizational politics and the international division of labour in MNCs. *International Journal of Human Resource Management*, 16(1): 1–21.

Gandhi, A., Chandan, K., Saha, P., Sahoo, B. K., & Sharma, A. (2011). *India Human Development Report*. Oxford University Press. Accessed October 1, 2013. (http://www.pratirodh.com/pdf/human_development_report2011.pdf)

Garavan, T., Costine, P., & Heraty, N. (1995). The emergence of strategic human resource development. *Journal of European Industrial Training*, 19(10): 4–10.

Garavan, T. N., McGuire, D., & O'Donnell, D. (2004). Exploring human resource development: A levels of analysis approach. *Human Resource Development Review*, 3(4): 417–441.

Gautam, D. K., & Davis, A. J. (2007). Integration and devolvement of human resource practices in Nepal. *Employee Relations*, 29(6): 711–726.

Ghosh, R., & Barman, A. (2014). Emerging trends, challenges and opportunities for HRD in India. In Rob F. Poell, Tonette S. Rocco and Gene L. Roth (Eds.), *The Routledge Companion to Human Resource Development*, 436–446. London: Routledge.

Haldar, U. K., & Sarkar, J. (2012). *Human Resource Management*. New Delhi: Oxford University Press.

Huda, K. N., Karim, R., & Ahmed, F. (2007). Practices of strategic human resource development in the RMG sector of Bangladesh: An empiritcal study. *International Business Management*, 1(1): 1–6. Accessed September 15, 2013. (http://docsdrive.com/pdfs/medwelljournals/ibm/2007/1–6.pdf)

ILO. (2002). *Decent Work and the Informal Economy*. International labor Organization Publications. Accessed October 10, 2013. (http://www.ilo.org/public/english/standards/relm/ilc/ilc90/pdf/rep-vi.pdf)

ILO. (2012). *Global Employment Trends*. International Labor Organization Publications. Accessed October 10, 2013. (http://www.ilo.org/wcmsp5/groups/public/@dgreports/@dcomm/@publ/documents/publication/wcms_171571.pdf)

International Labor Organization Press Release. (2012). *Decent Work in Afghanistan.* 29 November 2012, Accessed October 10, 2013. (http://www.ilo.org/asia/countries/afghanistan/WCMS_194524/lang—en/index.htm)

Islam, M. M., & Alam, M. A. (2013). Human resources development in the context of challenges of globalization with reference to teacher education in Bangladesh. *ASA University Review*, 7(1): 169–192. Accessed on September 15, 2013. (http://www.asaub.edu.bd/data/asaubreview/v7n1sl16.pdf)

Jhabvala, R., & Donane, D. (2011). Women home-based workers creating ties across South Asian countries: Experiences of SEWA and HomeNet. *SAARC Journal of Human Resource Development*, 2011: 95–104. Accessed on September 22, 2013. (http://www.shrdc.org/doc/sjhrd/2011/9.Renana-Jhabvala.pdf)

Khan, M. A. (2007). Role of human capital in attracting foreign direct investment: A South Asian perspective. *SAARC Journal of Human Resource Development*, 2011: 2–25. Accessed June 22, 2015. (http://www.shrdc.org/doc/sjhrd/2007/3.%20Dr.%20Aslam-Pakistan.pdf)

Khan, S. R. (2006). Learning from South Asian 'successes': Tapping social capital. *South Asia Economic Journal, 2006*, 7(2): 157–178. Accessed September 25, 2013. (http://sae.sagepub.com/content/7/2/157.full.pdf)

Khilji, S. E. (2001). Human resource management in Pakistan. In P. S. Budhwar and Y. A. Debrah (Eds.), *Human Resource Management in Developing Countries*, 102–120. London: Routledge.

Knight, P. T., & Wasty, S. S. (1991). *Comparative Resource Allocations to Human Resource Development in Asia, Europe, and Latin America*. Economic Development Institute, The World Bank. Accessed September 20, 2013. (http://documents.worldbank.org/curated/en/1991/12/699808/comparative-resource-allocations-human-resource-development-asia-europe-latin-america)

Lewis, D., & Ravichandran, N. (Eds.). (2008). *NGOs and Social Welfare: New Research Approaches*. Jaipur: Rawat Publications.

Maldives Civil Service Strategic Plan, 2011–17. Accessed September 15, 2013. (http://library.csc.gov.mv/lib/files/CSCStratPlan.pdf)

Mankin, J. (2011). *Rotten to the Core, Foreign Policy*. Accessed 22 October 2013. (http://www.foreignpolicy.com/articles/2011/05/10/rotten_to_the_core)

Ministry of HRD. *Government of India Website.* Accessed March 25, 2015. (http://mhrd.gov.in/about-mhrd)

McLean, G. N. (2004). National human resource development: What in the world is it? *Advances in Developing Human Resources,* 6(3): 269–275.

McLean, G. N., Kuo, Min-Hsun., Budhwani, N., & Yamnill, S. (2011). *Social Development through Human Resource Development.* Conference proceedings, AHRD 2012.

McLean, G. N., & McLean, L. D. (2001). If we can't define HRD in one country, how can we define it in an international context? *Human Resource Development International,* 4(3): 313–326.

Mustafa, U., Abbas, K., & Saeed, A. (2005). Enhancing vocational training for economic growth of Pakistan. *The Pakistan Development Review,* 44(4): 567–584. Accessed on September 22, 2013. (http://www.pide.org.pk/pdf/PDR/2005/Volume4/567-584.pdf)

Mustaghis-ur-Rahman. (2008). NGO management and operation: A South Asian challenge. In David Lewis and N. Ravichandran (Eds.), *NGOs and Social Welfare: New Research Approaches,* 219–234. Jaipur: Rawat Publications.

Nanavaty, R. (2011). *Women, Work and Peace: SEWA's Experience in Afghanistan,* 53–57. Accessed on September 22, 2013. (http://www.shrdc.org/doc/sjhrd/2011/5.Reema-Nanavaty.pdf)

National Human Resource Development Policy of the Kingdom of Bhutan, 2010. Accessed on September 20, 2013. (http://www.gnhc.gov.bt/wp-content/uploads/2011/05/NHRD.pdf)

National Human Resources and Employment Policy, 2011. Accessed on September 30, 2013. (www.nhrep.gov.lk)

Ozaki, M. (2012). *Worker Migration and Remittances in South Asia.* ADB South Asia Working Paper Series, No. 12, Asian Development Bank. Accessed on September 30, 2013. (http://www.adb.org/publications/worker-migration-and-remittances-south-asia)

Pandey, S. (2011). Managing for change: Organizational challenges for development organizations. In S. Anand, I. Kumar and A. Srivastava (Eds.), *Challenges of the Twenty First Century: A Trans-disciplinary Perspective,* 198–217. New Delhi: MacMillan India.

Pareek, U., & Rao, T. V. (1998). *Pioneering Human Resource Development: The L & T System.* Ahmedabad: Academy of HRD.

Pareek, U., & Rao, T. V. (2008). From a sapling to the forest: The saga of developing HRD in India. *Human Resource Development International,* 11(5): 555–564.

Qadeer, F., Rehman, R., Ahmad, M., & Shafique, M. (2011). Does ownership of higher education institute influence its HRM patterns? The case of Pakistan. *International Journal of Business and Management,* 6(10): 230–241. Accessed on September 22, 2013. (http://papers.ssrn.com/sol3/papers.cfm?abstract_id=2021751)

Rahman, M., Akhtar, R., Chowdhury, S., Islam, S., & Haque, M. R. (2013). HRM practices and its impact on employee satisfaction: A case of pharmaceutical companies in Bangladesh. *International Journal of Research in Business and Social Science,* 2(3): 62–67. Accessed on September 15, 2013. (http://www.ssbfnet.com/ojs/index.php/ijrbs/article/view/157)

Rao, T. V. (2003). *Future of HRD.* New Delhi: Macmillan.

Rao, T. V., & Pareek, U. (1992). *Designing and Managing Human Resource Systems.* (2nd ed). New Delhi: Oxford & IBH.

Ruona, W. E. A. (2000). Core belief in human resource development. In W. E. A. Ruona and G. A. Roth (Eds.), *Advances in Developing Human Resources: Philosophical Foundations of Human Resource Development Practice,* 1–27. San Francisco, CA: Berrett-Koehler.

SiliconIndia News. (2015). *My Priorities are Growth, Jobs: Modi to Investors.* (Feb 4, 2015). Accessed on April 15, 2015. (http://www.siliconindia.com/news/business/My-Priorities-Are-Growth-Jobs-Modi-To-Investors-nid-178466-cid-3.html)

Singh, M., & Vohra, N. (2005). Strategic human resources in small enterprises. *Journal of Entrepreneurship*, 14: 57–70.

Smillie, I., & Hailey, J. (2001). *Managing for Change: Leadership, Strategy & Management in Asian NGOs*. London: Earthscan.

Sofo, F. (2007). Transfer of training: A case study of outsourced training for staff from Bhutan. *International Journal of Training and Development*, 11(2): 103–120.

Stiglitz, J. E. (2002). *Globalization and Its Disconnects*. New York: W. W. Norton and Company.

The Economic Times. (2013). *Aadhaar Card Enrollment Sprints Ahead of Government-Run NPR, Courtesy Nandan Nilekani*. (April 30, 2013). Accessed March 26, 2015. (http://articles.economictimes.indiatimes.com/2013–04–30/news/38929970_1_biometrics-npr-nandan-nilekani)

The Economic Times. (2014). *India Has World's Largest Youth Population: UN Report*. (November 18, 2014). Accessed March 26, 2015. (http://articles.eco nomictimes.indiatimes.com/2014–11–18/news/56221890_1_demographic-divi dend-youth-population-osotimehin)

The Hindu. (2015). *National Skill Development Policy by April*. (Jan 13, 2015). Accessed March 23, 2015. (http://www.thehindu.com/news/cities/Thiruvanan-thapuram/national-skill-development-policy-by-april/article6782673.ece)

The Hindu BusinessLine. (2013). *AP Launches Aadhaar Linked Cash Transfer*. (Jan 6, 2013). Accessed March 26, 2015. (http://www.thehindubusinessline.com/news/states/ap-launches-aadhaar-linked-cash-transfer/article4279835.ece)

The Times of India. (2013). *Bangla Migration to India Largest in Developing World*. (Sep 13, 2013). Accessed September 14, 2013. (http://timesofindia.india-times.com/india/Bangla-migration-to-India-largest-in-developing-world/article-show/22528497.cms)

UN-DESA Report. (2013). *Number of international migrants rises above 232 million*. Accessed September 14, 2013. (http://www.un.org/en/development/desa/news/population/number-of-international-migrants-rises.html)

UN Website. (2015). *United Nations Milleneum Development Goals*. Accessed March 25, 2015. (http://www.un.org/millenniumgoals/)

Walton, J. S. (2003). How shall a thing be called? An argument on the efficacy of the term HRD. *Human Resource Development Review*, 2(3): 310–326.

Wang, X., & McLean, G. N. (2007). The dilemma of defining international human resource development. *Human resource Development Review*, 6(1): 96–108.

World Bank (2011). World Development Report. *Conflict, Security and Development*. The World Bank: Washington DC. Accessed on October 12, 2013. (http://siteresources.worldbank.org/INTWDRS/Resources/WDR2011_Full_Text.pdf)

World Bank. (2013). *South Asia Regional Brief*. Accessed October 12, 2013. (http://www.worldbank.org/en/news/feature/2013/09/26/south-asia-regional-brief)

5 Human Resource Development in China and North Korea

Judy Sun and Greg Wang

INTRODUCTION

While human resource development (HRD) has been a main theme in many parts of the world in recent decades, its role in most developing countries has not been fully understood (Wang et al., 2015). The People's Republic of China, a market-oriented socialist economy, contrasts greatly with the Democratic People's Republic of Korea (DPRK or North Korea) in terms of HRD evolution. China has become one of the most influential countries in the globalization process and is increasingly studied from a HRD perspective. DPRK, on the other hand, referred to as a hermit kingdom since the 1950s, has just recently opened its door to a very limited degree to its neighboring countries (Hassig and Oh, 2009). Due to the lack of understanding about the contexts of both China and DPRK and the roles of their HRD mechanisms, the literature tends to misinterpret information about the two countries. For example, Western commentators have repeatedly and incorrectly predicted DPRK's collapse in the last few decades (e.g., Eberstadt, 1990; Ricks and Glain, 1994; Bolton and Eberstadt, 2008); whereas HRD research on China has often focused on cultural influences without considering the sociopolitical context of HRD.

We cannot isolate our understanding and analysis of a nation's HRD system from its underlying historical, sociopolitical, and cultural contexts that have shaped its host system (Wang et al., 2015). China and DPRK are no exception to this. Existing scholarly work on HRD-related issues in the two countries has largely focused on their differences (e.g., Collins, Zhu, & Warner, 2012) and has overlooked the similarities and historical parallel paths of the two. Understanding the resemblance of the two from historical and sociopolitical perspectives is not only helpful to understanding their existing HRD status but also salient to predicting future evolution of HRD at the organizational and national levels. This chapter focuses on the uniqueness of the two nations' contexts and presents their latest developments in HRD as a way of proposing that HRD in China today is likely to be a predictor of what will happen in DPRK in the future.

HRD IN CHINA AND NORTH KOREA: POLITICAL, SOCIAL, HISTORICAL, AND CULTURAL CONTEXT

Essentially, DPRK has followed China's development path since the early 1950s. To understand the two nations' HRD systems and related roles in economic development, it is necessary to examine their historical evolutions from the cultural, historical, institutional, and sociopolitical contexts.

Cultural and Institutional Influences

From a cultural perspective, the similarity of China and Korea has been well documented (e.g., Hofstede and Bond, 1988; Zhang et al., 2005; Ryu and Cervero, 2011). Essentially, both nations are deeply rooted in Confucianism and Taoism which focus on social harmony under hierarchical order, conservatism, paternalism, and naturalness (Hofstede and Bond, 1988; Lee, 1999; Zhang et al., 2005). In DPRK, "even in the midst of institutionalized state reform, the cultural tendency of individual family groups was dominated by the basic principles and values of traditional Confucianism" (Kang, 2006, p. 34). Thus their Confucian roots determine that both societies view people as relational beings. Governance by social relationships is a strong force maintaining social order and stability (Barkema et al., 2015). Embedded in the cultures is a collectivism such that group interest takes precedence over individual interests and constitutes the combined interest of the two (Cho, 2006; Barkema et al., 2015). With such cultural backgrounds, China and DPRK have historically witnessed prolonged and stable dynasties, largely enforced by the interactions of the cultural elements and institutional arrangements (Tu, 2000).

Similarities in the cultural heritage, combined with their resemblance in sociopolitical systems and structures since the 1950s, have shown that China and DPRK experienced closely paralleled developmental paths, largely influenced by China's leading role (Kang, 2006). Their similarities in institutional arrangements can be seen in the following areas. First, as former Soviet Union communist allies in East Asia, both countries have followed and been affected by the then superpower, which has often been referred to as "big brother" in communist circles. Second, under big brother's umbrella, the two nations have developed a strong ideological bond between them with similar institutional arrangements associated with almost identical political principles and communist pursuits (Bradbury, 1961). For example, in orthodox Marxism ideology, "loyalty to the party and the leader" is constantly emphasized in both countries. In China, Marxism, Leninism, and Maoism have provided the guiding principles, whereas in DPRK, the principles of the Juche ideology, a variation of Marxism, have been dominant. In the earlier years, China publicly proclaimed the intimate association of the social, political, and ideological systems of the two countries. The *People's Daily*, the Chinese government official mouthpiece claimed,

> China and [North] Korea are separated by only a river. We are as dependent on each other as the lips and the teeth. What concerns one also concerns the other. We two have established unbreakable combatant friendship cemented with blood.
>
> (11 November 1953, p. 1)

Third, both nations are governed in a one-party system, the Communist Party of China (CPC) and Korean Worker's Party (KWP), respectively. Since the 1950s' Soviet Union era, they have followed an orthodox socialist system with its centrally planned economy where demand and supply of all output, including jobs and education opportunities, were controlled by the party-states. These economies focused on self-reliance and were closed to the outside world, whose economies were dominated by state-owned enterprises (SOEs) that left no room for the private sector. After China's open-door and economic transformation in the 1980s, DPRK also followed a similar path but at a much slower pace. Lastly, but not the least, DPRK has been economically dependent on China for most of its food and energy supplies. Since the early 1990s, China has served as DPRK's supplier, accounting for nearly 90% of its energy imports, providing 80% of its consumer goods, and 45% of its food (Bajoria and Xu, 2013). In recent years, DPRK's economic dependence on China has continued to grow, as indicated by the significant trade imbalance between the two countries (Nanto and Manyin, 2010). Given the similarities in cultures and institutional arrangements, it is not surprising that the two nations' development paths and major historical evolution have shared a similar, even identical pattern. The following section describes only a few major milestone events.

The 'Great Leap Forward' Versus the 'Flying Horse' Program

In the 1950s, China leader, Chairman Mao, attempted to replace moral and psychological incentives with material incentives and necessary skills as a major motivator for mobilizing national human resources. A typical statement of his reads: "Tomorrow we shall build a paradise of happiness never before attempted in the history of Communism" (People's Daily, 1958). As such, the nation promoted heavily the 'Great Leap Forward' movement to mobilize the entire population for 'native' production of iron and steel with the goal of "surpassing the UK and the US in 15 years" (Xing, 2013). At its extreme, the People's Daily (27 August, 1958) notoriously proclaimed a new national slogan: "the land can yield as high as we dare to imagine". Due to lack of skills and knowledge, this native production reached such a frenzy that millions of households donated their metal cooking utensils, doorknobs, and even locks as raw materials for steel and iron production. It was an era in which China's human resources experienced enthusiastic longing and dreaming, while diligently working for the happy tomorrow of communism. Some have characterized this period as "human resource exploitation" through ideological enthusiasm rather than HRD. Indeed, the literature has described the practice as "intensive exploitation of human labor to a degree unknown in modern history" (Bradbury, 1961, p. 17).

A few months later, inspired by China's glorious imagination and the 'Great Leap Forward', DPRK launched a similar 'Flying Horse' campaign in 1958 as its national five-year plan (Kuark, 1963). With the same focus on industrialization as China, even its motivational slogan appeared to be a close copy of China's: "surpassing Japan in 15 years" (Bradbury, 1961). The movement focused on amalgamating collective farms into political-economic township units, developing industries, which combined 'native' and modern technology (Winstanley-Chesters, 2015). The planned goal was to (a) more than triple industrial output and (b) to increase grain production by 50%. While the official figures claimed it reached the goal for industrial output two years ahead of plan, grain production lagged behind, resulting in insufficient food supplies (Li, 2012).

The Catastrophic Famines

Perhaps what these two nations resembled each other most in was their disastrous sufferings, particularly nationwide famines. While the famines occurred at different times, they were largely caused by failures in national policies (Peng, 1987; Haggard and Noland, 2007). In other words, the temporal progression of the two famines was fundamentally the same.

As a result of the 'exaggeration wind' for the 'Great Leap Forward' and excess grain procurement by the state Public Distribution System (PDS) based on exaggerated yields, China suffered three to four years of extended famines throughout the country from the 1950s to the 1960s. Combined with China's isolation from the international community at the time, no external assistance was sought to alleviate the famine, largely caused by the government's reluctance to admit the existence of adverse conditions. The literature estimates that death caused by the famine ranged from 23 million (Peng, 1987) to 45 million (Leong, 2012). For DPRK, the famine came about four decades later from 1995 to 1999 (Haggard and Noland, 2007). It was caused by failures arising from similar overzealous attempts to transform the farming system as well as social institutions to comply with Marxist ideology and exacerbated by natural calamities. That famine resulted in the deaths of 600,000 to 1 million people out of a pre-famine population of 22 million (Goodkind and West, 2001; Eberstadt, 2004). A more direct trigger of DPRK's famine was related to a disagreement in 1995 with China's ongoing economic reform. In response, China, which had taken up the former Soviet Union's role as primary supplier, significantly reduced its food supplies to DPRK. According to Noland (2004), "if there was a single proximate trigger to the North Korean famine, this was it" (p. 4).

To a certain degree, the famine sufferings in both countries were related to the former Soviet Union (Peng, 1987; Noland, 2004). For China, it was caused by the Soviet Union's disapproval of the 'Great Leap Forward' and its deviation from orthodox Marxism and Leninism, as well as its associated 'exaggeration wind' in reporting bogus high yields to please the leadership (Peng, 1987). In the case of DPRK, the famine was caused by the disintegration of the Soviet Union and its East European bloc, which resulted in a significant reduction in its external aids and resources (Noland, 2004). Additionally, both famines were officially disguised as 'natural disasters' in the government controlled media when they were indeed state induced (Peng, 1987; Noland, 2004).

The Cultural Revolution Versus the Nature Re-Making Program

The 1960s and the 1970s witnessed additional drastic change and damage in both countries. In China, the Cultural Revolution (CR), from 1966 to 1976, was a decade of national chaos. In this decade, China literally closed down fully the entire nation's higher education system and partially closed the secondary education system, sending 18 million middle school graduates to the countryside to be "re-educated by the poor and lower-middle peasant" (Gao, 1996). It was a decade when the notion prevailed that "the more knowledge one possesses, the more reactionary one would be". The overall knowledge creation and transmission systems were shut down during the political and economic chaos, all energies taken up by the cult of one person. By the end of the decade, after Mao's death, the CPC officially announced that the CR had led the national economy to the brink of collapse (Langley, 2008; Yan and Gao, 1996). Likewise, in 1973 the Worker's Party of Korea created a Cultural Revolution–type movement (Lee, 2003). Young communists were sent to the countryside to initiate ideological, cultural, and technical education of farming households. New rural educational institutions were established, and existing rural officials and staff were reassigned and required to enroll in these *juche* ideology–focused training programs. This social reengineering eroded knowledge of, respect for, and influence of traditional farming techniques; rural life was thoroughly regimented by the government, with all individual initiative stifled. At its peak in 1976, it was elevated to a mass 'Nature Re-Making Program' (Lee, 2003).

Because of their comparable political principles, ideology, and structural arrangements, both countries had adopted similar institutional policies in developing and controlling their human resources. In the Chinese central-planning system and present DPRK, the governments implemented regulations and mechanisms restricting unauthorized mobility of human resources. In China, it was the *hukou* system established in 1951, whereas in DPRK the *songbun* system was initiated in 1958, another learning from China, and intensified in 1993 (Collins, 2012). The direct English translation of both systems is "residence registration system". Under such systems, career choices are not made by individual choice or preference but by the demands of government planning and controls (Sun and Wang, 2009).

THE ECONOMIC CONTEXT OF HRD

After the Cultural Revolution, China undertook unprecedented economic reform for over three decades. Its accomplishment in economic development has been well documented and acclaimed in the literature (Collins et al., 2012; Wang, Rothwell, & Sun, 2009). In particular, this transition introduced market mechanisms with multiple ownership systems in the form of state-owned, private-owned, foreign-owned enterprises, and joint ventures (SOEs, POEs, FOEs, and JVs). These enterprises became major market competitors in all spectrums of economic activities and have been actively engaged in the global markets. From an HRD perspective, the multiple ownership systems have created new opportunities and incentives for individuals to pursue alternative career opportunities while contributing to economic growth (Sun and Wang, 2009).

Considering China's economic reform as a deviation from orthodox socialism, DPRK openly criticized China in the mid-1990s as "traitors to the socialist cause" and articulated a belief that DPRK was the only pure socialist state remaining to protect the original promise of the socialist revolution (Noland, 2004, p. 3; see also Schobell, 2004). Yet from the 1990s, DPRK appeared to start experimenting with a dual model, allowing limited free market and decentralization, but remaining politically controlling concerning ideology. This change came as a response to the collapse of the Soviet Union and its East European bloc and was also partially inspired by China's success. The shift was reflected in the establishment in 1991 of its first special economic zone (SEZ) in Rajin-Sonbong, known as Raseon, near the northwestern border with China. What turned out to be an unsuccessful Raseon SEZ experience plus China's repeated pressure on DPRK to initiate overdue market reform (Bajoria and Xu, 2013) prompted DPRK to reconsider the China model in the new millennium. From 2000 to 2011, the late leader, Kim Jong-il, visited China frequently (Wang, 2011) and investigated China's forefront provinces in economic reform, such as Guangdong and Shanghai together with other cities across China. The emerging economic reform in DPRK since 2000 may have reflected its learning from these visits. For example, in 2002, DPRK announced changes in its economic policy in agricultural product prices through its PDS and established additional SEZs (Lee, 2003; Hassig and Oh, 2009). Despite the repeated failure of SEZs since the 1990s, there are still plenty of incentives for DPRK to develop SEZs, because it would allow for experimentation with economic reforms in a manner that is "controllable, regional, and above all, containable" (Abrahamian, 2014, p. 3). Since 2013, DPRK has significantly increased its SEZs from 4 to 18 (www.sina.com.cn). It has also slightly relaxed the restrictions on the free market, mostly limited to farmers' markets. It is estimated that in the early 2000s, the average North Korean family drew 80% of its income from small businesses, which are still illegal (Lankov, 2011).

Limited reform in DPRK has resulted in some encouraging changes. For example, in more developed areas, such as the new Rason SEZ, one in five adults have access to a mobile phone (Abrahamian, 2014). More recent reports from DPRK also show the economy, at least in Pyongyang, as starting to open up. Shopping malls with luxury consumer goods are available to those who can afford them. KFC opened its first store in Pyongyang, and Coco-Cola can be purchased in stores accepting foreign currencies (Anonymous, 2013). However, according to Haggard and Noland (2007), North Korean "reform should not necessarily be interpreted as an effort to liberalize the economy. Rather, it can be interpreted as an effort to control a process of decentralization and marketization … as well as economic control" (p. 52).

THE INSTITUTIONAL CONTEXT AND STRUCTURES OF HRD IN CHINA AND NORTH KOREA

In China, the *hukou* system has effectively maintained a divide between rural and urban populations. The movement of individuals from rural to urban areas was permitted by the government only for joining the armed forces, colleges, state-owned enterprise (SOE), or government recruiting. Similarly, urban residents were not allowed to move to a different urban area without government approval. Associated with the system was the lifetime employment arrangement in the workplace. While economic reform allows multiple ownership forms in recent decades, employment within the state-owned sector is still *hukou*-based. Since the 1980s, the Chinese government has begun to relax the *hukou* restrictions in some cities in response to the challenge of skill shortages in some urban areas.

Compared to China, the *songbun* system in DPRK "is based on the economic conditions at the time of one's birth and influenced by one's family class foundation (*todae*, or the occupation and social status of one's parents prior to liberation)" (Colin, 2012, p. 3). *Songbun* is a combination of China's *hukou* and personal profiling systems (*chengfen* and *dang'an*). Following China, DPRK extended the system to the extreme. It divided the entire population into three major political categories: the loyalists, the waverers, and the hostiles. The three broad classes are further subdivided into 51 classes. "Kim Il-sung gave a public speech in 1958 in which he reported that the core class represented 25%, the waverer class 55%, and hostile class 20% of the population." (Collins, 2012). This classification system has had a profound impact on all aspects related to human resource development and beyond, including education and career opportunities, job assignments, and residential locations, as well as opportunities in marriage. For example, only those in the three highest 'lines' in the core *songbung*, the loyalists, are allowed to attend schools, to live and work in Pyongyang, the capital of DPRK (Goodkind and West, 2001); and no one from a family with a politically compromised background may reside in Pyongyang (Anonymous, 2012). Normally, a person with good *songbung* does not want to marry someone of a lesser *songbung* because they don't want their children to be negatively affected by the association. This is similar to China's *chengfen* (political status), once popular during the decade of the Cultural Revolution (Li, 2003; Sun, 2011).

With similar cultural, sociopolitical, and institutional contexts, both nations maintain dual systems of HRD to develop crucial human resources for two critical purposes: to maintain political control within the dominant ideology, and to ensure the societies have sufficient skills maintain productive activities within the confines of the political system. HRD-related legislation and policies also support these two purposes, because "in a democratic system, politics follows the law; in socialist systems, the law follows politics" (Zook, 2012, p. 135).

The Party School Systems and Governmental HRD Institutions

HRD systems in both countries have been clearly marked with similar ideological characteristics. In China, CPC's latest ideological principle is represented by its "three confidences": confidence in the (socialist) road taken, confidence in the (Marxist) theory, and confidence in the system (Xi, 2013). In DPRK, while maintaining the *juche* ideology, it revised the Ten Great Principles of the Monolithic Ideology in 2013, removing previous wordings such as, "communist" and "proletarian dictatorship" to reflect the KWP's determination to maintain a hereditary totalitarian state (Wang and Hu, 2013); whereas a similar wording of "people's democratic dictatorship" is highlighted in China's constitution (Wang, Lamond, & Verner, 2015). In terms of HR, these national ideological systems only tolerate qualified administrators with ideological purity. This task has been accomplished through respective party school systems, which create a path for the achievement of this ideal.

With the core function of developing the capability and capacity of the party, the party school systems in both countries play the following roles: (1) develops party officials' leadership in interpreting and implementing the ongoing policies; (2) develops selected cadres' management and leadership skills, which functions also in the career development of party members; (3) conducts policy-interpretation-related research for justification purposes. Similarly, the party schools are established at multiple levels. The Central Party Schools (termed Kim Il-sung Advanced Party School in DPRK) at the national level are intended for the training of ministry- or provincial-level senior officials. Party schools at the provincial level offer training for local officials. In China, different provinces also have their own party schools and township-level party leaders (Wang, 2012). Training targets include party or government officials and senior executives in SOEs.

In China, a parallel HRD system also exists under the government umbrella. For the central government, a Chinese Academy of Governance was established in 1994 to develop senior civil servants for national and provincial agencies (www.nsa.gov.cn). Meanwhile, equivalent governmental training institutions can be found within the ministry structure, such as the Academy for International Business Officials (AIBO) in the Ministry of Commerce, and the College for Managerial Cadres in the Ministry of Civil Affairs (www.mca.gov.cn). Because of the close association between the government and the party, government training institutions often organize and coordinate party school training programs according to ongoing political requirements (www.china-aibo.cn). By the same token, DPRK also has HRD institutes under the cabinet and the ministries intended for the training of administrators and officials, such as the Socialist Working Youth University, the Politics University of the North Korean CIA, and Kim Il-sung High Level Elite School (Reed and Kim, 2007).

HRD-Related Legislation

The Ministry of Education (MOE) in both countries is responsible for planning and coordinating vocational education systems. Consistent with the sociopolitical context in both countries, the training and education systems have two essential tasks: to maintain ideological purity and loyalty and to promote skill formation and knowledge learning. The goal is justified by a pithy aphorism once popular in China: "we'd rather maintain socialist weed rather than grow capitalist sprouts" (Wang et al., 2015). These two tasks are reinforced through legislation, party documents, and leaders' speeches. For example, in all education programs in China, 'political studies' is required on the curriculum from middle school to graduate education. On the skill development side, China's vocational education system is highly regulated based on government regulations and laws, such as the Vocational Education Law (1996), the Education Law (1995), and the Labor Law (1995). In 2010, MOE published the *Standards of Secondary Vocational School* to regulate all vocational schools from governance and finance; to student/instructor ratio; to campus size, sports facilities, libraries, and equipment; and to student/computer ratio, even as detailed as the available seats in a library in relation to student/instructor ratio (Ministry of Education, 2010). In this aspect, HRD activities are essentially similar to the pre-reform, central-planning tradition. Given China's ongoing economic transformation and emerging development of private sectors, HRD activities that related to economic activities and enterprises are largely based on a laissez-faire approach, leaving operations to respond to the free market.

A similar pattern is observed in North Korea. Due to Kim Il-sung's (1960) emphasis on the decisive role played by human consciousness in developing productive forces in the early years, the nationwide focus and priority in training has been to maintain the *juche* ideology as required by the constitution. For example, in the 1972 constitution, *juche* became the guiding principle of DPRK. *Juche* is commonly translated as 'self-reliance' but covers much more, especially calling for North Koreans to preserve the essence of pure socialism as an ideological foundation, as a distinctive path and guiding principle different from other nations in the communist bloc (Zook, 2012). The constitution further articulated that the *juche* ideology was a particular variant and "creative application" of Marxist-Leninist revolutionary ideology, one that was "national in form and socialist in content" (DPRK *Constitution*, 1972, as cited in Zook, 2002). *Juche* was later elevated to an exalted and exclusive status in all state practices, including culture, education, and the economy. In particular, training in *juche* is required for all HRD-related activities (Lee, 2003).

In 2001, DPRK passed its first ever Education Law. It highlighted the critical importance of education in determining the future of the nation, and reinstated 11-year compulsory education, stipulating that all education, including higher education and vocational education, be state-funded and free of charge to individuals. In 2011, it further passed the DPRK Higher Education Law (Zhou, 2012). From the skills development perspective, the vocational and general education in DPRK is also centrally controlled from the establishment of majors and curricula to student admission and enrollment. Given the fact that the private sector has not been formally developed, a free training market was not observed.

Vocational and Educational Base for HRD

Vocational education (VocEd) in China can be divided into a system of secondary and higher education. While both are focused on developing individuals' professional and technical skills in a given profession, the secondary VocEd system produces graduates with high school equivalence, and the higher VocEd develops graduates with college equivalence. According to China's Vocational Education Development Report, 2002–2012 (Ministry of Education, 2010), China has established the largest vocational education system in the world. In the last decade, the system has trained almost 73 million technicians. Among the graduates, 90% from secondary VocEd, and 20% from higher VocEd were state-funded. The employment rate of all graduates reached 87%, much higher than that of college graduates for the same period. To prepare for the ongoing urbanization process, the VocEd system has also trained 185 million (person/program) rural youths (Ministry of Education, 2010). The same report also documented that in 2011 alone, both secondary and higher VocEd formal education enrollment has exceeded 30 million; an additional 60 million people attended training programs offered by the VocEd system. However, VocEd diplomas are generally less valued or carry less prestige than college degrees among the Chinese influenced by Confucian culture.

During the recent decade, China has significantly expanded its higher education system. By 2013, its universities and colleges increased to 1,218 from 784, and the number of junior colleges increased to 1,266 from 429 in 2005. Meanwhile, the nation also encouraged the development of private colleges. By 2012, there were a total of 1,400 private universities, including 390 four-year colleges compared with only 20 in 2005 (Ministry of Education, 2010). There were also hundreds of satellite campuses operated by universities in the US and European countries in the 2000s.

In North Korea, aside from the formal education system, there are very potent and pervasive non-formal and informal systems promoting the *juche* principle that has become the defining factor of North Korean communism. *Juche* focuses on "the independent stance of rejecting dependence on others and of using one's own brains, believing in one's own strength and displaying the revolutionary spirit of self-reliance". It is a "scientific and revolutionary world outlook indispensable for men of a communist type" (Kim, 1977, p. 17). Similar to China, education in DPRK, including VocEd, has a key tenet focused on loyalty to the party in one person, the great leader, and in one thought, the leader's thought (Reed, 1997). Under the key tenet, most VodEd activities are part-time based or in the form of study while working in factory colleges, night schools, and correspondence learning (Reed, 1997). A factory college is a higher educational institute attached to a factory's workplace, "it allows factory workers to perform their duties during the day: after daily work they receive education related to the factory's required technical skills until they complete the training course" (Cho, 2006, p. 27). One of the advantages in this form of training is that it can make effective use of technical personnel, equipment, along with internal factory resources to develop the expertise needed by specific factories. Learning in factory colleges consists of two general tracks: technical and management. Both night tertiary colleges and factory colleges are administered by the state, with state appointed full-time faculty members supplemented by part-time instructors employed in the respective factories; the number of students is controlled by the state comprehensive plan in specific regions (Lee, 1993). In addition, these institutions offer job-related training under a Job Skill Learning System (JSLS). This system designates work groups as basic units of job-skill learning, which links production closely with training. The JSLS is basically structured according to the training objectives and workers' skill level.

Another similar aspect of the two countries in recent years is their expansion of higher education. In DPRK, the number of colleges and universities was significantly expanded to 270, with junior colleges increasing to 600 from 516 in 1989 compared with 170 in 1980. By 2003, the MOE reported that the number of universities had increased to more than 300 (Reed and Kim, 2007). In 2009, DPRK has approved the establishment of the first private Christian university, Pyongyang University of Science and Technology (Thompson, 2012).

ORGANIZATIONAL-LEVEL HRD

Parallel to the party and governmental training system, the training market in China has also witnessed significant expansion due to the growing needs in HRD in state-owned enterprises, (SOEs), private-owned enterprises (POEs), and multinational corporations.

In the Chinese context, human resources and human talents are differentiated, with the latter being a subset of the former. The CPC defines human talent as "those with specific professional knowledge and skills engaged in creative work to contribute to the society; they have high capacity and quality among all human resources" (CPC and State Council, 2010). After joining the WTO, CPC and the government established a strategy to "strengthen the nation through talent development (*rencai qiang guo*)" in the *National Plan for Developing Talents: 2002–2005*. It further emphasized the principle of "all human talents are to be managed by the party (*dang guan ren cai*)". The most recent talent strategy specified that by 2020, the country is to develop talent resources from the current 114 million to 180 million, a 58% increase, with the proportion of talents among human resources increasing by 16% (CPC & State Council, 2010).

With the support of the central government, coupled with increased market competition, Chinese organizational HRD activities have adopted a variety of strategies and approaches. Initially, the contemporary HRD approaches in China were introduced by Foreign Invested Enterprises (FIEs). For example, FIEs have brought in techniques in task and performance analysis, interactive training, and career development. HRD practices were also influenced by global consulting firms, such as McKinsey, HeyGroup, Boston Consulting Group, and other related multinational firms (Wang et al., 2009). Universities actively imported MBA programs, especially those in the US and Europe, to introduce new learning techniques and training content and methods. These Western influences, combined with Confucian learning culture, have created significant markets for HRD in the following areas. First, widespread certification programs in areas from engineering and IT to HRM and accounting have attracted millions of professionals in all organizations. Second, organizations have taken advantage of external consulting firms, especially Western ones in HRD-related areas of change management and training. Third, executive MBA programs have blossomed in every corner of the nation.

However, the latter two areas of HRD practices have recently been restricted by the party-state. SOEs were ordered to cut ties with US consulting firms. Some Western media speculated that this restriction had a twofold purpose, namely, to develop local indigenous consulting capacities and for security concerns (e.g., Lumsden and Zhou, 2014). On the EMBA front, the recent anticorruption campaign in China has cooled the market down significantly. "The government has barred 'leading cadres' in the party, the government and SOEs from signing up for costly business training unless they have official approval and pay their own fees. Those already on such programs must quit immediately" (Zhang, 2014). This was because the EMBA programs have become a central location for cadres to develop *guanxi* or personal network with peers and private entrepreneurs, thus vulnerable to potential corruption, which often costs the taxpayers as much as RMB 620,000 (USD 100,000) per person (Bradshaw, 2014). In the meantime, employees in the private sector were not restricted to participating in all forms of training and development opportunities. Given China's vast territory and imbalance in economic development, HRD practices, especially those consistent with the market economy, are generally more advanced in East China than in the western part of the country.

While there is only limited information available for DPRK on HRD activities in the emerging reform, sporadic reports reveal that the nation has sent ideologically reliable cadres to receive market-economics-related training both at home and abroad, particularly to China (Marumoto, 2007). Also employees in SEZs in joint venture (JVs) have been sent to receive training by foreign partners. Currently, almost all JV partners are from China or South Korea (Abrahamian, 2014). However, for the majority of SOEs, skill-based training is not a priority due to lack of available work. Hassig and Oh (2009) have reported that although official reports claim a zero unemployment rate, it is the practice that employees in SOEs leave their useless job assignment during workdays to engage in economic activities outside the socialist economy sector, working either on behalf of the SOE or for personal vending businesses. In these cases, employees are said to pay the SOE management a nominal fee to keep their absence from being recorded; some organizations that do not have enough work for their employees simply permit workers to sign in for work in the morning and then go out and produce something of value for the organization, such as homemade consumer goods, similar to Chinese SOE practices in the late 1970s and early 1980s. The workplace chaos and unofficial development of suppressed local markets has been repeatedly reported in the recent years (e.g., Everard, 2011).

DISCUSSION

In China and North Korea, HRD practices are deeply rooted in the cultural, historical, sociopolitical contexts, as well as in ideological propaganda. These cultural and historical roots explain their similarities today as 'relational' societies; the resemblance in sociopolitical areas is explained by their common paths in historical development and ruling by one party in an authoritarian or totalitarian governance style with strong ideological compliance. These contexts mean that HRD practices in China and DPRK fundamentally differ from the Western world. The paramount task and the first priority for HRD in the two countries is to maintain "thought unification"

(Tsai and Dean, 2013) with the purpose of sustaining the one-party dominance. A condition for HRD practice and growth is that common practices in skill building and knowledge transfer also ensure that individual thinking remains on the right ideological track. The uniqueness of HRD practices in both countries is best explained by the dominating role played by the party's Propaganda and Publicity Department (PPD) in both countries (Agitprop Department in DPRK), which extends downward from national to local levels, including all SOEs and public institutions. The PPDs are considered by both parties as legitimate tools for building and transforming society—a society with traditional values in harmony with and respecting hierarchy. As such, all of the following institutions are required to obey and follow the orders of the PPDs: (1) newspapers, radio and TV, publishing houses, magazines, and other news and media agencies; (2) universities, middle schools, primary schools, (3) vocational education, specialized education, cadre training, and other educational organs; (4) musical troupes, theatrical troupes, film production and theater, clubs, and other cultural organs; and (5) literature and art troupes, cultural amusement parks, cultural palaces, libraries, remembrance halls, exhibition halls, museums, and other cultural facilities and commemoration exhibition facilities (Encyclopedia on the Building of the CCP, 1992, p. 676; see also Winstanley-Chesters, 2015 for the case of DPRK). Clearly, all content areas related to learning, education, knowledge, information, and entertainment are under the control of the party's key organs. In recent years, Internet censorship has also become a focus of the party's control. China's Great Firewall effectively blocked all unwanted websites from its citizens. Google's recent withdrawal from China represents a typical case of what could happen if citizens disobey the party's ruling on information censorship (Wang, Lemond, & Verner, 2015). Furthermore, in the past two decades, the CPC has also promoted and expanded party branch offices to POEs and FIEs in order to more effectively influence POEs and FIEs (Wang et al., 2014).

The party's leadership and unification thought control has profound implications for HRD in both nations. First, given its surprising resemblance to China, it is anticipated that DPRK will follow the same path as China when embracing a more open policy to the outside world, including the enhancement of HRD practices, already proved to be valuable in improving the skill level of the labor force, and given the continuing political thought control to maintain unity and loyalty to the party. Second, China's success in economic development has demonstrated that the resulting outcomes of HRD are consistent with the host system design, because HRD still cannot operate above and beyond its functional role defined by the party. Chinese universities have recently received an order from the Minister of Education to never allow learning materials that spread Western values to enter in any classrooms without clearly defining what constitutes the Western values content (Yuan, 2015). While China has created an economic miracle in the last three decades by taking advantage of its low-cost labor, her future development is to be determined by its human resources' ability in creativity and innovation.

Third, and related to the creativity issue, the ideology mechanisms may have affected and suppressed human resources' creativity for greater societal benefits. While skill training and knowledge building are promoted within the sectors framed by the party, HRD's role in unleashing human expertise must be considered as essentially confined within an invisible box. To judge otherwise would require a demonstration that human potential can be developed to the fullest extent within certain ideological confines. The three-decades miracle has largely been based on effective learning and copying of existing technologies in the West with low-cost labor. As China faces the challenge of transforming itself from a labor-intensive economy to a technology-intensive economy, it is doubtful whether it can develop a creative workforce with novel ideas adequate for the necessary implementation and acceptance that would lead to significant economic gains. While existing research on cross-cultural creativity has focused mainly on cultural factors, more research is needed to study the relationship between thought control and creativity and the role of HRD in this relationship (Zhou and Su, 2010).

CONCLUSION

HRD activities and practices in China and DPRK with their similar contexts may be able to contribute to organizational and national goals in the defined domain. However, it is unlikely to develop world-class employees due to its restrictive ideological control and thought unification. While HRD has played an unprecedented role in recent years of economic reform, especially in China, its future role in developing innovation capacity and creativity in both countries will largely depend on how much HRD learning and development activities are given a free hand to explore. As suggested by Friedman (2015), the world economy is experiencing a paradigm shift: "the last 25 years was all about who could make things cheapest, and the next 25 years will be about who can make things smartest." We anticipate that HRD's role in this shifting paradigm is likely to be critical in shaping the future of these two countries.

REFERENCES

Abrahamian, A. (2014). The ABCs of North Korea's SEZs. US-Korea Institute, Baltimore, MD: School of Advance International Studies, John Hopkins University.

An Encyclopedia on the Building of the CPC. (1992). Chengdu: Sichuan People's Press.

Anonymous. (2012). *Pyongyang Elite Key to Regime's Survival*, CHOSUN ILBO. Retrieved from (http://english.chosun.com/site/data/html_dir/2012/01/04/20120 10400633.html) on November 24, 2014.

Anonymous. (2013). *New Pyongyang Mall Breaks Every Capitalist Taboo.* Accessed on November 26. 2013. (http://english.chosun.com/site/data/html_ dir/2013/08/06/2013080600435.html)

Bajoria, J., & Xu, B. (2013). *The China-North Korea Relationship.* Washington, DC: Council on Foreign Relations.

Barkema, H. G., Chen, X. -P., George, G., Luo, Y., Anne, S., & Tsui, A. S. (2015). West meets East: New concepts and theories. *Academy of Management Journal,* 58(2): 460–479.

Bolton, J. R., & Eberstadt, N. (2 October 2008). The world shouldn't fear the collapse of North Korea. *Wall Street Journal, Eastern edition,* A.19.

Bradbury, J. (1961). Sino-Soviet competition in North Korea. *China Quarterly,* 6: 15–28.

Bradshaw, D. (November 27, 2014). China's top business schools to pay back fees in EMBA crackdown. *Financial Times.* Online. Accessed on 2 April 2015. (http://www.ft.com)

Cho, J. -A. (2006). *North Korea's Human Resource Development System.* Studies Series: 06–06. Seoul: Korea Institute for National Unification.

Collins, N., Zhu, Y., & Warner, M. (2012). HRM and Asian socialist economies in transition: China, Vietnam and North Korea. In C. Brewster & W. Mayrhofer (Eds.), *Handbook of Research on Comparative Human Resource Management,* 598–619. Northampton, Mass.: Edward Elgar.

Collins, R. (2012). *'Marked for Life': Songbun, North Korea's Social Classification System.* Washington, DC: Committee for Human Rights in North Korea (HRNK).

CPC and State Council. (2010). *Outlines for National Mid-to-Long Range Talent Strategy, 2010–2020.* Beijing: People's Press.

Eberstadt, N. (June 26, 1990). The coming collapse of North Korea. *Wall Street Journal, Eastern Edition,* A18.

Eberstadt, N. (2004). The persistence of North Korea. *Policy Review,* 127: 23–48.

Everard, J. (2011). The markets of Pyongyang. *Academic Papers Series,* 6(1): 1–8. Seoul: Korea Economic Institute.

Friedman, T. (April 15, 2015). What's up with you? *New York Times,* D2.

Goodkind, D., & West, L. (2001). The North Korean famine and its demographic impact. *Population and Development Review,* 27(2): 219–238.

Haggard, S., & Noland, M. (2007). *Famine in North Korea: Markets, Aid, and Reform.* New York: Columbia University Press.

Hassig, R., & Oh, K. (2009). *The Hidden People of North Korea: Everyday Life in the Hermit Kingdom.* Lanham, MD: Rowman & Littlefield.

Hofstede, G., & Bond, M. H. (1988). The Confucius connection: From cultural roots to economic growth. *Organizational Dynamics,* 16(4): 5–21.

Kang, J. W. (2006). The "domestic revolution" policy and traditional Confucianism in North Korean state formation: A Socio-cultural perspective. *Harvard Asia Quarterly,* 10(2): 34–45.

Kim, I. -S. (April 15, 1960). *The "Flying Horse" Speed.* Pyongyang radio broadcast, NKHS.

Kim, I. -S. (1977). *Theses on Socialist Education.* Pyongyang: Foreign Language Press.

Kuark, Y. T. (1963). North Korea's agricultural development during the post-war period. *China Quarterly,* 14: 82–93.

Langley, A. (2008). *The Cultural Revolution: Years of Chaos in China.* New York: Compass Point Books.

Lankov, A. (2011). It's not all doom and gloom in Pyongyang. *Asian Times.* Online. Accessed 12 February 2014. (http://www.atimes.com/atimes/Korea/MI23Dg02.html)

Lee, E. (1993). *Research on North Korean Factory College.* Unpublished Thesis. Seoul: Seoul National University.

Lee, G. (2003). The political philosophy of Juche. *Stanford Journal of East Asian Affairs,* 105(3): 106–118.

Lee, Z. N. (1999). Korean culture and sense of shame. *Transcultural psychiatry,* 36:181–194.

Leong, C. K. (2012). A dynamic game of reputation and economic performances in nondemocratic regimes. *Dynamic Games and Applications,* 2(4): 385–400.

Li, C. (2003). Sociopolitical changes and inequality of educational opportunity: The impact of family background and system factor on education (1940–2001). *China Social Science,* 3:86–98 (in Chinese).

Li, J. (2012). North Korea economic development: Current status and future. *Contemporary International Relations,* 1: 49–52 (in Chinese).

Lumsden, A., & Zhou, W. (September 29, 2014). *The Truth Behind China's Ban on Foreign Consulting Firms. Thinking.* Sydney, Australia: Corrs Chamberu Westgarth.

Marumoto, M. (2007). *North Korea and the China Model: The Switch from Hostility to Acquiescence.* Korea Economic Institute, Academic Paper Series 2(5): 1–12.

Ministry of Education. (2010). *The Standards for Secondary Vocational Schools.* Beijing: People's Education Press.

Ministry of Education. (2012). *China's Vocational Education Development Report: 2002–2012.* Beijing: People's Education Press.

Nanto, D. K., & Manyin, M. E. (2010). *China-North Korea Relations Report* 7–5700, R41043. Washington, DC: Congressional Research Service.

Noland, M. (2004). Famine and reform in North Korea. *Asian Economic Papers,* 3(2): 1–40.

Peng, X. (1987). Demographic consequences of the great leap forward in China's provinces. *Population and Development Review,* 13(4): 639–670.

People's Daily. (November 11, 1953). *Long-Live the Successful Mutual Cooperative Cause between China and DPRK.* p. 1. (中朝两国互助合作的事业胜利万岁).

People's Daily. (February 3, 1958). *Gather Up All Forces, Striving for Higher Target.* p. 1. 《人民日报》社论《鼓足干劲，力争上游！》.

People's Daily. (August 27, 1958). *The Land can Yield as High as We Dare to Imagine.* p. 1. (人民日报，人有多大胆，地有多大产).

Reed, G.G. (1997). Globalisation and education: The case of North Korea. *Compare: A Journal of Comparative Education.* Vol. 27 Issue 2, p167-178.

Reed, G. G., & Kim, Y. -Y. (2007). Schooling in North Korea. In G. Postiglione & J. Tan (Eds.), *Going to School in East Asia,* 258–274. Westport, CT: Greenwood Press.

Ricks, T. E., & Glain, S. (11 July 1994). Death of Kim may be beginning of end for North Korea's Communist regime. *Wall Street Journal, Eastern edition,* A3.

Ryu, K., & Cervero, R. M. (2011). The role of Confucian cultural values and politics in planning educational programs for adults in Korea. *Adult Education Quarterly,* 61(2): 139–160.

Schobell, A. (2004). *China and North Korea: From Comrades-in-Arms to Allies at Arm's Length.* Washington DC: Strategic Studies Institute.

Sun, M. (2011). Family background and the acquisition of cadre status (1950–2003). *Society,* 31(5): 48–69.

Thompson, A. (September 2012). Teaching the dragon: Mission-minded Christian educators run fast-growing universities in North Korea and northeast China. *Christianity Today,* 56(8): 19–21.

Tsai, W. H., & Dean, N. (2013). The CCP's learning system: Thought unification and regime adaptation. *China Journal,* 69: 87–107.

Tu, W. (2000). Implications of the rise of "Confucian" East Asia. *Daedalus*, 129: 195–218.

Wang, G. G. (2012). Indigenous Chinese HRM research: phenomena, methods, and challenges. *Journal of Chinese Human Resource Management*, 3(2): 88–99.

Wang, G., & Hu, J. (2013). North Korea revises "the Ten Principles" to highlight the party's leadership. *China Global Times*, Online. Accessed 24 October 2013. (http://world.huanqiu.com/exclusive/2013–08/4236640.html)

Wang, G. G., Lamond, D., & Worm, V. (2015). It's the context all the way down! An institutional theory perspective on Chinese HRM Research. *Journal of Chinese Human Resource Management*, 6: 1–7.

Wang, G. G., Lamond, D., Zhang, Y., & Ke, J. (2014). Moving forward: Exploring unique Chinese phenomena and advancing HRM Research. *Journal of Chinese Human Resource Management*, 5: 2–13.

Wang, G. G., Rothwell, W. J., & Sun, J. Y. (2009). Management development in China: A policy analysis. *International Journal of Training and Development*, 13: 205–220.

Wang, G. G., Werner, J., Sun, J. Y., Gilley, W. J., & Gilley, A. (February 2015). Gateway to new frontier: Reconceptualizing the definition of HRD. *Proceedings of 2015 International Conference of AHRD*, St. Louis, MO.

Wang, W. (December 21, 2011). Kim Jong-Il's seven visits to China. Online Accessed 3 December 2013. (http://www.china.org.cn/world/2011–12/21/content_24211950.htm)

Winstanley-Chesters, R. (2015). *Environment, Politics, and Ideology in DPRK: Landscape as Political Project*. London: Lexington Books.

Xi, J. P. (March 2013). *Speech at the 12th Chinese National People's Congress*. Online. Accessed 10 December 2013. (http://www.cnr.cn/gundong/201303/t20130317_512169849.shtml).

Xing, H. (October 25, 2013). Mao's great leap forward for beating the UK and the US? *Elderly Daily*, A4. (in Chinese).

Yan, J. Q., & Gao, G. (1996). *Turbulent Decade: A History of the Cultural Revolution*. Honolulu: University of Hawaii Press.

Yuan, G. (2015). *MOE: Never Allow Learning Materials Spreading Western Values into Classrooms*. (教育部：绝不能让传播西方价值观念教材进课堂). Online. Accessed 5 April 2015. (http://news.xinhuanet.com/mil/2015–01/30/c_127438 444.htm)

Zhang, L. (5 September 2014). Xi's war on corruption spreads to China's executive MBAs. *Financial Times*, Online. Accessed 2 April 2015. (http://www.ft.com)

Zhang, Y. B., Lin, M. C., Nonaka, A., & Beom, K. (2005). Harmony, hierarchy and conservatism: A cross-cultural comparison of Confucian values in China, Korea, Japan, and Taiwan. *Communication Research Reports*, 22: 107–115.

Zhou, J., & Su, Y. (2010). A missing piece of the puzzle: The organizational context in cultural patterns of creativity. *Management and Organization Review*, 6(3): 391–413.

Zhou, Z. (January 2012). *North Korea Passes DPRK Higher Education Law*. Online. Accessed 15 November 2013. (http://www.people.com.cn)

Zook, D. C. (2012). Reforming North Korea: Law, politics, and the market economy. *Stanford Journal of International Law*, 48: 131–183.

6 Human Resource Development in Malaysia and Singapore

Maimunah Ismail and
Roziah Mohd Rasdi

INTRODUCTION

This chapter aims to analyze human resources development (HRD) issues in Malaysia and Singapore from historical, institutional, and societal perspectives. It also provides discussion on similarities and differences in HRD in the two countries as well as the challenges ahead in the face of globalization. These two countries were chosen to represent the Southeast Asia region because Malaysia and Singapore manifest some differences despite similarities in terms of history. Other countries in the region are Brunei, Darussalam, Indonesia, the Philippines, and Thailand, and together with Malaysia and Singapore they have comparatively high levels of per capita income compared with Cambodia, Lao People's Democratic Republic, Myanmar, Vietnam (referred to as CLMV), and Timor-Leste. The countries of Southeast Asia cover a total area of 4,500,000 km² (1,700,000 sq. miles) with an estimated total population of 610 million people, they achieve a gross domestic product (GDP) of $1.9 trillion, and have an average per capita income nearly equal to that of China (Brown, 2013). In addition, the region contains one of the most populous countries in the world, Indonesia, with a population of 250,585,668, as well as one of the least populated, Brunei, with a population of only 418,626.

Malaysia and Singapore have experienced significant growth, in pattern and rate. Malaysia has achieved one of the best economic records in Asia, with GDP growing at an average of 6.5% for almost 50 years. With its rich natural resources fueling the economy, Malaysia became a newly industrialized market economy at the turn of the century (Wikipedia, 2015, https://en.wikipedia.org/wiki/Economy_of_Malaysia). Singapore, well known as one of the 'Four Asian Tigers', has developed into an advanced and high-income economy, as well as being notable for maintaining exceptionally high growth rates and rapid industrialization within a relatively short period of time. The high-performing economies of Malaysia and Singapore feature the high-end growth of the Southeast Asian economies and represent the emergence of the Asian Economic Miracle alongside other countries, such as South Korea, Taiwan, and China (World Bank, 1993).

Malaysia and Singapore need to sustain their progress by developing systems in order to advance technological, economic, and human development. These countries are moving up the value chain through high-growth patterns in all technology sectors by raising productivity, improving competitiveness, and enabling human potential and by advancing education and training systems, with a special focus on technological intensification in all sectors. Continuous HRD is one of the key ingredients for the transformation of nation development and economic growth. Developing human resources is not an overnight task. It needs careful planning, effective strategies, operative policies, and vigorous implementation from the government, public, and private sectors as well as other nongovernmental organizations.

Malaysia and Singapore have all successfully entered into high-growth progression using HRD strategies. Taking these nations as representative of Southeast Asia, we provide in this chapter an insight into the complexity of the HRD process in both countries. We selected them due to their unique history and development of HRD, despite deficiencies in resources in certain sectors, plus their late development as capitalist countries compared to the developed countries in the West and Japan.

After an introductory section, we present the reviews of HRD components for each of the two countries. They cover the historical and socioeconomic backgrounds, training and education systems, the providers for HRD, the legislative and policy context, and the HRD practices. Indicators such as GDP per capita, years of schooling, gender inequality, labor force participation rates, R&D percentage to GDP, and phases of development experienced by each country are briefly highlighted to observe for similarities and differences in the two countries. The concluding section discusses comparisons between several aspects of the HRD, which are strongly influenced by the HRD and mainstream development initiatives in these countries. We base the reviews in this chapter mostly on data available from online sources, supplemented with secondary data collected from empirical studies of national and international sources.

MALAYSIA

The History and Development Contexts of HRD

HRD policies in Malaysia can be traced back to the colonial British administration in the region. Before the independence of Malaya in 1957, the major development policy was very economically oriented solely toward increasing productivity of the two major natural commodities, namely rubber and tin, for the purposes of meeting the high industrial demand in Europe. There was no specific usage of the term 'HRD' in policy and practice of the then Malayan Civil Service (MCS), whose policy was mainly to maintain peace through its 'break and rule policy' of the colonial administration in all states of the Malay Peninsula (Ismail and Osman-Gani, 2011). However, sporadic and limited 'training' for specific personnel in the public services did occur, such as for teachers, army personnel, police force, MCS officers, and British expatriates. There were also ad hoc programs called 'adult education classes' under the auspices of the Ministry of National and Rural Development, which aimed to eradicate basic adult illiteracy in the community (Mazanah and Associates, 2001). The program succeeded, but later the Adult Education Division of the ministry was renamed the Community Development Division (Bahagian Kemajuan Masyarakat or KEMAS), hence the emphasis also shifted to community development goals beyond illiteracy eradication.

An important milestone in terms of training during the colonial era in Malaya was the beginning of extension activities when the Department of Agriculture was set up in 1905. In 1945, however, when the department became active after long interruptions caused by World War I (1914–1918) and World War II (1939–1945), an important change happened, particularly the setting up of the Rural Extension Training and Development Centres (RETDC) by the Department of Agriculture in 1956. This was actually the beginning of the formalization of extension education for both extension workers and farmers in the country (Ismail, 1999). It was also the time when the concept of non-formal education seemed to be introduced as an alternative to formal education.

The training for human resources after independence is linked closely with the major development policies of the Malaysian economy (Ismail et al., 2007). The tragic event of May 13, 1969 resulted in the beginning of the New Economic Policy (NEP) (1971–1990) with its two-prong, long-term goal of eradicating poverty and the restructuring of society in order to correct interethnic economic imbalances. The specific HRD policies pursued in the NEP were: (i) the creation of preferential treatment in business, education, training, and job positions for disadvantaged groups of Malays and other indigenous groups and (ii) the creation of business-driven HRD policies that supported multinational and local companies' demand for labor. The growth of HRD is believed to be one of the consequences of the five-year affirmative development policies from 1971 to 1990 (Ismail, 1999).

From the 1990s then, the greater focus on HRD began with the Industrial Master Plan (1985–1995), which emphasized the upgrading of technology and human resources through institutional support. This continued right through to the Ninth Malaysia Plan (2006–2010), (Malaysia, 2006). But HRD under the New Economic Model (NEM) (2011–2020) faces more challenges. NEM consists of the four pillars of 1Malaysia, the Government Transformation Program (GTP), Economic Transformation Program (ETP), and the Tenth Malaysia Plan (2011–2015). The model is based on innovation, which is an important national agenda to make the country remain relevant in a competitive global economy. One of NEM's goals is to move toward a high-income economy, which implies the importance of high-skilled human capital. This measure will move the nation toward achieving more than a doubling of annual per capita income from the current USD 7,000 to USD 15,000, with a target of USD 20,000 in 2020. The rationale of this drive, according to Fong (2010) is that Malaysia should not be perpetually caught in the 'middle-income trap', a common phenomenon in many developing countries. Malaysian labor force statistics in relation to some Asian countries show Malaysia (25%) as the lowest in terms of highly skilled labor, putting Malaysia behind Taiwan (33%), Korea (35%), and Singapore (49%) (NEAC, 2010). These reasons certainly suggest the need for a strong HRD policy with programs in all services and in the manufacturing and financial sectors. Continuous efforts are being undertaken to train and improve the skills of the workforce to meet market demand, in the belief that the quality of the workforce will be enhanced through education and training.

One of the strategies under the Malaysian government's HRD initiative is called technical and vocational education and training (TVET) (Malaysia, 1997; Ibrahim and Associates, 2004). The key providers of TVET are the Ministry of Education, Ministry of Higher Education, and the Ministry of Human Resources (MHOR). The Ministry of Education, under the Department of Technical Education, runs technical-vocational schools for upper secondary students. Also important under this strategy is the role of PSD and specifically the National Institute for Public Administration (Institut Tadbir Awam Negara or INTAN) in providing professional training for public-sector managers. INTAN has also expanded its function as a training center for professionals in the region and for the commonwealth countries (Silong et al., 2011).

Manufacturing is one of the industries in the private sector that plays an active role in HRD. The industry contributed 25.8% to the country's GDP in 2010 (NEAC, 2010: 88), involving MNCs, SMEs, and Small-Medium Industries (SMIs). HRD in the manufacturing industry aims proactively to forge public-private partnership alliances with foreign multinational companies (MNCs) in the higher value-added forms of production, as well as encouraging companies to become the national driving force in the economic transformation process. HRD programs are also actively organized by private-sector trade organizations such as the Federation of Malaysian Employers, the Federation of Malaysian Manufacturers, the Malaysian Trade Union Congress, the Malaysian Federation of Bank Employees, and the Malaysian Institute of Management.

The Education System and the Malaysian Qualifications Framework

The education system in Malaysia consists of preschool (two years), primary (six years), secondary (five years), a total of 11 years of compulsory formal school education (excluding preschool) after which a school leaver receives a school certificate, called Sijil Pelajaran Malaysia or SPM (lately known as Malaysian School Certificate). After SPM, an individual will have a choice of pursuing Sixth Form Matriculation Classes (or Pre-University Classes) or Diploma Programs of various types (one to three years). SPM is a basic qualification for employment in administrative or nonprofessional positions; otherwise, an SPM holder may choose to go for higher qualification through tertiary education (minimum of two to three), which is explained next through the Malaysian Qualifications Framework (MQF).

MQF is Malaysia's declaration about its qualifications and their quality in relation to its higher education system. MQF is an instrument that develops and classifies qualifications based on a set of criteria that are approved nationally and benchmarked against international best practices. It clarifies the earned academic levels, learning outcomes for study areas, and credit system based on student academic load. These criteria are accepted and used for all qualifications awarded by recognized higher education providers. Hence MQF integrates with and links all national qualifications. MQF also provides educational pathways through which it links qualifications systematically. These pathways will enable the individual to progress through credit transfers and accreditation of prior experiential learning in the context of lifelong learning.

The MQF has eight levels of qualifications in three national higher education sectors and is supported by lifelong education pathways (Figure 6.1). The sectors come under three titles: Skills, Vocational and Technical, and Academic. Levels 1 to 3 are Skills Certificates awarded by the Skills Sectors.

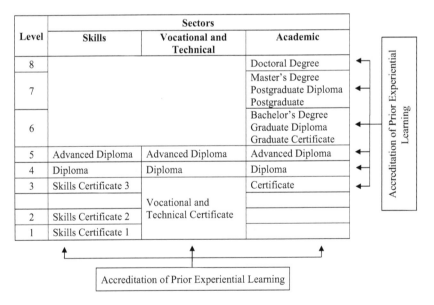

Figure 6.1   Malaysian Qualifications Framework

Academic and Vocational and Technical Certificates are at Level 3. Meanwhile, Diploma and Advanced Diploma are at Levels 4 and 5. Bachelor's Degree corresponds to Level 6, Master's Degree to Level 7, and Doctoral Degree to Level 8. These levels are differentiated by learning outcomes, credit hours, and student learning time. Lifelong education pathways cut across all levels of qualifications through accreditation of prior experiential learning.

Basic Regulatory Framework Governing HRD

Three main pieces of legislation important to Malaysian HRD practices are the Employment Act 1955, the Industrial Relations Act 1967, and the Human Resource Development Corporation Act 2001 (Omar, 2011). The Employment Act 1955 (EA) sets the minimum terms and conditions of employment to which every employer is legally obliged to comply (Omar, Chan, & Joned, 2009). Some of the basic terms are: a) payment of wages and deductions; b) termination of contract; c) employment of women and maternity protection; d) rest days, hours of work, overtime payment, public holidays, and leave; and e) terminations, layoffs, and retirement benefits. The act also governs the employment of domestic workers and foreign workers. The act does not prohibit employers and employees from agreement on terms and conditions that are more favorable, but parties cannot enter into any employment agreement on terms and conditions less favorable than stipulated in the EA. The terms and conditions of employment for employees not covered under the EA are governed by their employment contracts and negotiated individually based on market demand or are covered under a collective agreement (for unionized companies). Employees in the public sector, including statutory bodies, are excluded from the applications of the act.

The Industrial Relations Act 1967 (IRA) regulates the relationship between an employer and employee and their trade unions, stipulates provisions to help prevent and settle trade disputes, and regulates the termination of employment. The major concern of the act is in the settlement of any trade disputes between employer and employee. Unlike the EA, the IRA does not restrict an employee on the basis of his wages from seeking redress and justice under the act. This act also implicitly lays down matters considered as rights of the employer, often referred to as management prerogatives. These cover (a) promotion of employee, (b) transfer of employees, (c) employment of any person in the event of a vacancy, (d) termination by an employer of the services of an employee due to redundancy or reorganization, (e) dismissal and reinstatement of employees, and (f) assignment or allocation by an employer of duties or specific tasks to employees that are consistent or compatible with the terms of his employment. These prerogatives are predominantly related to HRD functions. The court recognizes the importance of giving employers certain prerogatives to enable them to run their business affairs and will not interfere in the exercise of these prerogatives if they are exercised in good faith (Omar, 2011).

The IRA is widely used by employees irrespective of wages or union membership to seek redress for unfair dismissal (including constructive dismissal). Employee termination and dismissal form an important component in HRD practice, as some activities related to HRD, such as organizational development intervention strategies, may result in termination of employment. An employee who considers himself dismissed without just cause or excuse by his employer may make representations in writing to the director general of Industrial Relations to be reinstated in his former employment. Reinstatement is an application in which an employee requests to be put back in law and in fact to the same position as he occupied before he was dismissed or terminated by his employer (Asghar, 2007). Any claims for unfair dismissal will be resolved by the Industrial Department through a conciliation process under the IRA.

The Human Resource Development Corporation Act 2001 (HRDC Act) provides for the imposition and collection of a HRD levy, referred to as the Human Resource Development Fund, for the purpose of promoting the training and development of employees, apprentices, and trainees. This act also regulates the administration of the fund (HRDF) by the Human Resource Development Corporation (HRDC or currently known as Pembangunan Sumber Manusia Berhad or PSMB), formerly known as the Human Resource Development Council prior to its corporatization in 1993. Employers listed in Part I of the First Schedule are required to pay a HRD levy at the rate of 1% of the monthly wages (basic salary and fixed allowances) of their employees. In addition to the compulsory contribution imposed on employers specified in Part I of the First Schedule, the act also allows for voluntary registration with the HRDC and contribution to the fund by employers specified in Part II of the First Schedule. Such employers shall pay a human resources development levy at the rate of 0.5% of their employees' monthly wages (Omar, 2011).

To date, the HRDC has introduced eight training grant schemes, namely,

- The SBL Scheme
- The SBL-Special Scheme
- The Annual Training Plan (ATP) Scheme
- The PERLA Scheme
- The Prolus Scheme
- The Joint Training Scheme
- The SME-OJT Scheme
- The Accreditation of Prior Achievement (APA) Scheme

Six other schemes related to employee training and upgrade of skills include:

- The Apprenticeship Scheme
- The Computer Based Training Scheme

- The English Language Program for Workers Scheme
- The SME Training Partners (SMETAP) Scheme
- The Purchase of Training Equipment and Setting up of Training Room Scheme
- The Information Technology and Computer-Aided Training Scheme

I Training Expet.com (2015). (www.itrainingexpert.com/hrdf-claim)
Continuing Professional Education: Providers and Programs

Continuing Professional Education (CPE) programs at the workplace are meant to expose employees to the organization's culture and update new skills according to the organization's needs. Professionals in Malaysia may arrange their own CPE programs in their domain by applying for permission from their professional associations. For example, medical doctors may apply for permission from the Malaysian Medical Association (MMA) to certify CPE providers and CPE credit hours before running a CPE program. The Judicial and Legal Training Institute is another example of workplace CPE for judiciary government staff in the country.

In Malaysia, there are more than 20 professional associations registered under the Malaysian Professional Centre (MPC), where all professional associations in Malaysia are pooled together (Hashim and Ahmad, 2011). Ten of the associations are:

- The Malaysian Bar and Judicial and Legal Training Institute
- The Institute of Engineers Malaysia (IEM)
- The Institute Kimia Malaysia (IKM)
- The Agriculture Institute of Malaysia (AIM)
- The Malaysian Dental Association (MDA)
- The Malaysian Medical Association (MMA)
- The Malaysian Architects Association (PAM)
- The Malaysian Pharmaceutical Society (MPS)
- The Veterinary Association Malaysia (VAM)
- The Institute of Surveyors Malaysia (ISM)

The law profession in Malaysia, for instance, follows professional development programs organized by the Malaysian Bar and Judicial and Legal Training Institute with cooperation of the Malaysian Bar Council. The Malaysian Bar organizes extensive talks, seminars, and conferences on current issues in the profession. Under the Malaysian Bar, law graduates who wish to practice in the private sector are required to enroll under a master (a private practicing lawyer), inform the Malaysian Bar, and file a petition to the state's high court where they are doing their chambering.

School administrators get their CPE at Institute Aminuddin Baki (IAB), which is the principal educational management and leadership-training center in this country. It was established based on a review result of the Implementation of Educational Policies in the Cabinet Report 1979 and has evolved in line with current developments in education and government policies. As the Ministry of Education's training wing, IAB takes pride in ensuring excellence in its national leadership and training courses conducted mainly for educational leaders and managers. IAB is committed to realizing the National Key Result Area (NKRA) by ensuring that educational administrators and leaders are well trained to keep up with the era of globalization and fast-paced technological changes.

The Board of Engineers Malaysia (BEM), as a provider of CPE to the engineering profession in Malaysia, has been responsible for providing CPE programs to the professional members on a voluntary basis since September 2003. The objective of CPE for professional engineers is the maintenance of technical knowledge and skill (i.e., competency) to do a job. The board states that a CPE program for professional engineers consists of six major groups of activities: formal education and training activities, informal learning activities, conference and meeting, presentation and papers, service activities, and industry involvement (for academicians). Every practicing professional engineer must submit his or her CPE records together with his or her application for renewal of registration with the BEM.

Universities provide professional education for the professional job market. After graduation, the graduates are required to go for internship (or industrial training) before they go into a proper job. The doctors need to go for internship and the lawyers go for their chambering. CPE collaborates with the professional associations, recognized places for apprenticeship, and the boards of the professions to certify for practice. In organizing CPE programs, the participants, trainers, professional associations, and workplaces collaborate in processes to seek for the needs for CPE, choosing the right experts to train, the workplaces to apply for permission to run the program, and to award CPE credit hours. Professional Architect Malaysia, for example, organizes the whole year's CPE workshops by collaborating with the professional associations, universities, and the experts in the field. Collaborations among providers also involve incentives given to professionals in the forms of study leave; scholarships by the government and professional associations provide opportunities for professionals to further their studies through post-graduate programs.

The Ministry of Higher Education established the Higher Education Leadership Academy (AKEPT) in January 2008, which aims to transform higher education in Malaysia, especially in the area of human capital development. AKEPT provides leadership development for the top- and mid-level management of Malaysian higher education institutions. AKEPT constantly strives to provide highly relevant and pragmatic courses that will lead to a certification program that is recognized by the global higher education community. With its clear vision, mission, and objectives, AKEPT, works with public and private universities and professional bodies in organizing conferences that bring together academia, professionals and students, and industrial experts to share current issues and research findings (Hashim and Ahmad, 2011).

The emergence of HRD as an academic discipline in Malaysia is worth noting briefly here. The birth of the HRD concept in Malaysia concurred with the rapid growth of HRD in Western contexts during the '80s. HRD was one of the areas of specialization in its parent field of extension education at the University of Agriculture Malaysia (beginning in 1997 and known as Universiti Putra Malaysia or UPM), a university that champions the growth of knowledge in agriculture and its related fields. UPM pioneered HRD in the country with its first master of science in HRD started at the university in 1987 (Ismail and Osman-Gani, 2011). HRD then expanded to several other universities, such as Universiti Teknologi Malaysia (UTM) (1991) and Universiti Malaysia Sarawak (UNIMAS) (1994). Then in 1997, UPM went on to offer HRD at the undergraduate level, long after the university had been successfully running a program at the master's level, begun in 1981. The years after 2000 were the time when HRD became a distinct discipline academically and in practice in Malaysia (Ismail et al., 2007). The setting up of HRDC in 1993 has been significant in bridging training activities among HRD affiliates, especially in the industrial sector.

HRD at the Organizational Level

We base this discussion of the organizational level of HRD in Malaysia on HRD initiatives conducted by the National Institute for Public Administration (Institut Tadbiran Awam Negara), also known as INTAN. The institute plays a fundamental role in the development of administrative and diplomatic officers (ADOs) who are the most prominent civil servants in the country (civil employees totaled 1.4 million or 10% of the total labor force in 2014). Historically, ADOs are equivalent to 'Malaysian Civil Service' officers, a term used during the British colonial administration. As a leading training institute in the public sector, the functions of INTAN are guided by the National Training Policy as contained in the Service Circular No.1/1970, dated 13 January 1970. The main features of the National Training Policy, as outlined in this circular are as follows (Silong et al., 2011):

- To achieve a progressive Public Service
- To facilitate the development of an administrative group and experts who are skillful, efficient, and advanced in line with scientific development and techniques of management
- To reduce transfers and depletion of Public Service personnel
- To achieve efficiency, effectiveness, and economy
- To achieve an equitable administration of training for all in the Public Service in line with government policy
- To provide fair and equitable training opportunities for all personnel in the Public Service

With the tabling of the Tenth Malaysia Plan and Vision 2020, HRD through education and training has become an important component in the country.

INTAN's general objective is to develop HR potential in the public sector toward excellence in service through training for national development through its seven regional campuses and one main campus in Kuala Lumpur. INTAN's operational objectives include (Silong et al., 2011):

- To provide training for public officials to increase their knowledge and skills and to enhance positive attitudes through training;
- To raise the quality of leadership and management of organizations in the public sector;
- To conduct research, publication, and provide consultancy services to instill corporate culture and values in the public sector;
- To provide a forum to encourage and promote ideas on and creativity in management in both the public and private sectors; and
- To establish linkages with local and international agencies and institutions.

Executive training in INTAN involves six major areas (ICT Management, Financial Management, Economic and Business Management, Urban and Environment Management, Human Resource Management, and Quality Management) and covers three organizational levels (individual, supervisory and management, leadership). The areas of emphasis are at the individual level where values and ethics, communication skills, basic computer skills, human relations skills, language and attitudes are the main concern. At the second level, the emphasis is on developing supervisory and management skills in the areas of ICT management, financial management, quality management, economic and business management, human resource management, as well as urban and environment management. At the highest level, the focus is on leadership development covering aspects of project development at town, district, and local government levels. To remain a competitive HRD provider in the public sector, INTAN continuously works with private partners, local and abroad, to bridge gaps in knowledge.

Malaysian Population Clock, http://countrymeters.info/en/Malaysia. Access on 24 April, 2015
Population Pyramids of the World from 1950 to 2100, http://populationpyramid.net/malaysia/2015/. Access on 24 April, 2015

SINGAPORE

History and Development Phases

Singapore is a small island on the tip of the Southern Malay Peninsula in Southeast Asia. A colony of the British Empire since 1819, Singapore first acquired independence in 1963 through a merger with Malaya, Sarawak, and

Sabah to form Malaysia. Singapore gained sole independence on August 9, 1965, when it was forcefully separated from Malaysia as a result of differences in political views between the leaders of Singapore and Malaysia. The city-state occupies an area of 710.2 square kilometers (274.2 square miles) (Low, 2001), with a total population of 5.6 million in 2015 (Table 6.1).

Singapore today is a modern city-state and global center for industry, business, finance and communications. Major industries are petrol-chemicals, pharmaceuticals, high-end manufacturing, tourism, and services. Key trading partners include Malaysia, the United States of America, China, the European Union, Hong Kong, and Japan. Per capita gross national income was US$45,374 in 2005, which increased to US$53,591 by 2012 (Table 6.1). As a young nation and with limited natural resources, one of Singapore's highest priorities has been education, training, and human capital development. The People's Action Party (PAP) has been the dominant political party, and the government is essentially a single-party dominant government. Since 1965, the PAP set policies and laws consistent with its rationale. The National Trade Unions Congress (NTUC) is the sole trade union center in Singapore and is politically supported. The purpose of the trade union is not so much to safeguard the rights and welfare of the workers but rather to preserve economic stability and, most importantly, to attract investors (Osman-Gani, 2004; Law, 2007).

Through the three phases of development, Singapore has also evolved from an 'Early Industrialization' economy to a 'Newly-Industrialized' economy, and on to the 'Globalized and Diversified' economy it is today (see Table 6.1). An important scenario concurrent with the change was the emergence of the vocational technical education (VTE) system in response to changing manpower needs (Law, 2007). This section on Singapore focuses on the economic, manpower, and VTE strategies implemented during these phases of development. TVE stands out as an important aspect of the HRD initiative becoming an alternative medium of education and training, complementary to the academic education offered by the secondary and university systems.

It is worth noting that in the early days of its economic development, the efforts at HRD came under the rubric of manpower development, general education, technical education, and training. The government embarked on more sophisticated HRD strategies as it moved from investment-driven economic growth to that which is driven by innovation, together with its emphasis on the regionalization and globalization of business. A small country with virtually no natural resources, Singapore has become one of the most developed countries in Asia, primarily due to its strong emphasis on developing human resources and for continuously making significant investments in its human capital (Low, 2001). Human resource development (HRD) has always been a core element in its strategic economic plans. The HRD strategies have been continuously revised and adjusted in conjunction with other national strategic economic policies. Singapore is thus

Table 6.1 Human Development Index (HDI) of Malaysia and Singapore

			HDI Indicators				5*			Phases of Development		
HDI Rank	Countries (Land Area/Population)	Years	1	2	3	4	F	M	6	1960s–1970s	1980s–1990s	2000s–2010s
64	Malaysia (329,847.0 km²; 30.8 million (2015))	2000	0.839	18,730	16					Investment-driven economy (education, labor-intensive technologies)	Innovation-led economy (R&D, expansion of education)	Factor-driven economy (knowledge-based)
		2005	0.875	22,783	16.5							
		2012	0.909	27,541	17.2	0.256	43.8	76.9	1.07			
18	Singapore (716.1 km²; 5.6 million (2015))	2000	0.826	38,063	14.4					Factor-driven economy (labor intensive)	Investment-driven economy (capital intensive)	Innovation-driven economy (toward maturation stage)
		2005	0.852	45,374	14.4							
		2012	0.895	53,591	14.4	0.101	56.5	76.6	2.09			

HDI Indicators: 1 –HDI Value, 4 –Gender Inequality Index (Data as of 2012)
2 –GDP per capita (USD) 5* –Labor Force Participation Rate—F: Female, M: Male (Data as of 2011)
3 –Expected Years of Schooling, 6 –R&D% to GDP (2005–2010)

(Note: *There is a discrepancy in statistics between the GDP per capita for Malaysia, which is targeted at USD 20,200 by 2020 based on NEM document*).

Sources: Human Development Report (2013, p. 144–159) and (http://hdr.undp.org/en)

a unique case that exemplifies the benefits of national HRD policies and strategies through a tripartite approach (involving employers, unions, and government) and a multidepartmental approach (Osman-Gani, 2004; Singapore Tripartite Forum, 2009). Several terminologies have been used in the past that emphasized the importance of HRD based on the changing perspectives of Singapore's national policy, terms such as human resource development, manpower development, people development, training and skills development, workforce development, and human capital development. However, these terms are interchangeably used in meaning and practice nowadays.

The education system in Singapore has five levels: preschool (three years), primary (six years), secondary (four to five years), postsecondary (one to three years) and university (three to four years). The diversification of education starts at secondary level, following through at the postsecondary and university levels. It combines academic, specialized, and integrated learning in both public and private institutions. Early diversification at the age of 13 years allows an individual to have an ample choice in the type of education according to interest, academic ability, and future vocational ambitions. The country also has pathways for the populations with special needs. Undeniably, Singapore's education curriculum is rigorous; but it is essential to maintain the country's human resource preeminence. The country's population needs to be well trained and ahead of the general curve in order to compete in a globalized world. It has been shown that Singaporean students rank highly in international education rankings, such as the Trends in International Mathematics and Science Study. This is evident by the fact that Singapore was placed fifth in reading, second in math, and fourth in science in the last round of the OECD's international tests in 2012—the Program for International Student Assessment (PISA)—in which OECD stated that the high-quality of teaching in Singapore is not accidental but rather the result of deliberate policy actions. It identifies the synergy among the schools and the Ministry and the National Institute of Education (NIE)(OECD, 2012).

It has recently been noted that the polytechnic has developed in tandem with Singapore's progress. The country's leader further highlighted polytechnics in Singapore as jewels in the country's educational system in offering a first-rate tertiary education to a large segment of the population. Polytechnics offer high-quality, practice-oriented technical training for jobs. They lay a solid academic foundation, especially in technical subjects like math and science, for those who go on to further their studies. An example is Ngee Ann Polytechnic, which collaborates with industry partners to create more opportunities for students to work and solve real-world problems. The scope for internship placements has also been expanded to include project components. These benefits of polytechnics to the nation contribute to Singapore's inclusive policy, through which the leader envisions everybody benefiting from the progress of the nation.

Vocational Technical Education in Singapore: The Path and Provider

ILO (1997) reported that VTE in Singapore is an important sector to expedite to ensure that the workforce has the basic vocational and technical skills to support labor-intensive manufacturing activities, such as ship repairing, sheet metal working, plumbing, and radio and TV maintenance and repair. The first vocational institute, the Singapore Vocational Institute (SVI), was established within the school system in 1964. In 1968, 84% of students in schools were enrolled in the 'academic' stream with only 8% in the technical, 7% in the vocational, and only 1% in the commercial stream (Law, 2007). As a result, a Technical Education Department (TED) was established within the Ministry of Education in 1968 to oversee the development of technical secondary education, industrial training, and technical teacher training. The secondary vocational schools were phased out in favor of vocational institutes. The apprenticeship schemes were transferred from the Ministry of Labor to the TED in 1969. By 1972, there were nine vocational institutes and the number of graduates had increased tenfold from 1968 to 1972. By 1973, the TED had developed a training infrastructure of sufficient strength for the next major phase of its development. Thus the first Industrial Training Board (ITB) was formally created in 1973 to centralize, coordinate, and intensify industrial training. In the early 1970s, another government agency, the Economic Development Board (EDB), whose mission is to promote foreign investment into Singapore, also played a significant role in strengthening the industrial training system. By partnering with multinational corporations, such as Tata of India, Rollei of Germany, and Philips of Holland, it established the so-called Joint Government Training Centers, which helped to enlarge the pool of trained technical manpower. This was an important milestone in the country's HRD (Law, 2007).

The new focus was the development of new industries, such as petrochemicals, biotechnology, and information technology, as well as manufacturing services in testing, financing, warehousing, and purchasing. In the area of VTE, a new stage was set for the establishment of the Vocational and Industrial Training Board (VITB) by the amalgamation in 1979 of the ITB and another existing board, the Adult Education Board (AEB). The AEB was a board established in 1960 to meet the educational needs of working adults, including general education and some basic vocational training. With increasing educational and training opportunities, it became apparent that the domains of AEB and ITB were complementary components of the same system of training for school leavers and working adults. A new certificate in business studies (CBS) was introduced in 1981. For the first time, a Centre of Vocational Training was set up within VITB to develop professional capability in areas such as curriculum development, training of trainers, and instructional media development. These were important areas of functional expertise necessary to develop and support a quality vocational training system. Economic restructuring had a direct impact on the capability of the existing workforce. What was expected of the workforce in terms of knowledge, education, and skills before was no longer adequate. National efforts were therefore directed toward developing a comprehensive continuing education and training system (CET) to facilitate upgrading and re-skilling of the workforce, especially those with lower education and skills. So between 1983 and 1987, three national CET programs were launched, namely, the Basic Education for Skills Training (BEST), Work Improvement Through Secondary Education (WISE), and Modular Skills Training (MOST). Focusing on English language and mathematics, BEST and WISE benefited a quarter of a million working adults in helping them to acquire a primary or secondary-level education, respectively (Law, 2007).

In 1990, the industrial training system was further strengthened with the introduction of a New Apprentice System, patterned after the well-known Dual System of Apprenticeship in Germany. In 1991, the government published a new economic plan in charting the next phase of Singapore's development. The goal was to turn Singapore into a first-league, developed nation within the next 30 to 40 years. The new direction was focused on building the manufacturing and service sectors as the twin engines of economic growth. Companies were encouraged to diversify, upgrade and develop into strong export-oriented companies and to invest in the regional economies. From the educational perspective, the stage was set for a critical review of the postsecondary education system, including the universities, polytechnics, and VITB. This review would ensure the availability of well-trained and qualified manpower in the high-technology, knowledge-intensive, and service industry sectors (Law, 2007).

In the knowledge-intensive economy, Singapore saw the need to increasingly develop into a globalized, entrepreneurial, and diversified economy. The response in the educational sphere was to position Singapore as an education hub by attracting foreign students and internationally renowned institutions to Singapore. In 1992, the Institute of Technical Education (ITE), a world-class postsecondary education institution, was established from the earlier Vocational and Industrial Training Board (VITB) (1960s–1970s). ITE was the first educational institution to win the prestigious Singapore Quality Award in 2005. Its mission, focused on the consistent use of five-year strategic plans, has created a unique brand of an ITE college education for a quarter of the school cohort in Singapore. Two plans were successfully completed over a ten-year period from 1995 to 2005. The first, "ITE 2000 Plan" (1995–1999), was aimed at positioning ITE as an established postsecondary education institution. The vision of the second plan, the "ITE Breakthrough" (2000–2004), was to build ITE into a world-class technical education institution. Under the current, third, five-year plan, the "ITE Advantage" (2005–2009), the vision is to be a global leader in technical education (Law, 2007).

HRD-Related Acts

Several HRD-related acts form part of the legislation in Singapore (Foo, 2009). The Employment Act covers workmen (defined as employees involved in manual labor). All executives and managers earning above S$2500 per month (approximately US$1700) are not covered under the act. However, executives and managers earning below S$2500 are covered only under the salary protection provision of the act.

The Skills Development Levy (SDL) Act was introduced in 1979 to encourage employers to upgrade the skills of their employees. This act, which came into effect October 1, 2008, states that employers must contribute either 0.25% of an employee's salary (capped at S$4500) or S$2, whichever is higher, into a Skills Development Fund (SDF), which comes under the Ministry of Manpower. The SDF provides a series of incentives to companies to upgrade the skills of their workers, such as funding for accredited training programs for employees.

In relation to this act, the Singapore Workforce Development Agency (WDA) was set up to retrain and upgrade the skills of Singapore workers so as to maintain a competitive workforce. The programs and benefits the WDA offers include: Lifelong Learning Endowment Fund, professional skills program, job placement programs, skill upgrading programs, career scholarships, job re-creation program, subsidized course fees for employers, and grants for employers who provide certified training (Foo, 2009).

The Organization of HRD in Singapore

HRD in Singapore is discussed here in terms of the initiatives of the Institute of Technical Education (ITE), a government-funded postsecondary institution focusing on vocational technical education. It plays a very significant role in Singapore's journey of transformation through HRD. It is unique because, despite the more difficult challenges in VTE, it has built a responsive world-class system of VTE in preparation for the future. Its mission is, "to create opportunities for school leavers and adult learners to acquire skills, knowledge and values for lifelong learning". There are clear demarcations with respect to the missions of the university, the polytechnic, and ITE. ITE's mandate is to provide an attractive pathway for those who do not progress to the junior colleges or polytechnics. All students receive at least ten years of general education in schools, comprising six years primary and four to five years secondary. Depending on their academic achievements, aptitudes, and interests, about 90% of a student cohort will progress to the junior colleges, polytechnics, or colleges of ITE (Hwa Chong Students' National Education Committee or SNEC, 2013).

The unique features of ITE's system of vocational technical education are several. First is the "One ITE, Three Colleges" system of governance. Under this initiative, to build a more responsive VTE system, the overall plan was to regroup existing smaller campuses into three mega regional campuses renamed 'ITE Colleges'. Under this system, the ITE headquarters continues to oversee the policy formulation and common functional areas of interest, such as curriculum development, student intake, examinations, quality assurance, and consistency of standards throughout the colleges. The economy of scale has helped to achieve synergy and resource savings through greater collaborations and yet promote competition among the colleges. The first regional campus, ITE College East, was built in 2005. The remaining two, ITE College West and ITE College Central, were completed in 2009 and 2011, respectively.

The second feature is the unique brand of ITE college education called 'Hands-On, Minds-On, and Hearts-On'. This is a holistic college education that has provided motivation, assisted student learning, and nurtured all-rounded graduates who are ready to take on the challenges of the global economy. 'Hands-on' training ensures that the students acquire a strong foundation in technical skills. 'Minds-on' learning develops independent thinking and flexible practitioners who are able to cope with changes. And 'hearts-on' learning develops the 'complete person' with a passion for what they do, with confidence and care for the community and society. These attributes underpin a comprehensive education where students integrate theory with practice through course work, projects, industry partnership, community service, and global education.

The third key element is pedagogy, the 'how' part of teaching and learning. The underlying objective in ITE's pedagogy is to develop 'thinking doers', graduates who can apply what they have learned to practice. Called the 'Plan, Explore, Practice, and Perform' or the 'PEPP' model, the approach is interactive and process based. The fourth unique feature of ITE is the creative and innovative teaching and learning environment. In particular, with the pervasive use of information technology (IT) in the society and knowledge economy, it is important that students learn in a rich IT-based environment that better prepares them for the real working world. The eTutor and eStudent were pioneering systems launched in 2002. Leveraged on the advances in IT and e-learning technologies, the web-based eTutor system has transformed ITE into a community of connected online learning campuses (Law, 2007).

Comparisons of HRD in Malaysia and Singapore

Based on the descriptions and the reviewed literature, a summary of comparisons of HRD in Malaysia and Singapore is shown in Table 6.2.

HRD Challenges in Malaysia and Singapore

Several issues and challenges in HRD in Malaysia and Singapore are worth highlighting here. First, with respect to skilled labor, Malaysia's productivity

Table 6.2 Similarities and Differences Between HRD in Malaysia and Singapore

	Malaysia	Singapore
Historical context	A British colony (originally Malaya) gained independence in 1957, and together with Sabah, Sarawak, and Singapore formed Malaysia in 1963. Rich in natural resources.	A British colony, separated from Malaysia in 1965 due to differences in political vision. Very limited natural resources, totally dependent on human resources and its strategic business location.
Development context (after 1960s within five decades)	From labor-intensive to knowledge-based economy. HRD has been in tandem with poverty eradication initiatives involving the socio-culturally and regionally diverse population.	From labor-intensive to innovation-driven economy or toward maturation stage. High investment in human capital development of its population, which is quite socio-culturally homogenous.
Scope of HRD	Wider scope of HRD started with adult illiteracy program within community development, training for specific employees in public sector, and now expanded to various professions in industries. National HRD policies are one of the Strategic Reform Initiatives (SRIs) (developing quality workforce) of the New Economic Model (NEM) involving relevant agencies and professional associations.	Vocational Technical Education (VTE) system has been the core of HRD as an alternative medium of education and training to manpower needs in manufacturing, engineering, services, and trade. Clear demarcations with respect to the missions of the universities, polytechnics, and ITEs. National HRD policies are addressed through the tripartite approach (involving employers, unions, and government) and a multidepartmental approach.
Providers of HRD	HRD or Training and Development (T&D) division of organizations	Institutes of Technical Education (ITE) and other polytechnics.

	Malaysia	Singapore
	and private companies, professional associations, and tertiary education institutions. Employers contributed to HRD fund (coordinated by HRDC under the Ministry of Human Resources).	Employers contributed to Skills Development Fund (SDF) (coordinated by the Ministry of Manpower).
Issues and Future Consideration	More HRD initiatives for specific types of employees (to achieve NEM goals of inclusivity, high income, and sustainability) based on rural-urban, interethnic, gender, generation cohort, and sector disparities. To double skilled workers from its current 30% by 2020. To reduce dependency on foreign labor (21% in 2015) through affirmative strategies to increase graduates numbers in science, technology, engineering, and mathematics (STEM) at college and university level.	To build positive image of VTE, which needs continuous and integrated systems of ICT, marketing, and rebranding of ITE. The country is continuously hungry for highly skilled foreign workers to develop Singapore into the talent capital of the global economy (migrants made up 25% of the workforce in 2012).

is lower than that of Singapore. Table 6.3 compares statistics of labor force participation with tertiary education, skilled labor force, and labor productivity per employee for Malaysia and Singapore and the first world. It is evident that Malaysia still faces a huge challenge in closing the gap with first-world talent. Singapore enjoys an economy built on the skills of its people; as shown in the table, labor productivity approaches the average of the Organization for Economic Cooperation and Development (OECD) countries.

The second challenge is that both countries are heavily dependent on foreign labor, particularly Malaysia, where foreign labor is high in construction, agriculture, and manufacturing, both at semiskilled and professional

Table 6.3 Closing the Gap to Achieve Characteristics of First-World Talent in Malaysia and Singapore

Country	Labor Force with Tertiary Education1 (%) (2007)	Skilled Two Labor Force (%) (2008)	Labor Productivity US$PPP3,000 per Employee
Malaysia	23.4	28.0	26.6
Singapore	35.0	51.0	60.8
USA	34.1	36.3	92.6
OECD (average)	27.4	37.6	64.8

Source: "The Economic Planning Unit," Tenth Malaysian Plan 2011–2015 (2010, p. 192)

[1] Tertiary education is the educational level following the completion of secondary education, i.e., after 11–12 years of basic schooling. Colleges, universities, institutes of technology, and polytechnics are the main institutions that provide tertiary education.
[2] Management, professional, and other skills occupations.
[3] Adjusted to Purchasing Power Parity.

levels. Singapore differs slightly in that it has invested highly to hiring expatriates; however, this is compensated by the high productivity per employee. The consequent challenge to HRD for both countries is providing migrants and expatriates with equal opportunities in training and development; hence they should be covered by any employee or employment act in the country. This leads to another challenge: for the countries to sustain competitiveness, they must continue developing more homegrown talent, not just on the office floor but also in the boardrooms.

The third challenge for Malaysia and Singapore is the move from quantity in HRD outcomes. For instance, in Malaysia, every employee in public services needs to undergo a minimum of seven days of formal training a year. Likewise in Singapore, one-third of Singapore employees receive some form of workplace training every year. But how much of this training is integrated into performance management or career development or individual learning needs poses a challenge to employers to quantify its return-on-investment in both nations.

Finally, a challenge to educators in HRD about transitioning from training to e-learning. The challenge will be to ensure that e-learning should add value to traditional classroom-based training rather than simply replace it. We cannot deny the strength of blended learning in upgrading the skills and knowledge of employees given that there are many factors affecting the effectiveness of learning at the workplace.

FUTURE DEVELOPMENT OF HRD IN MALAYSIA AND SINGAPORE

We discuss future developments of HRD in Malaysia and Singapore as follows: First, we propose Malaysia should intensify efforts to about double the pool of skilled workers from its current 30% by 2020. We need to reexamine and restructure the vital role of formal education in the science-based curriculum from the primary to secondary level. As for Singapore, the shortage of skilled labor is not that serious, as the country performs well by international standards.

Second, both countries should tap the skills and experiences of the returning professionals (remigration of Malaysian and Singaporean professionals) to the countries. In order for this to happen, efforts should be intensified to entice them to return by having attractive incentives that allow them to stay once they have come back. Malaysia should emulate the best practices of returnees or the reverse brain drain programs of countries such as China, Korea, and India (Ismail, Kunasegaran, & Mohd Rasdi, 2014) that have been successful in attracting a sizable number of professionals in science and technology to build their nations.

Third is to improve the image of vocational training programs at polytechnics and colleges as preparation of middle-level employees for various industries in Malaysia. Similarly, improve the image of the TVE system in Singapore, which has been the core of HRD as an alternative medium of education and training to manpower needs in manufacturing, engineering, services, and trade. This should be done through public advocacy and marketing campaigns; there should also be a similar path for both vocational and academic streams in terms of education and career development opportunities.

Finally, both countries should improve the image of HRD as an academic discipline at the university level. This could be possible by having a curriculum that emphasizes smart partnership with private companies in the various R&D initiatives. The ultimate aim of R&D should also be looked at from the human side of development in addition to scientific and technological advancement for these countries.

CONCLUSION

What can we learn from the experiences in HRD of both Malaysia and Singapore? Of those experiences that are transferable, the first is the early recognition by the Malaysian and Singaporean governments of the importance of investing in human capital development. Malaysia recognized this importance as the country gained independence in 1957 and as it followed through in the five-year development policies and the subsequent transformation initiatives in NEM. Singapore recognized that the surest way to building a strong nation and economy was to focus on the development of human resources, strengthened by strong administration and leadership. Second, both Malaysia's and Singapore's experiences show that deliberate government involvement in education and in HRD can bring long-term gain to the country materially and socioeconomically, despite differences in some development indicators, such as GDP per capita, gender inequality index, percentage of GDP spent on R&D, and female-labor-force participation. Finally, both countries realize that, together with their strategic position between the East and the West, they must emphasize and capitalize on the rich cultural contexts as they move toward becoming significant players in the global economy.

REFERENCES

Asghar, Ali. (2007). *Dismissal from Employment and the Remedies*. Kelana Jaya, Selangor: Lexis Nexis.
Brown, J. (2013). *Southeast Asia: Region on the Rise*. (http://www.inboundlogistics.com/cms/article/southeast-asia-region-on-the-rise/)
Fong, C. O. (February 7, 2010). Focus: Caught in middle-income trap. *Sunday Star*, 26–28.
Foo, S. (2009). *Singapore Public Policy*. Global policy brief no. 3. The Sloan centre of aging and work at Boston College. (http://www.bc.edu/content/dam/files/research_sites/agingandwork/pdf/publications/GPB03_Singapore.pdf)
Hashim, H., & Ahmad, S. (2011). Human resource development and continuing professional education. In M. Ismail & A. A. M. Osman-Gani (Eds.), *Human Resource Development in Malaysia*, 217–238. Pearson: Kuala Lumpur.
Human Development Report. (2013). *The Rise of the South: Human Progress in a Diverse World*. New York: United Nations Development Programme (UNDP). (http://www.hdr.undp.org)
Hwa Chong Institution Students National Education Council. (2013). *Theme of the Month: Education: An Introduction to Singapore's Education System*. Accessed 24 August, 2015. (http://hcisnec.wordpress.com/2013/05/19/theme-of-the-month-education/)
Hwa Chong Students' National Education Committee (SNEC). (May 19, 2013). *The Singapore Education Journey*. (http://hcisnec.wordpress.com/2013/05/19/theme-of-the-month-education/)
Ibrahim, Y., & Associates. (2004). *Training Guide in Malaysia* (7th ed.). Petaling Jaya, Malaysia: Challenger Concept (M) Sdn. Bhd.
International Labor Organization (ILO). (1997). *Human Resource Development for Continued Economic Growth: The Singapore Experience*. Act/Emp Publications. Paper presented at the ILO Workshop on Employers' Organisations in Asia-Pacific in the Twenty-First Century Turin, Italy, 5–13, May 1997. (http://www.ilo.org/public/english/dialogue/actemp/downloads/ ... /tanhrd1.pdf)
Ismail, M. (1999). *Pengembangan: Implikasi ke atas pembangunan masyarakat (Extension: Implication to community development)*. Kuala Lumpur: Dewan Bahasa dan Pustaka.
Ismail, M., Kunasegaran, M., & Mohd Rasdi, R. (2014). Evidence of reverse brain drain in selected Asian countries: Human resource management lessons for Malaysia. *Organizations and Markets in Emerging Economies*, 5(1): 31–48.
Ismail, M., & Osman-Gani, A. A. M. (2011). Conceptualizing human resource development and its emergence in Malaysia. In M. Ismail & A. A. M. Osman-Gani (Eds.), *Human Resource Development in Malaysia*, 241–274. Pearson: Kuala Lumpur.Ismail, M., Osman-Gani, A. A. M., Ahmad, S., Krauss, S. E., Ismail, I. A., & Hajaraih, S. H. (2007). Human resource development in Asia—thriving on dynamism and change: Reflection from 2006 Asian HRD Conference. *Human Resource Development International*, 10(2), 215–223.

I Training Expet.com (2015). *Claiming HRDF.* Accessed 21 June 2014. (www. itrainingexpert.com/hrdf-claim)

Jang, C. W. (n.d.). *Human Resources Development System, Policy and the Contribution of HRD to Economic Growth in South Korea.* (http://eng.krivet.re.kr/eu/index.jsp)

Law, S. S. (2007). *Vocational Technical Education and Economic Development— The Singapore Experience.* ITE Paper No 9, 2007. (https://www.ite.edu.sg/about_ite/ITE_Conference_Papers/Vocational)

Low, L. (December 2001). *The Political Economy of Singapore's Policy on Foreign Talents and High Skills Society.* Research Paper Series #2001–036 [BP]. Singapore: Faculty of Business Administration, National University of Singapore. Accessed on June 21, 2013. (http://www.fba.nus.edu.sg/fba/mscphd/01–36%2520Linda%2520Low.htm)

Malaysia. (1997). *Malaysia: Enterprise Training, Technology, and Productivity.* Washington: The World Bank.

Malaysia. (2006). *Ninth Malaysia Plan, 2006–2010.* Putrajaya, Malaysia: Government Printing Press.

Malaysia. (2010). *Tenth Malaysian Plan, 2011–2015.* Putrajaya, Malaysia: Government Printing Press.

Mazanah, M., & Associates (2001). *Adult and Continuing Education in Malaysia.* Hamburg & Serdang: UNESCO Institute for Education & Universiti Putra Press

National Economic Advisory Council (NEAC). (2010). *New Economic Model for Malaysia—Part 1.* Kuala Lumpur: Percetakan Nasional Malaysia Berhad. Retrieved from (http://www.neac.gov.my)

OECD. (2012). *PISA 2012 Results in Focus: What 15-Year-Olds Know and What They Can Do with What They Know.* Accessed 24 August, 2013. (http://www. oecd.org/pisa/keyfindings/pisa-2012-results-overview.pdf)

Omar, Z. (2011). Legal issues in human resource development. In M. Ismail and A. A. M. Osman-Gani (Eds.), *Human Resource Development in Malaysia,* 241–274. Pearson: Kuala Lumpur.

Omar, Z., Chan, K. Y., & Joned, R. (2009). Knowledge concerning employees' legal rights at work among banking employees in Malaysia. *Employee Right and Responsibility Journal,* 21(40): 343–362.

Osman-Gani, A. A. M. (2004). Human capital development in Singapore: An analysis of national policy perspectives. *Advances in Developing Human Resources,* 6(3): 1–12. doi:10.1177/1523422304266074

Silong, A. D., Ismail, I. A., Beh, L. S., Hassan, Z., Abdul Aziz, S. F., & Devadas, U. M. (2011). Human capital development in Malaysian public sector. In M. Ismail and A. A. M. Osman-Gani (Eds.), *Human Resource Development in Malaysia,* 33–67. Pearson: Kuala Lumpur.

Singapore Tripartite Forum. (2009). *National Wages Council—Singapore Tripartite Forum.* Accessed 24 July 2009. (http://www.tripartism.sg/ index.aspx?id=27).

Wikipedia (2015). *Economy of Malaysia.* Accessed 21 June 2013. (https:// en.wikipedia.org/wiki/Economy_of_Malaysia)

World Bank. (1993). *The East Asian Miracle: Economic Growth and Public Policy.* Oxford: Oxford University Press.

Section II
Africa and the Middle East

7 Human Resource Development in Sub-Saharan Africa

Fredrick M. Nafukho and
Helen M. A. Muyia

INTRODUCTION

As the second largest and second most populous continent on Earth, Africa is home to 54 sovereign states and countries, with an estimated population of 1.033 billion people (Africa Development Bank Report, 2012). One of the overarching objectives of any country's development is to improve the quality of life of its population, the people at the core of development. An outline of Africa's demographics gives an indication of just how Africa's demographic trends influence development of human resources. For example, it is projected that the African population will peak at 1.6 billion in 2030, which would represent 19% of the world's population (Africa Development Bank Report, 2012). This has significant implications for social and economic development, food security, and the sustainability of natural resources. In addition, the bulk of Africa's population is young, which implies that there is a large proportion of young adults in the working-age population and a rapidly growing school age population, with high rates of workforce growth indicators (Cincotta, 2010). Understanding these demographic trends is crucial for planning resource allocations and designing appropriate policy interventions that would lead to development in such areas as health, education, and labor.

The modern African continent is a product of European colonialism that began with Europe's partitioning of Africa at the Berlin Conference in 1884–1885, with consequences known as the 'Scramble for Africa'. This was an unfair and injustice policy, rationalized by the doctrine of discovery that had informed the European nations in their colonization. Following the end of the colonial era, many African countries had the desire to shape their own destinies. The focus on the localization of their public-sector policies through what was known as 'Africanization' became a rallying point for nationalists (Kirk-Green, 1972). Through Africanization, human resource capacity development was identified and developed by creating public service institutions. At the same time, the overseas training of key staff and the establishment of local universities was encouraged (Pallangyo and Ress, 2010). To address the hopes of the people, provision of public service became a key condition for consolidating the new continent. For example, the provision of services such as health care and education was considered fundamental to the overall development of the new African states. Investment in education was seen as a tool, not only for improving human capital but also for increasing productivity, innovation, and for the reduction of poverty (Kpessa, Be'land, & Lecours, 2011). As pointed out by Aina (2003), the economic health of the newly independent African states was assumed to hinge on the health of their people, whereas the knowledge and skills desperately needed for development were thought to depend on the quality of education provided to the citizenry.

It is important to point out that the African states' approach to nation building and economic development had its own challenges. For example, the demand for social services such as education, health care, and housing outstripped the supply capacity of such services. Other challenges included the presence of corruption, human rights abuses, and authoritarian rule (Mkandawire and Soludo, 1999). Clearly, the aforementioned discussion indicates that the African continent still has numerous challenges that make it difficult to design and deliver effective HRD programs. Today's challenges still include political instability; inadequate physical and financial infrastructure; poverty; and diseases, such as malaria and HIV/AIDS (Darley, 2012). Although these challenges vary from country to country, education on all levels is faced with serious crises as regards to quality and quantity of human capital. Difficult political decisions are needed for human resources to be developed in such a way that it will remain the engine for development in Africa, just as it has been for other continents (NORRAG, 2005).

Sub-Saharan Africa Region

Sub-Saharan Africa refers to the region of the continent of Africa that lies south of the Sahara Desert and consists of the following countries: Angola, Benin, Botswana, Burkina Faso, Burundi, Cameroon, Cape Verde, Central African Republic, Chad, Comoros, Congo, Cote d'Ivoire, Democratic Republic of the Congo, Equatorial Guinea, Eritrea, Ethiopia, Gabon, Gambia, Ghana, Guinea, Guinea-Bissau, Kenya, Lesotho, Liberia, Madagascar, Malawi, Mali, Mozambique, Namibia, Niger, Nigeria, Rwanda, São Tomé and Príncipe, Senegal, Seychelles, Sierra Leone, Somalia, South Africa, Swaziland, Togo, Uganda, United Republic of Tanzania, Zambia, and Zimbabwe. In 2012, the region had a total population of 910.4 million people, with the urban population consisting of 37% of the total population. The region's gross domestic product (GDP) stood at $1.290 trillion, the gross national income (GNI) per capita at US$1,351, with a GDP growth of 4.3% (World Development Report, 2014). The region is diverse and varies economically, politically, and socially, with significant cross-country differences. Understanding the diverse nature of these African countries helps the reader to understand what is happening in other countries and what other countries are doing in the development of adequate human resources to meet the development needs of their countries. In a short chapter such as this one, it is impossible to discuss all human resource development aspects of each sub-Saharan country, hence the need to select some exemplary countries in order to focus the discussion.

HRD in the Context of Sub-Saharan Africa

The ultimate measure of a country's progress is the quality of its human resources, hence the need to invest in human capital, especially in the sub-Saharan Africa region, with its very young population compared to other regions of the world. It is noted that increased investment in human capital increases the knowledge of individuals, thus generating capital necessary for development (Nafukho, Hairston, & Brooks, 2004; Sydhagen and Cunningham, 2007; Nafukho and Muyia, 2014). Education and training have long been recognized as key drivers of social and economic development. The need for skills development through education and training in sub-Saharan Africa cannot be overemphasized enough, especially in this new era of *ideas* and information. The growing complexity of the workplace impacted by globalization, technology, production, and trade has put the question of HRD at the heart of policy and development strategies of most African countries. Investing in people through improved education, training, and health ensures the availability of a skilled, motivated, and knowledgeable workforce that makes sustained economic growth possible (Richardson, 2007). Considering HRD's role in developing and unleashing human expertise (Swanson and Holton, 2009), this chapter highlights the past experience and the present status of HRD in sub-Saharan Africa. It explores the major challenges associated with HRD in supporting national and economic growth in the region. This chapter specifically examines the development of HRD in the Southern African Development Community (SADC). In addition, we suggest strategies that the SADC region should consider in enhancing the development of human resources. A chapter like this is anchored on the premise that HRD is well suited to addressing the economic and social challenges of the sub-Saharan region and also capable of offering solutions and policy changes for the long-term development and sustainability of the region (Lutta-Mukhebi, 2004; Nafukho, Wawire, & Lam, 2011).

Having made progress in the achievement of the Millennium Development Goals in primary education, gender parity, and the fight against HIV/AIDS, we can say that sub-Saharan Africa is a region on the move. It has seen commendable improvements in human development and has achieved sustained economic growth over the last decade in the midst of the international financial and economic crisis (UNDP, 2015). Despite these positive developments, the region continues to face a number of challenges that include poverty, food insecurity, joblessness, extreme weather events, political instability, conflict and civil unrest, and HIV/AIDS. In the Eastern

African region, countries such as Kenya, Uganda, Somalia, and Tanzania are faced with the challenge of terrorism. In view of the region's current and projected economic and social developmental activities and objectives, it is necessary and essential to build capacity through sustained human resources development and training (Nafukho and Muyia, 2014). As a priority on the human development agenda, any activity must be prioritized that contributes to progress in knowledge, skills, competency, institutional development, and the wider meeting of the region's needs. Driven by globalization and the accelerating shift to high-technology and information-technology economies, all of the sub-Saharan African countries face a huge challenge of developing a qualified human resource that has the capacity and flexibility to adjust to these rapid changes against the stark reality of decreasing resources. Because of its unique situation and position, sub-Saharan Africa provides a unique context for the study of HRD.

HRD IN THE SOUTHERN AFRICA DEVELOPMENT COMMUNITY

Given the diverse and large size of the sub-Saharan Africa region, we have purposely limited discussion of HRD issues to the Southern African Development Community (SADC) region. This region is composed of 15 member countries: Angola, Botswana, Democratic Republic of Congo, Lesotho, Madagascar, Malawi, Mauritius, Mozambique, Namibia, Seychelles, South Africa, Swaziland, Tanzania, Zambia, and Zimbabwe. Established in 1992, SADC is committed to regional integration and poverty reduction through investment in education. SADC has identified social and human development as one of the 11 themes to drive the economic development in the region. Key areas of social and human development include: employment and labor, education and skills development, science, technology and innovation, orphans, and vulnerable children and youth.

For this chapter, we rely on two important documents that provide the model guiding the development of human resources in the SADC region: the SADC Regional Indicative Strategic Development Plan (RISDP) and the SADC Protocol for Education and Training. RISDP gives strategic direction and focus to future SADC education and human resources development programs among the 15 member states. The focus and purpose of RISDP is to deepen regional integration across the SADC region and to provide member states with the long-term economic and social policies necessary for socioeconomic and human development. RISDP is a well-thought-out document, which identifies the role of education and training in the development of SADC member states. But most important is the SADC vision.

In reviewing the SADC Protocol for Education and Training for SADC, one is inspired by the dream or vision for the region as outlined in the document. SADC's vision is to improve economic growth and development, alleviate poverty, and enhance the quality of life of the people of the region. In short, the vision aims at promoting human development by SADC as a whole, supporting its socially disadvantageous areas through deeper regional integration, and by enhancing the quality of life of the peoples of the region. One of the ways of enhancing the quality of life of the peoples of SADC is to ensure that all population groups have adequate access to basic social services, of which education and training are central (SADC, 2007). SADC's vision focuses on the common future of a regional community that will ensure economic well-being, improve the standards of living and quality of life of its people, bring freedom and social justice, and work peace and security for the region. This shared vision is anchored in the common values, principles, and the historical and cultural ties existing among the people of the region.

PROTOCOL ON EDUCATION AND TRAINING

With an ultimate aim of harmonizing, standardizing, and establishing equivalence in the education and training systems across the region by 2020, the protocol stresses that these objectives are to be achieved through equitable participation, balance, and mutual benefit in regional collaboration and through the involvement of key stakeholders at the member-state level, including the private sector and nongovernmental organizations (NGOs). SADC (2007) pointed out that in 2000, the region adopted the Protocol on Education and Training to promote a regionally integrated and harmonized education system, particularly with regard to issues pertaining to access, equity, relevance, and quality of education. The protocol aimed at fostering regional integration and identity through promoting the values, history, and languages of the region in the education system. Key principles and objectives of the protocol emphasize regional approaches to educational development through the development of common systems, specifically policy-making capacity and regional policy frameworks, information and resource pooling, harnessing of regional expertise, and avoidance of duplication in the development of human resources.

In summary, the SADC Protocol on Education and Training was an agreement established and signed in 2007 to ensure cooperation in education and training as a strategy to develop human resources in the region. The protocol aimed at achieving the following objectives (SADC, 2012):

- To develop and implement a common system of regular collection and reporting of information by member states about the current status and future demand and supply, plus the priority areas for provision of education and training in the region
- To establish mechanisms and institutional arrangements that would enable member states to pool their resources to effectively and efficiently produce the required professional, technical, research, and

managerial personnel to plan and manage the development process in general and across all sectors in the region

- To promote and coordinate the formulation and implementation of comparable and appropriate policies, strategies, and systems of education and training in member states
- To promote and coordinate the formulation and implementation of policies, strategies, and programs for the promotion and application of science and technology, including modern information technology and research and development in the region
- To work toward the reduction and eventual elimination of constraints to better and freer access by citizens of member states to good quality education and training opportunities within the region
- To work toward the relaxation and eventual elimination of immigration formalities in order to facilitate freer movement of students and staff within the region for the specific purposes of study, teaching, research, and any other pursuits relating to education and training
- To progressively achieve the equivalence, harmonization, and standardization of the education and training systems in the region

SADC'S EDUCATION AND TRAINING IMPLEMENTATION PLAN

SADC's (2008) revised Regional Implementation Plan on Education and Training recognizes that *human centered development* is one of the most essential means by which to achieve the objectives of the SADC Treaty (See SADC Protocol on Education and Training, 2004). Regional cooperation in the area of education, training, and development was identified as necessary for developing knowledge, attitudes, appropriate and relevant skills, and human capacities, all prerequisites to promoting investment, efficiency, and competitiveness, as well as consolidating historical, social, and cultural ties and affinities of the people of the region. As mentioned earlier, in 2000, SADC adopted a Protocol on Education and Training to promote a regionally integrated and harmonized education system, particularly with regard to issues pertaining to access, equity, relevance, and quality of education. In addressing the access to education issue, the leaders of the region, including educators and policy makers, realized that there was an urgent need to develop open and distance learning (ODL) policies aimed at the provision of learner and instructor support materials, optimal utilization of information and communication technologies (ICTs), and improvement in education quality through the design and effective delivery of ODL programs at secondary, teacher education, technical and vocational education training, and higher education levels. This holistic approach of investment in education and training is considered an important strategy for developing human resources in the region. Thus in the SADC region, developing of human resources is looked at holistically and includes formal and informal education and training taking place in schools, teacher-training colleges, technical and vocational education institutions, and in the universities. Included also is training in the workplace as provided by for-profit enterprises, government agencies, and nonprofit organizations.

INVESTMENT IN EDUCATION AND ECONOMIC DEVELOPMENT FOR THE SADC REGION

Smith (1776) observed that the economic growth and development of any nation or region is determined by the availability of natural resources, growth in physical capital, organization (which relates to optimum use of factors of production in economic activities), division of labor, and scale production. Economic growth and development is also affected by structural changes, which imply the transition from a traditional agricultural society to the modern industrial economy and to the current knowledge economy. The process involves a radical transformation of existing institutions and social attitudes, including learning and motivation. These factors lead to increased employment opportunities, high labor productivity, increased capital stock, exploitation of new resources, and improvement in technology. Other noneconomic factors that affect economic growth include social attitudes, cultural values, institutions, efficient human resources development, political, administrative, and effective and caring leadership. However, key to the HRD process is the education and training of the people (Nafukho et al., 2011).

Based on SADC's (2007) revised Regional Implementation Plan on Education and Training, the eight-year, 2007–2015, priorities of the Second Decade of Education and other international commitments such as Education for All and the Millennium Development Goals (MDGs) are identified. The plan aims at addressing some of the key challenges affecting education and training development in the SADC region, such as limited access to secondary school, teacher education, TVET, and higher education levels; inequitable access to education and training especially by disadvantaged groups such as women, disabled people, and people from rural areas; the poor quality of education at all levels as indicated by the high repetition and dropout rates; the high levels of inadequately trained and qualified teachers; irrelevant curricula and the mismatch between the supply and demand in education; the negative impact of HIV and AIDS on the education and training sector; shortage of relevant and appropriate teaching and learning materials; and the lack of current and relevant data for planning and monitoring.

With respect to implementation, the plan focuses on nine priority areas: (1) education management information systems; (2) quality improvement and management; (3) higher education; (4) teacher education, technical and vocational education and training; (4) curriculum development, including teaching and learning materials; (5) quality assurance and qualifications frameworks; (6) open and distance learning; (7) mainstreaming of gender, culture; (8) HIV and AIDS; and (9) information and communications technology. The guiding principles of the implementation plan include: ensuring its alignment and integration into national plans, participation of all stakeholders, variable country-level specifications, fostering strategic partnerships with regional and continental organizations through the principle of subsidiarity, and maximizing the effective utilization of regional expertise and institutions. In the sections that follow, we examine the plan's goals of developing human resources through investment in education and training in secondary education, teacher education, technical-vocational education training, and higher education.

Need to Invest in Secondary Education as a Strategy to Develop Human Resources

Whereas the SADC 15 member countries have put in place the policy Education for All (EFA) for children attending primary schools, no policy exists for secondary education, teacher education, technical and vocational training, and higher education. Thus many students qualifying from primary schools are not able to proceed to other levels of the education system, which leads to internal inefficiency in the education system. To address this problem, open and distance learning is currently being rolled out to complement the conventional education system in the region. All four sectors of education are critical to the success of the education system in providing the population with the level of knowledge and skills required in the workplace.

According to the SADC (2006) report, secondary education access for most of the region is poor. Only two states, South Africa and Mauritius, have achieved a gross enrollment ratio (GER) above 50%. Most states provide places for fewer than 25% of the secondary age cohort. Secondary education systems in SADC also display high levels of inefficiency, wastage, and inequity. In Mozambique, for example, although 71% of those who graduate at the end of the primary cycle go on to the first grade of lower secondary, only 2% of that number enter the final secondary grade. In Malawi, the comparable figures are 87% and 18% and in Zimbabwe, they are 72% and 6%. The phenomenon is visible across the SADC region, but large populations of out-of-school youth are found in Angola (1 million), Mozambique (2.6 million), and Tanzania (3.5 million). These numbers are likely to have increased since 2006. A further three member states, Madagascar, Zambia, and Zimbabwe, each have over five hundred thousand children out of school (no figures are available for DRC).

Need to Invest in Teacher Education

According to the United Nations Educational, Scientific and Cultural Organization (UNESCO) estimates, sub-Saharan Africa will need about four million additional teachers by 2015 if the UNESCO's targets are to be reached. The SADC (2006) report noted that the SADC region will need at least one million additional teachers in the same time period. The same report observed that in 2003, the region had a total of approximately 804,800 primary teachers. About 45% were women, whereas 80% were trained. However, as no figures are available for Madagascar, DRC, Angola, or Zimbabwe, the actual percentage of trained teachers in the region is probably much lower. The situation with regard to secondary teachers is also incomplete, as no recent data is available on teacher numbers for three of the most populous countries (DRC, Madagascar, and Tanzania). The SADC (2006) report estimated that of a total number of secondary teachers in 2003 of about 220,000, 54% were trained; 32% of secondary teachers serving in the African Development Fund (ADF) countries are women. There are therefore about 160,000 untrained primary teachers and 100,000 untrained or undertrained secondary teachers working in the region. As demand for secondary education increases with the success of EFA, there will be a need to rapidly expand secondary teacher-training capacity in the region. At the higher education level, few states provide initial or systematic in-service training for their higher education teachers. The initial and in-service training of early childhood development (ECD) teachers and community assistants is another neglected area. Most ECD teachers working in the region are untrained. Given the high rates of return when investing in early childhood education, the training of ECD teachers represents an investment opportunity that could also use a mass ODL approach.

Need to Invest in Training and Development

Another critical form of developing human resources in the SADC region is through the technical and vocational education training provision. Across the SADC region, this form of training is fragmented, unevenly developed, underfunded, small scale, and generally neglected, which prevents the established graduate employment targets from being achieved (SADC, 2006). Women's representation in this sector is low (30%), particularly in the ADF countries. With the exception of South Africa, relatively small numbers of youth are catered to throughout the region. TVET development has been constrained by poor coordination, by a mismatch between training courses and programs and the economic needs, by the lack of institutional and curricular coherence, and by underfunding. The development of TVET is often the responsibility of several ministries and a plethora of private agencies offering both accredited and nonaccredited training. The relatively high cost of provision for workshops, tools, and teachers compared with general education is also a problem and results in much of the TVET provision being theoretical. Teachers are often untrained. Rarely are public or private employers involved in curriculum development or the provision of apprenticeship training. Provision is often supply driven rather than demand driven, resulting in a consequent mismatch between supply and demand. As a result, much of the provision is of low quality, and because of the under-developed nature of most SADC economies, many TVET graduates remain unemployed or underemployed.

Investing in Higher Education

According to the SADC (2006) report, participation in higher education across the SADC region is very low. In all nine ADF countries, higher education participation rates are lower than 5% of the eligible age group. Only three countries achieved any sizable higher education general enrollment ratings (GER): South Africa (14%), Mauritius (11.3 %), and Namibia (7.5%). South Africa accounts for 71% of the total higher education provision in the SADC (675,000 places). The ADF subregion as a whole accounts for only an additional 237,500 places. Malawi enrolls only 0.6% of the relevant eligible age group. The majority of students major in education, social science, business, law, and humanities. Very few students study the sciences or engineering subjects. At higher levels of education, women are less represented generally, and the subjects that are studied show a clear gender pattern, with more girls opting for social science and arts subjects. The report calls for an urgent increase in access to tertiary education across the region as a whole, the achievement of gender equity, and the upgrading of science and technology courses. Given the increasing pace of innovation and change and the need to improve the relevance and quality of higher education across the region, there is need for more university teacher training and access, especially with regard to the application of new methods of teaching and learning, such as open and distance learning and the use of ICTs.

DEVELOPING HRD AT THE ORGANIZATIONAL LEVEL

Training, like education, is a form of human capital development mainly offered at the organizational level. In sub-Saharan Africa, developing human resources through training at the organizational level takes place in for-profit, not-for-profit, and multinational organizations. In addition, all government ministries and agencies offer formal training and development to their employees. Nafukho and Kang'ethe (2002) observed that training is a form of education and that the differences between education and training can be explained in terms of the purposes for which education or training is provided and/or received. For instance, some employees go for training and coaching to acquire new competencies for successful job performance, whereas others undertake training and coaching to satisfy their curiosity or to improve their level of self-awareness (Nafukho, Wawire, & Lam, 2011). Regarding the meaning of training, Broad and Newstrom (1992, p. 5) defined training as, "instructional experiences provided primarily by employers for employees, designed to develop new skills and knowledge that are expected to be applied immediately upon (or within a short time after) arrival on or return to the job". Nafukho and Kang'ethe (2002) observed that training involves transfer of skills, knowledge, behavior, and attitudes. Thus training is a form of investment in employees with expected returns for both the employee and the organization where the employee works (Nafukho, Wawire, & Lam, 2011).

It is important to note that whereas training provides employees with new skills, knowledge, behavior, and attitudes for immediate use, education is concerned with the future development of the employee or the learner. Hakimian and Teshome (1993, p. 3), noted the following regarding the main differences between education and training: education focuses on broader objectives, whereas training normally has more narrowly defined objectives; education may open up career opportunities, whereas training helps to improve current job performance; and education deals mostly with knowledge and understanding, whereas training concentrates more on skills.

While the main differences between education and training can be explained by the purpose for which both are provided, the intended outcome is the *learning* that takes place and how it is transferred to the workplace or applied in real-life settings. "Looked at from this perspective, education and training are seen as deliberate investments that prepare the labor force and increase productivity of individuals and organizations, as well as encourage socio-economic growth and development" (Nafukho, Wawire, & Lam, 2011, p. 87). Therefore, given the importance of investing in people, sub-Saharan African governments and all organizations based in Africa are urged to demonstrate to policy makers and policy implementers through evidence-based work and research how much that investment in education and training benefits individuals, organizations, communities, and society.

DISCUSSION

Challenges

While investment in education was identified as being central to the achievement of the vision of the SADC member states, the region's education sector is faced with numerous challenges. The SADC (2006) report observed that, whereas SADC sought to increase economic growth, generate new jobs, and improve working conditions, particularly for youth, there were serious challenges across all parts of the SADC education sector. For instance, the region is struggling to achieve its EFA targets at both the adult basic and primary education levels. Secondary education provision averages just 25% of the eligible age group. Around 25% of the SADC adult population remains illiterate, and there are serious shortages of trained teachers at all levels of education. Educational access and performance at both the primary and secondary levels show wide variation across the region. On average, 68% of primary-aged children in the SADC region have access to the final primary grade. The figure falls to 57% for the ADF subgroup. In terms of completion, Angola recorded a 43% primary completion rate (PCR), whereas Mauritius achieved 100%. The transition rate from primary to lower secondary also varies from around 18% in Tanzania to 99% in South Africa. On average, just 20% of children complete the secondary cycle in the SADC region. At the higher education level, less than 5% of the eligible age group has access to tertiary education. In terms of the efficiency of the education system, according to SADC (2006), millions of children and young adults leave SADC education systems having failed to master basic skills, either because they have had insufficient time in school or because the quality of the education they received was inadequate. Thus several factors limit access to quality education in the region: absenteeism and drop out due to loss of opportunity costs; limited coverage of school catchment areas; the high cost of the conventional education systems, particularly at the secondary level; limited school infrastructure and consequently overcrowded classrooms; inadequately trained and qualified teachers; and irrelevant curricula. One of the ways SADC has identified for addressing these challenges is the adoption of open and distance learning (ODL)(SADC, 2006). ODL is not unique to SADC countries and is practiced worldwide as part of a strategy to meet the educational needs of citizens.

As for the rest of the sub-Saharan countries, the SADC region faces challenges in four educational sectors: secondary education, teacher education, technical and vocational training, and higher education. Students face obstacles related to access to and the high cost of education. As a means of responding to challenges of access, quality, and equity, online learning is increasingly considered within the region as a viable strategy especially in the provision of teacher preparation programs and higher education. In addition, the role of distance education in supporting out-of-school youth through the provision of formal open schooling or technical and vocational training, especially through e-learning, is now recognized, and such learning methods are being implemented across the region (SADC, 2006; Nafukho, 2007).

The role and importance of technology in developing human resources is strongly reflected in the SADC Protocol on Education and Training and in the SADC request to the African Development Bank for support for capacity development in open and distance learning. In the area of education and training, SADC Education and Training Protocol places special emphasis on developing technical and vocational education and training (TVET) across the region. It highlights the role of centers of specialization in harnessing regional expertise and developing regional frameworks and standardization as a measure to ensure quality education and training. Currently, TVET in the SADC region is underdeveloped, and its provision is small scale, fragmented, underfunded, and ill coordinated. South Africa is modernizing its further education and training (FET) and vocational education and training

(VET) college systems, whereas Botswana has embarked on developing a national open and distance education center for TVET at its Francistown TVET college. Mozambique initiated a TVET sector review with a view to restructuring its outmoded technical and vocational education system. In the case of higher education, online learning has been very effective in a number of SADC countries, including Botswana, South Africa, and Tanzania (SADC, 2006). At the higher education level, two main kinds of higher distance education organizational models are operational in the SADC region: the dedicated distance-teaching universities (DTUs—universities that admit only distance students), such as the Tanzania Open University, and dual mode universities (DMUs—universities that offer both face-to-face teaching and distance courses), such as the University of South Africa (UNISA).

To illustrate the importance of distance learning in developing human resources at the university level, the region has invested in three major distance-teaching universities. The University of South Africa (UNISA), which had over 200,000 enrollments in 2006 (There were 300,000 students enrolled in 2015. The higher number in 2015 was due to a merger with two other major distance education providers—Technikon South Africa and Vista University), Zimbabwe Open University (with 20,000 enrollments reported in 2001), and the Open University Tanzania (with 22,000 enrollments reported in 2006). A fourth Open University is being planned for Mauritius. In addition, many of the region's conventional universities also offers at least one distance-teaching program (operating as DMUs). Some, such as the University of Namibia, now have outreach campuses and several well-established programs, for example, in education, arts, nursing, and business studies. The DTUs, combined with the many dual mode operations in the region, provide very significant numbers of additional higher education study places.

There are some positive experiences of the deployment of e-learning in the SADC region, for example, the University of Dar es Salaam has a university-wide data communication network, connecting all 26 academic buildings on the main campus with a fiber optic cable, as well as two regional campuses with a wireless link. Likewise, the University of Namibia has a campus in the capital city, Windhoek, and a second campus in Oshakati with video-conferencing technology. The African Virtual University encompasses some of the SADC member states and serves as a model for other such networks, and it may well be extended to cover more of the SADC member states. Many more tertiary institutions throughout the region have ambitious plans to offer ICT-based programming, for example, the University of Dar es Salaam and the Zimbabwe Open University. However, although there is a higher level of computer and Internet use in the tertiary sector in the region than in the primary and secondary sectors, the use of new ICTs is still limited because of infrastructure constraints, lack of instructional materials, lack of skilled facilities, and also the newness for many of ICT-based pedagogy.

HRD and the Future of Sub-Saharan Africa

Clearly, the foregoing discussion indicates that sub-Saharan Africa as a region and the SADC region, in particular, still face numerous challenges that make it difficult for HRD. The region needs to adopt a more balanced, strategic, and holistic approach to HRD. In addition, effective leadership is an important factor influencing the successful management and development of human resources. Effective and strategic leadership requires that decision makers in the sub-Saharan countries consider short-, medium-, and long-term goals for their countries' HRD plans. Strategic leadership ought to be visionary in its effort to identify the skills needs, gaps, constraints, challenges, and opportunities with a view to efficiently maximizing the returns from human resource investment. There is need to adapt a new approach to training and development within the sub-Saharan region. The new approach entails identifying the vision, mission, and goals as far as HRD is concerned, followed by choice of strategic development and training initiatives in support. There should also be movement away from training toward learning in order to ensure employee performance improvement. Both formal and informal learning, coaching, and mentoring should be highly encouraged. Strategic development of human resources also entails integrating technology in learning and training functions of these countries.

Africa is now being referred to as a rising continent, mainly because of its investments in education and training. August (2013) observes that empirical evidence, looked at broadly, would suggest human development in sub-Saharan Africa has improved tremendously, partly because of investment in education. While many countries in Europe and other regions of the world have struggling economies, several African countries' economies are booming. For instance, according to August (2013, p. 1),

> Africa is the world's fastest-growing continent just now. Over the next decade its GDP is expected to rise by an average of 6% a year ... FDI has gone from $15 billion in 2002 to $37 billion in 2006 and $46 billion in 2012.

In the area of entertainment, Nigeria now produces more movies than the United States of America. Africa is projected to be the China of tomorrow or the new India. It is our hope that this chapter will not only stimulate further discussion but also become the starting point for subsequent critical analysis of the role of investment in human resources in the development of the sub-Saharan Africa region.

CONCLUSION

It has been argued that trade liberalization and direct foreign investments are the best alternatives for the development of sub-Saharan African countries (Moyo, 2010). We argue that without investment in education, training, and health, the region will remain disadvantaged. Thus the key to Africa's thriving is through investment in its people and the creation of income generation opportunities. In this era of knowledge and ideas, only those organizations and countries endowed with human capital will thrive in the twenty-first century and beyond. Empirical evidence has shown that even though Africa has vast physical and natural resources, intangible assets such as knowledge and information will determine the level of wealth creation in this century. African economies need people who possess the critical skills, knowledge, and virtues required for human development; without them the physical capital and natural resources will remain underutilized or will be exploited by others from outside sub-Saharan Africa. It is a truism that global wealth today is concentrated less and less in factories, land, tools, and machinery. Knowledge, skills, and the resourcefulness of the people are increasingly critical to the world and national economies. As the World Bank (2000) noted, knowledge acquired through education enlightens the lives of people and is crucial to any development effort. Economic equality within a population remains low without knowledge of available natural resources, possible alternative production techniques, necessary skills, existing market conditions, opportunities, and of institutions that might be created to promote economic activity. In summary, like many countries of the world, the African continent must invest in knowledge capital, human capital, and create supportive work environments for its people. Investment in these three areas is the key to Africa's human development.

REFERENCES

Africa Development Bank. (2012). *Africa Development Bank Annual Report 2012.* (http://www.afdb.org/fileadmin/uploads/afdb/Documents/Publications/Annual_Report_2012.pdf)
Aina, T. A. (2003). Introduction: How do we understand globalization and social policy in Africa. In T. A. Aina, C. L. Chachage, and E. Annan-Yao (Eds.), *Globalization and Social Policy in Africa*, 1–39. Dakar: Council for the Development of Social Science Research in Africa (CODESRIA).
August, O. (2013). Africa rising: A hopeful continent. *The Economist.* (http://www.economist.com/news/special-report/21572377-african-lives-have-already-greatly-improved-over-past-decade-says-oliver-august)
Broad, L. M., & Newstrom, W. J. (1992). *Transfer of Training: Action Packed Strategies to Ensure High Pay Off from Training Investments.* Reading and Massachusetts: Addison-Wesley Publishing Company.
Cincotta, R. (2010). *The Future of Sub-Saharan Africa's Tentative Fertility Decline.* Accessed April 27, 2015. (http://www.newsecuritybeat.org/2010/08/the-future-of-sub-saharan-africas-tentative-fertility-decline/)
Darley, W. K. (2012). Increasing Sub-Saharan Africa's share of foreign direct investment: Public policy challenges, strategies, and implications. *Journal of African Business*, 13(1): 62–69.

Hakimian, H., & Teshome, A. (1993). *Trainers Guide: Concepts, Principles and Methods of Training with Special Reference to Agricultural Development.* Rome: Food and Agricultural Organization.

Kirk-Greene, A. H. M. (1972). The new African administrator. *The Journal of Modern African Studies,* 10: 93–107.

Kpessa, M., Be'land, D., & Lecours, A. (2011). Nationalism, development, and social policy: The politics of nation-building in Sub-Saharan Africa. *Ethnic and Racial Studies,* 34(12): 2115–2133.

Lutta-Mukhebi, M. C. (2004). National human resource development policy in Kenya. *Advances in Developing Human Resources,* 6(3): 326–333.

Mkandawire, T., & Soludo, C. (1999). *Our Continent, Our Future: African Perspectives on Structural Adjustment.* Trenton, NJ: Africa World Press.

Moyo, D. (2010). *Dead Aid: Why Aid is Not Working and How There is a Better Way for Africa.* New York, NY: Farrar, Straus and Giroux.

Nafukho, F. M. (2007). The place of e-learning in Africa's institutions of higher learning. *Higher Education Policy,* 20(1): 19–43.

Nafukho, F. M. (2013). Capacity building through investment in people: Key to Africa's development. *European Journal of Training and Development,* 37(7): 604–614.

Nafukho, F. M., Hairston, N., & Brooks, K. (2004). Human capital theory: Implications for human resource development. *Human Resource Development International,* 7(4): 545–551.

Nafukho, F. M., & Kang'ethe, S. (2002). *Training of Trainers: Strategies for the 21st century.* Eldoret: Moi University Press.

Nafukho, F. M., Wawire, N. H. W., & Mungania, P. (2011). *Management of Adult Education Organizations in Africa.* Cape Town, South Africa: Pearson Education and UNESCO.

Northern Research Review and Advisory Group (2005). Accessed 29 April 2015. (http://www.norrag.org/en/publications/working-papers.html)

Pallangyo, W., & Rees, J. C. (2010). Local government programs and human resource capacity building in Africa: Evidence from local government authorities (LGAs) in Tanzania. *International Journal of Public Administration,* 33(12–13): 728–739.

Richardson, S. (2007). Forecasting future demands: What we can and cannot know. Accessed 21 April 2015. (http://files.eric.ed.gov/fulltext/ED499706.pdf)

SADC. (2006). *African Development Bank Appraisal Report on SADC: Capacity Building in Open and Distance Learning Project.* Gaborone: Botswana. Unpublished SADC Report.

SADC. (2007). *Revised Regional Implementation Plan on Education and Training.* Gaborone: Botswana. Unpublished SADC Report.

SADC. (2008). *Capacity Building in Open and Distance Learning Project Implementation Document.* Gaborone: Botswana. Unpublished SADC Report.

SADC. (2012). *Education and Training Protocol.* (http://www.unctadxi.org/sections/DITC/SADC/docs/SADC%20Regional/SADCProtocolonEducationandTraining.pdf) on February 8, 2014.

Smith, A. (1776). *The Wealth of Nations.* Accessed February 9, 2014. (http://www2.hn.psu.edu/faculty/jmanis/adam-smith/wealth-nations.pdf)

Southern African Development Community (2004). Accessed 23 April 2015. (http://www.sadc.int/documents-publications/protocols)

Swanson, R. A., & Holton III, E. F. (2009). *Foundations of Human Resource Development* (2nd ed.). San Francisco, CA: Berret-Koehler, Inc.

Sydhagen, K., & Cunningham, P. (2007). Human resource development in Sub-Saharan Africa. *Human Resource Development International,* 10(2): 121–135.

UNDP. (2015). *Human Development Report.* New York: UNDP.

World Bank. (2000). *Higher Education in Developing Countries: Peril and Promise.* Washington, DC: The World Bank.

World Bank. (2014). *World Development Report.* Washington DC Online. Accessed February 7, 2014. (http://data.worldbank.org/data-catalog/world-development-report-2014)

8 Human Resource Development in the Middle East

Hussain A. Alhejji and
Thomas N. Garavan

INTRODUCTION

The Gulf Cooperation Council (GCC) consists of six Middle East countries: Bahrain, Kuwait, Oman, Qatar, Saudi Arabia, and the United Arab Emirates (UAE). Besides their geographical proximity, there are several common features of history, economic resources, religion, culture, language, environment, and political systems that ameliorated the formation of the GCC (Ramady, 2010; Sidani and Al Ariss, 2014). The economies of the GCC countries rely heavily on natural resources, such as oil and gas productions, which represent the basis of the political and economic structures (Al-Waqfi and Forstenlechner, 2012). In order to support and sustain this growth in the wake of a shortage of supply of indigenous educated and skilled labor, expatriate and foreign workers are imported to fulfill this role. Over-reliance on expatriate and foreign workers in the GCC countries can have serious long-term political, economic, and social consequences for the region (Barnett et al., 2015). For example, the indigenous population in UAE and Qatar represent only one-fifth and one-quarter of the population in each country respectively (Scurry et al., 2013). In addition, the region is experiencing a rapid growth of its youth population, as well as high unemployment of youth and women, leading to more challenges to the national HRD systems. Consequently, the last decade has witnessed a dramatic change to the legal system (e.g., nationalization) and to organizational practices (e.g., training and development) aimed at overcoming these challenges (Salih, 2010; Al-Asfour and Khan, 2014).

The number of recent international studies on the nature and condition of HRD have increased in the past two decades; this output is bound to enhance the development of a comprehensive theoretical and methodological framework for the study of national HRD systems (Murphy and Garavan, 2009; McLean, 2012). Within the GCC countries, scholars have paid more attention to the mechanisms of the socioeconomic and political structure of society and their influence on management practices (Rutledge et al., 2011; Jackson and Manderscheid, 2015). In addition, given the nature of economic growth and large government spending, more and more multinational corporations (MNCs) have established joint ventures with local firms in the GCC countries (Mellahi et al., 2011). Although a large number of scholars have provided studies of a 'context-specific' nature on HRD, more research is still needed to cope with the political, economic, and social changes in the GCC region. Budhwar and Mellahi (2007) argue that there is a strong need to provide more on country-specific as well as region-specific aspects of HRD in the different parts of the world for which information is insufficient.

With this need in view, this chapter, therefore, will focus on the nature of HRD in GCC countries. We will provide an overall description of the historical, economic, and cultural contexts that have impacted National Human Resource Development (NHRD) systems. We will then describe how the legal system in GCC has played a major role in influencing HRD at the national and organizational levels. Finally, we will outline some of the similarities and differences between HRD practice in GCC in order to elaborate a general framework for future challenges and opportunities.

HISTORICAL, POLITICAL, ECONOMIC, INSTITUTIONAL, SOCIAL, AND CULTURAL CONTEXT IN THE MIDDLE EAST

During the periods from 1820 to 1971, the GCC countries were under British protection. Harry (2007) argues that the actual relationship was based on mutually beneficial terms: powerful people and tribal leaders benefited from British military protection as disputes among tribes were all too common at that time. In return, Britain had a de facto decision-making power on economic and political issues (Ramady, 2010). However, when anti-British sentiment arose, Britain decided to pull out by 1971, whereby the GCC countries gained formal independence from Britain. At the same time, most GCC countries signed an agreement with the United States (US). Forstenlechner and Baruch (2013) argued that, in order to fully understand the nature of HRD in the GCC countries, one needs to recognize that for each member state, the power to decide to invest in human capital only came in 1971.

Some years after independence, the institutional differences between the GCC countries became apparent. For example, Saudi Arabia was established and is still dominated by a religious group affecting all aspects of social life, including political decision making, the education system, labor law, etc. (Mellahi, 2007; Salih, 2010). Kuwait has led a liberal trade policy, particularly in the hydrocarbon industry, yet the rules on labor relations and citizenship for non-natives have been rigid. Bahrain and Oman have the most liberal policies toward nationalizing non-local workers (Rees et al., 2007). Qatar and the UAE have succeeded in relative terms at keeping political decision making separate from financial decision making, but they have not made progress in terms of the ratio of foreigners to locals. Although subsidization of local citizens by creating sufficient jobs is present in all the GCC countries, the degree and efficiency of subsidization differ across Gulf

States given the variation of revenues from oil and gas productions and the influence of values from the local tribal society (Rodriguez and Scurry, 2014; Sidani and Al Ariss, 2014).

Unlike most Arab countries, the GCC countries have a very unique political and economic structure. They are all monarchies, absolute in the case of Oman, Saudi Arabia, and Qatar; constitutional monarchies with elected parliaments in the case of Bahrain and Kuwait; and federal in the case of the UAE (Sidani and Al Ariss, 2014). In 1981, the Arab leaders of the Gulf met and signed an agreement to establish officially the Cooperation Council (Ramady, 2010). The purpose of this cooperation is to create a cooperative framework and a leaning toward unity. Further progress toward this unity intended to promote and facilitate economic and financial integration, including a common market, monetary union, as well the creation of employment and training opportunities for a rapidly growing national labor force. All GCC countries have significant oil and gas reserves, although the hydrocarbon reserves in Bahrain and Oman are moving toward depletion. Qatar, Saudi Arabia, and the UAE are still ranked among the top-ten countries because of their natural gas reserves (Rodriguez and Scurry, 2014). Table 8.1 provides more information on the GCC countries.

It is also important to note that not all countries neighboring the Persian Gulf are members of the GCC – Iraq had its membership discontinued after the invasion of Kuwait in 1990. There were also long negotiations regarding Yemen's GCC membership, which has resulted in partial accession to GCC membership, including, but not limited to, the Gulf Organization for Industrial Consultancy, the GCC Auditing and Accounting Authority, and the GCC Education and Training Bureau (Hvidt, 2011). There is, however, some resistance to full Yemeni membership due to its lack of natural resources, its unstable political system, and high poverty and illiteracy levels. It seems also possible that GCC membership will be extended to two other Arab monarchies: Jordan and Morocco (Hassi, 2011). The inclusion of these countries, along with Yemen, will bring the whole of the Arabian Peninsula into the GCC. However, for the rest of this chapter, we will only

Table 8.1   GCC Member States' Economic Indicators

Member State	GDP (PPP) US$ billion	GDP per capita US$	Land area km²	Oil reserves million bbl.	Gas reserves million m³
Bahrain	33.63	24,689	765	125	92,030
Kuwait	200.06	52,197	17,818	101,500	1,798,000
Oman	76.46	21,929	309,501	5,500	850,030
Qatar	181.7	93,714	11,571	25,382	25,200,000
Saudi Arabia	906.8	25,961	2,149,690	267,017	8,028,000
UAE	570	40,048	83,600	97,800	6,089,000

Source: World Bank (2013)

include in our analysis the six countries that have current GCC membership of HRD at the national and organizational levels.

Islam is the main religion practiced in all GCC countries. According to Showail, McLean Parks, and Smith (2013), Islam is not just a religious belief, but it is also central to the GCC way of life and the source of political, legal, social relations, and financial services. Islam is the basis of the constitution, employment relations, and management practices. Although international influences such as globalization, free trade, and labor migration have impacted the national culture in most countries, GCC countries still hold their strong cultural identities. For example, both Qatar and Saudi Arabia have Sunni Muslim majorities, those who practice the strict Wahhabi interpretation of Islam (Williams et al., 2011). However, in Qatar, unlike Saudi Arabia, alcohol is available and women enjoy more freedom. However, gender segregation in the workplace seems more problematic in Saudi Arabia than in other countries in the Gulf, a situation that has a direct impact on the structure of the HRD policies and practices.

In terms of the cultural context, the GCC countries have long been influenced by the traditions of tribe, household, and, more importantly, the Islamic religion (Metcalfe, 2008). These cultural factors also have a strong influence in the functioning of the HRD system at the national and organizational levels. Hofstede (1980) has described Arabic culture as a 'collectivistic culture' by which people work within a social structure where tribe and personal relationships dominate behavior and attitudes. Forstenlechner, Lettice, and Özbilgin (2012) note the potential conflict between the preferred decision making of an individual seeking to make a rational decision and the decision implicitly or explicitly indicated by the organizational culture in which that individual works. For example, GCC managers may feel bound to act in a way they perceive to be unprofessional. Many studies have found a direct relationship between organizational management practices and Arabic culture (Stalker and Mavin, 2011; Yaghi and Yaghi, 2013).

Arabic is the official language of the GCC countries. It is the formal language in communication and management practices. Arabic is one of six official languages of the United Nations and is spoken by as many as 422 million speakers in Arab countries (Hvidt, 2011). It is also the liturgical language of 1.6 billion Muslim speakers around the world. In addition to Arabic, English is considered to be a second official language, and it is widely spoken and studied by most GCC nationals. Other languages can be found but those are mainly related to foreign workers from Southeast Asia and Africa with temporary contracts in the GCC countries.

ECONOMIC GROWTH

Since the discovery of oil in the 1930s and its role as the main source of revenue, the economic and social structures, including the HRM/HRD system, have been influenced by the oil-based growth model adopted by GCC countries (Al-Waqfi and Forstenlechner, 2012). The massive exportation of oil has allowed GCC countries to enjoy substantial revenues from oil and gas productions. In 2012, for example, the hydrocarbon revenue in most GCC countries represented nearly 80% of the overall government revenues, with the exception of Qatar, for which gas revenues combined with oil accounted for 70% of government revenues (World Bank, 2012). According to the World Economic Forum's (WEF) Global Competitiveness Report (2013–2014), Qatar, the UAE, and Saudi Arabia, ranked thirteenth, nineteenth, and twentieth, respectively. These three countries are ranked among the top-20 most competitive economies in the world. The report also showed that whereas Switzerland was ranked the most competitive economy in the world for the fifth year, three GCC states headed the list of all Arab countries and most Asian countries in the rankings.

Ramady (2010) and Mellahi et al. (2011) underline that the success of GCC's economy depends on some other factors. For example, Qatar's is built on its strong institutional framework, stable macro economy, well-organized goods market, and its sophisticated business environment. UAE's economy is characterized by a high-quality infrastructure, macroeconomic stability, and a readiness to adopt new technologies (Barnett et al., 2015). Saudi Arabia, on the other hand, benefits particularly from the large size of its local market. It is considered to be one of the biggest among GCC countries. Kuwait, which, along with the UAE, improved its ranking in the 2011 index, climbing one place, boasts the most stable macroeconomic environment in the Arab countries (Al-Kazi, 2011).

During the past two decades, strong GDP growth was supported by rising financial investment, large government spending, and modernized infrastructure financed by rapidly increasing oil and gas revenues. In 2000, nominal GDP was around 422 billion USD and increased dramatically to 1,021 trillion in 2010 (World Bank, 2010). However, historically there was an overall relatively low level of economic diversification into productive and labor-intensive sectors. This distinguishes the GCC's economic path from that of most advanced economies, for which the transition to higher per capita income has generally been associated with greater diversification (Al-Waqfi and Forstenlechner, 2012). Additionally, large oil revenues have enabled the provision of free access to public services, including schools, universities, hospitals, etc. The government has also committed to securing their citizens' economic and social well-being by providing jobs in the public sector and subsidizing the social welfare systems.

However, reducing dependency on oil and gas revenues remains a key government priority (Rees et al., 2007). For example, Bahrain, as Oman, has limited oil and gas reserves that are expected to run out in the near future (Al-Hamadi et al., 2007); the oil and gas sector was 36% of GDP in 2012, the lowest in the GCC, reflecting a higher degree of economic diversification with large tourism and financial sectors (World Bank, 2010). For this reason, the economic diversification for the GCC countries has been recognized as an important key strategy in the region. According to Ramady (2010), the economic diversification would bring positive effects to the economic structures, as well as the HRD system, in a number of ways. First, it would reduce exposure of the economies to uncertainties in the global market. Second, it would help create new jobs in the private sector that are needed to absorb rapid growth of the youth population. Third, it would help increase productivity and sustainable growth. Fourth, it would help put in place the non-oil economy that will be needed many years down the road when oil revenues start to dwindle.

In addition, improving the competitiveness of the GCC countries will require addressing and removing a number of constraints generally common to all the countries in the region. These have been identified by Achoui (2009) and Ramady and Saee (2007), who report what respondents found were the most problematic factors of doing business in their countries. They listed restrictive labor regulations, lack of national manpower, an inefficient government bureaucracy, limited access to financing, and a poor work ethic among the national population as especially problematic. Harry (2007) argued that within GCC, the focus of the economy has not been on producing needed skills and attitudes and that the wealth brought from hydrocarbon products has not encouraged a productive work ethic of the type claimed by Asian economies. Due to lack of educated and skilled workers, GCC countries relied heavily on foreign knowledge and labor, which outnumbered the local population in some of the countries. The next sections will provide further details of the demographic changes in GCC countries and how it impacted the HRD system.

DEMOGRAPHIC CHANGE AND HRD SYSTEMS

The fast economic growth with modernization and diversification has resulted in a significant change in the demographic composition of the countries, which reflects the social and business structures within the GCC region. Labor inward migration began following the initial discovery of oil but increased significantly only after the 1973 oil boom (Rutledge et al., 2011). The decision to diversify the GCC economy posed major challenges in meeting market demand that could not be met by national workforces, either because they had small talent pools or were lacking in skills and expertise (Wilkins, 2001; Al-Dosary and Rahman, 2005). For example, in 1980, the population of the GCC countries was around 13.4 million, but after the rapid growth in the economy, the population increased dramatically to 21.3 million. With continued economy development, the population grew to reach 29.9 million in 2000 and 44.5 million in 2010, (World Bank, 2012). However, this increase of the population is more pronounced for non-nationals than nationals. In 2010, for example, there were 27 million foreigners in GCC countries constituting 59% of the total population. In UAE, Qatar, Kuwait, and Bahrain foreigners made up a majority (Yadapadithaya and Stewart, 2003); in the Qatar and UAE alone, foreigners accounted for around 88% of the population. Oman and Saudi Arabia, on the other hand, managed to maintain a relatively low number of foreigners: about 43% and 32%, respectively. See also Table 8.2.

In addition, the World Bank (2010) predicted that the population in the GCC countries would rise by a further third in the next few decades. Saudi Arabia is among the fastest-growing nations in the world in terms of population growth. The Saudi's population grew from 7.3 million in 1975 to almost 30 million in 2013, where non-nationals represent 9.7 million. By 2025, the GCC is expected to have a total population of 60 million, which is expected to increase by 14 million by 2050. As of 2011, the average age in Oman is the lowest in the GCC standing at 24 years, whereas the highest is 31 years in Qatar. The average age in the entire GCC region is 27 years with over 20% below the age of 15 (UNDP, 2013). Perceived as a serious challenge to future development of the region is the prediction that around 50% of the GCC population will soon be under 25, rating second highest in the world, after Africa. This trend raises significant questions for how the countries of the GCC will respond in terms of their HRD policies and practices to address the potential economic, cultural, and political instability from this growth (Al-Hamadi et al., 2007; Salih, 2010).

In terms of labor force statistics, expatriate and foreign workers continue to dominate jobs in private sectors, hitting 85% in 2008 (Yaghi and Aljaidi, 2014). In parallel, nationals were absorbed into the public sector, which commits to offering comfortable, well-remunerated jobs with high job security (Williams et al., 2011; Forstenlechner et al., 2012). Currently, non-national workers dominate the private sector, whereas national workers dominate the public sector. In 2008, for example, the non-national workers in private-sector organizations accounted for 95%, 97%, and 99%

Table 8.2   GCC Population

Country	Population 2000 (000s)	Population 2013 (000s)	Citizens (000s)	%	Foreigners (000s)	%
Bahrain	650	1,253	614	49.0	638	51.0
Kuwait	2,261	3,369	1,089	32.3	2,280	67.7
Oman	2,402	3,855	2,172	56.3	1,683	43.7
Qatar	613	2,269	278	12.0	1,991	88.0
Saudi Arabia	22,673	30,770	20,702	67.3	10,068	32.7
UAE	4,106	9,364	1,217	13.0	8,131	87.0
Total	32,705	50,880	26,072	51.2	24,791	48.7

Source: World Bank (2013)

in the UAE, Kuwait, and Qatar, respectively (World Bank, 2010). While at the same time, national workers in the public sector represented 85%, 87%, 94% in Oman, Bahrain, and Saudi Arabia, respectively (Al-Asfour and Khan, 2014). This stream of non-national workers has created serious problems according to Rutledge et al. (2011), including the segmentation of the labor market between nationals and non-nationals, unemployment among local citizens, over-reliance on outsider workers, government budget strains, and an outflow of local currency. Moreover, most people believe that the substantial imbalance in the composition of the population poses a threat to social as well as national security.

It is also becoming increasingly expensive for the public sector to employ only nationals. Swailes, Al Said, and Al Fahdi (2012) noted that the public sector has now become saturated, so the GCC governments have turned their attention to the private sector. While it meets the investment and opportunity needs of the domestic market (Mellahi, 2007), it employs few nationals. Instead, it depends on low-wage foreign laborers who generally work long hours, accept lower wages, tolerate poorer working conditions, and physically demanding jobs, which would not necessarily be accepted by the nationals (Bozionelos, 2009). Salih (2010) argued that within GCC countries, the profit-based organizations search for the cheapest unskilled labor (usually of Asian origin) and seem to have little interest in investing in national HRD. Nationals, on the other hand, are typically seeking education and training that prepares them for jobs in the public sector. As a consequence, the government wage bill has become large (in percentage of GDP). Ramady (2013) argued, however, with the GCC labor force projected to increase in the next 5 to 10 years, it will be difficult for the government to continue to absorb new labor market participants, and unless the employment of nationals in the private sector increases, unemployment will likely rise.

Moreover, the challenge of balancing between equipping citizens with suitable jobs while at the same time meeting market demands was considered an unresolved issue (Yaghi and Yaghi, 2013; Budhwar and Mellahi, 2007). The level of unemployment among nationals is high given the level of economic growth and large government spending. For example, in Qatar, youth unemployment, of both sexes, is estimated at 21% in Bahrain, 26% in Saudi Arabia, and 49% in Oman (World Bank, 2010). In this area of research, scholars are often faced with a lack of reliable data for the region (Rodriguez and Scurry, 2014). In total, Ramady (2013) estimates, there are over five hundred thousand people unemployed in the GCC or 15% of the total national workforce, and he believes that the ranks of the unemployed increase by over two hundred thousand a year. All these statistics represent only nationals seeking work, because expatriates who are not fully employed officially are meant to leave the country (Jackson and Manderscheid, 2015). Governments of the region, as the holders of major resources, used to be able to direct their budgets to the creation of public-sector jobs for citizens (Forstenlechner and Baruch, 2013). However, even when oil prices are high, it is becoming impossible for governments to make available enough public-sector jobs for all those entering the labor market. The rise in unemployment among young nationals has fueled resentment at the jobs being held by foreigners, even when the jobs are not ones attractive to citizens.

INSTITUTIONAL AND NATIONAL HRD SYSTEMS IN THE MIDDLE EAST

One of the major amendments to the GCC HRD system is the implementation of policies and practices that are focused on the nationalization of the labor force (Achoui, 2009; Karam and Afiouni, 2013; Al-Asfour and Khan, 2014). With an estimated 1 million unemployed nationals in the GCC and 24 million foreign workers (World Bank, 2010), governments have attempted to develop and improve the knowledge and skill gaps of home nationals. It has been contended that this action will lead to renationalization of the workforce—particularly within the private sector (Stalker and Mavin, 2011; Al-Waqfi and Forstenlechner, 2012). With the introduction of the employment quota system, it would seem that the replacement of expatriate and foreign workers with home nationals could become a reality within the next few years. The following is a summary of the localization policies that have been implemented in GCC countries.

Bahrainization

Initiated in 1998, Bahrain's nationalization program is the earliest example of a formal labor market strategy specifically designed to create employment opportunities for nationals within the GCC area (World Bank, 2010). Today, the program seeks to create as many as six thousand jobs a year for Bahrainis. Companies are now requested to increase their employment levels of nationals by 5% a year until half their labor force is Bahraini (Metcalfe, 2007), whereas new firms that develop within the area must employ a workforce that is 20% Bahraini. According to the Central Information Organization in Bahrain, a human resources development support program initiated in 1994 offers financial incentives to small and mid-sized firms in the manufacturing sector if they employ at least 30% Bahrainis in their workforce.

Omanization

This is a long-term program established in 1995 that seeks to promote competency and efficiency within both the public and private sectors. In recent years, increased emphasis has been placed on the private sector, as it represents a large occupational opportunity for locals to secure meaningful employment. The government views the private sector as the primary vehicle of growth and development, and as such, identifies it as the main area in which the employment of Omanis is most likely to occur. The current 'Vision 2020' plan created various labor market policies with the goal of creating new jobs each year and increasing the proportion of nationals from 30% to 40% within the current workforce (Al-Hamadi et al., 2007). The National Vocational Qualification Program, which was launched by the government in 1995 and is financed by the taxes of expatriate workers, is also designed to improve the skill set of Omani nationals (World Bank, 2010). According to Moideenkutty, Al-Lamki, and Murthy (2011), Oman is generally recognized to be the first GCC country to take steps toward reducing employment in the public sector.

Kuwaitization

The aim of the latest economic plan in Kuwait is to create ten thousand jobs a year for Kuwaitis during the next five years and raise the proportion of nationals within the labor force to 25% (World Bank, 2010). Policies to achieve these objectives include increasing the cost of expatriate labor through higher licensing fees, reducing employment of expatriates in certain businesses and endeavors, and improving the skills of nationals (see Salih, 2010). Some of these policies were classified in the new labor law of 2000, which also imposed a 2.5% tax on listed companies in order to finance the provisions of the law.

Qatarization

In 1997, the Qatari government issued a mandate to private businesses to ensure that nationals made up at least 20% of their employees. In sectors such as the oil and gas industry, the Qatarization program proposes 50% Qataris (Williams et al., 2011). The government made significant efforts to increase the nationalization of the labor force within the oil and gas sector, in the hopes of reaching 50% by 2005 (World Bank, 2010). Unfortunately, with a lower growth rate within the national labor force and an ongoing need for imported labor, nationalization efforts have not been as concentrated as in other Gulf States (Scurry et al., 2013).

Saudization

Saudi Arabia's sixth development plan employs a combination of inducements and targets in order to increase the percentage of home nationals in the private sector and simultaneously renationalize the workforce (Al-Asfour and Khan, 2014). Following the introduction of the employment quotas system, *Nitaqat*, every Saudi company was directed to reserve 30% of their jobs for the local population (Ramady, 2013). This system has proved highly effective and has greatly stimulated the number of jobs available to Saudi home nationals. The *Nitaqat* scheme insists that companies comply with the minimum local employment percentages if they wish to continue to enjoy access to valuable resources. Noncompliance can lead to companies facing financial penalties and other damaging restrictions. To boost compliance levels, the policy also includes financial support for firms that commit time and energy to training nationals, adhere to minimum targets for employment of nationals, and observe restrictions on the employment of skilled and semiskilled workers (see Achoui, 2009).

Emiratization

The policy for the Emirates was launched by the UAE government in early 2004, applying it to both the public and private sectors. It was first implemented through structural reform rather than specific measures (Rees et al., 2007). The aim of the program is to reduce the UAE's dependence on foreign workers and safeguard the rights of UAE citizens by ensuring that they benefit from the economic growth in the country. The Labor Law mandates that UAE nationals (followed by other Arab nationals) should be prioritized by employers over any other nationalities when seeking employees (Yaghi and Aljaidi, 2014). As part of its Emiratization program, the UAE has also attempted to identify specific industries that would be suitable for UAE national workers. Banking and insurance have been classified as two such industries. As a result, the companies operating within these sectors must now meet specific annual quotas. In addition, the government has established the National Human Resource Development and Employment Authority, which provides career guidance and training to UAE nationals. All employers in the UAE must be registered with this program (Stalker and Mavin, 2011). To ensure the efficacy of the program, the Ministry of Labor maintains the right to impose fines on companies that do not meet the Emiratization requirements.

Despite these major reforms, empirical studies have shown that most of these policies have not achieved the desired results. The goals were determined to be unrealistic and were dropped (Marchon and Toledo, 2014). Al-Asfour and Khan (2014) argue that focusing on representation alone might not overcome the challenges that are facing GCC. Harry (2007) claims that simply replacing expatriates with local citizens may not be a good strategy, as many jobs occupied by foreigners are traditionally perceived as low-status employment. The difference between employment in the public and private sectors has created a highly segmented labor market between nationals and foreigners (Forstenlechner and Mellahi, 2011). Ramady (2010) highlights that the issue of local participation in the private sectors is far beyond legal complaints. The majority of home nationals have negative perceptions of jobs in private sectors, lack adequate skills, as well social integration skills necessary to work in a multicultural environment. Al-Waqfi and Forstenlechne (2010) note that the majority of employers perceive the localization

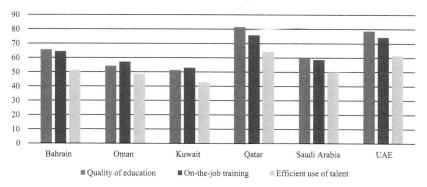

Figure 8.1 Level of Training and Development in GCC

polices as costly and as limiting organizations' capabilities to compete locally or internationally (see Figure 8.1).

COMMON CHALLENGES FACING HRD IN THE MIDDLE EAST

Despite the region's ability to profit from oil and gas production, the over-reliance on these two major resources has had a marked negative impact on HRD (Al-Kazi, 2011; Marchon and Toledo, 2014). Empirical evidence collected on the GCC has revealed several factors that significantly limit their capacity to absorb national workers. These factors in turn have contributed to the increase of the national unemployment rate and pose even more challenges to the HRD system. High-quality education, employment, and broadly accessible lifelong learning opportunities are seen as vital precursors to knowledge-based economic development. To varying degrees, many GCC countries are faced with similar human capital challenges that serve as formidable obstacles to their economic growth and development. The following is a summary of these challenges at both national and organizational levels.

Preference for Public-Sector Employment

GCC government-owned natural resources and government organizations have become the largest employers of nationals. For example, in countries such as Kuwait, Qatar, and the UAE, where national populations are relatively small, more than 80% of employed nationals work in government organizations (Salih, 2010). The ratio is also high in Saudi Arabia, whereas in Oman, about 50% of the employed nationals work in the public sector. At 35%, Bahrain appears to have the lowest proportion of nationals working in the public sector. Spurred on by the promise of highly paid government employment, many job seekers have applied for public jobs with minimal skill requirements. Barnett, Malcolm, and Toledo (2015) found that public-sector employment in some of the GCC countries often requires low-level skills to perform particular jobs. These social aspects of career choice have led to a slower rate of economic integration and decreased productivity in industries that import low-skill expatriate labor. As a result of this widespread preference for public-sector jobs, regional governments are now facing a crisis, whereby they are unable to create suitable employment opportunities for the youth population entering the labor market. Given that the current wage bill is already considerably high, it seems unlikely that GCC government budgets will be able to afford to create additional public jobs for nationals (Forstenlechner and Mellahi, 2011).

Job creation remains one of the major challenges in most GCC countries (Al-Dosary and Rahman, 2005). The public sector is the only area to have achieved progress; however, such a high rate of nationalization in the public sector may not necessarily be the result of a successful employment strategy (Salih, 2010). The government has put pressure on its departments to hire GCC nationals for less-needed jobs. Consequently, 65% of the government's annual budget is assigned to salaries, and that proportion is expected to increase (Rutledge et al., 2011). The private sector has not been able, or willing, to take on many of the unemployed young citizens. In reality, it is a complex, multifaceted problem that requires a large-scale economic reform strategy. The private sector appears to be resisting nationalization, complaining that home nationals are more expensive and less productive than non-nationals (Mellahi, 2007). Al-Asfour and Khan (2014) concluded that nationalization needs to be compatible with the economy's diversity, competitiveness, and growth potential.

Increasing Female Labor Market Participation

Within the GCC region, two of the more striking contrasts associated with HRD pertain to the 'inconsistency' or 'mismatch' between women's educational and skills levels and their limited employment opportunities (Tlaiss and Dirani, 2015). HRD scholars (e.g., Metcalfe, 2007) use the 'Islam Gender Regime' approach to explain this gender imbalance and the status of women in terms of the contradiction between social changes and cultural influence. This stream of research considers change as coming into conflict with the traditional values system that controls people's behavior. Advocates of this approach would argue that gender role in organizations reflects a conflict between job responsibility and the traditional attitude of people in the GCC region, which seems to have changed very little (Tlaiss and Dirani, 2015). While economic growth has been translated into high living standards, it has not yet significantly altered cultural norms, which still put a premium on large families and traditional gender roles. Advocates of this approach claim that the HRD system in the last two decades has partly contributed to several social distortions, leading to more gender gaps in employment and training opportunities.

According to GCC statistics, in 2012, the total number of higher education students exceeded 1.5 million, of whom at least 60% were women (World Bank, 2012). Given the fact that women outperform men in terms of graduation rates, the unemployment rate among women is greater than for men. For example, in 2008, the Saudi Arabian unemployment rate reached 25% for women compared to 8% for men. In Qatar and the UAE, the unemployment rate for women was 8% and 12%, respectively, whereas for men the rate only was only 2% in both Qatar and the UAE. In this region, therefore, the gender imbalance in employment has continued to pose enormous challenges to the development of HRD systems (Al-Kazi, 2011). Despite significant advances in educational attainment, the participation of females within the labor market is estimated to be as low as 22%, indicating high levels of female unemployment. While an increasing number of women have begun to enter the labor market, many are still struggling to find suitable jobs (Metcalfe, 2007). Rapidly evolving cultural values and changing perceptions of women's obligations within the family continue to be influential in labor market participation and the procurement of higher levels of education (Tlaiss and Dirani, 2015). Unemployment rates in Qatar and Kuwait have remained relatively low due to a small national population that is mainly employed in the public sector. In Saudi Arabia, unemployment among nationals has increased from 10.5% in 2009 to 11.5% in 2013 and is concentrated among highly educated women and less-educated men. For the UAE, unemployment was purported to be 14% among nationals in 2009. However, in Bahrain, labor market policies have supported a considerable reduction in the level of unemployment (Yadapadithaya and Stewart, 2003).

Increasing rates of female-labor-force participation are partly due to falling fertility rates and partly due to rising education levels among women. Women in GCC countries have traditionally been placed in government or education sectors (Bozionelos, 2009; Rutledge et al., 2011). However, high female unemployment levels persist as a result of limited employment opportunities. In all GCC countries, unemployment rates continue to be higher among women than among men, reaching as high as 30% in some countries, such as Saudi Arabia.

The Rapid Growth of the Youth Cohort

The HRD systems in the GCC are increasingly likely to face challenges in the near future because of large numbers of young people entering the education system and employment market (Al-Waqfi and Forstenlechner, 2012). Indeed, in 2010, the World Bank estimated that 54% of the GCC population was under the age of 25. For the same year, people under the age of 25 represented around 51% of the population in Oman, 50% in Saudi Arabia, 43% in Bahrain, 37% in Kuwait, 33% in Qatar, and 31% in the UAE. As these young people grow up and begin to seek employment, it seems inevitable that the pressures on the employment market will become even more severe. By 2020, GCC countries will have one of the fastest-growing populations in the world, and the majority will be under 25 years of age (World Bank, 2010). This rapid growth represents a major challenge, as well as an enormous opportunity for the development of national HRD systems in the region.

Unemployment in the region also seems to be particularly prevalent among the young. The low level of labor force participation denotes a significant challenge for GCC youth as they transition from school to work (Achoui, 2009). For example, recent figures estimate youth unemployment in Bahrain, Kuwait, and the UAE at nearly 30% (Barnett et al., 2015). Indeed, unemployment among the young is an issue that could become more serious should current labor market initiatives fail to remain effective. In addition, a substantial proportion of young Saudis, 18% of 15- to 24-year-olds, are categorized as being not well educated and lacking the proper skills necessary to secure meaningful employment. Addressing this challenge is a primary point of focus for the GCC; as a result, a large number of programs have been set up to support the upskilling of the young (Al-Waqfi and Forstenlechner, 2012). Through these endeavors, it is hoped that the young in these countries will be better prepared to meet the needs of the private sector in the future.

Failure to solve the problem has been attributed to the wrong treatment and the absence of a strategic vision by the government (Forstenlechner and Baruch, 2013). It seems impracticable that young GCC graduates can be attracted to the private sector without a clearly defined economic strategy. Over the last five decades, the economic model of GCC countries has relied heavily on the wealth accrued from oil revenue, which has transformed them into 'welfare states' (Salih, 2010, p.173). As a result, the economic activities within these countries have grown quickly but without proper policies to guide economic development. It seems apparent that a problem of this magnitude is likely to have long-lasting negative implications for the economy and for society as a whole. Furthermore, according to Bhuian, Al-shammari, and Jefri (2001), the growing number of GCC citizens who are ready to enter the labor market is largely viewed as a problem. It could, rather, be seen as an asset by being capitalized upon and used as a tool to aid development. This perception is attributed to the fact that the State has taken upon itself to provide all GCC citizens with public jobs, which has led to a rapidly growing public sector devoid of any standards for competency and required qualifications (Williams et al., 2011).

Misalignment Between Workforce Skills and Market Demands

Empirical evidence has shown that formal educational qualifications are frequently unrelated to current employment needs and that a high number of employees in the public sector believe their current jobs require skills and capabilities below their level (Mellahi, 2007). Ramady (2010) has claimed that the education system and vocational training institutions have not placed enough emphasis on developing soft skills, such as communication, teamwork, analytical skills, and innovative thinking. Some 80% of those who graduate do so in subjects such as geology, Arabic writing, and Islamic studies, with the remainder graduating in science, building, or from the medical schools (Williams et al., 2011). This pattern clearly does not meet the needs of the work market.

A recent survey of the private sector also found that 46% of regional managers do not believe that education and training systems in the GCC prepare students for the workplace (Bagadier, Patrick and Burns, 2011These findings are suggestive of an immense divide between current regional human capital levels and the skills demanded by private-sector employers. As the government aimed to renationalize the workforce, "citizens found themselves competing for positions in both the public and private sector, as they began to realize they could no longer expect to find abundant employment" (Forstenlechner and Baruch, 2013, 630).

In addition, although there is an ongoing tendency toward increased funding for education in the region, meeting the combined demands of increased access, assuring relevance, and improving quality in the face of finite resources remains a challenge (Baqadir et al., 2011). Despite improvements in the promotion of educational opportunity and increased national expenditure on education, regional human capital development and the ability of GCC countries to compete in the global economy continue to be hindered by poor quality education. The problem seems to lie with the region's higher-level education systems, which are failing to produce the right quality and mix of human capital needed for knowledge-based development.

MEETING THE CHALLENGES

To make a successful transition from the current oil-based economy to a knowledge-based economy, the GCC needs to make an enhanced effort to develop both cognitive and noncognitive skills (Harry, 2007). Investing capital in formal education, although necessary, is not the primary condition for a speedy improvement of individual competencies (Gallant and Pounder, 2008). Indeed, in countries with a high level of human capital, the education system is only one step in the process of spreading and developing cognitive and, to a lesser extent, noncognitive skills among the population. The other steps involve addressing cultural norms and tradition. The influence of national culture on the decision-making behavior of training managers in GCC countries has been the subject of many empirical studies (Al-Hamadi et al., 2007). For example, among all the GCC countries, Saudi Arabia has been found to be the most religiously conservative society. Given that women are still banned from driving in this country, this sexually segregated society has a long way to go if the problem of slow economic growth is to be tackled and effectively resolved.

Approximately one-third of the total GCC population are expatriates residing in the country on foreign worker visas (Stalker and Mavin, 2011). A sizable wage gap exists between GCC nationals and foreign workers, as the latter are economically more attractive. When implementing policies, it has become an important goal for GCC governments to promote the employment of GCC nationals in the private sector by either replacing low-cost foreign workers or creating new jobs specific to the GCC (Jackson and Manderscheid, 2015). At the same time, GCC governments and policy makers recognize the importance of foreign workers to the overall economy and strive to provide the best working environment possible for the foreign workers residing there. In general, there are a number of notable focus areas of GCC governments that have been acknowledged in the last few years, including increasing mobility, protecting wages, and providing tailored support and guidance to domestic workers.

The current level of female graduates highlights the large pool of underutilized human resources that currently exists within the GCC (Metcalfe, 2007). It is no surprise then that one of the key objectives of the GCC governments should be to focus on increasing female participation in the labor force, primarily through the running of several specific programs. A number of programs have been implemented but need further improvement by analyzing individual sectors, directly engaging companies to find suitable jobs for women, and providing them with practical assistance. Further measures include programs to provide or subsidize childcare, which would allow women increased opportunities to work outside the home. An efficient implementation of these efforts would serve to increase female participation in the workforce and enhance national HRD systems.

The GCC does not yet have a job-seeking system, but unless governments and business owners can meet the challenges of employment creation and localization, the region will face some serious problems across the board (Harry, 2007). The current high price of oil may be the key to helping the governments of the GCC find the resources necessary to confront these issues. However, without first addressing the underlying issues, simply throwing money at the problem is unlikely to produce any real change. The governments, employers, and citizens of the GCC will have to be tenacious in their approach and work together. Deporting foreigners and giving their jobs to nationals is not the solution either. The real, long-lasting solutions lie in the development of a capable indigenous workforce through high-quality education and changing expectations, as well as creating new worthwhile jobs for citizens that utilize all their skills and capabilities (Achoui, 2009). A focus on employment creation will enable the region not only to make the best use of its natural resources but also to make the best use of its human resources.

REFERENCES

Achoui, M. M. (2009). Human resource development in Gulf countries: An analysis of the trends and challenges facing Saudi Arabia. *Human Resource Development International*, 12: 35–46.

Al-Asfour, A., & Khan, S. A. (2014). Workforce localization in the Kingdom of Saudi Arabia: Issues and challenges. *Human Resource Development International*, 17: 243–253.

Al-Dosary, A. S., & Rahman, S. M. (2005). Saudization (Localization)—A critical review. *Human Resource Development International*, 8: 495–502.

Al-Hamadi, A. B., Budhwar, P. S., & Shipton, H. (2007). Management of human resources in Oman. *The International Journal of Human Resource Management*, 18: 100–113.

Al-Kazi, L. (2011). Women and non-governmental organizations in Kuwait: A platform for human resource development and social change. *Human Resource Development International*, 14: 167–181.

Al-Waqfi, M., & Forstenlechner, I. (2010). Stereotyping of citizens in an expatriate-dominated labour market: Implications for workforce localisation policy. *Employee Relations*, 32: 364–381.

Al-Waqfi, M. A., & Forstenlechner, I. (2012). Of private sector fear and prejudice: The case of young citizens in an oil-rich Arabian Gulf economy. *Personnel Review*, 41: 609–629.

Baqadir, A., Patrick, F., & Burns, G. (2011). Addressing the skills gap in Saudi Arabia: does vocational education address the needs of private sector employers?. *Journal of Vocational Education & Training*, 63: 551–561.

Barnett, A. H., Malcolm, M., & Toledo, H. (2015). Shooting the goose that lays the golden egg: The case of UAE employment policy. *Journal of Economic Studies*, 42: 285–302.

Bhuian, S. N., Al-Shammari, E. S., & Jefri, O. A. (2001). Work-related attitudes and job characteristics of expatriates in Saudi Arabia. *Thunderbird International Business Review*, 43: 21–32.

Bozionelos, N. (2009). Expatriation outside the boundaries of the multinational corporation: A study with expatriate nurses in Saudi Arabia. *Human Resource Management*, 48: 111–134.

Budhwar, P., & Mellahi, K. (2007). Introduction: Human resource management in the Middle East. *The International Journal of Human Resource Management*, 18: 2–10.

Forstenlechner, I., & Baruch, Y. (2013). Contemporary career concepts and their fit for the Arabian Gulf context: A sector level analysis of psychological contract breach. *Career Development International*, 18: 629–648.

Forstenlechner, I., Lettice, F., & Özbilgin, M. F. (2012). Questioning quotas: Applying a relational framework for diversity management practices in the United Arab Emirates. *Human Resource Management Journal*, 22: 299–315.

Forstenlechner, I., & Mellahi, K. (2011). Gaining legitimacy through hiring local workforce at a premium: The case of MNEs in the United Arab Emirates. *Journal of World Business*, 46: 455–461.

Gallant, M., & Pounder, J. S. (2008). The employment of female nationals in the United Arab Emirates (UAE): An analysis of opportunities and barriers. *Education, Business and Society: Contemporary Middle Eastern Issues*, 1: 26–33.

Harry, W. (2007). Employment creation and localization: The crucial human resource issues for the GCC. *The International Journal of Human Resource Management*, 18: 132–146.

Hassi, A. (2011). International briefing 23: Training and development in Morocco. *International Journal of Training and Development*, 15: 169–178.

Hofstede, G. (1980). *Culture's Consequences: International Differences in Work-Related Values*. Beverly Hills, CA: Sage.

Hvidt, M. (2011). Economic and institutional reforms in the Arab Gulf countries. *The Middle East Journal*, 65: 85–102.

Jackson, D., & Manderscheid, S. V. (2015). A phenomenological study of Western expatriates' adjustment to Saudi Arabia. *Human Resource Development International*, 18: 131–152.

Karam, C. M., & Afiouni, F. (2013). Localizing women's experiences in academia: Multilevel factors at play in the Arab Middle East and North Africa. *The International Journal of Human Resource Management*, 0: 1–39.

Marchon, C., & Toledo, H. (2014). Re-thinking employment quotas in the UAE. *The International Journal of Human Resource Management,* 25: 2253–2274.

Mclean, G. N. (2012). Invited response: Observations on modeling NHRD strategy. *Human Resource Development Review*, 1534484312458566.

Mellahi, K. (2007). The effect of regulations on HRM: private sector firms in Saudi Arabia. *The International Journal of Human Resource Management*, 18: 85–99.

Mellahi, K., Demirbag, M., & Riddle, L. (2011). Multinationals in the Middle East: Challenges and opportunities. *Journal of World Business*, 46: 406–410.

Metcalfe, B. D. (2007). Gender and human resource management in the Middle East. *The International Journal of Human Resource Management*, 18: 54–74.

Metcalfe, B. D. (2008). Women, management and globalization in the Middle East. *Journal of Business Ethics*, 83: 85–100.

Moideenkutty, U., Al-Lamki, A., & Murthy, Y. S. R. (2011). HRM practices and organizational performance in Oman. *Personnel Review*, 40: 239–251.

Murphy, A., & Garavan, T. N. (2009). The adoption and diffusion of an NHRD standard: A conceptual framework. *Human Resource Development Review*, 8: 3–21.

Ramady, M. A. (2010). *The Saudi Arabian Economy: Policies, Achievements, and Challenges*. New York, Springer.

Ramady, M. A. (2013). Gulf unemployment and government policies: Prospects for the Saudi labour quota or Nitaqat system. *International Journal of Economics and Business Research*, 5: 476–498.

Ramady, M. A., & Saee, J. (2007). Foreign direct investment: A strategic move toward sustainable free enterprise and economic development in Saudi Arabia. *Thunderbird International Business Review*, 49: 37–56.

Rees, C. J., Mamman, A., & Braik, A. B. (2007). Emiratization as a strategic HRM change initiative: Case study evidence from a UAE petroleum company. *The International Journal of Human Resource Management*, 18: 33–53.

Rodriguez, J. K., & Scurry, T. (2014). Career capital development of self-initiated expatriates in Qatar: Cosmopolitan globetrotters, experts and outsiders. *The International Journal of Human Resource Management*, 25: 1046–1067.

Rutledge, E., Al Shamsi, F., Bassioni, Y., & Al Sheikh, H. (2011). Women, labour market nationalization policies and human resource development in the Arab Gulf states. *Human Resource Development International*, 14: 183–198.

Salih, A. (2010). Localizing the private sector workforce in the Gulf cooperation council countries: A study of Kuwait. *International Journal of Public Administration*, 33: 169–181.

Scurry, T., Rodriguez, J. K., & Bailouni, S. (2013). Narratives of identity of self-initiated expatriates in Qatar. *Career Development International*, 18: 12–33.

Showail, S. J., Mclean Parks, J., & Smith, F. L. (2013). Foreign workers in Saudi Arabia: A field study of role ambiguity, identification, information-seeking, organizational support and performance. *The International Journal of Human Resource Management*, 24: 1–23.

Sidani, Y., & Al Ariss, A. (2014). Institutional and corporate drivers of global talent management: Evidence from the Arab Gulf region. *Journal of World Business*, 49(2): 215–224.

Stalker, B., & Mavin, S. (2011). Learning and development experiences of self-initiated expatriate women in the United Arab Emirates. *Human Resource Development International*, 14: 273–290.

Swailes, S., Al Said, L., & Al Fahdi, S. (2012). Localisation policy in Oman: A psychological contracting interpretation. *International journal of public sector management*, 25: 357–372.

Tlaiss, H. A., & Dirani, K. M. (2015). Women and training: An empirical investigation in the Arab Middle East. *Human Resource Development International*, 18 (4): 1–21.

Williams, J., Bhanugopan, R., & Fish, A. (2011). Localization of human resources in the State of Qatar: Emerging issues and research agenda. *Education, Business and Society: Contemporary Middle Eastern Issues*, 4: 193–206.

Wilkins, S. (2001). International briefing 9: Training and development in the United Arab Emirates. *International Journal of Training and Development*, 5: 153–165.

World Bank. (2010). Doing Business in the Arab World 2010. Accessed 1 May 2015. http://www.doingbusiness.org/reports/~/media/GIAWB/Doing%20Business/Documents/Special-Reports/DB10-ArabWorld.pdf

World Bank. (2012). World Development Indicators 2012. Accessed 15 May 2015. http://data.worldbank.org/sites/default/files/wdi-2012-ebook.pdf

Yadapadithaya, P., & Stewart, J. (2003). Corporate training and development policies and practices: A cross-national study of India and Britain. *International Journal of Training and Development*, 7: 108–123.

Yaghi, A., & Aljaidi, N. (2014). Examining organizational commitment among national and expatriate employees in the private and public sectors in United Arab Emirates. *International Journal of Public Administration*, 37: 801–811.

Yaghi, A., & Yaghi, I. (2013). Human resource diversity in the United Arab Emirates: Empirical study. *Education, Business and Society: Contemporary Middle Eastern Issues*, 6: 15–30.

9 Human Resource Development in North Africa

Hussain A. Alhejji and
Thomas N. Garavan

INTRODUCTION

Algeria, Morocco, and Tunisia are part of the eight North African countries defined by the United Nations. Although these countries share geographical boundaries, they differ in terms of scope and nature. For example, Drake (2006) indicated that whereas the Algerian economy is based on hydrocarbon productions, the Moroccan and Tunisian economies are still based on agriculture and tourism. Whereas Algeria and Tunisia were part of the Ottoman Empire, Morocco was not. The North African countries have also shown similar trends in relation to their HRD system, including a lack of unskilled manpower, young populations, a lack of training and skills development, gender imbalance in societies and workplaces, the predominance of Islamic law, and the power of tribes (Ali and Wahabi, 1995; Yahiaoui, 2015). These heritages have directly influenced the NHRD system. However, international HRD literature has shown a limited knowledge of how these factors are operating (Kamoche et al., 2015). A call for a legitimate extension to the field of HRD is extremely necessary, as globalization, transitioning economies, and political change have impacted large aspects of NHRD (Wang and Swanson, 2008).

Several theoretical frameworks in the context of HRD, such as the human capital theory, the resources-based theory, and behavior perspectives, have underscored the importance of developing human resources and HRD practices to suit individual and organizational performance (Ellis et al., 2015). The management literature suggests that HRD policies and practices are nationally specific and that organizations should have a full knowledge of how to align HRD practices with the national context in which they operate. Although a lot of HRD research exists, there is very little from a global perspective, particularly from non-Western countries (Kamoche et al., 2012). Although there is a growing amount of research on HRD in Africa (e.g., Cox et al., 2006; Sydhagen and Cunningham, 2007), most of the research outputs on HRD in Africa pale in comparison with the West and Asia (e.g., Calza et al., 2010; Gomes et al., 2014) or focuses on English-speaking countries, such as South Africa (e.g., Stuart, 2012) or Ghana (e.g., Arthur-Mensah and Alagaraja, 2013). Croucher et al. (2014), and therefore argues that the lack of theoretical and empirical knowledge on HRD in North African countries makes it very difficult to inform Western managers on how best to design and implement HRD practices. Yet the limited information on NHRD and factors that have shaped the policies and practices are scattered, and scholars suggested that HRD practices should follow a number of perspectives, such as the cross-convergence perspective or divergence perspective.

The aim of this chapter is to broadly discuss HRD in North African countries: Algeria, Tunisia, and Morocco. The focus of this study is appropriate because of the multicultural and multiethnic nature of the North African region. It will outline some of the historical, economic, and cultural contexts that have impacted HRD policies and practices. In the second section, we will discuss more specifically the HRD system at the national and organizational levels, followed by a discussion on how external and internal factors have influenced the outcomes of HRD. Throughout the chapter, we will outline some of the similarities and differences of HRD in these three countries.

THE CONTEXT OF NORTH AFRICA

Historical Context

The geographical limits of North Africa have been as difficult to define as those of the Middle East. Whether consisting of Morocco, Algeria, and Tunisia alone, or including Mauritania, the Western Sahara, and Libya, definitions of North Africa have depended on subjective criteria as much as the historical or political moment (Abun-Nasr, 1987). During the European colonial and protectorate period, which ended with the independence of Algeria in 1962, 'North Africa' or 'Maghreb' (in this context, meaning the states dominated by the French) became almost terms of defiance. For the rest of this chapter, we only include the Maghreb countries in our definition of North Africa.

Algeria, Morocco, and Tunisia share a common heritage with many postcolonial nation-states, which make them new in the novelty of their political independence. Although these countries were colonies, their citizens have had a cultural identity for centuries (Charrad, 2001). Morocco and Tunisia were protectorates rather that colonies of France, which means that the political traditions survived beyond their independence in 1956. Algeria had been colonized since 1930 and its traditional institutions wholly repressed by French institutions (Branine et al., 2008). After the achievement of independence from colonial rule, which ended with the independence of Algeria in 1962, the Maghreb region started to challenge the authority of institutions to overcome some critical factors, including a high level of demographic growth, uncertain economics, and Islamic radicalism (Abun-Nasr, 1987).

What these countries have had in common since independence are mainly centralized regimes. The power exercised by Maghreb's leaders has been focused on maintaining their regimes, which thwarted their development as modern nation-states. The leaders took the path of consolidating their own rule at the expense of building autonomous institutions of state. For example, the central power of the Moroccan regime under King Hassan II has been maintained by an elaborate system of divide and rule (Hoffman, 2008). In Tunisia, the first presidency with Habib Bourguiba had been forged out of a broad consensus among the elites of the main nationalist party in 1964 (Yahiaoui and Zoubir, 2006). In Algeria, by contrast, the lack of consensus among elites at independence made even the choice of the first president a matter for dispute, verging on civil war (Branine, 2006). However, in the 1980s, these formulas of political control were showing signs of strain in the face of rapid social and economic change (Abun-Nasr, 1987). At independence, the extensive use of patronage to co-opt elites was not so much a matter of choice as a reflection of behavioral patterns common to most of the region. Despite the management of incentives and coercion, the real political damage was wrought in the distancing of the mass population from the centers of power, which caused more local hierarchies and low social improvement (Charrad, 2001).

The lack of human capital in North Africa is rooted in the political context. For example, after independence, North Africa faced challenges due to the numbers of unskilled and uneducated indigenous workers (Cox et al., 2006). The HRD function then concentrated on improving the level of education and filling the skills gaps left by the departing French business leaders. At the beginning of the 1980s, the government's role focused on enhancing industrial development programs by establishing training institutions that helped them address the skills gap (Horwitz, 2014). However, the outcomes for the efforts of these institutions were limited, because they were government-based with little participation from private organizations. Early in the 1990s, two major forms were established (Charrad, 2001). The first forms allowed state firms full independence, which positively impacted the national economy and allowed more participation by the private sector in local skills development. The second major reforms of employment regulation were established to respond to global demands and the increased number of MNCs. In Algeria, for instance, there was a movement from a centralized system to a 'liberal system', which has positively impacted the social and economic situations (Tiliouine, 2014).

However, since 2010, when the Arab Spring started in Tunisia, Egypt, and Yemen, which was thought to be unavoidable for the rest of the countries in the region, both Algeria and Morocco have faced the uprising of more political demands for democracy and freedom (Yahiaoui, 2015). The Arab Spring has led the Maghreb's leaders to reform a number of policies that had been designed to maintain their control, while at the same time aiming to improve the social lives of their citizens. For instance, Tiliouine

(2014) highlighted that in Algeria there was a demonstration against unemployment and the cost of living. These demonstrations took on a harder political edge than any had witnessed before. The government responded by taking measures to help employment and support purchasing power, which resulted in increasing the participation of all political parties in the implementation of public policy.

Economic Context

The economic development pathways adopted after independence reflect the overriding concern of the Maghreb's leaders with political control. During the 1970s and early 1980s, the economic policy makers in the Maghreb, largely led by the public sector, were mainly preoccupied with putting in place the necessary infrastructure to support a development strategy (Ali and Wahabi, 1995). An important constraint was that none of the countries could break away completely from the export-oriented economics left by the French (Branine, 2006; Yahiaoui and Zoubir, 2006). They were hampered by the lack of skilled personnel at their disposal. For this reason, a large proportion of country funds had to be dedicated to the education of the younger generation. At independence, more than 50% of the population of each country was employed in the traditional and subsistence agricultural sectors (Bouzahzah and El Menyari, 2013). The industrial sector was not able to create new employment opportunities and revenues were limited. In Morocco, there were few alternatives available to the government but to promote the modern agricultural sector as the main source of foreign revenue (Gómez-Miranda et al., 2015). Tunisia faced similar problems in having limited resources apart from its largely rural workforce. Algeria, in contrast, had the advantage of hydrocarbon resources, exploited by the French since the 1940s and now accruing to the public sector (Calza et al., 2010). The neglect of other sectors resulted in shortages in consumer goods and low domestic agricultural production and consequent supplementary importation from Europe.

When the economic crisis affected many African countries in 1986, huge attempts were made to diversify economies and initiate policies to facilitate free trade (Ben Salha, 2013; Bouzahzah and El Menyari, 2013). A large number of public firms had been privatizing and attempting to create more market opportunities for foreigners. For example, most countries permitted foreign investors to hold between 50 to 100% ownership in ventures in order to increase employment and the transfer of technology. The free trade agreements resulted in a greater diversity and volume of exports, and they allowed for more flexible responses to fluctuations in international markets, particularly from Europe and the United States (US) (Gómez-Miranda et al., 2015). See Table 9.1 for more information.

The tourism and agricultural industries in Morocco and Tunisia have played a major role in economic development, and they are considered to

Table 9.1   Economic Indicators in Algeria, Morocco, and Tunisia

Countries	Population (million)	GDP ($ million)	GDP growth (annual %)	Gross national income (GNI) per capital (PPP $)	Poverty headcount ratio (% population)
Algeria	39.2	210,183	2.8	13,070	6.9
Morocco	33	103,835	4.4	7,000	8.9
Tunisia	10.9	46.993	2.5	10,440	15.5

Sources: UNDP, Human Development Report, 2013.

be two of the most vital sectors in both countries. According to the World Bank (2012), in 2011, the tourism sector contributed to some 8.9 % of gross domestic product (GDP) in Morocco and 6.6 % in Tunisia (The World Bank, 2014). In contrast, Algeria has been listed among the wealthiest countries in North Africa because of its natural resources, which have attracted much foreign direct investment. More than 50% of the Algerian government's revenue is currently derived from the hydrocarbon sector, whereas 97% of the country's total exports are derived from oil and gas productions. The World Trade Organization has estimated that Algeria has the world's third largest reserves in oil and gas.

Despite these positive outcomes and the overall economic improvement in North Africa, the countries are still experiencing a number of economic challenges (Horwitz, 2014). For example, Morocco has not been able to solve the problem of youth unemployment (ages 15–24), which reached 19.1% in 2013. In Algeria, the unemployment rate fell slightly to 9.8% in 2013; however, this reduction was more pronounced among men than among women. Tunisia, in contrast, is still facing a high percentage of university graduates dealing with few available job opportunities. The high unemployment rate, the lack of equality, and the poor living conditions of most Tunisian people led to dramatic political change in 2011 (Yahiaoui, 2015).

The literature also outlines several challenges that have contributed to the slow economic development of North Africa. These range from the deficient political system, dependency on foreign markets, the lack of capital to finance development, unhealthy economic conditions, the inadequate utilization of other natural resources, dominant public sectors, growing unemployment, gender unbalanced government systems, and widespread corruption (see Charrad, 2001).

Cultural Context

Although the societies in North Africa have been characterized by cultural and ethnic diversity, they are, however, united by the common adherence to the Islamic religion (Hassi, 2012; Afiouni et al., 2014). Islam is the main religion and the holy "Qur'an" and the "Hadith" are the main sources. The importance of learning and education are emphasized in the Qur'an with frequent injunctions, such as "O my Lord! Increase me in knowledge" (The Holy Qur'an 20:114) and "God will exalt those of you who believe and those who have knowledge to high degrees" (The Holy Qur'an 58:11). Such tenets provide a forceful stimulus for an Islamic society to strive for more education and learning. Muslim people consider the Qur'an as the core of, and gateway to, learning. Memorizing as well as understanding the Qur'an is highly encouraged and supported by these societies (Akdere et al., 2006). In the past, learning the principles and practices of Islam was given priority over academic institutions and study. Students at early ages learned the basic principles of Islam acquired general knowledge that allowed them to be good members of society. Thus the pursuit of knowledge in Islam was a religious duty. Even when formal schools were established by governments, most curricula were influenced and designed according to the Islamic perspective (Forster and Fenwick, 2015). Islam is a very important context in North Africa at many levels that connect to HRD. The example of the prophet Mohammed in terms of the concept of 'behavior modeling' is well understood in the context of HRD (Khan and Sheikh, 2012). Thus it is considered by many in the culture that HRD practices can be truly successful if they are linked to the Islamic behavioral role model represented in Mohammed. For this reason the management practices in Muslim countries have been distinguished from management practices in non-Muslim countries (Afiouni et al., 2014; Horwitz, 2014). For example, Ali (2010, p. 696) summarized the main principle of training and development in Muslim countries as:

> A morally anchored and performance based evaluation,[which] aims at allowing employees to consider their performance in line of their contribution to their organization and society; individuals are endowed with varying capacities to learn and develop, knowledge and experiences are essential for individual growth and utilization of potential.

These Islamic values have to be further developed in order to impact the legal frameworks in areas such as private law as well as law by norms and traditions (Hassi, 2011). It has always occupied an important position in the spiritual lives of millions of North Africans and constitutes an important part of their identities. Branine (2006) argued that, although European colonialism was certainly a destructive political, social, and economic force, the religious sentiments of the Muslim community have retained significant power within North Africa. The latest figures show that 99% of the population in North Africa is Muslim with a minority of Christian and Jewish citizens (Ramdani et al., 2014). Although the predominant language of the region is Arabic, historically, all North African countries have been affected by French dominance, which has resulted in the French language becoming the first foreign language (Drake, 2006). In Algeria and Tunisia, for instance, French is used in official government documents, by the business people, and in higher education.

Education and Training Context

The United Nations Human Development Index (HDI) provides a great source for analyzing the NHRD. A 2013 United Nations Development Program (UNDP) report confirmed that progress has been made. The HDI provided scores ranging from 0–1,000 and classified countries into low (<0.500), medium (0.500–0.700), high (0.700–0.800), and very high (>0.800) human development categories. In 2013, both Algeria and Tunisia were considered to be in the high bracket with a HDI score of 0.717 and 0.721, respectively. In contrast, Morocco was classified as medium with a HDI score of 0.617 (UNDP, 2013). It is also important to note that all of the Maghreb countries have shown great improvements in their human development over the last 30 years. For example, Morocco is still classified medium in its Human Development Index (see Table 9.2).

In terms of the population in North Africa, the total number has risen from 27.81 million in 1960 to 81.4 million, and the young population (under 25) represents almost 40% of the total population (UNDP, 2013). As the population increases each year, North African governments are required to improve the quality of human lives, eliminate mass poverty, and provide proper education and training. The gap between numbers and resources, particularly in Morocco and Tunisia, is all the more compelling because the greatest population growth is happening in poor and uneducated households.

Since independence, investing in education and vocational training has been a major trend in North Africa. Despite large government spending in education and vocational training, scholars argue that the efforts to expand access to education have often sacrificed quality for quantity. As a result,

Table 9.2   Living Standards in North Africa

Countries	HDI ranking*	Gender equality ranking	Labor force participation (%)	Unemployment rate (%)	Literacy rate (%)	Gross enrollment (%)*
Algeria	93	81	44	10.6	72.6	81
Morocco	129	92	51	9.7	67.1	65
Tunisia	90	48	48	15.2	79.1	78

Note:

HDI: Human Development Index Gross enrollment includes primary, secondary, and tertiary enrollment.

Sources: UNDP, Human Development Report, 2013.

academic institutions in North Africa are not internationally or regionally competitive. For example, Tunisia, the country with the most advanced education system in North Africa, has only an average score on the international student assessment scale that is 20% below the OECD average (The World Bank, 2012).

In analyzing the literacy rate, which reflects the government's spending on education (primary, secondary, and tertiary levels), all of the Maghreb countries have shown an improvement. Despite such improvement, empirical evidence has not shown a relationship between literacy skills and outcomes at both organizational and individual levels. At the organizational level, high literacy skills would have positive outcomes on productivity and innovation; for the individual, it would impact employees' performance and earnings. Yet all the Maghreb countries still suffer from high levels of unskilled workers.

Labor force participation in Morocco was the highest among the Maghreb countries. However, Tunisia scored the highest unemployment rate among the same group at 15.20%. and ranked 187th on the gender inequality index. With respect to health, empowerment, and the labor market, Tunisia, Algeria, and Morocco ranked forty-eighty, eighty-first, ninety-second, respectively (UNDP, 2013). The report also indicated that the number of female graduates from universities exceeded male graduates, but when it came to getting a job, women were in a much less favorable position, reflected by the high unemployment rate among women with university degrees (World Bank, 2014). The gender inequality in North Africa, as in most Arab societies, represents a serious problem to the NHRD system.

The high migration levels of skilled workers, particularly to Europe, is another important indictor (Sydhagen and Cunningham, 2007). For example, around 0.7% of the total population of Algeria has left the county, and the amount of international migration is expected to increase in the future. Since the post-revolution in Tunisia, more than 10% of the Tunisian population has left their home country because of political and religious persecution (Yahiaoui, 2015). In general, the NHRD is facing a lack of a sufficient number of workers with specific requirements and/or insufficient numbers to satisfy replacement demand.

TRAINING AND DEVELOPMENT: NATIONAL LEVEL

The rest of this chapter will focus on education and training at the national and organizational levels with a concluding summary on the similarities and differences of HRD in North Africa.

HRD in Algeria

At the beginning of 2000, the Algerian government invested a considerable amount toward improving the education system and vocational training in its country. In 2004, it established new reforms aimed to better integrate the Algerian education system into the global education system, as well as to enhance literacy and technical skills (Branine, 2006). The national figures show that around 1.5 million Algerian students are currently registered in 90 higher education institutions. By the end of 2015, the deputy minister of education estimates the number will have increased to three million students in the higher education system (Ramdani et al., 2014). The education system in Algeria is free for all citizens. The government and training institutions are endeavoring to meet the increasing demands being placed on the HRD system by the growing young population and attempting to improve educational outcomes.

For the last four years, the Algerian government has put more effort into creating an alignment between academic institutions, the public sector, and the private sector (Branine et al., 2008). As a result, a number of strategies have been drafted, including building partnerships with international academic, and training institutions; improving the level of English proficiency; establishing student exchange programs; supporting curriculum development for entrepreneurship; and creating more training opportunities in both sectors (Ramdani et al., 2014).

Despite the challenges that are facing the HRD system in Algeria, scholars argue that Algeria's economic system could help to fill the gaps (Kamoche et al., 2012; Stuart, 2012). The strong economic situation could support more cooperation between organizations and international academic institutions, a vital step to solving the skills gap. Studies have shown evidence that best practices shaping management and vocational training have had some success (Ramdani et al., 2014). Both the government and organizations understand the needs for better skills development and dedicated resources for partnership and knowledge sharing. However, there is still more demand to improve the alignment between schools and universities, as well as between universities and private sectors. The growing number of MNCs in Algeria has increased the need for more local workers with English language skills as well as technical skills (Branine et al., 2008). The success or failure of these initiatives depends on cooperation between universities and private-sector organizations.

HRD in Morocco

The education system in Morocco differs from that of Algeria and Tunisia. Students have to choose between two streams upon completion of high school (Boum, 2008). One stream allows students to study according to the French education model, whereby students must complete two years of work and then join a private university where they specialize in a particular area. In the second model, students join a public university overseen by the Moroccan government. Even within public universities, the French model has directly influenced the education and training system (Cox et al., 2005).

In total, there are 15 universities available for students as well as numerous vocational training and technical institutions. The vocational training institutions, for instance, offer a range of training programs for their academic faculty and organizational members. These institutions sometimes involve the designing and implementing of training programs. In the last few years, the government has implemented several evaluation measures to assess the outcomes of education, as well as job training (Forster and Fenwick, 2015).

One of the major challenges facing the education system in Morocco is the misalignment between graduates' skills and labor market demands, particularly in private sectors (Cox et al., 2006; Hassi, 2011). In fact, the education system in Morocco has not prepared students to join the job market and stay competitive at all. In addition, university graduates are not willing to work in jobs that are considered low-level jobs, resulting in a number of social and economic issues (Stuart, 2012). The country is also experiencing a high rate of university turnover. For these reasons, the government has started to plan for more exchange programs between Morocco and international universities, particularly in the USA (Boum, 2008). The government believes that these programs will allow students to be more knowledgeable and acquire the necessary skills to be competitive.

Although the exchange programs between Morocco and American universities have a long history and established some connections with local universities, there still remain HRD issues (Hassi, 2011). For example, French is still the primary language spoken at public universities and the level of English programs is insufficient. Local students are not able to communicate through English, which may slow the development of the exchange programs. In addition, there is still little emphasis on soft skills, such as analysis and management (Bouzahzah and El Menyari, 2013). These issues have affected the level of skills available at the national level, and although the government is still working to overcome these challenges, progress seems very slow.

HRD in Tunisia

Following the Tunisian revolution in 2011, the government has extensively focused on improving the level of education and vocational training. The new government has faced a number of external and internal pressures that have allowed them to enhance the education system and graduates' skills in order to decrease the unemployment rate and improve the standard of living (Ben Salha, 2013). In addition, since the ousting of President Zine El Abidine Ben Ali, the new government has faced big demands from Tunisian citizens, such as creating more job opportunities and increasing salaries, challenging, in turn, the HRD system (Bouzahzah and El Menyari, 2013). This challenge is even more acute in areas outside of the capital city where access to education and vocational training is particularly low.

In Tunisia, there are 13 universities, 24 higher institutions of technology, and 6 vocational training institutions (Yahiaoui and Zoubir, 2006). There are also a number of small education institutions operating under the cadre of the 13 universities. The Tunisian government has placed more emphasis on enhancing the education system through exchange programs with US institutions. These programs aim to improve the level of English language skills, the sharing of best practices in business training, and the expansion of research partnerships in particular areas, such as management, science, and engineering (Ben Salha, 2013).

Although the Tunisian educational and training system is considered to be better than the other countries in the region (Horwitz, 2014; Yahiaoui 2015), the new government recognizes the importance of not only relying on skills development but also of providing and supporting more critical thinking skills, as well as leadership skills. As the result of the revolution, the government has involved more stakeholders in decision making in order to create more innovation and skills building for students and graduates (Bouzahzah and El Menyari, 2013). However, these programs are only at an infancy stage, so there is still a major gap between the available skills and private-sector demands. Some studies shows that Tunisian graduates are still lacking sufficient training skills in research, communication, multi-cultural awareness, and management skills.

HRD Institutions and Actors

Despite the progress in many aspects as outlined earlier, the discrepancy between the HRD and the political systems, along with the socioeconomic stagnation overall, stands out for the region (Cohen and Jaidi, 2006). The Maghreb societies still manifest high social inequalities and limited access to training and development opportunities. There are increasing demands for social justice and human dignity by the citizens of North Africa (Yahiaoui, 2015), who are disillusioned by their regimes and affected by the negative social consequences of economic liberalization. Policy makers and HRD scholars have highlighted the importance of paying more attention to the role of HRD institutions as well as government actors as a way to understand this complexity; however, much remains to be done.

In order to improve the living standards as well as the HRD system, attempts have been made to diversify the economy and support the free trade market. After achieving independence from colonialism, the governments endeavored to nationalize resources, promote the local market, and attract international investment; however, these attempts did not encourage the development of competitiveness as part of human capital (Benson and Al Arkoubi, 2006). Despite the logic that economic development produces HRD, powerful economic and political groups resist the process of global market integration, as well as the development of the HRD system. International scholars have analyzed how different political and social parties respond to new market reforms. For example, the business elites who benefited from local markets resist the movement toward more open markets;

unions have also reacted against efforts to liberalize labor law and the HRD system. Cohen and Jaidi (2006) outlined how in Morocco and Algeria, specifically, the monarch can no longer impose a vision of authority to the detriment of all other parties.

In addition, politicized Islam now pervading the Muslim world has made its mark in North Africa; it acts as barriers to both free-market and HRD/HRM development. In fact, political Islam has been highly favorable to free-market and human development on the condition that Islamic core values are upheld in all policies and practices, including education and vocational training. Integrating political Islam into a HRD system as well as global market has raised high expectations and suspicions among institutions and government actors. This is because political Islam has only dealt with political and cultural rights and has paid little attention to economic and HRD strategic goals. In Tunisia, for example, although there was a high demand for better living standards, the new government has shown its limited expertise in negotiating with international bodies. The lack of technical knowledge as well as weak HRD institutions in Tunisia have negatively affected Tunisia's capacity to improve the national HRD system. In Algeria, Islam has deep roots and a long history of resistance, first to colonialism and later to the free market (Branine, 2006).

Scholars argue that the current circumstances in North Africa, particularly in Morocco and Tunisia, are unfavorable for free trade, because of the limited subsidies for local markets and limited competitiveness on the global market (Cox et al., 2006). There is also an absence of clear labor provisions that protect employees' rights. Benson and Al Arkoubi (2006), for instance, indicated that the Moroccan economy system remains fragmented and poorly structured. Many studies argue that in order to achieve a successful integration with global market, North African countries must ensure full respect of local and international labor regulations. Yahiaoui and Zoubir (2006) hold that the association agreement with the EU for a free-trade zone will eventually increase international competition and improve the HRD system; however, for this to happen, North African countries must change their policies and practices. This change will reveal the inevitability of the need for new competencies and the introduction of new HRD policies and practices, which, at the same time, must take into account North African's political and socioeconomic contexts.

TRAINING AND DEVELOPMENT: ORGANIZATIONAL LEVEL

Studies on HRD in Africa in general, or in North Africa in particular, are very scarce. Most of the literature has outlined the importance of understanding the national human resources development in emerging economies (Lynham and Cunningham, 2006; Wang and McLean, 2007; Wang and Swanson, 2008; McLean, 2012). The NHRD perspective suggested that political, economic, and institutional factors can directly influence the development of human resources in each country. A number of scholars have attempted to outline a region-specific-HRD analysis, see for example Sydhagen and Cunningham (2007). For country-specific HRD analysis in this region, see for example the works of Branine (2006) which provide insight into HRD in Algeria, Cox et al. (2006) present insights into HRD in Morocco and Yahiaoui (2015) analyse HRD in Tunisia. However, there is still limited research available related to the field of HRD in Algeria, Morocco, and Tunisia. This section will outline some of the main HRD-related works in these countries in order to identify some particular characteristics of HRD in North Africa and discuss how these might be affected by contextual factors (Ellis et al., 2015).

Training is one of the major HRM challenges confronting North Africa, and there exists a great need for programs to ensure that individuals and organizations can continue to develop. The nature of HRD in North Africa is highlighted by a number of trends that need to be considered in order to understand NHRD. As mentioned earlier, training and education in North Africa have been largely influenced by the French system (Gomes et al., 2014). In Algeria, for example, most of the academic institutions as well as teachers are either originally from France or have studied at French universities (Branine, 2006). Despite their independence, many people from North African countries travel to France to continue their education or to improve their technical skills, influencing in a major way the NHRD in North Africa.

In North Africa, training is recognized as a core element of HRM in both public and private organizations (Horwitz et al., 2002). The philosophy of HRD has not always succeeded in enhancing individual, group, and organizational outcomes (Chew and Horwitz, 2004). It has, therefore, been argued that the HRD rationale should change from the mere belief that training practices are the solution to individual and organizational performance, to a more explicit focus on "competence-creation" (Kamoche et al., 2015). Competence-creation originates from the assumptions that organizational performance will mainly depend on the possession of adequate human capital constituted by knowledge, skills, and abilities (KSAs), as well as the expertise of different members of organizations. HRD scholars argue that training practices in African countries that aim to enhance the skills of the group are more accepted and affective than training practices that target individual needs (Osabutey et al., 2015).

Organization type is an important aspect of NHRD. In North Africa, the level and form of training varies between public and private sector enterprises. Ellis et al. (2015) note that public-sector organizations invest in training and development more than private-sector organizations. The level of training in the public sector tends to be more formalized and tends to focus on improving the level of basic skills with less emphasis on leadership and management skills training (Cox et al., 2005). In contrast, private-sector organizations tend to emphasize informal workplace training and on-the-job training. This is because private organizations lack adequate resources to invest in training and development (Kamoche et al., 2012). In addition, given the large number of unskilled employees, most private organizations still believe that improving the skills of local people is a government responsibility and consequently the government should play a dominant role in training provision. Employers often consider training as a cost rather than a long-term investment. Budgets allocated to training and development are very limited, and people often lack the awareness of the benefits of training to the individual, to society, and to the organization (Calza et al., 2010). There is a general belief that people can acquire the necessary skills from school and university. Although most African countries extensively invest in vocational training and education, there is still a gap between what vocational training is offered and what managers are looking for (Ben Salha, 2013).

The process of identifying training needs at the individual, job, and organizational levels has been a major issue in the North African HRD system. It has been found that choice of selection for particular training by most organizations in North Africa tends to be based on relational aspects, such as on personal connection with people higher up in the organization and that the training is often conducted by the manager or supervisor, and not by the training department or training professionals (Hassi, 2011). For example, in a study of Tunisian subsidiaries, Yahiaoui (2015) found that the training focuses more on interpersonal relationships and loyalty rather than on skills development and work outcomes. Employees, on the other hand, usually attend training in order to ask for promotion or reward. Although some studies found a positive relationship between employee empowerment and trainee motivation with learning (Ramdani et al., 2014), few organizations in North Africa pay attention to the needs assessment process prior to training. There is still a bias against vocational training in most organizations, which has increased the employee skills gap.

The evaluation of training programs tends to be formal in most organizations operating in North Africa. Organizations often use a self-report evaluation process to evaluate the effectiveness of training at the individual level. Some organizations also implement some form of test after the training so that the employees can receive a certificate as proof of attending and completing the training. In a study of Algerian firms, for example, Ramdani et al. (2014) found that training is not associated with overall firm performance for two reasons: first, training in Algerian firms is poorly designed and does not account for efficiency; second, organizations tend not to consider training as a source of competitive advantage. Instead, they view training as costly and as a process that does not lead to better outcomes. Training in most Algerian firms is implemented for reasons other than improving their financial outcomes. Likewise, Osabutey et al. (2015) found that strategic HRD in most African countries is poorly implemented, which results in insufficient outcomes. They also indicated that most organizations in African countries do not view training as a source of competitive advantages.

In general, both the cultural background and the political system in North Africa have been considered major factors influencing the NHRD. The political system in North Africa is often described as Sheikho-capitalism (Ellis et al., 2015), which means that the HRD system will be influenced by a power hierarchy and tribal networks. The management literature has widely emphasized that the management practices in Arab countries are fueled by *wasta* or *ma'rifa* (the use of social connections to obtain benefits that otherwise would not be provided) (Berger et al., 2014). Nepotism and *wasta* still pose major problems to the development of NHRD and to the business setting. This is because organizations in North Africa are classified as communities in their own right that place a high value on personal relationships. Employees in the organization tend to relate more to the tribe than to the apparently abstract notion of country or nation-state. This family-oriented culture has not just impacted NHRD, but it has also affected the training programs as they transfer from parent companies to their subsidiaries in North Africa (Hassi, 2011). Most of the training programs transferred from Western MNCs often fail due to various socio-cultural and political institutions (Horwitz, 2014).

The increase of foreign investment by MNCs in North Africa has brought market opportunities; there are some opportunities and challenges for MNCs in North Africa. While the region provides access to cheap labor with low social restrictions, political instability and the lack of skilled workers represent a major challenge to MNCs (Kamoche et al., 2015). For example, Calze et al. (2010) found that Italian firms in Algeria face difficulties in motivating local employees and involving them in the decision-making process. They also found that managers would need to understand the cultural differences between Italy and Algeria in order to favor the establishment and longevity of business relationships.

Scholars who studied the NHRD have examined in depth the issue of management practice transfer from parent companies to subsidiaries in North Africa. For example, Yahiaoui (2015) examined the transfer of a number of HRM practices from French MNCs to Tunisian subsidiaries. Yahiaoui found that the relational context, type of practices transferred, the interest of different professional categories, and their social integration are factors that inhibit or foster the transfer of HRM/HRD practices to the foreign subsidiaries.

DIFFERENCES AND SIMILARITIES ACROSS THE NORTH AFRICA REGION

First of all, it is important to emphasize that North Africa is marked by diverse political systems, socioeconomics, and societies. With regard to the government-led political reforms, there still remains a lack of movement in Algeria and Tunisia (Ben Salha, 2013). In Morocco, the success of Mohammed VI in 1999 encouraged liberalization development; however, this promotion was less emphasized in the second year of the new king's reign (Cox et al., 2005). The centralized political system has a direct influence on the

NHRD system. This is because the king or president fully controls the development of human capital and the overall strategic vision.

Institutional dualism is also an important aspect to consider when studying HRD in North Africa. Within these countries, large numbers of foreign subsidiaries of MNCs function in a public-sector context characterized by formalism in roles and regulations. Although employment relations tend to move toward individualism, such as in Algeria, the general pluralism in employment relations is represented by the process of collective bargaining (Yahiaoui and Zoubir, 2006). In addition, there are also a large number of family-owned businesses, which represent the majority of firms in private sectors (Hassi, 2011). For this reason, networks and personal relationships are highly valued, which has affected the development of NHRD. Bischoff and Wood (2012) have noted that personal relationships can enhance individuals' employability and skills development in most African countries.

What these countries are more likely to have in common are their hierarchical economic structures with clear divisions of labor. Unions' representations tend to be very weak and focus on reducing the level of unemployment throughout the region (Gomes et al., 2014). Because high proportions of employees work in agriculture and in informal sectors, unions have only a very small influence on the labor market, other than in Algeria. Historically, when most of North Africa was colonized, unions were part of the government (Ellis et al., 2015). Since independence, most union movements regained their autonomy; however, they are faced with the challenge of poorly skilled workers. Even when unions had more chances to participate in decision making at the national level, their bargaining power was limited due to the increased level of international migration (Bischoff and Wood, 2012). Although MNCs in North Africa are facing pressure from national groups in their country of origin to improve the status of NHRD, the high cost associated with investing in HRD practices tends to win out (Mellahi et al., 2011).

The misalignment between universities' learning outcomes and organizational skills needs is still an issue. Boum (2008) noted that there is still a major gap between what universities teach and what organizations demand. Most academic institutions in North Africa are focused on improving the low-skills level and do not emphasize other important skills, such as communication and managerial skills. Graduates often do not possess the hard or soft skills necessary to be employed by local businesses or by MNCs and are not able to compete in the global market economy. Thus many HRD scholars have highlighted the importance of enhancing the linkage between universities and organizations in order to ensure that curricula and skills training meet employer demand (Cox et al., 2006; Hassi, 2011). Scholars have also outlined that this can encourage opportunities for students to engage with the organization directly through certain activities, such as internships, mentorships, coaching, and other informal training practices.

A major concern in the region is the lack of English language proficiency. As a result of globalization, the English language has become the official language of communication in the workplace, as well as in international business (Boum, 2008). Job seekers with a lack of English language skills are less likely to be hired by competitive firms. Within North Africa, available English-speaking teachers and students are in short supply. For this reason, the governments have implemented several practices in an effort to encourage students to improve their English skills.

In order to tackle these issues, the governments have implemented a number of regulatory frameworks consisting of national skills and training authorities (Drake, 2006). These, in effect, link the training practices at the national level with those at the organizational level. In addition, the governments in North Africa are reevaluating the level of education and vocational training and moving forward with new reforms with a particular emphasis on subsidiary education reform through international partnerships (Gómez-Miranda et al., 2015). Evidence, however, suggests that agendas implemented by the government alone often do not fully consider organizational skill demand and are therefore less effective.

Cox (2005) and Hassi (2011) outlined that skills emigration has continued to pose major challenges to the human capital development in Africa on the part of the government, which is responsible for improving the social well-being of their citizens. Attempts have been made by the Maghreb governments to solve this major issue. In Algeria, for instance, wages were raised in 2011 as part of a wider reform of the public sector in order to improve efficiency and to retain qualified professionals (Branine et al., 2008). However, in Morocco and Tunisia, progress is still very slow.

CONCLUSION

In this chapter, we attempted to analyze the context of HRD in Algeria, Morocco, and Tunisia. HRD policies and practices in the region have witnessed important transformations after independence from colonial rule. Given the lack of national manpower, governments have largely invested in public education and training, as well as initiated reforms to enhance the economic structure. Statistical analysis has shown positive improvement in literacy rates, labor participation, and in the human development index. Organizations, accordingly, have taken advantage of these changes and now import foreign HRD policies and practices that encourage more efficiency and human capital competitiveness.

However, two main constrains can be identified that are still facing the HRD system in North Africa. First, despite the large government spending in education and vocational training, most of these enterprises are government-owned and lack alignments with market demands from both local and MNCs. As such, these practices have not contributed to filling the skills gaps in all North African countries. Second, the role of Islam in post-independence North Africa cannot be diminished, as it has provided a foundation for HRD systems. Political Islam has been considered a counterforce to the development of HRD system. As the countries lack proper expertise in designing and implementing training programs, most of the Western-style HRD practices are resisted, because they do not align with Islamic principles. The current atmosphere represents a serious need for rethinking the HRD system being fostered in North Africa.

REFERENCES

Abun-Nasr, J. M. (1987). *A History of the Maghrib in the Islamic Period*. UK: Cambridge University Press.

Afiouni, F., Ruël, H., & Schuler, R. (2014). HRM in the Middle East: toward a greater understanding. *The International Journal of Human Resource Management*, 25(2): 133–143.

Akdere, M., Russ-Eft, D., & Eft, N. (2006). The Islamic worldview of adult learning in the workplace: Surrendering to God. *Advances in Developing Human Resources*, 8(3): 355–363.

Ali, A. J. (2010). Islamic challenges to HR in modern organizations. *Personnel Review*, 39(6): 692–711.

Ali, A. J., & Wahabi, R. (1995). Managerial value systems in Morocco. *International Studies of Management & Organization*, 25(3): 87–96.

Arthur-Mensah, N., & Alagaraja, M. (2013). Exploring technical-vocational education and training systems in emerging markets: A case study on Ghana. *European Journal of Training and Development*, 37(9): 835–850.

Ben Salha, O. (2013). Labour market outcomes of economic globalisation in Tunisia: A preliminary assessment. *The Journal of North African Studies*, 18(2): 349–372.

Benson, P. G., & Al Arkoubi, K. (2006). Human Resource Management in Morocco. In P. G. Budhwar and K. Mellahi (Eds.), *Managing Human Resources in the Middle East*, 273–290. London: Routledge.

Berger, R., Silbiger, A., Herstein, R., & Barnes, B. R. (2014). Analyzing business-to-business relationships in an Arab context. *Journal of World Business*, 50(3):454–464.

Bischoff, C., & Wood, G. (2012). The practice of HRM in Africa in comparative perspective. In C. Brewster and W. Mayrhofer (Eds.), *Handbook of Research on Comparative Human Resource Management*, 494–511. UK: Edward Elgar.

Boum, A. (2008). The political coherence of educational incoherence: The consequences of educational specialization in a southern Moroccan community. *Anthropology & Education Quarterly*, 39(2): 205–223.

Bouzahzah, M., & El Menyari, Y. (2013). International tourism and economic growth: The case of Morocco and Tunisia. *The Journal of North African Studies*, 18(4): 592–607.

Branine, M. (2006). Human resource management in Algeria. In P. Budhwar and K. Mellahi (Eds.), *Managing Human Resources in The Middle East*, 250–272. New York: Routledge.

Branine, M., Foudil Fekkar, A., Fekkar, O., & Mellahi, K. (2008). Employee relations in Algeria: A historical appraisal. *Employee Relations*, 30(4): 404–421.

Calza, F., Aliane, N., & Cannavale, C. (2010). Cross-cultural differences and Italian firms internationalization in Algeria: Exploring assertiveness and performance orientation. *European Business Review*, 22(2): 246–272.

Charrad, M. (2001). *State and Women's Rights: The Making of Postcolonial Tunisia, Algeria, and Morocco*. California: Univeristy of California Press.

Chew, I. K., & Horwitz, F. M. (2004). Human resource management strategies in practice: Case-study findings in multinational firms. *Asia Pacific Journal of Human Resources*, 42(1): 32–56.

Cohen, S., & Jaidi, L. (2006). *Morocco. Globalisation and its Consequences*. New York, USA: Routledge.

Cox, J. B., Al Arkoubi, K., & Estrada, S. D. (2006). National human resource development in transitioning societies in the developing world: Morocco. *Advances in Developing Human Resources*, 8(1): 84–98.

Cox, J. B., Estrada, S. D., Lynham, S. A., & Motii, N. (2005). Defining human resource development in Morocco: An exploratory inquiry. *Human Resource Development International*, 8(4): 435–447.

Croucher, R., Rizov, M., & Goolaup, R. (2014). The antecedents of direct management communication to employees in Mauritius. *The International Journal of Human Resource Management*, 25(17): 2420–2437.

Drake, C. (2006). Morocco, Tunisia, and Libya: Diversity within unity. *FOCUS on Geography*, 49(3): 1–9.

Ellis, F. Y. A., Nyuur, R. B., & Debrah, Y. A. (2015). Human resources management in Africa. In F. M. Horwitz and P. Budhwar (Eds.), *Handbook of Human Resource Management in Emerging Markets*,393–429. UK: Edward Elgar

Forster, G., & Fenwick, J. (2015). The influence of Islamic values on management practice in Morocco. *European Management Journal*, 33(2): 143–156.

Gomes, E., Sahadev, S., Glaister, A. J., & Demirbag, M. (2014). A comparison of international HRM practices by Indian and European MNEs: Evidence from Africa. *The International Journal of Human Resource Management*, (ahead-of-print), 1–25.

Gómez-Miranda, M. E., Pérez-López, M. C., Argente-Linares, E., Rodríguez-Ariza, L., Cornelius, N., & Kamoche, K. (2015). The impact of organizational culture on competitiveness, effectiveness and efficiency in Spanish-Moroccan international joint ventures. *Personnel Review*, 44(3): 364–387.

Hassi, A. (2011). International briefing 23: Training and development in Morocco. *International Journal of Training and Development*, 15(2): 169–178.

Hassi, A. (2012). Islamic perspectives on training and professional development. *Journal of Management Development*, 31(10): 1035–1045.

Hoffman, K. E. (2008). Purity and contamination: Language ideologies in French colonial native policy in Morocco. *Comparative Studies in Society and History*, 50(03): 724–752.

Horwitz, F. (2014). Human resources management in multinational companies in Africa: A systematic literature review. *The International Journal of Human Resource Management*, (ahead-of-print), 1–24.

Horwitz, F. M., Kamoche, K., & Chew, I. K. (2002). Looking East: Diffusing high performance work practices in the southern Afro-Asian context. *International Journal of Human Resource Management*, 13(7): 1019–1041.

Kamoche, K., Chizema, A., Mellahi, K., & Newenham-Kahindi, A. (2012). New directions in the management of human resources in Africa. *The International Journal of Human Resource Management*, 23(14): 2825–2834.

Kamoche, K., Siebers, L. Q., Mamman, A., Newenham-Kahindi, A., Cornelius, N., & Cornelius, N. (2015). The dynamics of managing people in the diverse cultural and institutional context of Africa. *Personnel Review*, 44(3): 330–345.

Khan, M. B., & Sheikh, N. N. (2012). Human resource development, motivation and Islam. *Journal of Management Development*, 31(10): 1021–1034.

Lynham, S. A., & Cunningham, P. W. (2006). National human resource development in transitioning societies in the developing world: Concept and challenges. *Advances in Developing Human Resources*, 8(1): 116–135.

McLean, G. N. (2012). Invited response: Observations on modeling NHRD strategy. *Human Resource Development Review*, 1534484312458566.

Mellahi, K., Demirbag, M., & Riddle, L. (2011). Multinationals in the Middle East: Challenges and opportunities. *Journal of World Business*, 46(4): 406–410.

Murphy, A., & Garavan, T. N. (2009). The adoption and diffusion of an NHRD standard: A conceptual framework. *Human Resource Development Review*, 8(1): 3–21.

Osabutey, E. L., Nyuur, R. B., & Debrah, Y. A. (2015). Developing strategic international human resource capabilities in Sub-Saharan Africa. In C. Machado (Ed.), *International Human Resources Management: Challenges and Changes* Springer, 37–51. Springer: Switzerland.

Ramdani, B., Mellahi, K., Guermat, C., & Kechad, R. (2014). The efficacy of high performance work practices in the Middle East: Evidence from Algerian firms. *The International Journal of Human Resource Management*, 25(2): 252–275.

Stuart, J. D. (2012). An examination of factors in adapting a technical and vocational education and training programme within South Africa. *Human Resource Development International*, 15(2): 249–257.

Sydhagen, K., & Cunningham, P. (2007). Human resource development in sub-Saharan Africa. *Human Resource Development International*, 10(2): 121–135.

Tiliouine, H. (2014). Gender dimensions of quality of life in Algeria. In E. Eckermann (Ed.), *Gender, Lifespan and Quality of Life: An International Perspective*, 63–82. Netherlands: Springer.

UNDP. (2013). *Human Development Report 2013*. Accessed 01 April 2015 (http://hdr.undp.org/en/2013-report).

Wang, G. G., & Swanson, R. A. (2008). The idea of national HRD: An analysis based on economics and theory development methodology. *Human Resource Development Review*, 7(1): 79–106.

Wang, X., & McLean, G. N. (2007). The dilemma of defining international human resource development. *Human Resource Development Review*, 6(1): 96–108.

World Bank. (2012). Accessed 03 April 2015. (http://search.worldbank.org/all?qterm=Africa&_Top/region=Africa)

World Bank. (2014). *At a Glance: Morocco*. [online]. Accessed 28 March 2015. (www.worldbank.org/ma)

Yahiaoui, D. (2015). Hybridization: Striking a balance between adoption and adaptation of human resource management practices in French multinational corporations and their Tunisian subsidiaries. *The International Journal of Human Resource Management*, (ahead-of-print), 1–29.

Yahiaoui, D., & Zoubir, Y. (2006). Human resource management in Tunisia. In P. S. Budhwar and K. Mellahi (Eds.), *Managing Human Resources in the Middle East*, 233–249. UK: Routledge.

Section III
The Americas

10 Human Resource Development in Canada and the United States

Gary N. McLean and Nadir Budhwani

INTRODUCTION

Canada and the United States of America (US) are among the two most northern countries of North America. With an area of almost ten million square kilometers, Canada is the world's second-largest country, after Russia, and the US is the fourth. Canada is bilingual (French and English, based on its historical origins) and culturally diverse as a result of its open immigration policies. The US is also multicultural (through both legal and illegal immigration) but has remained unilingual (English being its only official language), in spite of large numbers of Spanish-speaking inhabitants). Canada's population was an estimated 35 million in 2014 (Parliament of Canada, 2015), just a little over 10% of the US population. Unlike many countries being challenged by declining population, the population of the US is growing steadily, primarily through immigration. At the time of this writing, the population was 324,471,666, ranking the country third worldwide after China and India (Worldometers, March 28, 2015). Thus employers continue to have access to sufficient numbers to replace those leaving the labor force (retirement, death, emigration), although the HRD challenge is whether those coming into the labor force have sufficient skills to replace those leaving, especially high-skilled labor and those with significant intellectual capital. The US population is diverse. There is no longer a majority ethnicity, as whites accounted for 49.7% of the population in 2014, followed by Hispanics (25.1%), Blacks (12.7%), Asians (7.9%), Multiracial (3.7%), and other (0.9%) (Bradley, 2015).

While Canada and the US share the longest international border in the world (8,892 km), they are different in history, culture, economics, politics, institutions, education systems, geographic characteristics, even languages, and in many other ways. Those who do not know the backgrounds of these two countries often assume that they are similar, if not the same, in many aspects. However, whereas they belong in the same region of North America (along with Mexico, Greenland, Central America, and the Caribbean), the many differences in their features and cultures result in numerous differences between the two countries in human resource development (HRD) conceptualization and practice. Both countries share advanced HRD practices in corporate settings, but the US is one of the most advanced countries in developing and offering stand-alone HRD programs in academic settings (Roberts, 2014; McLean and Akaraborworn, 2015). Canada is more advanced than the US in using documented HRD in community settings and for societal development. Nevertheless, both countries fall into the category of the decentralized/free market model (Cho and McLean, 2004). The US has developed the only academic, individual membership HRD association (the Academy of HRD, AHRD) that has an international impact across the world with its three annual international conferences (Americas, Asia/MENA, Europe) and four scholarly journals (*Advances in Developing Human Resources, HRD International, HRD Quarterly, HRD Review*) with the plurality of their authors coming from the US. For example, for *HRDI*, about 30% of authors in the last three years were from the US, with the next highest country, the UK, at 15% (Alexandre Arcichili, HRDI Editor, personal communication, August 1, 2015); and for *HRDR*, in the same period, 73% of authors were from the US and 9% were from Canada (Julia Storberg-Walker, *HRDR* Editor, personal communication, August 4, 2015).

There are a number of challenges for HRD researchers and practitioners in Canada and the US, which include: (a) addressing HRD in increasingly multicultural and pluralistic societies; (b) applying HRD in countries that have abundant natural resources but lack a sufficient number of trained and skilled workers to capitalize on those resources; (c) handling issues related to fluctuating and differing regional/provincial economies within the countries; (d) planning strategically for HRD when driven not only by local and national but also immigrant talent pools; and (e) thinking creatively about managing HRD in countries where large urban areas are home to about 80% of each country's population: 80.7% in the US, according to the 2010 census (US Census Bureau, n.d.) and, almost identically, 80.0% in Canada in 2012 (Global Health Facts, 2012). In this chapter, we explore the pioneering efforts of HRD in these two countries and the challenges faced by them. Further, HRD and the factors affecting it are described within the historical, political, economic, social, and cultural contexts of both countries. We also describe the institutions and structures that support HRD and end with a comparison of HRD between the two countries.

THE HISTORICAL, POLITICAL, ECONOMIC, SOCIAL, AND CULTURAL CONTEXT OF HRD IN THE US AND CANADA

Any discussion of HRD must begin with a discussion of the context in which the theories, policies, and practices of HRD have evolved. We begin with a brief overview of the history, cultures, economics, politics, institutions, education, and systems of the US and Canada.

History

Canada's European influence shaped Canada's early history dating back to about 1000 AD when Leif Erikson, on his way to Greenland from Norway, veered off course and arrived in present-day Nova Scotia (BBC, 2015). Other explorers (French and British) followed during the late fifteenth and early sixteenth centuries, the beginning of a long period of colonization. In 1759, during the Battle of the Plains of Abraham, British forces defeated the French. At the end of the Seven Years' War in 1763, France surrendered its colonies, including those in Canada, to the British (The Canadian Encyclopedia, 2015c). This history set the stage for Canada's bilingualism. The Constitution Act of 1867 gave French-speaking citizens the right to practice their faith and French civil law, in addition to language rights (Mapleleafweb, 2015). Bilingualism presents a challenge for HRD, as all training materials and documents must be written in both languages.

Canada, with ten provinces and three territories, has its roots in Confederation, based on the Constitution Act, 1867, with a constitution inspired more by British parliamentary democracy. The Canadian Charter of Rights and Freedoms places Canada in the forefront of free, stable, and democratic societies (Parliament of Canada, 2015). Scots, who were among the first Europeans to settle in Canada, also contributed to Canada's development. Scots represent the third-largest ethnic group in the country after English and French. The number of Scots migrating to Canada continued, focusing, initially, on the Maritime Provinces. They included farmers, teachers, business professionals, and clergy, who mostly spoke English. They established schools and provided training opportunities in order to develop skilled workers. Their emphasis on education, training, and development strengthened the foundation for HRD in Canada.

Christopher Columbus is usually credited with opening the way to the US and North America in 1492, although he never actually landed on the mainland. The first British settlement was established in Jamestown, Virginia, in 1607, but it was short lived. The longest continually inhabited location by Europeans in the US was in St. Augustine, Florida, established by the Spanish in 1565. Twelve of the original 13 colonies joined together in Congress in 1774, declared independence in 1776 (a year after the beginning of the revolution), defeated the British in the Revolutionary War in 1781, and were officially acknowledged in the Treaty of Paris in 1783, with the Constitution being ratified in 1788 (Independence Hall Association in Philadelphia, 2014). The American Revolution also affected Canada. Thousands of United Empire Loyalists, Americans who supported the British during the War of Independence, migrated to British North America (later, Canada). Here they not only boosted the population but also influenced culture and politics. These loyalists set the foundation for an evolutionary instead of revolutionary approach to influencing the government (The Canadian Encyclopedia, 2015f).

The land mass that is now the US, originally populated by the Native Americans and subsequently occupied by Great Britain, France, Spain, the Netherlands, and Russia, now incorporates two formerly independent countries: the Republic of Texas and Kingdom of Hawaii. The country now consists of 50 states, plus the District of Columbia (Washington, DC), and 8 dependent and co-governed territories in the Caribbean and the Pacific Ocean. The country was torn apart by, and still suffers from the outcome of, the Civil War of 1861–1865, a conflict based on differing economics, slavery, and the view of the relationship between the individual states and the federal government. The US has been involved in many wars, which has affected HRD, especially its most recent, including military action in Vietnam, Iraq, and Afghanistan. For example, soldiers were to receive preferential hiring treatment, with many arriving at the workplace suffering from a range of disabilities, a situation that needed to be addressed by HRD (Humensky et al., 2013; Kleykamp, 2010).

Both countries experienced Prohibition and the Great Depression of the 1930s, which together with World War II still influence the work ethic of the post-war 'Baby Boomers'. The 1960s resulted in major progress in civil rights, leading to continuing efforts related to diversity in the workplace. The 1960s were also marked in both countries by the hippies, the Feminist Movement, and massive protests against the war in Vietnam, with many young men from the US migrating to Canada to escape the draft. Another major movement in the 1960s was the Black Panther Movement, under the leadership of Malcolm X, which focused on overcoming racial discrimination and on gaining equality for African Americans. The histories of Canada and the US show that the notion of HRD is not a recent phenomenon in these countries. However, there exist significant cultural differences between the two countries that have shaped and continue to influence HRD in various ways.

Cultures

The US and Canada differ significantly in their cultures and value systems. Canada is known for its pluralistic value systems and multicultural societies. Canada represents a mosaic of ethnicities: apart from those of European origin, three aboriginal groups in Canada—First Nations (Indians), Métis (First Nations and European mix), and Inuit (Eskimos)—have distinct histories, languages, spiritual beliefs, and cultural practices. Approximately 1.4 million Canadians are aboriginal. Aboriginal communities are located in rural areas (often referred to as "reservations"), some very remote, but also to be found in urban areas (Government of Canada, 2015). Based on Hofstede's cultural determinants (The Hofstede Centre, 2015), Canadians tend to be interdependent, and society places value on egalitarianism. Both individual and team work is valued. The Canadian culture is moderately masculine, indicating that gender roles are somewhat assigned, and people are more likely to live to work rather than work to live. The society focuses on work-life balance, caring for others, and quality of life. Tolerance of uncertainty is moderate. However, there may not be much emphasis on saving for the future. Rather, individuals may have a greater desire to spend resources on relaxation and entertainment. Caution must be exercised with these generalizations, however, because of the vastness of the country and the many variations that exist across regions.

The culture in the US is also diverse, due partially to the issues that led to the Civil War and to the clustering of immigrants from similar countries in particular areas. The differences in cultures between California, Minnesota, New York, and Alabama, for example, are as vast as between many countries. Nevertheless, this has not stopped researchers from trying to describe the US as having one culture. Hofstede (2008), for example, concluded that the US was the highest in the world on Individualism (91, compared with an average of 43), followed by Masculinity (62 vs. 50), Power Distance (40 vs. 55), Uncertainty Avoidance (46 vs. 64), and Long-Term Orientation (29 vs. 45). These results suggest that, in the US workplace, employees prefer to work alone rather than in teams, work best with few rules, have greater gender role differentiation (requiring successful females to move toward male models), accept change and ambiguity, and, with short-term orientation, do not plan far into the future. The GLOBE Study (Grove, 2005) resulted in similar conclusions.

Language diversity enriches the cultures of both countries. According to a 2006 survey, Canada's population includes people from more than two hundred ethnic origins who speak two hundred first languages (CMEC, 2015). In 2011, 58.7% and 22% of Canadians spoke English and French, respectively (CIA, 2015). Aboriginal languages are grouped into ten categories, including 60 indigenous languages. Only Cree, Ojibwa, and Inuit have enough numbers to remain viable languages into the future (The Canadian Encyclopedia, 2015a). For the US, not surprisingly, given its ethnic diversity, many different languages are used in US homes. The top-three languages are (calculated from Ryan, 2013): English, 79.2%; Spanish, 12.6%; and Chinese, 1.0%. From an HRD perspective, language differences can and do create challenges in the workplace. Some of these challenges concern team interaction, conflict resolution approaches, and corporate communications and training.

Overall, both the US and Canada have diverse populations. However, from a HRD perspective, it is important to understand that there exist significant inter- and intra-cultural differences between and within the two countries.

Politics

Canada is a parliamentary democracy, a federation, and a constitutional monarchy. The head of state is, nominally, Queen Elizabeth II. The prime minister (PM), the head of government, is not elected but is the leader of the party earning the largest number of seats in the House of Commons. The PM appoints federal ministers. The legislative branch is a bicameral parliament consisting of the Senate (105 senators appointed for life by the PM) and the House of Commons (308 elected members of parliament). Currently, the major political parties are Conservatives, New Democrats, Liberals, Bloc Quebecois, and Greens (CIA, 2015). A parallel structure exists for provinces with their own respective elections. Provinces in Canada are stronger than states in the US, with a subsequently weaker central government.

According to the Structure of the United States Government (n.d.), the US is a democracy with only two major parties—Democratic and Republican. The US has a tripartite governmental structure consisting of the executive branch (represented by the president and vice-president), The legislative branch (consisting of the Senate, with two senators per state, and the Congress, which proportionately represents the population), and the judicial branch (consisting of the Supreme Court, with its nine judges, members appointed for life by the president and approved by the legislature. In addition to the Supreme Court, there are other courts at district, appellate, state, and local levels, with the later two levels often elected. The president appoints senior government officials, with congressional confirmation, supported by an extensive civil service system.

In both countries, some parties are more likely to support business, whereas others are more likely to support workers. This becomes important when legislation is put forth affecting issues related to immigration, hiring of foreign workers, human capital, and its development. Thus politics in both countries are very important in influencing HRD at the individual and organizational levels.

Economic Contexts

Hunting, fur trading, and fishing supported the early communities of the indigenous people in both countries. The Europeans extended these economic activities through Atlantic fishing, transcontinental fur trading, and then industrialization, followed by rapid technological change. Canada's economy still relies on extensive natural resources. Its economy varies across regional economies that themselves provide important markets for each other (The Canadian Encyclopedia, 2015e). Canada's contemporary economic system is market oriented and is the tenth largest in the world. It is primarily industrial and urban, based on manufacturing, mining, and services. The 1989 US-Canada Free Trade Agreement (FTA), followed by the 1994 North American Free Trade Agreement (NAFTA), boosted Canada's economic growth. Canada is also a member of various international bodies, including G-7, G-8, G-20, and the Organization for Economic Cooperation and Development (OECD) (CIA, 2015). Abundant natural resources, a highly educated and skilled workforce, and a modern infrastructure have made Canada a high-tech industrial society that enjoyed consistent economic growth until the recession of 2008–2009. Conservative banking and capitalization practices enabled Canada's major banks to emerge strongly from the global recession. Canada's petroleum sector continues to expand, mainly because of Alberta's oil sands. In proven oil reserves, Canada now ranks third behind Saudi Arabia and Venezuela (CIA, 2015). The automotive industry represents the largest manufacturing sector in Canada. Pharmaceutical, agriculture, and energy industries also make significant contributions. It is considered a global leader in solar power research and its commercialization. It is also among the leaders in wireless, hydrogen, and fuel cell technologies. It also leads in retail and institutional banking, as well as in financial management and advisory services. Four of the ten largest banks in North America are in Canada. In addition, Canada is home to six of the world's 50 safest financial institutions (Canada FAQ, 2015). Expansion in the petroleum sector has encouraged the government to invest in HRD by attracting more skilled labor from within and outside Canada. With a backdrop of the 6.8% unemployment rate in 2015 for the whole of Canada, Newfoundland and Labrador have struggled with an unemployment rate of 13.3%, followed by the Maritime Provinces (Statistics Canada, 2015, Table 10.3). In 2013, Canada's per capita GDP was $51,958 USD, slightly below that of the US (The World Bank Group, 2015).

The US, as with Canada, is firmly committed to free enterprise. However, there exists a tension between government-driven policies and a *free market*, reflecting an individualist culture. However, in spite of the ideological, primarily driven by the two political parties, the extent to which a free market truly exists in the US is contested. The recession of 2008 had a dramatic impact on employment, but the economy has, as of February 2015, recovered significantly. The unemployment rate, overall, was 5.5% in February 2015 but with major differences among groups. Among teenagers, the unemployment rate was 17.1%; other jobless rates were: adult men (5.2%), adult women (4.9%), whites (4.7%), blacks (10.4%), Asians (4.0%), and Hispanics (6.6%) (BLS, 2015a). The US continues to struggle to prepare workers and provide comparable employment for blacks and Hispanics, a major challenge for HRD. The per capita GDP for the US in 2013 was $53,042, ranking tenth worldwide (The World Bank Group, 2015). The US ranks first worldwide for national GDP, at $17,416,253 million in 2014 (CIA, 2014). Contributors to the GDP in 2014 were services (45.7%, with dramatic increases in the financial and health-care industries), goods (just under 25%, with nondurable goods contributing twice that of durable goods), government spending (18.2%), business investment (18%), and exports/imports, with imports exceeding exports (-6.8%) (Amadeo, 2015). Recent advances in technology now allow the US to produce enough oil to be self-sufficient.

The economic systems of both countries have implications for HRD. Significant HRD-related challenges facing organizations in Canada include attracting and retaining employees in those regions that do not have a diverse and strong economic base. One way to address this might be to provide incentives to attract new immigrants. However, lack of growth opportunities makes it difficult to retain employees. Also, as organizations continue to move their manufacturing facilities to countries that offer lower labor costs, a HRD challenge faced by both countries is the preparation of a future workforce to run a knowledge-based economy.

HRD INSTITUTIONS AND ACTORS IN THE US AND CANADA

Business and industry, labor unions, government, community groups, non-government organizations, professional organizations, and education (covered in a separate section) are all institutions that drive the economy and have a significant impact on HRD.

Business and Industry

Large corporations in both countries have long had a focus on employee development, either in stand-alone departments of T&D or HRD (Haslinda, 2009) or as part of a broader department of HR. These have frequently evolved into corporate universities (CU) with a history beginning with General Motors in the 1920s, followed by General Electric in the 1950s (Ardichvili, 2015). CUs emerged out of large T&D or HRD departments. The literature reviewed by Alagaraja and Li (2015) suggest that CUs have grown dramatically during the past three decades, especially during the past decade. Their research concluded that, whereas some have questioned the effectiveness of CUs, CUs have been effective. However, given the institutional contexts in which HRD is embedded in organizations, CUs appear to be evolving into Talent Management (including talent development). According to Meister (2009, cited by Ardichvili, 2015), there were four thousand CUs in the US by 2008.

Similarly, in Canada, 23% of organizations engaged in formal learning and development activities provided by corporate universities (Conference Board of Canada, 2009a, Table 8). Also, various universities and colleges offered executive education programs that focused on nurturing high-potential employees and providing leadership development opportunities. "More than two-thirds (70%) of responding organizations identified high-potential employees and half (49%) provided them with greater learning opportunities" (Conference Board of Canada, 2009a, p. 29). The same study suggested that, "Eighty-two per cent of responding organizations made use of executive education programs offered by colleges and universities" (Conference Board of Canada, 2009a, p. 29). The programs were delivered in a variety of ways as, "Canadian organizations offer their employees a blend of training delivery methods as opposed to a single training activity" (Conference Board of Canada, 2009a, p. 27).

In addition to the focus on developing talent within large corporations, it is also common to find some focus in organization development (or organizational effectiveness or organizational change or change management). In the US, most HRD functions include some focus on both organizations and individuals (Fenwick, 2005; Heathfield, 2015).

Employer-sponsored training programs tend to focus on practical relevance in the workplace and change in behaviors and skills (Miller, 2014). A challenge with this approach is that HR and HRD activities and methodologies used in training programs tend to follow common practice rather than research that leads to evidence-based practice. Sadly, HR and HRD tend to be susceptible to the latest fads with little knowledge or use of evidence-based research findings (Joy-Matthews, Megginson, & Surtees, 2004,); Moats and McLean, 2009).

Goldenberg (2006) suggested that Canada's performance in workplace training and development, compared with that of other countries, is only average. According to the Conference Board of Canada (2007), at least 69% of Canadian full-time employees participated in workplace-related training programs. While Canada's economy is the best among the G-7 nations, there are concerns pertaining to Canadian organizations' commitment to investing in training, learning, and development (TLD) programs (Singleton, 2011). With increasing globalization and changing technology, it is important that Canadian organizations revisit their HRD strategies. In today's economic environment, it is unfortunate that access to workplace TLD programs is low. In contrast, almost every employee in the US receives some form of training during the year (99.2%) (BLS, US Department of Labor, 2015b, Table 9). Approximately 1.5% of Canadian organizations' payroll is used for TLD (The Conference Board of Canada, 2009a). This contrasts with 3.6% in the US, double that of Canada (Miller, 2014). Canadian companies need to rethink their expenditures for HRD activities. Many organizations in Canada consider TLD expenditures to be a cost rather than an investment in human capital. The percentage of organizations that considered themselves to be learning organizations was the highest in Canada in Québec (78%) and the lowest in Alberta (58%) (The Conference Board of Canada, 2007). Strangely, in spite of the fact that the concept of learning organizations and their benefits to organizations have been around for a long time, companies are challenged to implement the concepts underlying learning organizations (Garvin, Edmondson, & Gino, 2008).

In the US, "in 2013, organizations on average spent $1,208 per employee on training and development.... The number of learning hours used per employee also slightly increased to 31.5 hours" (Miller, 2014, para. 2). US corporations also reported that "the cost to have one hour of learning available was $1,798" (Miller, 2014, para. 8). According to the Canadian Chamber of Commerce (2013), direct learning expenditure per employee in Canada has been consistently low when compared with that of the US. According to Lavis (2011) in the Conference Board of Canada's 2011 report (cited in the Canadian Chamber of Commerce, 2013), on average, Canada spends 64 cents for each dollar that is spent on learning and development in the US. There are no statistics available for expenditures related to organizational development activities.

In Canada, 66% of all formal TLD activities took place in a classroom setting (The Conference Board of Canada, 2009a). Knowledge-based industries spent more on TLD per employee than did wholesale, retail, manufacturing, and construction industries. Informal learning was reported to be 56% of all learning activities. According to the Canadian Council on Learning (2009), non-formal training included coaching, mentoring, independent problem solving, and e-learning. In the US, more than two-thirds of organizations' formal learning hours involve an instructor, 55% take place in an instructor-led classroom, 9% are led online by an instructor, and 5% are led remotely by an instructor (Miller, 2014, para. 15). As for the content of training in the US, Miller (2014) reported that about one-third of the content is focused on managerial and supervisory skills, mandatory and compliance training, and profession- or industry-specific training. The remaining two-thirds of content covers topics such as processes and procedures, customer service, sales training, and executive development, to name a few.

According to Bélanger and Hart in a 2012 report of OECD (cited in Canadian Chamber of Commerce, 2013), legal requirements and regulatory compliance are the factors that drive organizations' investment in HRD in Canada. In this regard, they also state that occupational health and safety is the area with the biggest training expenditure. Lavis (2011, cited in Canadian Chamber of Commerce, 2013) notes that 80% of companies offer training on occupational health and safety compliance. The most common training content is related to management and supervisory skills (91%), followed by new employee orientation (85%). Percival, Cozzarin, & Formaneck (2013, cited in the Canadian Chamber of Commerce, 2013) found that the finance and insurance industry was the biggest investor in training, whereas the retail sector was at the other end of the spectrum. The 2012 Amex survey (American Express Small Business Monitor, cited in Canadian Chamber of Commerce, 2013) shows that, specifically in small and medium enterprises, 52% and 49% of training was on job-specific skills and company-specific knowledge, respectively. Other topics included sales, customer service, negotiation, communication, and time management.

In the US, Miller (2014) reported that training services provided externally by "consultants and services, content development and licenses, and workshops and training programs—account for 27 percent of expenditures, and tuition reimbursement accounts for 10 percent" (para. 12). In Canada, according to the Canadian Chamber of Commerce (2013), large firms tend to have in-house training departments. In general, there are various training providers and learning suppliers that include: (a) private-sector trainers and consultants, (b) government agencies, (c) educational institutions, (d) associate networks, and (e) unions.

Small and medium-sized enterprises (SME) have always played an important role in the US. However, their contribution to the GDP has been falling. In 2002, they contributed just over 48% of the GDP, but by 2010, this had fallen to just under 45% (Tozzi, 2012). Nevertheless, this is still a significant contribution. Because of the size of their personnel pools, such organizations often do not provide their employees with HRD benefits, especially in-house, so they must look to outside agencies to provide such services. Companies that offer public workshops and training thus benefit from enrollment of employees from SMEs.

Canada's GDP, which not only reflects investment in physical capital but is also indicative of the accumulation of human capital, knowledge and skills, can be used to identify the role played by small and medium-sized businesses in promoting HRD (Industry Canada, 2015b). Small businesses in Canada's public and private sectors have been contributing to the country's GDP in a consistent manner. During 2002–2011, small businesses' contribution to GDP remained in the range of 25–29% (Industry Canada, 2015d). Thus it can be deduced that almost 30% of Canada's GDP is driven by small businesses. In another study by Statistics Canada, in 2008, contributors to GDP included: small businesses (30%), medium-sized businesses (9%), large firms (36%), and public sector (25%) (Industry Canada, 2015d). Overall, from 2009–2013, the labor productivity in the Canadian economy increased 0.9% per year on average (Industry Canada, 2015c). A consistent increase in the labor productivity index is reflective of investments in various aspects related to and influenced by HRD, including human capital, organizational innovation, and technological change. The Conference Board of Canada (2009b) concluded that:

- Successful SMEs find an approach to learning that fits with their business models and organizational culture;
- Successful SMEs ensure that their learning activities are aligned with the needs of individual employees and current and future goals of the organization;
- Successful SMEs link workplace learning and training with performance management activities—which measure the effectiveness of performance, not the amount of learning or training completed;
- Successful SMEs leverage workplace learning providers and learning/training content that already exists in the market;
- Successful SMEs recognize the value of industry standards, credentials, and certifications;
- Successful SMEs always relate workplace learning and training activities back to the business issues that they are trying to address (p. 2).

Labor Unions

It was a struggle for labor unions to establish a role in business and industry, requiring several bloody battles before legislation mandated the right of workers to organize. The growth of labor unions came from dissatisfaction at work. The dissatisfaction continues, and most research focuses on the corporate perspective rather than the worker perspective (Bjorkquist and Lewis, 1994). There remains a paucity of research on HRD and labor unions. In spite of the benefits that labor unions have brought to workers in terms of apprenticeships, training and development, work environments, compensation, benefits, and work safety, in 2014, in the US, only 11.1% of workers were members of unions, down slightly from the previous year and down considerably from the high of 34% in 1956 (BLS, 2015c). This compares with 30% in Canada conditions (*Overview of Collective Bargaining in* Canada, 2015). In spite of the many HRD benefits to members, and thus contributions to the organizations, many in business are opposed to the labor union movement.

In spite of the declining participation of US workers in labor unions, labor unions still have an impact on worker development. According to the AFL-CIO America's Unions (2015), "training programs and apprenticeships are at the heart of unions' efforts to ensure that working men and women have a voice in our country's ever-changing economy. Every year, the labor movement trains more than 450,000 workers" (para. 1). Rubenstein (2001) highlighted several areas in which US unions have made a contribution to improving the workplace, including quality of work life, problem-solving teams, quality circles, labor-management committees, self-directed work teams, lean production systems, and worker suggestion plans. While unions have seen some of these transformations to be of high risk to them, they have participated because of the opportunities such changes have created in providing union members with an opportunity to influence their workplaces (Rubenstein, 2001).

Labor unions in the US have also played a role in instituting and administering apprenticeships, especially in the trades and crafts unions, although apprenticeships are not nearly as wide a form of training in the US as in most industrialized countries (Olinsky and Ayres, 2013). An import from Europe, they have been an effective but more costly way of providing on-the-job training combined with in-class instruction and advancing skills as workers acquire experience. Unions have been criticized, however, for exercising discrimination in apprenticeships, especially against minorities, women, and older workers. However, Berek and Bilginsoy (2000) explored the role of unions in providing training for women in the US. While women continue to be underserved, in spite of antidiscrimination laws, women who are admitted into apprenticeship programs jointly sponsored by unions and management are more likely to graduate than either men or women in unilateral apprenticeship programs sponsored only by management.

Government Policies

HRD in Canada is influenced by a government policy that takes an active and leading role in addressing and promoting HRD. Initially, the Department of Human Resources and Skills Development Canada (HRSDC) addressed HRD. HRSDC was renamed the Department of Employment and Social Development, Canada (ESDC). ESDC develops, manages, and delivers social programs and services. ESDC's objective is to improve Canadians' overall quality of life (ESDC, 2015). The Treasury Board of Canada Secretariat (TBS) addresses HRD for public service employees. The TBS is organized into more than ten branches and sectors, two of which, *Office of the Chief of Human Resources Officer* and *Human Resources Division*, focus exclusively on managing and developing human resources. Among other HR responsibilities, the TBS has responsibility for learning and leadership development (TBS, 2015). The Canadian government's approach to HRD is holistic and systematic. This approach benefits not only the public service but also enables the government in its HRD-related collaborative efforts with corporate, non-/not-for-profit, and community-based organizations. HRD in Canada also includes HRD initiatives in international settings where the focus has consistently been on knowledge transfer, investment in higher-level training, and sustainable development (Mundy, 1992).

The US is highly decentralized in its HRD practices, even in terms of efforts undertaken by the government, which occur at several levels—federal, state, regional, and local. Because of *states rights*, the federal government's role, as with education, is largely limited to the provision of funding to support HRD initiatives. Included are approaches at both micro and macrolevel (Cho and McLean, 2004; Kuiper, 2015).

The US government lacks coordination in its workforce development programs, resulting in considerable overlap and inefficiency. At least 12 departments, agencies, and other programs provide federal funding for job training (East-West Gateway Coordinating Council, n.d.). They offer 96 programs, with the largest number offered by the Department of Labor (42) and the Department of Health and Human Services (21 each). Ahn and McLean (2010) explored one example of a federal government–supported workforce development initiative. They conducted a case study of how Texas has implemented a decentralized federal initiative, the Workforce Initiative Act. The Manpower Development and Training Act (MDTA) in 1960 was a predecessor of this act, as were the Comprehensive Employment and Training Act (CETA) in 1970, the Job Training Partnership Act (JTPA) in 1980, and, since 1990, the Workforce Investment Act (WIA). Bradley (2015) also describes a program in Hennepin County, the largest metropolitan county in Minnesota, to prepare people of color for employment. Whereas the federal government frequently funds such programs, occasionally local municipalities, counties, states, and regional government organizations fund and offer workforce development programs.

Community Groups and Nongovernment Organizations

In Canada, Aboriginal Affairs and Northern Development Canada (AANDC) is responsible for HRD in aboriginal communities with inclusion of cultural, linguistic, economic, and spiritual perspectives. AANDC is an umbrella organization that builds healthy, stable, and sustainable communities. Another organization is the Centre for Aboriginal Human Resource Development (CAHRD), which focuses on aboriginal HRD in the province of Manitoba. There are both structured and unstructured HRD efforts in communities in Canada. The nature of these communities can be religious, spiritual, ethnic, or philanthropic. Unfortunately, information about HRD efforts in these communities is not easily available. Many NGOs (nongovernmental organizations) are active in Canada, headquartered in Canada and in other countries while active in Canada. Most of these have some components of community HRD, focusing on international development, aboriginal development, women's development, social justice, human rights, environmental issues, education, freedom of expression, humanitarianism, peace, education, health, and more (NGOs Based in Canada, NGOs Based in Other Countries, n.d.).

The case of the Ismaili Muslim community in Canada is an example of structured and pluralistic inter- and intra-community HRD efforts. The community's HRD efforts rest upon Canada's notion of creating a civil society that reflects a, "commitment to pluralism, to meritocracy, and to a cosmopolitan ethic" (Aga Khan IV, 2014, para. 63). Its inter-community HRD efforts, led by the Aga Khan Development Network, a nongovernmental and nondenominational organization, focus on various areas of development, including education and training (Aga Khan Development Network, 2014).

In the US (nongovernmental organizations) (Cordero-Guzman, 2014; see also the case that follows), community corporations or corporate foundations (through corporate social responsibility/CSR) (The Moody's Foundation, 2011; see also the case that follows), religious organizations (churches, temples, synagogues, mosques) (SHRM, 2008; SunTrust Foundation, 2015), charities (local, state, national, and international) (McCormick Foundation, 2014), and so on offer innumerable programs. For example, Summit Academy Opportunities Industrialization Center is a community-based effort focused on workforce development. Located in North Minneapolis, it is focused primarily on the development of people of color. Preparation for employment in construction industries is its major focus, as employers in these industries are less concerned about whether their hires have a record of incarceration. Programs are also offered in community-based health care. The mission of SAOIC is, "We exist to assist individuals in developing their ability to earn and to become contributing citizens in their community" (Summit Academy OIC, 2015, para. 3). Another example is Microsoft (2015), as one example of many companies doing CSR, which offers many types of programs related to workforce development. Some of the foci include empowering youth and nonprofits through training (as specifically related to HRD) and other activities.

Professional Organizations

HRD (often under the umbrella of HR) is addressed by a number of professional organizations. These organizations include career development, organization development, training and development, leadership development, and other components. The organizations in Canada with a primary focus on HRD include the Canadian Society for Training and Development (CSTD), Toronto OD Network, the Centre for Aboriginal Human Resource Development (CAHRD), and numerous local, provincial, national, and international organizations. Many professional organizations headquartered in the US are the source for considerable HRD opportunities. McLean and Akdere (2015, in press) summarize the role of numerous practitioner and academic organizations that provide both online and in-person workshops, webinars, professional journals and books, regional and national conferences, and certifications. As referenced earlier, consultancies also provide an extensive amount of HRD services. A comprehensive, but by no means complete, listing of HR consultancy firms in the US can be found at The Consulting Bench (2013). However, no criteria are provided for inclusion, but it appears that a firm must pay to have their company listed. A major challenge for organizations looking for a consultant is that there is no required licensure or certification for consultants. As a result, there is no guarantee of consultant competence. A similar listing of HR consultancy can be found in the Canadian Company Capabilities section of Industry Canada (2015a).

THE EDUCATION AND VOCATIONAL TRAINING SYSTEMS IN CANADA AND THE US

Canada

The education system in Canada comprises privately and publicly funded elementary and secondary schools, community colleges, technical institutes, colleges, university colleges, and universities. In general, public education is provided free to all Canadians, except for tertiary education (CMEC, 2008). Unlike in the US, parochial elementary and secondary schools receive public funding. According to the Canadian Constitution, education is the responsibility of provincial and territorial governments (CMEC, 2015). Whereas standards across the country are uniformly high, there are provincial differences. There is no Ministry of Education at the federal level (CICIC, 2015). This is similar to the US where there are huge differences in performance across states, and states are responsible for education. One difference is that, in the US, there is a secretary of education. The Department of Education in the US is primarily focused on funding and recommendations for education policy, sometimes tied to funding. Nevertheless, states can accept, reject, or modify such recommendations.

In general, in Canada, children begin kindergarten at age five. Secondary schools go up to Grades 11/12 depending on the provincial education system. Postsecondary education offers options, such as university, college, and Cégep studies. The Cégep system, which is found in Québec, refers to the French College of General and Vocational Education (CEC Network, 2003). Canada has one of the highest postsecondary education completion rates in the world (CICIC, 2015). In 2010, 25% of Canada's adult population had a college degree, followed by Japan and Belgium (The Conference Board of Canada, 2015). According to the US Census Bureau, in 2013, the comparable figure for the US was 28.8%.

Investing in HRD efforts is not a new phenomenon in Canada (CICIC, 2015). The university education system in Canada has a long history. At the time of Confederation (1867), there were 18 universities in Canada. New institutions were established in the post–World War II era. The history of most public colleges in Canada dates back to the 1960s when there was an increase in demand for vocational and technical training. In the 1990s, some institutions were awarded degree-granting status, and during the same decade, a system was created to expand college-university credit transfer mechanisms. According to an estimate, Canada has 163 recognized universities and 183 recognized colleges and institutes (CMEC, 2008). Female students tend to outnumber male students in universities and colleges; however, the opposite is the case in skilled trades training (CMEC, 2008). Canada ranks top among all OECD countries in spending per student in public postsecondary education. At least one-third of Canada's research is conducted at Canadian universities. More than 0.3 million international students chose Canada in 2013 (CMEC, 2015). The Council of Ministers of Education, Canada (CMEC, 2015), founded in 1967, assumes a national-level leading role for education in Canada. CMEC provides a platform for provinces and territories to work collaboratively on common objectives at various levels—elementary, secondary, and postsecondary.

Formal vocational education in Canada can be traced to the seventeenth century, whereas interest in and demand for vocational and technical education (VTE) increased during the nineteenth and twentieth centuries (Lyons, Randhawa, & Paulson, 1991). During the 1960s and 1970s, the federal government adopted an approach for developing what was then called 'manpower'. This enabled provinces to build a platform to establish a community college system. The responsibility for promoting HRD through VTE was gradually transferred to provinces and territories to overcome the gap between labor supply and labor demand. According to Fisher et al. (2006), the federal government was especially active in vocational and technical training during the 1980s and 1990s. The objective was to prepare a well-trained workforce to compete in the global economy. In the early 1990s, the terms manpower and human capital became human resources. Provinces and territories became more responsible for making decisions pertaining to VTE. Constant changes in demographics, technology, globalization, and labor market shifts influenced policies regarding VTE. In the most recent data available (2006), only 5.4% of secondary students were enrolled in pre-vocational and vocational programs, the lowest of any of the OECD countries (OECD, 2009). The explanation is that Canada has a very high percentage of students who pursue vocational education at the postsecondary level. This situation may be changing (Center on International Education Benchmarking, 2015). Vocational education at the secondary level is now offered either in comprehensive high schools, along with academic courses, or in separate vocational schools. Ontario has just begun a new program, " 'Specialist High Skills Majors,' which are programs of eight to ten classes in 18 industry or trade fields, including aviation, energy, transportation, hospitality and tourism, and health and wellness" (para. 1), offered by every secondary school in the province. Graduates receive both an industry certification and a high school diploma. They may enter the workplace, pursue a postsecondary program, or enter an apprenticeship. The Red Seal program approves vocational education across Canada, verifying that participating programs meet industrial standards; 52 occupations have been approved.

In 2010, almost 1.2 million students were enrolled in degree programs, of which 56% were women. From a HRD perspective, the demand for a highly skilled and educated workforce has played a pivotal role in the growth of university enrollment. Growth in employment for university graduates exceeded other levels of education. It was projected that, during 2008–2017, 1.4 million new jobs would be created in Canada, three-quarters of which would require postsecondary education (AUCC, 2011). During 2001 and 2007, the number of credentials granted increased at every level—master's degrees by 5.7%, bachelor's and first professional degrees by 5.2%, and doctoral degrees by 4.5% (Statistics Canada, 2009). In 2007, the highest number of university graduates were in law, social and behavioral sciences, management, business, and public administration. In community colleges, 23% of graduates obtained credentials in physical and life sciences and technologies; 18% in humanities; and 15% in health, parks, recreation, and fitness (Statistics Canada, 2009).

In Canada, the nature and delivery of adult education programs continue to change, especially with the rapid expansion and advancement in distance and online learning programs. Nearly 50% of adult Canadians are enrolled in adult education programs, and all provinces are making efforts to increase funding for adult education and higher education, especially "offering additional training for underserved populations, such as immigrants, rural workers, the unemployed and people with low literacy and numeracy skills" (Center on International Education Benchmarking, 2015). In the period 2000 to 2007, participation in apprenticeship programs experienced an 8.8% growth. The largest increase was in building construction trades. In 2007, 11% of completers of registered apprenticeship programs were women.

Preparation of professionals for HRD occurs primarily in adult education programs. Adult education, also referred to as lifelong learning, is not only a field of practice but also a field of study. Each province has at least one master's level program in adult education. Some of the earliest adult education efforts in Canada can be traced back to the 1800s when Mechanics'

Institutes in Nova Scotia, Québec, and Ontario provided learning opportunities to workers (The Canadian Encyclopedia, 2015b). The Canadian Association for Adult Education was established in 1935. During the 1930s through 1960s, various government, private, nonprofit, and community-based organizations increased their support for adult education. Four major national-level adult education associations were founded in Canada: the Canadian Association for Adult Education (1935, now defunct); Institut Canadien d'Éducation des Adultes (1952); the Canadian Association for University Continuing Education (1954); and the Canadian Association for the Study of Adult Education (1981) (The Canadian Encyclopedia, 2015b).

Several academic institutions offer degree, diploma, and certificate programs in human resources, HRM, HRD, labor relations, industrial relations, and organizational behavior. Preparatory courses are also offered for Certified Human Resources Professional (CHRP) exams. Two identified universities offer degree programs in HRD: the University of Regina, Saskatchewan (master of education and PhD in HRD) and the University of Prince Edward Island (bachelor of education in HRD). The Ontario Institute for Studies in Education (OISE), in Toronto, offers collaborative master's and PhD degrees in workplace learning and social change.

United States

Education in the US also is either public or private. The proportion of US students in private schools is 10% and declining (Jennings, 2013). In spite of the proven benefit of pre-Kindergarten (pre-K) education, only 69% of US four-year-olds are enrolled in preschool, compared with 97% in the UK. Compared with OECD countries, the US generally ranks twenty-fifth on measures related to pre-K education (Herman, Post, & O'Halloran, 2013). While the US has a relatively standard requirement of compulsory education through age 16, the high school completion rate is not laudatory as the US Department of Education, National Center for Education Statistics (2014, para. 1) report sets out:

> In school year 2011–12, some 3.1 million public high school students, or 81%, graduated on time ... Among all public high school students, Asians/Pacific Islanders had the highest graduation rate (93%), followed by Whites (85%), Hispanics (76%), and American Indians/ Alaska Natives and Blacks (68% each).

By 2012–2013, the US achieved an all-time high 81% graduation rate (Bidwell, 2015). In 2009, the last year for which statistics are available, 88.5% of secondary school students earned at least one credit in career/ technical education and 28.6% earned at least five credits (US Department of Education, National Center for Educational Statistics, 2009). Career/ technical education is directly related to employment skills and so is directly related to HRD.

At the tertiary level, students enroll in two-year vocational/technical, community, or junior colleges; four-year undergraduate colleges; and universities, including undergraduate and graduate education (representing master's, professional, and doctoral degrees). In 2010–2011, the latest figures available in 2015, the US had 4,726 Title IV-eligible, degree-granting institutions; 3,026 four-year institutions; and 1,700 two-year institutions (US Department of Education, National Center for Education Statistics, 2012, Table 5). The US had 21 million students in higher education, roughly 5.7% of the total population (US Department of Education, National Center for Education Statistics, 2014, Table 317.10). About 13 million of these students were enrolled full time. In 2009, 21.3% of the adult population above 18 years had attended college but had no degree; 7.5% held an associate's degree; 17.6% held a bachelor's degree; and 10.3% held a graduate or professional degree. By this time, male and female statistics were almost identical (Ryan and Siebens, 2012). As referenced earlier, by 2013, the percentage of adults with a bachelor's degree had increased considerably, and female students' numbers, by then, exceeded those of male students. Strangely, for such an advanced country, literacy rates for adults are discouraging and have a dramatic impact on the workforce. A recent OECD (2013) project found that 36 million US American adults have weak literacy skills. Further, the OECD argue that in the US education system,

> migration status and ethnicity remain important. One-third of the low skilled are immigrants. 35% of black and 43% of Hispanic adults have low literacy skills, compared with only 10% of whites. Racial differences in skills remain even among adults with similar levels of education.
>
> (2013, p. 11)

Determining the number and location of university HRD preparation programs has been difficult because of the varying definitions of HRD in the US. The Academy of HRD has published an annual inventory of HRD programs (Roberts, 2014). Based on respondents only, the 2014 inventory identified the following number of degree offerings in HRD: BA – 9, BS – 34, other bachelor's – 2, MA – 27, MEd – 20, MS – 60, other master's – 3, EdD – 14, and PhD – 28. An additional 165 nonresponding programs were included in the inventory. Especially in recent years, many proponents of national HRD have argued that education is a core component of HRD (McLean, 2014). Educational institutions that support HRD were described earlier. Explicit connection to HRD occurs through career (or vocational) and technical education programs in secondary and higher education. One could add professional education in colleges and universities to the list.

Postsecondary career, vocational, and technical education is most often pursued through one- or two-year postsecondary education programs in the US. The top-three fields in all sub-baccalaureate programs in 2011–2012, the last year for which statistics were available, were health sciences (36%);

business (17%); and manufacturing, construction, repair, and transportation (7%) (US Department of Education, National Center for Education Statistics, 2012). While universities are sensitive about the claim that their primary objective is vocational, there is no doubt that they are seen as serving the primary purpose of job preparation. Whereas liberal arts continues to have appeal for some, it is often seen as preparatory to moving into a job-specific field of preparation. The top-three majors in 2014, in order, were business administration and management, general psychology, and nursing (Stockwell, 2014).

COMPARISON OF HRD IN CANADA AND THE US

This chapter has highlighted some similarities between HRD in the two countries. HRD efforts are aimed at creating a better quality of life and a strong economy with a skilled workforce. HRD continues to evolve with changes in socio-cultural environment, demographics, economy, and technology. HRD is found at individual, community, organization (private, government, not-for-profit), and international levels. Both countries face the challenge of seeing HRD as a cost rather than an investment. And both countries have subgroup difficulties, especially related to minority groups and women. Both countries face regional differences and the problem of predicting future labor supplies and demands. In both countries, HRD is subject to fads rather than following evidence-based practices modified to meet the needs of the organization. Finally, much more information is needed in both countries related to HRD practices in all of its components, especially in organizational development. Both countries focus their public-sector HRD primarily on the unemployed and underemployed, whereas HRD in both countries seems solidly embedded in private-sector organizations. Statistics, however, suggest stability in both countries, with very little growth either in the amount of money spent for HRD efforts or the percentage of employees impacted by such programs.

But there are also major differences. The educational systems are quite different, with quality and success levels higher in Canada than in the US. Unions are stronger in influencing the training agenda in Canada than in the US. Indigenous peoples are treated differently, and the language distributions are quite different with Canada's bilingualism. Provinces, in general, are stronger than states, although both have primary responsibility for education. Professional preparation for HRD in Canada occurs through Adult Education programs and CHRP exams, whereas specific HRD programs dominate in the US. Both countries are committed to HRD for their populations, although cultural differences will continue to show differences in each country's journey toward improved HRD. Similarities between the two countries are summarized in Table 10.1, and differences are summarized in Table 10.2.

SIMILARITIES AND DIFFERENCES IN HRD BETWEEN CANADA AND THE US

Table 10.1 and Table 10.2 provide an overview of the similarities and differences in HRD between Canada and the US.

Table 10.1 Similarities in HRD Between Canada and the US

Theme	Similarities
Corporate-level HRD	HRD is addressed systematically by large corporations, and many have corporate universities. SMEs access public workshops. Academic institutions also offer corporate training.
Government-level HRD	Provinces/states receive funding from the federal government for micro- and macrolevel HRD initiatives.
Community level HRD	Structured and unstructured community-based HRD initiatives can be found in religious and charity organizations and philanthropic foundations. Community and international HRD is addressed by various NGOs. Corporations also participate in community HRD through CSR. Initiatives focus on various aspects, such as youth empowerment and job-related training.
Common training areas	– Management and supervisory skills – New employee orientation – Occupational health and safety – Mandatory and compliance training – Profession-/industry-specific training (Canadian Chamber of Commerce, 2013; Miller, 2014)
Role of unions in HRD	Where unions exist, they play a significant role in HRD, primarily in supporting apprenticeships.
Professional HRD organizations	Numerous local, provincial, national, and international professional organizations and consultancies.
Type and nature of investment in HRD	Investment in HRD is seen as a cost. Focus is more on fads and perceived relevance than on evidence-based HRD.
Instructor-led classroom training continues to dominate training activities	66% (the Conference Board of Canada, 2009) and 55% (Miller, 2014, para 15). There are opportunities to be more creative in designing, delivering, and evaluating HRD programs by using various aspects of technology.

(Continued)

Table 10.1 (Continued)

Theme	Similarities
Nonacademic professional development for HRD professionals	Preparation and exams are offered for certifications by professional organizations.
Key HRD challenges	– Aging population – Fluctuating provincial/ state economies – Widespread employee development and retention – Underemployment – Lack of trained and skilled employees – About 81% of population is in urban areas, making HRD difficult in other areas – Preparing workforce for knowledge-based economy – Effects of immigration policies on workforce development – Illiteracy in workforce – Responding to diversity in the workplace

Table 10.2   Differences in HRD Between Canada and the US

Theme	Canada	US
HRD higher education programs	Very few stand-alone HRD programs (three) with most academic programs embedded in other majors.	More stand-alone academic programs in HRD than in any other country.
Government-level HRD and funding	HRD at the government level is holistic and systematic, coordinating activities across the country and partnering with provinces and aboriginal groups.	Highly decentralized HRD programs with little coordination. Role is to set policy and distribute funding, giving states and local agencies considerable autonomy.
Professional HRD organizations and publications	Only one practitioner-oriented professional HRD organization (CSTD). No HRD-specific journal for scholarly publications.	Major scholarly professional organizations devoted to HRD (AHRD and others) and OD. Many practitioner journals in OD and T&D. US has leading HRD journals for scholarly publications.

Theme	Canada	US
Role of unions in HRD	Unions play a significant role in T&D, with 30% of workers belonging to unions (Overview of collective bargaining in Canada, 2015).	Unions are not as influential in HRD as in Canada. Only 11.1% of workers in USA belong to unions (BLS, 2015c).
Education system	Canada has better quality education and higher success rates in tertiary education.	Overall, quality of education is high; however, higher education attainment levels are low compared with other OECD countries.
Languages influencing HRD	Bilingual—English and French. Bilingualism offers opportunities for inclusive HRD efforts.	Unilingual—English is the only official language. This poses challenges for HRD programs, as they may lack a pluralistic approach and limit HRD opportunities for non-English workers.
Cultural differences	Canada tends to score low on masculinity and individualism. HRD programs promote inclusivity and pluralism.	US tends to place a higher value on individualism and masculinity. HRD programs address diversity but not pluralism.
Percent of payroll allocated to HRD	1.5% (the Conference Board of Canada, 2009). HRD in Canada needs more commitment from organizations.	3.6% (Miller, 2014). There may still be room for improvement but twice as much as Canada.
Information on HRD	Scattered and not easily accessible, which makes it challenging to explore and compare micro- and macrolevel HRD efforts. However, the government's HRD efforts are structured and well documented.	Surprisingly, there is also a lack of information on HRD practices, although there is considerable research information, especially in scholarly journals. However, it is challenging to gather information on public-sector HRD efforts and on statistics related to all aspects of HRD.

DISCUSSION

It has been interesting for both of us, with roots in both countries, to undertake this exploration of HRD in Canada and the US. We were most surprised by the difficulty in identifying information on the components of this chapter that we considered important, finding very few scholarly articles and, except for government websites, little other information. HRD is often seen as a strategic advantage for organizations; as a result, companies may be reluctant to share their information. This desire for confidentiality has been an ongoing barrier for researchers and serves as a barrier for improvement.

We are puzzled about why Canadian universities have not adopted HRD as an academic program. Given the commitment to HRD in Canada, one would expect universities to respond to this commitment by providing highly competent professionals for positions in corporations and government organizations. There is considerable cross-fertilization in education across the border, both in degree programs and in professional organizations. One of our recommendations, therefore, is that Canadian universities explore some of the best HRD programs in the US to implement such programs. Canada has extensive knowledge and experience that could be used for the purpose of offering HRD programs with an emphasis on international development. Reciprocal study abroad would be another way to enhance such cross-cultural understanding. Many Canadians study in the US (as do some Americans in Canada), but we are unaware of any programs designed for HRD students.

Both countries are challenged by the diversity that exists within their companies and communities. Language is a major issue given the large number of languages that are first languages in both countries. The illiteracy issues also present challenges to both countries. It is amazing that countries that are so healthy economically can have such problems with literacy in the workplace. Much more attention needs to be paid to adult basic education in both community education and in workplace training.

While the high number of employees who receive some form of training in the workplace appears encouraging, and although the US percentage is much higher than that in Canada, a closer look at the type of training received is more discouraging. The details behind the types of training received indicate that much of the training is oriented toward new employee and mandatory training related to legal and regulatory requirements. To be truly competitive in the global economy, employers need to be much more serious about providing in-depth training and more development activities. Also, we recommend that organizations evaluate the impact of HRD on employee learning and productivity and on organizational improvement. In Canada, "in 2008, almost half of organizations did not evaluate the impact of formal or informal learning on their employees" (The Conference Board of Canada, 2009, p. 46).

It is our perspective that systems' thinking, implemented through organization development and being a learning organization, have the most impact in improving an organization's productivity. Yet, surprisingly, we were unable to identify any summary information about the extent to which organizations took advantage of these aspects of HRD. There are lots of case studies and research on specific aspects of organizations. Yet parallel data for organizations' development, such as we found for training and development, seems unavailable. This is troubling. If our bias is correct, we clearly need to have more information about this aspect of HRD.

The contribution of various sectors to a country's GDP has implications for organizational and national-level HRD. Perhaps more HRD efforts are needed to increase the growth of medium-sized businesses. Also, studying HRD efforts of small businesses and large firms might help in understanding reasons why these businesses' relative contribution to GDP is not significantly different from each other. In addition, we need to ask what type of HRD efforts are needed in the future if the interest in small businesses continues to increase, especially with an increase in aging in the population and virtual businesses.

Within both countries, there are huge differences across states and provinces. Such regionalism is a problem for the economic development and talent development and management of both countries. The regionalism is also seen in ignorance of the human resources available nationally, as well as the cultures that affect such human resources. This regionalism is also seen in ignorance between the two countries, especially in the US about Canada. Given population differences, little attention is paid to Canada in the US education system and in the US media. Thus cooperation that could occur through the existing trade treaties is seriously impaired. Mandating learning units in the curriculum that focus on the other country throughout the education system would do much to overcome biases, prejudices, and lack of knowledge. Addressing cultural differences between the two countries in international field trips or international education courses in academic settings could also be a valuable stepping-stone toward overcoming such ignorance.

Further, the immigration policies of both countries make it difficult for mobility between the two countries, impairing the meeting of talent requirements for the improvement of organizations in both countries. Both countries would benefit greatly if reciprocal immigration policies were put in place, allowing for free movement between each other. Given the education systems in place, there would be little downside to such an agreement, and talent on both sides of the border would be enhanced. Further, AHRD, for some time, has wanted to hold its annual Americas conference in Canada. But existing immigration laws make this difficult, if not impossible, although the Academy of Management held its 2015 conference in British Columbia, suggesting that the existing barriers might be manageable. AHRD has many students and scholars from outside of the Americas attending its conference, and visa restrictions make conference participation nearly impossible for many such students and scholars. We recommend that AHRD explore the possibility of organizing its conference in the Americas in Canada for the purpose of jointly addressing HRD issues in the two countries.

Where is HRD likely to go in both countries? Perhaps the answer lies in a multidimensional approach to understanding and promoting HRD in both countries. We would hope much less attention would be paid to fads and more paid to research and existing evidence. We are cautiously optimistic, however, that this will happen. We do expect that there will be a growth in the use of virtual technologies, for both training and organization development. And we anticipate the continuing impact of globalization and diversity, requiring HRD professionals to be much more aware of culture and language in the development and implementation of their HRD programs. As both countries evolve into knowledge economies, we also expect more depth in the training content, with less emphasis on the rudimentary components of orientation and regulations. Innovation is essential for the survival of companies today. One of the major requirements for innovation is domain expertise (McLean, 2011) to which content-rich HRD can contribute. Thus increasing partnerships between HRD professionals and subject matter experts is also likely to increase. Hence we recommend that such partnerships take place between professionals and organizations in the two countries, perhaps under the auspices of the Scholar-Practitioner Special Interest Group of AHRD.

Another hope is for a future in which HRD can influence management. We know a lot about what contributes to successful management. But, in spite of the large investments made in leadership and management development, we still find managers behaving more from their own experiences and personal preferences than from the evidence available about how managers can truly influence productivity in a positive way.

In both countries, but particularly within the public sector in the US, management has to find better ways to partner with unions to improve working conditions and, ultimately, performance. Unions (and, conversely, management) must be seen as necessary and useful, not as adversaries but as partners working together for the benefit of employees and the organization.

CONCLUSION

We believe that Canada and the US have much to offer to the world in the way of talent development, education, and talent management. Cooperation between the two countries would enhance these contributions to the benefit of everyone involved. Creating a closer bond, especially as it relates to HRD, will not only create synergy and true benefits to humanity but will also prepare the two countries in their respective journeys toward creating knowledge-based economies. Finally, from an international development perspective, many organizations and institutions, especially in developing countries, look to Canada and the US for evidence-based practices and cutting-edge research in HRD. Thus improvements in HRD in the two countries will enhance not only their national but also their international HRD efforts.

REFERENCES

AFL-CIO America's Unions. (2015). *Training and Apprenticeships*. Accessed 7 April 2015. (http://www.aflcio.org/Learn-About-Unions/Training-and-Apprenticeships)

Aga Khan IV. (February 27, 2014). *Address of His Highness the Aga Khan to both Houses of the Parliament of Canada in the House of Commons Chamber. Ottawa*. Accessed 28 April 2015. (http://www.akdn.org/Content/1253/Address-of-His-Highness-the-Aga-Khan-to-both-Houses-of-the-Parliament-of-Canada-in-the-House-of-Commons-Chamber-Ottawa)

Aga Khan Development Network. (2014). *Human Resource Development*. Accessed 9 August 2015. (http://www.akdn.org/akf_issues.asp)

Ahn, Y. S., & McLean, G. N. (2010). Regional human resource development systems and policies in the USA: Focus on the Workforce Investment Act. *Journal of Lifelong Education and HRD*, 6(1): 221–239.

Alagaraja, M., & Li, J. (2015). Utilizing institutional perspectives to investigate the emergence, rise, and (relative) decline of corporate universities. *Human Resource Development Journal*, 18(1): 4–23. doi:http://dx.doi.org/10.1080/13678868.2014.979003

Amadeo, K. (2015). What are the components of GDP? The four major things the US is good at producing. *Aboutnews*. Accessed 27 April 2015 from: (http://useconomy.about.com/od/grossdomesticproduct/f/GDP_Components.htm)

American Express Small Business Monitor. (2012). *Investing in Talent: Skills Training and Development*. (http://www.profitguide.com/news/investing-in-talent-35853) Cited in: Canadian Chamber of Commerce. (2013). *Upskilling the Workforce: Employer-Sponsored Training and Resolving the Skills Gap*. Ottawa, ON: Author.

Ardichvili, A. (2015). Editorial. *Human Resource Development International*, 18(1): 1–3. doi:http://dx.doi.org/10.1080/13678868.2014.979007

AUCC (The Association of Universities and Colleges of Canada). (2011). *Trends in Higher Education*. Accessed 30 April 2015. (http://www.aucc.ca/wp-content/uploads/2011/05/trends-2011-vol1-enrollment-e.pdf)

BBC. (British Broadcasting Corporation). (2015). *Leif Erikson*. (11th century). History. Accessed 28 April 2015. (http://www.bbc.co.uk/history/historic_figures/erikson_leif.shtml)

Bélanger, P., & Hart, S. A. (2012). *Leveraging Training and Skills Development in Smes an Analysis of Two Canadian Urban Regions: Montreal and Winnipeg*. Organisation for Economic Cooperation and Development. (http://www.oecd.org/canada/Canada%20report%20FINAL%20formatted.pdf). Cited in: Canadian Chamber of Commerce. (2013). *Upskilling the Workforce: Employer-Sponsored Training and Resolving the Skills Gap*. Ottawa.

Berek, G., & Bilginsoy, C. (2000). Do unions help or hinder women in training: Apprenticeship programs in the United States. *Industrial Relations*, 39(2): 600–624.

Bidwell, A. (February 12, 2015). High school graduation rate hits all-time high. *US News*. Accessed 10 April 2015. (http://www.usnews.com/news/blogs/data-mine/2015/02/12/us-high-school-graduation-rate-hits-all-time-high)

Bjorkquist, D. C., & Lewis, T. (1994). A model for training research from the workers' perspective. *Human Resource Development Quarterly*, 5(2): 111–129.

BLS. (Bureau of Labor Statistics), US Department of Labor. (2015a, February). *The employment situation—February 2015*. USDL-15-0325. Accessed 28 March 2015. (http://www.bls.gov/news.release/pdf/empsit.pdf)

BLS. (Bureau of Labor Statistics), US Department of Labor. (2015b). *Percent of Employees Receiving Benefits from Completing Formal Training Activities while Working for Current Employer*. Accessed 10 July, 2015 (http://www.bls.gov/news.release/sept.t09.htm)

BLS. (Bureau of Labor Statistics), US Department of Labor. (2015c, January). *Union Members Summary*. Accessed 28 March 2015. (http://www.bls.gov/news.release/union2.nr0.htm)

Bradley, J. (March 17, 2015). The challenging face of the Heartland: Preparing America's diverse workforce for tomorrow. *The Brookings Essay*. Accessed 29 March 2015. (http://www.brookings.edu/research/essays/2015/changingface oftheheartland#)

Canadian Council on Learning. (2009). *2008 Survey of Canadian Attitudes toward Learning: Results for Learning Throughout the Lifespan*. Accessed 30 April 2015 (http://www.ccl-cca.ca/pdfs/SCAL/2009/SCAL2008_EN.pdf)

Canada FAQ. (2015). *Economy. Canada Questions and Answers*. Accessed 28 April 2015 from: (http://www.canadafaq.ca/what+are+the+top+industries+in+c anada/)

CEC Network. (2003). *The Education System in Canada. About Canada*. Accessed 14 April 2015. (http://www.studycanada.ca/english/education_system_canada. htm)

Center on International Education. (2015). *Benchmarking: Learning from the World's High Performing Education Systems. School-to-work Transition*. Accessed 2 May 2015. http://www.ncee.org/programs-affiliates/center-on-international-education-benchmarking/top-performing-countries/canada-overview/canada-school-to-work-transition/)

Cho, E. S., & McLean, G. N. (2004). What we discovered about NHRD and what it means for HRD. *Advances in Developing Human Resources*, 6(3): 382–393.

CIA. (Central Intelligence Agency). (2014). *List of Countries by GDP Sector Composition: The World Factbook*. Accessed 28 March 2015. (http://en.wikipedia. org/wiki/List_of_countries_by_GDP_sector_composition)

CIA. (Central Intelligence Agency). (2015). *Canada: The World Factbook*. Accessed 14 April 2015 (https://www.cia.gov/library/publications/the-world-factbook/geos/ca.html)

CICIC. (The Canadian Information Centre for International Credentials). (2015). *Ministries/Departments Responsible for Education in Canada*. Accessed 14 April 2015. (http://www.cicic.ca/1301/Ministries-Departments-responsible-for-education-in-Canada/index.canada)

CMEC. (Council of Ministers of Education). (2008). *Education in Canada*. Accessed 15 April 2015. (http://www.cmec.ca/Publications/Lists/Publications/Attachments/64/Education-in-Canada2008.pdf)

CMEC. (Council of Ministers of Education). (2015). *Canada's Education Systems*. Accessed 15 April 2015. (http://www.educationau-incanada.ca/educationau-incanada/systems-systemes.aspx?lang=eng)

Cordero-Guzman, H. R. (2014). *Community-Based Organizations, Immigrant Low-Wage Workers, and the Workforce Development System in The United States*. New York, NY: Baruch College and the City University of New York.

Accessed 9 August 2015. (https://www.gcir.org/sites/default/files/resources/Cordero-WorkerCenters-WorkforceDevelopment-3–14-out.pdf)

East-West Gateway Coordinating Council. (n.d.) *Federal Funding Streams for Workforce Development Planning and Programming*. St. Louis, MO: Author. Accessed 17 April 2015. (http://www.doleta.gov/usworkforce/communityaudits/docs/Files%20for%20CA%20Website/MO-St%20Louis/MO-St%20Louis-Product-Federal%20Funding%20Streams%20Directory.pdf)

ESDC. (Employment and Social Development Canada). (2015). *Government of Canada*. Accessed 15 April 2015. (http://www.esdc.gc.ca/eng/home.shtml)

Fenwick, T. (2005). Conceptions of critical HRD: Dilemmas for theory and practice. *Human Resource Development International*, 8(2): 225–238.

Fisher, D., Rubeson, K., Bernatchez, J., Clift, R., Jones, G., Lee, J., & Trottier, C. (2006). *Canadian Federal Policy and Postsecondary Education*. Winnipeg, MB: Printcrafters.

Garvin, D. A., Edmondson, A. C., & Gino, F. (2008). 'Is yours a learning organization?'. *Harvard Business Review*, 86(3), 109–116.

Global Health Facts. (2012). *Urban Population (Percent of Total Population Living in Urban Areas)*. Accessed 1 August 2015. (http://kff.org/global-indicator/urban-population/)

Goldenberg. M. (2006). Employer investment in workplace learning in Canada. *Canadian Policy Research Networks*. Accessed 30 April 2015 (http://www.ccl-cca.ca/NR/rdonlyres/4F86830F-D201–4CAF-BA12–333B51CEB988/0/EmployerInvestmentWorkplaceLearningCCLCPRN.pdf)

Government of Canada. (2015). Aboriginal peoples and communities. *Aboriginal Affairs and Northern Development Canada*. Accessed 14 April 2015. (https://www.aadnc-aandc.gc.ca/eng/1100100013785/1304467449155)

Grove, C. N. (2005). *Worldwide Differences in Business Practices and Values: Overview of Globe Research Findings*. Accessed 27 March 2015. (http://www.grovewell.com/pub-GLOBE-dimensions.html)

Haslinda, A. (2009). Evolving terms of human resource management and development. *The Journal of International Social Research*, 2(9): 180–186.

Heathfield, S. M. (2015). *What is Human Resource Development?* Accessed 8 August 2015. (http://humanresources.about.com/od/glossaryh/f/hr_development.htm)

Herman, J., Post, S., & O'Halloran, S. (2013). *The United States is far behind other countries on pre-K*. Accessed 27 March 2015. (https://www.americanprogress.org/issues/education/report/2013/05/02/62054/the-united-states-is-far-behind-other-countries-on-pre-k/)

Hofstede, G. (2008). *Geert Hofstede on the Dimensions of Cultural Differences*. Accessed 27 March 2015. (http://www.edbatista.com/2008/02/hofstede.html)

Humensky, J. L., Jordan, N., Stroupe, K. T., & Hynes, D. (2013). Employment status of veterans receiving substance abuse treatment from the US Department of Veterans Affairs. *Psychiatric Services*, 64(2): 177–180.

Independence Hall Association in Philadelphia. (2014). *The American Revolution*. Accessed 2 August 2015. (http://www.ushistory.org/us/11.asp)

Industry Canada. (2015a). *Canadian Company Capabilities*. Accessed 11 July 2015 from: (http://www.ic.gc.ca/eic/site/ccc-rec.nsf/eng/home)

Industry Canada. (2015b). *Canadian Economy (NAICS 11–91): Gross Domestic Product (GDP)*. Accessed 11 July 2015. (https://www.ic.gc.ca/app/scr/sbms/sbb/cis/gdp.html?code=11–91&lang=eng)

Industry Canada. (2015c). *Canadian Economy (NAICS 11–91): Labour Productivity*. Accessed 11 July 2015. (https://www.ic.gc.ca/app/scr/sbms/sbb/cis/labourProductivity.html?code=11–91&lang=eng)

Industry Canada. (2015d). *SME Research and Statistics*. Accessed 11 July 2015. (https://www.ic.gc.ca/eic/site/061.nsf/eng/02812.html)

Jennings, J. (2013). Accessed 27 March 2015 (http://www.huffingtonpost.com/jack-jennings/proportion-of-us-students_b_2950948.html)

Joy-Matthews, J., Megginson, D., & Surtees, M. (2004). *Human Resource Development*. London, UK: Kogan Page.

Kleykamp, M. A. (2010). *Women's Work after War*. Upjohn Institute Working Paper No. 10–169. Kalamazoo, MI: W.E. Upjohn Institute for Employment Research. Accessed 11 August 2015. (http://research.upjohn.org/up_workingpapers/169)

Kuiper, A. M. (2015). *Theory of Change*. Unpublished manuscript, available from Dr. Kuiper at (AKuiper@saoic.org)

Lavis, C. (2011). *Learning and Development Outlook 2011: Are Organizations Ready for Learning 2.0?* Conference Board of Canada. (http://www.conference-board.ca/e-library/abstract.aspx?did=4490.) Cited in: Canadian Chamber of Commerce. (2013). *Upskilling the Workforce: Employer-Sponsored Training: and Resolving the Skills Gap*. Ottawa, ON: Author.

Lyons, J. E., Randhawa, B. S., & Paulson, N. A. (1991). The development of vocational education in Canada. *Canadian Journal of Education*, 16(2): 137–150.

Mapleleafweb. (2015). History of bilingual politics in Canada. *Official Bilingualism in Canada: History and Debates*. Accessed 28 April 2015. (http://mapleleafweb.com/features/official-bilingualism-canada-history-and-debates)

McCormick Foundation. (May 13, 2014). *McCormick Foundation Grants $900,000 for Citywide Workforce Development Programs through Chicago Tribune Charities*. Accessed 13 August, 2015. (http://www.prnewswire.com/news-releases/mccormick-foundation-grants-900000-for-citywide-workforce-development-programs-through-chicago-tribune-charities-259057151.html)

McLean, G. N. (2014). National human resource development. In N. E. Chalofsky, T. S. Rocco, & M. L. Morris, (Eds.), *Handbook of Human Resource Development*, 243–260. Hoboken, NJ: Wiley.

McLean, G. N., & Akaraborworn, C. (2015). HRD education in developing countries. *Advances in Developing Human Resources*, 17(2): 213–238. doi:10.1177/1523422315572622

McLean, G. N., & Akdere, M. (2015) (In press). Enriching HRD education through professional organizations. *Advances in Developing Human Resources in Developing Human Resources*. doi:10.1177/1523422315572650

McLean, L. D. (2011). *Understanding Creativity in Organizations: The Relationships Among Cross-Level Variables and Creativity in Research and Development Organizations*. Unpublished doctoral dissertation, University of Minnesota, Minneapolis, MN.

Meister, J. C. (2009). Corporate universities 2.0: The future networked learning organization. In A. Romano & G. Secundo (Eds.), *Dynamic Learning Networks: Models and Cases in Action*, 137–149. New York, NY: Springer Science.

Microsoft. (2015). *Corporate Citizenship*. Accessed 27 April 2015 from: (http://www.microsoft.com/about/corporatecitizenship/en-us/serving-communities/)

Miller, L. (2014). *2014 State of the Industry Report: Spending on Employee Training Remains a Priority*. Alexandria, VA: ATD (Association for Talent Development). Accessed 30 March 2015. (https://www.td.org/Publications/Magazines/TD/TD-Archive/2014/11/2014-State-of-the-Industry-Report-Spending-on-Employee-Training-Remains-a-Priority)

Moats, J. B., & McLean, G. N. (2009). Speaking our language: The essential role of scholar-practitioners in HRD. *Advances in Developing Human Resources*, 11(4): 507–522.

Mundy, K. E. (1992). Human resource development assistance in Canada's overseas development assistance program: A critical analysis. *Canadian Journal of Development Studies*, 13(3): 385–409.

NGOs Based in Canada, NGOs Based in Other Countries. (n.d.). Accessed 4 May 2015 (http://www.chatt.hdsb.ca/~menkac/classes/NGOs.htm)

OECD. (2009). How many students enroll in vocational programmes? *Highlights from Education at a Glance 2008*. OECD Publishing. Accessed 2 May 2015. (http://dx.doi.org/10.1787/eag_highlights-2008–7-en)

OECD (Organization for Economic Cooperation and Development). (2013). *Time for the US to Reskill? What the Survey of Adult Skills Says*. OECD Skills Studies. OECD Publishing. Retrieved on March 28, 2015 from: (http://skills.oecd.org/documents/Survey_of_Adult_Skills_US.pdf)

Olinsky, B., & Ayres, S. (2013). *Training for Success: A Policy to Expand Apprenticeships in the United States*. Center for American Progress. Retrieved on August 8, 2015 from: (https://www.americanprogress.org/wp-content/uploads/2013/11/apprenticeship_report.pdf)

Overview *of collective bargaining in Canada*. (2015). Retrieved on April 30, 2015 from: (http://www.labour.gc.ca/eng/resources/info/publications/collective_bargaining/collective_bargaining.shtml)

Parliament of Canada. (2015). History of Canada. *Parliamentary Treasure—A Glimpse Inside the Archives of the Senate of Canada*. Accessed 2 April 2015 (http://www.parl.gc.ca/About/Senate/ParliamentaryTreasures/history-canada-e.htm)

Percival, J. C., Cozzarin, B. P. & Formaneck, S. D. (2013). Return on investment for workplace training: the Canadian experience. *International Journal of Training and Development, 17*: 20–32.

Roberts, P. B. (Ed.) (2014). *2014 Human Resource Development Directory of Academic Programs in the United States*. Tyler, TX: The University of Texas at Tyler.

Rubenstein, S. A. (2001). Unions as value-adding networks: Possibilities for the future of US unionism. *Journal of Labor Research*, 22(3): 581–598.

Ryan, C. (2013). *Language Use in the United States: 2011*. Retrieved on March 27, 2015 from: (https://www.census.gov/prod/2013pubs/acs-22.pdf)

Ryan, C. L., & Siebens, J. (February, 2012). *Educational Attainment in the United States 2009: Population Characteristics Report*. Washington, DC: United States Census Bureau.

Singleton, S. (November 4, 2011). Canada not spending enough on learning, development. *The Barrie Examiner*. Retrieved on April 30, 2015 from (http://www.thebarrieexaminer.com/2011/11/04/canada-not-spending-enough-on-learning-development-2)

SHRM (Society for Human Resource Management). (2008). *Religion and Corporate Culture*. Retrieved on August 11, 2015 from: (http://diversityinc.com/medialib/uploads/2011/12/08–0625ReligionSR_Final_LowRez.pdf)

Statistics Canada. (2009). Postsecondary enrollment and graduation. *Statistics Canada Catalogue no. 11–402-X*. Accessed 30 April 2015 (http://www.statcan.gc.ca/pub/81-599-x/81-599-x2009003-eng.pdf)

Statistics Canada. (March 2015). *Labor Force Characteristics by Province—Seasonally Adjusted*. Retrieved April 30, 2015 from: (http://www.statcan.gc.ca/daily-quotidien/150410/t150410a003-eng.htm)

Stockwell, C. (2014). *Same as it Ever was: Top ten Most Popular College Majors*. Retrieved on April 15, 2015 from: (http://college.usatoday.com/2014/10/26/same-as-it-ever-was-top-10-most-popular-college-majors/)

Structure of the United States government. (n.d.) Retrieved on August 2 from: (http://www.theusgov.com)

Summit Academy OIC. (2015). *Training for Life*. Retrieved on March 30, 2015 from: (https://www.saoic.org/about/)

SunTrust Foundation. (July 13, 2015). *SunTrust Foundation Supports Community Strengthening Work of Catholic Charities USA*. Retrieved on August 13, 2015 from: (http://www.prnewswire.com/news-releases/suntrust-foundation-supports-community-strengthening-work-of-catholic-charities-usa-300112304.html)

TBS (Treasury Board of Canada Secretariat). (2015). *Human Resources*. Retrieved on April 29, 2015 from: (http://www.tbs-sct.gc.ca/tbs-sct/cmn/activity-activites-eng.asp#hr-rh)

The Canadian Chamber of Commerce. (October, 2013). *Upskilling the Workforce: Employer-Sponsored Training and Resolving the Skills Gap*. Accessed on July 11, 2015 from: (http://www.chamber.ca/media/blog/131009_Upskilling-the-Workforce/131009_Upskilling_the_Workforce.pdf)

The Canadian encyclopedia. (2015a). *Aboriginal Languages of Canada*. Accessed 22 April 2015 (http://www.thecanadianencyclopedia.ca/en/article/economic-history/)

The Canadian encyclopedia. (2015b). *Adult education*. Accessed 22 April 2015 (http://www.thecanadianencyclopedia.ca/en/article/adult-education/)

The Canadian encyclopedia. (2015c). *Battle of the Plains of Abraham*. Accessed 28 April 2015 (http://www.thecanadianencyclopedia.ca/en/article/battle-of-the-plains-of-abraham/)

The Canadian encyclopedia. (2015d). *Economic history*. Accessed 22 April 2015 (http://www.thecanadianencyclopedia.ca/en/article/economic-history/)

The Canadian encyclopedia. (2015e). *Loyalists*. Retrieved on April 28, 2015 (http://www.thecanadianencyclopedia.ca/en/article/loyalists/)

The Conference Board of Canada. (2007). *Learning and Development Outlook: Are We Learning Enough?* Retrieved on April 30, 2015 from (http://www.wln.ualberta.ca/en/Events/Archives/Seminar%20Archives/~/media/wln/Documents/Events/Seminars_2008/LearningandDevelopmentOutlook2007.pdf)

The Conference Board of Canada. (2009a). *Learning and Development Outlook: Learning in Tough Times*. Retrieved on July 11, 2015 from (http://www.ntab.on.ca/wp-content/uploads/file/LearningDevelopment2009v1.pdf)

The Conference Board of Canada. (2009b). *Workplace Learning in Small and Medium-Sized Enterprises: Effective Practices in Improving Productivity and Competitiveness*. Accessed 8 August 2015 (http://www.ccl-cca.ca/pdfs/OtherReports/CBofC-WorkplaceLearning-SME-OverviewReport.pdf)

The Consulting Bench. (2013). *Human Resources Consulting Firms*. Accessed 27 April 2015 (http://www.consultingbench.com/consulting-firms/human-resources-consulting-firms)

The Hofstede Centre. (2015). *What about Canada?* Accessed 15 April 2015 (http://geert-hofstede.com/canada.html)

The Moody's Foundation. (2011). *Moody's Corporate Social Responsibility Report*. Retrieved on August 10, 2015, from: https://www.moodys.com/sites/products/ProductAttachments/CSR%20Report.pdf

The World Bank Group. (2015). *GDP per capita (current US$)*. Accessed 28 March 2015 (http://data.worldbank.org/indicator/NY.GDP.PCAP.CD?order=wbapi_data_value_2013%20wbapi_data_value%20wbapi_data_valuelast&sort=aschttp://data.worldbank.org/indicator/NY.GDP.PCAP.CD?order=wbapi_data_value_2013%20wbapi_data_value%20wbapi_data_value-last&sort=asc)

Tozzi, J. (2012). Small business share of economy, job growth shrinks. *Bloomberg Business*. Accessed 27 April 2015 (http://www.businessweek.com/smallbiz/running_small_business/archives/2012/01/small_business_share_of_economy_job_growth_shrinks.html)

US Census Bureau. (n.d.). *2010 Census Urban and Rural Classification and Urban Area Criteria*. Retrieved on August 1, 2015 from: (http://www.census.gov/geo/reference/ua/urban-rural-2010.html)

US Department of Education, National Center for Education Statistics. (2009). *High School Transcript Study*. Washington, DC: Author. Retrieved March 27, 2015 from: (https://nces.ed.gov/surveys/ctes/tables/h123.asp)

US Department of Education, National Center for Education Statistics. (2012). *2011–12 National Postsecondary Student Aid Study (NPSAS:12)*. Washington, DC: Author. Accessed 27 April 2015 (http://www2.ed.gov/rschstat/eval/sectech/nacte/career-technical-education/final-report.pdf)

US Department of Education, National Center for Education Statistics, Common Core of Data. (2012). *Higher Education General Information Survey (HEGIS)*. Washington, DC: Author. Retrieved on April 14, 2015 from: (http://nces.ed.gov/programs/digest/d12/tables/dt12_005.asp)

US Department of Education, National Center for Education Statistics. (2014). *Digest of Education Statistics*. Washington, DC: Author. Accessed 14 April 2015 (http://nces.ed.gov/programs/digest/d13/tables/dt13_317.10.asp?current=yes)

US Department of Education, National Center for Education Statistics. (2014). *Public High School Graduation Rates*. Washington, DC: Author. Retrieved on March 27, 2015 from: (https://nces.ed.gov/programs/coe/indicator_coi.asp)

Worldometers. (March 28, 2015). *US Population (Live)*. Retrieved on March 28, 2015 from: (http://www.worldometers.info/world-population/us-population/)

11 Human Resource Development in Latin America

Consuelo L. Waight, José Ernesto Rangel Delgado and Johana Lopez

INTRODUCTION

Human resource development, as a field of practice, is catalytic to the successful analysis, execution, evaluation, and institutionalization of economic development policies and strategies regardless of sector or context in Latin America. HRD has moved from superficial inclusion or complete exclusion in economic plans to being a core requirement. Today, although HRD continues to be riddled by historical misalignment of capital, infrastructure, science, technology, education, and capacity building, it commands attention and discussion. These conversations are due to the multiplicity of HRD discussions held across all sectors by multiple stakeholders. The United Nations, for example, considers HRD strategies as increasingly part of national development planning, crucial to enlighten policy (www.un.org, 2015). Latin America, driven by Millennium Development Goals (MDGs) and local, regional, and global competition, is taking slow but concrete steps toward integrating HRD into the social and economic fabric of its communities, institutions, and enterprises.

This chapter will first provide an overview of the relevance of HRD in Latin America. The historical, political, economic, institutional, social, and cultural context of HRD in the region will be presented with emphasis on Bolivia, Nicaragua, Costa Rica, Peru, Argentina, Colombia, Belize, and Mexico. The interface of enterprise and HRD in Latin America will also be examined and the general vocational and educational base for HRD will be explored and subsequently discussed.

THE RELEVANCE OF HRD IN LATIN AMERICA

HRD in Latin America is impacted by inequality, especially among the indigenous populations. Limiting political ideologies, divergent economic policies, and social challenges such as hunger, poverty and inadequate education and health care take their toll. The eight countries discussed in this chapter, Mexico, Costa Rica, Nicaragua, Belize, Colombia, Peru, Bolivia, and Argentina, provide a clear sense of how HRD has emerged in the region. Historically HRD has been focused in the primary, secondary, and tertiary education systems. Despite this emphasis, access to and quality of education continues to be a challenge (United Nations Economic and Social Council, 2010). The differences in the characteristics of the schools attended by children from advantageous backgrounds and those attended by children from poor socioeconomic backgrounds are considerable (Ferreira et al., 2012). Although vocational and technical education has been in existence, it has remained a lesser priority for governments, evidenced by a fragmented approach, limited investment, and a neglect of outdated curriculum and equipment. From the economic and social perspective, HRD could only bring small incremental changes.

In the last three decades, however, governments have become active in defining and implementing national HRD strategies that go beyond education. The HRD momentum has been triggered by foreign investment, Millennium Development Goals (MDGs), private enterprises, associations, international technical assistance furnished by organizations, such as the Pan American Health Organization (PAHO), the World Health Organization (WHO), the United Nations (UN), the United Nations Development Program (UNDP), the Inter-Development Bank and the World Bank. Today HRD is more than education, as governments, in their role as the primary agents of change, integrate the efforts of education and training institutes, religious organizations, business and industry, unions, NGOs, and nonprofit organizations toward a more inclusive HRD.

THE HISTORICAL, POLITICAL, ECONOMIC, INSTITUTIONAL, SOCIAL, AND CULTURAL CONTEXT OF HRD IN LATIN AMERICA

Although governments have moved forward with devising HRD strategies, the implementation of such strategies is riddled with misalignment, lack of accountability, accessibility, and results. In El Salvador, for example, where there is an overproduction of health workers in certain categories, the country still faces the challenge of meeting the health needs of the country. One of the challenges is the lack of health-care workers who are adequately trained for the implementation of the current health-care strategy. This challenge accentuates the weak coordination and cooperation between health-sector institutions and health-care training institutes (Ministerio de Salud De El Salvador, 2010). These challenges are not unique to El Salvador or to health-care systems. In 2011, Costa Rica, one of the few vibrant knowledge economies in Latin America, created a working group led by the Ministry of Trade and the Ministry of Science and Technology to identify and implement actions toward closing the gaps between skills demand and supply (OECD Development Centre, 2012).

Bolivia

Given that HRD is strongly aligned with the social and economic fabric of the nations in the region, it remains underwritten by political ideologies. For example, Bolivia's president, Evo Morales, a democratic socialist, has implemented land confiscation, redistribution, and nationalization of industries. Indigenous rights and empowering the poor are cornerstones of his leftist policies. He emphasizes the importance of decolonizing the Bolivian culture and asks his people to live in the "communitarian socialism of living well" (Fidler, 2013). The People's Trade Agreement, for example, was signed in 2006. This agreement promotes HRD through the lens of literacy programs, scholarships, and the exchange of medical professionals (Kennedy, 2011). In addition to investing over 217 million in primary education over the last ten years, the government has provided cash incentives so that families can keep their children in school, as well as providing incentives to pregnant women and mothers with babies two years or less to maintain regular medical appointments (Kennedy, 2011). The People's Trade Agreement (PTA) is not unique to Bolivia. It resulted from the Bolivian Alliance for Our Americas (ALBA), which was first created in 2004 by Fidel Castro and Hugo Chavez. In 2007, Nicaragua signed the PTA for the first time, ratifying it along with Venezuela, Ecuador, and some of the Caribbean Islands. Unlike Bolivia, whose PTA focuses on the people, the new ratification does not emphasize the people as much as the 'grand national companies' that run their businesses in virtual currency called SUCRE, a Bolivarian bitcoin (Rogers, 2013).

Nicaragua

Nicaragua's focus on HRD, like Bolivia, is framed by religious, socialist, and community perspectives. The government of Nicaragua published the 2012–2016 national plan for human development and made it explicitly clear that human development is not only about education and competency development but also about offering and providing the guarantee to people that they will not only have the necessary opportunities to live and survive but also the freedom to realize their human potential (Plan Nacional de Desarrollo Humano, 2012). The plan is diverse and addresses concerns such as internal and foreign political affairs, economics, banking, health, poverty, and education, among others. The education section describes basic, preschool, primary, secondary, tertiary, and special education. In addition, the plan focuses on literacy and technical education for the poorest population. Technical education offers students a general or technical baccalaureate in areas such as automotive mechanics and rural tourism. The plan also describes the importance of science, technology, innovation, and entrepreneurship to the economy and highlights the vacuum that presently exists. One has to note, however, the minimal research on technology and innovation and the nonexistence of science and technology as human capital. It was noted that international companies import their talent and very little knowledge and technology transfer occurs between expatriates and host country nationals. Also cited was the limited research and innovation partnerships between the universities, business and industry, and the limited investment by the government for research and innovation. As is, Nicaragua's economy is primarily based on basic manual production with little global reach; the challenge is to develop knowledge-based products and services that could serve the region and beyond (Plan Nacional de Desarrollo Humano, 2012).

Costa Rica

Unlike Nicaragua, Costa Rica's science, technology, and innovation platforms are vibrant. This vibrancy results from a solid education system, strong international investment, local technology companies, and integrated human capital initiatives by the government, business and industry, and universities. Intel, Abbott, Baxter, and Proctor & Gamble, for example, have manufacturing plants in Costa Rica, made possible in large part by the free trade zone legislation and subsidies that were introduced in the 1980s (Rodriguez-Clare, 2001). Intel, in particular, has been recognized for its workforce development programs and for its university partnerships that have generated new degrees and curriculum changes, especially for teacher training in technical areas (Rodriguez-Clare, 2001). In addition, Costa Rica has the highest software exports per capita in Latin America (Rodriguez-Clare, 2001).

Costa Rica's success, however, is not an overnight phenomenon. Its development is rooted in its commitment to democracy and education. In 1870, Costa Rica was the first country in Latin America to introduce free, universal primary education for girls and boys (OECD Investment Policy Review 2013). The first public university opened in the 1940 (Rodriguez-Clare, 2001); the National Institute for Learning, which provides technical training for the industrial workforce, was created in 1965 (OECD Development Centre, 2012). In 1980, computer laboratories were installed in schools, a bold education initiative for this time period (Rodriguez-Clare, 2001). Technical education has been a major lever in developing a steady stream of technicians and professionals needed in the competitive and emergent economic sectors (Rodriguez-Clare, 2001; OECD Development Centre, 2012). Costa Rica realizes, however, that education and its training resources need periodic assessment and alignment to remain competitive in the knowledge economy.

In response, Costa Rica established an interministerial working group on skills to identify mechanisms and lines of action to elaborate supply and demand projections and align skills development and training with the changing needs of the labor market. The working group includes representatives from the ministries of foreign trade, science and technology, and education, as well as the National Institute for Learning, the Technical Secretariat of the Council for Competitiveness, the Private Council for Competitiveness, the National Council of University Deans, and from the main public universities (OECD Development Centre, 2012). The Ministry of Public Education and the National Apprentice Institute are collaborating on technical programs in plastic processing, productivity, quality and administrative, and logistics and distribution (OECD Investment Policy Review, 2013). The government also recently implemented the 'Young Talent' program, which advises young talent on career choices. In addition, the government is allotting resources to increase second-language acquisition and to update training programs at universities and technical institutes (OECD Development Centre, 2012). Despite Costa Rica's strong education system, there are still challenges. The OECD (2012), for example, reports that not a single PhD in engineering was awarded during the 2007–2009 period. Costa Rica is focused on increasing the number of science, engineering, and technology PhD graduates to remain viable in the knowledge economy (OECD Development Centre, 2012).

Peru

Costa Rica's progressive strides toward a knowledge economy are not readily matched in other countries. Peru's economy has been growing by an average of 6.4% per year since 2002, and it is expected that by 2050, Peru will most likely climb from forty-sixth to twenty-sixth place in the global economic ranking list (HSBC Global Research). HRD is still in the process of definition at the national level. Workplace practices and initiatives are strongly regulated by the Peruvian Ministry of Labor. The main goal of this ministry is to develop and enforce labor legislation. This ministry promotes workplace practices and standards that are essential to the social and economic development of the Peruvian people, such as occupational health and safety, employment rights and responsibilities, and labor relations. The Ministry of Labor also supervises HR practices, such as selection, recruitment, and compensation. HRD practices are not explicitly identified among the ministry regulations, although there are many regulated areas directly connected to HRD. For example, productivity and effectiveness regulations, workers' development initiatives, educational training, employability, employee benefits, health and safety in the workplace, and all union-related areas. Peru does not have an authentic HRD policy, only policies and strategies that reflect initial development projects (Talleri, Llinas-Audet, & Escardíbul, 2012). Consequently, each company internally promotes training practices, a practice that started in the 1990s through fiscal bonuses in some training contracts.

Various institutions offer training services for specific industries. For example, the National Services for Training in Industrial Jobs collects a training levy of 0.75% of the total cost to the employee in order to develop training programs. The National Service for Training in Construction Jobs collects 0.002% of total billing of construction companies to train employees (Talleri, Llinas-Audet, & Escardíbul, 2012, p. 63). Human Dynamics/ APPROLAB is a project that contributes to the development, competitiveness, and quality of the workforce in order to promote economic development and reduce poverty in Peru. The goals of the project include, but are not exclusive to, capacity development of local authorities, restructuring of training in technical and vocational centers, the strengthening of management skills of directors, and establishing a fund for micro-projects relating to the promotion of the pedagogical and technological innovation.

In the public sector, there are many programs to help underrepresented people to obtain a job. The Ministry of Labor promotes an employability program that consists of three months of training and three months of work experience to help socially disadvantaged young people and women. In addition, the Centre of Services for Labor Training and Development (CAPLAB) is a voluntary and nonprofit organization for human development. One of the main goals is to help young people and women obtain vocational qualifications and to create job opportunities through education, technical training, and job placement support.

Argentina

Like the rest of South America, Argentina is not immune from social and political challenges. Once the third-strongest economy in Latin America, it now holds the fourth spot due to political problems, weak economic growth, and high inflation (Maellén, 2014). As Argentina resolves its economic and political challenges, HRD as a concept and practice continues to evolve. HRD, frequently integrated with human resource management (HRM), became popular during the late nineteenth century when the industrial era appeared with the development of transportation, commerce, industry, and finance. (Aldao-Zapiola, 2014). The emergence of HRD was due to the organized effort by groups to support the new economies and their workers. An early organized effort, Sociedad de Tipografica Bonaerense (Typography Society of Buenos Aires), was establish in 1857 to promote the progress of typography art, to help members who were ill or who were unable to work, and to ensure that members were paid in accordance with their knowledge and skill in a way that guaranteed their survival (Aldao-Zapiola, 2014). These organized efforts marked the beginning of the trade unions and the use of the term 'personnel administration'. While trade unions' focus remained solely on collective bargaining, the influx of foreign companies such as the Standard Oil Corporation and Nestlé, heightened the importance of training (Aldao-Zapiola, 2014). The cross-pollination of management and training practices between foreign and local companies had begun, and Alpargatas, a leading Argentine textile company, was among the first to train managers in house and, in 1920, to create the personnel function grounded in Taylorism and welfare (Aldao-Zapiola, 2014). The Taylorism and welfare era lasted until 1940 (Aldao-Zapiola, 2014).

As the private sector continued to espouse HRD practices, unions recognized the importance of size and influence, with union mergers becoming prevalent. In 1930, for example, the Confederación General del Trabajo (CGT, the General Labor Confederation) was formed and remains in existence today. After four decades of military coup d'états, political instability, and economic turmoil, Argentina finally split into two trade union federations in 1968. In 2007, however, under the reign of President Cristina Fernandez de Kirchner, who is presently serving her second term, the CGT split again, and the power of the unions resurfaced (Aldao-Zapiola, 2014).

As unions pivot their presence and prominence amid the present economic challenges, HRD continues to evolve and align with practices in the USA. Today, the terms 'human resources' have prominence and 'industrial relations' is used minimally (Aldao-Zapiola, 2014). The focus of human resources includes, but not exclusively, leadership and employee development, organization change, knowledge management, career development, and organization culture. In addition, as in the USA, the importance of HRD metrics and alignment with business is visible in academic programs as well as in the private sector, as is the delivery of training programs through e-learning. An important anchor in HRD's evolution has been the HR Association, Asociación De Recursos Humanos de la Argentina (ADRHA), which has been in existence for 47 years and continues its partnership with private, public, and academic organizations with the purpose of developing HR professionals (ADRHA, 2014).

Whereas the private-sector drives the identity of HRD, the government considers it an economic lever. Argentina is well known for its strong education system, which is free at the pre-primary, primary, secondary, and undergraduate levels. Like most Latin America countries, Argentina has implemented the Chilean Joven Program (ILO, 2010). This program was created as a response to the long-term negative effects of the economic downturn of the previous decade. Subsequent programs in other Latin American countries were designed to address the problems faced by poorly educated young people from low-income backgrounds trying to enter the labor market (ILO, 2010). The government also encourages small and medium-sized enterprises (SMEs) to train their workers by applying a tax credit. These enterprises can finance training projects up to the equivalent of 8% of total remuneration. They can also be reimbursed for costs incurred in undertaking the assessment of skills and certification in addition to actual training. This is an incentive to boost recognition of skills learned informally or on the job. This feature helps make the program, which began in 2007, attractive to SMEs, which comprise 70% of beneficiaries (ILO, 2010). Overall, whereas this is not an exclusive review of HRD in Argentina, it provides a glimpse of the strong role the private sector plays in defining and applying HRD. It is also clear that the education system and other government programs are focused on capacity building. Finally, the unions have and continue to be the protectors of worker employment and wages.

Colombia

Colombia, like Argentina, has had its fair share of social and political instability. It has had three military coup d'états and manifests major social and economic inequalities. In the 1980s, approximately 20% of the population controlled 70% of income (Hanratty and Meditz, 1988). In 1999, unemployment decreased from 20.3% at the end of 1999 to nearly 13% percent in 2003 (DANE, 2004). Last year, Colombia surpassed Argentina and now has the third-strongest economy in Latin America (Maellén, 2014).

Unlike Argentina, unions are not as prevalent and powerful due to violence and other pressures, which saw the the percentage of unionized workers drop from 15% 20 years ago to about 4% in 2013 (Franklin, 2013). In 2014, the AFL-CIO together with the most important labor federations in Colombia, and the largest labor federations in the Americas, issued a declaration criticizing Colombia's Labor Action Plan and the Colombian government for its failure to protect workers' rights and safety. The declaration also asks the US and Colombian governments to make commitments to guarantee that labor rights in Colombia are respected (Gonzalo, 2014).

Similar to Argentina, Colombia also transitioned from using terms such as 'personnel function', 'industrial relations' to using 'human resources'. HRD is framed within the context of human resources and HRM. Ogliastri, Ruiz, and Martinez (2005) reported that as early as 1965, terms such as 'organizational development' were used in companies and that performance evaluation, personality testing, and internal consulting were also applicable in companies. In the 1990s, competency-based performance, talent management, and organizational learning, among other practices, were applied in companies to encourage foreign investment and global competition. Whereas these practices seemed parallel to those in the US, the extent and frequency of practice was discontinuous. Training and development, for example, was not strategic and few companies had a training strategy. Of 90 companies surveyed in 2002, only 39% had some form of a training strategy, and most of those companies were in the service sector (Lucero and Spinel, 2002; Ogliastri, Ruiz and Martinez, 2005). Limited training opportunities continue to persist. In 2014, the Workforce 2020 report by Oxford Economics and SAP reported executives of Colombian companies as reckoning that better and more training and opportunities for education would benefit their businesses as well as their employees. These limitations are a symptom of the inadequate efforts at HRD by the government. Unequal access to education is a core cause of social inequality in Colombia. This inequality is played out by social status, ethnicity, and gender, especially in rural areas (UNESCO, 2012). In addition, although Colombia has a strong adult literacy rate, it provides minimal continuing education opportunities.

The Colombian government, alongside private and not-for-profit institutions, is tasked with providing quality education and access because for-profit education is forbidden by law (Isakson de Carvalho et al., 2013).

In the face of all the challenges, the government should be commended for the HRD efforts achieved through its National Training Service (El Servicio Nacional de Aprendizaje, SENA), established during the rule of the military junta by Rodolfo Martinez Tone and after the resignation of General Gustavo Rojas Pinilla, by Decree-Law 118 of June 21, 1957. Its function, defined in Decree 164 of August 6, 1957, was to provide training to workers, youth, and adults of industry, commerce, agriculture, mining, and ranching (SENA Website, 2014). At that time, SENA was categorized as 'non-formal education' under the general law of education. This categorization was replaced with the phrase 'education for work and human development' by Act 1064 of 2006 (UNESCO-UNEVOC, 2013). Today SENA's mission is to "invest in the social and technical development of Colombian workers, offering and implementing comprehensive training for the incorporation and development of people in productive activities that contribute to social, economic and technological development" (SENA Website, 2014). SENA is presently affiliated with the Ministry of Labor and serves as an advisor to the Ministry of Education for the design of technical programs and comprehensive training (SENA Website, 2014).

Belize

Belize is the smallest and the only English-speaking country in Central America. Belize is also the youngest independent nation in Central America, having broken away from Great Britain in 1981. Although Belize has the advantage of English, it competes poorly in the knowledge economy. Most of its revenue comes from tourism and agriculture. The education system provides a strong foundation for a seamless transition to undergraduate and graduate programs in the US, UK, and the Caribbean. The preparation does not, however, prepare for a strong school-to work transition or, for that matter, contribute to job creation. Despite the gains in education enrollment, Belize still has not harnessed its domestic capacity effectively to significantly grow its own economy (Millennium Development Goals Report, 2013). Belize also has a limited graduate education. The University of Belize offers baccalaureates in education, nursing, business, tourism and social sciences, and science and technology education. It also offers a graduate degree in biodiversity conservation and sustainable development, the university's first, which was initiated in 2011 and is a collaboration of four Caribbean universities. Engineering is only offered at the associate level. Over the last 20 years, the University of Belize and Galen University, a private institution, have had dual undergraduate and graduate degree programs in collaboration with universities in the US and the Caribbean, but none of these, however, have endured.

Given that Belize does not possess a strong knowledge economy, most HRD initiatives are led by the government or nonprofits and NGOs. Organizations such as PAHO, UNICEF, USAID, and UNDP, for example, have provided training and education leadership and support in areas related to health, poverty, gender, youth equality, adult education, formal education, and the environment. The government, for example, in the last 12 years has provided a quarter of public resources to education. These resources have helped tremendously in primary education access, teacher training, provision of textbooks, subsidized school feeding programs, and transportation in rural areas (Millennium Development Goals Report, 2013). The involvement of business and industry in human resource development varies across industries.

Most of Belize's companies are family owned and have less than 50 employees. Consequently, few have training departments or internal HRD initiatives. Organizations such as the Chamber of Commerce, the Belize Business Bureau, and the Belize Trade and Investment Development Service (BELTRAIDE) serve as brokers of HRD initiatives. Membership in these organizations primarily provides interpersonal training opportunities for employees. Few of these training initiatives, however, are linked to core performance problems faced by these organizations. Over the last five years, the hospitality industry has led the human resource development efforts within the business and industry sector. This is due to efforts by the government through the Tourism Board, the Belize Tourism Industry Association, individual companies, and other associations. The human resource development initiatives have helped tremendously to transform the tourism industry and the overall customer experience. In 2006, oil was discovered in Belize, and this has become an emergent sector for HRD. Although small at this time, if the petroleum industry is to grow in Belize, it will require specialized training in geophysics, geology, and petroleum engineering, among other areas. As is, the universities are not equipped to offer these certificates or degree programs. In addition to the technical needs, basic education on the impact of the oil industry on Belize's natural resources is essential. Presently, Oceana Belize is leading the education effort on how to safeguard the barrier reef, the second largest in the Western hemisphere, from offshore drilling.

Despite Belize's limited involvement in the knowledge economy, the government, with the help of organizations such as the Inter-American Development Bank, Central American Integration System (SICA), and Caribbean Community and Common Market (CARICOM) has made initial attempts to define a national HRD policy and strategy. The HRD strategy is expected to inform the future development and design of tertiary-level programs, as well as those at TVET and secondary levels (Belize Education Sector Strategy 2011–2016, 2012).

Today Belize struggles with basic needs, such as youth development, quality health care, and poverty alleviation (National Development Framework for Belize, 2010–2030). In 2009, 41.3% of the population lived below the poverty line, and this trend has not improved (Millennium Development Goals Report, 2013). A central issue for Belize in 2015 is turning the tide for its youth. There is a rapid deterioration of identity roles among youths caused by high unemployment, strained family structures due to poverty, crime, and limited education. The unemployment rate among youths between the ages of 14 and 24 years was 30% in 2012 (Millennium Development Goals Report, 2013). The government of Belize has the challenge of reframing the social structure so that young people can grasp, feel, and attach new meaning to their roles. Reitzes and Mutran (1994) propose that roles link individuals with the social and material resources of social groups and institutions and thereby provide these individuals with external sources of rewards and opportunities. Reitzes and Mutran also note that roles provide individuals with an internal framework on which to develop a sense of meaning, purpose, and agency.

National HRD policies and strategies in Belize are multipronged, but HRD efforts have to remain at the grassroots level with performance perspective in the backdrop. The focus has to be on social justice, poverty alleviation, and access to quality health care, as well as the education of the poor, the indigenous, women, and the young. Although there are more demands for results and accountability, the performance perspective of HRD is minimal in the overall implementation of public and private HRD strategies.

Mexico

The story of HRD in Mexico has to be told in tandem with that of the industrialization, which happened there in the years 1930–1958. Mexico undertook a process of industrialization based on import substitution. After 1930, it consolidated the existence of national companies based on the use of national resources and emerging national companies for the generation of productive chains. The expropriation of oil in 1938 meant for Mexico a break with the US as the technology resource. This resulted in an economic mess whose correction was subsequently reflected in the consolidation of the Mexico oil system. From 1946 to 1958, the industrialization process was reorganized and included the petrochemical, pharmaceutical, cosmetics, automotive, household appliances, and light electrical machinery industries. Also, there was a more active participation of foreign capital, particularly in the form of direct foreign investment (Ángeles and Rangel, 1996).

However, in 1958–1970 the presence of foreign capital began to reduce in response to tighter state control. So the government began a new phase of industrialization in the economic history of Mexico, and although questions arose about the effective contribution of foreign capital to the technological progress of a society, the lack of progress was directly linked to the inadequate education system. The problem, however, still remains of the absence of an education strategy as a significant component of the industrialization policy. (Fonseca, 1994).

With the development of the capital goods industry from 1970 to 1980, the process of import substitution developed along with the new oil production. The opening of international credit attracted a high flow of currency, which later resulted in the dismantling of Mexican industry. Debt became the most serious consequence of the eighties. It forced a new direction in economic policy, resulting in a change in strategy that created a greater openness to international trade. The application of adjustment policies and trade liberalization countered inflation and promoted political change. This change also boosted foreign investment and reduced tariffs on imports of capital goods. This marked the beginning of a new policy aimed at linking the country to foreign markets, a short-lived move because the policy did not address international competition (Ángeles and Rangel, 1996).

At the end of the '90s, industrial policy remained unclear, but an interest in HRD resumed with "the consideration of labor competencies and the performance evaluation of individuals and workgroups linked to process certification and organizational processes" (Brown, Rangel, & Cassa, 2015, p. 429). This interest in HRD, however, is challenged by the persistent limitations in the technological and economic infrastructure. Approximately 90% of companies, for example, qualify as small and medium, curtailing their ability to effectively develop a competitive workforce. In many ways, to this day, HRD efforts in Mexico remain laissez-faire. The lack of a clear industrial policy does not help to effectively align a strategic national HRD policy.

HRD AND ENTERPRISE IN LATIN AMERICA

Throughout Latin America, HRD at the enterprise level is more similar than dissimilar. Most companies are small and medium-sized enterprises (SMEs). These SMEs are limited by their technology, finance, and human resources. Although SMEs account for around 99% of businesses and employ around 67% of employees, they contribute relatively little to GDP, which reflects their low levels of productivity (OECD, 2013). Whereas only about 10% of Latin American SMEs engage in export activities, 40% of European SMEs do so (OECD, 2013). In addition, these SMEs are primarily heterogeneous; this means their business models range from mere trade to microenterprise to innovative company exporting services or products. This heterogeneity limits collaborations and partnerships across the region (OECD, 2013).

These SMEs live within countries where HRD is discussed and practiced within the context of HRM. This means that HRD falls within the nonstrategic to strategic continuum. The SMEs also operate within countries where social and economic challenges persist. The governments are challenged by gender and indigenous inequality, by limited access to education, structural poverty, and by limited technological infrastructure, to name a few. These challenges are the fundamentals that SMEs depend on to effectively compete globally.

As mentioned earlier, Mexican companies apply a laissez-faire approach to HRD due to the lack of a strong economic policy that speaks specifically to human resource development as a core strategy. Interestingly, in Belize, most of the companies are family owned and are also limited by archaic economic perspectives on HRD. Consequently, HRD practices are basic and operate in silos or are nonexistent. Colombia, Argentina, and Costa Rica, on the hand, have benefited from foreign investment. Foreign companies such as Standard Oil and Nestlé in Colombia and Intel in Costa Rica have played a major role in influencing the HRD practices within the private and public sectors in their respective countries. Peru, Nicaragua, and Bolivia have also benefited from foreign companies, although to a lesser degree than Colombia, Argentina, and Costa Rica.

The evolution of HRS at the enterprise level parallels the growth of SMEs and competitiveness in Latin America. This means that HRD is still being defined in concept and practice by its dependence on the broader development in the respective countries. Whereas this dependence is inevitable, SMEs have the potential to redirect and accelerate HRD practices, and in so doing, they assist with the social and economic challenges faced by these Latin American countries. For example, OECD (2013) reported that 75.9% of the people employed in SMEs in Latin America had not completed secondary school. SMEs, with the appropriate policies and incentives, such as the tax credit for training in Argentina, have the potential to lead HRD efforts that can accelerate capacity building, structural change, and economic development.

THE GENERAL VOCATIONAL AND EDUCATIONAL FOUNDATION FOR HRD

Given the critical perspectives of HRD in Latin America, technical-vocational education training (TVET) is direly necessary to increase employment rates, to meet labor market needs, and to provide education access to the disadvantaged and at risk populations. The World Bank report autored by Ferreira, Messina, Rigolini, Lopez, Calva, Lugo & Vakis (2013) showed that for the first time, more people in Latin America were part of the middle class than living in poverty. Despite this improvement, however, approximately 80 million people still live in extreme poverty, half of which exists in Brazil and Mexico. Chile, Colombia, Costa Rica, and Peru were cited as the top middle-class advocates (Ferreira et al., 2013). This poverty to middle-class continuum is the result of an increased focus on improved quality of and access to education and support systems. Latin Americans are spending more time in the classroom, an average of eight year versus five years a few years ago (Ferreira et all., 2013).

The first technical and vocational institutions were introduced in South America in the early twentieth century through the adaptation of the Spanish '*escuela de artes y oficios*' or school of arts and trades, which has a long tradition in Argentina, Brazil, Colombia, Chile, Peru, and Uruguay (Salazar, 2005; Sánchez, 2007; Orellana, 2013). Today TVET is influenced by French 'instituts universitaires de technologie', American community colleges, and the Australian Technical and Further Education (TAFE) system (Bernasconi, 2006; Ruiz, 2009; Orellana, 2013). In Latin America, TVET has two disciplines: one that awards a secondary school diploma and prepares students for university, although not all attend and the other that prepares students for work (De Moura Castro, Carnoy, & Wolff, 2000; Briasco, 2010). TVET has two components: technical education (TE) and vocational training (VT), designed as two different programs and operating separately.

Historically, technical education (TE) has always been aligned with the Ministries of Education and Labor and designed to assist in meeting market labor needs, preparing students for employment. It was conceived as a subsystem forming part of the secondary education program but also offered technical qualifications in the different market sectors. The structure adopted a Taylor-Ford style of organization (De Moura Castro, Carnoy, & Wolff, 2000; Briasco, 2010). On the other hand, VT, defined in its origins as a final training system for workers, is characterized by three distinctive elements: (a) independence from the regular education system; (b) flexibility, establishing it as a non-formal system of education; and (c) tripartite governance (the state, business, and workers), although this is the result of an initiative from the state. Moreover, the program was centralized in large decision-making and implementing organizations and is known as the 'S and I' system (De Moura Castro, Carnoy, & Wolff, 2000; Briasco, 2010). The following paragraphs describe TVET in Argentina, Colombia, Belize, and Costa Rica.

Argentina

Gallart (1986) noted that the evolution of technical education in Argentina has not been so much a process of 'vocationalization' of academic education as a process of 'secondarization' of vocational education. Argentine technical schools are the product of a process of amalgamation of terminal trade schools, vocational schools, and industrial technological school. This has resulted in an educational system with a dual purpose (to foster mobility toward higher education and to teach vocational skills) and in a nonintegrated curriculum. This amalgamation was necessary due to mass enrollment and massive diversification of private and public institutions of both university and non-university types in the 1960s and 1970s (Marquis and Martinez, 1992; Orellana, 2013).

In the 1990's the enrollment and diversification trend continued; quality, however, was becoming an obvious problem (Orellana, 2013). In addition, technical schools and vocational training centers along with other secondary schools were transferred to provinces, Briasco, 2010). Briasco also notes that during this period, the Federal Education Law 24.195/93 changed the education system, from seven years at primary school and five in general secondary school or six in technical school to a structure where primary education lasted for nine years and secondary or poly-modal education for three years. A technical qualification was obtained following the poly-modal education system, with vocational technical an extra-curricular option. The introduction of this reform led to a high level of fragmentation in the TVET program (Briasco, 2010).

The focus of the non-university sector institutions moved from teacher training to tourism management, computer science and trade. In recent years these institutions have seen the greatest growth and have shifted to offering short technical programs that align with labor market needs (Villanueva, 2007; Orellana, 2013). In 2005, the Ministry of Education instituted new framework agreement for the humanities, and for the social and technical-vocational areas of the so-called 'non-university sector' to safeguard quality, diversification and alignment with market needs.

According to Orellanna (2013)

> the agreement established an institutional and organizational structure for the non-university sector consisting of guidelines for planning the offer, institutional development and management. It moreover laid down criteria for curricular organization, including definitions of institutional target groups, professional profiles and occupational areas, types of qualifications, and program lengths.

Quoting from the agreement text itself, Orellana (2013) describes the new order:

> the subsystem [is] composed of non-university higher education institutions devoted to teacher training and artistic, humanistic, social and technical-professional (vocational) education. It has the following basic functions: to provide training for teachers at the non-university levels of the education system; to provide comprehensive advanced scientific and technological training; and to provide training in humanistic social and technical-vocational fields related to local and national culture and production with a view to raising living standards.

Briasco (2010) argues that

> the new law established that the secondary-level TVET study program should last for a minimum of six years and be structured according to the criteria adopted by each province. In addition, it created the National Fund for Technical and Vocational Education, which guarantees the investment required to improving the quality of institutions. The funds are awarded as the improvement plans presented by the respective institutions are approved.

Colombia

The National System of Education for Work (El Sistema Nacional de Formación para el Trabajo) (SNFT) was established by SENA (UNESCO-UNEVOC, 2013). The National System of Education for Work is defined as a structure that oversees and combines companies, associations, educational, and technological development centers, technical and professional educational institutions, and the state. Its purpose is to define and implement policies and strategies for the continuing development and qualification of the national workforce (UNESCO-UNEVOC, 2013).

The SNFT consists of three subsystems that provide for the following:

- Standardization of work competencies
- Evaluation and certification of work competencies
- Establishing an education system based on work competencies

SENA provides free comprehensive training and is self-funded by levy contributions from companies (Briasco, 2010; UNESCO-UNEVOC, 2013). Companies benefit at all technological levels from an extensive infrastructure of laboratories and workshops. The board of directors and technical committee of its training centers include employers and trade unions. Labor market trends are continuously analyzed and training is aligned with the production sector (UNESCO-UNEVOC, 2013).

SENA is decentralized and serves approximately 43 regions within Colombia (SENA Website, 2014). It offers programs organized in four semesters. Upon completion of the full four semesters, a graduate is awarded a qualification in arts and business, which is equal to the bachelor's degree. Those completing a minimum of one year of the full four-semester program are awarded a certificate of occupational skills. Graduates with the qualification in arts and business may apply for further studies in technical-professional institutions of higher education (UNESCO-UNEVOC, 2013).

It should be noted that secondary education is either academic or technical, leading to the baccalaureate, and is not compulsory. It is directed at 16- and 17-year-olds and offers two levels of training: Grade 10 and Grade 11. The academic program is aimed at providing more detailed studies in a specified field of the sciences, arts, and humanities; the technical program prepares students for employment in one of the production or service sectors (Briasco, 2010).

SENA plays a major role in TVET, although secondary education and higher education institutions also provide training for work in Colombia (Briasco, 2010; UNESCO-UNEVOC 2013). Higher education in the field of TVET is provided by technical-professional institutions that offer programs of two to three years, which lead to the qualification of 'professional technician' in a given occupation. TVET programs in universities or technological schools last for three years and lead to a qualification in a respective occupation (UNESCO-UNEVOC, 2013).

Belize

In comparison with Argentina and Colombia, Belize's TVET efforts are in their infancy. The Education Act (1990), amended in 2000, stipulated the establishment of the National Council for Technical and Vocational Education and Training. It outlined its composition, general functions, and the governance of the TVET Council Schedule. The Education and Training Act (2010) stipulated the establishment of the National Council for Technical and Vocational Education and Training (UNESCO-UNEVOC, 2013). TVET is affiliated to the Ministry of Education, Youth, and Sports and the Ministry of Labor and is funded by the government. TVET aims to improve quality and relevance of technical and vocational education and training so that more graduates can gain access to appropriate employment. The provision of TVET remains problematic, and despite substantial investment, increase in enrollment has been disappointing. The four centers established in 2001 have seen no increase in enrollment, according to the Belize Education Sector (Strategy 2011–2016, 2012). TVET is perceived as inferior and is not aligned with the secondary or junior colleges. The inferior perspective of TVET is connected to the subsector's lack of integration with secondary education and the prevalent and persistent view that TVET options are for the less academically inclined student who must opt for TVET as a last resort, having failed to secure a place in a junior college or in regular secondary school. The government of Belize has made TVET enrollment a priority and recently implemented a marketing campaign to boost enrollment. This campaign is funded by CARICOM Education for Employment (News 5, 2014). In addition, the government, per the Education Sector Strategy 2011–2016, has listed changes with a view to increasing enrollment at six institutes of technical and vocational education and training (ITVET). In addition, the government is focused on improving coordination and collaboration between high schools, continuing education programs, and ITVET.

It is evident that much needs to be done for TVET to be successful and for it to have an impact on workforce development and economic prosperity in Belize. The changes proposed, especially those of formal and non-formal integrations with secondary and tertiary institutions, are important to TVET access, perceived value, quality, and usability. All the changes proposed by the government are in alignment with changes that other TVET programs in the region have undergone in their pursuit of social, educational, economic, cultural, and technical development.

Costa Rica

Technical and vocational education and training is divided into the formal and non-formal sector in a similar way to Argentina and Colombia. The formal TVET initiative is embedded in the education system and controlled by secondary academic colleges (academic study centers for advancement within the formal system) and professional technical colleges, which offer the chance to get a diploma as a 'medium technic' with the mention of the specialty followed. This is called third-cycle and diversified education (tercer ciclo y educación diversificada) and is composed of different specialties, such as agricultural, industrial, commercial, secretarial, accounting, crafts, family, and social education (UNESCO-UNEVOC, 2012).

The non-formal TVET initiative is developed at a national level through the national INA and its regional centers. The National Institute of Apprenticeship (Instituto Nacional de Apprendizaje, INA) is autonomous and acts as one of the main TVET bodies in Costa Rica (UNESCO-UNEVOC, 2012). Zuniga (2010) notes that before the creation of the INA, vocational learning in Costa Rica was initiated by religious organizations, various social groups, individual or business willingness but was not long lasting. When private initiatives arose, like commercial branches, the work was uncoordinated and there was no state control. Zuniga added that the deciding factor for the emergence of the INA was the pursuit of an innovative institutional plan to solve the need of high-level technical quality labor with the utmost urgency, with a view to initiating the industrialization process. INA's regional centers are divided into the following sectors: agricultural, food industry, crafts processes, graphic industry, fisheries, textile and industrial clothing, materials technology, car mechanics, electricity, metal and trade and services (UNESCO-UNEVOC, 2012).

The INA Certification Service sets tests and examinations related to the technical-professional specialty to be certified and formally recognizes knowledge and skills (UNESCO-UNEVOC, 2012; INA Website, 2014). INA's mission is to provide for people over 15 years old, with all citizens being legally entitled to avail of their vocational training programs, and thereby promote productive work in all sectors of the economy and contribute to the improvement of living conditions and the socioeconomic development of the country (Zuniga 2010; INA Website, 2014).

According to the Law of 1965, funding of the INA is achieved in the following way (INA Website, 2014):

- All companies engaged in industrial, commercial, mining, or service activities that have the capital of no less than 50,000 Costa Rican colons and employ at least ten workers, pay 1% of their total payroll to the budget of the INA.
- The government contributes 1,000,000 colons annually to the budget of the INA.
- The government contributes the annual sum of 500,000 colons intended for the needs of Vocational Colleges under the Ministry of Public Education.
- Additional income may come from donations, subsidies, service charges, etc.

The 1993 Law on financing and development of technical and professional education in Costa Rica decrees that the financing of technical and professional education is distributed to administrative boards of TVET institutions and amounts to 5% of the annual budget of the INA. The funds are taken from the accumulated budget surplus of the INA or, when it is not available, from the INA's annual income (UNESCO-UNEVOC, 2012). The mission and vision of TVET in Costa Rica has changed over the last 48 years. This change is reflected in and aligned to Costa Rica's economic and industrialization journey. Today, TVET continues to evolve through INA's Institutional Strategic Plan 2011–2016.

Mexico

The structure of education in Mexico is as follows: a) preschool education, b) primary education, c) secondary education, d) indigenous education, e) compensatory programs, f) adult education, g) upper secondary education, h) higher education, and i) special education (SEP, 2000).

The 2013 Current Education Act addresses issues pertaining to students, teachers, and parents; educational authorities; teacher professional service; plans, programs, methods, and educational materials; educational institutions of the state and its decentralized agencies; private institutions authorized or official certification of studies; higher education institutions to which the law grants autonomy; educational evaluation; educational information system and management; and educational infrastructure (DOF, 2013).

Generally in Mexico, the vocational approach is not aligned to developing a global workforce. The relationship between the education institutions and the private sector is not results oriented. Despite good intentions, society remains unclear about the benefits of vocational education. As a result of new policies and economic needs, from the late '40s, education policy was oriented to limiting the social character of education to its mere 'technical' function. That meant technical education ceased to be an instrument to prepare a proletariat, as the intellectual approach had tried to in the 1930s, but rather to become an instrument to prepare staff to establish functional and complementary links between workers and the private sector (Ángeles and Rangel, 1996). However, the correspondence between education and work failed to establish that linkage directly, especially because the government kept responsibility for defining the functionality of the education system, despite the pressures from business sectors.

In the late forties, as a result of the enrollment in Mexico City's Regional Technology Institutes (TI), the National Politechnic Institute (IPN) emerged and was integrated into the structure of the Ministry of Education (SEP). During the period 1955–1970, training centers for work were established throughout the country; the government also set up the Center for Research and Advanced Studies (CINVESTAV), and for the first time, IPN had the largest number of technical staff and researchers.

During the seventies, the technological education system was extended to multiply and diversify the number and type of colleges and high schools.

At the high school level, two basic forms of training were identified: the 'terminal' (vocational) and the 'bivalent', which prepared students for a professional career.

Higher education in the '90s saw the development of technological education at the national level, including TI and IPN. In 2005, the national education system was restructured at all levels; TI and IPN were integrated and became the Department of Higher Education (SES), called the Directorate General of Higher Education Technology (DGEST). According to a campaign promise made by the current president of Mexico, Mr. Enrique Peña Nieto, the Directorate General of Higher Education Technology ceased to exist, which consequently gave rise to the creation of a decentralized agency of the Ministry of Education called Mexico National Technology (DOF, 2014). Mexico National Technology is responsible for overseeing the development of competitive human resources for the industrial sector and overseeing the inclusion of engineering and of science and technology programs in universities. In addition, Mexico National Technology works with other levels of education, especially high school, to contribute to the development of the workforce.

DISCUSSION

In Latin America, it is clear that HRD efforts remain fragmented, and their primary outcomes are alleviating poverty, hunger, and increasing access to and quality of education and health care. Human resource development also reflects the economic development of the region and formal and non-formal education and training strategies and programs. Weller (2008) notes that the generation of skills and knowledge plays a vital role in economic, political, and social contexts and discourse in Latin America. Brazil, Colombia, and Honduras rank as the worst on inequality and access to education in Latin America (Maellen, 2013). In Peru, as in many other countries, severe horizontal inequalities persist between indigenous populations and those of European descent (Cortina, 2010). Peru is not the only country with very high levels of economic inequality, but it does have the highest social inequality in the world, which is strongly reflected in social exclusion of minorities. Indigenous women, in particular, have experienced significant exclusion from the education system. Most women in indigenous communities endure long-term unemployment, work in part-time jobs or low-paid occupations, and experience wage discrimination when they do work (Cortina, 2010).

The alignment between HRD and economic development remains fragile, although countries such as Mexico, Colombia, and Argentina, which are among the largest economies in the region, strive to compete globally. Access to employment is largely limited by the number and size of companies. Foreign rather than local companies lead the way when it comes to strategic workforce development. Local companies do not always have the resource bandwidth to champion HRD efforts. In addition, the different political ideologies portray differing attitudes toward HRD. Presently, Venezuela, for example, has a grim economic outlook, and embedded within this chaos is the deterioration and underutilization of a skilled workforce.

In the theory of development (endogenous growth, human capital, social cohesion, widening and deepening participation in democracy) and also in development policy (Millennium Development Goals), it is recognized that skills generation plays a key role. The application of HRD in the region underscores both the critical and performance lenses. In cases such as Belize, Peru, Honduras, and Nicaragua, the critical perspective stands out.

CONCLUSION

If systemic HRD change is to occur in Latin America, we must address leadership and culture. At the national level, Latin Americans are proud of their heritage and culture. The core values at the regional level are relationship, status, hierarchy, and religion. Although the family is considered the foundation of society in Latin America, Chile, and Argentina, for example, also value individualism and risk taking. These core values work for and against HRD.

Given the strong relationship-based culture, voting is not always a critical decision. A vote can be an ancestral decision, meaning that you vote as did your parents. This means that government officials are not always elected based on competence but on relationship. For leaders to become knowledgeable about HRD contributions to social and economic development, government leaders need to be coached so that they can envision the multiple futures of human resource development in the region. If government leaders understand HRD, the probability is high that they will consider and include HRD in the abundance of policies and decisions that they will make throughout the course of their years of elected office.

HRD needs government leaders who are transparent and who will act with consistent advocacy, not just tactically. The development of such leadership is pivotal for HRD's future and success in Latin America, because the government is HRD's primary change agent. Leadership development, regardless of political ideology, must be continuous, because governments change. And as such, HRD efforts risk being discontinued. Gropello (2006) cautioned that consistent policies for secondary education, for example, are important so they strengthen and complement, rather than undermine, one another. Like secondary education, TVET suffers from discontinuous efforts. The United Nations Economic and Social Council (2010) noted:

> . . . despite recent efforts to link together existing institutions, the TVET sector remains very poorly articulated; there are significant

differences in approach and distances between for the formal education system, the professional training system, and institutions in the production sector. Policies and programs are often discontinuous, beset with duplications, and lacking in relevance for young people's entry into the workforce.

Given this tenuous context, in the absence of knowledge, skills, and values about HRD, government leaders may continue to dismiss and mismanage HRD efforts and alter the progressive course toward social and economic development in their respective countries.

The region overall is slowly moving toward meeting the 2015 goals based on the UN MDG Progress Report (2010) for Latin America and the Caribbean. For example, with regard to achieving full and productive employment and decent work for all, the report notes that from 1990 to 2008, the indicators have evolved relatively well, although the low productivity growth and structural heterogeneity in the region have impeded real wages and income distribution from improving sustainably (UN MDG Progress Report, 2010). The report also indicates that the region has made significant progress in terms of coverage and access of education. Most countries have registration rates close to or over 90%, similar to developed countries. However, there is still much to do in coverage and quality of high school education (UN MDG Progress Report, 2010).

This chapter remains one story in the pluralistic discourse regarding HRD in Latin America. It is limited by the fact that it does not explicitly detail every HRD effort or program in all countries of the region. It is also limited by its sources, primarily international organizations such as UN, UNESCO, PAHO, and UNDP and government strategy documents. Nevertheless, the chapter sheds light on HRD's constitution, challenges, and opportunities.

In conclusion, it has to be reiterated that the primary stakeholders and shareholders of HRD in Latin America are individual governments. While the private sector plays a role in developing HRD at the level of enterprise, its success completely depends on government efforts to sustain it and to keep it competitive and relevant. Consequently, HRD in Latin America is about leaders and policy makers making conscious efforts to enhance HRD in any strategy, process, program, or activity intricately tied to the alleviation of poverty and hunger, access to quality education, access to quality health care, and gender and ethnic equality.

REFERENCES

(ADRHA) Asociación De Recursos Humanos de la Argentina (2014). ¿Que es ADRHA? Accessed 10 March 2014. (http://www.adrha.org.ar/quienes-somos/)

Aldao-Zapiola, C. (2014). A century of human resource management in Argentina. In B. E. Kaufmann (Ed.), *In the Development of Human Resource Management across Nations: Unity and Diversity*, 21–45. UK: Edgar Elgar Publishing Limited.

Ángeles, Ofelia, & Ernesto, Rangel (1996). Formación de Recursos Humanos en Corea del Sur, Taiwan y México. Comercio Exterior Vol. 46, NUM. 12, Mexico, Diciembre de 1996. Retrieved from (http://revistas.bancomext.gob.mx/rce/magazines/329/3/RCE3.pdf)

Belize Education Sector Strategy 2011–2016. (2012). Government of Belise Ministry of Education and Youth Policy and Planning Unit. Retrieved from (http://www.moe.gov.bz/index.php/belize-education-sector-strategy)

Bernasconi, A. (2006). Donde no somos tigres. Problemas de la formación técnica en Chile en el contexto latinoamericano. Expansiva, 72, 1–24. Retrieved from (http://www.oei.es/etp/problemas_formacion_tecnica_chile.pdf)

Braisco, I. (Ed). (2010). *Trends in Technical and Vocational Education and Training in Latin America.* Paris, France: IIEP-UNESCO.

Brown, T, C., Rangel, Delgado, J. E., & Bronwyn, C. (2015). HRD in North America. In R. F. Poell, T. S. Rocco and G. L. Roth (Eds.), *The Routledge Companion to Human Resource Development*, 425–435. London: Routledge

Cortina, R. (2010). Gender equality in education: GTZ and indigenous communities in Peru. *Development*, 53(4): 529–534.

DANE (National Department of Statistics. (2004). Balance of the evolution of the Colombian Labor Market in the fourth quarter of 2003. Accessed 11 November 2014 (http://www.dane.gov.co/inf_est/empleo.htm)

De Moura, Castro, C., Carnoy, M., & Wolff, L. (2000). *Secondary Schools and the Transition to Work in Latin America and the Caribbean.* Sustainable Development Department, Inter-American Development Bank, Washington DC Retrieved from Eric Database (ED474307)

De Moura, Castro, C., Navarro, J. C., Wolff, L., & Carnoy, M. (2000). *Reforming Primary and Secondary Education in Latin America and Caribbean: An IDB Strategy.* Sustainable Development Department, Inter-American Development Bank, Washington DC Retrieved from Eric Database, (ED474669).

Diario Oficial de la Federación DOF. (2013). Ley General de Educación. México. Retrieved from (http://dof.gob.mx/nota_detalle.php?codigo=5313841&fecha=11/09/2013)

Diario Oficial de la Federación DOF (2014). Decreto que crea el Tecnológico Nacional de México DOF : 23/07/2014. Retrieved (http://www.dof.gob.mx/nota_detalle.php?codigo=5353459&fecha=23/07/2014)

Ferreira, F. H., Messina, J., Rigolini, J., López-Calva, L. F., Lugo, M. A., Vakis, R., & Ló, L. F. (2012). *Economic Mobility and the Rise of the Latin American Middle Class.* World Bank-free PDF. Retrieved from (https://openknowledge.worldbank.org/bitstream/handle/10986/11858/9780821396346.pdf?sequence=5)

Filder, R. (2013). Evo Morales historic speech at the Isla del Sol. Retrieved from (http://lifeonleft.blogspot.com/2013/01/evo-morales-historic-speech-at-isla-del.html)

Fonseca, M. A. (1994). Política de industrialización y crisis en México (1930–1970), in América Saldívar et al., *Estructura económica y social de México*, Textos Universitarios, Ediciones Quinto Sol, México.

Franklin, Stephen. (2013). *Death Stalks Colombia's Unions.* Retrieved from (http://pulitzercenter.org/projects/south-america-colombia-labor-union-human-rights-judicial-government-corruption-paramilitary-drug-violence-education)

Gallart, M. A. (1986). *The Secondarization of Technical Education in Argentina and the Professionalization of Secondary Education in Brazil in a Comparative Perspective.* Vocationalising Education Conference. London, England. Retrieved from Eric Database, (ED280971).

Gonzalo, S. (2014). *Afl-Cio Report Exposes Persistent Violence against Colombian Trade Unionists.* Retrieved from (http://www.aflcio.org/Press-Room/Press-Releases/AFL-CIO-Colombia-Unions-Condemn-Colombia-s-Labor-Action-Plan-73-Colombian-Trade-Unionists-Murdered-since-the-Plan-Went-into-Effect)

Government of Belize, Ministry of Finance and Economic Development. (2013). *Millennium development goals report and post 2015 agenda: Belize 2013*. United Nations Development Programme in Belize. Accessed 24 January 2014. (http://www.bz.undp.org/content/belize/en/home/library/mdg/publication_31.html)

Gropello, E. D. (2006). Meeting the Challenges of Secondary Education in Latin America and South East Asia. The International Bank for Reconstruction and Development. London: The World Bank.

Hanratty, D. M., & Meditz, S. W. (1988). *History of Colombia*. Retrieved from (http://countrystudies.us/colombia/)

ILO. (2010). *A Skilled Workforce for Strong, Sustainable and Balanced Growth: A G20 Training Strategy*. Retrieved from (http://www.ilo.org/skills/pubs/WCMS_151966/lang—en/index.htm)

INA Website. (2014). Instituto Nacional de Aprendizaje. Retrieved from (http://www.ina.ac.cr/)

Izecson de Carvalho, A., Looi, Y., Saad, F., & Sinatra, J. (2013). *Education in Colombia: Is There a role for the Private Sector*. Retrieved from (http://knowledge.wharton.upenn.edu/article/education-in-colombia-is-there-a-role-for-the-private-sector/)

Kennedy, J. (2011). Evo morales and the global economy: Sustainable development in Bolivia. *Latin American Studies*, 39(1): 151.

Lucero, P. M., & Spinel, F. (2002). Estudio sobre la estructura y necesidades de capacitació'n en la corporació'n industrial "Las granjas" de Bogota´ [Study of the structure and necessities in the industrial corporation "Las granjas" in Bogota´], unpublished thesis in Business Administration, Universidad de los Andes, Bogota´.

Mallen, P. R. (2013). Latin America's inequality is improving. The US is the most unequal country in the west. *International Business Times*. Retrieved from (http://www.ibtimes.com/latin-americas-inequality-improving-usis-most-unequal-country-west-1278679)

Mallen. P. R. (2014). *Colombia Surpasses Argentina as Latin America's Third-Largest Economy Due to Inflation, Currency Changes and GDP Growth*. Retrieved from (http://www.ibtimes.com/colombia-surpasses-argentina-latin-americas-third-largest-economy-due-inflation-currency-changes-gdp)

Marquis, C., & Martínez, L. (1992). Universidade e Integraçao No Cone Sul. Porto Alegre: Editora da Universidade.

MDG Progress Reports: Latin America and Caribbean. (2010). Retrieved from (http://www.undp.org/content/undp/en/home/librarypage/mdg/mdg-reports/lac-collection.html)

Ministerio de Salud De El Salvador. (2010). *Situacion de los Recursos Humanos en Salud en El Salvador*. PAHO, San Salvador. Retrieved from (http://new.paho.org/hq/dmdocuments/2010/RH_ELS_EstudiodeCaso_Taller_ELS_mayo2010.pdf)

National Development Framework for Belize 2010-2030. Accessed 29 January 2014. (http://www.cdn.gov.bz/belize.gov.bz/images/documents/NATIONAL%20DEVELOPMENT%20FRAMEWORK%202010-2030%20USER%20FRIENDLY%20VERSION.pdf)

OECD Development Center (2012). *Attracting knowledge-intensive FDI to Costa Rica: Challenges and policy options*. OECD Development Centre. Accessed 29 January 2014. (http://www.oecd.org/countries/costarica/E-book%20FDI%20to%20Costa%20Rica.pdf)

OECD Development Center (2013). *Latin American Economic Outlook 2013: SME Policies for Structural Change*. Retrieved (http://www.oecd.org/dev/americas/)

OECD Investment Policy Review (2013). Accessed 29 January 2014. (http://www.oecd.org/daf/inv/investment-policy/costa-rica-investment-policy-review.htm)

Ogliastri, E., Ruiz, J., & Martínez, I. (2005). Human Resource Management in Colombia. In A. Dávila and M. Elvira (Eds.), *Managing Human Resources in Latin America*, 165–178. London: Routledge.

Orellana, N. (2013). *Diversity between Higher Education Institutions: The Cases of Argentina, Chile and Uruguay.* Retrieved from (http://www.guninetwork.org/resources/he-articles/diversity-between-higher-education-institutions-the-cases-of-argentina-chile-and-uruguay). Accessed October, 2013.

Plan nacional de desarrollo humano 2012–2016 (2012) Nicaragua. Retrieved from (http://www.ni.undp.org/content/nicaragua/es/home/library/mdg/publication_1.html)

Reitzes, D. C., & Mutran, E. J. (1994). Multiple roles and identities: Factors influencing self-esteem among middle-aged working men and women. *Social Psychology Quarterly*, 313–325.

Rodríguez-Clare, A. (2001). Costa Rica's development strategy based on human capital and technology: How it got there, the impact of Intel, and lessons for other countries. *Journal of Human Development*, 2(2): 311–324.

Rogers, T. (2013). Nicaragua ratifies ALBA 'fair treaty'. *The Nicaragua Dispatch*. Retrieved from (http://nicaraguadispatch.com/2013/04/nicaragua-ratifies-alba-fair-trade-treaty/)

Ruiz, E. (2009). Advanced university technicians: Educational differentiation, social stratification and labor segmentation. *Revista Mexicana de Sociología*, 71(3): 557–584.

Salazar, J. (2005). *Estudio sobre la Educación Superior No Universitaria en Chile.* Santiago de Chile: IESALC/UNESCO. Retrieved from (http://unesdoc.unesco.org/images/0014/001404/140427s.pdf)

Sánchez, J. (2007). De las escuelas de artes y oficios a la Universidad obrera nacional: Estado, elites y educación técnica en Argentina, 1914–1955. *Cuadernos del Instituto Antonio de Nebrija de Estudios sobre la Universidad*, 10(1): 269–299.

SENA Website. (2014). Sistema Nacional de Formación por el Trabajo. Enfoque Colombiano. Bogota: SENA Retrieved from (http://www.sena.edu.co/Paginas/Inicio.aspx)

SEP. (2000). La estructura del sistema educativo Mexicano. Dirección general de acreditación, incorporación y revalidación. unidad de planeación y evaluación de políticas educativas, Retrieved from (http://www.sep.gob.mx/work/models/sep1/Resource/1447/1/images/sistemaedumex09_01.pdf)

Talleri, V. A., Llinas-Audet, X., & Escardíbul, J. (2012). International briefing 27: Training and
development in Peru/International. *Journal of Training and Development*, 17(1): 61–75.

UNESCO. (2012). EFA Global Monitoring Report. *Youth and Skills: Putting Education to Work.* Retrieved from (http://unesdoc.unesco.org/images/0021/002180/218003e.pdf)

UNESCO-UNEVOC. (2012). *TVET in Chile.* Retrieved from (http://www.unevoc.unesco.org/worldtvetdatabase1.php?ct=CHL)

UNESCO-UNEVOC. (2012). *TVET in Costa Rica.* Retrieved from website (http://www.unevoc.unesco.org/worldtvetdatabase1.php?ct=CRI)

UNESCO-UNEVOC. (2013). *TVET in Belize.* Retrieved from (http://www.unevoc.unesco.org/worldtvetdatabase.php)

UNESCO-UNEVOC. (2013). *TVET in Colombia.* Retrieved from (http://www.unevoc.unesco.org/worldtvetdatabase1.php?ct=COL)

UNESCO-UNEVOC. (2013). *TVET in Paraguay.* Retrieved from website (http://www.unevoc.unesco.org/worldtvetdatabase1.php?ct=PRY)

United Nations Economic and Social Council. (2010). *Challenges for Education with Equity in Latin America and the Caribbean.* United Nations. Retrieved from (http://www.un.org/en/ecosoc/newfunct/pdf/6.challenges.for.education.with.equity.web.pdf)

Villanueva, E. (2007). Transnational commercial provision of higher education: The case of Argentina. In M. Martin (Ed.), *Cross-Border Higher Education: Regulation, Quality Assurance and Impact*, 7–119. Argentina, Kenya, Russia. Paris: UNESCO.

Weller, J. (2008). The recent economic, political and social context of education and training for work in the region. In C. Jacinto and J. Sassera (Eds.), *The Role of International Cooperation in Education and Training for Work in Latin America*, 13–14. The International Labor Organization. Retrieved from (http://www. norrag.org/fileadmin/Working_Group/Paper13.pdf)

Workforce. (2020). *Building a Strategic Workforce for the Future*. Retrieved from (http://www.oxfordeconomics.com/workforce2020)

12 Human Resource Development in Brazil

Renato Ferreira Leitão Azevedo,
Alexandre Ardichvili, Silvia Casa Nova,
and Edgard B. Cornacchione Jr.

INTRODUCTION

With a population of more than 202 million and a territory of 8,515,767 sq km, Brazil is the fifth-most populous country in the world. Its economy, at Purchasing Power Parity, has a GDP of $3.073 trillion and is the seventh largest (CIA, 2015). Brazil is one of the world's largest exporters of commodities and agricultural products and has diversified into robust industry sectors as well.

As noted by Griesse (2007), the intersections of geography with economic, political, and sociological factors form a mosaic of conditions for people to live and work in. Each country in South America is unique and Brazil presents a particularly distinctive country within the region thereby calling for specific attention in reviewing Human Resource Development (HRD) in the region. First of all, unlike the majority of the countries of the continent, Brazil was colonized by Portugal, not by Spain, and therefore, Portuguese is the official language, not Spanish. Second, from a racial point of view, Brazil is one of the most diverse nations on Earth: whites comprise only 53.7% of the population, whereas the mulatto (mixed white and black) population accounts for 38.5% and blacks for 6.2%. There are also large Japanese, Lebanese, Korean, and Chinese diaspora and a substantial group of Amerindian descendants. Third, in terms of its economy, Brazil is much more influential than any of its neighbors because of its large internal markets and its booming trade in commodities, mostly destined for the fast-growing Chinese economy (Kingstone, 2012; Hirst and Lima, 2015).

In terms of human capital development, Brazil's Human Development Index of 0.73 puts it into the category of countries with high HDI (UNDP, 2013). Data from the OECD (2013) show that Brazil has a highly favorable employment picture overall: it has one of the highest employment rates for the population aged 25–54 (76.9%) and one of the lowest unemployment rates among the total labor force (6.7%). On the other hand, 14% of the youths of 14 to 19 years of age are neither enrolled in any educational institutions nor employed, and this percentage rises to 23.3% for youths between 20 and 24 years of age (OECD, 2009). Only 10% of the Brazilians have higher education and 32% of the undergraduate students are functionally illiterate, yet the country has large numbers of young people following business-related careers, getting proper education, and moving up the social ladder (Azevedo, 2013).

This chapter starts with an overview of Brazil's culture and sociopolitical environment with a description of their impact on HRD. Further, a separate section is devoted to a discussion of the educational system (including K–12, vocational, and higher education) as the basis of HRD. Next, we discuss the institutions responsible for HRD, including government, employer bodies, labor unions, and NGOs. As part of this overview, we consider government legislation, policy context, and other actions aimed at increasing the quality of education in general and focused on improving HRD in the country. We also cover enterprise-level HRD programs. The concluding section presents our reflections on the current state and possible future trajectories of HRD in Brazil and the implications of this analysis for business and human development policies.

THE CULTURAL, SOCIOPOLITICAL, AND INSTITUTIONAL BACKGROUND

In cultural terms, what has had the greatest impact on the business environment in Brazil is *jeitinho*, explained by Tanure and Duarte (2005, 2026) as "a middle path between what is allowed by numerous laws and regulations, and what is practically possible and makes sense". This middle path emerges as an adaptation mechanism, which allows both businesses and private individuals to function despite cumbersome legislative systems, massive bureaucracy, hierarchical management, and an oligarchic economy dominated by powerful interest groups (Ardichvili et al., 2013). Amado and Brasil (1991, p. 53) viewed *jeitinho*, "as a hermeneutic key for the Brazilian culture" and "a special way of managing obstacles in order to find a way out of bureaucracy". Amado and Brasil (1991, p. 10) defined *jeitinho* as "a rapid, improvised, creative response to a law, rule, or custom that on its face prevents someone from doing something". *Jeitinho* cannot be reduced to just an illegal or immoral practice; rather, it serves as an example of a practice in a society that values human relationships, where the special way of managing obstacles out of the constraints is based on networking and the development of genuinely warm interpersonal relations.

In addition to *jeitinho*, Brazilian workplace culture is also characterized by: (a) paternalism, which is defined as a dyadic relationship between superiors and their subordinates in which superiors provide protection and guidance in exchange for loyalty and deference on the part of subordinates (Kjellin and Nilstun, 1993); (b) power concentration based on networks of personal relationships between executives and top managers; (c) the loyalty of employees to peers and leaders; and (d) flexibility in work arrangements. As a consequence, organizational cultures are based, as a rule, on the preference for reducing conflict and enhancing social cohesion. Employees are expected to demonstrate unconditional loyalty to leaders; the leaders, on the other hand, are expected to care for the well-being of group members. However, as pointed out by Ardichvili et al. (2012), this web of reciprocal obligations can lead to both positive and negative outcomes. On the positive side, it can result in high performance on the part of individual employees, if they are loyal to the group and to the leader. On the other hand, such loyalty is associated with fear of making a mistake and, in so doing, hurting the whole group, thus leading to a lack of initiative and autonomy thereby reducing creativity and innovation.

To understand the roots of the aforementioned cultural traits, we need to refer to Page (1995), who describes the historical factors that shape the Brazilian socioeconomic system and explain how paternalism, power concentration, and flexibility as described earlier serve to make a pathway for business. On the one hand, the Portuguese rulers of the colonial period created a rigid and cumbersome bureaucracy. On the other hand, because the colony was too large to control from the center (and separated from Lisbon by a vast ocean), local authorities developed a "cavalier attitude toward legality that still exists today" (1995, 124). *Jeitinho*, as a way of life, was a result of the attempt to satisfy the dictates of bureaucratic rules while still finding ways to accomplish business (and personal) goals (Ardichvili et al., 2012).

When considering the socio-cultural background for HRD in Brazil, it is important to recognize that the history of labor includes a legacy of coercion and slavery and that the country's cultural heritage includes customs and values brought not only by immigrants from Portugal and other European countries but also by millions of slaves, forcefully relocated there from Africa. It also incorporates strong influences from the cultures of dispossessed native Indians. Furthermore, Brazilian society carries as a persistent part of its social structure significant income disparity and concentration of wealth in the hands of a small portion of the population. According to Griesse (2007), Brazil is among ten countries in the world with the greatest disparity in wealth distribution. The country is rich in natural resources and has experienced a succession of booms, triggered by the discoveries of new sources of wealth, from earlier cycles of sugarcane, gold, coffee, and rubber, to the more recent production and export of soybeans, iron ore, chemicals, oil, fuels, food and beverages, aeronautics, and transportation materials (Baer, 2008; Mueller and Baer, 1998, p. 1995). Each one of these booms has created new waves of powerful dynasties that control a disproportionate share of the country's wealth.

In terms of its more recent history, the period from 1930 to 1945 (the Vargas Era) was very important in terms of the government's influence on the development of labor markets and the emergence of the HR systems.

This era was characterized by strong state intervention in labor relations with the creation of the Ministry of Labor and the Consolidation of Labor Laws (CLT—*Consolidação das Leis do Trabalho*. During this period, the government kept a tight grip on the population, but also as first steps toward industrialization created the first steelwork, developed the mining industries, and built large seaports, thus providing new employment opportunities for large numbers from low-income groups.

The post–World War II period was highly turbulent, with five different presidents holding office between 1946 and 1964 and then a long period of military government (1964–1985). Juscelino Kubitschek's (JK) government from 1956–1961 was one of the most important. His economic policies created a strong manufacturing base and opened the country to multinationals, especially in the automotive industry. These multinationals in turn contributed significantly to the development of human resources, as they brought to the country the traditional North American model.

Any analysis of Brazil's sociopolitical realities needs to take into account the fact that the country is a relatively young but vibrant democracy. The democratic reforms started only after the end of the military dictatorship in 1985. During the dictatorship, political dialogue was repressed and many intellectuals left the country. Soon after the end of the dictatorship, the constitution of 1988 was crafted (Constituição-Cidadã). It must be noted that until the end of the 1980s, the Brazilian economy was highly regulated and shielded from global competition by the protectionist policies of the military government. After liberalization, Brazil suffered from hyperinflation and many of the other economic problems common to Latin American countries. President Fernando Henrique Cardoso (FHC) was elected in 1994 in part because, as Minister of Finance in the former administration, he had created an economic plan that brought the hyperinflation from 2000% down to less than 20%. Cardoso privatized some large state-owned companies and used some of the funds to implement desperately needed social reforms, especially in education.

Government policies to encourage the development of new technologies and new industries required better-educated workers. The model of a small, highly educated elite and uneducated masses proved inadequate to coping with the labor demands of a country opening itself to world trade and competition. The growing demand for social mobility through education and dissatisfaction with the levels of corruption and taxation in the country led eventually in 2013 to protests at a level never before observed in Brazil, a clear signal for change. Ignited by a reaction against high public transportation fares in large cities and the confusion over increasing public spending on the eve of the 2014 FIFA World Cup (along with the lack of effective policies in other areas such as health and education), Brazilian citizens started to voice their opinions as a group and in very specific ways (Saad-Filho, 2013). The protests continued in 2015, mainly in major cities, bringing to the streets a different group of protesters with different demographics and with a more conservative agenda. Political analysts affirm that Brazil is facing a political polarization, with a clash of interests between the working classes and some sectors of the upper and middle classes. On the other hand, many agree that the country is embracing the need for political reform. That could allow the replacement of oligarchical political groups (referred to earlier as political dynasties) by more progressive and technocratic political representatives.

THE EDUCATIONAL FOUNDATION FOR HRD

The biggest current challenge for education and HRD in Brazil is to raise the level of functional literacy and professional preparation of its citizens to a level high enough to enable them to take commerce and industry to competitive levels on the global market (UNESCO, 2009). In the last five decades, the country has made significant progress in developing its educational system. However, Brazil stands at the lower end of the scale with respect to levels of literacy and educational attainment when compared with other large emerging economies, such as Mexico, China, Russia, and India (OECD, 2013).

The history of the federal education system of Brazil can be traced back to 1930, when the federal Ministry of Education and Culture (MEC) was created. At about the same time, education for children aged seven to ten was made universal and mandatory (Schwartzman, 2004). The MEC established a curriculum for high schools as a preparation for college, although few students were able to reach high school. In an economy based on raw materials and commodities, very few employers believed that the majority of students needed any more than a few years of limited practical education. In the 1950s, 64% of Brazilians lived in rural areas and over 50% were illiterate. During the subsequent 50 years, the population of the country nearly quadrupled, with many moving from rural to urban areas, but the pace of improvement of the quality of education was inadequate. It was not until 1972 that MEC expanded mandatory education to include children from 7 to 14 years of age.

The election of Cardoso as president of Brazil set the stage for a radical change in education policy. In 1996, the Law of Directives and Bases of National Education (LDB) was developed with the involvement of professional educators and other stakeholders. It clarified the roles of municipal, state, and federal education systems. The federal government had the responsibility of overseeing the entire education system; and the states were responsible for the quality of education in each state. Because school principalships were traditionally a political appointment awarded regardless of educational expertise, the LDB called for the democratization of school governance, including involvement of the community in the election of principals. The law also provided schools with greater autonomy by decentralizing funding and decision making, by making curricula more flexible and by encouraging higher teacher qualifications.

In 1996, the Constitutional Amendment, No. 14, created the Fund for Primary Education Administration and Development and for the Enhancement of Teacher Status, or FUNDEF (Fundo de Manutenção e Desenvolvimento do Ensino Fundamental e de Valorização do Magistério). This fund was a major step toward a more equitable distribution of state and municipal tax funds. It replaced a population density formula that left the majority of funds in large cities, leaving little funding for smaller municipalities and their schools. With the addition of federal funding for resource-poor states, FUNDEF raised all elementary schools to minimum per-pupil allocations. With additional funds, states in the north and northeast regions could expand their school offerings and move toward universal elementary education. In addition, the federal government provided R$1 billion (Brazilian real) to support high schools by compensating the poorest states for their contribution to FUNDEF. With assistance from the Inter-American Development Bank (IDB), the Cardoso administration created the Program for Improvement and Expansion in High School (Programa de Melhoria e Expansão no Ensino Médio—Promed), a R$850 million fund from which grants were given to states to support high school education.

As a way toward increasing the quality of education at the various levels, the government implemented general examinations for those completing secondary and tertiary education. On the secondary level, the Brazilian National High School Examination (ENEM—Exame Nacional do Ensino Médio) was established in 1998 aiming "to assess student performance at the end of the basic school cycle, to assess core competencies necessary to the full exercise of citizenship" (INEP, 2013). Year after year since then, ENEM has grown in relevancy and scale, becoming the main entrance examination to higher education and the main access point to scholarships granted by the Federal Program 'University for All' (PROUNI—Programa Universidade para Todos) (Schwartzman, 2010).

The Brazilian Nationwide Postsecondary Student Evaluation System (ENADE—Exame Nacional de Desempenho de Estudantes) is a part of the National System of Higher Education Evaluation (Sinaes—Sistema Nacional de Avaliação da Educação Superior), which was established in 2004. A large-scale examination is applied for both first-year and graduating students of all three-year programs with the aim of assessing students' knowledge, skills, and competencies.

The other important social policy implemented in the early 2000s was the *Bolsa Escola* (School Allowance), introduced in April 2001 (Glewwe and Kassouf, 2012). *Bolsa Escola* added stipends for children to encourage higher enrollment and attendance in schools where attendance was the lowest. The combination of the *Bolsa Escola* and FUNDEF has made high school education a priority on both the supply and the demand sides.

In 2004, the government of President Luiz Inácio Lula da Silva (known as Lula) amalgamated the *Bolsa Escola* program and a number of conditional cash transfers for health and nutrition into one program, *Bolsa Família* (Family Allowance), which offers cash payments to parents. At the same time, the government increased federal expenditures on this program from R$314 million in 2006 to R$4.5 billion in 2009. While this increase may be seen as a positive trend, the government has removed the important requirement of school attendance for receiving the funds. Therefore, *Bolsa Família* is seen as creating some collateral effects, and it has also been criticized for reaching mostly cities governed by mayors from Lula's party (PT—Workers Party). Despite its shortcomings, this program (along with higher minimum wages) has helped shift 40 million people out of the lowest-income level category.

One of the key problems of the Brazilian education system is the quality of training of its 1.5 million teachers. The size of the country and regional inequalities in levels of development lead to significant regional differences in the quality of teachers' education. In many areas of the country, schoolteachers have only had high school education themselves, and even at the higher education level, many faculty members at federal universities do not hold doctoral degrees. Working conditions for teachers in most cases includes teaching two shifts a day, often in different schools. The majority of teen and older students have to work during the daytime and so reserve evenings for their formal education. Teacher absenteeism is high, partly because of the difficulties of getting from one school to the other, especially in big cities with heavy traffic or along rural roads.

There are also differences in the quality of education between public and private schools, the latter offering much better education as the Brazilian National High School Examination (ENEM), conducted in 2011, revealed. The ranking of the ENEM assessment shows that the average test score, achieved by students in private schools was 569.2 points, whereas students in public schools had an average score of only 474.2. Among the top-100 schools, only ten are public (two state and eight federal schools).

This discrepancy between private and public results in inequality, which persists beyond the high school level into working life. Students from families with upper- and middle-class income tend to study at private schools and receive better quality education; consequently, they are able to enter high-quality public universities through the competitive *Vestibular* (the Brazilian entrance exams for higher education).

The public universities in Brazil are fully supported by government funding and are legally forbidden to charge tuition, to raise private funds, or even receive donations. Private institutions, with very few exceptions, cannot receive government subsidies and depend on tuition to survive. Because public universities attract the best-qualified students, typically coming from richer families who can afford private high schools, private higher education institutions, with rare exceptions, find themselves catering to low-income families who cannot pay much.

In Brazil, law, medicine, and engineering colleges have existed since 1822. The first state-owned university, the University of São Paulo, was established in 1934. In 1937, several colleges came together in Rio de Janeiro as the first federal university in the country. Higher education institutions (HEIs) run by the federal government, as well as those created by private initiative, are regulated and supervised by MEC. The National System for the Evaluation of Higher Education (SINAES) periodically assesses students, degree programs, and institutions, the results of which serves as the basic yardstick for the regulation and supervision of MEC (INEP, 2013).

Comparing data on graduate education in various countries, we conclude that the Brazilian graduate education system is highly competitive on the international higher education scene. Brazil is one of the ten countries that granted the largest number of PhDs in the world in 2004 (Centro de Gestão e Estudos Estratégicos, 2008). The Brazilian government considers graduate education as 'the jewel in the crown' of its educational system and has invested heavily in various graduate-level programs over the last 10 to 15 years.

As an example, one of the priority initiatives of the current president, Dilma Rousseff, was a massive effort called Science Without Borders (Ciência sem Fronteiras), which includes undergraduate, graduate, and post-doctoral scholarships for study abroad, programs to attract foreign scientists to the country, and programs for professional and technical qualification development. The program has the goal of promoting the consolidation and expansion of science, technology, and innovation in Brazil by means of international exchange and mobility. According to the Science Without Borders website, it aims to increase the presence of students, scientists, and industry personnel from Brazil in international institutions of excellence; to encourage young talent and highly qualified researchers from aboard to work with local researchers on joint projects; and to encourage the internationalization of universities and research centers in Brazil by the establishment of partnerships with foreign institutions of higher learning (Ciência sem Fronteiras, 2013).

According to Cornacchione, HRD in higher education programs is not yet clearly established as a separate field of scholarship, although HRD is taught as part of many business degree programs under headings such as 'people management', 'talent management', or 'organizational behavior'(Azevedo, 2013). In addition, topics that would be typically classified as HRD (e.g., career development) are covered in various programs in departments of psychology and colleges of education.

THE GOVERNMENTAL INSTITUTIONS WITH RESPONSIBILITY FOR HRD

The Vargas Era (1930 to 1945) saw the birth of the first professional training centers and the establishment of vocational courses in public schools in 1938. In 1942, the National Industrial Learning Center (SENAI) was created, and it still plays an important role in the training of professional technicians for manufacturing firms. Following SENAI, in 1946, the National Service for Commercial Learning (SENAC) was created with the goal of preparing young apprentices to enter the job market. The creation of the Social Service for the Industry (SESI), also in 1946, generated a network of nationwide private institutions with the goal of promoting social well-being, cultural development, and improvements in the quality of life of manufacturing workers, their families, and the communities in which they lived. Also in 1946, President Eurico Gaspar Dutra authorized the National Confederation of Trade to create the National Service of Trade (SESC), offering the same benefits as SESI but this time to workers in the business world.

During the military dictatorship (1964 to 1985), the Brazilian economy was largely closed to multinationals and to foreign technologies. Labor unions were suppressed. In addition to a growing supply of cheap labor, due to the natural increase in the fertility rate and the influx to the cities of unemployed people from rural areas, wages froze and HR focused on cost reduction and on combating low productivity. On the positive side, 1960 and 1970 saw the emergence of federal technical schools, which had high standards of education and were able to provide big private and state-owned enterprises with trained employees for highly skilled jobs. In 1972, the Brazilian Small and Medium Company Support Service (SEBRAE) was created, boosting national entrepreneurship.

ENTERPRISE-LEVEL HRD IN BRAZIL: EVOLUTION AND CURRENT CHALLENGES

The rise of importance of HRD in Brazil can be traced to the 1980s, when the military dictatorship came to an end. During the dictatorship, the state controlled and regulated labor relations, leaving little opportunity for HRD. Labor syndicates were closely supervised and elections of employee representatives monitored and manipulated by the state. The net result of all this was low wages and a high turnover of the workforce. The models for industrial organization and management of work were Taylorism and Fordism (Tonelli et al., 2003). According to Lacombe and Bendassolli (2004), during the military regime, HR management was carried out through the Departments of Personnel (DP). This model depended on paternalistic authority and authoritarianism on the part of managers, on the one hand, and obedience and docility of low-skilled employees, on the other. This system assumed that managing people is the same as managing any other resource. Of course, the HR function in large Brazilian companies has gone through a major transformation since the 1980s, yet in many small enterprises or family businesses the old personnel model of HR persists.

In the 1980s, organizations worldwide, in light of growing global competition, began to feel a need to encourage creativity, quality, workplace communication, and cooperation and to reduce absenteeism. In many countries of the developed world, more and more employers started to grant more control and autonomy to workers in the execution of their tasks, utilizing semiautonomous work teams, total quality (TQM) practices, worker participation in planning and coordination of their activities, and flexible work arrangements. In Brazil, these trends took more time to take hold, but since the early 1990s, the economy became more open to outside influences and industry—less protected by the government—which resulted in the introduction of more contemporary HR systems and more flexible labor relations. The management of HR became more decentralized, taking on a role of supporting management's strategies. One exception was the experience of Ricardo Semler, who implemented a radical form of industrial democracy combined with innovative business management policies in his company, fully described by Semco in a best-seller book *Virando a prórpia mesa* (meaning *Turning Your Own Table* and published in English as *Maverick*).

The publication of ABTD's (Brazilian Training & Development Association) *Training and Development Manual* in 1980 made this a landmark year in the field of training & development (T&D) in Brazil. The manual brought together 32 articles from various researchers and professionals grouped into seven sections: the role of T&D; the training process; training methods, techniques, and resources; the clients of T&D; workforce forming systems; training and its relationship with like procedures; and the general aspects of training. The second edition of the manual was published in 1994 (Boog, 1995). An additional impetus for the legitimation of HRD as an area of work and research was provided in the mid–1980s when Rio de Janeiro hosted Brazil's first worldwide T&D convention.

In the 2000s, increased technological progress and globalization have enabled the rise of individualism and competition and also led to the emergence of virtual companies, requiring the development of multiskilled professionals and further decentralization of HRM. The traditional designation of HR as the 'Personnel Department' was being replaced by various new labels, such as People Management, Talent Management, and Strategic Management of Human Resources. The focus changed to one that saw recruitment and selection, as well as pay and continuous education, as based on the relationship between individual performance and enterprise-level outcomes (Fischer, 2002). These trends led large Brazilian companies to adopt management and HR technologies and approaches, which were popular in other countries, especially in the US.

In recent years, investment in HRD has been steadily growing. For example, in 2013, enterprises intended to invest 14.3% more in T&D compared to the previous year, according to the report "The Portrait of Training in Brazil", published annually by ABTD's T&D Magazine. At the same time, HRD as an area of professional practice and as a subject of research has not yet assumed the same important role as in North America or in some European countries. Whereas HRD is present in large organizations and also practiced by numerous consultants under various labels (T&D, leadership development, talent management, human capital development, etc.), HRD as an integrated system combining T&D, OD, career development, management development, and other functions is rarely found and rarely acknowledged as such. In Brazil, the most advanced HRD systems are found, as a rule, in innovative and internationally competitive companies in areas such as aeronautics, banking, petrochemicals, natural gas, mining, steel, paper and pulp, ethanol, and meat production. These companies have a workforce that averages nine years of education, with on-the-job training provided in most cases internally by the employer or supplied by partnerships with higher educational institutions that provide MBA and executive programs (Além and Giambiagi, 2010).

The Brazilian branch of PricewaterhouseCoopers, a multinational consultancy, has conducted research based on in-depth investigations in 36 large companies in a variety of sectors in Brazil in order to understand challenges in human capital and talent retention (PWC, 2011). The CEOs of participating companies reported that they believed the country's educational system was unable to generate the needed talent at the pace required to compete internationally. Interestingly, the major concern about talent shortages was related to companies' inability to find qualified skilled production workers and technicians, not managerial talent or white-collar professional employees (PWC, 2011).

Another important finding of the PWC (2011) study was that three top factors, important for talent attraction and recruitment (based on employees' perceptions), were Work Environment (66%), Learning and Professional Development (65%), and Opportunities for Growth and Career Planning (62%). All three areas are arguably within the writ of HRD. It would make sense, therefore, to coordinate the work of HRD by bringing all these areas under one roof in a single HRD department.

Since the early 2000s, as happened in many countries around the world, large Brazilian firms also started to create corporate universities (CUs) (Alperstedt, 2001). In many cases, corporate universities took over the training and development of employees at all levels. According to recent reports by the Brazilian Association of the Corporate Universities (Associação Brasileira de Educação Corporativa, EDUCOR/Brazil), the industry is still booming (EDUCOR, 2015).

Another trend in HRD is the growing focus on talent management. Attracting talent, stimulating, developing, and maintaining it is becoming an issue of major concern to Brazilian companies. A recent doctoral study with a sample of 541 (mostly large) organizations found that many companies are strategically reorienting their HR efforts toward talent management (Freitag, 2012).

Employment agencies and word of mouth are used for hiring professionals and online services to fill technical, management, and temporary positions. As pointed out by Nery-Kjerfve and McLean (2015), the personality-dominated nature of Brazilian society also often creates a situation in corporations in which managers develop personal relationships with in-group members that go beyond the limits of workspace. It is not uncommon that a manager would have to socialize after work hours, attend their employees' children's parties, and assume that they will protect and guard members of the group from harm (Nery-Kjerfve and McLean, 2015). Organizational development and performance are often hindered by privileging personal ties in lieu of accurate assessment of employee performance.

With respect to work-life balance, Brazil might be described as having a 'work hard, play hard' culture. About half of both men and women in the workforce work between 40 and 44 hours per week. Despite the legal maximum of 44 hours, almost 40% of men and 25% of women work more than 45 hours weekly. Brazilians value work, but they also value family and leisure time. During the annual Carnival period and the FIFA World Cup (every four years), work can effectively come to a halt. Spontaneous national holidays may be declared as the Brazil team advances toward the finals of the World Cup. Companies often create lounge spaces for the employees to watch the games together in the office. There is a 50% premium for overtime, although some collective bargaining agreements require overtime pay up to 100% on normal work days and up to 200% for weekends or holidays. Trade unions have resisted platforms supporting flexible work arrangements in favor of reduced work hours (Sorj, 2003).

Acknowledging the need for increased investment in HRD and, at the same time, realizing that a massive investment, required to compete in the global economy, may be beyond the means of most individual companies, most forward looking Brazilian business organizations enter into partnerships focused on human capital development of whole industry sectors. A number of the country's productive sectors of the economy have created the so-called 'S-Systems', which focus on the formation and qualification of workers in respective sectors. These entities are privately owned, non-profit, legal entities, and they count on the support of SEBRAE; SENAI; SENAC; SENAR and SENAT (same as SENAC but to rural and transport workers); SESI; SESC; SEST (same as SESI and SESC but to transport workers); SESCOOP (National Cooperative Learning Service), which provides development to cooperatives and professional development to their members; and IEL (Euvaldo Lodi Institute, Instituto Euvaldo Lodi), which provides business training and supports industrial research and technological advancement.

DISCUSSION

Despite significant progress made over the past decade, Brazil still needs to overcome numerous challenges in the areas of general education, vocational education, and enterprise-level HRD if it is to develop human resources capable of competing on the global market. K–12 education has moved to a more universal approach (with about 60 million students enrolled annually) but still faces challenges associated with inadequate investment in the infrastructure, quality of teacher preparation, and regional disparities.

At the same time, the country has a number of significant advantages it can capitalize on. First, unlike most developing countries and large emerging economies, Brazil is characterized by a favorable demographic situation, with an expanding rather than a shrinking workforce pool. Second, the country's strong export-oriented industry and agriculture, coupled with huge reserves of natural resources, can provide the necessary financial basis for investment in education and HRD for years to come. Third, the generally positive and collaborative nature of human relations in Brazil makes it one of the most diverse and tolerant societies of the world. As a fourth advantage, Brazil has great geographic diversity, with abundant and varied natural resources and ecosystems. As such, Brazil has the potential to contribute to HRD with new models of sustainability that take into account not only the profit considerations but also the needs of the people and the planet (the so-called 'triple bottom line'). The fifth advantage that could further enable the development of HRD in Brazil is the robustness of Brazilian higher education, not only in size but also in quality. Brazil has numerous well-funded federal and state universities, producing large numbers of high-quality graduates in critical areas of engineering, math, and sciences.

Tanure and Duarte (2005) have demonstrated how a large Brazilian company has successfully utilized a combination of uniquely Brazilian cultural traits such as flexibility, creativity, power concentration, importance of personal relationships, and innovative managerial institutional arrangements to create an effective system of HR management and an organizational culture that is both effective and humane at the same time. Therefore, instead of trying to borrow HRD models from developed countries, Brazilian business organizations and educators could try to understand what could be uniquely Brazilian approaches to developing its workforce and talent.

While this chapter focused mostly on the role of the government, educational institutions, and of business organizations, in recent years, there has been a growing discussion of alternative ways of providing services needed to secure a high quality of life and work for citizens. Recent massive protests and national debates about the future development of the country are driven, in large part, by the widespread perception in Brazil that the government is not able to provide the necessary conditions for further development of the welfare of its citizens; meanwhile, corruption reveals the severe contradictions of a very rich country that wastes public resources.

Also, as a result of these protests, there is a growing realization of the urgency of political reform. In recent years, companies, civil organizations, and various state agencies have been forging new groups and alliances in order to offer new models of cooperation. The mantra of *Cidadania* (citizenship) increasingly guides the discourse on civil rights and participation in

Brazil. The success of this discourse will involve the development of the necessary institutions, procedures, and systems, both formally and culturally, that will allow for the full participation of all citizens in national and local affairs and will strengthen the space for political debate, collective decision making, and the fight against corruption. Part of this transformation is further development of the so-called *terceiro setor* (third sector), which involves cooperative arrangements and the creation of private initiatives through which industry can invest in social programs. It goes without saying that HRD, considered in its entirety, not only at the level of companies but also at the national level and at the local and community levels, has a major role to play in this massive transformation.

CONCLUSION

As pointed out by Cornacchione (Azevedo, 2013), Brazil can contribute to the development of HRD in Latin America and beyond as a country that has a unique combination of such socioeconomic factors as a large dynamic economy, cultural diversity, a young and fast-growing population, a resilient democracy, abundant natural resources, social cohesion, large internal markets, favorable for foreign investment policies, a highly developed financial infrastructure, and geographic diversity.

REFERENCES

Além, A. C., & Giambiagi, F. (2010). *O BNDES em um Brasil em transição*. BNDES. Online. Available (http://www.bndes.gov.br/SiteBNDES/export/sites/default/bndes_pt/Galerias/Arquivos/conhecimento/livro_brasil_em_transicao/brasil_em_transicao_completo.pdf) Accessed October 10, 2013.

Alperstedt, C. (2001). 'Universidades corporativas: discussão e proposta de uma definição',

Amado, G., & Brasil, H. V. (1991). Organizational behaviors and cultural context: The Brazilian 'Jeitinho'. *International Studies of Management and Organization*, 21(3): 38–61.

Ardichvili, A., Jondle, D., Wiley, J., Cornacchione, E., Li, J., & Thakadipuram, T. (2013). Building ethical business cultures: BRIC by BRIC. *The European Business Review*, March–April, 2013. Retrieved from: http://www.europeanbusinessreview.com/?p=2215

Ardichvili, A., Zavyalova, E. and Minina, V. (2012) 'Human capital development: comparative analysis of BRICs', *European Journal of Training and Development*, 36(2): 213–33.

Azevedo, R. F. L. (2013). Renato F. L. Azevedo, A conversation with Edgard Cornacchione: understanding the HRD field in Brazil through his lens and perspectives, Human Resource Development International, 16(2), 220–235.

Baer, W. (2008). *The Brazilian Economy: Growth and Development*. (6th ed.). Boulder, CO: Lynne Rienner.

Boog, G. G. (1995). Manual de treinamento e desenvolvimento. São Paulo: Makron Books do Brasil.

Centro de Gestão e Estudos Estratégicos (2008). *Características do emprego dos doutores brasileiros: Características do emprego formal no ano de 2004 das pessoas que obtiveram título de doutorado no Brasil no período 1996–2003*. Brasília. Online. Available (http://www.inovacao.unicamp.br/report/inte_relatorio-doutores080825.pdf) Accessed November 10, 2013.

CIA. (2015). *The World Factbook, 2014–15*. Washington, DC: Central Intelligence Agency.

Ciência sem fronteiras (2013). Online. Available at: (http://www.cienciasemfronteiras.gov.br/web/csf/o-programa) Accessed 10 November 2013.

EDUCOR. (2015). Práticas de Educação Corporativa. Available at: (http://www.educor.desenvolvimento.gov.br/universidades) Accessed April 29 2015.

Freitag, B. B. (2012). Talentos em gestão e gestão de talentos: análise da literatura acadêmica e de práticas corporativas. Master's Thesis. São Paulo: University of São Paulo.

Glewwe, P., & Kassouf, A. L. (2012). The impact of the Bolsa Escola/Familia conditional cash transfer program on enrollment, drop out rates and grade promotion in Brazil. *Journal of Development Economics*, 97: 505–517.

Griesse, M. A. (2007). The geographic, political, and economic context for corporate social responsibility in Brazil. *Journal of Business Ethics*, 73: 21–37.

Hirst, M., & Lima, M. R. S. (2015). Challenges in Brazilian foreign policy. In J. I. Domingues and A. Covarrubias (Eds.), *Routledge Handbook of Latin America in the World*, 139–152. New York, NY: Routledge.

INEP. (2013). *Instituto Nacional de Estudos e Pesquisas Educacionais Anisio Teixeira*, SINAES. Online. Available (http://portal.inep.gov.br/superior-sinaes) Accessed November 10, 2013.

Kingstone, P. (2012). Brazil's reliance on commodity exports threatens its medium- and long-term growth prospects. *Americas Quarterly*, 6(3): 18.

Kjellin, L. and Nilstun, T. (1993). Medical and social paternalism Regulation of and attitudes towards compulsory psychiatric care. Acta Psychiatrica Scandinavica, 88(6): 415–419.

Lacombe, B. M. B., & Bendassolli, P. F. (2004). Cinco décadas de RH. Fator Humano: GV Executivo, 3 (3): 65-69.

Mueller, C., & Baer, W. (1998). The economy: Historical background and economic growth. In R. Hudson (Ed.), Brazil: A Country Study, 157–208. Washington, DC: Federal Research Division.

Nery-Kjerfve, T., & McLean, G. N. (2015). The view from the crossroads: Brazilian culture and corporate leadership in the twenty-first century. *Human Resource Development International*, 18(1): 24–38.

OECD (2009). OECD Economic Surveys: Brazil 2009, OECD Publishing.

OECD (2013). OECD Economic Surveys: Brazil 2009, OECD Publishing.

Page, J. A. (1995). *The Brazilians*. Reading, MA: Addison-Wiley.

PWC. (2011). Tendências em Capital Humano: Retenção de Talentos, 1-34. São Paulo: PriceWaterhouseCoopers.

Saad, Filho, A. (2013). Mass protests under 'left neoliberalism': Brazil, June-July 2013. *Critical Sociology*, 39(5): 657–69.

Schwartzman, S. (2004). The challenges of education in Brazil. In C. Brock and S. Schwartzman (Eds.), *The Challenges of Education in Brazil. Oxford Studies in Comparative Education*, 1–30. Oxford, UK: Triangle Journals.

Schwartzman, S. (2010). *Benchmarking Secondary Education in Brazil*. Paper prepared for the International Seminar on Best Practices of Secondary Education (idB/oced/Ministry of Education), Brasilia.

Sorj, B. (2003). A luta contra a desigualdade na Sociedade da Informação. 85–92, Rio de Janeiro: Jorge Zahar Ed.; Brasília, DF: Unesco, 2003.

Tanure, B. & Duarte, R. G. (2005). Leveraging competitiveness upon national cultural traits: The management of people in Brazilian companies. *International Journal of Human Resource Management*, 16: 2201–2217.

Tonelli, M., Caldas, M., Lacombe, B., Tinoco, T. (2003). Produção acadêmica em Recursos Humanos no Brasil: 1991-2000. Revista de Administração de Empresas, 43(1): 105–122.

UNESCO. (2009). *Youth and Adult Literacy in Brazil: Lessons from Practice*, UNESCO, Brasilia office. Online. Available (http://unesdoc.unesco.org/images/0016/001626/162640e.pdf) Accessed November 12, 2013.

Central and Eastern Europe, Russia, and the Former Soviet Union

13 Human Resource Development in Central and Eastern Europe (CEE)

Maura Sheehan and Beata Buchelt

INTRODUCTION

Central and Eastern Europe (CEE) is a region that includes the European countries that were under Soviet economic and political influence before 1990 and often referred to as the 'Eastern Bloc'. Since the fall of the Berlin Wall and the collapse of the Soviet Union, the economies of the CEE region have frequently been referred to as in 'transition' and more recently as 'transformed' or 'post-transition'. The 'transition' from state socialism has been viewed as one of the most significant economic, political, and social processes in recent history (McCann and Schwartz, 2006). The CEE region has provided an engine of growth, dynamism, and mobility often lagging in the EU-15 (Ederer, Schuler, & Willms, 2007).

Critical to the transformation of CEE was membership of the EU in the first wave of eight accession countries that joined on May 1, 2004: the Czech Republic, Estonia, Hungary, Latvia, Lithuania, Poland, Slovakia, and Slovenia. The lead-up to European Union membership contributed to additional substantive changes within these countries, especially in terms of their labor markets, including labor mobility and macroeconomic policies. Indeed, for the countries that have joined the EU, according to the World Bank, "the transition [which began in the early 1990s] is over" (World Bank, 2008). This chapter focuses on these eight CEE countries.

Remarkable transformations have taken place over the past quarter century, not only at the level and nature of competition within the region but also in the associated evolution of the role and contribution of the HR function, which includes the increased level of investment in HRD to attract and retain ever-increasingly talented and mobile workers. As of January 1, 2014, there are almost no restrictions on labor mobility within the EU (European Commission, 2014).

Much of this economic growth is attributable to significant flows of foreign direct investment (FDI) into the region, especially post-2004. In the case of Poland and Hungary, the number of FDI projects rose 40% and 38% respectively from 2009 to 2010 (Allen and Overy, 2011). Given that FDI can be so vital to the fortunes of these economies, the progression out of the financial crisis, and the secure employment of thousands of people, there is considerable competition among CEE countries for such investment. In addition to generous tax and capital incentives offered by regions and governments, the level and quality of human capital that investors can avail of through their location decisions provides another key resource that can be leveraged to attract FDI. Given the value of human capital, the importance of HRD for enhancing micro and macrolevel competitiveness is generally well recognized within the region. However, reflecting, at least in part, the historical legacy of socialism/communism in the region, CEE countries still lag behind Western Europe in terms of the use of formal HRM systems and resources targeted at HRD (Cranet, 2011).

The CEE region provides an extremely important example for analyzing the interaction between economic, social, and cultural influences in relation to HRD policies and outcomes. This chapter provides such an analysis in six main sections: Section 1 provides an overview of the history, culture, social, and economic factors that are likely to influence HRD in the region. Section 2 examines the vocational and educational training (VET) systems. Section 3 examines the extent of social cohesion, labor market and business regulation, and the extent of trade union membership in the eight countries. Section 4 utilizes Cranet data on training and development and helps to illustrate how HRD has changed between 2005 and 2011 at the organizational level. Finally, Section 5 provides a discussion on some issues arising, and Section 6 makes some concluding remarks.

CONTEXT OF HRD IN THE REGION

History and Culture

The eight countries in the region have very different historical backgrounds. Each country also has its own language and unique cultural traditions. Given these complex and highly diverse historical contexts, only a brief historical overview is presented. Even though all eight countries were under Soviet influence from the early 1940s until the late 1980s/early 1990s, the degree of influence varies significantly. Estonia, Latvia, and Lithuania became independent from Russia after the First World War but then fell under Russian rule again after World War II and experienced significant reprisals, including mass deportations and substantial repression of language and culture. There was also a large 'plantation' of Russians during the Soviet era, and this legacy continues to have influence today, especially in relation to language and labor market opportunities for the Russian-speaking minorities in these countries. The history and culture of Hungary was heavily influenced by the legacy, until 1918, of being part of the vast Austro-Hungarian Empire; then in 1956, Hungary was the first country to rebel against the Soviet rule and, as a result, economic reforms were introduced as early as

1968. Czechoslovakia was also, until 1918, part of the Austro-Hungarian Empire, then fell under Soviet rule and finally separated peacefully in 1993 into the two independent countries of the Czech Republic and Slovakia. Slovenia was part of the former Yugoslavia, which had a unique relationship with the Soviets, especially under Josip Tito's reign, but was less influenced directly by the Soviets and communism compared with the other countries in the region. Slovenia's move to independence predated by almost one year the Revolutions of 1989 in the rest of the CEE region, and its early years of independence were heavily influenced by tensions arising in the Balkans during this period.

Finally, Poland, perhaps because of the size of its population and a continued strong commitment to Catholicism, even under Soviet rule, experienced very significant repression during the communist period. Student protesters in 1968 and workers who had been shot at in 1970 joined forces in efforts that gave rise to Solidarity, both as a movement and a trade union. After the selection of a Polish Pope in 1978, the emergence of Solidarity—which did not have the backing of the Soviets—led millions of Polish people to emerge from silence, caution, and oppression. Nearly a third of the nation joined Solidarity and hundreds of thousands, mostly young workers, resigned from the Communist Party. Poland gained independence from the Soviets in 1989. It is the sixth most populous member of the EU, as well as being its most populous post-communist member. Since late 2014, the former prime minister of Poland, Donald Tusk, has been president of the influential European Council. Poland was also the only EU country that did not enter into recession during the global and financial crisis of 2007–2008.

Perhaps not surprisingly, given the countries' different and complex histories, culturally they are also very diverse according to Hofstede, using Hofstede and Minkov's (2010) six dimensions of national culture: PDI (power distance), IND (individualism), MAS (extent of masculinity with a lower score indicating a less masculine culture), UAI (uncertainty avoidance), LTO (long-term orientation), and IVR (indulgence vs. restraint) (Hofstede, Hofstede, & Minkov, 2010; see also www.geert-hofstede.com). The variation between the study countries is generally greater than their similarities—for example, Slovakia has an extremely high PDI (100) compared to Estonia (4); and perhaps most striking is Latvia's high degree of femininity/low masculinity (9) compared with Slovakia's score of 100.

It may be expected that both an individual's and a firm's likelihood of investing in HRD would be positively influenced by a long-term orientation (LTO), reflecting that it often takes time to benefit from HRD investment. Estonia and Lithuania both score high on LTO (82), whereas Poland is the lowest (38). Higher levels of restraint compared to indulgence (IVR) is likely to be reflected in the fact that for learners, HRD often requires short-term sacrifice to devote time to training and educational opportunities; so it may be expected that higher levels of restraint will be associated with higher levels of HRD. Latvia has the highest level of restraint (13) and Slovenia the lowest/highest degree of indulgence (48). For individuals, HRD may be a way to reduce uncertainty in terms of the labor market, reflecting that higher levels of human capital should enhance their labor market competitiveness. For firms, the expected relationship with uncertainty avoidance is not clear-cut—HRD always involves some risk due to labor turnover—however, similar to individuals, it raises the firm's level of human capital, which should enhance competitiveness in uncertain and volatile markets. Poland has the highest level of uncertainty avoidance (UAI) (93) and Slovakia the least (51). We now turn to examine broader social and economic indicators.

Society

The basic social indicators that characterize the CEE countries are listed in Table 13.1 below.

Critical for HRD assessment are the academic achievement levels in the various countries. We shall first look at the two 'extremes' of achievement: the population percentage with low academic achievement (i.e., individuals with less than upper secondary studies) and the percentage of university graduates. The ranking of the countries for low achievement is as follows: 1. Hungary (22% of the population has low academic achievement), 2. Slovenia (18.4%), 3. Latvia (16.1%), 4. Poland (15.5%), 5. Slovakia (15.2%), 6. Estonia (15.1%), 7. Lithuania (14.2%), and 8. Czech Republic (only 12.4% of the population have low academic achievement).

The ranking for university graduates is as follows: 1. Czech Republic (only 26.7% of the population have university degrees), 2. Slovakia (26.9%), 3. Hungary (32.3%), 4. Slovenia (40.1%), 5. Poland (40.5%), 6. Latvia (40.7%), 7. Estonia (43.7%), and 8. Lithuania (51.3%, reflecting that more than half the population aged 30–34 are university graduates). In countries where academic achievement is low (e.g., Hungary and Slovenia), firms may need to invest more in HRD so that human capital shortfalls are addressed. In contrast, where academic achievement is high (e.g., Lithuania and Estonia), returns to HRD may be higher because the investment is being made in a higher stock of human capital in the first place (assuming that diminishing returns to HRD investment are not present) and, moreover, there is likely to be considerable competition for talent in countries with high academic achievement and HRD investment is one way to attract and retain scarce talent (Pocztowski and Buchelt, 2008).

While educational attainment rates are important indicators of the stock of human capital in a country, the quality of human capital and the importance that governments afford to education in terms of spending as a percentage of GDP are also important measures in terms of contextualizing potential levels and returns to HRD investment.

Figure 13.1 shows the educational spending as a percentage of GDP (2002–2004). Among CEE countries, Hungary and Slovenia rank highest for education spending as a percent of GDP (6%). The other countries'

Table 13.1 Basic Educational Indicators in CEE

	Czech Republic	Estonia	Hungary	Latvia	Lithuania	Poland	Slovakia	Slovenia
Population with low academic achievement (2014)	12.4%	15.1%	22%	16.1%	14.2%	15.5%	15.2%	18.4%
Upper secondary studies (2014)	68.5%	51.2%	57.7%	57%	54.3%	60.70%	66.70%	56.50%
Tertiary education (2014)	19.1%	33.7%	20.20%	26.90%	31.40%	23.80%	18.1%	25.1%
University graduates, age 30–34 (2013)	26.70%	43.70%	32.30%	40.70%	51.30%	40.50%	26.90%	40.1%

Source: Compiled from Eurostat and World Bank databases (2015)

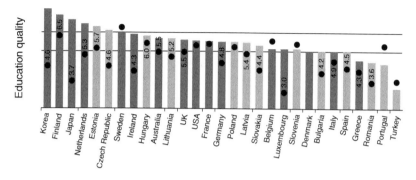

Figure 13.1   Secondary Schooling in CEE

spending is as follows: Poland (5.8%), Estonia (5.7%), Lithuania (5.2%), Czech Republic (4.6%), and Slovakia (4.4%). It therefore appears that Slovenia is actively attempting to improve the quality of secondary schooling, critical for future competitiveness. With the exception of the Czech Republic and Slovakia (both higher), the remaining CEE countries have similar percentage spending on education as the UK (5.5%) and US (5.9). Nevertheless, given the human capital shortfall among many over the age of 35 (see details in the following section), the CEE countries should perhaps significantly increase levels of educational expenditure—targeted at adults—to try to narrow this shortfall in the future.

Figure 13.1 also illustrates the quality of secondary education in CEE countries compared with Western European and other advanced economies (the calculations are based on international comparisons of the Pisa & Timms tests). Using the UK and US as benchmarks, the quality of secondary education in four CEE countries (Estonia, Czech Republic, Hungary, and Lithuania) exceeds that of the benchmarks, whereas four countries fall below (Poland, Latvia, Slovakia, and Slovenia). The poorest performer, Solvenia, with a quality percentage of 86, only lags behind the UK by three percentage points. This analysis shows that there is generally a high level and high quality of human capital in the region for VET and HRD interventions to build upon. However, it is critical that these standards are maintained and enhanced to help contribute to the future competitiveness of the region, especially in terms of remaining attractive to foreign investors.

Economy

Key economic indicators that are of particular relevance to HRD for the CEE countries are presented in Table 13.2.

Long-term unemployment is a significant problem for this region with the majority of countries above the EU average of 44.6% (the two exceptions are Poland at 34.8% and the Czech Republic at 43.4%). In Slovakia,

63.7% of the population is long-term unemployed. The picture is slightly better for youth unemployment, with only four of the eight countries having a rate higher than the EU average of 23.4% in 2013. Government-sponsored HRD investment may be an important policy tool to help reduce unemployment and to ensure that the skills base and competency of the labor force become more competitive (Eichhorst et al., 2014). In terms of income equality/inequality, half of the countries are below the EU average of 30.5 (Slovenia, Slovakia, Czech Republic, and Hungary) and half are above this average (Lithuania, Estonia, Poland, and Latvia, with Latvia having the highest degree of income inequality at 36.03).

This section has highlighted the high level of heterogeneity in terms of history, culture, social, educational, and economic indicators of the eight CEE countries. These differences are perhaps not surprising given their very different histories—for example, the Baltic States only gained independence—and briefly—from Russia in 1918; Hungary and Czechoslovakia were part of the long-established Austro-Hungarian Empire; and Slovakia was part of the former Yugoslavia. Each of the countries had very different experiences during the two world wars and thereafter very different experiences in terms of the influence of the Soviet Union on their respective political and economic systems. Despite these differences, there are four striking similarities: a relatively smooth and peaceful transition to parliamentary democracy during the 1990s; the introduction of significant privatization and pro-market reforms during the 1990s; EU membership since 1 May 2004; continued evidence of economic development, especially a strong track record of attracting FDI, albeit somewhat slowed by the global financial and economic crisis of 2007–2008. These differences and similarities should be carefully considered when analyzing how context is likely to influence HRD patterns in this region.

OVERVIEW OF THE VOCATIONAL EDUCATION AND TRAINING (VET) PROVISION IN THE CEE REGION

The changes in the education and training systems in the region since transition have been substantial. From the central-planning period, these economies inherited a relatively well-developed education system, school enrollment was almost universal (the significant exceptions were Romani children and children with disabilities), and enrollment rates in secondary and tertiary education were well above those in countries with a similar level of economic development (Micklewright, 1999).

Since the start of the transition period in the region, general trends have involved vocational education moving from firms to schools, thus weakening the links between schools and enterprises (Eichhorst et al., 2014). There has also been declining enrollment in vocational and technical schooling, often offset by rising general secondary school participation rates and expanding

Table 13.2 Basic Economic Indicators in CEE

	Czech Republic	Estonia	Hungary	Latvia	Lithuania	Poland	Slovakia	Slovenia
Unemployment (2013)	7%	8.6%	10.2%	11.9%	11.8%	10.3%	14.2%	10.1%
Change in unemployment (2009–2013)	6.7% to 7% +4.48%	13.5% to 8.6% −36.30%	10% to 10.2% +2%	17.5% to 11.9% −32%	13.8% to 11.8% −14.49%	8.1% to 10.3% 27.16%	12.1% to 14.2% 17.36%	5.9% to 10.1% 71.19%
Long-term unemployment (2012)	43.40%	54.10%	46.30%	51.90%	49%	34.80%	63.70%	47.90%
Youth unemployment (2013)	18.9%	18.7%	27.2%	23.2%	21.9%	27.3%	33.7%	21.6%
Public debt (2014)	42.6%	10.6%	76.90%	40%	40.90%	50.10%	53.60%	80.90%
External debt (2014)	−7.1%	NA	57.4%	31.1%	29.2%	20.1%	27%	38.7%
Gini index (2011)	26.39	32.69	28.94	36.03	32.63	32.78	26.58	24.87

Source: Compiled from Eurostat and World Bank databases (2015)

tertiary education (Saar, Unt, & Kogan, 2008). These trends reflect changes to both demand and supply factors. On the supply side, transition saw closure of publicly owned and/or no longer competitive enterprise-based schools, and on the demand side, there was a shift of students into general secondary schools, likely reflecting the view that obtaining a broader education would be more appropriate in market economies (Micklewright, 1999). Prior to transition, vocational schools produced more than 50% of all secondary school graduates in most CEE countries, but during transition, the vocational system collapsed very quickly (Eichhorst et al., 2014). While students left vocational schools in favor of general secondary education, often with the aspiration of pursuing a tertiary degree, employers frequently emphasized that it has become increasingly harder to find graduates with technical skills (Sondergaard and Murthi, 2012). Despite this overall trend toward a school-based system characterized by a clear distinction between education and work, elements of the dual German-influenced system remain visible in the Czech Republic, Hungary, and Slovenia, with some elements still present in Poland and Slovakia (Matkovic, 2008).

There is considerable consensus among authors that the post-transition VET system has severe limitations (e.g., see; Bejakovic, 2004; World Bank, 2005; Bartlett, 2009; Eichhorst et al., 2014), which can be summarized under five points: subject-specific specialization occurs too early; a narrow curriculum focuses too much on subject-specific skills and competencies; VET provision is too highly decentralized and unregulated across government ministries and regions; training systems lack flexibility and are not able to respond to rapidly changing labor market conditions, especially changes arising from the inward flow of FDI; and, finally, there exists a lack of institutional links between schools and employers. Thus there are considerable challenges and opportunities for both governments and employers in relation to future VET and HRD levels and the types of investment in the region. The European Centre for the Development of Vocational Training (Cedefop) data provides a rich source from which to analyze and compare the types and levels of vocational education and training (VET) and lifelong learning in CEE countries.

Table 13.3 shows there is considerable variance in VET across the CEE countries. Incidence and participation are frequently used indicators in continued vocational training (CVT) research and policy analysis. *Incidence* indicates the most fundamental information about whether an enterprise provides CVT at all. This indicator is binary: either a firm provides training or it does not. The *participation* indicator refers to the chances of the workforce receiving employer-provided CVT (see CEDEFOP, 2010 for a detailed methodological discussion of the variables in Table 13.3). CVT that corresponds to training during working hours or being paid for at least partially by the employer (for instance, evening courses) is a critical indicator of HRD interventions.

Table 13.3 VET Scores in CEE Countries in 2010

Indicator Label	Czech Republic	Estonia	Hungary	Latvia	Lithuania	Poland	Slovakia	Slovenia	EU
Employees participating in continued vocational training (CVT)%	61	31	19	24	19	31	44	43	38
Employees participating in on-the-job training (%)	31	14	12	21	25	11	21	25	21
Adults in lifelong learning (%)	–	10.9	2.8	–	4.0	5.3	2.8	16.2	9.1
Enterprises providing training (%)	72	68	49	40	52	22	69	68	66
Innovative enterprises with supportive training practices (%)	47.1	52.6	37.6	35.7	60.6	55.4	61.3	44.4	41.5
Workers helped to improve their work performance by training (%)	86.9	90.7	91.6	94.6	95.3	91.0	88.1	89.2	89.7
Workers with skills matched to their duties (%)	61.4	52.6	47.0	47.2	60.5	59.6	52.4	47.7	55.3

Source: CEDEFOP (2010)

Employee participation in CVT ranges from a high of 61% in the Czech Republic to a low of 19% in Hungary and Lithuania. Of concern is that CVT participation is below the EU average of a 38% participation rate for five of the eight CEE countries (Estonia, Hungary, Latvia, Lithuania, and Poland). In terms of incidence—that is, the percentage of enterprises providing training—the Czech Republic again scores the highest at 72% and Poland the lowest at 22%. Half of the countries in the region score above the EU average of 66% for this measure (the Czech Republic, Estonia, Slovakia, and Slovenia), whereas half are below (Hungary, Latvia, Lithuania, and Poland).

A similar pattern is found for employees participating in on-the-job training. This percentage is again highest in the Czech Republic (31%) and is lowest in Poland (11%). Two CEE countries are at the EU average of 21% participation for this measure (Latvia and Slovakia), three are above (Czech Republic, Lithuania, and Slovenia), and three below (Estonia, Hungary, and Poland).

Given the concern about the human capital shortfall among those aged 35 and older, the percentage of adults participating in lifelong learning is an important indicator. The EU average for this measure is 9.1%. Slovenia is significantly above this average at 16.2%, followed by Estonia at 10.9%. The rates for the other countries in the region where data is available for this measure is quite low: 5.3% in Poland, 4.0% Lithuania, and 2.8% in Hungary and Slovakia.

An encouraging indicator for the region is the results for 'innovative enterprises with supportive training practices'. The EU average for this variable is 41.5% and only two CEE countries (Hungary and Latvia) are below this average. Over 60% of enterprises in Slovakia and Lithuania are providing training to support innovation. Such patterns may help the region to overcome its low rate of innovation as reported by the Community Innovation Surveys (CIS). Potential links between HRD and innovation are considered in the conclusion.

Further encouraging indicators are found in relation to the variable 'workers helped to improve their work by training' with five countries (Estonia, Hungary, Latvia, Lithuania, and Poland) scoring above the EU average of 89.7%. In contrast, in Estonia, Hungary, Latvia, Slovakia, and Slovenia, the response to the question on whether workers' skills were matched with their duties was below the EU average of 55.3%.

This section has shown that there have been significant changes to post-transition VET provision in the region. A general pattern of fragmentation in the provision of VET has emerged that presents challenges for the level and quality of VET services provided. Table 13.3 presents data on different types and levels of VET provision. Of the 54 outcomes where comparisons can be made to overall EU-level data, the CEE countries fall below EU levels in 53.6% of the outcomes (for 26 outcomes, and they are level for 2 other outcomes (3.7%)). Hungary and Latvia lie below the EU average for six out of the seven possible outcomes, whereas the Czech Republic and Slovenia lie above the EU level for five of the seven possible outcomes.

While these first two sections provided context for understanding VET and HRD patterns in the region, no clear trends emerge in terms of academic achievements, quality of education, and the level and nature of VET provision and take-up.

VARIETIES OF CAPITALISM AND HRD SYSTEMS

Whether there is intervention and regulation of a country's VET and HRD systems will be heavily influenced by the Variety of Capitalism (VoC) in which the system operates (Amable, 2003; Hall and Soskice, 2001). Hall and Soskice's (2001) original typologies (e.g., liberal market economies (LMEs), such as the UK and US, or coordinated market economies (CMEs), such as Germany and Japan) are highly appropriate for countries in the CEE region. Knell and Srholec (2007) utilized data from 20 OECD countries and 31 'transition'/'post-socialist' countries (n = 51) over the period of 2001–2004 to examine three modified dimensions of VoC:

- **Social Cohesion:** inequality/equality (Gini coefficient, see Table 13. 2), taxation of income and public spending (highest marginal personal and corporate income tax rate and government final consumption as a percentage of GDP).
- **Labor market regulation:** regulation in relation to hiring and firing employees (cost of, weeks of wages) and rigidity of working hours (index).
- **Business regulation:** barriers to entry (number of start-up procedures to start a business) and exit (time to resolve insolvency), number of procedures to register property, and stock market relative to the banking sector in the financial system.

Table 13.4 indicates that in terms of all four measures of regulation, Slovenia is consistently within the coordinated range and has a GDP at purchasing power parity (PPP) consistently above the average. This would suggest that VET and HRD are likely to be higher and more regulated in Slovenia compared with the other seven countries. Indeed, for VET outcomes (Table 13.3), Slovenia is above the EU level and the second highest (behind Czech Republic). Also, broadly consistent with coordination and regulation, Slovenia has the highest share of public debt (80.9%) and the lowest Gini coefficient (24.87) of all of the countries in the region (Table 13.2). Moreover, broadly consistent with Hofstede's indicators, Slovenia has the lowest score of the eight countries in terms of individualism (27) (the next lowest score is Slovakia's 52).

In terms of HRD, the regulation of labor markets is likely to be important. First, if the cost of hiring and firing employees is high, there should be lower rates of involuntary labor turnover, which should have a positive

Table 13.4   Varieties of Capitalism in Post-Communist/Transitioned Economies

	Liberal	Between the two typologies	Coordinated
Social Cohesion (−6 highest liberal to +6 highest coordinated)	Estonia (highest liberal = −4.5 in region), Hungary, Latvia, Lithuania, Poland, Slovakia [all *below* average GDP per capita, PPP]		Slovenia (+3) [*above* average GDP per capita, PPP]
Labor Market Regulation (−6 highest liberal to +7 highest coordinated)	Slovakia (highest liberal = −4.8 in the region), Czech Republic, Poland [all *below* average GDP per capita, PPP]	Hungary and Lithuania [and *below* average GDP per capita, PPP]	Slovenia (+2) [*above* average GDP per capita, PPP] Estonia and Latvia [and *below* average GDP per capita]
Business Regulation (−7.5 highest liberal to + 6 highest coordinated)	Lithuania (highest liberal = −2.9 in the region), Hungary, Estonia [all *below* average GDP per capita, PPP]	Poland [and *below* average GDP per capita, PPP]	Slovenia (+1.5) [*above* average GDP per capita, PPP] Latvia and Slovakia [and *below* average GDP per capita, PPP]
Overall Index of Coordination (−10 highest liberal to +12 highest coordinated)	Estonia (highest liberal = −5.9 in the region), Lithuania, Hungary, Slovakia, Poland [all *below* average GDP per capita, PPP]		Slovenia (+6.5) [*above* average GDP per capita, PPP] Latvia and Czech Republic [Latvia *below* average GDP per capita, PPP. Czech Republic at *midpoint* between low and high]

Source: Developed from Knell and Srholec's (2007) factor analysis

influence on employer's HRD investment decisions. Second, greater work-ing-hour rigidity means less scope for employers to compete on hourly flexibility, such as zero hours contracts, and should also stimulate HRD investment, reflecting more pressure to compete through the quality of employees. Estonia and Latvia are both at the low end (all under two out of a possible range of seven) of a coordinated labor; and whereas Estonia is higher than the EU average for four of the seven possible VET outcomes (Table 13.2), Latvia is higher for just one outcome. Slovakia, the Czech Republic, and Poland all fall into the liberal spectrum of labor market regulation. Poland and Slovakia are slightly higher than the EU average for three of the seven possible VET outcomes, whereas the Czech Republic is higher for five out of a possible six outcomes (no data are available for lifelong learning) (Table 13.3). No pattern emerges in relation to Hungary and Lithuania that lie between the two typologies (Hungary is higher than the EU average for one outcome only, but Lithuania is higher for four of the seven possible VET outcomes).

Finally, there is considerable debate in the literature about the relationship between trade union density and training and development (Freeman, 2005). Trade unions in the CEE region are quite weak and are highly fragmented, nor have they been actively involved in advocating training for their members (Dimitrina and Vilrokx, 2005). Trade union density varies from a high of 23.12% of the workforce in Slovenia to a low of 6.41% in Estonia (OECD, 2011 and 2012). The fact that Slovenia has the highest rate of trade union density is consistent with its coordinated approach to the management of capitalism. Interestingly, Estonia is the least coordinated in terms of overall coordination of the countries in the region, which is consistent with it having the lowest trade union density for the six countries where data are available. Trade union densities in the remaining four countries (reliable data are not available for Latvia and Lithuania) are as follows: Czech Republic (13.40%), Hungary (10.55%), and Slovakia (16.76%). Trade unions may have scope to advocate greater VET and HRD interventions by both governments and employers, which could also help with their post-transition regeneration efforts.

TRAINING AND DEVELOPMENT WITHIN ORGANIZATIONS

Shifting our focus away from the macrolevel, this section analyzes training and development systems at the level of organizations utilizing data. Cranet is a network of scholars from universities across the world, representing over 40 countries. It conducts a survey of HRM in member countries approximately every four years, inquiring into policies and practices in people management through a series of common questions (see Lazarova, Morley, & Tyson, 2008). The data used for the analysis presented below focus on questions asked about training and development from the 2005 and 2011 surveys for participating CEE countries.

Table 13.5 presents findings from Cranet on the amount of money spent as a percentage of annual payroll costs on training and the number of annual training days various types of employees have undertaken. Only

Table 13.5 Cranet Data—Annual Training Days, 2005 and 2011

Country	Training cost (%) 2005	2011	Management 2005	2011	Professional/Technical 2005	2011	Clerical 2005	2011	Manual 2005	2011	Average, 2011
Czech Republic	2.58	2.04	7.98	8.15	8.0	8.0	3.67	5.35	3.21	3.56	6.26
Estonia	3.55	5.51	8.11	12.66	7.65	13.10	5.88	6.78	4.39	5.11	9.41
Hungary	3.65	4.12	5.75	6.81	5.86	6.63	3.80	3.53	3.62	1.98	4.74
Lithuania	−4.17		−8.17		−10.04		−5.18		−5.37		7.19
Slovakia	2.19	4.83	6.10	10.11	4.94	10.45	4.21	7.10	1.75	5.50	8.29
Slovenia	2.82	3.55	6.72	7.97	6.5	10.45	2.71	3.89	2.75	6.25	7.14
EU Average	2.99	3.72	6.24	7.20	6.22	7.88	4.14	4.71	3.67	4.14	5.98

two countries (Czech Republic and Slovenia) were below the EU average of 3.72%. While training monies spent increased across the EU in this six-year period by 24%, the average increase among the CEE countries with an increase—and data in both periods—was 53.6%. The most significant increases were in Slovakia (120.5%) and Estonia (55.2%).

There is also quite a significant upward trend in terms of average training days across all occupational grades but most significantly for managers, with an increase of 32% for average training days compared to an increase of 15.4% across the EU. Moreover, only one country (Hungary) was below the EU average of 5.98 for overall training days across all occupations in 2011, with Estonia topping this measure at 9.41 days. With the exception of Hungary (primary responsibility has been devolved to line managers), the delivery of training and development is the responsibility of both HR and line managers.

Formally evaluating training and development is critical for assessing whether training budgets have been spent effectively (Cascio and Aguinis, 2005). On average across the EU, just over 50% of Cranet survey organizations evaluated training effectiveness. With the exceptions of Hungary (42.4%) and Lithuania (31.1%), the remaining four CEE countries were above the EU average on this measure, with just over 72% of sample companies in the Czech Republic evaluating training effectiveness. In terms of methods used to formally evaluate training, return of investment is probably the most rigorous, and, again, four CEE countries (the Czech Republic, Estonia, Hungary, and Slovakia) were above the EU average of 15.3% for this measure.

In sum, the analysis of the Cranet data show that most CEE countries have increased their spending and days allocated to training and development, especially for managers. This is an important trend, especially given the severe financial and economic crisis experienced by all of these countries in 2007 and with many still struggling to emerge from pre-crisis levels of economic activity and employment levels. Indeed, it appears that for many companies, sustained investment in training and development can no longer be viewed as a nonessential expenditure and must be retained and even increased to ensure sustained competitiveness, despite a volatile and uncertain macroeconomic environment (similar findings are reported by Cascio, 2014 for the US; Sheehan, 2014 for the Czech Republic, Hungary, and Poland). It also appears that CEE countries are careful in their evaluation of R&D expenditures, which bodes well for sustained efficiencies with this type of expenditure.

DISCUSSION

It is important to emphasize that HRD and HRM are rarely analyzed as separate constructs in CEE countries and are often used interchangeably

(Cseh et al., 2015). This may reflect that North American/Western European HRM has really only been in place for less than 25 years. The HR function in this region has a historical legacy of being limited to executing communist ideology and keeping control over employees through administration and monitoring (Hetrick, 2002). Over the past 25 years, HRM/HRD has undergone three periods of quite profound change. During the first period—the transition period throughout the 1990s—companies in the CEE region struggled to restructure and survive. Commenting on the role of HR managers in the region during transition, Pocztowski (2011) observes that:

> [HR managers] ... acted as forerunners of the new way of thinking about the organization, and they were among the first to implement new solutions. Unfortunately, however, especially in the cases of Polish companies, such changes usually involved large headcount reductions.
> (Pocztowski, 2011, p. 16)

In the second period, at the turn of the century, HR specialists were commonly responsible for HR decentralization as well as social accountability in the business. Other issues that arose at the time were connected with the strategic importance of HRM function and the numerous HR challenges arising from EU candidacy in 2004. It was during this period that HRD began to emerge as a separate function and began to be differentiated by academics and practitioners from HRM. At present, most of the CEE countries are in the third stage, whereby more emphasis is being given to HRD activities to attract and retain talent, especially by MNCs, which have an ever-growing importance in the region. Moreover, as wage rates increase in the post-recovery period and higher value-added companies are attracted into the region, the importance of VET and HRD will continue to increase. Indeed, HRD interventions inherently influence the level and nature of human capital within companies, industries, and countries. The attraction and retention of FDI and a talent pool is inherently linked to a country's and to the region's level and quality of human capital. Given that Central and Eastern European countries fall below the EU-14 average on the human capital index, the contribution of HRD interventions is of particular importance for this region (Ederer, Schuler, & Williams, 2007).

This chapter has presented an overview of the historical, cultural, social, and economic context in which VET and HRD take place in the CEE region, with a focus on the eight countries within this region that joined the EU in 2004. Perhaps the most striking finding was how highly heterogeneous countries within this region are in relation to almost all measures examined. In Section 3, we used the lens of 'Variety of Capitalism' to provide a theoretical underpinning for the patterns found in the first two sections of the chapter. A somewhat consistent story emerges in relation to the theory and the empirical pattern only for Slovenia, which follows a more coordinated approach to regulating labor markets and business and has a higher degree of social cohesion compared with the other countries in the region. This approach is likely to contribute to the higher levels of VET outcomes, human capital endowments, and perhaps the high percentage of manual workers who receive training in Slovenia relative to other countries in the region. Interestingly, it is also the only country in the region that was not under direct Soviet influence, as it was part of the former Yugoslavia, which, under Josip Tito's leadership, pursued a more socialist rather than communist approach to managing institutions and markets. Slovenia also has the highest degree of income equality (lowest Gini coefficient). Section 4 examined HRD at the organizational level; here there is more consistency across the region. In particular, there is an upward trend in training within organizations and also a more rigorous approach being taken in relation to evaluating the effectiveness of HRD interventions. It is likely that these trends are influenced quite significantly by the growth of FDI in the region.

In terms of the future outlook for the region, the role of innovation is likely to be of great importance, and it is widely acknowledged that there is a strong correlation between innovation rates, human capital, and HRD. The percentages of enterprises in the CEE region that introduced an innovation activity based on the 2008 Community Innovation Survey (CIS) are as follows: Estonia (57%), Czech Republic (56%), Slovenia (50%), Slovakia (38%), Hungary (28%), Poland (27%), and Latvia (23%) (Note: Lithuania did not participate in the 2008 CIS). The EU average was 51.5%, so only two CEE countries are above this average. These low rates of innovation are potentially a very significant threat to the region's future competitiveness. The changes made to VET systems—post-transition—are almost certainly a contributing factor to the low rates of innovation. In addition, culturally, the countries in the region tend to be highly risk averse: Poland (93), Slovenia (88), Hungary (82), Czech Republic (74), Latvia (63), Estonia (60), and Slovakia (51). This is also likely to negatively impact on innovation propensities, as almost all innovations have some inherent risk of failure. To ensure the future sustainability of the region, it is imperative that innovation rates in the region rise and that VET and HRD policies can have a critical role in enhancing this objective (Sheehan, Garavan, & Carbery, 2014).

CONCLUSION

Central and Eastern Europe recently celebrated two important anniversaries in 2014: 25 years since the beginning of post-communist transition (1989) and 10 years since the first wave of EU Eastern Enlargement. However, if not implemented soon, the thirtieth anniversary of transition and fifteenth anniversary of the first EU Eastern Enlargement may be celebrated more pessimistically. Even if CEE economies manage to return to the convergence path with relatively strong economies, such as Germany and the

UK, its speed will likely be slower than it was before 2007/2008, as the expected rate of inward FDI slows, reflecting, in part, rising wage costs in the region and the rise of other attractive regions, for example, Southeast Asia. Another very significant challenge relates to the steadily decreasing cohorts of working-age populations and the impact of outward migration, especially a 'brain drain' from the CEE region to other parts of Europe. A well-designed reform agenda that can boost productivity and innovation growth rates is needed for the region. Fortunately, as the chapter has highlighted, the region's labor force is relatively well educated, yet it is critical that VET and HRD interventions are adjusted to be more consistent with the needs of contemporary labor markets, including the requirements of foreign investors. Policies to slow and even reverse the very significant 'brain drain' in the region should also be considered carefully.

REFERENCES

Allen, & Overy (2011). *Cee you there- Foreign Direct Investment in Central and Eastern Europe*. Available from: (http://www.allenovery.com/SiteCollectionDocuments/Foreign%20direct%20investment%20in%20Central%20and%20Eastern%20Europe.PDF) Accessed April 11, 2015.

Amable, B. (2003). *The Diversity of Modern Capitalism*. Oxford: Oxford University Press..

Bartlett, W. (2009). The effectiveness of vocational education in promoting equity and occupational mobility among young people. *Economic Annals*, 54(180): 7–39.

Bejaković, P. (2004). How prepared is Croatia for a knowledge-based society?" In Katarina Ott, ed., *Croatian Accession to the European Union: Facing the challenges of negotiations*, 109–28. Zagreb: Institute of Public Finance.

Cascio, W. Y. (2014). Investing in HRD in uncertain times now and in the future. *Advances in Developing Human Resources*, 16(1): 108–122.

Cascio, W. Y. & Aguinis, H. (2005). *Applied Psychology in Human Resource Management*, 6th Ed. New Jersey: Person Prentice Hall.

CEDEFOP. (European Centre for the Development of Vocational Skills). (2010). *Skills Supply and Demand in Europe: Medium-Term Forecast up to 2010*. Luxembourg: Publications of the European Union.

Cranet Survey on Comparative Human Resource Management. (2011). *International Executive Report. Cranfield Network on Comparative Human Resource Management*. Available from: (http://www.cranet.org/home/Pages/default.aspx.) Accessed December 3, 2013.

Cseh, M., Rozanski, A., Nemeskeri, Z., & Krisztian, B. (2015). HRD in Hungary and Poland. In R. Poell, R. Rocco & G. Roth (Eds.), *The Routledge Companion to Human Resource Development*, 492–505. London: Routledge.

Dimitrina, D., & Vilrokx, J. (Eds.). (2005). *Trade Union Strategies in Central and Eastern Europe: Toward Decent Work*. Geneva: International Labor Organization.

Ederer, P., Schuler, P., & Willms, S. (2007). *The European Human Capital Index: The Challenge of Central and Eastern Europe*. Brussels: The Lisbon Council.

Eichhorst, W., Rodríguez-planas, N., Schmidl, R., & Zimmerman, K. (2014). *A Roadmap to Vocational Education and Training around the World*. IZA Discussion Paper 7110. Bonn: IZA-Institute for the Study of Labor.

European Commission. (2014). *EURES: The European Job Mobility Portal.* Available from: (https://ec.europa.eu/eures/page/homepage?lang=en) Accessed April 11, 2015.

Freeman, R. B. (2005). What do unions do? The 2004 M-Brane Stringtwister Edition. *Journal of Labor Research,* 26: 640–668.

Hall, P. A., & Soskice, D. (2001). An introduction to varieties of capitalism. In P. A. Hall and D. Soskice (Eds.), *Varieties of Capitalism– The Institutional Foundations of Comparative Advantage,* 1–68. New York: Oxford University Press.

Hofstede, G., Hofstede, G. J., & Minkov, M. (2010). *Cultures and Organizations: Software of the Mind. Revised and Expanded.* 3rd Ed. New York: McGraw-Hill.

Knell, M. & Srholec, M. (2007). Diverging pathways in Central and Eastern Europe. In D. Lane and M. Myant (Eds.), *Varieties of Capitalism in Post-Communist Countries,* 40–65. Houndsmill: Palgrave.

Lazarova, M., Morley, M., & Tyson, S. (2008). International comparative studies in HRM and performance—the Cranet data. *The International Journal of Human Resource Management,* 19(11): 1995–2003.

Matkovic, T. (2008). *Recent Developments in the Education System and School-to-Work Transitions in Croatia.* Working Paper 138. Mannheim: Mannheimer Zentrum für Europäische Sozialforschung.

McCann, L., & Schwartz, G. (2006). Terms and conditions apply: Management restructuring and the global integration of post-socialist societies. *The International Journal of Human Resource Management,* 17(8): 1339–1352.

Micklewright, J. (1999). Education, inequality and transition. *Economics of Transition,* 7(2): 343–376.

OECD. (2012/2011). *Trade Union Density.* Available from: (https://stats.oecd.org/Index.aspx?DataSetCode=UN_DEN) Accessed May 22, 2015.

Pocztowski, A. (2011). Transformation of the HR function. In A. Pocztowski A. (Ed.), *Human Resource Management in Transition. The Polish Case,* 13–31. Oficyna a Wolters Kluwer business: Warszawa.

Pocztowski, A., & Buchelt, B. (2008). Trends and issues in human resource management in Polish companies Zarządzanie Zasobami Ludzkimi, 1: 51–66.

Saar, E., Unt, M., & Kogan, I. (2008). Transition from educational system to labor market in the European Union: A comparison between new and old members. *International Journal of Comparative Sociology,* 49(1): 31–59.

Sheehan, M. (2014). Investment in training and development in times of uncertainty. *Advances in Developing Human Resources,* 16(1): 13–33.

Sheehan, M., Garavan, T., & Carbery, R. (2014). Innovation and human resource development (HRD): Guest editorial. *European Journal of Training and Development,* 38(1/2): 2–14.

Sondergaard, L., & Murthi, M. (2012). *Skills, Not just Diplomas- Managing Education for Results in Eastern Europe and Central Asia.* Washington, DC: World Bank.

World Bank. (2005). *Expanding Opportunities and Building Competencies for Young People: A New Agenda for Secondary Education.* Washington, DC: World Bank.

World Bank. (2008). *Unleashing Prosperity: Productivity Growth in Eastern Europe and the Former Soviet Union.* Available from: (http://siteresources.worldbank.org/ECAEXT/Resources/publications/UnleashingProsperity.pdf) Accessed April 11, 2014.

14 Human Resource Development in Russia and the Former Soviet Union

*Alexandre Ardichvili, Elena Zavyalova
and Oleksandr Tkachenko*

INTRODUCTION

This chapter considers the evolution and the current state of HRD in Russia and the post-Soviet states, also commonly known as the former Soviet Union (FSU). After the dissolution of the USSR, 15 republics of the union became independent states. The largest of these (in territory, population, and the size of the economy) is Russia. This group of countries also includes Ukraine, Belarus, Moldova, five countries of Central Asia (Kyrgyzstan, Kazakhstan, Turkmenistan, Uzbekistan, and Tajikistan), three countries in Transcaucasia (Armenia, Azerbaijan, and Georgia), and three Baltic States (Latvia, Lithuania, and Estonia). While sharing a sociopolitical legacy (all these republics had been part of the Russian Empire prior to the revolution of 1917 and later became part of the USSR), these countries do not form a homogenous entity. The region is characterized by an amazing array of ethnic and linguistic groups, religious groups, and levels of economic development and prosperity.

This chapter explores emerging forms of HRD in selected FSU countries, identifying commonalities as well as unique features of HRD systems. We start our analysis by discussing the common historical, political, economic, institutional, social, and cultural factors influencing HRD in the region. The next sections discuss, for each of the four countries, the economic, educational, social factors that shape skills development and the main HRD and VET trends and related government policies. The section on Russia also includes a more detailed analysis of enterprise-level HRD in large Russian corporations. The concluding part of the chapter discusses similarities and differences within the region, formulates our conclusions related to the current problems and successes of HRD systems in countries of the region, and outlines possible trajectories for the evolution of HRD in the future.

Because it is impossible to provide a meaningful discussion of HRD systems on all 15 nations of this large and diverse region in a single chapter, we focus on a sample of countries that represents major geographic and cultural clusters and also cover a range of levels of socioeconomic development found in the region. Our sample includes Russia (the largest, most prosperous, and politically and economically the most influential country of the group), Ukraine (the second-largest FSU country in population, possessing diversified industry and a large agricultural sector but located at the opposite end to Russia on the income level continuum), Azerbaijan (representing the Transcaucasia and belonging to the small country category, both in the size of population and in territory), and Kazakhstan (one of the largest of the FSU in territory and natural resources representing the Central Asia region). We did not include the Baltic countries, because these states are now part of the European Union and are discussed in the chapter on HRD in Central and Eastern Europe.

RUSSIA AND THE FSU: POLITICAL, ECONOMIC, AND INSTITUTIONAL CONTEXTS

The current political, economic, and institutional contexts of Russia and the FSU countries were shaped by a common legacy of the socialist regime that existed for more than 70 years. During that period, the regulative and normative institutional frameworks were directed by communist ideology, and economic life was governed not by market mechanisms but by centrally developed five-year plans. Enterprise-level management was controlled by the Nomenklatura, an elite group of administrators who, in most cases, did not have business or management education, but instead were trained in political disciplines and party ideology. Over the years, the inefficiencies of the centrally planned economy resulted in chronic shortages of food and consumer goods, enormous waste of resources in all sectors of the economy, and gradual deterioration of the infrastructure.

However, in the human capital domain, the centrally planned system has produced notable positive outcomes, because the government was investing heavily in education at all levels. The former USSR has achieved some of the highest levels of literacy in the world; a wide network of vocational training and professional development institutions was created; and impressive results were achieved in science, math, and engineering, as well as related disciplines in higher education institutions.

After the dissolution of the USSR in 1990–1991, all 15 newly independent countries went through major institutional upheavals, which resulted in "the dismantling of the central planning regime, a need for a new property-rights based legal framework, and the transition from 'state-policed firms' to market-based mechanisms restricting opportunistic behavior of firms" (Roth and Kostova, 2003, p. 315). In the HRD domain, one of the results of this institutional upheaval was the dissolution of the network of state-controlled VET establishments and management development institutes, and the emergence of numerous private professional development and higher education institutions that attempted to fill the created void.

Despite sharing a common institutional legacy, all four countries followed somewhat different paths of economic and political development over the past 25 years. Thus after experimenting with both political and economic liberalization in the 1990s and early 2000s, Russia is showing signs of developing a new form of authoritarian state, with a 'statist economy', dominated by centralized control mechanisms and large state-owned companies. Azerbaijan and Kazakhstan seem to rely more on market mechanisms in the economic sphere, but are heavily dependent on the energy and extractive sectors and, in the political sphere, have authoritarian governments. Finally, in Ukraine, the new leadership recently made a commitment to political and economic integration with the European Union and signed the Association Agreement with the EU in 2014. However, at the time of this writing, the pursuit of this goal was being severely jeopardized by the conflict in the east of the country.

HRD POLICIES, SYSTEMS, AND INITIATIVES IN FOUR COUNTRIES

In this section, we discuss for each of the four countries: a) the economic, educational, and social factors shaping skills supply and demand and b) the main HRD/VET trends and related government initiatives. As mentioned earlier, the section on Russia includes a more detailed analysis of the enterprise-level HRD in large Russian corporations.

Azerbaijan

Azerbaijan is the largest country in the Transcaucasia region, located at the crossroads of Eastern Europe and Western Asia. Azerbaijan has a territory of about 88,600 sq km, with a population of 9.7 million people (WB Databank, 2015). The country is rich in natural resources, especially in oil and gas. Azerbaijan has a dynamic growing economy in which the industry sector contributes about two-thirds of the country's GDP. At the same time, agriculture remains an important source of employment in Azerbaijan: while contributing only 5.7% of GDP, it employed about 38% of the working population in 2014 (CIA, 2015a). With a steady rise in income and a drastic reduction in poverty over the last decade, Azerbaijan has rebounded much better from the economic crisis of 2008–2009 than other CIS countries have. Compared with the rest of the countries in our sample, Azerbaijan's PPP GDP is the smallest. Its 2013 HDI rank was 76, which put Azerbaijan in third position among the countries covered in this chapter (see Table 14.1).

Azerbaijan has experienced rapid economic and social development over the last decade. Much of the growth is attributed to the revenues gained from the export-oriented oil and gas sector. During this period, the economy of Azerbaijan often outperformed the economies of the EU and FSU countries. In some years, GDP growth reached 25%. Seizing the opportunity

Table 14.1   Economic and Demographic Characteristics of Russia and the FSU in 2013

Country	Population (in millions)	GDP (billion dollars)	GNI per capita PPP (dollars)	GDP annual growth rate (%)	Life expectancy at birth (years)	HDI ranking
Azerbaijan	9.4	73.6	16.180	6	71	76
Kazakhstan	17	231.9	20.680	6	70.5	70
Ukraine	45.5	177.4	8.970	2	71	83
Russia	143.5	2.097	24.280	1	71	57

Source: World Bank Databank (2015); UNDP (2015)

afforded by the oil boom, Azerbaijan initiated large public-sector programs and institutional reforms aimed at modernizing the economy (WB, 2010). Despite the deterioration of living standards and human development indicators following the breakup of the Soviet Union, Azerbaijan managed to improve the situation considerably during the last decade. This economic growth and stability led to a steady improvement in the quality of life. In particular, average life expectancy increased by more than five years in the last 15 years. The country experienced a significant decline in poverty rates from 49% in 2001 to 7.6% in 2011. In the same period, income per capita in purchasing power parity increased by 450% (ETF, 2012a). Although the macro indicators have shown considerable growth during the last decade, many economic and social challenges still exist in Azerbaijan. Several population groups, mainly young people (age 15–25), internal migrants, internally displaced persons (IDPs), and immigrants are particularly vulnerable and could significantly benefit from integration and retraining (ETF, 2012a).

Contrary to the trends in many other FSU countries that have experienced decline in population since the '90s, the population of Azerbaijan has increased almost 28% since the breakup of the Soviet Union and the labor force has grown by 25% (ETF, 2012a). The growth in population creates pressures on the education system and the labor market, as more young people need schooling and employment. Given that the majority of young people do not receive a specialization upon leaving the education system, they often find employment in the informal sector (ETF, 2012a). Although a large informal economy somewhat buffers the lack of formal jobs, informal employment often creates obstacles for social mobility and career development for young people. Those who have found employment in the informal sector and received some basic training on the job are often at risk of being trapped in low-income categories and may experience significant difficulties in finding jobs in the formal sector afterward.

The divide between urban and rural populations is significant in Azerbaijan. The increase of employment opportunities in urban areas has resulted in internal migration from rural areas. The migration processes were strongly amplified after the Nagorno Karabakh conflict of 1991–1994. More than half a million people were driven from their homes, and most of these internally displaced persons (IPDs) went to the metropolitan areas looking for jobs. After 20 years of unemployment and inadequate livelihood, opportunities still remain a problem for the IPDs. According to the World Bank (2010), about 11% of the population of Azerbaijan reported themselves as internally displaced in 2008. Over half of the IDPs were not active participants in the labor force (either working or looking for jobs), compared to only 36% for the general population. Finally, in addition to IPDs, Azerbaijan has become a receiving country for foreign migrants, mainly from other Asian countries.

With regard to the provision of training in companies, as it is the case in many FSU countries, large indigenous companies and MNCs operating in the region increased training of their employees as the economy started to grow. Thus from 2003 to 2009, there was a 32% increase in enterprise employee training in Azerbaijan (Bardak, 2011). The level of training provision, however, differed across sectors. For instance, the 2009 EBRD-World Bank study indicated that only about 12% of Azerbaijani enterprises declared skills and education of workers as important for growth (ETF, 2011b). At the same time, the results of the Skills@Work Survey (British Council, 2009) showed that skills appeared to be a major concern in the tourism sectors. In particular, the survey results indicated that 56% of employers reported that young people lacked the skills needed in the hotel business. The vast majority of the employers in the tourism sector provided training on the job (ETF, 2011a).

The government of Azerbaijan has taken important steps aimed at enhancing HRD in recent years. In particular, the State Program on Technical and Vocational Education Development 2007–2012 set forth the provisions for modernization of the VET system and the increase of its responsiveness to labor market needs. In 2009, the Law on Education established a new legal framework that emphasized the importance of lifelong learning (ETF, 2012a). In 2012, a national development strategy for Azerbaijan 2020 formulated the Vision of the Future strategy. It emphasized the importance of a balanced export-oriented economy, which would be more knowledge-oriented and less dependent on fossil energy revenues. The strategy also stressed investment in human capital as one of the keys to achieving this goal.

Another initiative—the establishment of a Workforce Development Agency—was focused on the enhancement of the skills-needs-identification and the development of occupational standards (ETF, 2013a). With the support of the DIOS project (2013), the Ministry of Labor and Social Protection developed two hundred occupational and training standards for seven priority sectors: construction, hospitality and tourism, agriculture; manufacturing; transport; trade, business administration, and individual services; and energy. The development of a National Qualifications Framework for lifelong learning is currently in process. It builds on the Law on Education of 2009 and ongoing reforms in various sectors of education and in adult learning.

In addition to the progress in policy formulation and legislative framework development, the ongoing modernization of vocational schools and innovative practices in VET are reported as contributing to the improvement of the image of vocational education in Azerbaijan. One such innovation is the establishment of VET centers in Gabala and Ismayilli that function both as schools and adult learning centers. The centers were developed with a clear regional focus and in close cooperation with local stakeholders (ETF, 2012a). This successful practice is being emulated in other regions and additional centers are expected to open their doors in the near future. The analysis of the participation trends in VET, conducted by the Ministry of Education in 2012, pointed to the increasing number of applications, which was often higher than the available number of places, particularly in the modernized institutions. However, it is worth noting that this increase may be in part due to other regulatory policies as the government tightened access to higher education in Azerbaijan (ETF, 2012a).

With regard to IDPs and migrants, several state programs were introduced in recent years to address the needs of these categories of population. In particular, the Public Employment Service of Azerbaijan provided training for about five thousand people in 2009. Although the number was twice more than reported in 2007, the need for training still remains significant (ETF, 2012a). The General Employment Department of Azerbaijan has created two centers dedicated to the training of the unemployed and the creation of two more centers is being planned. The development of training curriculum is supported by the International Labor Organization (ILO), which supports the development of training curriculum, particularly through the adaptation of the ILO Modules of Employable Skills.

Kazakhstan

Kazakhstan is the ninth-largest country in the world, with a territory equal to the land area of Western Europe. With a population of 17 million, Kazakhstan has one of the lowest population densities globally. The country possesses enormous fossil fuel reserves and is rich in minerals and nonferrous metals. Extractive industries have been playing a crucial role in the growth of Kazakhstan in recent years. At the same time, agriculture still remains an important source of jobs, employing 25.8% of the working population (CIA, 2015b). Kazakhstan is often considered among the most successful former Soviet States in transitioning from a centrally planned to a free-market economy. During the transition, Kazakhstan achieved a significant decrease in poverty rate, from 46.7% in 2001 to 6.5% in 2010 (World Bank, 2013a). In 2009, Kazakhstan ranked first on UNESCO's 'Education for All Development Index', reaching nearly universal levels of primary education, gender parity, and adult literacy (World Bank, 2013a). Kazakhstan's

2013 HDI, with the rank of 70, places the country in the high human development group globally and, after Belarus and Russia, third highest in the group of the FSU states (cf. Table 14.1).

Following a period of instability after the breakup of the USSR, Kazakhstan has demonstrated an exceptional economic performance over the last decade, with GDP increasing by around 10% annually during 2000–2007 (UNECE, 2012). The rapid growth was in part attributed to the development of extractive industries. During that period, Kazakhstan experienced strong investment activity, with the ratio of investment to GDP of about 33.5% in 2005–2007 (UNECE, 2012). Although the rapid expansion was hampered in 2008–2009 by the global economic crisis, Kazakhstan weathered the crisis better than most other countries of the FSU, with 7.5% growth of GDP in 2010 (World Bank, 2013a). Despite these impressive results, the fast-growing economy faces several challenges that shape the skills supply and demand. The challenges are mainly related to economic restructuring, competitiveness, and sustainable development, according to the Ministry of Labor and Social Protection (ETF, 2012b). With regard to the supply of skills, Kazakhstan is experiencing favorable demographic and labor market trends. At the same time, these trends are impacted by migration and there are discrepancies in employment and training opportunities across regions.

The demographics of Kazakhstan have undergone significant changes over the last 20 years. Following the decrease in population by almost 1.5 million between 1992 and 2002, mainly attributed to high levels of emigration, mortality, and low fertility, the country's population has been on the rise since 2004 and exceeded the 1991 level by 1.9% in 2011 (ETF, 2012b). Overall, the economically active population rose by 15% in 2001–2010, while employment increased by 21% over the same period (UNECE, 2012). In addition to natural growth, the population increase was due to the growing number of migrants, mainly from other Central Asian countries. The net migration was reported to be positive in 2010, after a long period of being negative during the 2000s (ETF, 2012b). Although this fact may indicate the increasing attractiveness of the Kazakh economy, the growing influx of illegal migrants, mainly low-skilled workers, has forced the government to create legal frameworks aimed at managing the migration processes. In addition to the transnational migration, Kazakhstan is experiencing internal migration from rural to urban areas, as many young people from rural and less developed areas move to urban regions trying to find jobs in large cities. According to ETF (2012b), there is an imbalance in the distribution of funding between regions, which may also contribute to the discrepancies in opportunities for employment and practical training in the regions. Overall, the problems of employment and training are more evident in rural areas of the country.

Over recent years, a variety of measures have been taken to support the development of the country's human resources. Specifically, in 2011, the Kazakh Parliament issued an amendment to the Law on Education to form a new model of TVET, the cooperative VET. The new legal framework introduced norms of social partnership and cooperative learning as a form of VET organization, which is based on corporate responsibility of the state, enterprises, and educational institutions (EFT, 2013b). The developments in Atyrau (A city of about 150,000 inhabitants located on the Caspian Sea.) may serve as an example of such partnerships. An agreement to provide internship opportunities to students and to cooperate in developing the VET curricula and methodologies was signed by 232 companies in Atyrau (ETF, 2012b).

Since 2012, VET has become the focus of government attention as one of the strategic initiatives. In June 2012, the Ministry of Education and Science and the National Welfare Fund's joint stock company, 'Samruk-Kazyna', signed a memorandum on cooperation in training, retraining, and skills development. The Ministry of Labor and Social Protection is currently implementing the Employment 2020 program that "seeks to provide subsidized trainings to self-employed, unemployed and poorer people, and facilitate entrepreneurship in rural areas through respective consulting services, micro-credits, and trainings on small business basics" (Government of Kazakhstan, 2011). During the first year, the Employment 2020 program established about 500 educational centers nationwide, which provided nearly 63,000 Kazakhs with job training and created about 52,000 jobs (Embassy of Kazakhstan, 2013).

Ukraine

Ukraine, located in Eastern Europe, has the territory of 603,550 sq km (slightly larger than France) and a population of 45.5 million people. It is rich in a variety of natural resources. After Russia, the Ukrainian economy was the second largest in the Soviet Union with a production output four times larger than the next-ranking republic (CIA, 2015b). Historically, the processing industry (metallurgy, in particular), machine building, and chemical industries have constituted the key sources of revenue in the country. However, after the dissolution of the USSR, some sectors of Ukrainian's heavy industry lost sources of raw materials and markets for their output and went into decline. With this decline, the service sector has become more important, employing about 68% of the working population and generating 58.8% of GDP in 2014 (CIA, 2015b). Ukraine's 2013 HDI rank is 83, which is currently the lowest among the four countries discussed in this chapter, although the country is still classified as part of the high HDI group worldwide (Table 14.1).

In spite of its great potential, Ukraine is regarded as one of the least successful transition economies (ILO, 2010). After the dissolution of the USSR, the Ukrainian economy began its recovery only in the early 2000s. In 2009, the country's economy was severely hit by the global economic crisis, when GDP declined by 14% in real terms in just one year (ILO, 2010). The crisis had a serious impact on the labor market. In particular, the unemployment rate increased to 9.5% at the beginning of 2009 (World Bank, 2013b). In some industries, changes in employment were especially dramatic, decreasing by 26% in the construction and nonmetallic mineral products industries and 21% in the machinery and equipment industries (ILO, 2010). The slow recovery the Ukrainian economy has been experiencing since 2009 was interrupted by the conflict in the east of the country, which disrupted economic activity in the region and was expected to result in 8% GDP decline in 2014 (World Bank 2014). This conflict has intensified already existing economic hardships in the country and amplified the social and demographic challenges that Ukraine has been facing.

According to the World Bank's (2014) report, the labor market in Ukraine is characterized by excessive levels of informal employment and severe skills mismatch. The situation is exacerbated by a high percentage shadow economy, accounting for 28 to 39% of GDP from 2007 to 2009 (ETF, 2012c). Informal employment accounted for 22–23% of total employment in 2009–2011. Informal employment is especially high in rural areas and among young workers and workers with low qualifications (ETF, 2012c).

The severe skills mismatch and unemployment appear to be interrelated trends: many of the unemployed lack the skills that employers need; the higher the skill level required, the more difficult it is to fill a position. Over the years of growth, there has been a strong shift in the demand for labor from predominantly low-skill sectors to high-skill sectors (World Bank, 2009). Twenty percent of enterprises in Ukraine view the skills of workers as a major obstacle to their successful operation and growth (World Bank, 2014). It is symptomatic that the lack of skilled employees is seen as a more important obstacle than access to capital, corruption, or difficulties in obtaining business permits (EBRD-World Bank, 2009). High-technology and high-growth companies seem to be the main victims of the skills shortage (World Bank, 2009).

Demographic trends also pose significant challenges. Between 1991 and 2011, Ukraine experienced a significant population decline from 51.7 million to 45.5 million. The workforce is also aging. The situation is exacerbated by the emigration of skilled workers, leading to an even higher skills mismatch. In addition to these hardships, the demographic and social situation has been significantly worsened in the recent times as a result of Russia's annexation of Crimea and an armed conflict in the east of the country. More than a million people have been driven from their homes and became internally displaced persons (IDPs) (UNOCHA, 2015). These negative social and demographic trends, together with the economic hardship, present significant challenges to sustaining and developing the country's human capital. To combat the aforementioned negative trends, the government is seeking assistance from the international community and is also committed to structural reforms in various sectors of the economy.

With regard to VET and adult education, some efforts have been made in reformulating and updating related policies and practices over the recent

298   Alexandre Ardichvili, Elena Zavyalova and Oleksandr Tkachenko

years. Regarding the improvements in legislative and regulatory frameworks, several recent laws are worth noting, in particular, the laws on the Professional Development of Employees (Verkhovna Rada, 2012a) and on the Development and Placement of the State Order for Training Specialists, Scientists, Scholars, Educationalists, and Workers, as well as for Skills Upgrading and Retaining of Labor Force (Verkhovna Rada, 2012b). Specifically, the law on the Professional Development of Employees, for the first time in Ukrainian legislation, defined the concept of informal education (ETF, 2012c).

In addition, several important strategic documents and regulations have been developed in recent years: the State Targeted Program of VET development for 2011–2015 (Cabinet of Ministers of Ukraine, 2011a), the National Strategy of Education Development in Ukraine (Cabinet of Ministers of Ukraine, 2011b), and the Strategy of State Personnel Policy for 2012–2020 (President of Ukraine, 2012). Finally, the development of the National Qualifications Framework in 2011, in turn, was an important step in the establishment of a new regulatory model of VET and standardization of the VET content (ETF, 2012c).

There have also been some improvements in the cooperation among various stakeholders ('social partners') involved in adult education over the recent years (ETF, 2012c). This primarily concerns the collaboration between the employment services and VET schools. Continuing education and training in VET schools accounts for about 25% of the total number of graduates (as opposed to initial vocational education and training, or IVET). Vocational schools in Ukraine also participate in training of unemployed people. During the academic year of 2011–2012, 315 vocational schools provided training to unemployed people in 478 occupations (ETF, 2012c).

The increased involvement of enterprises in the development of occupational standards, design of curricula and programs, as well as the modernization of the technical capacity of VET schools indicates another positive trend. Several examples are worth noting here, for example, the cooperation between the Ministry of Education, Science, Youth, and Sports of Ukraine (MESYSU) and a group of large enterprises in the chemical industry. The cooperation between MESYSU, the Confederation of Employers of Ukraine, and a group of employers represented by the LLC System Capital Management, one of the largest business groups in Ukraine with over one hundred enterprises, provides another example. The partners agreed to work on developing and implementing new professional standards in the metallurgy, energy, and mining industries (ETF, 2012c). There is also close collaboration between the Jewelry Association and a Kyiv vocational school of jewelry in providing training for workers from all regions of Ukraine and resulting in 100% employment for all graduates (ETF, 2012d). Despite these positive examples, systemic involvement of social partners still remains an exception rather than a norm (ETF, 2012c).

Russia

In terms of its landmass, Russia is the largest country on Earth. Russia's GDP, in excess of two trillion dollars, is the ninth largest in the world; its population at 143.5 million people is also the ninth largest (WB Databank, 2015). Russia has some of the world's largest reserves of natural resources, especially natural gas and oil. Whereas not all sectors of Russian industry are competitive on the world markets, it possesses a full range of modern industries, from aerospace to car manufacturing and electronics.

Russia's HDI, at 57, puts it in the group of countries with high HD levels worldwide (Table 14.1). The country's pattern of economic development over the last 25 years was characterized by significant ups and downs: an abrupt fall in the 1990s (after the dissolution of the USSR) was followed by a rapid improvement between 2004 and 2007, with a sharp decline during the economic crisis of 2008–2009. Since then the economy has recovered, and the 2013 growth rate rose to about 1% (WB Databank, 2015).

Referring to the educational foundation for HRD systems, Russia shows one of the highest levels of primary education enrollment in the world—almost 99%. However, the regional differentiation in educational enrollment numbers is very high. The Russian government has made concerted efforts to develop the country's human resources over the last 10 to 15 years. The strategy for the country's long-term development, formulated in 2000, included an explicit emphasis on rebuilding national human capital (UNDP, 2015). Some of the high-priority issues in that strategy were: elimination of the existing disparities among regions and within the regions; monitoring the indicators of primary and secondary education, which include the number of children currently not covered by the educational system and children requiring special education services; the development of strategies to eliminate cases of exclusion of children from the educational process; and reforming the system of administration and financing of the educational system.

As in other republics of the Soviet Union, until the collapse of the union in 1991, VET in Russia was provided by an extensive system of state-owned professional technical colleges (PTUs). PUs had close collaboration agreements with state-owned enterprises, which provided guaranteed access to apprenticeships and job placement for students. However, after the breakup of the USSR, the VET system in Russia lost most of its state funding and went into decline. An additional blow was the loss of apprenticeships, workplace learning opportunities, and funds from the state-owned factories; the majority of which were closed or privatized. Thus it is not surprising that many PUs disappeared, whereas those that remained open were preparing students for nonexistent jobs in industries in decline (Walker, 2006; Ardichvili et al., 2012).

The late 1990s to early 2000s witnessed some positive changes. The VET system recovered somewhat through a combination of efforts by the Russian government, international development agencies, and projects funded by the European Union. Some of the most important changes were the increased focus on marketable skills, a more manageable number of professions, for which students were trained (e.g., whereas there were more than 1,200 types of professional certificates in late 1980s, in the late 1990s, there were only about 300), and a shift from training predominantly for the manufacturing sector to focusing on the service industry (Walker, 2006).

ENTERPRISE-LEVEL HUMAN RESOURCE DEVELOPMENT IN RUSSIA

In this section, we will discuss the current state of HRD in large Russian private and state-owned companies. It must be noted that industrial training and development in Russia are not recent phenomena. Prior to the beginning of market-oriented reforms, the Soviet Union had a highly developed system of vocational education colleges, continuous professional education, and management development institutions, all sponsored by the government. For example, each industry sector had its own management development institute attached to the corresponding government ministry, and top-level executives and senior managers of industrial enterprises participated in various professional development programs on a regular basis. However, with the beginning of market reforms, most of the state-sponsored system was disbanded. Individual enterprises, nonprofit institutions—funded by international agencies—and newly created private educational institutions had to shoulder the bulk of the burden of providing training and professional development for employees and managers of both private and state enterprises. Enterprise-level HRD at private firms has only emerged fairly recently (mostly in the mid-1990s) and is still in early stages of formation and development.

It must be noted that even when Russian companies have well-developed HRD strategies, they still tend to adhere to the functionalist approach, with education and training events focused on developing employees for specific jobs in separate functional domains and without taking into consideration the interconnections between various organizational functions. In many cases, training is delivered and managed by functional departments (e.g., Finance or IT) and not by a centralized HRD function (Zavyalova and Ardichvili, 2013).

A study conducted by the research center Amplua Insights identified leading trends in HRD in Russian firms (Trainings.ru, 2012). Study participants included HRD and HR managers from 81 large companies—the consumers of HRD services—and 45 provider companies (HR and HRD consulting companies). The study showed that the development of functional skills takes precedence. Thus sales training and management skills development were the top choices (with 38 and 36% respectively of respondents selecting these as top-priority areas), followed by customer service training, leadership development, and project management (15, 14, and 12% respectively). At the same time, more general soft skills, such as motivation, communication, and decision making, or more abstract topics, such as seminars and interventions related to corporate culture or enterprise-level strategy development, were less popular.

According to an online survey of HR executives in companies with advanced HRD, more than half of responding companies had some form of competency modeling in place (Konovalova, 2008). However, if all Russian companies were taken into consideration, this percentage would be much lower. A related trend is the creation of programs for the development of talent pools. Such programs were found in 40% of companies responding to the survey (Konovalova, 2008).

Another trend is the growing realization that traditional forms of education and development (e.g., classroom training sessions) are insufficient and that managers and employees need to learn on the job and from experience. Increased attention is paid to such methods as mentorships, job rotations, and action learning. Yet another trend is the decrease of the share of training programs conducted outside the workplace context. Firms with advanced HRD systems are increasingly using mini-training sessions in the workplace, company-based internal conferences, and encourage self-development and continuous learning.

Despite the fact that individual coaching has a fairly long history in Russia, organizational implementation of this approach is limited. There are only a handful of experts who can train coaches for this market, and whereas the culture of coaching is evolving, this evolution has been so far very slow.

Likewise, e-learning, despite being a popular training delivery method in Western countries, is only slowly being adopted in Russian companies. Some barriers to the adoption of e-learning in Russian corporate training are: high cost of initial development and implementation, absence of related technological solutions on the Russian IT market, and low levels of self-directed learning readiness among Russian managers and employees. However, a number of successful Russian companies have become early adopters of e-learning and have created sophisticated e-learning platforms and large libraries of online training courses. For example, the largest Russian bank, Sberbank, has numerous online training courses, simulations, and games and trains thousands of employees online every year (Sberbank, 2014). Overall, there is a growing realization that it is necessary to use e-learning to train a geographically widely distributed workforce, especially in banking, transportation, and telecom industries (Khodak, 2012).

Another trend is the growing importance of managing knowledge resources. We could not find examples of Russian companies with what can be called a comprehensive knowledge management system. At the same time, a number of firms have implemented low-cost approaches aimed at facilitating knowledge sharing among employees, including company-wide conferences, seminars, and communities of practice (E-xecutive, 2008).

Corporate universities are becoming a popular solution, especially among large Russian companies. Some observers indicate that the growth of corporate universities is related to the realization that there is a link between HRD, managed through a centralized entity such as a CU, and strategic outcomes. In addition, corporate universities strengthen companies' brand image, giving them recognition as best places to work. Surveys show that in large Russian companies, corporate universities are perceived as a major vehicle for disseminating corporate values and strengthening corporate culture (Fursova, 2011; Genkin, 2012). Our research at five large Russian firms, MTS (МТС), Group VTB (ВТБ), Gasprom (Газпром), Sberbank (Сбербанк), and Vimpelkom (Вымпелком) showed that all five had corporate universities offering training on multiple levels (ranging from entry-level employees to executives), and some of these universities were established back in the mid-1990s (Zavyalova and Ardichvili, 2013).

One of the major obstacles to faster growth of enterprise-level HRD in Russia is the deficit of qualified T&D managers. As the importance of HRD is gaining recognition, more and more companies are searching for top talent in this field. At the same time, many HRD managers are leaving corporations to pursue more lucrative opportunities as outside consultants. It must be noted that surveys suggest that employers are rating the professionalism and effectiveness of Russian T&D professionals as being fairly high. However, the supply of new HRD professionals is limited: there are no dedicated HRD academic programs in Russia, and the number of programs that prepare HRM generalists (who also get some training in HRD) also remains inadequate.

DISCUSSION

The four countries discussed in this chapter face similar problems and each also has unique challenges to overcome. All four nations experienced radical restructuring of their economies and of their sociopolitical institutional frameworks after the dissolution of the USSR. In all, numerous state-owned enterprises and whole sectors of industry lacked competitiveness on the world market and had to be closed or radically restructured. In three of these countries, state budgets became overly dependent on extraction and export of natural resources, especially natural gas and oil.

In addition, all four countries faced major demographic challenges. In Azerbaijan and Kazakhstan, population in general and the share of young people of employable age has been growing, due both to the internal population growth and to immigration. Russia and Ukraine, on the other hand, experienced a sharp decline in population and an aging workforce. In Russia, even the significant influx of migrants from the neighboring countries, attracted by favorable job prospects, could not reverse this trend. Azerbaijan and, more recently, Ukraine are facing a massive problem created by the need to absorb and accommodate large numbers of internally displaced people. Typical for developing economies, all four countries face a gap between urban and rural populations, overcrowding of cities (due to the influx of migrants from impoverished rural communities), and problems of pollution and congestion brought about by rapid growth in car registrations and increased demand for electricity and heating in urban agglomerations.

Each country's responses to the aforementioned challenges resulted in different paths of socioeconomic development. Russia's transition was rather abrupt, with radical privatization of most state-owned enterprises; Ukraine opted for a much slower, gradual transition; and Azerbaijan and Kazakhstan relied mostly on their natural resources and did not focus on diversification of their industry base.

The differences in national economic policies were mirrored in different approaches to developing human capital. While all four countries have relatively high levels of HDI, they all had periods of significant growth of poverty, deterioration of health-care services, and declining educational standards during the first years of the transition from centralized planning to the market economy. And while all four countries have rebounded from sharp economic decline in subsequent years, the levels of investment in education in general and in higher and vocational education in particular remain inadequate to meet the challenges of globalization and transition to the knowledge economy. For example, the VET systems of these countries lack efficiency and responsiveness to the demands of the market due to the radical shift from a Soviet-era system, where there was a strong link between enterprises and schools (including apprenticeships and work-based learning), to an almost exclusively school-based VET system. The apprenticeship systems no longer exist in Russia; they are present only in the informal sector in Azerbaijan and somewhat present in Kazakhstan. Only in Ukraine are they still widely popular: in 2011, close to two hundred thousand people were enrolled in some type of apprenticeship or work-based learning programs (ETF, 2011b).

Reflecting on our comparisons of government-level HRD efforts in the four countries of the FSU, we observe that all four governments play an important role by investing in the development of the infrastructure in support of VET, higher education, and other forms of human capital development and by trying to regulate related activities by issuing laws and developing midterm plans. In Russia, a hybrid model has emerged under which centralization and top-down regulation of the skills formation system is combined with free-market-regulated, enterprise-level HRD provision. In Ukraine, Kazakhstan, and Azerbaijan, a model of collaboration between the government and private enterprise seems to be emerging. In the case of Azerbaijan and Kazakhstan, the role of foreign entities (either foreign private companies or international development agencies) is prominent in sponsoring workforce development projects.

Turning our attention to enterprise-level HRD, we conclude that, given heavy dependence of three of the four countries on revenues from natural resource extraction and processing, it is not surprising that notable examples of developed enterprise-level HRD systems are available mostly in the larger companies of these industries. In Russia, however, HRD is undergoing a fairly rapid evolution toward the creation of rather sophisticated HRD systems in a range of industries, including banking, high-technology manufacturing, telecommunications, transportation, and aerospace (RUIE, 2013). While the majority of Russian firms are still at the stage where HRD is not a recognized independent function and still relies mostly on outsourced T&D services, the number of firms with advanced HRD is steadily growing. These firms have enterprise-level HRD strategies supported by top executives. Modern practices, among them corporate universities, talent management and development, knowledge sharing, competency modeling, and e-learning are becoming a norm among the early adopters of HRD. There are, however, some significant barriers. Among them are the lack of recognition of HRD as separate from HRM function, the lack of qualified HRD professionals and dedicated HRD academic programs, ingrained cultural assumptions that make the adoption of learning technology difficult, and the emphasis on functional and technical skills as opposed to strategic thinking and innovation-related skills and knowledge.

Speaking about prospects for future development of HRD at national and enterprise levels in the four countries, it is important to consider the potential long-term impact of geopolitical conditions emerging in the region. The conflict in Eastern Ukraine and EU sanctions against Russia have already resulted in economic recessions in both countries and could lead to long-term decline in investment in education at all levels. If Russia continues on the path of confrontation with its neighbors and the West, we can expect more resources to be diverted into the military-industrial sector to the detriment of other sectors of the economy. However, whereas under this scenario the progress of national-level HRD initiatives may be seriously curbed, we expect that enterprise-level HRD will continue to expand due to the increasing efforts of both private and state-owned companies to strengthen their competitiveness both in regional and global markets.

REFERENCES

Ardichvili, A., Zavyalova, E., & Minina, V. (2012). Human capital development: Comparative analysis of BRICs. *European Journal of Training and Development*, 36(2): 213–33.

Bardak, U. (Ed.). (2011). *Labour Markets and Employability: Trends and Challenges in Armenia, Azerbaijan, Belarus, Georgia, Moldova and Ukraine*. European Training Foundation, Luxembourg: Publications Office of the European Union.

British Council. (2009). *South Caucasus Skills@Work Survey*. Online. Available (http://www.britishcouncil.org/survey_-_matching_needs_employer_and_learner_perceptions_of_vet_in_the_hotel_sector_eng.pdf) Accessed October 10, 2013.

CIA. Central Intelligence Agency. (2015a). *The World Factbook: Azerbaijan*. Online. Available (https://www.cia.gov/library/publications/the-world-factbook/geos/aj.html) Accessed October 15, 2013.

CIA. Central Intelligence Agency. (2015b). *The World Factbook: Ukraine*. Online. Available (https://www.cia.gov/library/publications/the-world-factbook/geos/up.html) Accessed October 17, 2013.

DIOS. (2013). *Development of Improved Occupational Standards According to Isco08 And Relevant Training Standards*. Online. Available (http://dios.az/wp/en/progress/) Accessed October 9, 2013.

Embassy of the Republic of Kazakhstan. (April, 2013). *New "Employment 2020" Initiative Off to Great Start*. Online. Accessed 5 October 2013. (http://www.kazakhembus.com/article/new-employment-2020-initiative-off-to-great-start)

ETF. (European Training Foundation). (2011a). *Torino Process 2010: Azerbaijan*. Report. ETF. Turin.

ETF. (European Training Foundation). (2011b). *The Torino Process—Evidence Based Policy Making for Vocational Education and Training*. Report. ETF. Turin.

ETF. (European Training Foundation). (2012a). *Torino Process 2012: Azerbaijan*. Report. ETF. Turin.

ETF. (European Training Foundation). (2012b). *Torino Process 2012: Kazakhstan*. Report. ETF. Turin.

ETF. (European Training Foundation). (2012c). *Torino Process 2012: Ukraine*. Report. ETF. Turin.

ETF. (European Training Foundation). (2012d). *Torino Process 2012: Eastern Europe*. Report. ETF. Turin.

ETF. (European Training Foundation). (2013a). *Country Project Azerbaijan*. Online. Available (http://www.etf.europa.eu/web.nsf/pages/PRJ_2013_WP13_31_08_AZB) Accessed October 12, 2013).

ETF. (European Training Foundation). (2013b). *Country Project: Kazakhstan*. Online. Available (http://www.etf.europa.eu/web.nsf/pages/PRJ_2013_WP13_30_11_KAZ) Accessed October 16, 2013.

E-xecutive. (2008). *Non-Standard Approaches to Developing Top Managers: Results of An E-Xecutive Survey*. [Нестандартные подходы к развитию топ-менеджеров. Результаты опроса E-xecutive]. Online. Available (http://www.e-xecutive.ru/publications/ratings/article_6081/) Accessed October 21, 2012.

Fursova, I. (2011). *Back to School: Corporate University is Not for Everybody*. [in Russian]. Russian Business Newspaper 787, no. 5. February 8. (http://m.rg.ru/2011/02/08/sberbank.html) Accessed December 23, 2014.

Genkin, A. (2012). *Corporate University: Employer's Choice*. [in Russian]. Kadrovik. no. 7. June 13, (http://www.hr-portal.ru/article/korporativnyy-universitet-vybor-rabotodatelya?page=0) Accessed December 23, 2014.

Government of the Republic of Kazakhstan. (February 2011). *Kazakhstan's Government Focuses on Employment Programs and Housing Construction*. Online. Available (http://en.government.kz/site/news/022011/03) Accessed October 5, 2013.

International Labour Organization (2010). Promoting Economic Diversity in Ukraine: The role of the business enabling environment, skills policies and export promotion. Online. Available HTTP: <http://www.ilo.org/budapest/what-we-do/publications/WCMS_168801/lang--en/index.htm> (accessed 21 October 2013).

Khodak, E. (2012). *Distance Education: Opportunities and Limitations*. [Дистанционное обучение: возможности и ограничения]', Working with Personnel, Online. Available (http://www.hr-journal.ru/articles/op/op_879.html) accessed October 21, 2012.

Konovalova, V. (2008). *World Trends in Education and Training of Personnel and the Current Situation in Russia*. [Мировые тенденции обучения и развития персонала и ситуация в России]', Kadrovik, 9. Online. Available (http://www.case-hr.com/statiyi-i-otcheti/35008.html) Accessed August 17, 2012.

President of Ukraine. (2012). Decree No 45/2012 of 1 February 2012. *On a National Personnel Policy Strategy 2012–2020*. Online. Accessed 21 October 2013 (http://zakon4.rada.gov.ua/laws/show/45/2012)

Roth, K., & T. Kostova. (2003). Organizational coping with institutional upheaval in transition economies. *Journal of World Business*, 38: 314–330.

RUIE. (2013). *Cadres for Business: Company Practices in the Area of Education and Development* [in Russian]. Moscow: Russian Union of Industrialists and Entrepreneurs.

Sberbank. (2014). *Employee Development* [in Russian]. (http://sberbank-talents.ru/Info/learning) Accessed December 27, 2014.

Trainings.ru. (2012). *Trends in Personnel Education and Training* [Тенденции обучения и развития персонала 2012]', Online. Available (http://www.trainings.ru/library/reviews/?id=14402) Accessed August 17, 2012.

UNDP (2015) *Human Development Index (HDI) - 2013 Rankings*. Online. Available *Accessed 15 April 2015*. (http://hdr.undp.org/en/statistics/) *Accessed April 15, 2015*.

UNECE. (2012). *Innovation Performance Review of Kazakhstan, United Nations Economic Commission for Europe*. United Nations: New York and Geneva.

United Nations Office for the Coordination of Humanitarian Affairs. (UNOCHA). (2015). *Ukraine: Situation Report No.35 as of 10 April 2015*. Online. Available (http://reliefweb.int/report/ukraine/ukraine-situation-report-no35–10-april-2015) Accessed April 15, 2015.

Verkhovna Rada of Ukraine. (2012a). Law 4312–17 of 12 January 2012. *On Professional Development of Employees*. Online. Available (http://zakon4.rada.gov.ua/laws/show/4312–17) Accessed October 21, 2013.

Verkhovna Rada of Ukraine. (2012b). Law 5499–17 of 20 November 2012. *On the Development and Placement of State Order for Training Specialists, Scientific, Scientific-Pedagogical and Regular Labor Force, Training and Retraining*. Online. Available (http://zakon1.rada.gov.ua/laws/show/5499–17) Accessed October 21, 2013.

Walker, C. (2006). Managing vocational education and the youth labor market in post-Soviet Russia. *International Journal of Human Resource Management*, 17(8): 1426–40.

World Bank. (2009). *Ukraine Labour Demand Study*. World Bank, Washington, DC.

World Bank. (March, 2010). *Azerbaijan, Living Conditions Assessment Report*. No. 52801-AZ.

World Bank. (2013a). *Kazakhstan Overview*. Online. Accessed 15 October 2013. (http://www.worldbank.org/en/country/kazakhstan/overview).

World Bank. (2013b). *Ukraine Overview*. Online. Accessed 15 October 2013. (http://www.worldbank.org/en/country/ukraine/overview)

World Bank. (2014). *World Bank Group—Ukraine partnership: Country Program Snapshot*. October 2014. Online. Available (http://www.worldbank.org/content/dam/Worldbank/document/Ukraine-Snapshot.pdf) Accessed April 15, 2015.

World Bank Databank. (2015). *World Bank Open Data*. Online. Accessed 15 April 2015. (http://data.worldbank.org)

Zavyalova, E., & Ardichvili, A. (February 2013). *Enterprise-level Human Resource Development in Russia: Trends and Barriers*, refereed abstract presented at the 2013 AHRD International Research Conference in the Americas, Washington, DC.

Section V
Western Europe

15 Human Resource Development in Ireland and the UK

Alma M. McCarthy

INTRODUCTION

This chapter examines HRD in Ireland and the United Kingdom (UK). Ireland refers to the Republic of Ireland comprising the 26 counties in the South of Ireland. The UK comprises England, Scotland, Wales, and Northern Ireland. Ireland and the UK provide an interesting region in which to analyze and understand HRD policy and practice. The five countries are geographic neighbors located on the western periphery of Europe, many with contiguous borders. At a political, cultural, and institutional level, Ireland, England, Wales, Scotland, and Northern Ireland share a similar history heavily influenced by British rule. Furthermore, Ireland and the UK are classified as Anglo-Saxon countries. Mead (2007,p. 15) argues that Anglo-Saxon countries are characterized by a "slowly evolved liberal political system focused on innovation, a pluralist approach to society, and a capitalist system preoccupied with material wealth not for its own sake but because of a passion for growth, for achievement, for change". Notwithstanding this similar historical, economic, and cultural backdrop, different national approaches to HRD and VET can be found within the region today while accepting that some general commonalities are also prevalent.

This chapter examines the HRD landscape in the Ireland and UK region, taking into account its historical, economic, social, and cultural backdrop. Particular attention is given to the development of the vocational and educational training context in the region. The chapter reviews the key institutions, actors, and stakeholders in the HRD landscape in the region and assesses organization-level HRD policy and practice. The chapter assesses the key similarities and differences in HRD across the countries examined in the region and concludes with a discussion of current issues and challenges for HRD in Ireland and the UK in the coming years.

HRD IN IRELAND AND THE UK: THE HISTORICAL, POLITICAL, ECONOMIC, SOCIAL, AND CULTURAL CONTEXT

Ireland

Ireland is a small country with a population of 4.6 million (CSO, 2014) located on the western periphery of Europe. Ireland is a developed economy and ranked forty-fifth globally with a GDP in 2013 of $232 billion according to the IMF (2014) Global Economic Outlook. At eleventh place globally, Ireland is ranked as 'very high' in the UN Human Development Index 2013, which is a composite statistic of life expectancy, education, and per capita income indicators used to rank countries into four tiers of human development. Modern-day Ireland's culture has been influenced heavily by Gaelic culture, British rule, Americanization, and elements of broader European culture. Historically, religion has played a significant role in the cultural and political development of Ireland since the seventeenth century plantations resulting in political identity and divisions based on religion. However, modern-day Ireland, religion plays almost no role in politics, and there is a concerted move to ensure greater separation between church and state.

Ireland gained independence from Britain in 1922. The Irish political system is a parliamentary democracy based on the constitution of 1937 (Bunreacht Na hÉireann). Ireland has experienced considerable economic, social, and cultural development over the past century. It has developed from being an inward-looking country focusing on an economic development strategy of self-sufficiency and isolation for the first few decades of its independence to being one of the most globalized, dynamic, and innovative economies in the world in 2015.

Ireland adopted an isolationist and protectionist approach to economic development from 1932 to 1958 based largely on the agricultural sector. However, the late 1950s saw a small 'modernizing elite' successfully change its isolationism strategy (O'Donnell, Garavan, & McCarthy, 2001), when Ireland embarked on a process of export-led-industrialization based on foreign direct investment (O'Malley, 1989). This policy shift changed the nature of Irish society in the intervening years and is widely considered a catalyst for Ireland's progressive economic development. Ireland's economic performance over the past decade has seen her reach the pinnacle of economic success, culminating in Ireland's characterization as the 'Celtic Tiger' during the mid-2000s but then rapidly falling victim to the global financial and banking crisis of 2007 that resulted in an EU/IMF bailout. The GDP for Ireland was 4.9% in 2014 and is estimated to be 5.0% in 2015, representing a significant increase from a figure of -0.9% in 2011 (Duffy et al., 2014). Thus, at the time of writing, Ireland's economy is starting to recover and predictions for growth are positive.

United Kingdom

The United Kingdom (UK) has a population of over 64.1 million (ONS, 2014), with 53.9 million in England, 5.3 million in Scotland, 3.1 million in

Wales, and 1.8 million in Northern Ireland. The UK is a developed economy ranked fifth globally with a GDP in 2013 of $2,945 billion in the IMF (2014) Global Economic Outlook. The UK's culture has developed as a result of many different influences, including its history as a major colonizing power, its Western liberal democracy, and its being a union of four countries in which each retains distinctive traditions, cultures, customs, and symbolism (Rebellato et al., 2011). The UK political system is a constitutional monarchy. Whereas there is no written constitution in the UK, the constitution resides in established conventions, traditions, and judicial precedents that can be changed by Acts of Parliament. The UK Parliament operates in London with devolved powers for some decision making to the Scottish and Welsh Assembly and more recently in Northern Ireland following the Good Friday Agreement of 1998.

Following World War II, the UK Labor government implemented a radical program of reforms, which had a significant effect on British society in the following decades (Francis, 1997). Francis (1997) enumerates the reforms as including the nationalization of major industries and public utilities and the establishment of a welfare state with a publicly funded national health-care system (now the National Health Service or NHS). The rise of nationalism in the colonies resulted in the inevitable policy of decolonization (Lee, 1996). In 1947, independence was granted to India and Pakistan, and during the following 30 years, most colonies of the British Empire gained their independence.

Following a period of widespread economic slowdown and industrial strife in the 1970s, Dorey (1995, p. 15) reports that the Conservative government of the 1980s initiated a policy of "monetarism, deregulation, particularly of the financial sector (for example, Big Bang in 1986) and labor markets, the sale of state-owned companies (privatization), and the withdrawal of subsidies to others". While this policy led to economic growth, it also led to high unemployment and social unrest. Around the turn of the new millennium, the establishment of devolved administrations for Scotland, Wales, and Northern Ireland resulted in major changes in UK governance. The 2008 global financial crisis severely affected the UK economy, and in 2010, the government introduced austerity measures intended to tackle the substantial public deficits. Like Ireland, its recent economic growth and growth projections are more positive. The Office of National Statistics in the UK (ONS, 2015) reports that GDP was estimated to have increased by 2.8% in 2014, compared with 2013.

HRD INSTITUTIONS, POLICY, AND ACTORS IN IRELAND AND THE UK

An informative approach to understanding the institutional context of HRD in any region is to assess whether national government plays a voluntarist or interventionist role in HRD policy and practice (Stewart and McGuire, 2012; Stewart et al., 2013). In Ireland and the UK, the institutional context is a mix of both, with national government policy in each country accounting for various dimensions of the HRD landscape but where HRD activity is also very much determined at the organizational level.

Ireland

Since the late 1950s, major changes and expansion of both the industrialization process and the education system have taken place in Ireland (O'Donnell et al., 2001). In this period, the Irish class and occupational structure changed from one primarily based on property ownership to one based on educational credentials and wage employment (Breen et al., 1990; Fahey, 1995). O'Connell and Rottman (1994, p. 219) outline how "family resources rooted in the old agrarian class structure facilitated acquisition of the credentials and qualifications that governed access to the new class positions in services, industry and the welfare state". Those who adapted to the new regime of credentialism obtained the major benefits.

The advent and growth of foreign direct investment (FDI) into Ireland is widely regarded as a turning point for HRD practices at the firm level. Since the early 1960s, Irish governments have adopted a policy of 'industrialization by invitation' expressly focused on attracting FDI through various tax and financial incentives (Gunnigle et al., 2003). Heraty and Collings (2006) argue that Ireland's national HRD framework commenced in earnest in the 1960s, having been limited only to apprenticeship training up to that time. The establishment of a national training authority under the Industrial Training Act in 1967 pointed to a significant change in government training and development policy and the move toward more of an interventionist approach. Following the 1967 Act a new national training authority was established called An Comhairle Oilun (AnCo), whose activities covered three key areas: training advisory service, training for individuals, and apprenticeship training.

During the 1970s and 1980s, the increase in foreign direct investment to Ireland, as well as sustained efforts to heighten the importance of training and development at a political and policy level, resulted in a myriad of reports and policy papers that influenced HRD policy and practice in Ireland. The 1986 *White Paper on Manpower Policy*, the 1987 Labor Services Act, and the 1988 Advisory Committee on Management Training all heralded a new era for training and development, arguing that investment in human capital was key to Ireland's future economic development and success, including addressing the needs of the long-term unemployed. Heraty and Collings (2006) argue that the publication of both the *Galvin Report on Management Development* in 1988 and the *Culliton Report* in 1992 acted as a critical starting point for Ireland's national training and development infrastructure and as a catalyst for subsequent reform. The *Culliton Report*

(1992) strongly advised that greater workplace training was necessary and that the national training agency, FÁS, should refocus its efforts toward workplace and employee-level training and development. In response to continued criticism of the state's role in Ireland's training infrastructure, the government produced a policy document entitled the *Human Resource Development White Paper* in May 1997 (Heraty and Collings, 2006). The white paper identified three critical pillars for developing effective HRD strategies at a national level: promotion of investment in the development of skills and knowledge of the workforce; promotion of gainful employment by helping people develop their knowledge and skills to full potential; and achievement of high levels of efficiency, effectiveness, and value for money in delivery of state training interventions. This white paper strongly argued a move from program or provider-led training and development to demand-led approaches focused on requirements of learners, employers, and industries. These various policy papers and reports were instrumental in influencing the institutional context of HRD in Ireland and in establishing many of the bodies and organizations with responsibility for training, learning, and development in the country.

The qualification framework in Ireland is overseen by Quality and Qualifications Ireland (QQI), which was formed in 2012 through the merger of the Higher Education Training Awards Council (HETAC) and the Further Education Training Awards Council (FETAC). QQI establishes the standards of awards from the secondary level, which include the Junior Certificate at the age of 15 or 16 and the Leaving Certificate two years later at the age of 17 or 18, through to third-level certificates, diplomas, degrees, master's and PhD level. Third-level education in Ireland is available from a range of providers, including 14 state-funded institutes of technology, seven state-funded universities, colleges of education, and various other private-sector learning and development organizations and bodies. The Higher Education Authority is the statutory agency responsible for the funding of universities, institutes of technology, and certain other higher education institutions. It has an advisory role in relation to the whole sector of third-level education. Apart from the various statutory bodies and educational and training institutions providing learning and development programs, there are a number of important representative groups and policy-led bodies that impact the HRD landscape in Ireland, as the next section sets out.

The Management Development Council (MDC) was established in 2007 to advise the government on the adequacy and relevance of management development provision in Ireland. The aim of the MDC was to promote a coordinated approach to building awareness and appreciation in small and medium-sized businesses for the value of and need for upgrading leadership and management skills. In its 2010 report entitled *Management Development in Ireland*, a number of demand-side reforms were called for, including participation in relevant management development programs among SMEs not currently catered for by either the local government level through

County Enterprise Boards (now called Local Employment Organizations) or by Enterprise Ireland (the government organization responsible for the development and growth of Irish enterprises in world markets). The report also called for a number of supply-side reforms, arguing that the third-level sector should play a greater role in the area of management development, particularly in the area of continuing and professional development. The report also strongly argues that state funding should be used to drive the use of best practice among management development training providers and that regular research should be conducted to ensure that the best practice guidelines highlighted in the report remain relevant and up-to-date. The County Enterprise Boards, now Local Employment Offices, should continue to address management development in companies employing up to ten people, and the state should provide a funding allocation starting at €10–12 million per annum from the National Training Fund to fund management development networks. The Skillnets Program has been in operation in Ireland since 1999, a state-funded, enterprise-led support body tasked with promoting and facilitating training and upskilling as key levers for achieving Ireland's national competitiveness. Skillnets supports and funds networks of companies wishing to work together to design, manage, and deliver specific sectoral or industry-level training that they require. Due to funding constraints, many of the Skillnets member companies may not be able to provide this training on their own, and there is a synergy to working as a group that defrays design and delivery costs. Eight hundred networks have been supported during the first ten years of the Skillnets program, and over 240,000 employees have participated in Skillnets training (Indecon, 2014). The Expert Group on Future Skills Needs (EGFSN) was set up in 1997 and advises the Irish government on the current and future skills needs of the economy and on other labor-market issues that impact on Ireland's enterprise and employment growth. EGFSN has a central role in ensuring that labor market needs for skilled workers are anticipated and met.

At present, the *Further Education and Training Strategy 2014–2018* report argues that the further education and training sector in Ireland has developed from a combination of educational policies and different workforce employment and development strategies across a range of government departments and agencies characterized by an absence of "coordinated strategic direction". The adoption of the Further Education and Training Act (2013) heralded the replacement of the national training agency formerly known as FÁS with a newly created agency, SOLAS. The new strategy aims to provide for more coordinated and integrated FET arising from the streamlining of 33 existing Vocational Education Councils into 16 Education and Training Boards (ETBs). The former FÁS employment services function transferred to the Department of Social Protection in January 2012. SOLAS, the Further Education and Training Authority, comes under the aegis of the Department of Education and Skills. It is responsible for the strategic coordination and funding of the further education and training sector, as set out in the *Further Education and Training Strategy 2014–2018*. Therefore, a number of important changes have occurred in the institutional and policy context that set an agenda for national learning, training, and development in Ireland in the coming years.

United Kingdom

A wide range of policies and institutions have impacted the development of the HRD field in the UK. The weak economic performance of the UK in the post-war period resulted in greater intervention and policy development in the area of training (Wilson, 2012) not present in the UK up to that point. One of the seminal training policies in the UK was the 1958 Carr report on apprenticeships and the subsequent setting up of Industrial Training Councils. This was then followed by a 1962 white paper and the influential Industrial Training Act of 1964 (Holmes, 2012). The 1972 white paper reviewing the 1964 Act was an important precursor to the adoption of the Employment and Training Act in 1973. The Employment and Training Act in 1981 led to the abolition of most of the Industrial Training Boards. The review of vocational qualifications lead to the establishment of the National Council for Vocational Qualifications in 1986; and in 1989, it led to the establishment of locally based Training and Enterprise Councils in the UK and the Local Enterprise Companies in Scotland. The Investors in People initiative of 1991, originally administered by Investors in People UK and now administered by UK Commission for Employment and Skills, is quoted by many HRD commentators as an important move in encouraging organizations to invest in learning and development.

The Leitch (2006) report stands as one of the most important HRD policy developments in HRD in the UK in recent times (Harrison, 2009). It was commissioned following various criticisms about skills development and how it was inadequately aligned with economic growth and development. For example, the 2005 white paper entitled *Skills: Getting on in Business, Getting on at Work* (DfES) and the 2006 Engineering Employers Federation report both criticized the supply, relevance, and structural and provisional nature of HRD in the UK. The Leitch (2006) report paved the way for significant change in learning, training, and development in the UK and formed the basis for the government's revised national VET targets, plans, and delivery framework to meet the targets of the 2003 Skills Strategy (Harrison, 2009). The UK Commission for Employment and Skills (UKCES) was set up in 2008 following Leitch's (2006) recommendations and is tasked with providing strategic leadership for skills and employment areas across the four countries in the UK. The commission is a social partnership with representation from a broad range of organizations, further and higher education, large and small employers, trade unions, and the third sector.

Sector Skills Councils (SSCs) were established in the mid-2000s with responsibility for skills and workforce development of all those employed across the 21 existing SSCs. SSCs are employer-led skills organizations and cover a broad range of sectors from professional staff to tradesmen and women, administrative staff, support staff, and other ancillary workers. They also cover all sizes of employer, from large firms to micro-businesses and the self-employed. They work with over 550,000 employers to define skills needs and skills standards in their industries, to support employers in developing and managing apprenticeship standards, and to reduce skills gaps and shortages and improve productivity.

More recently, the Scottish government's (2010) *Skills for Scotland: Accelerating the Recovery and Increasing Sustainable Economic Growth* report sets out a framework to ensure that citizens and employers have the opportunity to access the right advice, support, and opportunities for skill development that can contribute to and benefit from future economic success. The report also sets out a strategy to simplify the skills system to ensure that it is more coherent and easy to understand for individuals and employers as well as strengthening partnerships and collective responsibility between public, private, and third sectors to improve skills and economic success. In the UK, the Department for Business, Innovation & Skills and the Department for Education launched the *Rigour and Responsiveness in Skills Policy* report (2013), which lists the achievements since the 2010 National Skills Strategy and sets out measures to raise standards by making the system more professional, by intervening in poor provision, as well as creating traineeships to prepare young people for work. The 2013 report focuses on reforms and improvements needed in the quality of apprenticeships and on how the UK can make qualifications more relevant and more highly valued by using funding to make skill development provision more responsive.

In terms of the education system in the UK, there are five stages: early years, primary, secondary, further education (FE), and higher education (HE). Education is compulsory for all children between the ages of 5 (4 in Northern Ireland) and 16 (www.gov.co.uk). FE is not compulsory and covers nonadvanced education, which can be taken at further (including tertiary) education colleges and HE institutions (HEIs). The fifth stage, HE, comprises study beyond GCE A levels and their equivalent, which, for most full-time students, takes place in universities and other HEIs and colleges. On completion of lower secondary education, students typically take the General Certificate of Secondary Education (GCSE) exams, which are a prerequisite for entering upper secondary education. The majority of students enter upper secondary education for two years leading to A-level exams, which form the main basis for entry into third-level education. Musset and Field (2013) argue that vocational education and training routes are much less structured and less clear-cut than academic qualifications in the UK. Students who do not continue to HE after secondary school can follow a variety of training programs, such as apprenticeships, that are sometimes at a lower level than upper secondary education. The programs and qualifications, which span a broad range of progression routes to postsecondary VET programs, are also highly diverse (Musset and Field, 2013). There is no automatic right to progression from one level to the next in the UK system (UKCES, 2013). Further education colleges are the main providers of sub-bachelor-degree-level professional and technical education and training in the UK.

In summary, the institutional and policy context of HRD in the UK shares common features, but there are also important differences given that each of the four countries that make up the UK can determine national-level approaches. Raffe et al. (1999) present a comparative treatise of education across the four UK countries. They report similarities in terms of nationally prescribed curriculum to the age of 16 years. Raffe et al. (1999) argue that the four systems are interdependent to a much greater extent than for entirely separate national states. This interdependence is an expected outcome of devolution. However, they conclude that the similarities are more important than the differences across the four UK countries and that each has distinctly 'British' features. These features include similar institutional structures of schools and third-level providers, similar structures in terms of secondary education and certification, as well as third-level certification, and a growing recognition for the need for flexibility and relevance of learning, training, and development at national level, which enables economic growth and development.

VET BASE FOR HRD IN IRELAND AND THE UK

The VET systems in Ireland and the UK share, in general, many similarities; although some divergence of activity exists in terms of VET policy and VET stakeholders. The VET system in any country involves a range of stakeholders, including government, VET providers, trade unions, employee representative groups, regional and local governmental authorities, and accreditation and professional agencies and bodies. In Ireland and the UK, the HRD actor landscape is broad ranging (Stewart et al., 2013), which has the potential to strengthen HRD in the region but also can result in tensions across the various stakeholders depending on their power, interests, and values. The OECD has recently published a number of reports on VET in Ireland and the four UK countries in its series entitled *Skills Beyond School: The OECD Study of Postsecondary Vocational Education and Training*. This series of reports informs the discussion in this section of the chapter.

Ireland

The history of VET in Ireland can be traced back to 1930 when the most important legislation within the vocational education system, the Vocational Education Act, was passed, which led to the establishment of 33 regionally based Vocational Education Committees (VECs) (Barry, 2007). The Vocational Education (Amendment) Act, 2001, broadened the representative element of VECs to include public representatives, parents, teachers, local businesses, and a requirement for the VECs to adopt education plans (Barry, 2007). In the 1960s–1970s, the most significant legislation in vocational training was the establishment of a number of public bodies with responsibility for VET, including AnCO (the Industrial Training Authority), which became FÁS (the National Training and Employment Authority) in 1998 and is now SOLAS. Fáilte Ireland is a significant HRD actor in the tourism and hospitality sectors and Teagasc is the agriculture and food development authority that supports training in the science-based innovation in the agri-food sector and the broader bio-economy.

The majority of young adults (usually entering at 15 or 16 and exiting at 17 or 18) in Ireland complete the Leaving Certificate at secondary level, which is designed around offering students a broad education, while also providing the opportunity for some specialization, in particular subject lines, e.g., science, business, and arts. The Leaving Certificate is used as the basis for selection into further education, employment training, or higher education through a national central admissions process. The traditional Leaving Certificate curriculum, which is quite academic in nature, has broadened over the past couple of decades into a new stream that offers a much more applied and vocational focus. The Leaving Certificate Vocational Program (LCVP) focuses on developing enterprise and entrepreneurship by developing students' interpersonal, vocational, and technological skills (DES, 2015). LCVP caters for students who do not wish to pursue third-level education. It is designed around three areas: vocational preparation, vocational education, and general education.

In Ireland, further education and training (FET) is broad ranging with numerous agencies, actors, and stakeholders involved in the system. The roles and responsibilities for the Irish education system, which includes vocational education and training, are distinct from the vocational training system, the latter being the remit of the labor-market authorities (Barry, 2007). Barry outlines three levels of responsibility in the publicly funded VET sector in Ireland: government departments that set policy and overall direction, including providing the public funding for VET; intermediate organizations that may be involved in implementing government policy, channeling funds, or acting as a provider of VET programs; and VET provider bodies such as SOLAS (formerly FÁS), which is the National Training and Employment Authority. Responsibility for the provision of early vocational education in schools and centers and institutes of further education is devolved from the Department of Education and Skills to 16 Education and Training Boards (ETBs), which replaced the 33 national Vocational Education Committees (VECs) in 2013. In terms of VET courses and provision in Ireland, full-time programs in FE include: Post Leaving Certificate (PLC) courses; Vocational

Training Opportunities Scheme (VTOS); Youthreach, part-time programs that come under the remit of the Back to Education Initiative (BTEI); Adult Literacy; and Community Education.

Apprenticeship training is the key approach used for developing craft-based skills in Ireland. Apprenticeship training in Ireland is regulated by legislation, with SOLAS as the regulatory authority. The current apprenticeship model is founded on the AnCO legislation (the Industrial Training Act), enacted in 1967, as amended by the National Training Fund Act 2000 and the 1987 Labor Services Act, which are based on the 1986 *White Paper on Manpower Policy* and the 1991 Program for Economic and Social Progress (PESP Agreement). DES carried out a review of the apprentice training system in Ireland in 2013, and in June 2014, the Minister for Education announced the establishment of a new Apprenticeship Council to oversee apprenticeship training in Ireland. The council is enterprise-led and has representatives from business, trade unions, further and higher education bodies, and the Department of Education and Skills.

Lifelong learning has been a priority focus of a number of recent governments in Ireland. A *White Paper on Adult Education, Learning for Life* was published in 2000, and the National Framework of Qualifications was established in 2001 under the Qualifications (Education and Training) Act 1999, in order to improve access, transfer, and progression within the VET system.

In 2000, Ireland's labor, employment, training, and development agenda formed a significant part of the government's National Development Plan (NDP) for 2000–2006, which became the principal government framework for the allocation of funding for all VET programs provided by the state. The EHRD OP for this period set out a range of programs and services to be provided to improve access to employment opportunities, address skills and labor shortages, and tackle social exclusion. The NDP for 2007–2013 retained investment in human capital as one of its five strategic investment priorities. Today, at a policy level, responsibility largely rests with the Department of Education and Skills and the Department of Social Protection. In 2014, the Department of Education and Skills provided €826m to support further education and training provision in Ireland (SOLAS, 2014).

United Kingdom

After 1945, the UK started to expand small-scale provision of secondary education, which involved dismantling senior elementary education (roughly, 10–15 years phase) by setting a universal age of transfer to secondary schools and determining how technical education should be provided at secondary level (Richardson and Wiborg, 2010). In the 1960s, various day-release courses, complementary to apprenticeships, had been established in further education colleges. These courses resulted from the work of the Industrial Training Boards that were set up under the 1964 Industrial Training Act. The courses were mainly in the areas of craft construction, engineering, and manufacturing industries and were offered by City & Guilds of London Institute (CGLI).

In the 1970s, the Business Education Council and its parallel Technician Education Council (which subsequently merged and became the Business and Technician Education Council, BTEC in 1983) offered courses in broader vocational areas than CGLI, with an express focus on more general education and designed to enable progression from secondary to sub-degree level while offering higher national certificates (West and Steedman, 2003). BTEC went on to offer full-time courses, issuing diplomas rather than the part-time certificates (Richardson and Wiborg, 2010). By the late 1980s, a system of substantial full-time vocational education courses was available, ranging from the first level (level 2 equivalent in the National Qualifications Framework), through the advanced level National Diploma, to the Higher National Diploma (HND). These programs were offered in colleges of further education and in polytechnics. The other major body offering vocational education courses was the Royal Society of Arts Examinations Board (RSA), which mostly delivered secretarial and administrative courses. Richardson and Wiborg (2010) argue that whereas these courses and providers prevailed over time, the offerings did not add up to a unified system of vocational education. The offerings of each body differed substantially in design, quality, assessment, and size. There were issues with progression across different programs and from different levels; and with the dismantling of many Industrial Training Boards in the 1980s, the degree to which these qualifications had recognition with employers became unclear. Richardson and Wiborg (2010) enumerate the key government initiatives that have impacted vocational education in the UK in the 1980s and early 1990s: the Technical and Vocational Employment Initiative (TVEI), announced in 1982, was intended to develop dedicated pathways of largely vocational education for nonacademic routes; the introduction of the Certificate of Pre-Vocational Education (CPVE) in 1985 aimed at addressing the issue of high youth unemployment; the development of National Vocational Qualifications (NVQs) aimed at developing curriculum, a syllabus based on standards of performance (outcomes) and a new assessment regime; General National Vocational Qualifications (GNVQs) were introduced at three levels (Foundation, Intermediate, and Advanced) and aimed at replacing HNDs and intended to provide more general education rather than forcing learners into early specialization with new GCSEs in vocational subjects; the establishment of the Further Education Funding Council, which took over the funding of colleges from local education authorities in 1993; and the development of vocational options in the 14–16 age phase, which enabled the introduction of expanded vocational education and training for some at the lower secondary level. In 1992, a tripartite system of academic A levels, general vocational qualifications, and work-based vocational NVQs were created, providing an alternative to academic qualifications for students not suitable for A levels (Gleeson and Hodkinson, 1995).

In terms of qualifications and certification in the UK, the National Vocational Qualifications (NVQs) in England and Northern Ireland, the Credit and Qualification Framework (CQFW) in Wales, and the Vocational Qualifications (SVWs) in Scotland cover most professional areas and set out the expected outcomes required for effective performance in a particular role (Stewart et al., 2013). National Occupational Standards determine the level of skills and knowledge required at different levels of achievement on the NVQs. They range from low-level skill requirements at Level 1 to complex skills and knowledge at Level 5. The NVQ system is, therefore, a competence-based system where the knowledge, skill, and ability requirements of various jobs are determined among employers, educational policy makers, and representative groups. The failure to link vocational qualification with the higher education Qualifications and Credit Framework is a key problem within the UK VET system (Lester, 2011).

A number of different governance, quality assurance, and regulation bodies operate in the VET landscape in England, Scotland, Wales, and Northern Ireland. There is a complex institutional framework in the UK VET sector, with the Department for Education (DfE) and the Department for Business, Innovation, and Skills (BIS) sharing policy-making responsibilities in England. The policy-making authorities for VET in Northern Ireland are the Department of Education (DE) and the Department for Employment and Learning (DEL), and the Scottish and Welsh governments in Scotland and Wales, respectively (CEDEFOP, 2012). Government policies and private interests jointly drive the qualifications market in the UK. This has led to a large choice of qualifications and awarding organizations (CEDEFOP, 2012). Some criticism has been leveled at the NVQ system in England, arguing that the content of the qualifications does not adequately cater for employer needs (Gold and Thorpe, 2008). Stewart et al. (2013) argue that there are perceptions of lack of rigor with the VET and NVQ qualifications compared with the higher education sector and universities. A VET policy paper published by the Conservatives in 2008 argued that the UK VET system had become one driven by the requirements of the government's funding regime rather than the needs of individuals and the economy (Fuller and Unwin, 2011). Wolf (2011) argues that employers valued low-level NVQs very little, and yet such qualifications are taken by a large number of 16- and 17-year-olds.

Stewart et al. (2013) argue that the VET system in the UK is informed by a demand-led model and characterized by some common features that indicate its mature development: a single framework for transparency of competencies and qualifications, a system of credit transfer for VET, common criteria and principles for quality in VET, common principles for the validation of non-formal and informal learning, and information for lifelong learning. An issue that exists in the broader HRD educational provision context in Ireland and the UK is the two-tier nature of vocational versus academic qualifications and skill development. Gold et al. (2013) argue that historical and cultural influences result in perceptions of a lack of equivalence based on which route learners have taken and which institutions they attended rather than assessing the outcome of those qualifications in terms of skills acquisition. Likewise, the SOLAS (2014) report confirms that status differences between further education and training and higher education remain an issue in the Irish context. The SOLAS (2014) report refers to the expected growth in partnerships enabling higher levels of progression from further to higher education in the Irish system, as well as calling for greater employee development programs at the workplace level. Wilson (2012, p. 136) concludes that the UK VET system consists of a "complex range of agencies and initiatives that, in spite of some rationalization, appear to be diversifying as the various countries of the UK develop their own system".

HRD IN IRELAND AND THE UK: ORGANIZATION-LEVEL PROVISION

In late 2012, the Irish Business and Employers Confederation (IBEC) conducted a survey of 445 member organizations to assess training and development provision and training priorities (IBEC, 2013). The findings report that nearly two-thirds of respondent organizations (63%) conduct training audits within their organization, more likely in larger organizations than in smaller companies. In terms of training and development content, IBEC (2013) reports that management skills, occupational health and safety, and leadership skills are the most common skills included in training and development programs in member organizations. Furthermore, the survey found that many organizations predict that over the next five years management and leadership will continue to be important, along with performance management. The IBEC survey also reports changes in training methods being employed by member organizations, increased use of technology being a key feature of these changes, with many companies reporting increased use of e-learning, online courses, webinars, podcasts, etc. The average cost of training as a percentage of payroll was 2.59% according to the 2012 IBEC survey. Furthermore, training spent as a percentage of payroll was highest in large companies with over 500 employees (3.20%) and lowest in companies with fewer than 50 employees (2.84%).

Since 1999, Ireland has operated the Skillnets program (see earlier discussion), which plays a significant role in organizational-level training for organizations that are members of a Skillnet. The programs, funded from the National Training Fund (NTF) through the Department of Education and Skills, operate on the basis of a networks model, whereby networks of enterprises engage in the design, management, and delivery of specific train-ing programs to employees as well as to jobseekers across a broad range of industry and service sectors nationwide. The Indecon (2014) report evaluated the activity and impact of these 64 operational Skillnet training networks for 2013. The enterprise-led approach to Skillnets is evidenced by the involvement across the networks of a total of 10,145 member companies, which provided industry matching funding amounting to €10.4 million in 2013. Indecon (2014) reports that in 2013, 45,878 trainees participated in Skillnets training and the total number of training days was 280,175 within the Skillnets program. The report goes on to conclude that the key strategic challenges for Skillnets include the need to maintain a rigorous ongoing focus on the relevance and quality of the training provided in line with its mission to further education and training policy in Ireland.

The recent Annual Learning and Development 2015 survey by the Chartered Institute of Personnel and Development (CIPD) provides useful information regarding organizational-level HRD structures and provision in the UK. The findings are drawn from the survey responses from 541 learning and development (L&D) specialists in the UK, with half of the respondents working in the private sector, a quarter in the public sector, and the remainder evenly split between manufacturing and production and nonprofit organizations. In terms of the role and purpose of L&D, in over 40% of respondent organizations, L&D is a specialist function within the HR department; about 20% of respondents report that L&D is an activity within a generalist HR activity set; and in the remaining 40% of respondents, L&D activities are split between HR and another area of the business or are completely separate from the HR function. The report found that L&D is extremely aligned with business needs in only 25% of respondent organizations, with 40% indicating broad alignment. The most common barriers to alignment cited in the CIPD (2015) report are: L&D practitioners' lack of clarity regarding business strategy, lack of resources, and lack of interest or understanding of the purpose and capability of L&D from business leaders. In terms of organizational-level HRD provision, on-the-job training, in-house development programs, and coaching by line managers or peers are the most popular L&D methods deployed. Delivery of training and learning through learning technologies is more common in larger organizations. Seventy-five percent of organizations currently offer coaching or mentoring, and an additional 13% plan to offer it in the next year. The survey found that there are a number of L&D capability gaps (such as analytical and technological skills) that need to be addressed. In line with previous findings in HRD studies, evaluation of L&D investment and impact is still weak, and the CIPD (2015) report found that only 30% of organizations try to quantify the impact of L&D on productivity. In terms of L&D investment at the firm level, the economic recession has had a deleterious impact, with more than 50% of public-sector respondents indicating that their L&D budget had decreased over the previous year. The private sector showed a mixed landscape with 25% reporting decreased L&D budgets, whereas 25% reported increased budgets in the previous year.

HRD IN IRELAND AND THE UK: SIMILARITIES AND DIFFERENCES

The sections heretofore in this chapter are helpful for understanding the historical and current HRD landscape in Ireland and the UK. Building from that base, a key question that emerges is how similar or different HRD is within the region. In addition to the discussion in the earlier sections, which draws out similarities and differences, Table 15.1 provides an outline of how Ireland and the UK compare when exploring their HRD institutional and policy context, post-war development context, state of VET development, and providers of HRD. This chapter, and Table 15.1, demonstrates that there are more similarities than differences across the Ireland and UK region in terms of its HRD history, landscape, institutions, actors, opportunities, and challenges. The analysis in this chapter supports Raffe's (1999) assertion that any comparison across the four countries in the UK education system could be best described as representing 'variations upon common themes' rather than being uniquely distinctive. The inclusion of Ireland as another country within the region and the HRD analysis presented in this chapter for all five countries indicates that variations upon common themes is also an appropriate lens through which to examine HRD in the Ireland and UK region.

Table 15.1   Similarities and Differences in HRD in Ireland and the UK

	Ireland	UK
Institutional and policy context	Multi-actor institutional context. Ireland provides an infrastructure for the supply of skills, but the market for skills is demand-led by employers. This represents a mix of interventionism and voluntarism in HRD policy and practice and a mix of centralization in terms of skills supply through the QQI but decentralization at the firm level.	The UK provides an infrastructure for the supply of skills, but the market for skills is demand-led by employers. This represents a mix of interventionism and voluntarism in HRD policy and practice and a mix of centralization in terms of skills supply through the NQF framework but decentralization at the firm level. A complex and where criticism is leveled at the lack of integration of various institutions and actors in determining joined-up HRD and VET policy.

	Ireland	UK
Post-war development context	Move from agrarian and labor-intensive sectors to a knowledge-based economy. Education and investment in HRD is seen as a critical lever for economic growth and development.	Move from manufacturing and labor-intensive sectors to services sectors. Education and investment in HRD is seen as a critical lever for economic growth and development.
State of VET development	A well-developed National Qualifications Framework (NQF) with many providers and provisions for skill development from entry- and medium-level skills across different industries served by the FE sector to more advanced, high-level skill formation through the HE sector. Vocational Education and Training (VET) in Ireland is seen both in policy and structural terms as one of the main pillars for building and maintaining of a skilled workforce.	VET system in the UK is informed by a demand-led model and characterized by some common features that indicate its mature development: a single framework for transparency of competencies and qualifications, a system of credit transfer for VET, common criteria and principles for quality in VET, common principles for the validation of non-formal and informal learning, and information for lifelong learning.
Providers of HRD	Organizational-level through HRD or learning and development functions of organizations and private companies, professional associations, educational institutions, national Skillnets program, IBEC, and other sectoral (e.g., Teagasc) or statutory bodies (e.g., SOLAS and Skillnets).	Organizational-level through HRD or learning and development functions of organizations and private companies, professional associations, educational institutions, national Sectoral Skills Councils, employer groups, and government bodies.

This chapter reviewed the historical, political, social, and institutional influences that have impacted HRD in Ireland the UK. The current state of play with HRD in the region shows many similarities in terms of overall structures and espoused objectives, which are ultimately aligned with the enhancement of the citizen and for the overall economic growth and development of each country within the region. However, the chapter also demonstrates that the region suffers from a lack of joined-up thinking across the various institutions and actors. The development of the National Vocational Qualifications (NVQs) in the UK, National Qualifications Framework (NQF) in Ireland, the Scottish Vocational Qualifications (SQF) framework in Scotland, and the Credit and Qualification Framework (CQFW) in Wales is an essential component of the skills and qualifications elements of HRD in Ireland and the UK. These frameworks allow for identification of skill requirements, competence levels, and comparisons of assessment of qualification and skill equivalence across different national systems. While the development of VET qualification frameworks has significantly advanced the HRD field in the region, some concerns exist about their impact and effectiveness. Gold et al. (2013) argue that vocational qualifications are regularly criticized for their lack of rigor compared with more traditional third-level, university-based academic degrees and qualifications. Further, Stewart et al. (2013, p. 17) state that "VET in the UK is characterized by a lack of consistency, in that changes are fairly frequent and there are swings between the extent to which institutions operate at regional, sub-regional and local authority levels". Similar concerns have been echoed in Ireland.

The focus, content, and appropriateness of educational, HRD, and VET provisions are other areas that need attention in future policy development in the UK in particular. The low-skills equilibrium (Wilson and Hogarth, 2003) in the UK, where the economy is trapped in a vicious cycle of low-skilled work and wages leading to a fall in demand for high-skilled, value-added jobs, presents a challenge for HRD policy makers. Government policy and organizational skill requirements focus on the more pressing and immediate lower-skilled labor supply at the expense of developing a more high-skilled workface. Yet it is the latter that is increasingly seen as the source of national economic growth and development. The ability of HRD policy makers to both focus on the short-term HRD and skill requirements while ensuring the longer-term development of a highly skilled workforce necessary for sustained economic growth and development is an important balance that must be achieved in HRD policy and practice (UKCES, 2010).

Another key HRD debate in Ireland and the UK is the value of a more focused development strategy, for example, at the sectoral or functional level. Sambrook and Stewart (2007) argue that HRD policy and practice can vary depending on sector, e.g., public versus private and profit versus nonprofit. Therefore, HRD policy makers stakeholders need to ascertain if HRD within the region should also engage in sectoral-level analysis, which would complement generic national-level approaches. At a functional level, the HRD field now features many academic- and practice-based contributions in areas such as leadership development, front-line/supervisory development, coaching and mentoring. The impact of funding reductions due to the global financial crisis has also affected functional based HRD initiatives at the firm level so that HRD practitioners need to focus on ensuring they can make the case for increased investment (McCarthy and Sheehan, 2014). MacKenzie et al. (2012) have articulated strong criticism of the financial bottom line taking precedence over any real considerations of HRD focused on employee development and career enhancement in organizations post the global financial crisis (GFC) of 2008. Furthermore, Keeble-Ramsey and Armitage's (2015) study of middle and front-line managers in the UK concludes that post-GFC HRD is silenced or absent and associated solely with low-cost-based e-learning rather than playing a strategic role in support of sustainable business objectives. A challenge for HRD in Ireland and the UK is to ensure that HRD's role in HRM at the organizational level will regain its potential to influence skill development in the workplace strategically and to argue convincingly the necessity for investment in HRD in a challenging financial context. The CIPD (2015) L&D survey in the UK found mixed views regarding the future of L&D funding at the organization level, with over 25% of the private-sector respondents forecasting an increase in the overall funding of L&D over the next 12 months but 15% expecting a decrease. However, the public-sector organizations report much more pessimistic projections, with more than half expecting a decrease in L&D investment. Therefore, challenges remain in terms of HRD investment.

CONCLUSION

HRD in Ireland and the UK shares many similarities in policy and practice due to the common cultural and historical circumstances out of which it emerged. For example, the VET system in Ireland and the UK developed from broadly similar contexts with broadly similar objectives and expected outcomes. However, the extent to which various HRD stakeholders have influenced systems and policy at a national level and practice at organizational level is mixed. The CIPD (2015) report found that learning and development (L&D) professionals in the UK are increasingly aware of how important it is to understand business needs, to be commercially aware, and to align learning and development with strategic decision making in organizations. While L&D has improved its alignment with business strategy, there is still much that needs to be done to ensure that L&D is seen as a critical lever of organizational success. At a policy level, significant progress has been made in terms of VET and HRD policy in the region, but further work needs to be done in terms of ensuring that the various institutions and actors are aligned in delivering an integrated and joined-up approach to HRD in the region.

REFERENCES

Barry, M. (2007). *Vocational Education and Training in Ireland: Thematic Overview*. Dublin: FÁS.

Breen, R., Hannan, D. F., Rottman, D. B., & Whelan, C. T. (1990). *Understanding Contemporary Ireland: State, Class and Development in the Republic of Ireland*. London: Macmillan.

CEDEFOP. (2012). *Spotlight on VET in the United Kingdom*. Athens, Greece: CEDEFOP.

CIPD. (2015). *Learning and Development*. London: CIPD.

CSO. (2014). *Population and Migration Estimates Statistical Release*. Cork, Ireland: CSO. August 26, 2014.

DES. (2015). *Department of Education and Skills*. (http://www.education.ie).

Dorey, P. (1995). *British Politics Since 1945. Making Contemporary Britain*. Oxford: Blackwell.

Duffy, D., FitzGerald, J., McQuinn, K., Byrne, D., & Morley, C. (2014). *Quarterly Economic Commentary*. October. Dublin: ESRI.

Fahey, T. (1995). Family and household in Ireland. In P. Clancy, S. Drudy, K. Lynch and L. O'Dowd (Eds.), *Irish society: Sociological Perspectives*, 205–234. Dublin: IPA.

Francis, M. (1997). *Ideas and Policies under Labor, 1945–1951: Building a New Britain*. UK: Manchester University Press.

Fuller, A. and Unwin, L. (2011). Vocational education and training in the spotlight: back to the future for the UK's Coalition Government? *London Review of Education*, 9: 2, 191–204

Gleeson, D., & Hodkinson, P. (1995). Ideology and curriculum policy: GNVQ and mass post-compulsory education in England and Wales. *Journal of Education and Work*, 8(3): 5–19.

Gold, J., Holden, R., Stewart, J., Iles, P. and Beardwell, J. (2013). *Human Resource Development: Theory and Practice*, 2nd ed. London: Palgrave Macmillan.

Gold, J., & Thorpe, R. (2008). Training, it's a load of crap: The story of the hairdresser ad his suit. *Human Resource Development International*, 11(4): 385–399.

Gunnigle, P., Heraty, N. and Morley, M.J. (2003). *Human Resource in Ireland*. Dublin: Gill and Macmillan.

Harrison, R. (2009). *Learning and Development*. 5th ed. London: CIPD Publishing.

Holmes, L. (2012). *Re-examining National HRD in the UK: The Potential Utility of a Governance Perspective*. Paper presented at the University Forum for HRD, UK.

IBEC. (2013). *Management Training Survey 2013*. Dublin: IBEC.

IMF. (2014). *World Economic Outlook Database*.

Indecon. (2014). *Evaluation of TNP, Finuas and Management Works in 2013*. Dublin: Indecon International Economic Consultants.

Keeble-Ramsay, D. R., & Armitage, A. (2015). HRD challenges faced in the post-global financial crisis period—insights from the UK. *European Journal of Training and Development*, 39(2): 86–103.

Lee, S. J. (1996). *Aspects of British Political History 1914–1995*. London, New York: Routledge.

Leitch, S. (2006). *Prosperity For All in the Global Economy—World Class Skills*. London, H M Treasury.

Lester, S. (2011). The UK qualifications and credit framework: A critique. *Journal of Vocational Education and Training*, 63(2): 205–216.

MacKenzie, C. A., Garavan, T. N., & Carbery, R. (2012). Through the looking glass: Challenges for human resource development (HRD) post the global financial crisis—business as usual? *Human Resource Development International*, 15(3): 353–364.

McCarthy, A. and Sheehan, M. (2014). Uncertainty and On-Going Economic Turbulence: Implications for HRD. *Advances in Developing Human Resources,* 16(1), 3–12.

Mead, W. R. (2007). *God and Gold: Britain, America, and the Making of the Modern World.* New York: Alfred A. Knopf.

Musset, P., & S. Field. (2013). *A Skills beyond School Review of England,* OECD Reviews of Vocational Education and Training. OECD Publishing: OECD.

O'Connell, P. J., & Rottman, D. B. (1994). The Irish welfare state in comparative perspective. In J. H. Goldthorpe and C. T. Whelan (Eds.), *The Development of Industrial Society in Ireland,* Proceedings of the British Academy, Vol. 79, 205–239. Published for the British Academy by Oxford University Press.

O'Donnell, D., Garavan, T., & McCarthy, A. (2001). Understanding the Irish VET system: Beyond neo-classicism. *International Journal of Manpower,* 22(5):425–445.

O'Malley, E. (1989). *Industry and Economic Development: The Challenge for the Latecomer.,* Dublin: Gill and Macmillan.

ONS. (2014). *Population Estimates for UK, England and Wales, Scotland and Northern Ireland, Mid-2013.* (http://www.ons.gov.uk/ons/rel/pop-estimate/population-estimates-for-uk—england-and-wales—scotland-and-northern-ireland/2013/index.html)

ONS. (2015). *Statistical Bulletin: Second Estimate of GDP, Quarter 1(Jan to Mar) 2015.* London: ONS.

Raffe, D., Brannen, K., Croxford, L., & Martin, C. (1999). Comparing England, Scotland, Wales and Northern Ireland: The Case for 'Home Internationals' in Comparative Research. *Comparative Education,* 35(1): 9–25.

Rebellato, D., Horn, E., Mjøen, L., Williams, J., Barrow, S., Turner, A., Clifton, N., Gray, C., & Bjorvand, E. (2011). The cultural superpower: British cultural projection abroad. *British Politics Review,* 6(1): 1–12.

Richardson, W., & Wiborg, S. (2010). *English Technical and Vocational Education in Historical and Comparative Perspective: Considerations for University Technical Colleges.* London: Baker Dearing Educational Trust.

Sambrook, S., & Stewart, J. (2007). HRD in health and social care. In S. Sambrook & J. Stewart (Eds.), *Human Resource Development in the Public Sector,* 3–15. London: Routledge.

SOLAS (2014). Further Education and Training Strategy 2014 – 2019. Dublin: SOLAS.

Stewart, J., & McGuire, D. (2012). Contemporary developments in human resource development. In J. Stewart and K. Rogers (Eds.), *Developing People and Organizations,* 121–143. London: CIPD.

Stewart, J., Beardwell, J., Gold, J., Iles, P., & Holden, R. (2013). The scope of HRD and national HRD policies and practice. In J. Gold, R. Holden, J. Stewart, P. Iles and J. Beardwell (Eds.), *Human Resource Development: Theory and Practice,* 3–25. 2nd ed. London: Palgrave Macmillan.

UKCES (2010). Skills for Jobs: Today and Tomorrow. London: UK Commission for Employment and Skills.

UK Commission for Employment and Skills. (UKCES). (2013). *OECD Review: Skills beyond School. Background Report for England.* Briefing Paper February 2013. UK Commission for Employment and Skills. (http://www.ukces.org.uk/publications/oecd-skills-beyond-school-england)

West, J., & Steedman, H (2003). *Finding Our Way: Vocational Education in England.* London: Centre for Economic Performance.

Wilson, J. P. (2012). *International Human Resource Development: Learning, Education and Training for Individuals and Organizations.* London: Kogan Page.

Wilson, J. P., & Hogarth, T. (2003). *Tackling the Low Skills Equilibrium: A Review of Issues and Some New Evidence.* London: DTI.

Wolf, A. 2011. *Review of vocational education – the Wolf report.* London: Department for Education.

16 Human Resource Development in the Nordic Countries

Britta H. Heidl and Indravidoushi C. Dusoye

INTRODUCTION

This chapter discusses HRD in the Nordic countries, which include the Scandinavian countries and Iceland. These countries form a specific cluster, not only because of their geographic location in the north of Europe but also due to common political, cultural, demographic, and economic factors (Olofsson and Wadensjö, 2012). The Nordic countries are represented in the Nordic Council, which ties them together into common educational and labor market policies. What this means is that whereas each country has its own legislation, the political decisions of one directly affects the HRD developments in the others. Furthermore, the Nordic countries all have relatively small economies and small populations (Eurostat, 2015). Compared to European countries, people in the Nordic countries have a more 'feminine culture', where competition and winning is less important than quality of life and enjoying what they are doing (The Hofstede Centre, 2015). All of these indicators impact on HRD, and hence it makes sense to review the situation of HRD in these countries as a group. The purpose of this chapter is to discuss both the contextual influences on HRD at a macrolevel as well as at the organizational level. In examining the similarities and differences between the Nordic countries, this chapter aims to show that there is a common Nordic model of HRD.

The chapter is structured in eight sections. The first discusses the context of HRD and looks at the political and demographic environment. The second considers economic developments as they form the basis on which labor market institutions and organizations make their decisions and implement policies. The third and fourth sections deal with the current state of the labor market, exploring similarities and differences in some labor market indicators, but also looking at the main institutions that play a role in labor market regulation. The fifth section looks at the educational systems that determine the educational level of people entering the labor market and discusses the involvement of private organizations, especially through vocational education. The sixth section then looks at HRD at the organizational level. The main trends, similarities, and differences with respect to HRD in Nordic countries is discussed in section seven, and the final section finishes with some concluding remarks.

NORDIC CONTEXT

The term 'Nordic countries' commonly refers to five countries, namely Denmark (including Greenland and the Faroe Islands), Sweden, Finland (including Aland), Norway, and Iceland. These countries are grouped together, on the one hand, because of their geographic position, and on the other hand, because of their similarities in political, social, and economic approaches (Olofsson and Wadensjö, 2012). Furthermore, these countries are organized in a common council, the Nordic Council, which regulates their interstate relationships. Because of their close economic relationships, the Nordic countries are often considered an extended home market with similar institutional, historic environments, and even a common labor market that allows free movement and employment in all Nordic countries (Norden, 2015). The relationship between the Nordic countries and the European Union differs among these countries. Finland, Denmark, and Sweden are all members of the European Union. However, Finland is the only one of these countries to also be a member of the Eurozone. Norway and Iceland are completely outside the European Union but belong to the European Economic Area (Norden, 2015). The Nordic countries are among the world's 20 most affluent nations. According to figures from the IMF data (International Monetary Fund, 2009), in terms of GDP per capita (PPP) in US dollars, Norway (53,451), Iceland (40,025), Denmark (37,266), Sweden (37,245), and Finland (36,217) ranked number 3, 10, 16, 17, and 20, respectively, in world wealth (Lin and Edvinsson, 2011).

The Nordic countries consist of a total area of 3.5 million sq km. Even excluding Greenland and the Norwegian islands of Svalbard and Jan Mayen, the Nordic countries cover a vast area of 1.3 million sq km, which is equal in size to Germany, France, and Italy together. The five Nordic countries cover five time zones and are bordered by Russia on the east, Germany and Poland to the south, and the Arctic Ocean to the north. Yet the population of Nordic countries totals 26 million, one of the lowest population densities in the world. This is mainly because the Nordic countries have large marginal areas where habitation is difficult due to the region's natural landscape. Denmark has the highest population density. Around 20% of the population in four out of the five Nordic countries is normally found within regions close to the capitals; however, this percentage is low compared with Iceland where the majority (60%) of inhabitants live close to the capital. Iceland, Norway, and Aland have experienced an increase in population compared with some regions of Sweden, Finland, Greenland, and Faroe Island. Overall, however, the Nordic countries have experienced growth in population numbers (Nordic Statistical Yearbook, 2012).

Economic Developments in the Nordic Countries

The Nordic economies share certain similarities. All of them are small and open economies that depend on foreign trade. Coming from a strong agricultural economy, they have developed into modern economies and are often considered a hub for innovation, change, and creativity (Gaude, 2015). In recent decades, the sectoral structure has changed significantly in most of the Nordic countries (Worldbank, 2015). In Sweden, Denmark, and Finland a decrease in both agricultural and industrial contributions to the GDP can be seen, whereas the services sector shows constant growth since the 1990s in the whole of the Nordic countries. In 2012, the services sector dominated the Nordic economies, 67.8% in Iceland and over 70% in Finland, Sweden, and Denmark. Whereas with 56.8% the services sector is also the biggest contributor to the economy in Norway, the Norwegian industrial sector is considerably stronger than in the other Nordic countries, reaching over 40% of the GDP. This is at least partly due to the high influence of Norway's oil and gas sector. Iceland, on the other hand, is an exception as to the agricultural sector, which with 7.73% of GDP remains relatively strong.

Despite those recent structural changes, the Nordic economies remain successful (Magnusson, L. 2007; Steinacher, 2015). The GDP per capita, one of the widely accepted measures of the success of an economy, shows that all the Nordic countries perform over the European average, with Norway's GDP per capita being nearly three times higher than the average of the European Union. The financial crisis in 2008/2009 hit the Nordic countries hard, but the effects were particularly strong in Iceland. However, the growing GDP per capita in the post-crisis years suggests economic recovery in all five Nordic countries (Eurostat, 2015).

The Labor Market in the Nordic Countries

In order to understand HRD in the specific context of the Nordic countries, it is essential to consider the labor market their organizations operate in. The Nordic countries have to some extent created a common labor market. Since 1983, this allows citizens from Nordic countries to work in any other Nordic country without the need for special working permits (Nordic Council of Ministers, 1983). Furthermore, employee mobility between Nordic countries is supported by additional agreements, such as acknowledging higher education degrees awarded by all institutions located in one of the Nordic countries (Nordic Council of Ministers, 1998). However, there are differences in terms of employment and labor market policies that distinguish the individual labor markets from each other. Table 16.1 gives an overview of some labor market indicators for the Nordic countries.

In general, the employment level in the Nordic countries is fairly high (Olofsson and Wadensjö, 2012). However, the employment rates within the Nordic countries vary considerably. Whereas in Iceland over 80% of the population aged 15 to 64 is in employment, in Finland, the employment rate is significantly lower with only 68.7%. The employment rate needs to be interpreted in the context of each country, as it does, for example, not

Table 16.1   Labor Market Indicators in the Nordic Countries in 2014

	Denmark	Sweden	Finland	Norway	Iceland
Employment rate 2014 (15–64 years)*	72.8%	74.9%	68.7%	75.2%	81.7%
Unemployment 2014*	6.6%	7.9%	8.7%	3.5%	5.0%
Youth unemployment 2014 (under 25 years)*	12.6%	22.9%	20.5%	7.9%	10.0%
Part-time contracts 2014 (% of employment)*	25.5%	26.2%	15.4%	26.7%	20.4%
Temporary contracts 2014 (% of employment)*	8.5%	17.5%	15.5%	7.9%	13.4%
Employment rate females 2014 (15–64 years)*	69.8%	73.1%	68.0%	73.4%	79.3%
Gender Inequality Index Rank 2014**	5th	4th	11th	9th	14th

Sources: *Eurostat, 2015; **UNDP, 2015

take into account that, especially among younger people, many are still in further or higher education and not active in the labor market. Looking at the unemployment rate, and hence those who are looking for work, there are considerable differences as well. Norway reports a very low unemployment rate of only 3.5%, whereas in Finland, 8.7% are unemployed. In all Nordic countries, the unemployment rate among young people is higher than the total unemployment rate, indicating that young people leaving school or higher education have more difficulties finding jobs. Attempts to reduce youth unemployment are being made. The Swedish government, for example, declared its intention to tackle this issue by investing more into the creation of graduate jobs through training (Steinacher, 2015).

Temporary contracts, which give employers more flexibility, are common in the Nordic countries. However, the rates of employees in temporary employment vary. The use of such contracts is highest in Sweden, where 17.5% of all employees are in temporary contracts. In contrast, Danish companies make less use of temporary contracts for only 8.5% of employees. However, in Denmark, the regulations concerning hiring and firing employees (Euromonitor International, 2015a) are looser than in other Nordic countries, which implies that employers do not need to use temporary contracts to keep their flexibility. Compared with temporary contracts, the use of part-time contracts is high. Apart from Finland, all Nordic countries report that over 20% of the workforce is in part-time employment.

In terms of diversity and equality, the Nordic countries are often considered a benchmark for the rest of the world. One reason for this is extensive public funding for childcare and elder care (Olofsson and Wadensjö, 2012).

Paid maternity and paternity leave with payment levels of up to 100% of the salary are available in all of the Nordic countries. Women can take maternity leave for up to 18 weeks, paternity leave varies between 2 weeks and 3 months, and additional parental leave or family leave is possible in all Nordic countries with the exception of Iceland (O'Brien, 2013). This helps to retain both mothers and fathers in the workforce and results in a high female employment rate. Hence women participate to a great extent in the Nordic economies. The gender inequality index, which measures inequality under three parameters, reproductive health, empowerment, and labor market, ranks all Nordic countries within the top 15 out of 187 countries (UNDP, 2015), indicating comparably low levels of gender inequality across all the Nordic countries.

THE INSTITUTIONAL CONTEXT OF HRD

The Nordic countries are often located within the coordinated market economies (Gooderham et al., 2015), which means, compared with Anglo-Saxon countries where most of the wages and employment conditions are negotiated between employer and employee, the Nordic labor markets are highly regulated. Legislation and collective agreements largely build the basis for employment conditions, hiring and firing policies, as well as education and development. This leaves employers with less flexibility; however, it also results in fewer conflicts between employer and employees, low wage spreads, and long-term employment (Olofsson and Wadensjö, 2012). The focus on long-term employment increases the need for human resource development. New skills cannot simply be acquired through hiring new employees, rather the talent and potential of the current workforce needs to be used and developed within the organization. On the one hand, that gives employees a career perspective, but on the other hand, it helps organizations as well as employees to keep up with changes in knowledge, technology, and processes.

As collective agreements play a major role, it is not surprising that labor unions have a high impact on the labor markets in Nordic countries. The high level of collective bargaining in the Nordic countries is also reflected in the high levels of unionization. With the exception of Norway, where just around 50% of employees are unionized, this percentage stands much higher in other Nordic countries. The influence of unions is, however, not limited to employees' being actual members of the unions: in all of the Nordic countries, the proportion of employees covered by collective agreements is higher than the actual membership. Collective agreements in the Nordic countries have a similar status to legislation, applying not only to local organizations but also to a certain extent to international companies (Steinacher, 2015), hence their impact is far-reaching. Labor unions in the Nordic countries stress, for example, the importance of training and re-education; the regulation of wages, as well as the hiring and firing decisions; and the negotiating of employment related issues, such as working hours, holidays, and holiday pay (Steinacher et al., 2014).

The other major force in the Nordic labor markets is the government, which exerts its influence on the labor market through laws and regulations, as well as public investment in labor, in the labor market, and, in particular, education. In the Nordic countries, public support has traditionally been strong (Tomé, 2005), resulting in a strong welfare state that provides high levels of support in terms of unemployment, health care, childcare, and education. Denmark reports the highest levels of governmental spend on the labor market, where public spending on the labor market activities exceeded nine billion Euros in 2012, which constitutes 3.7% of the GDP.

These investments in social welfare are funded by relatively high taxes in the Nordic countries; however, whereas it is often argued that high levels of unemployment support actually increase unemployment, in the case of the Nordic countries, it actually increases employment and employee mobility. In general, the relationship between governmental agencies, labor unions, and employers in the Nordic countries is characterized as very open and consultative (Gooderham et al., 2015). Despite similarities in the way the labor market is organized in the Nordic countries, there are some differences. Norwegian legislation, for example, regulates the employment relationship in a way that is more far-reaching than in the other Nordic countries by demanding the satisfaction of employees' psychological needs, such as task autonomy and task variation (Ramirez, 2004). Denmark, on the other hand, has implemented a system that differs from the rest of the Nordic countries. Known as 'flexicurity', it involves, on the one hand, a greater degree of flexibility for employers by loosening the regulations on, for example, redundancy, but on the other hand provides employees that might suffer from those loose regulations a stronger security net in increased social security (Gooderham et al., 2015). Flexicurity aims at ensuring welfare, an effective labor market, high productivity, and competitiveness and ultimately high overall employment rates in the long term and on the national level. However, it can lead to a more short-term approach when it comes to individual employment. As organizations are more flexible in terms of hiring and firing, the responsibility of training and development now lies in the hands of the employees and government rather than the organization. However, in the long term, flexicurity develops a high level of social capital among employees, which benefits both the organization and the individual (Hilson, 2008; Kvist and Greve, 2011).

EDUCATION IN THE NORDIC COUNTRIES

The Nordic countries share the same values in terms of teaching and education (see Table 16.2). Their focus is on long-term training and development, democracy-oriented learning programs, and educational curriculum around independence and critical awareness. Similarly, the Nordic countries, share the same views regarding the state's role in education, as in financing of comprehensive schooling, which is compulsory in all of the five countries. Compulsory schooling in Denmark and Finland, however, comes with more flexible approaches, such as learning at home. After nine to ten years of compulsory schooling, most students pursue further or higher studies (Nordic Council of Ministers, 2014). However, all programs offered in the different countries vary: some educational programs, for example, support academic development, whereas others support vocational development for specific professions. Vocational programs in Denmark, Sweden, Norway, and Iceland do not automatically aim at preparing students for higher education, so students need to take additional courses to be eligible for higher-level education. On the other hand, secondary education students in Finland can enter university after completing any of the secondary educational programs.

Iceland differs from the other Nordic countries in that its average education attainment rates are low compared with the other Nordic countries, but there has been significant improvement in these scores at the secondary and tertiary levels (OECD, 2010a). The Icelandic Strategy 2020 has been supporting this mission of improvement (Ministry of Economic Affairs, 2011). An additional attribute of the Icelandic educational system is its higher percentage of school dropouts compared with other Nordic countries. However, some of these school dropouts aim at achieving their secondary education at a later stage in their lives, allowing them to pursue either their tertiary education or move forward in their career paths. This suggests that the Icelandic educational system is not as seamless and linear as in the other Nordic countries (OECD, 2012; Blöndal et al., 2011)

According to European statistics (Eurostat, 2015), the most popular areas of study in all the Nordic countries in 2012 were the social sciences, business, or law, followed by health and welfare programs in Denmark, Sweden, Iceland, and Norway and more technical subjects such as engineering in Finland. The smallest proportion of students graduate from services-related studies, as well as from agricultural and veterinary study programs.

In conclusion, the population in the Nordic countries is well educated, and the percentage of the workforce with higher education degrees is increasing. With between 29.4% in Denmark and 36.1% in Norway of the workforce holding a college or university degree in 2014, all Nordic countries rank above the European average of 26% (Eurostat, 2015). Such high levels of college and university attendance lead to a generally well-skilled population. Social mobility is high in the Nordic countries (OECD, 2010b). That means that students' economic backgrounds do not influence, to a large extent, their achievements or their eventual economic status.

HRD AT THE ORGANIZATIONAL LEVEL

Although Nordic countries share similar approaches to labor market regulation and education, differences occur when looking at HRD on the

Table 16.2 Education in the Nordic Countries

	Compulsory School Education in the Nordic Countries				
Country	Denmark	Sweden	Finland	Norway	Iceland
Years of compulsory education	9	9	9	10	10
Government influence	High, government sets standards	High, government sets standards	High, government sets standards	High, government sets standards	High, government sets standards
Involvement of private institutions	around 10%	around 7%	> 5%	> 5%	around 6%
Tuition fees	No fees	No fees	No fees	No fees	No fees
	Secondary School Education in the Nordic Countries				
Integrated system	No	Yes	No	Yes	No
Main programs	– General preparatory school – Business and technical schools – Vocational training programs	– General preparatory school – Vocational training programs	– General preparatory school – Vocational training programs – tenth year of compulsory school	– General preparatory school – Vocational training programs	– Grammar Schools – Vocational training programs – Comprehensive schools

(*Continued*)

Table 16.2 (Continued)

			Compulsory School Education in the Nordic Countries			
Country	Denmark	Sweden	Finland	Norway	Iceland	
VET gives access to further studies	No	No Supplementary courses optional	Yes	No Supplementary courses optional	No	
Apprenticeships included in VET	Yes	No	Optional	Yes	Yes	
VET financed by	Government, individual employers and employers collectively	Mainly government	Mainly government (national and municipal tax)	Mainly government	Mainly government	

Source: Based on Icelandic Ministry of Education, Science and Culture (2008); Olofsson and Wadensjö (2012); EURYDICE (2015); Icelandic Ministry of Education, Science and Culture (2015); Statistics Iceland (2015)

organizational level. A remarkable characteristic of the HRD system in Nordic countries is its strong and long-standing performance in adult education, training, and lifelong learning. Nordic countries have strong traditions and high participation rates in adult education. They share a high level of social capital that leads to a high level of trust between employers and employees, thus increasing the ability to compete. Furthermore, Nordic countries are very efficient at knowledge diffusing and learning in organizations with a strongly developed absorptive capacity (Hall and Soskice, 2001). They have demonstrated greater success in learning-oriented work programs than Europe in general, and this can be ascribed to the cooperation between the labor market stakeholders and the national political authorities, leading to trust between management and workers at a local level (Gustavsen, 2007).

According to the European Working Conditions Survey in 2010, organizations in the Nordic countries benefit from a well-educated workforce (Martinaitis, 2014). However, the Nordic labor market has been suffering from a mismatch between workforce qualifications and qualifications demanded by emerging sectors (Magnusson, D., 2007). The skills mismatch becomes more problematic, especially because the labor supply in Nordic countries is already limited. The Euromonitor International Reports (2014; 2015a; 2015b) show that Denmark, Sweden, and Norway are still facing skills shortages in health care and engineering, although Norway particularly needs engineers for the mining and petroleum industry.

Skills development in managerial programs is very specific to each of the Nordic countries. Management development is as dependent on managers' personalities as their experience in both Denmark and Norway (Mabey, 2008; Mabey and Ramirez, 2004; Ramirez, 2004; Ramirez and Mabey, 2005). Whereas Norwegian organizations use firm-specific, in-house training linked to organizational strategy, Danish organizations rely more on vocational education, as well as on experiential and informal learning. Similarly, Norwegian companies align their management development programs more with organizational strategy compared to Danish organizations. Although both Norwegian and Danish organizations possess management development programs that support high potentials, no established evaluation of these programs exists. The reasons for investments in training and development of managers in Norwegian and Danish companies are fairly similar. General practices in management development in firms of both countries include regular appraisals, career planning, discussion of development needs and special routes, and support for high potentials (Ramirez and Mabey, 2005). General practices in management development in firms of both countries include regular appraisals, career planning, discussion of development needs and special routes, and support for those with high potentials; however, the evaluation of management development practices themselves was found to be quite weak. The reasons for investments in training and development of managers in Norwegian and Danish companies are fairly similar. The main emphasis is on promoting managers from within the organization, which offers employees career opportunities and helps retaining staff in the long term.

Training approaches in Iceland are mostly on the job rather than classroom based. In fact, one of the most useful programs in Iceland is a small long-term internship program where the Icelandic employment services pay a stipend to a company to train unemployed workers for six months. This stipend lowers the cost of hiring a new worker for the first six months and can act as a type of marginal employment subsidy that may represent the best trade-off for money spent (OECD, 2010a). To avoid problems of firms firing high-paid workers to hire lower-paid ones, the subsidy can only be claimed by firms that have not fired workers in the past six months. At the end of the program, most of the workers stay with the company that they interned with. However, this high-value program can accommodate the small number of seven hundred unemployed because the demand for workers in organizations is low. Iceland also provides numerous skills-training classes for the unemployed so that they are continuously refining their skills and competencies in line with the market demand.

The theory and practice of HRD in Finnish organizations can be described as a transformational form of traditional training with continuous learning and development. Finnish HRD experts, influenced by the Anglo-American HRD literature and practices, have embraced the concepts of 'learning organizations'. HRD experts constantly act as change and learning agents by linking developmental needs in line with the organization's objectives. Even though HRD has been considered a special focus for adult education, it was seen as an activity that was focused on intentional and formal learning and even incorporated an andragogical perspective into management. Educational attainment in the 1960s in Finland was low; only one out of ten adults had completed more than nine years basic education, which was similar to countries such as Malaysia and Peru and left it lagging behind its Scandinavian neighbors. However, in 2010, Finland emerged as OCED's leading country in educational achievement due to the country's excellent educational system taking teacher preparation, professional learning and development, and decision-making systems and practices for curriculum and assessment into account (Sahlberg, 2010). Finland has strengthened its position on workforce development in recent years, too, through the Finnish Workplace Development Program, which supports the development of working practices in Finland under the auspices of the Finnish Funding Agency for Technology and Innovation. The program is based on the view that for a small country such as Finland to cope with the globalizing economy, the most effective way of generating organizational learning is through close cooperation and interaction between workplaces, researchers, consultants, public authorities, and social partners (Cseh and Manikoth, 2012).

Norway and Sweden have experimented with job redesign and efforts to enhance workplace democracy since the 1960s (Alasoini, 2009). The tradition of action research that saw light from the creation of programs such as

Leadership, Organization, and Co-Determination (LOM) lasted from 1985 to 1990 in Sweden followed by the Enterprise Development Program in 2000 in Norway. The central concepts of the LOM program was to promote network, learning, and democratic dialogue. These developmental programs moved the focus from intraorganizational to interorganizational, inviting organizations to collaborate together with researchers (Gustaven, 1992). More recently, Norway has been guided by Value Creation 2010, a program designed to develop new forms of cooperation and work organization through strong social partnerships (Alasoini, 2009).

DISCUSSION

Whereas the EU has been looking for solutions to solve the EU 2008 crisis, the Nordic countries, with the exception of Iceland, were only slightly touched by this world event (Veggeland, 2012). These five countries have topped the list as the 20 most affluent nations with high GDP per capita and outstanding economic performance. There has been a shift in the importance of certain sectors and, consequently, changes in employment opportunities, which has had an impact on both skill demand and supply in the labor market. Skills and knowledge that used to be high in demand for industrial jobs might be less relevant for the services sector. As a result, training and education will need to respond to this shift. However, the strong economic status of the Nordic countries indicates that the economy has adapted successfully to these economic developments.

The strength of these countries lies in their active welfare state and their labor-focused policy (Veggeland, 2012). The strong coordination of the labor market through unions along with governmental legislation restricts the range of decision making for employers and HRD professionals in organizations. While some of the regulations might not directly fall into the area of HRD, such as minimum wages, hiring and firing decisions, and other employment conditions mentioned earlier, these can have far-reaching effects on HRD functions and hence indirectly affect HRD strategies. Other areas, such as education, directly impact on national HRD, which provides the skills and knowledge set employees bring into organizations, thereby providing the starting point for organizational HRD. On the other hand, strong regulation that decreases flexibility brings standardization benefits for employers. Not every single contract needs to be negotiated; this saves companies time and resources. Furthermore, both employers and employees know the benchmark and hence conflicts based on inequality are reduced (Olofsson and Wadensjö, 2012).

Coupled with that, the Nordics have invested in their inimitable asset: their human capital. The Nordic countries have strong developmental programs, tertiary education enrollment, and compulsory schooling. Both compulsory and further and higher education have a big impact on the skills and knowledge available to the labor market and hence heavily influence organizational HRD. A well-educated workforce, as in the Nordic countries, brings a wide range of skills and knowledge into the workplace. HRD can then focus on enhancing these skills instead of providing basic training. Apprenticeships offered in many areas serve to give students training before they are hired. The usually lower wages that are paid to apprentices and the possibility to evaluate candidates over a longer period of time make apprenticeship an interesting option for organizations (Olofsson and Wadensjö, 2012). Although the Nordic countries are quite similar in terms of long-term learning, democracy, and state financing for schooling, some countries provide more of an academic pathway compared with others, where focus is more on the vocational. The key here is a mixture of both, in a system that ensures that both employees' and employers' needs are cared for.

As Nordic countries operate within a common market pool (Norden, 2015), free mobility of labor can alleviate the issue of unemployment in some of the Nordic countries. Someone unemployed in one of the countries can find a job in another. However, youth unemployment follows the global trend, with higher levels also in Nordic countries

Despite general similarities, there are differences between the countries in the Nordic group and these pull them in different directions. Denmark has developed into a services-based economy. However, compared with the other Nordic countries, the sectoral changes during the last decades were rather small. The changes in the skills demand could, as a result, be tackled over a longer period of time. One way in which Denmark has addressed this is in its 'flexicurity' policy, which differentiates Denmark from the other Nordic countries. It gives employers more freedom in hiring and firing decisions and hence employers can instantly react to changing demands. This ensures, on the one hand, that employers have the most appropriate talent in their workforce and, on the other hand, that continuous development becomes an imperative for employees (Gooderham et al., 2015). However, it leads to a more short-term orientation, which implies less development and fewer career opportunities within organizations. Instead of developing employees for the future, organizations rely on the educational system to develop the future workforce. In order for this to work, employers and government work closely together in developing and funding secondary education and vocational education that corresponds to the needs of employers.

Finland and Sweden share fairly similar characteristics. They are the two Nordic countries with the highest unemployment rates in both total and youth unemployment, which results in fewer career opportunities for employees. This, together with the high amounts of temporary employment contracts, paints a picture of oversupply of labor, in which even skilled and well-educated people struggle to find employment. While work-based learning and development are a part of vocational education in the other Nordic countries, that is not the case at all in Sweden, and it is only optional in Finland. Hence employers do not engage in the basic development of skills and knowledge. However, by not engaging they also miss out on the benefits such as directing the focus to core skills or to needed new skills.

In contrast to Denmark, Sweden, and Finland, training and development in Iceland is mainly work-based (OECD, 2010a). Apart from training and development for employees, organizations also engage in long-term internships for the unemployed that are funded by the government. This could be partly due to higher dropout rates from secondary and tertiary education, but it ensures that developmental initiatives are in line with employers' needs and hence organizational goals. Despite still recovering from the economic crisis, Iceland shows the highest employment rates, the highest female employment rates, and one of the lowest unemployment rates of the Nordic countries.

Norway differs from the rest of the Nordic countries in that its background and resources are different. Whereas in the other Nordic countries the importance of industry is declining and the services sector is growing, the economic analysis for Norway paints a different picture. Relying heavily on its natural oil and gas resources, Norwegian industry has grown over the last decades. This boom of the oil and gas sector is reflected in the highest GDP per capita of the Nordic countries and strong economic growth (Eurostat, 2015). In this context, both total and youth unemployment rates are considerably lower than in the other Nordic countries, and the use of temporary contracts is comparably the lowest. It is therefore not surprising that the skills demand is high and employers report labor shortages especially in the oil- and gas-related engineering professions. In order to attract and develop necessary knowledge and skills, organizations respond with extensive development programs and career development within the organization (Mabey, 2008). Governmental legislation is more restrictive than in other Nordic countries, which poses additional pressure on Norwegian employers. However, with a unionization rate of only around 50%, the influence of labor unions is smaller than in the other Nordic countries. In a nutshell, the main issue for Norwegian HRD is the skills shortage in a strong economy. Developing talent early on through the educational system and offering further career-related development in employment seems to be the key issue and the route chosen.

CONCLUSION

Drawing on the findings of this chapter, it seems to be reasonable to consider the Nordic countries as a cluster from an HRD perspective. Relatively similar economic developments are paired with regulated labor markets and an emphasis on a strong education—accessible to the majority of the population—which lead to high levels of human capital and development. This forms the basis of HRD on the organizational level, which means that employees joining the workforce already possess a high level of knowledge and skill. The free movement of the workforce in a common labor market further highlights the strong connection of the Nordic countries. And still more, the high participation rates and high female participation in all the Nordic countries suggest a similar culture and value with respect to work. As such, at a macrolevel, the Nordic countries reflect a more 'feminist' approach in terms of Hofstede's cultural dimensions compared to other countries with HRD models that are more paternalistic. However, at a micro level, within the organizations across the different countries, the HRD practices tend to differ, especially in their degree of strategic alignment of HRD and the approaches to employee and managerial development. As such, the presence of a converging macrolevel 'feminist' culture, coupled with divergent HRD practices at the micro level, makes the existence of one Nordic model of HRD highly questionable. The question hinges on the fact that HRD practices are different, whereas we could expect them to be shared across organizations in the Nordic countries. It is not really possible to have a specific Nordic model, although there are commonalities at the macro level between countries. There is, however, such divergence in terms of HRD practices that, in this sense, it would be too simplistic to speak of one Nordic model of HRD.

REFERENCES

Alasoini, T. (2009). Strategies to promote workplace innovation: A comparative analysis of nine national and regional approaches. *Economic and Industrial Democracy*, 30(4): 614–642.

Blöndal, K. S., Jónasson, J. T., & Tannhäuser, A. (2011). Dropout in a small society: Is the Icelandic case somehow different? In S. Lamb, E. Markussen, R. Teese, N. Sandberg and J. Polesel (Eds.), *School Dropout and Completion: International Comparative Studies in Theory and Policy*, 233–251. London: Springer.

Cseh, M., & Manikoth, N. N. (2011). Invited reaction: Influences of formal learning, personal learning orientation, and supportive learning environment on informal learning. *Human Resource Development Quarterly*, 22(3): 259–326.

Cseh, M. & Manikoth, N. (2012). The Future of Human Resource Development: Shaping National Human Resource Development Policies in the Global Context. Paper presented at University Forum of Human Resource Development, Portugal. doi: http://www.ufhrd.co.uk/wordpress

Euromonitor International. (2014). *Business Environment: Norway*. Online. Accessed 25 June 2015. (http://www.portal.euromonitor.com)

Euromonitor International. (2015a). *Business Environment: Denmark*. Online. Available (http://www.portal.euromonitor.com) Accessed June 25, 2015.

Euromonitor International. (2015b). *Business Environment: Sweden*. Online. Available (http://www.portal.euromonitor.com) Accessed June 25, 2015.

Eurostat. (2015). *Your Key to European Statistics*. Online. Available (http://ec.europa.eu/eurostat/data/database) Accessed May 20, 2015.

EURYDICE. (2015). *Countries: Description of National Education Systems*. Online. Available (https://webgate.ec.europa.eu/fpfis/mwikis/eurydice/index.php/Main_Page) Accessed, June 22, 2015.

Gaude, E. (2015). *Erfindergeist in Europas Hohem Norden*, Bonn: Germany Trade and Invest.

Gooderham, P. N., Navrbjerg, S. E., Olsen, K. M., & Steen, C. R. (2015). The labor market regimes of Denmark and Norway—one Nordic model? *Journal of Industrial Relations*, 57(2): 166–186.

Gustavsen, B. (1992). *Dialogue and Development*. Assen: van Gorcum.

Gustavsen, B. (2007). Work organization and the Scandinavian model. *Economic and Industrial Democracy*, 28(4): 650.

Hall, P., & Soskice, D. (2001). *Varieties of Capitalism: The Institutional Foundations of Comparative Advantage*. Oxford: Oxford University Press.

Hilson, M. (2008). *The Nordic Model: Scandinavia since 1945*. London: Reaktion Books Ltd.

Icelandic Ministry of Education, Science and Culture. (2008). *The Upper Secondary School Act No 91/2008*. Online. Available (http://eng.menntamalaraduneyti.is/media/MRN-pdf_Annad/Upper_secondary_school_Act.pdf) Accessed, June 22, 2015.

Icelandic Ministry of Education, Science and Culture. (2015). *Education*. Online. Accessed 22 June 2015. (http://eng.menntamalaraduneyti.is/education-in-iceland/Educational_system/)

International Monetary Fund. (2009). *World Economic Outlook: Crisis and Recovery Survey*. International Monetary Fund Publications Services.

Kvist, J., & Greve, B. (2011). Has the Nordic model been transformed? *Social Policy and Administration*, 45(2): 146–160.

Lin, C. Y., & Edvinsson, L. (2011). *National Intellectual Capital: A Comparison of 40 Countries*. New York: Springer-Verlag.

Mabey, C. (2008). Management development and firm performance in Germany, Norway, Spain and the UK. *Journal of International Business Studies*, 39: 1327–1342.

Mabey, C., & Ramirez, M. (2004). *Developing Managers: A European Perspective*. London: Chartered Management Institute.

Magnuson, D. (2007). The perils, promise, and practice of youth work in conflict societies. In D. Magnuson and M. Baizerman (Eds.), *Work with Youth Individed and Contested Societies*. Rotterdam: Sense Publishing.

Magnusson, L. (2007). *The Swedish Labor Market Model in a Globalised World*. Stockholm: Friedrich Ebert Stiftung.

Martinaitis, Ž. (2014). Measuring Skills in Europe. *European Journal of Training and Development*, 38(3): 198–210.

Ministry of Economic Affairs. (2011). Iceland; Pre-accession Economic Programme. Accessed 28 July 2015. http://ec.europa.eu/economy_finance/international/enlargement/pre-accession_prog/pep/2011-pep-iceland_en.pdf

Norden. (2015). *Business and the Economy*. Online. Available (http://www.norden.org/en/fakta-om-norden-1/business-and-the-economy) Accessed May 20, 2015.

Nordic Council of Ministers. (1983). *Agreement Concerning a Common Nordic Labor Market*. Online. Accessed 20 May 2015. (http://www.norden.org/en/om-samarbejdet-1/nordic-agreements/treaties-and-agreements/labor-market/agreement-concerning-a-common-nordic-labor-market)

Nordic Council of Ministers. (1998). *Agreement on a Nordic Labor Market for Persons Who Have Received Higher Education for at Least Three Years, Qualifying Them to Exercise a Profession*. Online. Accessed 20 May 2015. (http://www.norden.org/en/om-samarbejdet-1/nordic-agreements/treaties-and-agreements/labor-market/agreement-on-a-nordic-labor-market-for-persons-who-have-received-higher-education-for-at-least-three-years-qualifying-them-to-exercise-a-profession)

Nordic Council of Ministers. (2012). *Nordic Statistical Yearbook.* Copenhagen: Rosendahls-Schultz Grafisk Publishers.

Nordic Council of Ministers. (2014). *Nordic Statistical Yearbook.* Online. Available (http://norden.diva-portal.org/smash/record.jsf?pid=diva2%3A763002andd swid=-3023) Accessed May 18, 2015.

O'Brien, M. (2013). Fitting fathers into work-family policies: International challenges in turbulent times. *International Journal of Sociology and Social Policy,* 33(9/10): 542–564.

OCED. (2010a). OCED *Employment Outlook in OECD Economic Surveys: Iceland 2011.* OECD Publishing.

OECD. (2010b). *Generation Shift in the Swedish Labor Market.* Online. Available (http://www.oecd.org/employment/leed/OECD-Sweden-report-Final.pdf) Accessed May 16, 2015.

OECD. (2012). *Education at a Glance 2012: OECD indicators.* OECD Publishing.

Olofsson, J., & Wadensjö, E. (2012). *Youth, Education and Labor Market in the Nordic Countries: Similar but not the same.* Berlin: Friedrich Ebert Stiftung.

Ramirez, M. (2004). Comparing European approaches to management education, training, and development. *Advances in Developing Human Resources,* 6(4): 428–450.

Ramirez, M., & Mabey, C. (2005). A labor market perspective on management training and development in Europe. *International Journal of Human Resource Management,* 16(3): 291–310.

Sahlberg, P. (2010). Rethinking accountability for a knowledge society. *Journal of Educational Change,* 11(1): 45–61.

Statistics Iceland. (2015). *Compulsory Schools.* Online. Available (http://www.statice.is/Statistics/Education/Compulsory-schools) Accessed June 22, 2015.

Steinacher, H. (2015). *Skandinavien in Fokus 2015.* Bonn: Germany Trade and Invest

Steinacher, H., Danielsen, N., & Huber, A. (2014). *Lohn- und Lohnnebenkosten— Dänemark.* Copenhagen: Germany Trade and Invest.

The Hofstede Centre. (2015). *Country Comparison.* Online. Available (http://geert-hofstede.com/countries.html) Accessed June 22, 2015.

Tomé, E. (2005). Human resources policies compared. *Journal of European Industrial Training,* 29(5): 405–418.

UNDP. (2015). *Gender Inequality Index.* Online. Available (http://hdr.undp.org/en/content/gender-inequality-index-gii) Accessed May 20, 2015.

Veggeland, N. (2012). Social capital in a Nordic context. *Beijing Law Review,* 3(2): 24–30.

Worldbank. (2015). World Data Bank: World Development Indicators. Online. Available (http://databank.worldbank.org/data/views/reports/tableview.aspx#) Accessed May 20, 2015.

17 Human Resource Development in Germanic Europe

Regina H. Mulder and
Loek F. M. Nieuwenhuis

INTRODUCTION

This chapter provides insight into the current state of human resource development (HRD) in the Germanic countries, more specifically: Germany, Austria, the Netherlands, and Switzerland. These four countries possess a well-developed public-private system for vocational education and training (VET) at the secondary level, by which youngsters are prepared to enter the labor market with a solid foundation of labor-oriented skills achieving a level 2 or higher on ISCED. In contrast, these countries achieve mediocre scores on the lifelong learning (LLL) scale (Desmedt et al., 2006; Nieuwenhuis et al., 2011 suggest the same relationship, but a hypothesis has yet to be proved). HRD in the Germanic countries appears to be limited to functioning as a vehicle for VET (except for Switzerland) as it prepares young people to enter the initial labor market. In this respect, we can say that VET covers the main core purposes of HRD: improving individual or group effectiveness and performance; improving organizational effectiveness and performance; developing knowledge, skills, and competencies; and enhancing human potential and personal growth (cf. Hamlin and Stewart, 2011).

In this chapter, we develop a typology of HRD policies. On that basis, the Germanic countries can then be considered as a group, characterized by a transitional model, in which HRD is directed through a collaboration between government, employers, and unions (Cho and McLean, 2004). The Rhineland model (Jaap and Weggemans, 2010) is distinctive for these countries: social partners and governments working together to steer and support economic processes and social conflicts dealt with by deliberation and common steering. The Rhineland model differs from the Anglo-Saxon model, which is much more market driven and laissez-faire. It also differs from the Scandinavian model in which government leads in the promotion of social welfare.

In addition, the type of labor markets largely dictates the delivery of education and training. Countries within an internal labor market are characterized by an ill-developed system for VET. In these countries, education is targeted at generic skills and knowledge. Training for firm-specific skills is carried out internally or production is organized in a low-skilled way. Within internal markets, occupational skills are firm specific and have little impact on the external labor market. Occupational labor markets, however, are characterized by well-developed systems for VET at the intermediate level. Within occupational labor markets, several VET-system varieties can be discerned with respect to the interplay between government and social partners. Commitment of government and social partners is related to the governance of the system (definition of outcomes, accountability, financing, training markets), and the delivery of qualifying pathways (work-based models versus school-based models). We can discern two major clusters of VET systems:

(1) *Corporatist systems* (VET is delivered by social partners, mainly employers; dual trajectories are mainstream). Germany and Switzerland are examples of such corporatist systems for dual VET;

(2) *State-based systems* (government has the lead in VET delivery). In some countries, VET is mainly school based; whereas in other state-based systems, a high involvement of social partners is evolved. In the Netherlands (but also in other countries, such as Denmark and Norway), VET systems are developed that are publicly governed but with a high involvement of social partners, both nationally as well as regionally.

VET systems and LLL activities seem to be inversely interdependent: the investments in initial labor market-oriented skills negate the need for company investments in basic skill training. Nieuwenhuis et al. (2011) argue that the high participation in further education in the UK can be explained by the low skills of workers as they enter the labor market. Further education functions as a kind of compensation for the nonexistence of VET. So to understand HRD development in the Germanic countries, a description of their VET systems is needed.

These countries have certain similarities in historical background, political, social, and cultural developments. This may explain similarities in VET and HRD systems in these countries. However, these countries also manifest differences both in their development as well as in their systems. The aim of this chapter is to give insight into the HRD and VET systems in the countries, including the typical ways these countries develop employees. Therefore, we will give insight into the specific characteristics of HRD and VET systems for the larger region of the Germanic countries, relating them also to the historical, economic, social-cultural, and institutional contexts with related developments in their HRD systems. In addition, general information on the HRD and VET systems will be provided, followed by more information on the VET systems in the Germanic countries, with a section on the HRD systems in each of the four countries. A section on HRD at the organizational level will be presented followed by one on similarities and differences between them. A discussion and conclusion will close the chapter.

HISTORICAL, INSTITUTIONAL, SOCIAL, ECONOMIC, AND CULTURAL CONTEXT

Historical Context

Compared with other countries worldwide, all four countries have a long tradition in democracy, especially since the 'Renaissance' of the seventeenth and eighteenth centuries, as evidenced not only in the federal republics of Germany, Switzerland, and Austria but also in the constitutional monarchy of the Netherlands. Democratic governance at the level of *Länder* (states) and cantons has a long tradition in these countries, whereas the Netherlands have had republicanism in their genes since the Eighty Years' War (1568–1648), which aimed at liberation from Spanish (Habsburg) rule. The Dutch Republic stood as an inspiration for both the American Declaration of Independence and the French Revolution. The Germanic countries have been a politically stable region since World War II. West Germany and the Netherlands were founding countries of the European Union (EU); Austria joined the EU in 1995. Switzerland, however, has kept its policy of neutrality and did not join the EU. But because of the strong cultural and economic interdependency over the years, Switzerland has signed many agreements with the EU. Most important of the recent transforming happenings in this region are the destruction of the Berlin Wall in 1989 and the successive opening up of the countries of Eastern Europe. For Germany, that has resulted in the reunification of East and West Germany. Eastern Germany had at that time 16.4 million inhabitants and was economically in a bad state.

Economic Context and Labor Market

Austria has 8.4 million inhabitants (2012), with a rather stable birth rate between 2005 and 2012 (Statistik Austria, 2015). In 2011, about 18% of the population was 65 years old or older, and this has increased since. In 1990, it was less than 15% (Statistik Austria, 2015). GDP was €246 billion in 2010, of which 5.7% was spent on education (Bruneforth and Lassnigg, 2012). Germany is the largest country in the region with about 82 million inhabitants (Statistisches Bundesamt, 2013, with a federal government consisting of 16 *Länder*. Economically, Germany suffered relatively little from the worldwide economic crisis. It remains very strong internationally, for instance, in industry, with a GDP of €2592 billion in 2011 (Statistisches Bundesamt, 2012). In Germany, there has been a decline in the birth rate since 1997, moving from 812,000 then to 663,000 in 2011 (Statistisches Bundesamt, Wissenschaftszentrum Berlin für Sozialforschung, 2013). It is considered that the increasing percentage of elderly in the population will become a major problem in the future. In 2011, about 20% were older than 65 (Statistisches Bundesamt, 2013).

In the Netherlands, the population is estimated at c. 17 million people (16.7 in 2012) (Statistics Netherlands, 2014). The birth rate was 179,933 in 2012 (Statistics Netherlands, 2014) and declining (Eurostat, 2015). In 2012, 16.2% were 65 or older (Statistics Netherlands, 2014) and increasing. GPD was US\$838, 11 billion in 2011, with 6.8% spending on education (in 2012). Until 2013, the Netherlands was one of the five economically most prosperous countries worldwide (Eurostat, 2015).

Switzerland has eight million inhabitants (2012), with an increasing birth rate between 2009 and 2012 (from 78,286 to 82,164), and, in 2012, 17% were 65 or older (Statistik Schweiz, 2015). GDP was US\$585, 102 million, with 5.4% spending on education in 2010 (Eurostat, 2015). It is a very wealthy state. Recent overviews indicate that it stands as number one worldwide (Allianz Global Wealth Report, 2014), with a very strong bank sector. There is a relatively strong inward migration (around 16%) from Germany (Statistik Schweiz, 2015). Switzerland has three national languages and is divided into 26 federally organized cantons, with education systems organized accordingly.

Basic economic indicators of the four countries are listed in Table 17.1. From the data presented, we can conclude that all four countries are economically strong in comparison with other countries. The unemployment rates are relatively low, especially in Switzerland. The long-term unemployment is very low, although youth unemployment has increased in the last few years.

Table 17.1   Basic Economic Indicators in Germanic Countries

	Germany	Netherlands	Austria	Switzerland
Real GDP per head (In 1000 € 2013)	30.2	32.3	32.2	45.0
GDP ranking (Europe 2013)	1	6	11	7
GDP growth (2012–2013)	0.4	−0.8	0.3	0.6
Unemployment (% 2014)	5.0	7.4	5.6	3.2
Unemployment evolution (percentage point 2010–2014)	−2.0	+2.4	+0.8	−0.3
Long-term unemployment (2014)	2.2	3.0	1.5	1,7
Youth unemployment (2014)	7.7	10.5	10.3	8.6
LTU evolution (percentage point 2010–2014)	−1.1	+1.6	+0.3	+0.2
Public debt (2014% of GDP)	74.7	68.8	84.5	48.1
External debt	−1.4%	28.4%	20.4%	24.3%
Gini index 2013	30	25	27	29

Source: Eurostat (2015); Statistik Schweiz (2015); World Bank (2015)

Cultural Context

The latest surveys, using the Hofstede cultural dimensions (The Hofstede Centre, 2015), show that these four countries are rather similar in the dimensions of power, individualism, uncertainty avoidance, and of long-term orientation, all represented on a scale from 1–100. For *power*, Austria, Germany, the Netherlands, and Switzerland rate 11, 35, 38, and 34, respectively. These scores for the four countries indicate the general idea that inequalities should be minimized and that equal rights are important. Power is decentralized and control is disliked. In Switzerland, the French-speaking cantons score higher on power, similar to France. The scores for *individualism*, with respective values of 55, 67, 80, and 68, are rather high, which suggests these countries highly prefer a loose social framework. People are considered capable of taking care of themselves and their families. Labor relations are based on contracts of mutual advantage; hiring and promotion are based on merit. Communication is honest and clear. The Netherlands, especially, is considered as a very individualist country. In Switzerland, the same can be said of the German and French-speaking parts. The scores for *uncertainty avoidance* stand at 70, 65, 53, and 58 respectively. Austria has the highest score, meaning a strong preference for avoiding uncertainty. A need for rules, time is money attitude, an inner urge to work hard, precision and punctuality are important; innovations may be resisted, such as unorthodox behavior and ideas, and security is important. The Netherlands show only a slight preference for avoiding uncertainty. The scores for *long-term orientation* are all high: 60, 83, 67, and 74, respectively. Germany, even more than the other countries, takes a pragmatic approach: encouraging efforts in education as a way to prepare for the future. These countries have pragmatic orientations, they adapt traditions to changing conditions, and show a strong propensity to save and invest and for thriftiness and perseverance in achieving results (The Hofstede Centre, 2015).

Many critics exist of the Hofstede dimensions. Nevertheless, in these countries, scores based on these dimensions are more similar than between other countries. However, we have to beware that regional differences exist, sometimes strongly so, within each country. For instance, in the examples mentioned regarding Switzerland, but also in the other countries, and especially in such a large country as Germany. These differences may be partly due to differences in history (e.g., the former Eastern European situation in East Germany). In addition, migration streams in Central Europe have influenced diversity within countries.

Cultural context is influenced by migration. Germany and the Netherlands, especially, have a long tradition of immigration. Because of the trading character of its economy, Dutch society has been an open one since the Dutch Republic of the 1600s. French Huguenots and Portuguese Jews have been integrated into Netherlands' society since that time. Since World War II, immigration increased both in Germany and in the Netherlands in three waves: (1) in the Netherlands, immigrants from former colonies such as Indonesia fled to

Europe because they took the side of the Dutch in the Indonesian Independence War; (2) in the 1970s, labor immigration grew, especially from Turkey, Greece, Italy, as well as immigration from former colonies, especially in the Netherlands, combined with immigrants from Morocco and Turkey. In Germany, in 2014, there were about three million people with a Turkish background (Auswärtiges Amt, 2015); and (3) labor migrants from Poland, Rumania, and Bulgaria form the most recent wave of immigration, both in Germany and the Netherlands. Austria and Switzerland do not know immigration on this scale, but in all four countries, right wing politicians try (and sometimes succeed, although hardly in Germany and Switzerland) to incite anti-immigrant sentiments, especially during the last years of the financial crisis.

Societal Context

The basic social facts in Table 17.2 indicate that life expectancy is high, the health system is good, and the education level outperforms all other regions in the world. These countries do not differ significantly in their basic social indicators. The main difference indicates that Switzerland is wealthier and more expensive.

Germanic countries show high education levels in comparison with other European countries. The proportion of the population aged 30–34 with completed higher education (university, university of applied sciences, polytechnics) is in all countries relatively high, with the lowest percentage in Austria. 'Lifelong learning' refers to the percentage of persons aged 25 to 64 who stated that they received education or training in the four weeks preceding the survey. The information comes from the EU Labor Force Survey and relates to all education or training whether or not relevant to the respondent's current or possible future job.

Institutional Context

The Rhineland model, with its strong institutional cooperation between social partners and governments, has its roots in the region's long tradition of local democracy. The Dutch 'polder model' is world famous because of its consensus institutions, but also because of its slow way of decision making. A decentralized decision-making process in which the cantons play a major role also characterizes Switzerland. In Germany, too, there is the system of *Föderalismus* (Federalism), whereby the *Länder* have more influence than at the country level. Furthermore, the Austrian system of economic and social partnership is based on voluntary cooperation between statutory and voluntary interest groups, including government representatives (EQAVET, 2015). Statutory interest groups are representatives of employers, employees, and agriculture. Voluntary interest groups include the Austrian Trade Union Federation and the Federation of Austrian Industry. So the countries in the Germanic region can be considered as democracies at a regional level, focused on collaboration

Table 17.2 Basic Social Indicators in Germanic Countries

	Germany	Netherlands	Austria	Switzerland
Life expectancy 2012	W: 83.3 M: 78.6	W: 83.0 M: 79.3	W: 78.4 M: 83.6	W: 84.9 M: 80.6
Doctors per 1 000 inhabitants#	3.7	2.9	4.9	4.1
Infant mortality (per 1000, first year)	3.3	3.7	3.2	3.6
Expenditures in health per inhabitant 2012 (in Euro)	3,670.86	4,350.35 (2011)	4,051.72	7,055.97
Lower secondary educational attainment 25–64 year* ~	13.4	26.6	17.1	13.7
Upper secondary studies, at least *	86.6	73.4	82.9	86.3
Tertiary educational attainment, age 30–34 2013*	32.9	43.1	27.1	46.1
Lifelong learning age 25–64 in 2012*	7.9	16.5	14.1	29.9

Source: #World Bank (2015); Eurostat (2015); * = %; ~ European mean = 25.7.

Table 17.3 Broad General Vocational and Educational Base for HRD in Germanic Countries

Education		Germany	The Netherlands	Austria	Switzerland
Secondary	Compulsory education (years)	13	13	10	9
	Upper secondary or tertiary educational attainment (%, age 20–24, 2014)	77	79	86	86
	Upper secondary or tertiary educational attainment (%, age 25–64, 2014)	87	79	90	86
	Secondary vocational education (% Pupils in upper secondary education enrolled in vocational stream) 2012	56	71	80	71
Higher Education / Tertiary Education	population with HE (%, age 30–34, 2014)	31	45	40	49
	Population with HE (%, age 25+, 2014)	26	29	18	32
Continuing vocational / adult training	Lifelong learning (% of adults in education, 2014)	7,9	17,8	14,2	31,7
	*Public expenditure in active LMP (% of GDP, 2012)	1,7	2,9	2,0	1,2
	Expenditure on education (% of GDP, 2011)	5,0	5,9	5,8	5,3

Source: Eurostat (2015); *OECD (2012)

between several civic interest groups, such as employers, trade unions, and local administrators. Decisions are made after ample public debate (In Switzerland there is even a tradition of politics by referenda.), and the political arena is formed by participation of its citizens. This open, interactive policy-making tradition has recently been challenged by attempts to exclude immigrants from economic and social activities and to obstruct the European movement. It is not clear yet, whether these attempts will succeed or not.

VET IN THE GERMANIC COUNTRIES

The VET systems of the four countries in the region are summarized in Table 17.3. The table provides some key VET statistics and an overview of the educational level in the different countries. From available international data, the VET picture for the Germanic countries is becoming clearer. The four countries all opt for an occupational labor market, whereby youngsters are expected to train at least up to ISCED level 2–3 before entering the labor market. Dual trajectories for vocational training supply young workers for the employment market in Germany, Switzerland, and Austria; and for those young people not entering dual trajectory schools, school-based vocational education is obliged to deliver that training. In the Netherlands, dual trajectories are more rare, and more than half of young people follow vocational courses in a school-based system in combination with internship (OECD, 2010).

Main Institutions Responsible for VET

Germany, especially, has a long tradition of the dual system. About 9% of GPD was spent on education in 2011. About €20 billion for vocational education and €20 billion for other kinds of (adult) education such as vocational training was spent in 2009 (Statistisches Bundesamt, 2012). The responsibility for education is shared between the federal government and the 16 *Länder* (states). The Vocational Education and Training Act of 2005 was crucial for VET development. The act reformed VET comprehensively by amending and combining previous acts: the Vocational Education and Training Act of 1969 and the Aid for Vocational Trainees Act of 1981. The aim was to improve the quality of VET and youth training opportunities. All legislation on schools is under *Länder* (state) legislation, not federal. The Ministers of Education of the *Länder* cooperate in a Standing Conference (KMK) to ensure some kind of uniformity and comparability. The *Länder* have committees for vocational training, with equal representation of employers, employees, and the *Länder* authorities. They advise the *Länder* governments on vocational training issues in schools.

The students in the dual system work part time within companies, which includes educational support through part-time schooling. The federal government is responsible for in-company, non-school VET. The Federal

Ministry of Education and Research is responsible for general policy issues of VET, including the act, the legal supervision and funding of the Federal Institute for Vocational Education and Training (BIBB), and the implementation of programs to improve VET. BIBB is the core institution at the national level for consensus building between all parties involved in VET, stimulates innovations, works to identify future challenges in VET, etc. There exists a procedure in this field for close coordination and cooperation between the federal government and the *Länder*, which also involves the social partners.

The dual system forms the core of the German VET system. At the moment, 348 training occupation possibilities are available. Enterprises select trainees and pay the costs of in-company training and trainee salaries. To support the training in the company, training in part-time vocational schools provides the required knowledge and skills. Competent bodies monitor in-company training. Quality assurance has traditionally been provided through supervision and monitoring of education and training (EQAVET, 2015). Here also, the *Länder* are largely autonomous.

In Austria, vocational education is the responsibility of the Austrian Federal Ministry for Education, Arts, and Culture. The General Directorate for VET, Adult Training, and School Sport of responsible for curriculum development; continuing and further training of teachers; issues of location and facilities; school development and research on education, training, and qualifications; international cooperation; etc. In the field of school-based vocational education, the social partners are involved in legislation and the adoption of ordinances (e.g., new curricula). Partnership with businesses is important for curriculum development, requirement of economy, and placement at work. Governmental school authorities implement school legislation (i.e., regional education boards at the provincial level) in conjunction with regional school inspectors. VET schools and colleges provide initial VET and, with the exception of private schools, VET attendance is free. More than 80% of the over-14s opt for a VET pathway. The federal government bears the costs of facilities and maintenance of public VET schools and pays the salaries of the teachers. Evaluation exists in the form of self-evaluation (internal evaluation). Other ministries have responsibilities in the VET system: the Federal Ministry of Economy; Family and Youth for On-the-Job Training; the Ministry of Health (think of schools for health care and nursing); and the Federal Ministry of Agriculture and Forestry, Environment. and Water Management (EQAVET, 2015).

VET is the main supplier of employees in the Netherlands. The Ministry of Education, Culture, and Science takes care of the (legal) conditions. The law on education and training, 'WEB', has provided the legal underpinning since 1996, with its successive amendments. The entire VET system is characterized by strong partnerships, including educational institutions and the social partners. Provision is decentralized and there are 43 regional, multisectoral vocational colleges that provide the training in school. Centers of Expertise are organized according to industry type, according to function and sector, and they represent over 220,000 accredited work placement firms. These centers take care of accreditation, assist with work placements in companies, manage development and maintenance of the qualification structure, and provide labor market research. After a recent alteration of law in 2014, these Centers of Expertise have been merged together into one multisectoral organization bridging education and labor. Although quality assurance is carried out by internal assessment, it is monitored by the Inspectorate of Education, which is responsible for the external assessment (EQAVET, 2015). There are several quality networks consisting of the VET providers or their representatives for organizational peer assessment and feedback.

In Switzerland, the vocational education system is the responsibility of the state, the cantons, and the social partners (work organizations), with the state playing the lead role. Cantons as well as the state consider the employers an important partner (Bildungsgewerkschaften, 2015).

Vocational education trajectories also consist of different elements: in-company and in school, with additional 'trans-company' (*überbetriebliche*) courses whose objective is to integrate the company and the learning settings. At a national level, there is legislation (*Regelungskompetenz*) for the whole of VET, and the possibility to make laws (*Grundsätze*) for continuing education and training. The cantons carry out the law (*Bundesgesetzgebung*) and are responsible for financing the system. They are organized into the Swiss Conference of Cantonal Education Directors (EDK). EDK is an agent of cooperation with the federal system and takes care of harmonizing the relations between national government and the cantons, while seeking to maintain the autonomy of the cantons (Bundesamt für Statistik, 2013). The reverse side of this coin of complex structures is that it takes a rather long time to respond to needed change in course content. The Vocational Education Act (*Berufsbildungsgesetz*) has been the operative legislation since 2004.

Thus in all Germanic countries, we can conclude that the various social partners are highly involved in the delivery and design of vocational courses, which guarantees the occupational relevance of the courses.

Comparison: VET Commonalities and Differences

The OECD (2010) promotes mixed models for VET systems in which dual trajectories are combined with school-based trajectories and social partners are highly involved, as well as public institutes. Educational systems in all four countries are geared to participation in and qualification for the labor market. VET is highly developed, especially in Germany and Switzerland, and highly esteemed. Globally seen, the Germanic countries are the exception in this domain: in many countries, even OECD member states, VET is not well developed at the secondary level.

VET systems show large differences in participation rates and in combinations of work and learning. In some countries, such as the US and the UK, VET is nonexistent or hidden as minor subjects in community colleges; vocational subjects are delivered, but an institutional bond with social partners is missing. On the other side of the spectrum, mid-European countries

(Germany, Czech Republic, the Netherlands) have highly developed VET systems, sometimes work based, sometimes school based. Participation in secondary VET makes a huge impact on participation in LLL; public investments compliment private investments in occupational and professional skills. In order to understand participation in LLL, we need to explore this complementary role of public and private systems for vocational and professional education and training.

Social systems evolve over long time and can be understood as constituted by societal rules and expectations (institutions), which regulate individual and organizational behavior. Rules and expectations are sometimes laid down in laws but are often implicit. Institutions are important, as they engender social trust; and in economic terms, they decrease transaction costs, because with them there is less need for permanent negotiation. Within public social systems, organizations are mandated to implement the public intentions of the system and to defend the institutions. The evolution of social systems is not a blueprint exercise but a historical, path-dependent process. VET systems have their roots in the medieval guilds, but also in societal developments, both in the world of work and the world of education. In each country, and in each industrial sector, adaptations have taken place at different moments and out of different instances, resulting in a complex quilt of varieties. Because of the high amount of stakeholders and societal debates, VET systems tend to be more scattered than systems for general education or higher education.

HRD IN THE DIFFERENT COUNTRIES

HRD has many dimensions, such as informal learning, training, knowledge development, skills and competences, and personal growth enhancement (c.f. Hamlin and Stewart, 2011). Of those dimensions, very little empirical data is available except for training. On informal learning, systematic quantitative large-scale research has not been undertaken. Therefore, we focus here on the information that can be provided on the participation in formal training.

Table 17.4 lists the percentages of the population that participate in training in the four countries. For comparison, we include the data for 15 EU countries with a norm of 13%.

Participation in post-initial training in the Netherlands is lower than in the leading EU countries (De Grip et al., 2008), where only 16% of the population is following a post-initial training module or course. Furthermore, in Germany and Austria, the participation in (formal) LLL is lower than in the Netherlands. These two countries lag behind in respect to EU targets. In Germany, the proportion of 15–66-year-olds participating in some form of additional training is almost 13% (Autorengruppe Bildungsbericht, 2014. EU data (Moraal et al., 2007) show that average participation in training for older workers in EU25 is 8.5%, with high variance between countries.

Table 17.4 Participation in Training in Germanic Countries

	Germany	Netherlands	Austria	Switzerland	EU-15
1999	5	13	9	31	8
2007	7	16	13	27	11 norm:13

Source: Eurostat (2015)

On the other hand, from Table 17.4, we can see that Switzerland has a very high percentage participation in training.

It needs to be mentioned that because of the differences in definitions by each, that these kinds of statistics are very difficult to compare between countries. For instance, there is variance in the use of the term LLL, which in some countries refers to work-related training only but in others includes all other adult education courses as well. In addition, within countries, definitions have sometimes changed over time. Roughly, the trend is as follows: the Netherlands and Austria are rather at EU levels in participation, Germany strongly below, and Switzerland above (Nieuwenhuis et al., 2011).

Institutions and Political Context

In all four countries, a public system for LLL is missing, and the debate on further training is left to the arena of collective agreements bargaining on labor conditions between employers and trade unions. Austria and Germany lag behind the European targets for LLL, whereas the Netherlands is playing its role in the middle group. There is low public concern regarding VET systems in the Germanic countries and HRD, as this area is considered by that public as belonging to the influence sphere of the HR(M) officers and of managers of companies but not to the sphere of public policy.

In relation to continuing VET (CVET), in the Netherlands (EQAVET, 2015) there is a distinction between general adult education and vocationally oriented continuing training. Corporate training for employed people constitutes a large part of this sector; however, it is very difficult to define. There is no distinct difference between initial vocational education training (IVET) and CVET. They happen in both publicly funded and private schools. The Netherlands has a long history of policy reports directed to the captains of industry and leaders of the trade unions, who consider themselves as responsible for enhancing LLL and in-company training and development. Golsteyn (2012) shows that the Dutch government is trying to implement all kinds of stimulating and facilitating measures, but the impact on enrollment and participation in LLL remains low. The same observations count for agreements made by trade unions and employer organizations: in the collective labor agreements, funds are allocated at the sector/branch level to enhance training participation, but most of these funds are not utilized

Table 17.5 Main Institutions for HRD in Germanic Countries

	Germany	Netherlands	Austria	Switzerland
Government	• Sets the legal framework (e.g., *Bildungsfreistellungsgesetz, Weiterbildungsgesetze*) • Certifies providers • Provides financial support (e.g., *Gesetz zur Förderung beruflicher Aufstiegsfortbildung*)	• Sets the legal framework • Initiate experiments with financial schemes, Ιnterdepartmental initiatives project (2005–2011) • Tax reduction for LLL • Τraining obligation for employers (qualifying duty in case of firing) • Starting experiments with flexible provision of LLL in higher education (2015)	• Promotes training programs (e.g., *Erwachsenenweiterbildungs-Förderungsgesetz*) • Sets the legal framework (Ministry of Labor, Social Affairs, and Consumer Protection)	• Certifies providers • provides training (subsidiarity principle) • Sets a wide legal framework (e.g., *Berufsbildungsgesetz, Arbeitsrecht*) nearly according to free-market economy
Governmental agencies	• *Bundesagentur für Arbeit* provides training	• Labor market service facilitates training • Εxpertise center APL (approval of prior learned competencies) • Regional support desks for LLL • Certificate for work experience	• Labor market service does not provide, but finances, training programs • State institutions provide training (e.g., universities)	• IKW (*Interkantonale Konferenz für Weiterbildung*) elaborates suggestions on the topic

Labor unions and employers	• Co-arrange the framework for HRD with the collective bargaining law • work council has a say	• Collective labor agreements • Collective sectoral training funds (O&O) • Branch organizations provide training	• Promotes and provides training
Economy / Providers	• Provide training (e.g., Chambers such as IHK)	• Many private providers • Declining provision by HPE and VET	• Many private providers • Predominant private providers • Supply of providers nearly according to market economy • Prodivers can apply for governmental certification

Source: Ondraschek (2013); EQAVET (2015); Eurydice (2015)

over long periods. So at the national level, the awareness of the urgency of stimulating LLL and HRD is clear, both for policy makers and social partners; but on the local level, inside companies and organizations, it is difficult to promote LLL. This might be partly explained by the number and importance of SMEs in these countries, which find it difficult to organize training and to give employees the time for participation in training (e.g., Gonon et al., 2005). And in addition, it might be (partly) explained by the high productivity rates, which render the situation such that it is difficult to reserve time for training.

For CVET in Austria (EQAVET, 2015), there are no legal or educational policy supervisory functions for the whole sector. The Federal Ministry of Education, Arts, and Culture is responsible for CVET in schools, but for higher education, it falls to the Federal Ministry for Science and Research. All other providers are largely autonomous within the framework of legal specifications and depend mainly on market conditions of supply and demand.

CVET in Germany (EQAVET, 2015) is characterized by a pluralism of providers, has a largely market character, and a relatively small degree of state regulation. Only a small part of the training leads to formal vocational qualifications by law or to awards from industry's self-governing organizations, their Chambers of Commerce (*Deutscher Industrie- und Handelskammertag*). Providers can be vocational colleges, trade and technical schools, *Volkshochschulen*, higher education institutes, and private organizations.

The roles of the state in the field of continuing education are, for the most part, restricted to laying down principles and issuing regulations relating to organization and financing. Such principles and regulations are enshrined in the legislation of the federal government and the *Länder*. State regulations are aimed at establishing general conditions for the optimum development of the contribution of continuing education to LLL. HRD in companies is not regulated and remains a matter for the companies themselves in negotiation between employers and employees. In some domains (e.g., specific industries or parts of health care), employers strive for and realize HRD agreements at a national level.

In Switzerland, continuing training is the private responsibility of companies themselves. In some domains, there is some financial support (subvention) by the national government (Eurydice, 2015) and there is a great diversity with regard to responsibility, regulation, programs offered, and financing. CVET is largely market based. Private bodies often provide CVET with courses and programs. Providers can be public providers, private (profit oriented) providers, companies, associations, umbrella organizations, etc. CVET is largely privately funded. The Federal Vocational and Professional Education and Training Act regulates job-related CVET. The cantons regulate job-related CVET in cantonal implementing laws under this act.

HRD AT ORGANIZATIONAL LEVEL

In addition to the relatively low amount of training in companies, we see that the number of small companies offering training is relatively even lower. Data from 2005 (Perspective 25, Bundesagentur für Arbeit, 2011) indicate that the number of small enterprises (10–49 employees) providing training varies from 50% in Germany, to 63% in Austria, to 65% in the Netherlands, with an EU average of 47%. In Switzerland, however, a survey showed 62% of the participating SMEs reported training provisions (Gonon et al., 2005). The EU average for large companies is 86%. Germany lies behind with 78%. A higher percentage of the large companies in the Netherlands (94%) and Austria (98%) offer training.

In Germany, public measures such as financial incentives and training standards have had hardly any effect on the training (policy) in companies. In addition, there are only a few contracts between the social partners (companies, unions, and government) that contain any statements on content, amount of training, and training policy (Vollmar, 2013). In the Netherlands, this is the domain of negotiations between social partners, both on the national as well as on the company level. Private training companies mostly provide training, with public institutions filling only 5% of the training market (yearly about €3000 million).

In Austria (Statistik Austria, 2015), a survey among companies showed that about a quarter of the companies reported that financial incentives (part payment by government) influenced their training policy, planning, and practice. About 20% of the companies mentioned the influence of tax incentives, and the same percentage mentioned influence of training norms and standards (e.g., certification). Measures for qualification of trainers (16%) were indicated and fewer companies (6%) mentioned public support, such as analyses of need for training or development of training.

DISCUSSION

Germanic Countries: Strong VET

The four countries in the Germanic region can boast a strong VET system and a relatively unstructured system of LLL, further education (CVET), and formal training. Apart from these similarities, there are differences. An important difference stands out between a VET system primarily in-company with the support of school in the dual system and a school-based VET system with internships. With its strong VET system, discourse about LLL differs in these German countries with other countries; for instance, the UK where LLL is a natural part of education in society and a way of training for specific jobs in industry. Because the VET system is responsible for the preparation of young citizens for their life and work, LLL at a later age is considered far more as something 'in addition' rather than a natural process for which individuals themselves are considered to be (mainly) responsible. Some consider, however, that the boundaries between CVET, HRD, and LLL are weakening (Mulder, 2012). The participation in LLL in the Germanic countries is low, except for Switzerland, compared with Sweden (32%), Denmark (26%), Finland (23%), and the UK (21%).

International Comparison of HRD Systems: Relation with Structure of Labor Market

Björnavold (2000) discerns six different learning models in EU member states. We opt, however, for a more global distinction between systems. Following Van Lieshout (2008), we start from the structure of labor markets for intermediate skills. In the economic literature, a distinction is made between occupational labor markets and internal labor markets (Marsden, 1999; De Grip and Wolbers, 2006; cf. Culpepper & Thelen, 2008). This distinction in labor markets is closely related to the structure of the various economic systems: liberal market economies versus coordinated market economies. In an occupational labor market, the entrance to work is organized through a system of vocational courses and trainings, whereas in an internal labor market, the entrance to work is unregulated. This has huge consequences for public and private investments in intermediate skills (Van Lieshout, 2008) and for the expected returns of learn-work trajectories. Within an internal labor market, workers aim for generic competences to increase labor market prospects, whereas employers opt for company-specific competences in order to avoid free-rider behavior of competitors. For the occupation labor market, the balance between generic and specific competences is more complicated: on the one hand, both employers and workers have interests in high, occupation-specific skills for labor market entrance; on the other, broad generic competences are needed to deal with high-speed innovation. De Grip and Wolbers (2006) show different outcomes for low-skilled workers: in an internal labor market, they have more chance of decent work compared to occupational labor markets because that system's demand for high skills at intermediate levels works against them and acts as a selective threshold. Personnel selection by companies is based on the outcomes of the VET systems: youngsters are expected to have obtained a vocational qualification. This implies that, because of this selective threshold, low-skilled youth have more difficulties finding a decent job in occupational markets (cf. De Grip and Wolbers, 2006).

The variation in formal LLL in countries shows an opposite pattern to VET; especially in the UK, LLL acts as compensation for low-entrance skills of workers on the intermediate level (cf. Nieuwenhuis et al., 2011). Within an internal labor market, firms have to invest in training in order to establish a minimum of firm-related competences but they can choose for a low-skill production process (cf. Brown and Keep, 1999, who conclude that the majority of UK companies still use a low-skill production concept). Within an occupational context, the point of departure is different: higher-skills entry levels lead to high-skill production processes with different investment considerations by both employers and employees. Institutional configurations operate within an occupational labor market, establishing connections between the educational system, social security system, and labor market regulations. Different outcomes are not always easy to correlate directly to the skills system.

The distinction between internal and occupational labor markets also has consequences for participation in LLL and firm-specific training of workers. Comparable data on informal learning at work are scarce. Existing figures indicate that many people learn at work (e.g., Felstead et al., 2005). Borghans et al. (2007) show that employees can learn from 31% of the work they do. For young workers, this figure is higher (40%) than for older workers (25%). Firm culture and organization play an important role in establishing informal learning. Higher participation of unemployed people in Sweden could be promoted by activating labor-market policy in that country (cf. Desmedt et al., 2006). Low participation of older workers (over 50) can be due to early retirement policies that lack an 'active aging' dimension (cf. Montizaan and De Grip, 2008)

The Germanic countries are challenged to complement their strong VET systems with a strong LLL investment. Until now, only Switzerland has succeeded in establishing both initial and continuing VET. Policy makers, both in government and with social partners, are aware of the urgency of organizing LLL and collective HRD strategies, but the impact of this awareness is negligible (Golsteyn, 2012). The success of Switzerland is comparable to that of Denmark and other Scandinavian countries (Nieuwenhuis et al., 2011), but there is no recipe to copy that success. Public organizations for IVET delivery are not well suited to delivering tailor-made CVET programs, so, for example, in the Netherlands, only 5% of company training is delivered by public institutions for VET or higher professional education (Nieuwenhuis et al., 2011). In Germany, the same figures count. Figures are only provided on the basis of participation in labor force surveys and not based on a company's policies on internal training, and international data are difficult to compare (cf. Nieuwenhuis et al., 2011). Large companies do provide training themselves, whereas small and medium-sized companies tend to organize collective training facilities.

Public institutes for dual or state-based VET are constrained by public regulations, which hinder them in adapting to market conditions for CVET. On the other hand, companies and employees seem to rely on the quality of IVET delivery. These two processes enhance a vicious circle, difficult to break down, of noninvestment and nondelivery of public CVET (cf. Golsteyn, 2012).

The future labor market demands are rather uncertain: the rate of job change is increasingly rapid, whereas economic and global developments are rather unpredictable. Relying on flexibility delivery in the IVET system is a risky strategy. Building a stable CVET system offers better options for the uncertainty of future developments. Switzerland is the only Germanic country that has developed a two-edged sword for this purpose. Investigating the sources of success of the Swiss model could be a wise strategy for future VET policies in the Germanic countries.

REFERENCES

Allianz Golbal Wealth Report 2014. München: Allianz SE. Online. Available (https://www.allianz.com/v_1411376188000/media/economic_research/publications/specials/de/AGWR14d.pdf). Accessed June 30, 2015.

Auswärtiges, Amt. (2015). *Beziehungen zu Deutschland,* Online. Available (http://www.auswaertiges-amt.de/DE/Aussenpolitik/Laender/Laenderinfos/Tuerkei/Bilateral_node.html) Accessed July 06, 2015.

Autorengruppe Bildungsberichterstattung (2014). *Bildung in Deutschland 2014: Ein indikatorengestützter Bericht mit einer Analyse zur Bildung von Menschen mit Behinderungen,* Bielefeld: wbv. Online. Available (http://www.bildungsbericht.de/daten2014/bb_2014.pdf) Accessed July 31, 2014.

Bildungsgewerkschaften. Online. Available (http://www.bildungsgewerkschaften.ch/) Accessed July 04, 2015.

Bjornavold, J. (2000). *Making Learning Visible.* Cedefop reference series, Luxembourg: Office for official publications of the EC.

Borghans, L., Golsteyn, B., & De Grip, A. (2007). Werkend leren. *Economisch-statistische berichten,* 92: 260–263.

Brown, A., & Keep, E. (1999). *Review of Vocational Education and Training Research in the United Kingdom.* COST A11 report. Luxembourg: Office for official publications of the EC.

Bruneforth, M., & Lassnigg, L. (2012). *Nationaler Bildungsbericht Österreich 2012,* Graz: Leykam.

Bundesagentur für Arbeit (2011). *Perspektive 2025: Fachkräfte für Deutschland,* Online. Available (http://www.arbeitsagentur.de/web/wcm/idc/groups/public/documents/webdatei/mdaw/mtaw/~edisp/l6019022dstbai398619.pdf?_ba.sid=L6019022DSTBAI398622) Accessed January 31, 2014.

Bundesamt für Statistik (2013). *Personen in Ausbildung,* Neuchâtel: Office fédéral de la statistique (OFS).

Culpepper, P., & Thelen, K. (2008). Institutions and collective actors in the provision of training: Historical and cross-national comparisons. In K.U. Mayer and H. Sorga (Eds.), *Skill formation: Interdisciplinary and Cross-National Perspectives,* 21–50. Cambridge and New York: Cambridge University Press.

Desmedt, E., Groenez, S., van den Broeck, G., Lamberts, M., & Nicaise, I. (2006). *Onderzoek naar de systeemkenmerken die de participatie aan levenslang leren in de EU-15 beïnvloeden.* Leuven: HIVA.

De Grip, A., Kirschner, P., & Nieuwenhuis, L. (2008). *Waarom stagneert in Nederland de deelname aan een leven lang leren?* Heerlen: Open Universiteit.

De Grip, A., & Wolbers, M. H. J. (2006). Cross-national differences in job quality among low-skilled young workers in Europe. *International Journal of Manpower,* 27: 420–433.

EQAVET, Online. Available (http://www.eqavet.eu/gns/what-we-do/implementing-the-framework/netherlands.aspx) Accessed July 04, 2015.

Eurostat, Online. Available (http://ec.europa.eu/eurostat) Accessed May 29, 2015.

Eurydice, Online. Available (https://webgate.ec.europa.eu/fpfis/mwikis/eurydice/index.php/Main_Page) Accessed May 29, 2015.

Felstead, A. Fuller, A., Unwin, L., Ashton, D., Butler, P., & Lee, T. (2005). Surveying the scene: Learning metaphors, survey design and the workplace context. *Journal of education and work,* 18: 359–383.

Golsteyn, B. (2012). *Waarom groeit leven lang leren in Nederland niet sterker, ondanks de vele adviezen erover.* Onderzoek ten behoeve van de Onderwijsraad. Maastricht: Netwerk sociale innovatie universiteit Maastricht.

Gonon, P., Hotz, H.-P., Weil, M., & Schläfli, A. (2005). *KMU und die Rolle der Weiterbildung: Eine empirische Studie zu Kooperationen und Strategien in der Schweiz,* Bern: Hep.

Hamlin, B., & Stewart, J. (2011). What is HRD? A definitional review and synthesis of the HRD domain. *Journal of European Industrial Training,* 35: 199–220.

Jaap, P., & Weggeman, M. (2010). *The Rhineland Way.* Amsterdam: Uitgeverij Business Contact.

Marsden, D. (1999). *A Theory of Employment Systems: Micro-Foundations of Societal Diversity.* Oxford: Oxford University Press.

Montizaan, R., & de Grip, A. (2008). *Pensioenverwachtingen en menselijk kapitaal,* Heerlen: ABP/ROA.

Moraal, D., Schönfeld, G., & Schöpe, T. (2007). 'Betriebliche Weiterbildung von älteren Arbeitnehmerinnen und Arbeitnehmern in KMU und Entwicklung von regionalen Supportstrukturen (Leonardo da Vinci-Projekt)', unpublished final report, Bundesinstitut für Berufsbildung.

Mulder, M. (2012). European vocational education and training. In J. P. Wilson (Ed.), *International Human Resource Development: Learning, Education and Training for Individuals and Organizations,* 3rd ed., 155–177. London, Philadelphia, New Delhi: Kogan Page.

Nieuwenhuis, L., Gelderblom, A., Gielen, P., & Collewet, M. (2011). *Groeitempo Leven Lang Leren: een internationale vergelijking,* Tilburg, Rotterdam: IVA/SEOR.

OECD. (2010). *Learning for Jobs: Oecd Policy Review of Vocational Education and Training: Initial Report.* Paris: OECD/CERI.

OECD. (2012). *Public expenditure and participant stocks on LMP.* Accessed 29 May 2015. (http://stats.oecd.org/index.aspx?queryid=28935

Ondraschek, R. (2013). *Statuten und Geschäftsordnung des Österreichischen Gewerkschaftsbundes,* Wien: Verlag des Österreichischen Gewerkschaftsbundes GmbH.

Statistics Netherlands. (2014). *Population forecasts: key §s 2010–2060,* Online. Available (http://statline.cbs.nl/StatWeb/publication/?VW=T&DM=SLEN&PA=03766eng&LA=EN) Accessed January 31, 2014.

Statistik Austria, Online. Available (http://www.statistik.at) Accessed July 06, 2015.

Statistik Schweiz, Online. Available (http://www.bfs.admin.ch) Accessed July 06, 2015.

Statistisches Bundesamt. (2012). *Bildungsfinanzbericht 2012,* Online. Available (https://www.destatis.de/DE/Publikationen/Thematisch/BildungForschungKultur/BildungKulturFinanzen/Bildungsfinanzbericht1023206127004.pdf;jsessionid=728AEC3DC4928781A98659A867752769.cae2?__blob=publicationFile) Accessed January 31, 2013.

Statistisches Bundesamt, Wissenschaftszentrum Berlin für Sozialforschung (2013). *Datenreport 2013: Ein Sozialbericht für die Bundesrepublik Deutschland,* Bonn: Bundeszentrale für politische Bildung.

The Hofstede Centre, Online. Available (http://geert-hofstede.com/countries.html) Accessed July 04, 2015.

Van Lieshout, H. (2008). *Different Hands: Markets for Intermediate Skills in Germany, the U.S. and the Netherlands.* Groningen: Hanze Hogeschool.

Vollmar, M. (2013). Gestaltung der beruflichen Weiterbildung in Unternehmen 2010, In Statistisches Bundesamt (ed.) *Wirtschaft und Statistik.* Wiesbaden: Statistisches Bundesamt.

World Bank, Online. Available (http://www.worldbank.org/) Accessed May 29, 2015.

18 Human Resource Development in Southern Europe

Eduardo Tomé

INTRODUCTION

The aim of this chapter is to review the situation of HRD in the Southern part of Europe, namely in Italy, Spain, Portugal, France, and Greece. These countries are known to be culturally very specific, forming what will be defined as the "Latin part" of Europe sharing religion (Roman Catholic or Orthodox), family as a core value in society and conservative political ideologies, a historic legacy (all these countries were once world rulers), and varying levels of democratization. These countries experienced specific political evolutions since World War II and all the challenges of the latest economic developments worldwide—namely, the globalization process, the financial crisis, and the Eurozone experience.

HRD in Latin countries has come late and has been much smaller and less efficient than in the other European countries. The commitment to HRD is directly related to the economic fortunes and misfortunes these countries have faced, particularly in the last decade. HRD is also a predictor for the future evolution of these countries. This chapter examines HRD under the following headings: Context and Background, Broad V&T Systems, Institutional Actors, Political Context, Training and Development Systems at the National Level, Organizational-Level Developments in HRD, Impact, Summary, Discussion, and Conclusion.

CONTEXT AND BACKGROUND

Italy and France joined the European Community from its inception in 1957. Portugal, Greece, and Spain only became democratic in the early 1970s, joining the European Union in the 1980s. Crucially, all the five countries were founding members of the Eurozone in 2002.

Economy

The basic figures characterizing each one of these countries in 2012 are shown in Table 18.1. Some differences exist between their per capita incomes

Table 18.1 Basic Economic Indicators in the Southern European Region

	France	Greece	Italy	Portugal	Spain
GDP per head	€36104	€25331	€33111	€25411	€32682
GDP ranking	5	42	9	44	13
GDP growth	0%	–6.4%	–2.5%	–3.2%	–1.6%
Unemployment	10.2%	24.3%	10.7%	15.9%	25%
Unemployment evolution (2008–2012)	+2.4%	+16.6%	+4.0%	+7.4%	+14.7%
Long-term unemployment	4%	9%	4.5%	6%	8%
Youth unemployment	25%	56%	35%	38%	53%
Public debt % of GDP	127%	157%	90%	124%	86%
External debt	–5%	–3%	–1%	–3%	–1%
Troika Agreement	No	Yes	No	Yes	Yes
Gini index	30	34	32	35	35

Note: Average GDP of high-income countries and high-middle countries.

Source: Eurostat (2015), World Bank (2015), and United Nations (2015)

(about 30% more in France than in Portugal) and also in their current evolution (France having been much less hurt by the recession than Portugal and Greece). It should be underlined that even considering those differences, the five countries lay well inside what is considered to be the 'developed' and 'high-income' world, as their positions in the world rankings show.

In relation to unemployment, Greece, Spain, and Portugal present current values and evolution, which differ by huge margins from Italy and France (by 6–15%). The same separation exists between Greece, Portugal, and Spain and Italy and France in terms of long-term unemployment and youth unemployment, with differences between 5 and 20 percentage points on average. Unemployment in this analysis is interesting, as it is closely related to the main economic goal of HRD, i.e., employability.

The recession of 2007–2014 and the resultant unemployment in the labor market are factors in and causes of the massive public debt and external debt facing these countries, mainly Greece, Portugal, and Spain, in that order. These debt problems were addressed in three agreements on macroeconomic stability with the so-called Troika Partnership (European Commission, European Central Bank, and International Monetary Fund). However, the economic problems of Greece, Portugal, and Spain were aggravated by the fact that they have inequalities, measured by the Gini index, which are higher than those of Italy and France.

The Southern European region is not as affluent as North or Central Europe, but its position in world rankings is good, and its countries must be considered as belonging to the 20% wealthiest countries of the world. The differences that do exist, however, were put to an increasingly severe test since the Eurozone came into existence in 2002. Since then, all five countries

Table 18.2   Basic Social Indicators in the Southern European Countries

	France	Greece	Italy	Portugal	Spain
Life expectancy	82	80	83	80	82
Doctors (per thousand)	3	6	4	4	4
Infant mortality (per thousand)	3	3	3	3	3
Health expenditure	€3997	€3069	€3046	€2729	€3057
Population with low academic achievement	27%	34%	43%	62%	45%
Upper secondary studies, at least	72%	66%	57%	38%	54%
University graduates, age 30–34	44%	31%	22%	28%	40%
Lifelong learning	6%	3%	7%	11%	11%

Source: Eurostat (2015), World Bank (2015), and United Nations (2015)

have had difficulties keeping pace with the German-led and Euro-centered European Union, with those difficulties being more evident in Greece, Portugal, and Spain. Crucially, the authors of the chapter defend the thesis that one root of the recession in the southern countries, if not the main cause, lies in the HRD field.

Society

The basic social indicators that characterize these countries are listed in Table 18.2.

The figures regarding health are slightly better in France than in the other five countries. This is also true of education and training. These figures are analyzed in more detail in the next section. The importance that sports and particularly football have in these societies is related to the conservative culture and the idolization of the father, the boss, or the great football player. This is actually an important cultural backdrop for the development of HRD systems in these countries, and the place of HRD in these countries as will be discussed further in the next section.

BROAD V&T SYSTEMS

Table 18.3 summarizes the broad general vocational and educational base for HRD for each country, which includes the involvement of the public and private sectors. Today, all five countries possess a more homogeneous educational system than in the past, due to successive aligning adjustments made within a European Union context (European Commission, 2014).

Since 2002, all five countries have formally required at least 11 years of compulsory education. Those 11 years are divided in four parts: a primary

Table 18.3 Broad General Vocational and Educational Base for HRD in the Southern European Countries

		France	Greece	Italy	Portugal	Spain
Primary and secondary education						
	Compulsory education number of years	11	11	11	12	11
	Year CE definition	1959	1983	1999	2012	2000
	Population with CE (20–24)	84%	85%	78%	67%	63%
	Population with CE	72%	65%	37%	57%	54%
	Private share	21%	18%	15%	13%	15%
Higher education / tertiary studies						
	Population with HE (30–34)	43%	31%	22%	22%	40%
	attainment	27%	22%	13%	16%	29%
Vocational training						
	Lifelong education	5.7%	2.9%	6.6%	10.6%	10.7%
	Public expenditure in active LMP	2.3%		1.7%	1.9%	3.6%
	CSFs investment	5395	4384	6950	6843	8057

Source: Eursotat (2015)

cycle of four or five years and three parts of a secondary cycle with six or seven years, and usually divided in at least two parts (OECD, 2012). At the end of the secondary education, the student should be able to attend university; however, it is also possible to arrive at the university by being successful at a third type of secondary studies with a professional and vocational profile (OECD, 2012).

Since 2007, all five countries adjusted their university studies to the Bologna Process guidelines (European Commission, 2014). Those guidelines meant that higher education was divided into three cycles: graduation (three years), master's (two years), and PhD (three years).

Since at least 1990, the vocational systems of the five countries, above all Portugal, Greece, and Spain, have been framed and defined by the Community Support Framework (CSF) of the European Union (EU). The CSF are in fact financial packages that support programs made with EU financial support, essentially through the European Social Fund (ESF). The CSFs follow some sparse annual guidelines that have existed since 1960 and have been in practice for the periods 1990–1993, 1994–1999, 2000–2006, and 2007–2013 (Tomé, 2013). At the time of this writing, the CSFs for the period 2014–2020 are being defined and put in place under the umbrella of Horizon 2020 (European Commission, 2012). In addition, following EU guidelines, levels of compulsory vocational education have been introduced (European Commission, 2014), with an explicit commitment to increasing the levels of lifelong learning within the population (European Commission, 2014).

In practice, however, there is no such equality between the educational systems of the five countries. History certainly plays a part in this differentiation, and it is important to note that the countries that long have had compulsory secondary studies (France and Greece) have much higher figures in all measures of attainment at the secondary level (around 20% for the total population and around 10% for the younger generations).

The differentiation also exists in terms of the major players in the secondary scene. For those countries that long have had compulsory secondary studies, the private presence in the market is higher, an indication that compulsion stabilizes the market and increases the chances of private agents in the market. Even after the installation of the Bologna guidelines, the differentiation between the five countries is much greater with respect to higher education than to secondary studies, with the values of the top-two countries doubling those of the last two. France, Spain, Greece, Italy, and Portugal demonstrate, in that order, higher to lower values regarding the percentage of attainment in universities and the percentage of the younger generation with HE. Also, the public presence in HE provision is higher in the countries that have lower values of HE in the population. This seems to be an indication that the provision of HE has to be a social phenomenon and not only a public responsibility.

The differences are also important in what relates to vocational training (VT). In fact, the indicator on lifelong learning investments is much influenced by the presence of the ESF in the countries. Spain and Portugal lead Italy and France, with Greece lagging behind. This fact seems to point to the importance of European guidance in the investment in VT. When the ESF is not counted, Spain and France have more public expenditure than Portugal and Italy. However, and finally, the investments guided by the EU with the support of the ESF have been a major financial force in those countries, particularly in Greece and Portugal (Tomé, 2013). Also, since the 1990s, the EU worked toward Greece and Portugal increasing public expenditures on labor-market programs.

Overall, what has been shown in this section leads to two basic conclusions: (i) In legal and broad terms, these five countries have quite similar legal systems regarding the implementation of educational and vocational policies. Therefore, it might be said that the broadest base of educational and vocational systems in these five countries is similar. This similarity is due to the EU regulations. And (ii) in practical terms, the broad vocational and educational base for HRD differs considerably within the region. France, Italy, Spain, Portugal, and Greece have, in that order, developed from large and strong to relatively weak and medium-sized education and training (E&T) systems. This discrepancy exists even if the European Union tried decisively to balance the 'European Social Space' by using the ESF as a financial instrument, along with EU legislation as a nonfinancial instrument. With this broad basis in mind, the following sections analyze the institutions, the political settings, and the programs that materialize and operationalize the HRD systems of the five countries of the region.

INSTITUTIONAL ACTORS IN HRD

The major institutions operating in each one of the five countries are listed in Table 18.4.

In France, the public presence in the HRD system is felt at two levels: At a national level the Ministry of Education is the major responsibility for vocational education; however, the Ministry of Employment promotes HRD for private-sector employees, adult job seekers, and young people; other Ministries support HRD in the areas for which they are responsible. Each one of the 26 French regions have Regional Committees for Employment and Vocational Training to make policy analysis, monitoring, research, and evaluation (Rodgers, 2001); furthermore, each region develops its plan of continuing VT relying on regional monitors of E&T. The National Council for Lifelong Vocational Training exists to promote cooperation between the various agencies involved. Private bodies, profitable or nonprofitable, provide continuous VT mostly through training plans, individual entitlements to training, apprenticeship programs, training leave, or professionalization courses. The nonprofit organizations may also organize VT in the same conditions. Labor and employers organizations are partners in the definition of HRD policies. Finally, all the HRD operations should promote the instauration of a European Lifelong Learning Area.

In Greece, the Ministry of Education is responsible for organizing initial vocational education and training, whereas the Ministry of Labor organizes continuing vocational training (Vetrakou and Rousseas, 2003). This situation followed the establishment in 1992 of the National Vocational and Educational Training System (ESEEK). At the same time, the Organization for Vocational Education and Training (OEEK) and Institutes for Vocational Training (IEKs) were set up. The National Organization for the Certification of Qualifications & Vocational Guidance (EOPPEP) and the Manpower Employment Organization (OAED), restructured in 2001, are also important

Table 18.4 Main Institutions for HRD in the Southern European Countries

	France	Greece	Italy	Portugal	Spain
Government	Ministries of Education and Employment Regional bodies	Ministry of Education for Initial Vocational Training and of Employment for Continuous Vocational Training	Regional and state authorities in VET	Ministry of Employment with the support of the Ministries of Education and Economy	Guidelines defined by the central government Supervision and implementation by local governments
Government agencies	National Council	OEEK and IEKs, EOPPEP and OAED	Commission for the study of the future of VT	Institute for Employment	Serviço Publico de Empleo Estatal
Employer bodies	Support in policy definition	Provide training	Promote participation	Partners in the social dialogue	Promote participation
Labor unions	Same as employer bodies	Promote participation	Promote participation	UGT and CGTP	Promote participation
NGOs	Same as private companies	Provide	Provide	Private institutions of social solidarity	Nonspecified
Private companies	Provision through training plans, the individual entitlement to training and through the apprenticeship programs, training leave or professionalization courses	Provide	Provide	Major banks and companies, consultancy firms	Providers of VT in working context
External bodies	European Lifelong Learning Area	European Social Fund	European Social Fund and CEDEFOP	European Social Fund and multinationals	European Social Fund and EU legislation

public agencies. Despite the efforts of the European Union to involve the employers and labor unions in some form of partnership in promoting the Greek HRD system (European Commission, 2014), the main steps those partners have taken consist in the provision of courses by the employers and encouragement to participate in them by the unions. Private companies and NGOs have also mainly participated as providers and promoters.

In Italy, the regional authorities are responsible for vocational education; by contrast, the school system is the responsibility of the state. Vocational education is defined as education and training that is related to the labor market (Marchetti and Seveso, 1991). Vocational training is typically categorized as 1) training at the workplace for young people who have yet to be recruited, 2) on-the-job training for new and existing workers, and 3) training in accordance with legislative requirements (e.g., licensing). Marchetti and Seveso in 1991 (p.51), in a study for the European Center for Development of Vocational Training, found "virtually no social research" regarding training in Italy and, furthermore, that few reliable statistics were available. Much later in 2013, La Marca (2013) noted the situation had not changed dramatically, a fact that is in itself dramatic: the system is weak, fragmented, and the social partners' roles are based on provision.

In Portugal, the major institution involved with vocational education is the IEFP (Institute of Employment and Vocational Training), which is also a government agency, mainly a responsibility of the Ministry of Employment. But it should be noted that the Education Ministry defines educational policy, including the vocational options in the secondary studies. Also, the management of the European Union Structural Fund allocations has been traditionally spread over several ministries and nowadays is a feature of the Ministry of the Economy. Labor unions had a major role in the provision of vocational training but were tainted, however, by some scandals. The main employer partners, currently on the Council for Social Dialogue, also have an important role as vocational training providers. The nonprofitable private sector is also present in the form of the so-called private institutions of social solidarity. But it is important to stress the importance of the private sector as provider of vocational training—namely, through the big banks and major companies. Also in Portugal is the existence of a very large and important network of consultants who effectively support the management and provision of HRD and whose operations are mostly carried out with the support of the European Social Fund. Finally, the Portuguese description of the main agents in the HRD market would be very incomplete if the investors of external origin, namely the European Social Fund itself and private multinational companies, were not mentioned.

In Spain, education is the responsibility of the Ministry of Education (WEBVT, 2013), but since 2006, the 'New Vocational Training' became a responsibility of the public administration at the national or local level (BOE, 2006). Central government plays an important role in the formulation of guidelines for V&T policies, such as those found in the Qualifications and Training Act, of major plans such as the Training and Employment Integration Plan. It also plays a major role in the management institutions such as the National Institute for Employment and in discussion with the European bodies. However, the autonomous regional governments of Spain also have a decisive role in defining and implementing HRD policy. In this context, the central government defines guidelines and the supervision and implementation by local governments. The implementation of a dual system of VT is the responsibility of the Autonomous Communities (Governo de Espana, 2013). It is stressed, however, that companies have a fundamental role in providing training in a working context (Governo de Espana, 2013b). The participation of NGOs is not specified, and it is understood that labor unions and employer bodies should promote participation in training. As in all the other countries of the zone, the ESF and the EU provided the background for the implementation of this new legislation.

POLITICAL CONTEXT

The legislative and policy context within the various countries of the region are summarized in Table 18.5.

In France, the legislation has been somewhat dirigistic (interventionist) (CEDEFOP, 2008), with many specific rules and regulations defining the framework for HRD in the country. These were effective even after the regionalization of the VET system. The roots for the conception of laws and their application by the public bodies and other actors lie in the French 'raison d'etat', according to which laws are to be obeyed.

In Greece, a myriad of institutions exist to ensure the management of HRD, particularly for VT (Vetrakou and Rousseas, 2002), and the practice of policy has been essentially estate led. In theory, the system should promote a vast and strong system of HRD; in practice, the operations are centralized in public bodies. The difference has to do with the weakness of the private bodies as promoters and the importance of the EU as a funder.

In Italy, the legislation defined a broad legislative setting (Adams and Nibauer, 2000), put in place with a high degree of liberty and decentralization. The nature of the Italian conception of state, with its tendency to decentralization and liberalism, explains the situation.

In Portugal, the norms and legislation originate mainly from the European Union and, above all, through the European Social Fund. Even if the EU proclaims to be a market economy, the rules that govern ESF operations in Portugal are strong and reflect some dirigisme and the importance of the state as the definer of the programs (see next section). However, when the programs are put to practice, the enormous dimension of the operations and the absorption logic (see "Impacts" section), which in fact forms the basis of the HRD operations in Portugal, implies that the control system is completely overwhelmed. This fact in turn means that the thousands of

Table 18.5 Legislative and Policy Context in the Southern European Countries

	France	Greece	Italy	Portugal	Spain
Theory	Dirigisme	Institutionalized	Broad guidelines	Dirigisme	Regionalism
Practice	Regionalized dirigisme	Estate-led	Liberty and decentralization	Laissez-faire	Social partners involvement with European background
Difference	Small	Significant	Small	Big and significant	Small
Causes	French conception of state	Weak private promotion and strong EU funding	Italian conception of state	Absorption logic	National concern over VET and HRD

consultants who manage the HRD operation can use the ESF funds in a different (and more useful) way than the one they were awarded for, provided the consultant prepares an administrative file that hides the divergence.

In Spain, the more recent rules (Homs, 2009) proclaim a deep regionalism. In practice, that idea has proved fruitful, and with the involvement of the social partners and the guidance of the European Union, Spain has built and advanced an up-to-date system of HRD provision.

T&D SYSTEMS AND PROGRAMS

The main programs and systems of HRD provision in each of the countries of the region are described in Table 18.6.

In France, private provision is high (Cedefop, 2008), but it is also complemented by a strong public presence, which in turn is increased by the fact that France has tried to obtain important funds from the ESF. The programs are extensive and cover all the areas of training and HRD facets. In Greece, the main programs serve the employed and the unemployed, separately, and are sponsored by the European Union (Vretakou and Rousseas, 2002). Moreover, the level of employer provision and its efficiency stands as the lowest in Europe (Eichhorst et al., 2012). However, the level of public intervention through the ESF appears as the second highest since Greek entry into the EU (Tomé, 2013). Italy's provision of HRD by private companies lies low in the European index of levels (Adams and Nibauer, 2000). A strong difference exists, however, between the north and the south of the country. However, with respect to public provision, the opposite is the case with European funds playing a major role. Public provision has also been connected to the unemployment situation and the role of private provision in the retraining and qualification of employees.

In Portugal, there exists a divide between public provision and privately funded programs. The ESF has been funding programs related to disadvantaged social economic groups, such as young people (Tomé, 2007), unemployed, or unskilled adults (Tomé, 2012). Those main target groups have been defined by the EU legislation (Tomé, 2012). However, since EU entry in 1986, the private sector has been providing training for its employees, mostly for requalification but sometimes also for initial training; those training operations are usually small and geared to company needs. The level of private funding is substantial. The main programs promoted have been for young people between 1986 and 1990, for the active population between 1990 and 1993, and for human capital development since 1994 (Tomé, 2012). Finally, in Spain, the main concern has been skills acquisition by the labor force (Holms, 2009). The problem arose when the unemployment levels soared as high as 20% in the '90s. Until then, in spite of all the discourse, Spain and companies relied on low labor costs and a not-so-skilled workforce. Since then, companies have tried to use EU money to make sensible investments.

Table 18.6 Major HRD Programs and Systems in the Southern European Countries

	France	Greece	Italy	Portugal	Spain
Main programs	Extensive: for a huge variety of economic and social purposes e.g., apprenticeship, job seekers, and current workers	EU funded for employed and unemployed	Company for employees and unemployed by the state	Young people until 1990, labor force in the '90s, reinforcement of human potential since 2000	Skills promotion
Private firm provision	Among the highest in Europe	Lowest in Europe	North high, south low	Small, labor centered for requalification	Increasing
State provision	Important and supported by the ESF	Second to Portugal using the ESF	South high, north low	Huge, socially oriented to eliminate unemployment and maintain employment	Basing and based in the European Funds with strong regional input

ORGANIZATIONAL-LEVEL DEVELOPMENTS IN HRD

The main characteristics for the five countries in what concerns organizational HRD are shown in Table 18.7:

In France, as late as 2005, research studies (Well and Woodall, 2005) concluded that French companies lacked a clear understanding of HRD, which led to the fact that a wide range of activities were considered HRD. At that time, an emerging interest existed in management development, career development, and skills forecasting but training evaluation was neglected. Also, growing evidence existed about the involvement of line managers in human resource development activity with a strong commitment to the strategic significance of human resource development.

In Greece, in 2000, a study of best practices (Papalexandris and Nikandrou, 2000) showed that training could no longer be treated as a method to cure skills deficiencies but rather as a continuous, lifelong learning process with considerable impact on the growth of firms; acquiring human skills presented the greatest challenge for training; and adaptability and self-learning were necessary elements that need to be incorporated in the educational system from its early stages. More than a decade later (Panagiotakopoulos, 2011), it was found that training in industrial micro firms is significantly affected by the business strategy, the owner commitment toward employee training and development, and the way work was organized. In this context, it would be important to facilitate changes in owner attitudes, as well as to change the current institutional framework, encouraging micro firms to adopt higher value-added strategies and consequently improve their training efforts.

Regarding Italy, a recent study (Guerci and Solari, 2012) found that in the Italian context, talent is managed for very different organizational objectives, with the general aim to foster a segmented approach to the workforce and to commit top and line managers to HRD activities. In Portugal, training has been common in big companies, particularly if they fund their own programs. In these cases, the goal has been to promote competitiveness (Tomé, 2007, Tomé, 2008, and Tomé, 2012). SMEs and the public sector rely very much on EU funds to provide training for employees, and the HRD operations in these organizations have been to upgrade skills for survival (Tomé, 2007, Tomé, 2008, and Tomé, 2012). In Spain, for the strategic tourism sector, previous staff qualification is not an option, and training actually is a determining factor for companies to achieve a differential positioning within the sector (Ubeda-Garcia et al., 2013).

IMPACT OF HRD

In France, the evaluation of vocational training in regard to employment has been a common practice since the 1980s (Heckman, Lalonde, &Smith, 1999) with respect to levels of productivity (Laulhe, 1990) and the IT sector

Table 18.7 Main Characteristics of Organizational HRD in the Southern European Countries

	France	Greece	Italy	Portugal	Spain
Positive	Emerging interest, wide range of activities, involvement of line managers, strategic significance	Continuous, lifelong learning process with considerable impact on growth of the firms	Fosters segmented approach to the workforce and to commit top and line managers to HRD activities	Big companies funding some excellent programs and good practices otherwise	Training a determining factor for companies to achieve differential positioning
Negative	Lack of clear understanding, neglect of evaluation	Significantly affected by business strategy, owner commitment toward employee training and development and the way work is organized	Very varying organizational objectives	SMEs lacking HRD staff, facilities and even perspective; public sector spending ESF funds	Staff qualification may not be an option

(Cooper, 1986), and it continues to the present (Bailly et al., 2013; Lambert and Vero, 2013). Public policies have been analyzed (Greenhalgh, 1999 and 2002). The implementation and monitoring of the funds have been analyzed also for a long time (Barbier and Simonin, 1997; 1999); however, there seems to be no study available to date exploring the impact of ESF on the French experience. The authors are also unaware of any major assessment study on Greece regarding ESF operations or on private investment in training. The assessment of the structural funds was designed long ago (Christodoulakis et al., 1998) and has been estimated as slightly more than 1% annually (Eurobank, 2011). Therefore, the available evidence about HRD in Greece is partial and based on cases studies on learning (Zambarloukos and Constantelou, 2002), knowledge and multinationals (Manolopoulos et al., 2007), and micro firms (Panagiotakopoulos, 2011).

The situation regarding Italy is somehow better: the analysis reported in Euréval (2010) found positive but small impacts for the ESF in the period 2000–2006. Those findings were in line with the results from Conti (2005) for the private sector and followed other more abstract works from Lion et al. (2004, 2006), Gularte (2003), or Marchetti and Seveso (1991). In Portugal, evaluations of impact of HRD have seldom been done (Tomé, 2012). There is study on the impact of privately funded training, with the exception of basic wages functions (Tomé, 2007). Some studies exist on ESF operations, which show some positive impact in employability but no effect on wages (Tomé, 2007). No macroeconomic studies have been done on the impact of ESF on the Portuguese economy, even if the global effect of the structural funds has been found to be positive. Finally, in Spain, the evaluation of ESF operations started long ago (Ballart, 1998; Saez and Toledo, 1996) and have continued to be carried out (Cueto and Mato, 2009), followed by other studies on the private sector (Nijhof, 2004).

HRD SIMILARITIES AND DIFFERENCES ACROSS SOUTHERN EUROPEAN COUNTRIES

The main HRD similarities and differences across Southern European countries are summarized in Table 18.8. In France, the HRD system leads to high performance and is the most advanced and balanced of the five countries analyzed. The level of supply is high, as described by the data exposed in Tables 18.6 and 18.7 and the corresponding sections (Cedefop, 2008). However, demand for training is also high, which implies that the unemployment situation in France is average in European terms; emigration is not a problem, although, in fact, France faces integration problems of immigrants; furthermore, poverty rates are low, and the country's standard of living is high by world levels. To continue to remain near the top of the ranking list in world terms, France needs to attend further to HRD; however, it seems

Table 18.8 Summary of HRD in the Southern European Countries

	France	Greece	Italy	Portugal	Spain
Supply	High, private and public	Very high, public	Private in the North, public in the south	High, public	Strong and increasingly private and in quality
Demand	High, private and public	Very low, private	Northern based	Low, private	Considerable, increasing
Needs	Large, but met	Large, but not met	North: to maintain economic edge, south: to achieve prosperity	Very large, almost not met	Important
Impacts	Assessed and significant	Unknown in micro, economic disaster in macro	Important	Positive employment effect at micro level Recession at macro level	Strong

to have an adequate HRD system to achieve that result having had a long history of HRD. France stands out among the five countries analyzed for its 'French singularity'. French singularity refers to France's long-standing competition with the UK and Germany for a position of power in Central Europe. French governments have long understood that a strong HRD system is an essential social feature in order to win that position. The fact that evaluation practices were developed following the implementation of projects is not surprising—it also happened in other countries such as the USA (Tomé, 2001).

The failure of the Greek experience is explained by the divide between the weak private provision (Eichhorst et al., 2012) and the enormous public provision (Tomé, 2013). Whereas private companies tried to fund HRD according their own needs, which were weak and reflected the incipient level of development of the Greek economy (Eichhorst et al., 2012), the European Social Fund provided huge funds for the education of the Greek population and mostly the young. When the 2007–2008 financial crisis hit Greece, and when the effects of participating in the Eurozone became defining and too strong (Tomé, 2013 b), these young people were found to be too skilled for the Greek companies and had to choose between several bad alternatives: low-paid and low-skilled jobs, emigration or unemployment.

Italy has an unbalanced system of HRD, with variations from region to region. The north has an HRD system that is similar to the best in Northern Europe and compares to France. But the south reassembles more the situation in Greece and Portugal. Both parts of Italy need strong HRD: the north must continue to be at the front of the developed regions in Europe, and the south must obtain the average European level of wealth, income, and employment. The EU has helped the south. Evaluations have been made, both of private and public experiences, with some positive results.

The case of Portugal is very similar to Greece, because it follows the same pattern of imbalances between private and public provision and between supply of skills and demand for skills. As a consequence of the ESF funding, in both countries, the supply of HRD has been much higher than the demand. Even if the needs for HRD were obviously very big (Tomé, 2009), there was no economic platform put in place to meet these needs and to guarantee that the investment in HRD would have an important positive impact. The only major fact that differentiates, only slightly, the two countries is that in Portugal, private training was higher and slightly more efficient than in Greece; also, in Portugal, the private bodies had some presence in the management of the partnership institutions that ruled the ESF. But all in all, these two countries illustrate absolutely the case of an estate-led HRD system with low participation and relevance of the private sector. Also, both countries relied on EU money and programs to solve their problems, something that somehow exonerates the internal bodies from the possible failure of that investment; furthermore, the investment tends to be seen as a gift sent by the European Union. Therefore, even if the effects of the investment will be positively felt in the long run by the young generations, who will certainly profit from a higher level of HRD in the new Europe and Eurozone of the twenty-first globalized and English-speaking century, for now, in the short run, what is seen is a massive waste of funds, energy, money, and an enormous social problem. The situation only gets worst because the current powers that govern the two countries do not see HRD imbalances and shortages as a cause of the crisis (Tomé, 2013d) and are only interested in the macroeconomic, budget-related aspect of this crisis (Tomé, 2013c).

In Spain, the supply of HRD was always strong, but its quality was low for a long time. In the last 15 years, the private sector has been more conscious of promoting HRD. This resulted, for a while, in an important decrease in unemployment, helped by the economic bonanza of the turning of the century. However, following the economic crisis of 2007–2008, Spain also felt the hardship of Eurozone membership and unemployment levels rose again. However, the Spanish problems were not of the same degree as those of Greece and Portugal, because the Spanish labor market had more HR and was therefore based on a more competitive economy. The strong relationship of Spain with Spanish-speaking Latin American countries and even with the USA, where more and more people speak Spanish these days, also helped the Spanish economy profit from HRD investment.

DISCUSSION

The analysis presented here points to the value of classifying the five Southern European countries under investigation in this chapter as low skilled, medium skilled, and high skilled (Ashton and Green, 1996). Crucially, a high-skills equilibrium coincides with a positive cycle of investment, with good jobs matched by highly qualified personnel, and vice versa. A high-skills equilibrium is characteristic of rich countries, and the 'North of the North' corresponds to this type of situation. A high-skills equilibrium is also characterized by high wages and exports in intersectoral or intrasectoral goods and services of high quality, indicative of high-tech industries or services. Emerging countries tend to manifest a medium-skills equilibrium. The achievement of a high-skills equilibrium, in fact, requires some sort of social agreement between major forces representing the government, the workers, the companies, the education and training system itself, and even the elites. The concept is interesting because the five 'South of the North' countries may be ranked in a continuum of middle skills to high skills: Greece, Portugal, Spain, Italy, and France with Portugal and Greece on one side of a spectrum, namely the ones closer to a middle-skills equilibrium, with high and unfulfilled needs, very high support from the EU, and low private capacity. These two countries are similar to the south of Italy. The fact that EU support remains very essential indicates the absence of a true social agreement on HRD, even if the EU tries to implement its programs through partnerships between the main social forces. That lack of agreement results in low wages and low private investment. It is a measure of the importance of this middle-skills equilibrium that these two countries faced big adjustment problems between 2010 and 2015, and this process is not finished. A middle-income equilibrium in these countries has to face the mounting challenge of the emerging Brazil, Russia, India, China, and South Africa (BRICS) on one side, and of the 'North of the North' on the other side, a very tough task.

On the other end of the spectrum is France, Italy, particularly in the north, and Spain. In these three countries, the private intervention is stronger, demand and supply are more balanced, and the needs, even if important, are less than in the other two countries. Curiously, it is in these three countries that HRD is more evaluated, a sign of the social importance of HRD and of the aforementioned social agreement. In these countries, investment, particularly private investment, is higher, wages are higher, and compulsory education is not recent. The administration of HRD is much more guided by national bodies and not by the urgency of spending EU funds. Interestingly, these countries are big but very regionalized—a fact that adds to the performance of the investment in HRD. In Portugal, the formulation of HRD policies tends to be more national, and this proves not to be beneficial.

In any discussion on HRD in these five countries, the fact that all are members of the Eurozone cannot be ignored. We sincerely believe that the Eurozone puts a heavy burden on each of these five countries, because, in the first place, it highlights daily and increasingly their level of competitiveness in relation to the other Eurozone members, and, second, it highlights competiveness in relation to the other developed countries and even to BRICs. It is in the context of this socioeconomic struggle for survival that HRD will prove to be of immense importance for the future of these five countries. Most probably, they will only achieve or maintain high levels of income and strong levels of sustained growth if their HRD systems, as described in national and organizational terms in this paper, become big and reach high performance.

As it is, France is the better prepared of the five countries, followed by Northern Italy, then Spain, then Southern Italy, then Portugal, and finally Greece. Therefore, three countries should fight to maintain and improve their high-skills equilibrium and two others should struggle to bridge definitively the gap between the actual situation of middle skills and the desired situation of high skills.

The role of the EU itself should also be in question, as its HRD policies have not helped to alleviate the crisis in the weaker regions of these countries. In fact, we believe that EU policies have been misguided and have been part of the problem of the current crisis.

In the countries studied here, and mainly in Portugal and Greece, the interesting and quite impressive EU guidelines must be applied with increasing private involvement at all levels, including the funding of the programs to improve the social impact of HR and HRD investments, thereby increasing its reach in the short run and its impact in the long run. This would eliminate the 'low-cost' mentality and replace it with the consideration that HRD, although an expensive investment, brings high returns by generating high skills and prosperous equilibriums. Indeed the failure of Southern Europe is somehow the failure of taking seriously that HR and HRD are really central, although expensive and time-consuming investments. France has known this since at least the 1960s, and Northern Italy accepts it too. Spain understood this around 2000. Greece and Portugal are still coming to terms with it. The correlation of HRD to economic development in each of these countries is straightforward.

CONCLUSION

The five countries analyzed in this chapter (France, Greece, Italy, Portugal, and Spain) share geographic and social history. They are 'the South of the North'. All are traditional and conservative societies that were once world powers that entered the Eurozone in 2002 as founders. These countries have achieved some relative levels of economic prosperity in world terms, being objectively ranked among the industrialized or rich regions of the world. However, and crucially, they have not focused their success on the development and upgrading of nationwide skills with the exception of France and Northern Italy. As a whole, these countries had more cheap labor and a lower investment in HR and HRD than Central and Northern Europe where labor was always more valued.

With the integration of the European countries, the EU decided to help weaker countries through the European Social Fund mechanism, which included subsidizing HR almost at full cost. That practice in turn increased the perception that HR was a cheap investment. The first consequence of that perception was that, in spite of the political discourse, which insisted in the valorization of HR and HRD, the investments were made more to absorb the funds than with a view to the lasting economic effect. Another consequence in these weaker regions was that a significant number of young people had more academic degrees than any of their predecessors, yet were paid lower wages and were put to work in low-skilled and routine services, such as call centers. HR was perceived as a cheap investment because it was essentially funded by public money: free cost studies from primary school to university and free cost training through the ESF but little sense of what to do with the fruits of HRD which resulted. The more private money was involved in the provision of all kinds of HR, the less the national HR market was classified as low cost. In the long run, it turns out that the more affluent the economy the more sustainable the society.

Somebody said once that Europe will be united or will not exist. A corresponding way of giving HRD its societal importance in Europe is to say: Europe will be made with HRD or it will not exist. HRD will be needed to ensure competitiveness and social well-being and as a complement to education. The economy will need a strong private sector to use HRD for competitive and strong public and third sectors to care for social well-being. At the end of the day, HRD will be central for the prosperity of all five countries into the future.

REFERENCES

Adams, M., & Nibaue, R. (2000). *The Vocational Training System in Italy*, ISFOL.

Ashton, D., & Green, F. (1996). *Education, Training and the Global Economy*. Cambridge, UK: Edward Elgar.

Bailly, F., & Chapelle, K. (2013). *The Training of Jobseekers by Non-profit Organizations: An Analysis Based on Data from the Upper Normandy Region of France. Metroeconomica*. Nov 2013, 64(4): 645–682.

Ballart, X. (1998). Spanish evaluation practice versus program evaluation theory. *Evaluation*, 4(2): 149–170.

Barbier, J. C, & Simonin, B. (1997). European social programmes can evaluation of implementation increase the appropriateness of findings? *Evaluation*, October 1997 3(4): 391–407.

BOE. (2006). Lei Organica de la Education, 4 mayo de 2006, n 106.

Cedefop. (2008). *Vocational Education and Training in France, Short Description*. Thesalonika, Greece.

Christodoulakis, N., & Kalyvitis, C. (1998). A four-sector macroeconometric model for Greece and the evaluation of the community support framework. *Economic Modelling*, Oct 98, 15(4): 575.

Conti, G. (2005). Training, productivity and wages in Italy. *Labour Economics*, August, 2005. 12(4): 557–576.

Cooper, J. (1986). Industrial training in France (with Reference to the new microelectronic technology). *Journal of European Industrial Training*, 10(5): 26–31.

Cueto, B., & Mato, F. (2009). A nonexperimental evaluation of training programmes: Regional evidence for Spain. *Annals of Regional Science*. Jun2009, 43(2): 415–433.

Eichhorst, W., Rodríguez-Planas, N., Schmidl, R., & Zimmermann, K. (2012). *A Roadmap to Vocational Education and Training Systems Around the World*. IZA, DP.No 7110.

Euréval. (2010). *Study on the Return on ESF Investment in Human Capital*, Final Report. Brussels.

Eurobank. (2011). Euro structural funds in Greece, more necessary than ever. *Greece Macro monitor*—December, 22.

European Commission. (2014). Education and Training—Strategic framework: (http://ec.europa.eu/education/policy/strategic-framework/index_en.htm)

Goberno de Espana (2013b) El portal de la formacion professional http://www.todofp.es/ as accessed in November 2013 and November 2015.

Greenhalgh, C. (1999). Adult vocational training and government policy in France and Britain. *Oxford Review of Economic Policy*. 99.15(1): 97.

Greenhalgh, C. (2002). Does an employer training levy work? The incidence of and returns to adult vocational training in France and Britain. *Fiscal Studies*. Jun2002, 23(2): 223.

Guerci, M., & Solari, L. (2012). Talent management practices in Italy—implications for human resource development. *Human Resource Development International*, Feb2012, 15(1): 25–41.

Gularte, M. (2003). *Workforce Development and HRD in the European Union and Italy: Exploring the Literature*. UFHRD Conference Proceedings.

Heckman, J., Lalonde, R., & Smith, J. (1999). The economics and econometrics of active labour market programs. In Orley Ashenfelter and Robert Lalonde (Eds.), *Handbook of Labour Economics*, 3A (31): 1865–2097. North Holland.

Homs, O (2009). *Vocational Training in Spain, Toward the Knowledge Society—La Obra Social*. Social Studies Collection, 25.

La Marca, T (2013). *Investing in Lifelong Learning: A Chance to Give a Future Back to the Italian Citizens*. (http://www.infonet-ae.eu/en/background-reports/to-invest-in-life-long-learning-a-chance-to-give-back-future-to-italian-citizens-1279). Assessed October 29, 2013.

Laulhe P. (1990). La formation continue: un avantage pour les promotions et un accès privilégié pour les jeunes et pour les techniciens. *Economie et statistique*, 228 (1) pp. 3-8.

Lambert, M., & Vero, J. (2013). The capability to aspire for continuing training in France: The role of the environment shaped by corporate training policy. *International Journal of Manpower*, 34(4): 305–325.

Lion, C., Martini P., & Volpi, S. (2004). The evaluation of European social fund programs in a new framework of multilevel governance: The Italian experience. *Regional Studies*, 38: 207–212.

Lion, C., Martini, P., & Volpi, S. (2006). Evaluating the implementation process: A contribution within the framework of the European social fund (ESF) programme. *Evaluation July*, 12: 313–329.

Manolopoulos, D., Papanastassiou, M., & Pearce, R. (2007). Knowledge-related competitiveness and the roles of multinationals' R&D in a peripheral European economy: Survey analysis of Greece. *Management International Review (MIR)*, 5th Quarter, 47(5): 661–681.

Marchetti, A., & Seveso, F. (1991). *Continuing Training in Firms and Trainer Development in Italy*. Berlin: European Centre for the Development of Vocational Training (CEDEFOP).

Nijhof, W. (2004). Training in Spain: An evaluation of the continuous training agreements (1993-2001) with particular reference to SMEs. *Human Resource Development International*. Mar2004, 7(1): 23–37.

OECD. (2012). *Education at Glance*, 2012. Paris.

Panagiotakopoulos, A. (2011). What drives training in industrial micro-firms? Evidence from Greece. *Industrial & Commercial Training*, 43(2): 113–120.

Papalexandris, N., & Nikandrou, I. (2000). Benchmarking employee skills: Results from best practice firms in Greece. *Journal of European Industrial Training*, 24(7): 391–402.

Rogers, V. (2001). *The Regionalization of Youth Training in France Regional Studies*. May2001, 35(3): 259–264.

Saez, F., & Toledo, M. (1996). Formation, Mercado de Trabajo e Empleo. *Economistas*, 69: 351–357.

Tomé, E. (2001). The evaluation of vocational training: A comparative analysis. *Journal of European and Industrial Training*, 25(7): 380–388.

Tomé, E. (2007). Employability, skills, and training in Portugal (1988–2001): Evidence from official data. *Journal of European Industrial Training*, 31(5): 336–357.

Tomé, E. (2008). The Portuguese youth labor market, a critical approach. *Journal of European Industrial Training*, 32(7): 510–527.

Tomé, E. (2009). HRD in a Multipolar world: An introductory study. *Chinese Business Review*, 8(12): 17–26.

Tomé, E. (2012). European social fund in Portugal: A complex question for human resource development. *European Journal of Training and Development*, 36(2-3): 179–194.

Tomé, E. (2013). The European Union HRD policies: A very specific case of HRD. *European Journal of Industrial Training*, 4: 336–356.

Tomé, E. (2013b). *Innovation, Knowledge and Incompetence: The Case of the Eurozone Macroeconomic Policies*. ECKM 2013 Kaunas.

Tomé, E. (2013c). *Explaining the Economic Crisis Through Human Resources Development Policy: A comparison between the USA and the European Union*. Academy of HRD Conference, February, Washington.

Tomé, E. (2013d). *HRD in Times of Turbulence: The Case of Southern Europe*. A study on low cost HRD economies. UFHRD 2013, Brighton, 5–7 June.

Úbeda-García, M., Marco-Lajara, B., Sabater-Sempere, V., & Garcia-Lillo, F. (2012). *International Journal of Human Resource Management*, Dec 2013, 24(15): 2851–2875.

Úbeda-García M, Marco-Lajaraa, B. García-Lilloa F & Sabater-Semperea V. (2013). Universalistic and Contingent Perspectives on Human Resource Management: An Empirical Study of the Spanish Hotel Industry. *Journal of Human Resources in Hospitality & Tourism*, 12: 26–51.

Vetrakou, V., & Rousseas, P. (2002). *Vocational Education and Training in Greece*. Short Description. Cedefop, Panorama Series, Luxembourg.

Vetrakou V. and Rousseas P. (2003). *Vocational education and training in Greece: Short description*. Luxembourg: Office for Official Publications of the European Communities.

Weil, A., & Woodall, J. (2005). *Journal of European Industrial Training*, 29(7): 529–540.

Zambarloukos, S., & Constantelou, A. (2002). Learning and skills formation in the new economy: Evidence from Greece. *International Journal of Training Development*, Dec 2002, 6(4): 40–253.

Section VI
Emerging Markets

19 Human Resource Development in CIVETS

Thomas N. Garavan and Mesut Akdere

INTRODUCTION

Our knowledge of human resource development (HRD) in Colombia, Indonesia, Vietnam, Egypt, Turkey, and South Africa is sparse. These emerging economies, which the economist have termed CIVETS, are unified by a number of characteristics, including: a) dynamic and growing economies, b) the adoption of free-market principles, c) a young and growing population, and d) relative political stability (Hoskisson et al., 2000; Guerra-Baron, 2012). They also share a strong explicit intention to develop human capital and have in various ways committed to enhancing institutional arrangements to support HRD. Culturally they have a number of national cultural characteristics in common, and their governments have given particular emphasis to the attraction of foreign direction investment (FDI) and to the development of strong international trade relationships. However, as we illustrate in this chapter, they differ in their success in creating an environment for the development of human capital, the strength of their institutional arrangements for HRD, and both the quality and comprehensiveness of organization-level HRD practices.

This chapter contributes to our understanding of HRD in CIVETS countries by exploring, from a comparative perspective, the HRD system of each country. We first consider their political, historical, cultural, and economic characteristics, which will provide a rich contextual background to understanding the approach to HRD in each country within the grouping. We then consider the institutional arrangements that support HRD in each country followed by a discussion of organizational-level HRD practices. In the final section, we discuss the extent of convergence and divergence in approaches to HRD across the CIVETS as well as a consideration of the HRD challenges that face each country.

COMPARING CIVETS HISTORICAL, POLITICAL, CULTURAL, ECONOMIC, AND INSTITUTIONAL CONTEXTS

The CIVETS countries represent an economic rather than a political grouping. They are among the biggest and fastest-growing emerging markets and account for 50% of the world's population, 40% of its geographic area, and 50% of global GDP (CIA, 2013). CIVETS countries contain a large youth population (Indonesia having the largest population and Egypt the fastest growth rate). Indonesia, Vietnam, and Egypt are categorized as middle-income countries with the remainder categorized as in the middle-to upper-income category. Politically, Indonesia, Turkey, Egypt, and South Africa are viewed as pivotal states, whereas Colombia is viewed as a secondary regional player behind Brazil, and Vietnam is viewed as a middleweight political player in Southeast Asia (Nolte, 2010). They have unique historical, political, and cultural characteristics, and yet share a plethora of similar economic challenges.

COLOMBIA AND SOUTH AFRICA

Historical and Political Context

Both Colombia and South Africa share a similar historical and political trajectory. Both countries have experienced a long period of conflict and violence (Murillo, 2009), and they both made the decision politically to liberalize their economies utilizing a combination of constitutional and legal measures. The transition process in Colombia began under the presidency of César Gaviria (1990–1994) and continued under subsequent presidents, Ernesto Samper (1994–1998) and Andrés Pastrana (1998–2002). Under the presidency of Alvaro Uribe (2002–2010), Colombia started to focus on FDI provision by initiating major reform of its trade and domestic policies. Major investment climate reforms were also implemented. Juan Manuel Santos came to power in 2010, and he has continued to develop Colombia's image internationally and make the economy more attractive to foreign investment. He implemented a National Development Plan with 'International Relevance' as its central political goal (Guerra Baron, 2012). He has significantly diversified the trade agenda to include Asian and African countries as well as CIVETS countries.

South Africa experienced a major period of diplomatic isolation during apartheid. President Mandela (1994–1999) brought South Africa into the international arena through the adoption of neoliberal political ideas and a strong focus on FDI as a strategy to achieve economic growth (Alden and Vieira, 2007). Mandela placed a strong emphasis on social equality and full access to the benefits of economic growth (Hirschsohn, 2008). He also promoted multi-literalism and new economic blocks, such as the Southern African Development Community. President Mbeke (1999–2009) continued the emphasis on equitable access to the benefits of economic growth and focused on developing South Africa as a key political leader through the implementation of a butterfly trade strategy that included both Brazil and India. Under Mbeki's presidency, South Africa became a key regional power with participation in various global governance forums. President Jacob

Zuma (2009–current) continues a political and economic agenda similar to his predecessors, focused on enhancing South Africa's political stature internationally (Mantzikos, 2010).

Economic Context

Colombia benefits immensely from its significant natural resource base, including oil, coal, and natural gas and industries, including textiles, coffee, nickel, and emeralds. Its main export is oil, it is the third-largest exporter of oil in Latin America and the largest source of US coal imports (CIA, 2014a). About 94% of the population is classified as literate, and expenditure on education constitutes 5% of GDP. And yet there is a high level of gender inequality in areas such as wages and employment conditions. Its economy has expanded significantly; unemployment has reduced to under 10% (2013) and it has a rapidly growing middle class (Whittington, 2011). Its primary economic goals focus on strengthening competitiveness, raising productivity, and investment in training and retraining (Cruz et al., 2010b).

South Africa is considered economically to be one of the most developed nations on the African continent. It has a very young population—28% are between 15–24 years of age. Almost 80% of the population is black, with only 9% categorized as white. Like Colombia, South Africa has vast natural resources, as well as strong financial, legal, communication, energy, and transport sectors. GDP per capita is $11,500 with a large number of primary industries including corn, wheat, sugar, fruits, vegetables, and beef. It suffers, however, from significant poverty, racial inequality, and very high levels of unemployment (about 25%). Unstable power supplies remain a significant challenge to South Africa's economic growth.

Cultural Context

Culturally, the Colombian population consists of a racial mixture of Native American peoples and decedents of Spanish conquerors. In terms of leadership, the style has been described as closed and elitist. On the Hofstede scale (2001), culturally Colombia is classified as high on group orientation, high on the elitist scale, medium-high on uncertainty avoidance, and oriented toward 'masculine' values. The role of women in Colombia is strongly influenced by religion. Ogliastri and the GLOBE Study (2007) found that Colombia is less able to tolerate uncertainty and is one of the most aggressive countries in the world. There is a growing tendency toward a performance orientation and the traditional Catholic values of charity and resignation to one's destiny are a strong part of Colombian culture. The culture is also characterized by values of personalism (sense of connection and respect for individual dignity), particularism (legitimacy of using personal connections for one's personal benefit and advancement), and paternalism (Osland, De Franco, & Osland, 1999).

South Africa is, as Colombia, a culturally diverse nation. It consists of many ethnic groups with differing religious, cultural, and linguistic characteristics (Statistics South Africa, 2010). The concept of *ubunto* is widely respected particularly among the black population. *Ubunto* emphasizes people's allegiances and relationships with each other. This is reflected in cultural values, such as mutual respect and support, interdependency, unity, collective work, and responsibility. Morris and Schindehutte (2005) suggested that South Africa is very high on collectivism, low on uncertainty avoidance (with a fatalistic ethos), low masculinity, and high power distance with a collective recognition that power is based on age and wisdom. South Africans have mixed attitudes toward organizations and organizational members; workers are more dedicated to ancestors and the land rather than to organizations and will be committed to the company if it is embedded in the community and has a special attachment to the land. South Africans value orderly ways of doing things, especially where there are established values. Loyalty is paramount and overrides other social rules and regulations. Teamwork and consensus building in organizations are influenced by strong group identity and loyalty.

Institutional Context

HRD in both Colombia and South Africa happens in complex institutional contexts. For Colombia, the legal framework supporting its education and training system includes both the 1991 revised constitution and a number of acts such as the General Education Act 1994, the Higher Education Act 1992, and the Higher Education Act 2002. The 2002 act focuses on professional and technical education. Colombia has a unitary higher education system with no distinction made between academic and professional education. Primary education is compulsory for all children aged 6–14. Secondary education lasts only two years and students may choose between general and vocational education. Technical institutions provide postsecondary education. Both private and public institutions provide higher education, and universities are free to offer programs at any level, up to and including the doctoral level. Higher professional education is provided by both universities and technological institutions and prepares graduates for entry into the labor market. Colombia does not have an established national qualification framework; national qualifications are not referenced to an overarching national framework.

A number of laws enacted in 2006 and 2007 regulate education for employment and HRD. These laws provide for technical education, the development of technical skills and competencies. There is also a Colombian strategy to standardize and certify human resource skills, and in recent years, the Colombian government has been promoting competence development as an alternative to university education. This type of training is provided by SENA (National Service for Learning), CESDE, and INCAP.

By law, Colombia must spend a minimum of 10% of its annual budget on education. The Ministry of Education has responsibility for public education policy. The Ministry of Education also administers secondary and technical education. Local governments have educational secretariats that have responsibility for their respective areas. These 94 education secretariats provide both policy, guidelines, and funding; however, they are not obliged to follow standards or policy set by central government.

Over the past two decades, Colombia has begun to reform its HRD system with the state having an increasingly important role in financing but much less in providing training. The Colombian National Apprentice Service (SENA) was established in 1957 and offers services to different sectors. In 1991, Colombia established the Youth in Action Program to provide training to young people living in urban areas who were unemployed. HRD policy in Colombia is specifically focused on socially disadvantaged populations that experience difficulty in participating in the formal labor market. However, the unitary nature of the Colombian state combined with an emphasis on decentralized governance and a diverse set of regions making the implementation of national HRD policies difficult. The Ministry of Education sets out general policy and guidelines. Local authorities have significant power and influence around their implementation. Local governments, for example, have been incentivized to implement a national competencies approach.

In South Africa, schooling is compulsory; however, under the National Qualifications Framework (NQF), students may opt out upon successful completion of Grade 9 with a General Education and Training Certification to pursue employment or technical training in further education and training (FET) institutions. Students who continue senior secondary school take nationally set and moderated examinations at the end of Grade 12 with a National Senior Certificate. Twenty-three publicly funded institutions provide higher education in South Africa. The Higher Education Act 1997 stipulates that all higher education institutions come under the national government, whereas FET colleges report to regional or provincial governments.

Lynham and Cunningham (2004) highlight some of the more important legislative provisions in South Africa supporting HRD. The Employment Equality Act specifies that employers who have more than 50 employees or who meet specified turnover requirements are required to prepare an Employment Equity Plan. The Skills Development Act 1998 addresses the development of skills in the workplace and the transformation of workplaces into sites for learning. The act focuses on increasing the level of investment in education and training by employers, as the implementation of measures to enable employees acquire new skills and help the unemployed find work. The act also established an institutional and financial infrastructure for training. The SDA Act (1998) also created statutory bodies such as Sector Education and Training Authorities (SETAs) to regulate training and education within specific industrial sectors. Employees pay 1% of their payroll as a tax-deductible levy to fund the administration of SETAs and the creation of jobs and 'learnerships' for the unemployed and disadvantaged. Companies are also required to register a skills development facilitator and provide a workplace skills plan. Otherwise they forfeit the levy. The Skills Development Levies Act (1999) was introduced to manage the skill development levy and impose penalties for failure to pay the levy. The South African Qualifications Act (1995) established a national qualification framework and the SA Qualifications Authority (SAQA). This body accredits education and training providers and the development of standards for qualifications.

INDONESIA AND VIETNAM

Historical and Political Context

Both Indonesia and Vietnam have pursued a political agenda of strengthening trade and financial cooperation and relationships with a variety of countries. In Indonesia, for example, President Sukarnoputri (2001–2004) focused on the need to coordinate and cooperate with ASEAN policies focused on transforming member states into attractive FDI host countries. President Yudhoyono (2004–current) has adopted a market-oriented approach. He has also prioritized ASEAN but also focused on the Asia-Pacific Economic Cooperation (APEC) and the East Asia Community (EAC).

Vietnam has had significant political transformation in the past 30 years. It traditionally had a very strong and excessive dependence on the Soviet Union; however, this dependence ended abruptly with the collapse of the Soviet Bloc in 1989. Following this collapse, Vietnam initiated a major reform process largely inspired by the Chinese experience (Toh and Gayathri, 2004; Painter, 2005). In 1986, Vietnam introduced a reform program called *Doi Moi* (Renovation). This was designed to liberate the economy from socialism to a more market-oriented approach (Edwards and Phan, 2013). The government restricted state intervention in private enterprise and implemented major structural reforms to modernize the economy. FDI was a central plank of *Doi Moi* combined with significant efforts to develop better trade and investment relationships with Japan (Beresford, 2008; Dinh, 2009). In terms of foreign policy, Vietnam has placed strong emphasis on developing relationships with the great powers, including the US, Russia, Japan, and India. President Mink Trict (2006–2011) focused on developing a strong relationship with the US and negotiated a trade and investment treaty.

Economic Context

Indonesia has a young population with a median age of 29 years. Almost 26% of the population is under the age of 14, 17% aged between 15–24, and 42% between 25–54. Twelve percent of the population lives below the poverty line. Indonesia has the largest economy in Southeast Asia and both the private and public sectors play a significant role in the Indonesian economy. It possesses vast natural resources (Bergers, Permana, & Tu, 2011) and enjoys very strong economic ties with China, South Korea, Taiwan, and Japan (Gupta and Hanges, 2004). Almost 48% of its workforce is employed in the services sector, with 38% employed in agriculture. It has an unemployment rate of about 6%, which is related to rural migration to urban areas (Dhanani, Islam, & Chowdhury, 2009), and it has experienced major difficulties in making the transition to a highly skilled workforce. There are major deficits in investment in education, workforce development, and training (Blondal, Hawksworth, & Choz, 2009).

Vietnam has a population of over 93 million, with a median age of 29. Almost 24% of the population is under 14 years of age and 18% are aged between 14–18 years old. It has a GDP per capital of $1.527 (IMF, 2014c), with 6% allocated to education. During the period 1991–2010, Vietnam achieved steady growth in GDP and average annual income increased from US$98 to US$1,174 (Ohno, 2009). It reduced poverty levels from over 58% to 10% (Asian Development Bank, 2011). It is the second fastest-growing economy behind China, and it is forecast to be the seventeenth largest world economy by 2025 (Karmel, 2010). Even though there is a high level of investment in education, Vietnam suffers from a major scarcity of skilled labor. Only 10% participate in higher education (Hayden and Thiep, 2007), and there is a very significant mismatch between education output and the needs of industry. Industrially, Vietnam has moved away from agriculture to food processing, garments, shoes, mining, coal, steel, chemical fertilizer, and mobile phones. Manufacturing, information technology, and high technology are fast-growing sectors of the national economy. It has significantly increased its oil production and is now the third-largest oil producer in Southeast Asia and the eighth largest in the Asia-Pacific region.

Cultural Context

Culturally, Indonesia is very diverse with each province having its own language, ethnic makeup, and religions. However, at the macro level, harmony and cohesiveness are highly valued, hierarchical relationships are respected and emphasized. It also emphasizes friendliness, while avoiding negative feelings and confrontation. It places less emphasis on punctuality, and it is viewed as disrespectful to show annoyance. Therefore, Indonesians tend not to directly disagree or say 'no', and it is important that blame is not publicly directed at a particular individual or group. Vance (1992) highlights four characteristics of management culture in Indonesia: a) a strong collectivist focus with a heavy emphasis on groups, b) a focus on group rather than individual performance, c) a strong emphasis on maintaining strong positive work relationships, and d) a tendency to shy away from negative feedback. In the context of managing people, Indonesian managers focus on the past rather than the present; there is a clear distinction between gender roles, a strong preference for stability, a dislike of highly ambiguous conditions, and deference to seniority.

As a country, Vietnam derives its cultural values from a Confucian belief system. It generally values harmony, hierarchy, collectivism, and personal relationships. Vietnamese culture is also patriarchal. Hofstede (2008) found that Vietnam is high on power distance, high on collectivism, mid-range on masculinity, low on uncertainty avoidance, and they have a very short-term orientation. In a business context, Vietnamese place great importance on developing a relationship and talking about family and other non-business issues (Kohl, 2007). The Vietnamese language takes different forms to reflect age, gender, and marital status. A relationship culture is particularly strong given the focus on the village in Vietnam; people need to build strong relationships to work effectively with each other. Kamoche (2001) highlights two cultural characteristics that have important implications for the way people are developed. First, Vietnamese employees view the firm as a family with a focus on a long-term employment relationship. Second, the concept of face is central to the Vietnamese culture. Therefore, Vietnamese will emphasize trust and are less likely to do anything that would give them a bad name.

Institutional Context

Both Indonesia and Vietnam have a variety of institutional arrangements that support HRD. The Indonesian education and training system is both immense and extremely diverse. Overall, responsibility for education resides with both the Minister of Education and Culture and the Ministry of Religious Affairs. However, many of the institutional structures operate at the level of the district. Law 32 of 2004 and Law 33 of 2004 set out the overall framework for the decentralization of the management and implementation of education, and they also specify how education is funded. Government Regulation 19, 2005, defines national education standards, including graduate competency, funding, and assessment.

Vocational education in Indonesia is extremely fragmented. A variety of institutions provide vocational education, including community colleges, polytechnics, and universities. The Ministry for Manpower and Transmigration has issued national competency standards for works in collaboration with industry stakeholders. The National Council for Accreditation provides certification for individuals. Training providers are certified to provide particular courses through the International Organization for Standardization (ISO). The Higher Education Law No. 12 of 2012 specifies standards for higher education. However, the general standard of universities is poor, with few universities of international standard.

In Vietnam, education and training are considered a top priority. Both are viewed as strategies to address poverty and central to developing the skills necessary to transform the economy. The country's Socio-Economic Development Strategy accords education a major role in facilitating economic growth. However, there are major concerns about the quality of Vietnamese education. Vocational training is significantly less popular than higher education and as a consequence, the number of 19–21-year-olds who participate in vocational training has remained stagnant (World Bank, 2013). There appears to be a disconnect between schools and universities and the needs of industry.

The Ministry of Labor, Invalids, and Social Affairs has responsibility for vocational training and technical teacher training. The law on vocational training requires three levels: primary, secondary, and college. In addition, a variety of sectors based on training initiatives have been developed. These initiatives have been directed at particular sectors, such as telecommunication and electronics. The system has moved from a supply to a demand-driven system. The government has implemented a mixture of policies and measures, such as the formulation of training orders to meet enterprise demand with the required adjustments by vocational training organizations. However, the institutional context is complex and there is an unclear demarcation of responsibility and accountability for both VET and education. There are over one thousand training institutions, including universities, colleges, and employment centers.

EGYPT AND TURKEY

Historical and Political Context

Politically, Egypt has played a major role in the creation of the Arab League and the Non-Aligned Movement. President Nassar ruled the country from 1956–1970 but made little progress in modernizing the economy. President Anwar-as-Sadat (1970–1981) was more successful in opening up the Egyptian political and economic system. Hosni Mubarak (1981–2011) pursued a policy of opening the country both politically and economically; however, his term was considered a failure. It resulted in very little inflows of FDI (Farah, 2009). Mubarak adopted a 'unique policy' in 2003 in order to accelerate structural reforms, enhance the investment climate, and eliminate inequality, again with very little success. Since the military coup of 2013, Egypt has been under military rule and has made little progress in returning the country to normality.

Turkey is recognized politically as a key state due to its population, geographic location, its economic and military potential, and its impact as a regional power. During the 1980s and 1990s, Turkey experienced a major economic crisis. As a consequence, it sought stronger ties with the IMF, significant liberalization of its economy, and enhanced development of trade relations. Turkey has a key political objective, the desire to achieve EU membership, resulting in major economic reforms in areas such as DFI protection, competition, and intellectual property rights. It has also given significant priority to the development of trade relations with the Middle East, North Africa, and Eastern Europe. It has prioritized the development of industrialization centers with major emphasis on trade and investment. However, FDI targets have not been met due to political and economic crises.

Economic Context

Egypt has a population of 87 million people with 33% under the age of 14. In 2014, Egypt's GDP per capital was $6,600 with 47% of its workforce in services, 29% in agriculture, and 24% in industry (CIA, 2014). Egypt is a major producer of corn, wheat, and cotton, and its main industries are food processing, tourism, pharmaceuticals, construction, and light manufacturing. In 2014, Egypt announced a wide range of economic reforms that included new taxes and reduced energy subsidies. The economy has benefited from financing from Saudi Arabia, Kuwait, and UAE. In 2015, the government implemented an economic reform program focused on driving economic growth, restoring fiscal stability, and attracting foreign investors.

Turkey, as Egypt, has a very young population but has relatively low levels of unemployment and a very high level of labor market participation (51%). It is primarily a free-market economy. Agriculture accounts for about 25% of employment; however, significant growth has occurred in industry and service sectors. State involvement in industry, banking, communication, and transportation has declined significantly in the past five years. Turkey's primary export partners are Germany, Iraq, Iran, and the UK. It has a labor force of approximately 28 million and almost 17% of the population lives below the poverty line.

Cultural Context

Egypt is a Muslim country and its culture is shaped by the Islamic moral and legal code. Parnell and Hatem (1999) argued that the Egyptian culture is a blend of Arab and Middle Eastern influences. Hofstede (1980) did not investigate cultural values in Egypt; however, he classified Arab countries as having high power distance, low individualism, moderately strong uncertainty avoidance, and moderate masculinity. Organizations tend to be hierarchical and controlled, and HRD practices have both a relationship and team focus. Nydell (1996) highlighted the importance of seniority in Egypt and the importance of loyalty to the group. Parnell and Hatem (1999) emphasize the central role of friendships as a cornerstone of Egyptian culture. Employees show a strong preference to working with the same organization. Hickson and Pugh (1995) found that in Egyptian organizations, job roles are less clearly defined, because employees are likely to do what they are told, out of both respect for authority and loyalty to the organization.

The Islamic work ethic emphasizes hard work, which is viewed as a source of personal growth, self-fulfillment, satisfaction, and respect (Yousef, 2001; Akdere, Russ-Eft, & Eft, 2006). There is also a latent fatalism in Egyptian culture by which the future is considered best left to Allah (Kanango and Jaeger, 1990; Akdere and Salem, 2012).

Culturally, Turkey is considered the cradle of civilization, where West meets East. It has inherited its cultural and social norms from the Ottoman Empire. Modern Turkey is built upon a secularism foundation, which is a very unique governmental and societal structure for a Muslim country. The secular culture in Turkey has introduced some conflicting elements to organizations—both governmental and private, as well as the society at large. Turkish culture is characterized by high collectivism, high power distance, and uncertainty avoidance. Turkish managers favor top-down communication, strong paternalism, and a strong focus on the organization as a family (Wasti, 1998; Tuzuner, 2014). Kanungo and Aycan (1997) found that Turkey had strong paternalistic values and ranked above average on values such as conservatism, hierarchy, egalitarian commitment, and harmony. The GLOBE Study found strong in-group collectivism and power distance. Turkey was also below average on gender egalitarianism, humane and future orientation. Ronen (1986) found that Turkish organizations have high-centralized decision making, limited delegation, and highly personalized, strong leadership.

Institutional Context

Egypt has a complex, fragmented, and inefficient institutional context for HRD. The 2011 Global Competitiveness Index Report ranked Egypt 94 out of 142 countries, due primarily to its weak labor and HRD institutions. There is an almost total lack of coordination between the various ministries that manage technical and vocational training. The Ministry of Education manages technical and vocational schools, whereas the Ministry of Higher Education supervises technical institutions, and the Ministry of Industry has responsibility for the supervision of vocational training centers. Technical and vocational education is considered as second-best education, vastly inferior to higher education.

Third-level education in Egypt is structurally inefficient. A major mismatch exists between education outputs and the needs of the labor market. Educational institutions have not kept pace with the economic needs of the country, and the development of soft skills and technology skills are largely ignored (OBG, Egypt Report, 2013). Numerous reports have identified deficiencies in the institutional structure supporting HRD. Overall, the system is not sufficiently demand driven with little involvement from the private sector. Labor Law 12, 2003, regulates the Egyptian labor market. This law prescribes regulations related to the content of employment contracts and imposes lots of restrictions that are not necessarily favorable to HRD.

Egypt established the Supreme Council for Human Resource Development (SCHRD) in 2000. This body is charged with the formulation of national human resource development policy. However, this institution is deemed ineffective. A MENA OECD Report (2010) highlights the need to establish a single institution to coordinate a workforce skills development strategy, bring about greater involvement of stakeholders and ensuring a more holistic approach to HRD.

The Turkish education and vocational training and development system is extremely complex. As in Egypt, this system has resulted in low levels of educational attainment, with 60% of the Turkish labor force having incomplete education or even the most basic education. The government formulated the Ninth Development Plan (2007–2013) with a view to establishing an integrated, single-structure vocational training system, to developing industrial zones, to creating an environment where organizations could work collaboratively to develop vocational skills, and to developing a national qualifications network.

Third-level education outcomes have been very disappointing: returns in terms of learning outcomes are poor, and despite high levels of public expenditure, efficiency and effectiveness are very poor. Public spending is only about 3% of GDP compared to an OECD average of 5% (OECD, 2010). Education policy is greatly fragmented with a lack of coordination between the Higher Education Council and the Ministry of National Education. There is a strong focus on investment in inputs rather than on learning outcomes, with very limited evidence of business-education partnerships. As a consequence, like Egypt, the link between education and the needs of the labor market is suboptimal. An overall challenge concerns the need to engage the workforce in lifelong learning activities and the implementation of decentralized approaches both to general education and vocational education. The Ministry for National Education has initiated a number of structural reforms to make HRD in Turkey more fit for purpose. Particular focus is placed on strengthening the role of the Quality Assurance and Accreditation Agency to ensure effective program and institutional accreditation in line with international best practice.

ORGANIZATION-LEVEL HRD IN CIVETS COUNTRIES

An analysis of organizational-level HRD practices within the CIVETS grouping reveals a fragmented and disjointed picture. In the following section, we consider each pair of countries in turn.

Colombia and South Africa

The sophistication of HRD in Colombian organizations depends on whether they are public-sector organizations, SMEs, or subsidiaries of multinationals. Overall, HRD has not achieved a level of strategic development in

Colombian organizations. Training and development tends to have a strong individual focus and is not oriented toward the development of human capital, intellectual capital, and knowledge management (Ogliastri, Ruiz, & Martinez, 2004). HRD activities primarily focus on issues of competency development and quality enhancement. Competency approaches have pro-liferated in subsidiaries of MNCs. Individual development and training in basic skills are common in SMEs. Most of HRD activity is conducted in the workplace (Arbelaez et al., 2003), delivered on the job, and it tends to be less formal and unstructured. Approaches to HRD tend to be centralized and hierarchical with very few formal training and development policies. Lucero and Spinel (2002) found that 39% of organizations did not have a formal training policy. Formal policies were more frequently found in the services sector and in organizations with over one hundred employees. HRD priorities are generally decided without consultation with supervisors and employees. Training and development in SMEs is commonly initiated reactively and lacks neither plan nor budget. In large organizations and sub-sidiaries of MNCs, the HR function has responsibility for organizing HRD. Training and development needs are primarily determined on the basis of performance evaluation, training needs surveys, 360 degree evaluations, and employee competency development plans. Training in public-sector organizations tends to focus on a variety of technical and behavioral compe-tencies. A central HRM body generally determines HRD policy and leaves it to line departments. Overall, HRD in public-sector organizations tends to be focused on the needs of individuals rather than the strategic priorities of the organization. Linkage of competency frameworks with the strategic needs of the organization is poor (OECD, 2013). Overall, MNCs and pub-lic-sector organizations have more rational and bureaucratic approaches to HRD. In SMEs and family firms, there is a strong sense of paternalism in the provision of HRD, with limited long-term vision. HRD is essentially viewed in organizations as a support activity with very little emphasis on HRD as a strategy to achieve organizational goals.

South Africa has many similarities to Colombia when it comes to orga-nizational-level HRD; however, approaches to HRD tend to vary consider-ably depending on the type of organization and sector. The approach is essentially strategic in public-sector organizations and in subsidiaries of MNCs, whereas informal approaches tend to be more common in SMEs (Webster and Wood, 2005; Debrah and Ofari, 2006). Training and develop-ment activities are more frequently focused on managerial employees and professionals rather than on operational and front-line employees (Coetzee et al., 2012). Approaches to HRD in general tend to be more reactive rather than strategic, and there is limited evidence of a long-term approach. Orga-nizations in general are slow to implement planned approaches and adopt more sophisticated HRD practices, even though South African MNCs view the development of capability as a key HRD challenge and priority (Thite, 2015). While skills development legislation does provide for sectoral train-ing and a training levy, there remain major sectoral imbalances in investment in HRD. This system has failed because employers have not taken up the challenge and are not incentivized to directly provide HRD. HRD in SMEs is generally informal, ad hoc, and unsystematic (Rogerson, 2009). Many South African SMEs suffer from a major lack of managerial skill and do not possess the expertise to deliver HRD (Bezuidenhout and Nenungwi, 2012). Most of HRD is provided informally and takes place on the job. In contrast, the experience in South African MNCs is significantly different. Horwitz (2012) identified the influence of Asian MNCs on African MNCs and the adoption of more humanistic approaches to HRD, with a focus on the extended family and individual development processes.

Human resource development in public-sector organizations is characterized as centralized and bureaucratic in how it is managed and delivered. Personal development plans are frequently completed for the sake of compliance rather than genuinely identifying and prioritizing development needs. Individual government departments tend to be slow in adopting strongly strategic approaches. A study by the Public Service Commission (2010) found four key practices: a) an overuse of self-reflection as the key way of identifying HRD priorities, b) ineffective use of performance management processes to identify HRD priorities, c) poor prioritization and management of HRD activities, and d) low levels of commitment by managers to HRD.

Indonesia and Vietnam

Research on HRD in Indonesian and Vietnamese organizations is nascent. The picture that comes shows significant fragmentation and sectoral differences across organization types and sectors. Habir and Rajendran (2008) observed that a significant shift has occurred in how organizations view human resources, from being viewed as a factor of production to being viewed as human capital. Other research highlights the growing awareness of the need to pay attention to strategic HRD (Rhodes, Walsh, & Lok, 2008). Thorat (2013), for example, found that Indonesian organizations have shifted their perspective on how HRD should be organized. Lake (2008) found that manufacturing firms had low investment in HRD. Managers in these firms perceived that there were relatively few benefits to be derived from investment in HRD resulting in a legacy of significant underinvestment. Drost et al. (2002) found that Indonesia scored lowest in investment in HRD technical skills development. Indonesian organizations have not made significant efforts to develop employees at all organizational levels and have yet to embrace the idea that human resources are key elements of organizational success. SMEs primarily use on-the-job training as the primary strategy to develop employees (Chandrakumara, 2013). In public-sector organizations, HRD has a more individual and personal development focus (Rhodes, Walsh, & Lok, 2008) with a high level of centralization with limited transparency in how decisions are made about HRD investment.

In Vietnam, the evidence indicates major organizational and sectoral differences (McDaniel, 1999; Thang and Quang, 2007). Many Vietnamese organizations acknowledge the importance of HRD; however, there is a significant lack of resources for HRD implementation. King-Kauanui, Ngoc, and Ashley-Cotleur (2006) found SMEs provided some training for employees, although it was largely informal. They also had limited resources for HRD and achieved poor outcomes due to inadequate expertise and systems. MNCs on the other hand, invested considerably more in HRD than SMEs or the public sector. Thang and Quang (2007) found that MNCs understand the lack of skills and qualifications in Vietnam and therefore make HRD a priority. They use HRD as a strategic tool and as a mechanism to support strategy implementation. Reid, Collins, & Singh (2014) found that managers placed greater priority on personal rather than technical development with a focus on developing moral standards.

Vietnamese organizations demonstrate significant variation in HRD practices depending on ownership, stage of technology development, and extent of internationalization. Local MNCs are less effective than global MNCs. High-tech and export-oriented organizations are likely to have more formal HRD systems. Local firms are significantly less receptive to adopting HRD practices due to resource and expertise constraints.

Egypt and Turkey

Egypt is exceptionally uneven and fragmented when it comes to organizational-level HRD, and the research of HRD practices in organizations is embryonic. Managers in Egyptian organizations are less willing to participate in HRD research. They face numerous challenges, including major competition, the challenge of new technology, privatization, and issues with child labor and gender discrimination. Studies highlight the inability of Egyptian organizations to develop human resources as a critical weakness. Where organizational HRD is provided, it is sensitive to local cultural norms and the influences of the Islamic work ethic and principles (Budhwar and Mellaki, 2007; Leat and El Kot, 2007). HRD preferences tend to be job specific, to focus on the group rather than on the individual, to develop specialized career paths, and emphasize internal development of job skills. Kanungo and Jaeger (1990) found that employees in Egyptian organizations are receptive to the acquisition of new skills, even though it may conflict with the culture's high uncertainty and ambiguity avoidance.

In Turkish organizations, managers generally make decisions about training policy and programs with limited focus on the needs of employees. Sozer (2004) found, for example, that in Turkish firms, HRD efforts were determined by organizational priorities. The Cranet Study (Cranet, 2011) found that Turkish firms rely on on-the-job training and make significant use of external trainers. They conduct significantly fewer evaluations of the effectiveness of HRD.

Aycan (2006) reported that HRD is one of the most important functions of HRM departments in Turkey. However, there are sectoral and organization differences. Financial sectors provide much more HRD than manufacturing organizations. A significant number of large organizations have a dedicated HRD department with a separate budget for HRD activities. Cetinel, Yolal, and Emeksiz (2009) found that HRD in SMEs was informal due to a lack of financial supports and a poor level of management skill and understanding of HRD. The majority of businesses in Turkey are classified as SMEs and account for 82% of total employment (Elci, 2011). HRD practices in SMEs lack sophistication compared to MNCs. They have significantly more sophisticated approaches to HRD. Local firms in Turkey have adopted more Western HRD approaches (Sayim, 2010); however, they lack the expertise and flexibility to manage these systems effectively. In contrast, MNCs in Turkey use more standardized approaches and implement HRD practices that address the needs of a diverse workforce.

CONVERGENCE AND DIVERGENCE OF HRD IN CIVETS COUNTRIES

The CIVETS countries have in common the objective of internationalization and the development of their economics in a manner to attract FDI. The characteristics of CIVETS HRD are explained by a multiplicity of historical, cultural, institutional, and systemic factors. Economic and financial events have the process for these countries to become more open economies. As an umbrella label, CIVETS does not suggest convergence; the label was not conceived on that basis. However, an analysis of the HRD institutional context and the evidence of HRD practices in organizations suggest commonalities as well as differences between these countries. The CIVETS countries are projected to experience levels of economic development that will rival the BRIC nations; they share a large young population, very significant national resources, and major service sector growth. The CIVETS countries are viewed as second-generation emerging markets whose economies are dynamic and rapidly changing (S&P, 2014).

Institutionally, all CIVETS countries exhibit to varying degrees significant literacy poverty, numeracy and basic skills gaps. They differ, however, in their investment in education, vocational training, and HRD. Their institutional arrangements for HRD are complex, fragmented, inefficient, and poorly aligned with the needs of businesses and employers. This has resulted in the lack of skilled professionals required to address and meet talent gaps and in a major reliance on migrant labor. Countries such as Egypt, South Africa, and Indonesia have struggled to reform their institutional arrangements, making them fit for purpose.

The CIVETS countries share a number of common cultural characteristics, such as low individualism, high power distance, and high levels of uncertainty avoidance. These characteristics are reflected in their approaches to HRD. There is a particularly strong emphasis on HRD that addresses the needs of individuals rather than organizations. Organizations themselves prefer internal development to the buying in of these skills. Many HRD practices are consistent with the socio-cultural context of these countries. However, the growth in MNCs has resulted in the influence of Western HRD practices becoming more prominent. Local HRD practices are in some cases influenced by MNC practices. Therefore, we can say that HRD practices in CIVETS countries reflect a mixture of international and local institutional and cultural influences. However, consistent with theoretical arguments by Budhwar and Sparrow (2002), it is difficult to identify the unique influence of various cultural and institutional influences.

Each country has some significant, unique challenges and issues. Colombia is a country that has suffered significantly from civil unrest, and large parts of the country are still considered to be unsafe due to control by rebel forces. A major misalignment exists between the growth of the Colombian economy and investment in HRD. Colombia needs to achieve greater oversight and control of its HRD institutions and invest considerably more in education. The cultural focus of HRD is toward individual development, a strong sense of paternalism, and the notion that the organization is a family. South Africa is a country that is still coming out of the apartheid system, while socially transforming itself into a developed nation. Culturally it is an extremely diverse country. Its HRD infrastructure is inefficient, and there is a significant gap between rhetoric and reality. There are major variations in how HRD is approached in different types of organizations and sectors, and a major misalignment exists between the needs of business and the outputs of the education and VET systems.

Indonesia is a country that has experienced growth and development, has the largest population of the CIVETS countries, and it has been greatly impacted by the global financial crisis. The country has become a popular location for FDI; however, it suffers from an uneducated population, a poor education and HRD infrastructure, and a lack of a workplace culture of HRD. It also experiences major issues related to diversity, innovation, and the integration of technology. Its HRD system is highly fragmented and overly decentralized. There is poor coordination among HRD stakeholders and actors. MNCs practices have not yet impacted local organization approaches to HRD as in other CIVETS countries. Vietnam was also greatly been impacted by the global financial crisis, which has driven it away from a dependence on Russia and increased its participation in ASEAN and toward the development of relations with a variety of trade partners. There is a major gap between the Vietnamese cultural value system and the demands of the capitalist system. HRD approaches are strongly hierarchical, and there is a strong focus on maintaining harmony (Mabey and Finch-Lees, 2008). Increasingly, Vietnam has embraced the practices found in MNCs, while also retaining a unique and culturally constructed notion of HRD. Due to the weaknesses of the education, VET, and HRD systems, Vietnam is increasingly reliant on MNCs to improve skill levels.

Egypt and Turkey share a number of common features as well as having important differences. Egypt's efforts at economic growth have been undermined by political turmoil. Its HRD institutional context is both complex and inefficient. It suffers from low levels of literacy, a lack of technological infrastructure, and challenges in attracting FDI. Egypt's approach to HRD in organizations is extremely reactive and lacks any semblance of a strategic model. MNCs appear to have a limited influence on local organization HRD practices. As a consequence, there is a major shortage of skilled labor in new occupations and technologies. Turkey has strategically focused on FDI as a way of dealing with its financial problems and its desire to join the EU. It has grown steadily over the last decade both in terms of attracting foreign investment, lowering unemployment, increasing educational opportunities, and investment in education and technology. It needs to make major strides in investment in human capital, and there are major disparities between local and foreign firms. Turkey implemented a national HRD policy almost a decade ago (Akdere and Dirani, 2014); however, its HRD system lacks coherence and a demand-led focus.

CONCLUSION

CIVETS refers to a group of emerging economies that are focused on internationalizing their economies and moving toward developed country status. They present an interesting context in which to study HRD. They reveal both convergence and divergence. Each country has unique cultural, economic, historical, and institutional characteristics that shape its approach to HRD. However, each country is to varying degrees subjected to the influences of internationalization and the Westernization of their approaches to HRD. They have major deficiencies in their institutional arrangements for HRD, and their organizational-level HRD is ineffective and not sufficiently strategic. They share a common set of future challenges to improve the quality of their respective education systems, decrease the fragmentation of institutional support and policies for HRD, and align HRD better with sectoral and business needs.

REFERENCES

Akdere, M., & Dirani, K. (2014). Human resource development in the Middle East. In R. Poell, T. Rocco and G. Roth (Eds.), *Routledge Companion to Human Resource Development*. New York: Routledge.

Akdere, M., Russ-Eft, D., & Eft, N. (2006). The Islamic worldview of adult learning in the workplace: Surrendering to God. *Advances in Human Resource Development*, 8(3): 355–363.

Akdere, M., & Salem, J. M. (2012). Islamic perspectives on work-based learning. In P. Gibbs (Ed.), *Learning, Work and Practice: New understandings*, 207–217. Springer.

Alden, C, & Vieira, M. (2007). 'La nueva diplomacia del Sur: Brasil, Sudáfrica, India y el trilateralismo'. In: Tokatlian, J. G. (Ed.). *India, Brasil y Sudáfrica: El impacto de las nuevas potencias regionales*. Buenos Aires: Libros del Zorzal.

Arbelaez, M. A., Zuleta, L. A., & Velasco, A. (2003). *Las micro, pequenas y medianas empresas en Colombia: Diagnostico general y acceso a servicios financieros [Micro, small, and medium businesses in Colombia: General diagnosis and access to financial services]*. Colombia: Fedesarrollo

Asian Development Bank. (2011). ADB Annual Report 2011. Accessed 1 November 2015. (http://www.adb.org/documents/adb-annual-report-2011).

Aycan, Z. (2006). Human resource management in Turkey. In P. Budhwar and K. Mellahi (Eds.), *Human Resource Management in the Middle East*. London: Routledge

Beresford, M. (2008). Doi moi in review: the challenges of building market socialism in Vietnam. *Journal of Contemporary Asia*, 38(2): 221–243.

Bezuidenhout, A., & Nenungwi, A. L. (2012). A competency framework for the small business sector in Johannesburg South Africa. *African Journal of Business Management*, 6(47): 11658–11669

Bl4ndal, J. R., Hawkesworth, I., & Choi, H. D. (2009). Budgeting in Indonesia. *OECD Journal on Budgeting*, 9(2): 1–31.

Budhwar, P., & Mellahi, K. (2007). Introduction: Human resource management in the Middle East. *International Journal of Human Resource Management*, 18: 2–10.

Budhwar, P. S., & Sparrow, P. R. (2002). An integrative framework for understanding cross-national human resource management practices. *Human Resource Management Review*, 12(3): 377–403.

Burgers, P., Permana, R. P., & Tu, T. N. (2011). Fuelling Conflicts: overcoming asymmetry between global interests in Vietnam and Indonesia. *Development*, 54(1): 77–84.

Central Intelligence Agency (CIA). (2013). *World Factbook*. Available at: (https://www.cia.gov/library/publications/the-world-factbook/geos/eg.html) Accessed August 20, 2015.

Çetinel, F., Yolal, M., & Emeksiz, M. (2008). Human resources management in small-and medium-sized hotels in Turkey. *Journal of Human Resources in Hospitality and Tourism*, 8(1): 43–63.

Chandrakumara, P. M. K. (2013). Human resources management practices in small and medium enterprises in two emerging economies in Asia: Indonesia and South Korea. *Annual SEANNZ Conference*. Australian Technology Park, 11–12 July. Sydney, Small Enterprise Association of Australia and New Zealand 1–1, 5.

CIA. (Central Intelligence Agency). (2014). List of Countries by GDP Sector Composition: The World Factbook. Accessed 1 November 2015. (https://www.cia.gov/library/publications/the-world-factbook/fields/2012.html)

Coetzee, M., Botha, J., Kiley, J., Truman, K., & Tshilongamulenzhe, M. C. (2012). *Practicing Training and Development in South African Organisations*. Cape Town: Juta.

Cranet. (2011). Cranet Survey on Comparative Human Resource Management. International Executive Report. Cranfield Network on Comparative Human Resource Management. Accessed 1 November 2015. (http://www.ef.uns.ac.rs/cranet/download/cranet_report_2012_280212.pdf)

Cruz, R. P., Villa, T., Villa, A.M. T., Valdivieso, J. J., Gomez, L. M., & Ortiz, Y. G. (2010). 'Colombia BIT 2007 survey results: general report'. In: Karmarkar, U. and Mangal, V. eds. *The UCLA Anderson Business and Information Technologies (BIT) Project: A global study of business practice*. Singapore: World Scientific.

Debrah, Y. A., & Ofori, G. (2006). Human resource development of professionals in an emerging economy: The case of the Tanzanian construction industry. *The International Journal of Human Resource Management*, 17(3): 440–463.

Dhanani, S., Islam, I., & Chowdhury, A. (2009). *The Indonesian labour market: Changes and challenges.* London: Routledge.

Dinh, H. L. (2009). Vietnam-Japan relations in the context of building an East Asian community. *Asia-Pacific Review,* 16(1): 100–129.

Drost, A. E., Frayne, C. A., Lowe, K. B., & Geringer, M. J. (2002). Benchmarking training and development practices: a multi-country comparative analysis. *Human Resource Management,* 41(1): 67–86.

Edwards, V., & Anh Phan (2013). *Managers and Management in Vietnam: 25 years of Economic Renovation (doi moi).* Routledge: London and New York.

Elci, S. (2011). Leveraging training skills development in SMEs: an analysis of OSTIM Organised Industrial Zone, Turkey. *OECD Local Economic and Employment Development (LEED).* Working Papers, 2011/16, OECD Publishing.

Farah, N. R. (2009). *Egypt's Political Economy: Power Relations in Development.* Cairo: American University in Cairo Press.

Guerra-Barón, A. (2012). Colombia y Brasil: un análisis desde la perspectiva económica. *Colombia y Brasil: ¿ socios estratégicos en la construcción de Suramérica,* pp. 387–420.

Gupta, V., & Hanges, P. J. (2004). Regional and climate clustering of societal cultures. In R. J. House, P. J. Hanges, M. Javidan, P. W. Dorfman and V. Gupta (Eds.), *Culture, leadership, and organizations: The GLOBE study of 62 societies,* 178–218. Thousand Oaks, CA: Sage.

Habir, D., & Rajendran, K. (2008). The changing face of human resource management in Indonesia. In C. Rowley and S. Abdul-Rahman (Eds.), *The Changing Face of Management in South-East Asia,* 30–53. London: Routledge.

Hayden, P.M., and Thiep, L. Q. (2007) 'Institutional autonomy for higher education in Vietnam', *Higher Education Research and Development,* 26(1), pp. 73–85.

Hickson, D. J., and Pugh, D. S. (Eds.). (1995) *Management worldwide: The impact of societal culture on organizations around the globe.* UK: Penguin.

Hirschsohn, P. (2008). Regulating the animal spirits' of entrepreneurs? Skills development in South African small and medium enterprises. *International Small Business Journal,* 26(2): 181–206

Hofstede, G. (1980). *Culture's Consequences: International Differences in Work-Related Values.* Thousand Oaks, CA: Sage.

Hofstede, G. (2001). *Culture's Consequences: Comparing Values, Behaviors, Institutions and Organizations across Nations.* Thousand Oaks, CA: Sage.

Hofstede, G. (2008). *A Summary of my Ideas about National Culture Differences.* Available at: (http://www.uigarden.net/english/national_culture_differences) Accessed August 19, 2015.

Horwitz, F. M. (2012). Human resource management in Southern African multinational firms: considering an Afro-Asian nexus. *The International Journal of Human Resource Management,* 23(14): 2938–2958.

Hoskisson, R. E., Eden, L., Lau, C. M., & Wright, M. (2000). Strategy in emerging economies. *Academy of ManagementJjournal,* 43(3): 249–267.

IMF (2014). World Economic Outlook Report. Accessed 1 November 2015. (http://www.imf.org/external/pubs/ft/weo/2014/01/pdf/text.pdf).

Kamoche, K. (2001). Human resource in Vietnam: the global challenge. *Thunderbird International Business Review,* 43: 625–650.

Kanungo, R. N., & Aycan, Z. (1997). Organizational cultures and human resource practices from a cross cultural perspective. *The 58th Convention of the Canadian Psychology Association.* Toronto, 7–9 June. Toronto: Canadian Psychological Association.

Kanungo, R. N., & Jaeger, A. M. (1990). Introduction: The need for indigenous management in developing countries'. In A. M. Jaeger and R. N. Kanungo (Eds.), *Management in developing countries.* London: Routledge.

Karmel, R. S. (2010). *The Vietnamese Stock Market*. Available at: (http://www.fwa.org/pdf/Vietnam _posttrip_article.pdf) Accessed August 18, 2015.

King-Kauanui, S., Ngoc, S. D., & Ashley-Cotleur, C. (2006). Impact of human resource management: SME performance in Vietnam. *Journal of Developmental Entrepreneurship*, 11(1): 79–95.

Kohl, K. S. (2007). Americans doing business in Vietnam: communication differences. *COM 9656: International Business Communication*: pp. 1–5.

Lake, H. (2008). *Unravelling Performance: Work Organization and Human Resource Management in the Indian Export Garment Industry*. IZA Discussion Paper Series.

Leat, M., & El-Kot, G. (2007). HRM practices in Egypt: The influence of national context? *The International Journal of Human Resource Management*, 18(1): 147–158.

Lucero, P. M. & Spinel, F. (2002). *Estudio sobre la estructura y necesidades de capacitacio´n en la corporacio´n industrial "Las granjas" de Bogota´ [Study of the structure and necessities in the industrial corporation "Las granjas" in Bogota´]*. Unpublished thesis. Universidad de los Andes, Bogota

Lynham, S. A., & Cunningham, P. W. (2004). Human resource development: The South African case. *Advances in Developing Human Resources*, 6(3): 315–325.

Mabey, C., & Finch-Lees, T. (2008). *Management and Leadership Development*. Thousand Oaks, CA: Sage.

Mantzikos, I. (2010). The good multilateralists: Brazil and South Africa in the new area of multilateralism. *Meridiano 47*, 11(118): 6–14.

McDaniel, D., Schermerhorn, J. R., & Cuoc, H. (1999). Vietnam: The environment for management development in the twenty-first century. *Journal of Management Development*, 18(1): 79–93

MENA, OECD (2010). Investment Program; Business Climate development Strategy. Phase 1 Policy Assessment. Available at (http://www.oecd.org/globalrelations/psd/47248312.pdf) Accessed August 20, 2015.

Morris, M., & Schindehutte, M. (2005). Entrepreneurial values and the ethnic enterprise: An examination of six subcultures. *Journal of Small Business Management*, 43(4), 453–479.

Murillo, M. V. (2009). *Political Competition, Partisanship, and Policy Making in Latin American Public Utilities*. UK: Cambridge University Press.

Nolte, D. (2010). How to compare regional powers: analytical concepts and research topics. *Review of International Studies*, 36(4): 881–901.

Nydell, M. (1996). *Understanding Arabs: A Guide for Westerners*. Boston: Intercultural Press.

OBG. (2013). Oxford Business Group The Report: Egypt 2013. Accessed 1 November 2015. (http://www.oxfordbusinessgroup.com/egypt-2013)

OECD. (2010). OECD Economic Surveys 2010: Turkey, OECD, Paris, September, 2010

OECD. (2013). OECD Economic Surveys 2013: South Africa, OECD, Paris, March, 2013

Ogliastri, E. (2007). Colombia; The human relations side of enterprise. In Chhokar, J., Brobeck, F., & House, R. eds. *Culture and Leadership Across the World: The GLOBE Study of 62 Societies* (Translated by Bayless, S. W). CA:Sage Publications.

Ogliastri, E., Ruiz, J., & Martinez, I. (2004). 'La Gestion Humana en Colombia'. In *Symposium au 15 e congrès annuel de l'AGRH. Montréal*.

Osland, J. S., De Franco, S., & Osland, A. (1999). Organizational Implications of Latin American Culture Lessons for the Expatriate Manager. *Journal of Management Inquiry*, 8(2): 219–234.

Oxford Business Group. (2013). *The Report, Egypt*. Accessed 17 August 2015. http://www.oxfordbusinessgroup.com/country/Egypt

Painter, M. (2005). The Politics of State Sector Reform in Vietnam: Contested Agendas and Uncertain Trajectories. *Journal of Development Studies*, 41 (2): 261–283.

Parnell, J. A. & Hatem, T. (1999). Cultural Antecedents of Behavioral Differences between American and Egyptian Managers. *Journal of Management Studies*, 36: 399–418.

Public Service Commision (2010). *Assessment of the State of Human Resource Management in the Public Service*. Commission House, Cnr. Hamilton and Ziervogel Streets, Arcadia, South Africa. Accessed 21 August 2015. (http://www.psc.gov.za/documents/2010/PSC_March_2010_Review.pdf)

Reid, C., Collins, J., & Singh, M. (2014). *Global Teachers, Australian Perspectives*. Singapore: Springer.

Rhodes, J., Walsh, P., & Lok, P. (2008). Convergence and divergence issue in strategic management—Indonesia's experience with the Balanced Scorecard in HR Management. *International Journal of Human Resource Management*, 19(6): 1170–1185.

Rogerson, C. M. (2009). Strategic review of local economic development in South Africa. Final report submitted to Minister Sicelo Shiceka (Department of Planning and Local Government (DPLG) Commissioned by the DPLG and Afrikaanse Handelsinstituut (AHI) Supported by the Strengthening Local Governance Program of GTZ.

Ronen, S. (1986). *Comparative and Multinational Management*. New York: John Wiley and Sons.

S&P CIVETS 60. (2014) http://us.spindices.com/indices/equity/sp-civets-60-index [Accessed on 21 August 2015].

Sayim, K. Z. (2010). Pushed or pulled? Transfer of reward management policies in MNCs. *The International Journal of Human Resource Management*, 21(14): 2631–2658.

Sozer, S. (2004). *An Evaluation of Current Human Resource Management Practices in the Turkish Private Sector*. Unpublished PhD thesis. Middle East Technical University.

Statistics South Africa (2010). *Labour Force Survey*. (http://www.statssa.gov.za/publications/P0211/P02113rdQuarter2010.pdf) Accessed August 20, 2015.

Thang, N. N. & Quang, T. (2007). International briefing: Training and development in Vietnam. *International Journal of Training and Development*, 11(2): 139–149.

Thite, M. (2015). International human resource management in multinational corporations from emerging economies. In F. Horwitz, and P. Budhwar (Eds.), *Handbook of Human Resource Management in Emerging Markets*, 97–121. Cheltenham, UK: Edward Elgar.

Thorat, P. (2013). HRM in Indonesia. *International Journal of Enterprise and Innovation Management Studies*, 4 (1): 1–9.

Toh, M. H., & Gayathri, V. (2004). Impact of regional trade liberalization on emerging economies: the case of Vietnam. *ASEAN Economic Bulletin*, 21(2): 167–182

Tüzüner, V. L. (2014). Human Resource Management in Turkey. In B. E. Kaufman (Eds.), *The Development of Human Resource Management Across Nations: Unity and Diversity*. R.T. Edwards, Inc. Edwards, Inc. Elgar Publishing, Glos: Ingiltere

Wasti, S. A. (1998). Cultural barriers in the transferability of Japanese and American human resources practices to developing countries: The Turkish case. *International Journal of Human Resource Management*, 608–630.

Webster, E., & Wood, G. (2005). Human resource management practice and institutional constraints: The case of Mozambique. *Employee Relations*, 27(4): 369–385.

Whittington, J. M. (2011). Go South, young men (and women…): Key investment considerations in Latin America. *Real Estate Issues,* 36(2): 27–32.

World Bank. (2013). The World Bank Annual Report 2013. Accessed 1 November 2015. (https://openknowledge.worldbank.org/bitstream/handle/10986/16091/9780821399378.pdf?sequence=1).

Yousef, D. A. (2001). Islamic Work Ethic: A Moderator between Organizational Commitment and Job Satisfaction in Cross-Cultural Context. *Personnel Review,* 30: 152–169

Contributors

Mesut Akdere, Purdue University

Mesut Akdere is an Associate Professor of Human Resource Development in the Department of Technology Leadership & Innovation at Purdue University. His research focuses on leadership, technology innovation, quality management, leadership, and human resources. He conducts research both in the US and internationally. He has published in business, management, technology, and education journals. He is the recipient of the 2012 Early Career Scholar Award of the Academy of Human Resource Development.

Hussain A. Alhejji, University of Limerick

Hussain Alhejji, PhD, is Research Assistant in Edinburgh Napier University Business School. Hussain has a Bachelor of Business Studies from King Faisal University, Saudi Arabia, and a Master of Human Resources and Employment Relations from The University of Western Australia, Perth. He completed a Doctorate of Human Resource Development at the University of Limerick, Ireland. His research focuses on diversity at work from institutional and cross-cultural perspectives. He has authored a number of publications on diversity management practices in organizations and lectures on diversity in organizations, cross-cultural work, international human resources management/development and research methodology.

Alexandre Ardichvili, University of Minnesota

Alexandre Ardichvili is Professor of HRD and Hellervik Endowed Chair in Leadership and Adult Career Development at the University of Minnesota. He holds an MBA from the University of Minnesota and a PhD in management from Moscow State University. Ardichvili has published an edited book and more than 70 peer-reviewed articles and book chapters in HRD, international HRD, entrepreneurship, business ethics, leadership, and knowledge management. Alexandre is President-Elect of the University Council on Work and Human Resource Education. He has consulted and researched at Caterpillar, 3M, Honeywell, the Carlson Companies, ADM, ADC, BI Worldwide, Target, and numerous other businesses and nonprofits.

Renato Ferreira Leitão Azevedo, University of Illinois at Urbana-Champaign

Renato Ferreira Leitão Azevedo is a PhD Student in Educational Psychology (Cognitive Sciences of Teaching and Learning) at the University of Illinois at Urbana-Champaign (UIUC). He holds a MSc in Accounting Education and Research from the University of São Paulo (USP, 2008–2010), a BS in Information Systems (2003–2006), and a BS in Accounting (2004–2007). Renato has been an MBA FIPECAFI Instructor for Business Strategy Games and Management Accounting Cases Courses and Research Fellow at University of São Paulo (USP) since 2009. Among other experiences, he was a Visiting Graduate Student at University of California, Los Angeles (UCLA) and Visiting Scholar at Mercer University (Atlanta, GA), with research grants from these institutions. He has published scholarly papers in Argentina, Brazil, US, France, Finland, Italy, Switzerland, and Turkey, and lectured at universities in Brazil, Mexico, South Korea, and the US. He is the author of "O profissional da contabilidade: desenvolvimento de carreira, percepções e seu papel social" ("Accountants: Career Development, Perceptions and Their Social Role"].

Beata Buchelt, Cracow University of Economics

Beata Buchelt is a Reader at Cracow University of Economics, Faculty of Economics and International Relations and a Member of the Polish Economics Society. Her research interests are human capital theory, human capital management, labor market policies and trends, strategic HRM, international HRM, and HRM in health care. She was Visiting Scholar at the Grand Valley University, USA. She has received a number of prizes from the President of CUE for her teaching and research and also by national academic organizations in Poland.

Nadir Budhwani, Fanshawe College Canada

Nadir N. Budhwani is a professor in the Lawrence Kinlin School of Business, Fanshawe College, London, Ontario (Canada). He obtained his PhD in HRD from the University of Minnesota, USA. He has experience teaching in Canada, USA, Morocco, and Pakistan. He also designs and facilitates executive development programs using case method pedagogy. His research areas include HRD in community development, international HRD, spirituality and HRD, and organization development.

Silvia Casa Nova, University of São Paulo

Silvia Pereira de Castro Casa Nova is Associate Professor in the Department of Accounting and Actuarial at the University of São Paulo. She received her baccalaureate in Public Administration from the São Paulo Business Administration School at Getulio Vargas Foundation (EAESP / FGVSP). She earned both her master's and doctoral degrees in Accounting from the School of Economics, Business, and Accounting at the University of São Paulo (FEA-USP). She developed her postdoctoral research in Quantitative Methods applied to Accounting at EAESP/FGVSP. She has been a visiting scholar at the Department of Organizational Leadership, Policy, and Development at the University of Minnesota (UMN). She is currently a visiting researcher at the Business Research Unit at Instituto Universitário de Lisboa (BRU-IUL), Portugal. Her research interests are: gender in higher education, feminism, gender in accounting, accounting education, accounting profession, teaching accounting in higher profession accounting for small businesses, and financial management for small businesses.

Edgard B. Cornacchione, University of São Paulo

Edgard Cornacchione, PhD, is Full Professor at the University of São Paulo (USP, Brazil), where he served as the Chairman of the Department of Accounting and Actuarial Sciences (2010–2014). Dr. Cornacchione is a Brazilian chartered accountant and holds a PhD in Accountancy from USP and a PhD in Human Resource Education from the University of Illinois at Urbana-Champaign (USA). He acted as Scientific Director of ANPCONT/Brazil and as Member of the Scientific Development Committee of CRC-SP (Brazilian accounting professional body). He is currently a Member of the IAAER Council (2013–2015) and of the board of FIPECAFI (Research Foundation). He has published many studies and books with a record of successful grant applications and funded projects (e.g., FIPSE/CAPES). He acts as editorial board member and reviewer for journals and conferences in the US, Europe, and Brazil. Based on the management accounting framework, his research interests gravitate toward organizational development and human performance improvement by focusing on accounting education along with its evaluation, including effects of advanced technologies.

José Ernesto Rangel Delgado, University of Colima

José Ernesto Rangel Delgado, PhD, is a full-time Professor in the Faculty of Economics, Coordinator of the Transpacific Relations PhD, and Director of the Pacific Basin Studies Center and APEC Study Center at the University of Colima, Mexico. He earned his PhD from the Academy of Sciences of

Russia (1991). He was Pacific Circle Consortium President (2007–2009); Chairman of the Mexican APEC Study Centers Consortium (2009–2011; 2014–2016), Korea Foundation Fellowship (2010), and Visiting Professor of Southern Baja California Autonomous University (2012–2013). His research is focused on human resource development, economics of education, and employment and education in Asia Pacific.

Indravidoushi C. Dusoye, Edinburgh Napier University

Indravidoushi Dusoye is a Doctoral Student at Edinburgh Napier University. Her PhD thesis focuses on knowledge brokering in multinationals. Indra is a Lecturer in Human Resource Management at the University of Mauritius, Reduit, where she has taught Human Resources, Managing Transition and Change, Ethics CSR and HRM, Cross-Cultural Management, and International Human Resource Management. She has practitioner experience working in major multinationals in Mauritius, including Accenture, Ceridian, Orange Business Services, and Capfor.

Thomas N. Garavan, Edinburgh Napier University

Thomas Garavan is Research Professor of Leadership, specializing in leadership development, HRD and leadership, CSR and leadership, and cross-cultural leadership in Edinburgh Napier University Business School. Thomas graduated from the University of Limerick, Ireland, with a Bachelor of Business Studies and completed a Doctorate of Education at the University of Bristol. He is Editor of the *European Journal of Training and Development* and Associate Editor of *Personnel Review*. He is a Member of the Editorial Board of *Human Resource Management Journal*, *Human Resource Development Quarterly*, *Human Resource Development Review*, *Advances in Developing Human Resources*, and *Human Resource Development International*. He is the recipient of the Academy of Human Resource Development, Outstanding HRD Scholar Award 2013. His research interests include CSR and transformational leadership, cross-cultural dimensions of diversity training, tacit knowledge in manufacturing, international human resource management standards, and human resource management in MNCs. He is currently involved in two major research projects on tacit knowledge in manufacturing firms in the pharmaceutical and health care industries and the role of CSR in the tourism sectors.

Britta H. Heidl, Edinburgh Napier University

Britta Heidl is a Doctoral Researcher at Edinburgh Napier University and teaches in the area of Human Resource Management. Her current research focuses on ethical leadership and its impact on organizational outcomes. Previous research includes studies on gender diversity in various cultural backgrounds.

Gertrude I. Hewapathirana, Ashford University

Gertrude I. Hewapathirana is currently an Assistant Professor in the College of Business and Professional Studies at Ashford University. Prior to this, she was an Assistant Professor at the Suffolk University in Boston, USA. She received her PhD in Work Human Resource Development from the University of Minnesota, where she was a Fulbright Scholar and a Hubert Humphrey Fellow. During her tenure there, she completed a Mid-Career Executive Development Program and specialized in International Business and Marketing. She has an MA in Comparative International Development Education and an MSc in Scientific and Technical Communication at the University of Minnesota. She was specially trained in teaching International Entrepreneurship at the University of the Philippines, the University of Twente in the Netherlands, and the International Center for Entrepreneurship and Career Development in India. She has 20 years of professional work, teaching, and research experience. She worked as a Researcher at the United Nations, Managing Director of the Business Management Bureau, Project Director of Agromart Foundation, Deputy Executive Director of the Business Development Center, and Statistical Officer of the Industrial Development Board in Sri Lanka. She has published a book and several book chapters, book reviews, and peer-reviewed articles and dozens of conference proceedings.

Maimunah Ismail, Universiti Putra Malaysia

Maimunah Ismail is Professor in the Faculty of Educational Studies, Universiti Putra Malaysia (UPM). Her current research interests include work adjustment of self-initiated expatriates, career development, and the human side of mergers and acquisitions of organizations from the perspective of the intergenerational workforce. She has authored 12 books and numerous articles in international journals. She sits on the Editorial Advisory Board of *Human Resource Development International, European Journal of Training, and Development, Gender in Management*, and *Organizations and Markets in Emerging Economies*. She is a Member of the Academy of Human Resource Development and the British Academy of Management.

Robin Kramar, Australian Catholic University, Sydney

Robin Kramar is Professor of Human Resource Management at the Australian Catholic University in North Sydney, Australia. She has been interested in issues in the labor market and in the workplace for more than 35 years. Her research interests include sustainable HRM; social justice in the workplace, including discrimination issues; diversity management; and corporate social responsibility. She has published more than 60 refereed journal articles and book chapters as well as a number of books. Her most recent book *Capstone HRM: Dynamics and Ambiguity in the Workplace,* coauthored with Peter Holland, examines the outcomes of HRM practices and the reasons espoused HRM policies are not implemented.

Johana Lopez, Independent Consultant/Coach

Johana Lopez received her Doctoral degree in Organizational Leadership and Supervision from Purdue University, she holds a BA in Psychology from Javeriana University in Colombia, and a MA in Administrative Dynamics from Western Kentucky University. Dr. Lopez consults in the areas of leadership, training, organizational development, and human resource development. She is currently working as a Leadership Coach for a global consulting company and is the Mentorship Program Director for a nonprofit organization in the US. Her research focuses on organizational and workforce development practices that affect job satisfaction and success in the workplace.

Alma M. McCarthy, National University of Ireland, Galway

Alma McCarthy is Head of the Department of Management and Senior Lecturer in Management in the J. E. Cairnes School of Business and Economics, National University of Ireland, Galway. She has taught previously at the University of Limerick and Waterford Institute of Technology. She lectures in the areas of Human Resource Development, Human Resource Management, Organizational Behavior, and Leadership. Her research interests include performance management, human resource development, work-life balance, and multi-rater (360°) feedback systems. Alma's publications include articles in journals such as the *International Journal of Human Resource Management, Human Resource Management Review, Personnel Review, Advances in Developing Human Resources*, the *European Journal of Training and Development*, the *Journal of Managerial Psychology*, the *International Journal of Manpower Studies*, and the *Journal of Vocational Educational Training*; papers at national and international conferences including the Irish Academy of Management, the European Academy of Management, the American Academy of Management, and the American Society for Industrial and Organizational Psychology; and coauthored books and several chapters in edited books. She is a Chartered Member of the Chartered Institute of Personnel and Development (CIPD) and served as elected Chair of the Irish Academy of Management (IAM) from 2010–2013.

Peter McGraw, University of Technology, Sydney

Peter McGraw, PhD, is an Associate Professor in the Faculty of Business at the University of Technology, Sydney, where he teaches subjects in human resource management, leadership, and change management. He is the author of over 60 academic articles and book chapters, as well as two HR textbooks. His current research interests include HR in multinational companies, leadership, and employee training and development. Peter is a well-known consultant and executive educator and has worked with many large Australian and international companies running programs in management and leadership.

Gary N. McLean, McLean Global Consulting, Inc.

Gary N. McLean (Ed.D., Ph.D. hon.) is President of McLean Global Consulting, Inc. As an OD practitioner, he works extensively globally, especially in Asia. He recently worked in the Graduate School of Management in the International Islamic University of Malaysia as "Renowned Scholar." He teaches regularly in the PhD program in HRD at NIDA (National Institute for Development Administration) in Thailand. Previously, he was a Senior Professor at Texas A&M University. He is professor emeritus and co-founder of the HRD program at the University of Minnesota. He served as President of the Academy of Human Resource Development and the International Management Development Association, in addition to serving as an editor of five refereed journals. His research interests are broad, focusing primarily on organization development and national and international HRD.

Roziah Mohd Rasdi, Universiti Putra Malaysia

Roziah Mohd Rasdi, PhD, is Senior Lecturer at the Department of Professional Development and Continuing Education, Faculty of Educational Studies, Universiti Putra Malaysia. Her teaching and research focus on the areas of Human Resource Development, Career Development, and Gender in Human Resource Development. The findings of her studies have been presented at various national and international conferences, as well as published in journals and other outlets. She has received eight best paper awards at international conferences. She is a Member of the Academy of Human Resource Development and British Academy of Management.

Michael J. Morley, University of Limerick

Michael J. Morley is Professor of Management at the Kemmy Business School, University of Limerick, Ireland, where he has variously served as Head of the Department of Management and Marketing, Head of the Department of Personnel and Employment Relations, and Assistant Dean of Research. He has held Visiting Appointments at several universities, including, most recently, at IESE Business School, Barcelona, where he spent academic year 2010/11. In conjunction with his collaborators, he has published some 20 books, 24 guest-edited journal special issues, and over 100 journal articles and book chapters. Among his recent edited volumes are *Manager-Subordinate Trust: A Global Perspective* (with P. Cardona) (Routledge, 2013); *International Human Resource Management: Policy & Practice* (with M. Lazarova and S. Tyson) (Routledge, 2011); and *Managing Human Resources in Central and Eastern Europe* (with N. Heraty and S. Michailova) (Routledge, 2009). He served as Associate Editor of the *Journal of Managerial Psychology* from 2007 to 2012. He is a Member of the Editorial Board of 15 other international journals, including the *International Journal of Cross Cultural Management, Human Resource Management Review, International Journal of Human Resource Management, British Journal of Management, Leadership and Organization Development Journal* and the *International Journal of Emerging Markets*. He was the 2007–2010 Chair of the Irish Academy of Management and is the 2012–2014 President of the International Federation of Scholarly Associations of Management.

Regina H. Mulder, University of Regensburg, Germany

Regina H. Mulder is full Professor in Pedagogy/Educational Science (University of Regensburg, Germany) since 2004. She acquired her MA degree in Sociology and her PhD in Social Sciences in the Netherlands. She researches and publishes on topics in vocational education and training (VET) including learning in organizations, design and evaluation of VET, innovative work behavior, feedback, learning from errors, informal learning at work, learning of older workers, team learning, diversity in teams, and leadership and research methods. She has a number of co-edited books, is Member of Editorial Boards for international journals, including *Educational Research Review and HRDQ* and reviews for other journals, such as *Vocations and Learning*.

Helen M. A. Muyia, Texas A & M University

Machuma (Helen) Muyia is a Clinical Associate Professor, Human Resource Development, Department of Educational Administration and Human Resource Development, Texas A&M University. She holds an EdD in Workforce Development Education/Human Resource Development, and an MEd (Adult Education/ Human Resource Development) from University of Arkansas, Fayettville, an MPhil (Educational Planning), and a BEd (Economics and Geography) from Moi and Kenyatta University, respectively. She teaches Training and Development, and Organization Development, and has published, copublished, and presented several articles and papers. Dr. Muyia also serves as a reviewer for several journals and is a member of several associations in her field. She is a recipient of the spring

2011 Teaching Excellence Award, Board of Regents, Texas A&M University System.

Fredrick Muyia Nafukho, Texas A&M University

Fredrick Muyia Nafukho serves as Professor and Department Head in the Department of Educational Administration and Human Resource Development, College of Education and Human Development at Texas A&M University. He earned his PhD in Human Resource and Leadership Development from Louisiana State University, MEd in Economics of Education, and BEd in Business Studies and Economics from Kenyatta University, Kenya. He attended Harvard's Management Development Program (MDP) offered by Harvard Institutes for Higher Education. He has received numerous awards in recognition of his scholarship, including the Fulbright Scholarship in 1996, Distinguished International Scholar Award, Louisiana State University in 1997, Arkansas Business Teacher Educator of the Year Award in 2004, Cutting Edge Award for the Outstanding Papers, Academy of Human Resource Development (with his student Dr. Carroll C. Graham) in 2005 and Outstanding New Faculty Award, CEHD at Texas A&M University in 2008. Prof Nafukho's research foci is on adult learning, emotional intelligence and leadership development, organizational learning, e-learning, performance improvement, evaluation in organizations, and investment in human capital development. He is author, coauthor/co-editor of *Handbook of Research on Innovative Technology Integration in Higher Education* (2015, IGI Global), *Governance and Transformation of Universities in Africa* (2014, IAP), *Foundations of Adult Education in Africa* (2005, Pearson Education & UNESCO), and *Management of Adult Education Organizations in Africa* (2011, Pearson Education &UNESCO). In addition, he has authored numerous books, book chapters, and refereed journal articles. He has served as a Consultant with the UNDP, WHO, and UNESCO and as a Lead Consultant for 15 SADC countries on a Four Sector Open and Distance Learning (ODEL) Research Project. He has received numerous grant funding to support his research and graduate students.

Loek F. M. Nieuwenhuis, HAN University of Applied Sciences

Loek F. M. Nieuwenhuis is full Professor in Professional Pedagogy at HAN University of Applied Sciences in Arnhem and Nijmegen (the Netherlands), and he holds a Chair at Welten-Institute, Research Center for Learning, Teaching and Technology at the Dutch Open University. He has a MA degree in Educational Psychology and a PhD in Social Sciences. His field of research and publication is vocational and professional education and lifelong learning. His main research interests are workplace learning and learning for socioeconomic innovation. He is an active Member of the Dutch Association of Educational Research, and its division on professional education, company training, and skill development.

Satish Pandey, Pandit Deendayal Petroleum University(PDPU)

Satish Pandey is currently working with School of Petroleum Management (SPM), Pandit Deendayal Petroleum University (PDPU), Gandhinagar, as Associate Professor in Organizational Behavior and HRM area since August 2007. He completed his PhD in Psychology from Gurukul Kangri Vishwavidyalaya, Haridwar (Uttarakhand) in 1995. Prior to joining SPM, he worked with reputed institutions, such as Mudra Institute of Communications Ahmedabad (MICA), Nirma Institute of Management, Ahmedabad, Institute of Banking Personnel Selection-Mumbai (IBPS), and BITS-Pilani. He has over 17 years of teaching and research experience at various institutions. He has presented papers in national and international academic conferences; published papers in refereed journals; and edited books on topics related to stress management, personality, organizational culture, cross-cultural management, organizational turnaround, organizational learning, and behavior change communication. His most recent book is entitled *Stress and Work: Perspectives for Understanding and Managing Stress* (Co-editor: D. M. Pestonjee, Publisher: Sage Publications, India).

Dinyar M. Pestonjee, Pandit Deendayal Petroleum University(PDPU)

D. M. Pestonjee is currently associated with the School of Petroleum Management, Pandit Deendayal Petroleum University, Gandhinagar, as GSPL Chair Professor since July 2009. He was also associated with CEPT University, Ahmedabad as Dean, Faculty of Applied Management. He has served eminent institutions, such as IIM Ahmedabad and Banaras Hindu University. He is a psychologist having earned his PhD in Industrial Psychology from the Aligarh Muslim University and he was conferred the DLitt (Honoris Causa) by the Banaras Hindu University in April 2003. In November 2000, he was conferred the title of Honorary Professor of the Albert Schweitzer International University, Geneva (Switzerland). He was awarded the Albert Schweitzer Medal for Science and Peace in April 2004. He has over four decades of teaching and research experience. Among his better known works are, *Organization Structure and Job Attitudes* (1973), *Behavioral Processes in Organization* (1981), *Second Handbook of Psychological and Social Instruments* (1988), *Third Handbook of Psychological and Social Instruments* (1997), *Studies in Organizational Roles and Stress and Coping* (1997), *Studies in Stress and Its Management* (1999), and the celebrated *Stress and Coping: The Indian Experience* (1992, 2002). His most recent book is entitled *Stress and Work: Perspectives for Understanding and Managing Stress* (Co-editor: Satish Pandey, Publisher: Sage Publications, India).

Maura Sheehan, Edinburgh Napier University

Maura Sheehan is Professor of International Management at Edinburgh Napier University Business School. Before joining Napier, she was Professor of International Management at NUI Galway, and before that, Maura was a Reader at the University of Brighton. Previously, she was an Associate Professor at the Graduate School of Management, University of Dallas. From 1993–2000, Maura taught at the Queen's University of Belfast. She taught at St. Catharine's College Cambridge, Birkbeck College, University of London, University of Graz, Austria (as an Erasmus exchange professor), and was a Visiting Research Fellow at the ESRC Centre for Business Research, University of Cambridge. Maura has a BSc in Economics from New York University and a PhD in Economics from the University of Notre Dame, USA. Maura recently completed an EU Marie Curie Fellowship (2009–2012). She investigated the determinants and performance of foreign direct investment (FDI) in the emerging economies of the Czech Republic, Hungary, and Poland. The project also compared how labor is managed and by whom in foreign and domestic subsidiaries of the same organizations. The importance of country and organizational culture in understanding differences in HRM and the delivery of HR were central to this investigation. This project represented a synthesis of Maura's expertise in industrial and labor economics, human resource management, and international management.

Judy Sun, University of Texas at Tyler

Judy Y. Sun, PhD, is an Assistant Professor of Human Resource Development at the University of Texas at Tyler. Her research interests include career development, HRD theory building, management development, and international HRD with a focus in China and Asia. She was recipient of the AHRD Dissertation of the Year Award in 2012. Prior to her doctoral studies, she worked for multinational corporations, such as Motorola, KPMG, and ABB as a Senior Consultant for over a decade.

Oleksandr Tkachenko, University of Minnesota

Oleksandr Tkachenko is a Doctoral Student in Human Resource Development (HRD) at the Department of Organizational Leadership, Policy, and Development, University of Minnesota, US. Oleksandr is a recipient of the Edmund S. Muskie Graduate Fellowship (US Department of State, 2004–2006). Prior to joining his PhD program, Oleksandr worked as a trainer, manager, and consultant in Ukraine and in the Netherlands. His research interests include international HRD, organization development, workplace learning, and leadership development. Oleksandr has published articles in such journals as *Human Resource Development International, Journal of Workplace Learning*, and *Zarządzanie Zasobami Ludzkimi* (HRM/ZZL).

Eduardo Tomé, Universidade Europeia Lisbon

Eduardo Tomé completed his PhD in Economics in 2001 at the Technical University in Lisbon, where he completed his dissertation on Vocational Training and the European Social Fund. Since then, he has published 34 papers in peer-reviewed journals, 6 chapters in books, and presented 60 papers at International Conferences. He also led the organization of four well-attended international conferences, which resulted in three special issues in international journals. His main interests are HRD, knowledge management, intellectual capital, and international economics and social policy. Since 2013, Eduardo works for Universidade Europeia, Laureate Group, in Lisbon, Portugal.

Consuelo L. Waight, University of Houston

Consuelo L. Waight is an Associate Professor of Human Resource Develop-ment (HRD), Director of the Executive HRD Program and Coordinator of the Graduate HRD program at the University of Houston. Dr. Waight's research interests include e-learning, learning and mergers and acquisition, and international human resource development. She has worked on learning and development projects in Nicaragua, Belize, Jamaica, St. Lucia, Belize, Thailand, Mozambique, Angola, and the US. Consuelo serves on the edi-torial boards of the Human Resource Development International, Human Resource Development Review and New Horizons in Adult Education and Human Resource Development journals.

Greg Wang, University of Texas at Tyler

Greg G. Wang, PhD, is a Professor of Human Resource Development at the University of Texas at Tyler. His research interests include HRD theory development, HRD research and practice assessment and evaluations, and HRD in China and international settings, among others. He has both HRD research and practical experience in China and the US as an internal HRD practitioner and external consultant with ARAMARK, CIGNA, GE, IBM, and Motorola, among others. He also served as the Editor of *Journal of Chinese Human Resource Management* from 2010 to 2015.

Elena Zavyalova, St. Petersburg State University

Elena K. Zavyalova (Dr. Psychol.) is a Professor and Head of Organiza-tion Behavior and HR Management Department, Graduate School of Man-agement, St. Petersburg State University. Her scientific interests include problems of HRM and HRD, peculiarity of HRM/HRD in Russia, IIRM/ HRD in BRICs, HRM/HRD, and Innovative Work Behavior. She has published over 90 articles, reports, and books, mainly about problems of HRM and HRD. She teaches a range of course, including Psychology of Success, Motivation and Reward Systems, and Human Resource Development. She has conducted consulting with several Russian and international companies, including Shell, Lenenergo, and Admiralteyskie Shipyards. She is recipient of the prestigious award Honorable Worker of Higher Professional Education of Russia. She is a Member of Editorial Boards of the *International Journal of HRM* and *Human Resource Development International*. She is a Member of the Academy of Human Resource Development and of the International Association for Research in Economic Psychology.

Index

Note: Italicized page numbers indicate a figure on the corresponding page. Page numbers in bold indicate a table on the corresponding page.